THE ORIENTAL RENAISSANCE

The Oriental Renaissance

Europe's Rediscovery of India and the East, 1680–1880

RAYMOND SCHWAB

Translated by
Gene Patterson-Black
and
Victor Reinking

Foreword by Edward W. Said

New York   Columbia University Press   1984

Library of Congress Cataloging in Publication Data
Schwab, Raymond.
The oriental renaissance.

Translation of: Renaissance orientale.
Bibliography: p.
Includes index.
1. Europe—Civilization—Oriental influences.
2. Europe—Civilization—Indic influences.   3. Europe—
Intellectual life.   4. East and West.   I. Title.
CB253.S3813 1984   909'.09811   83-25279
ISBN 0-231-04138-1 (alk. paper)

The Foreword by Edward W. Said is reprinted by permission of *Daedalus,*
Journal of the American Academy of Arts and Sciences,
where it appeared in slightly different form under the title
"Raymond Schwab and the Romance of Ideas" in the issue "In Praise of Books"
(Winter 1976), vol. 105, no. 1, Boston, MA.

First published in French as *La Renaissance orientale,*
copyright 1950 by Editions Payot, Paris

English-language translation copyright © 1984 by Columbia University Press

Columbia University Press
New York   Guildford, Surrey

*Clothbound editions of Columbia University Press books are Smyth-sewn and
printed on permanent and durable acid-free paper.*

Contents

Foreword

Edward W. Said

POET, biographer, man of letters, novelist, editor, translator, and scholar, Raymond Schwab is not known (to most of the standard Anglo-American authorities on the Romantic movement, for example), and except for this excellent version of *La Renaissance orientale*, none of his works has been translated into English. For a man whose interests observed no national boundaries and whose capacities were deeply transnational, this is a depressing irony. He was born in Nancy in 1884 and died in Paris in 1956. The little that is easily discovered about his life and personality comes from three issues of *Mercure de France*, where some of his hitherto unpublished poetry and his memoirs appeared, along with reminiscences written by his friends.[1] He seems to have been a quiet and rather modest man who spent most of his life in the service of letters. Between 1936 and 1940 with Guy Lavaud he edited *Yggdrasil*, a journal devoted to poetry; its catholicity of interests and openness to currents in poetry other than those either European or fashionable were noteworthy. Schwab leaves behind the impression that he had the tastes of a fastidious man and that he was intensely meditative by nature and withdrawn in his habits, with a kind of powerful, yet muted, religious sense that would cause him to translate the Psalms or write an epic poem on Nimrod without his necessarily having been committed to an organized faith.

In many ways Schwab resembles Borges, if not also a character in one of Borges' *Ficciones*. When he dealt with literature, Schwab would produce books about little-known figures such as Elémir Bourges; when asked to write a preface to a French translation of the *Thousand and One Nights*, he would write instead a three-hundred-page work on Antoine Galland, a late seventh-century personality who was the *Nights'* first French translator. We are reminded of Borges' interest in such odd figures as John Wilkins and G. K. Chesterton, who benefited from the rather surprising seriousness displayed in his studies of them, since unknown books and shadowy writers do not often command this kind of attention. Both Schwab and Borges reveal a fundamental personal reticence married to an almost Mallarméan idea of The Book—the quest for it, its life, the gentleness and calm heroism to be found in it, despite the almost unthinkable effort expended on its behalf. One always has a sense in Schwab, as of course in Borges, of a sort of library of humanity slowly being discovered, walked into, and described, but valued less for its ponderous classics than for its surprising eccentrics.

Endless detail is the mark of Schwab's major scholarly work, of which *La Renaissance orientale* is the greatest achievement. The underlying theme of this work is the European experience of the Orient, which is in turn based on the human need for absorbing the "foreign" and "different." To his description of this experience, Schwab brings a rare gift for dealing with very concentrated and meticulously gathered detail. In Schwab's view, the Orient, however *outré* it may seem at first, is a complement to the Occident, and vice-versa. The vision, as one admirer of Schwab has put it, is that of an integral humanism.[2] Its style—its verbal idiom as well as its angle of vision—is both subtle and difficult, since Schwab manages always to depict a phenomenon as it is in itself and as something that affected many lives over a long period of time. He is up to the painstaking effort required to document cultural interchanges. But he can also create fascinating nooks, sheltered from the broad outline of his large theme, in which new, often intimate spaces appear.

The detail in such instances is the detail of influence—how one writer or event bears on another. Like Erich Auerbach, however, Schwab is stingy about giving a theoretical explanation for what he does; like Auerbach discussing in *Mimesis* the classical notion of high and low literary styles, he is content to take on an almost ingenuously obvious motif, the influence of the Orient in the West, and to let the imprints of that motif appear in myriad places in a vast body of later literature. Indeed, the analogy with Auerbach, and an even more compelling one with Ernst Robert Curtius, press home Schwab's *philological* learning, especially its capacity for revealing how enormous unities (the Latin cultural *imperium* or the Orient) inform, live, and take textual body in consequent ages and cultures. For to a very great extent Schwab, like Auerbach, Curtius, and Borges, is possessed by the image of the text as a locus of human effort, a "text-ile" fertility gathering in cultural identity and as a result disseminating human life everywhere in time and space. The importance to Schwab of the Oriental Renaissance (the phrase is taken from Edgar Quinet's neglected work, *Le Génie des réligions*) is that, whereas the classical Renaissance immured European man within the confines of a self-sufficient Greco-Latin terrain, this later Renaissance deposited the whole world before him. The second Renaissance, as Schwab puts it in one of the compact generalities with which his work abounds, combined India and the Middle Ages and thereby displaced the centuries of Augustus and Louis XIV. The job of displacement was apportioned to the great capitals: Calcutta provided, London distributed, Paris filtered and generalized.

So profound and beneficent is Schwab's view of the Orient that one is doubtless more accurate in describing him as an *orienteur* than as an *orientaliste,* a man more interested in a generous awareness than in detached classification.[3] Insofar as European awareness of the Orient can be said to have had an effect, Schwab believes it was a productive one, since oriental influences in pre-Romantic and Romantic cultures are everywhere to be found. Yet two recent scholars of the Romantic period, Harold Bloom and W. J. Bate, have advanced the opposite thesis that all influence produced anxiety, a sense of inferiority and belatedness, in the writers of the time, for whom an uninfluenced originality was the highest (and least possible) goal. Schwab takes the position that Romanticism welcomed the Orient as an influence benefiting poetry, prose, science, and philosophy. So here already is one major theoretical and scholarly contribution of Schwab's work: influence in Romantic literature is seen as enrichment and useful persistence rather than a diminishment and worrying presence. But again Schwab sees and plentifully provides detail to back up the generalization. He seems to be saying that if so much work—which he chronicles with vertiginous minuteness—went willingly and consciously into the discovery of the Orient, then we must regard influence finally as supplying something that would otherwise be felt as absence. What results is not that violent contest among writers for time and space sketched by Bloom with such urgency, but rather an endless accommodation similar to the one Schwab sees in the Asian temperament, which does not contrast novelty with latecoming but instead sees all time as the poet's possession: "He repeats the same interwoven patterns endlessly, not to save time at his disposal that there is no danger of his using up in necessarily transient little details."[4]

Schwab's, then, is a criticism of sympathetic cast. Dualities, opposition, polarities—as between Orient and Occident, one writer and another, one time and another—are converted in his writing into lines that criss-cross, it is true, but that also draw a vast human portrait. A year before his death, he mused that what was needed was a "History of Universal Poetry," but unfortunately he did not write it. He had attempted a physiognomy of literature as a step in that direction.[5] The human image always dominates in Schwab's criticism, but what provokes its interest for us is that, when we perceive it, such an image is the writer's achievement, never his given. There are the details of human effort, then their organization, finally their total portrayal. In its attempt to appropriate and reproduce the subject of its study, Schwab's criticism belongs with that of Georges Poulet, Albert Beguin, Albert Thibaudet, Jean Starobinski, and others like them, whose patient and engaged imagination dominates the business of industrious fact-gathering. Unlike all of them, however (except perhaps the Starobinski of *L'Invention de la liberté*), Schwab is continually guided by events, privileged historical moments, and large movements of ideas. For him, consciousness is a cultural affair, heavily laden with empirical experience in and of the world. Whether he is describing the rise of linguistics attendant upon the numerous discoveries made in Avestan, Sanskrit, Semitic, or Indo-European languages or the fabulously rich interlacing of oriental themes in English, French, German, and American writing, or even the precise data involved in scientific or artistic activity during the years 1771 to roughly 1860, his work is always a treasure of insight and information. Most of all, it deepens our appreciation for a particular and extremely rare type of unhurried scholarship, whose role is too infrequently examined by theorists of either criticism or literature.

Appearances notwithstanding, Schwab is no Taine or Lanson. Historical criticism for him is not science, even though facts must of course command respect. But human history gets its impulses from the desire for truth, not simply from its establishment: history "teaches us that establishing truth is less important than making a particular truth desirable. What great inventor has even found a new truth without first looking for it in the wrong place?"[6] Schwab wrote this about the early orientalists, but it applies as well to his own work. The tremendous cultural drama with which all his scholarship was concerned is the struggle between either acquired or felt certainties (and not facts) that takes place both within a culture and between cultures. His view reinforced by his own background, Schwab sees the Judeo-Christian component in Western culture as being forced to submit to the discovery of an earlier civilization; thus Indo-European linguistics rival the primacy of Hebraic society in the European mind. Later that mind will accommodate the discovery, making the world into a whole again. But the gripping drama of Orientalism, as Schwab puts it in the superb opening pages of *La Renaissance orientale*, is the debate it initiates about the meaning of "the primitive," how different worlds are seen as claimants to originality and genius, how the notions of civilization and savagery, beginning and end, ontology and teleology, undergo marked transformation in the years between 1770 and 1850: "Thus, at the moment when a thirst for discord was spreading throughout Europe, fomenting the crises that spawned political revolution, oriental studies, masses fundamentally at odds with the West, began their own revolt" (p. 23). His task therefore is to study the progress by which the West's image of the Orient passes from primitive to actual, that is, from disruptive invigoration to condescending veneration. There is a saddening impoverishment, obviously, from one image to the other. Yet so judicious and modulated is the rendering and so encyclopedic the scale that we feel the impoverishment less as sentiment than as a law of cultural change. From being a "library" without divisions, the Orient becomes a scholarly or ideological province: revelations slide into the niches provided by specialization. Before 1800, Europe possessed *le monde du passé*, with Homer its first and final classical perfection; after 1800, a new secular world intrudes, the "dissident." Gone is the dependence on fables, traditions, and classics. Instead texts, sources, and sciences resting on difficult, tiring, and troublesome work thrust a strange new reality on the mind. Schwab's concern is how this occurs and how quickly even the novelty is transformed into orthodoxy.

A peculiar feature of Schwab's scholarship, however, is that he takes little explicit note of the sheer folly and derangement stirred up by the Orient in Europe. For, as a subject, the Oriental Renaissance is no less bizarre a current in the Romantic imagination than those currents documented by Mario Praz, and Schwab is no less equipped than Praz to comment on them. Yet he does not, even when he is recording in detail—for instance, the madness of Anquetil-Duperron's life, as he trekked through steamy jungles enduring impossible physical hardships, unrecognized even as a scholar until his very last years. The asceticism of scholars is only partly useful as explanation for such men. What they saw and felt about the Orient in many cases literally took their minds, but Schwab is more concerned with demonstrating the humanistic symmetry between this Renaissance and the earlier one than he is with the crazy enthusiasms that could produce a Beckford, Anquetil, Renan, or Rückert. Conversely, Schwab's Oriental Renaissance, while it avoids the disorienting aspects of the European experience in the East, also tends to shun the other great Romantic appetites of nature, the macabre, heightened consciousness, folk culture.

La Renaissance orientale is in fact the apogee of Schwab's scholarly career, although chronologically it stands more or less at its center. Just as its subject matter is the preparation for, the encounter with, then the absorption of the Orient by the West, so too it is already suggested by Schwab's earlier work as well as assumed by his later. I shall speak briefly here of a circle of historical and scholarly books and monographs surrounding and informing *La Renaissance orientale*, a circle that must exclude the substantial body of his poetry, fiction, and translation: Schwab's alternation between linear, or genealogical, fidelity to his subject and his encompassing structural ambitions to show prefiguration, latency, refraction, metalepsis despite linear history—in short, the alternation in his method between filiation and affiliation as modes of perceiving and conducting cultural history.

Schwab's first book was the *Vie d'Anquetil-Duperron* (1934), a biography of the French scholar, theoretician of egalitarianism, and ecumenist of beliefs (Jansenist, Catholic, and Brahman), who between 1759 and 1761 transcribed and later translated the *Zend Avesta* while in Surat. This event for Schwab prefigures the spate of translated documents that would appear in the West during the Oriental Renaissance. Aside from an uncritical analysis of Anquetil's strange follies and enthusiasms, we find in the book an adumbration of most of Schwab's later motifs. First among them is "abnégation des érudits," selflessness during the quest for a manuscript, total commitment to the cause of learning: "What we would regard as calamities were in his eyes just one more chance to learn something"[7] Second is Schwab's penchant for telling detail, as when he describes the real conditions of shipboard life in the eighteenth century or when he chronicles Anquetil's relations with Grimm, Diderot, William Jones, and Herder. Third is Schwab's attention to the contest in the European mind between oriental priority and biblical "history." Both Anquetil and Voltaire were interested in India and the Bible, but "the one to make the Bible more indisputable, the other to make it more unbelievable."[8] Schwab's epigrammatic flair will strengthen in his later work into passages of extraordinary poetic beauty.

Yet the motif to which Schwab's imagination is mostly dedicated is the life of images and forms in the human consciousness, which is always located existentially in a specific historical context and is never left to float freely here and there. Cultural history is drama because the ideas that derive from archetypal images, on the one hand, cause men to struggle in their behalf and, on the other, induce in men a kind of entranced passivity or even, as in Anquetil's case, a disconcerting appetite for all ideas or faiths, regardless of contradiction. Images are historical, quasi-natural artifacts created out of the interaction of *nous a tous*. Moreover, they are limited in number, so economical is the imagination and so powerful their range: Orient, Occident, community, the human, the Origin, the divine. Among themselves they form a matrix that generates cultural romance and adventure, expressed as ideas in conflict or in concert with each other. Although idea and image seem to move freely, they are first the product of men and the texts men make; then they become the focal points of institutions, societies, periods, and cultures. For images are constants in human experience; the ideas they legitimate take different forms and varying values. Here, in a passage from the *Vie*, Schwab illustrates the interplay that will dominate his writing: "He goes to find in Asia a scientific proof for the primacy of the Chosen People and for the genealogies of the Bible: instead it happened that his investigations soon led to criticism of the very texts which had hitherto been considered revealed, a process Assyriology would subsequently prove irreversible."[9]

These ideas of necessity have a physical dimension, which conveys not only the alternation in culture between the limited and the limitless (as when Schwab talks of pre-Anquetil Orientalism: "l'exotisme sort du bibelot")[10] but also the metamorphoses of notions of distance, time, relationship, memory, society, language, and individual effort:

In 1759 Anquetil finished his translation of the *Avesta* at Surat; in 1786 that of the *Upanishads* in Paris—he had dug a channel between the hemispheres of human genius, freeing the old humanism from the Mediterranean basin. Less than fifty years earlier, his compatriots were asking how one could be Persian, when he taught them how to compare the monuments of the Persians to those of the Greeks. Before him, one looked for information on the remote past of our planet exclusively among the great Latin, Greek, Jewish, and Arabic writers. The Bible was regarded as a lonely rock, an aerolite. A universe in writing was available, but scarcely anyone seemed to suspect the immensity of these unknown lands. The realization began with his translation of the *Avesta*, and reached dizzying heights owing to the exploration in Central Asia of the languages that multiplied after Babel. Into our schools, up to that time limited to the narrow Greco-Latin heritage of the Renaissance, he interjected a vision of innumerable civilizations from ages past, or an infinity of literatures. Moreover, the few European provinces were not the only places to have left their mark in history; "the right direction of the universe" ceased to be "fixed between northern Spain and Northern Denmark in one direction and England and the borders of western Turkey in the other."[11]

Schwab's portrait of Anquetil goes very far in attempting to dispel "the obscurity that always hides the beginnings of discoveries."[12] Ultimately Schwab locates the beginning in a change of focus generated by a mysterious fragment of the *Zend* that appears in Oxford; whereas "the scholars looked at the famous fragment of Oxford and then returned to their studies; Anquetil looked, and went to India."[13]

Although in the end Schwab was to voice some misgivings about the fetishized Western biographical mode, his next work, *La Vie d'Elémir Bourges*,[14] is governed by the life-and-works framework. Bourges' dates are 1852 to 1925, and even though he was admired by a number of authors—among them Edmond Jaloux and Henri de Regnier—he will probably remain an obscure and minor writer. The book on Bourges is the least distinguished of Schwab's output; one wonders why—except for the undeveloped personal connections hinted at between Bourges and Schwab—he took on this particular chore for his complementary thesis at the Sorbonne. Occasionally we get glimpses of the authentic Schwab, notably in his analyses of Bourges's eclecticism, as well as in his capacity for spiritual renovation within an otherwise episodic life. Nor should we overlook the fact that Schwab was in his early sixties when he undertook formal petitioning for the doctorate; like the subject of one of his own studies, he transformed himself from a man of letters into an academic scholar. The *méandre* of Schwab's work—that attractive expanding sweep within which occurred the very alchemy of ideas he was so expert at describing—allowed him the maximum of self-transformation with the maximum of coherence and intelligibility. So it is hard to believe that the inward-tending intensity of Bourges' life is not really Schwab's own, rendered with comradely loyalty by Schwab as belonging to Bourges.

The contrast with *La Renaissance orientale*, which was to follow two years later in 1950, is immediately obvious. Its itemized subtitle reads like an encyclopedia, if not also like a doctoral program in East-West literatures (incidentally, the book was the principal thesis for Schwab's doctorate): "La decouverte du sanscrit—le siècle des écritures dechiffrées—l'avenement de l'humanisme intégral—grandes figures d'orientalistes—philosophies de l'histoire et des réligions—sciences linguistiques et biologiques—l'hypothèse aryenne—l'inde dans la littérature occidentale—l'asie et le romantisme—Hindouisme et Christianité." This was followed in turn by two works, both of them logical outcomes. One, a two-hundred-page portion of the *Pléiade Histoire de Littératures,* was entitled "Domaine Oriental" and modestly subtitled "Le Porche oriental." Schwab here turned his attention to all that material whose effects he had so assiduously recorded earlier. It was as if Mallarmé had finally decided to write about the object whose absence had previously engaged him (for of course *La Renaissance orientale* is a work of scholarship wirtten from a symbolic standpoint). Then posthumously, in 1964, the *Vie d'Antoine Galland* appeared. A less exciting work than the Anquetil-Duperron, it nevertheless complemented the earlier book, as well as rounding out Schwab's career, by treating the phenomenon of pre-Orientalism as style and literature at the moment before the Orient succumbed to Western science.[15]

A principal feature of all of Schwab's mature work is his interest in what he calls *le secondaire,* the smaller figures—the translators, the compilers, the scholars, whose unflagging effort make possible the major work of the Goethes, Hugos, and Schopenhauers. Thus the major cultural renaissance called "oriental" by Schwab is inaugurated by the translations made by two practically forgotten men, Anquetil and Galland—the one opening the road to linguistic and scientific revolution in Europe, the other initiating the stylistic literary exoticism associated in Europe with Orientalism.[16] What clearly fascinates Schwab in such men is that they have none of the finish of the major literary or cultural figures, no easily discernible shape to their careers, no fully appreciated role in the larger movements of ideas they serve. Rather they are like fragments contributing, Schwab once said, to an imaginary manuscript whose will they obey[17] and whose totality resembles what Foucault would call the archive of a particular period. Moreover, their abnegation exerts a sort of inverse reaction in the contemporary scholar, who will not allow their modesty to disappear behind the major works or figures to which they have so obviously contributed. One of Schwab's successful restorations of justice occurs when he demonstrates how Galland's style, more than being a straight transcription of an Arabic original, in fact creates the ambience within which the achievements of the *Princesse de Clèves* are made.

There is another aspect of Schwab's interest in the secondary: his appreciation, evident throughout the "Domaine Oriental," for the anonymity of Asian literature and the comparative disregard for strong ego-individuality it displays. How much this appreciation derives from Schwab's impressions of the literature he discusses and how much it is a real factor in it (since one is disappointed to discover that Schwab knows oriental literature mainly through translation), I cannot tell. I suspect, though, that as he grew older he was searching for—and in his own way finding—other means of communicating cultural history, new unities sought by the exacting and original scholar, more effective generalizations. For his work starts the process that will bridge the gap between the polymathic historians—formalists all of them, such as Elie Faure, Henri Focillon, and André Malraux and, to their left, the systematic verbal and institutional materialism of Foucault's archaeological investigations. There is, of course, a political meaning to this kind of work, although in the East-West context Schwab himself rarely makes it explicit. Early in the "Domaine Oriental" he does say, however, that Europe, or Western culture, needs to be reminded that it, its achievements, and its heroes are at most a particular case in the transcendental generality of human culture at large.[18]

The avoidance of ethno- and anthropocentric attitudes dictates an interest in oriental literature for its own sake. And the "Domaine Oriental," within the limits indicated above, is a marvelous prose-poem meditation. A much worked-over prose such as Schwab's moves from large generalizations about Asian literature to nuanced instances of its variety. And, indeed, one of that literature's characteristics continuously asserted by Schwab is its exemplification of unity combined with infinite variations. The Bachelardian side of the "Domaine Oriental" demonstrates, for instance, how certain figures—shepherds, laborers, trees, voyagers, riders, walkers—give Asian literature its strong anchor in actuality. But it is in his consideration of aesthetic and verbal means that Schwab is most impressive. Starting from the notion that oriental literatures view historical reality as something to be transformed into "mythical parabolas" by transgression, he investigates the predominance of the nominative mode in oriental artistic grammar, the typology of rhythmic accent, the poetics of length, time as a meditative category, the use of *mot-germes* in the structure of rhythmically obsessive poetry, the interplay between infinite particularity and infinite generality, and the frequently employed festival mood in what he calls oriental oceanic epics. All this, with a wide range of illustration, is subordinated to the proposition that Western literature attempts to turn all the means at its disposal into verbality and articulation, whereas oriental literature seeks to transform everything, including words, into music.

The comparative rarefaction of the "Domaine Oriental" is a function of limitations imposed on Schwab by the collective general work to which he was contributing and by the unimaginable scope of the subject he was attempting to treat. No such limitations exist for him, however, in *La Renaissance orientale*. There he disposes of enormous amounts of detailed information, all of which is obviously treated at first hand. Read both as a prefiguration of and as an important complement to Foucault's *Les Mots et les choses*, the book is of great importance for understanding the great transformation in culture and learning that took place at the end of the eighteenth century and the beginning of the nineteenth. But where Foucault is rather ambiguous, that is, in assigning a particular set of causes to the change, Schwab is uncompromising and more unstinting with information supporting his case for the Orient-as-cause. Yet both men see how it was that the acquisition of knowledge, its institutions, and its currency determine not only cultural praxis generally but aesthetic praxis as well. For neither of these scholars is the hagiolatrous view of the "poet" sufficient for understanding literary production; nor is it their view that literary works can be studied in unheeding isolation from those conditions of verbal production and textual revolution that were more or less commanding all types of verbal activity during a given period. Schwab gives flesh to such of Foucault's statements as are unquestionably true— for instance, that near the beginning of the nineteenth century we have a period in which philology as well as biology was invented. Still more, Schwab demonstrates with inexhaustible patience what it means in Foucault's sense (formulated nineteen years after *La Renaissance orientale* in *The Archeology of Knowledge*) literally for an archive to be formed.

The agents and the heroes of cultural change and formation are scholars, according to Schwab, since cultural transformations take place because of men's appetites first to know and then to organize new things. The formula is perhaps simple, but it encompasses in *La Renaissance orientale* the reeducation of one continent by another. The work is divided into six main sections with dozens of smaller subdivisions and a conclusion. Just as its subject matter seems to have operated by dilation and contraction, so too does *La Renaissance orientale*. Part One identifies and asserts the phenomenon of the European awareness of the Orient—how geographical discovery, the prestige of Egyptology, and the various colonial missions to India fortified the oriental challenge and the predisposition for dealing with it systematically in European society. Part Two details the movement of integration by which Europe received the Orient into the body of its scientific, institutional, and imaginative structures. This section includes the wave of Sanskrit studies that swept the Continent, with a base in Paris primarily, and the enthusiasm that, in Schwab's happy phrase, multiplied the world. In Part Three Schwab doubles back over the first two sections in order to show the active changes that take place in knowledge of the Orient. Central here is the metamorphosis in knowledge about language from a religious issue to a linguistic, scientific, and even a racial one. Accompanying this change is the one by which India acquired a whole figurative dimension in Western literature, from the pre-Orientalism of Milton and Dryden through the Lake Poets to Emerson, Whitman, the Transcendentalists, Richter, Novalis, Schelling, Rückert, Heine, Goethe, and of course Friedrich Schlegel.

Part Four is an elaborately constructed mosaic of "case histories," items of personal witness to oriental effect drawn from forty or so lives. Schwab's interest is to give an intimate as well as a panoramic vision of reorientations in the work of scholars, scientists, critics, philosophers, and historians. Each portrait multiplies the complexity of Orientalism as a phenomenon of reception and transmission. The treatment of subject matter is scenic, which is to say that whether he examines Balzac, Cuvier, Jules Mohl, Sylvestre de Sacy, Ampère, Ozanam, or Fauriel, Schwab also represents the changing conceptions of time and space brought forward by each. Concurrently Schwab's antennae sort out shifts in informal relations among people affected by the Orient (salons, paraoccult leagues, gossip factories) and among disciplines (linguistics, geology, biology). His investigations of discursive formations can show, for example, that the library, the museum, and the laboratory underwent internal modifications of paramount importance. Dotting Schwab's web are countless dates, names, journals, works, exhibitions, and events (for instance, the Nineveh exposition of 1846 in Paris) that give his narrative its gripping immediacy.

Parts Five and Six lift all the myriad details of Orientalism from the plane of schools, scholars, academies, sciences, salons, and ideologies into the more discriminating dramas enacted within the careers of major imaginative writers. Part Five concerns French writers wrestling with the travail of creation as erudition impinges upon it: Lamartine, Hugo, Vigny,

Michelet, Leconte de Lisle, Baudelaire. In addition, there is a section on what Schwab calls the "external Orient," the exotic East so influential in the work of Nerval, Gautier, and Flaubert. There are some especially fine comments on Flaubert's *roman archéologique,* whose matter is adopted from Quinet but whose tone flatly contradicts him. Part Six, "Detours and Continuations," focuses for the most part on German (among them Nietzsche, Wagner, and Schopenhauer) and Russian writers later in the century. Gobineau is to be found in these pages, along with his doctrine of the inequality of races. For, as his study nears its end, Schwab attends to the often pernicious divisions (Iran versus India, Aryans versus Semites, East versus West) that filter through the gigantic cultural mass created, during almost a century of "comparatism," by the Orientalist consciousness. These divisions are all traceable to the two *techniques spirituelles* facing each other from West to East.

A concluding section, written in a complex and compact style, affirms that the Oriental Renaissance was fundamentally a phenomenon of difference, generating comparative techniques, whereas the first Renaissance was essentially assimilative in that it flattered Europe without disturbing Europe's self-affirming cultural centrality. Thus the second Renaissance multiplied, rather than decreased, the points of comparison and the techniques available to Western culture and its "invisible interlocutor," the more so because the later Renaissance was a verbal event, not a verbal and plastic one as the earlier one was. Orientalism made possible a "premier tour du monde parlé," which in turn initiated a linguistic theory of constantly receding and impossible origins. Standing between history and faith, such a theory was a significant event:

the linguists believed they had found the answer to Babel, the poets expected the return of Eden; a passion for origins rose up in the hearts of men with each new archaeological excavation, a little as if, with each new formula produced by a chemist came the illusion that he had created new life: the postulate of a mother tongue produced linguistics by parthenogenesis. But the notion of the primitive could be confirmed only by distorting it; it could no longer be regarded as the starting point of history, but only as an increasingly lower point on its scale. It was movable and it therefore brought into play notions about change; history no longer provided a bulwark for all time, and certainly it could not provide a foundation. At the same time, both aesthetic canons and scientific theories renounced their claims to permanence; each worker in what had been the ancient verities felt that he had been betrayed if he pursued or acquired anything durable. The Romantic aesthetic movement, the biological dogma of evolution, the imperialism of language in the intellectual empires, these were now the new and important things that one could agree upon. In our day, the heirs of the poets of instability, the metaphysicians of the unconscious, and the doctors of myth, the most revolutionary manipulators of language and literature, speak of "free words" as of a "spiritual experience"—

they are confirming without knowing it Burnouf's formula: *Nomina numina. (477–78)*

The coincidence of the advent of Romanticism and Orientalism in the West, as Schwab so carefully portrays it, gave the former its complex dimensions and led it to the reformulation of human limits—indeed, to that frontier where the unconscious and even the monstrous can claim the title of natural. Governing the coincidence are two laws: the "odds of the ages" and the "mission of the generations" (p. 482). Therefore Schwab's conception of cultural history in *La Renaissance orientale* is cosmological, because he sees himself as mediating between the two laws and their claims on cultural understanding.

In part systolic, in part diastolic (the images are Schwab's), *La Renaissance orientale* is a virtual education in the meaning of intellectual adventure, a species of vital detective work that neglects neither the material clues nor the higher speculations involved in formulating general observations. Schwab's monumentality lies in never letting us doubt that philology, as he uses it in the large Nietzschean sense and studies it in the philological archaeology through which oriental texts were brought into European knowledge and consciousness, is the study of texts as constantly worked-upon monuments, arranging and rearranging the culture's sense of its identity. Recent studies of Romantic literature—as the world of Abrams, Bloom, Hartman, de Man—would find their inescapable underpinning in Schwab; for, as Romantic writing seems best understood as a prolonged investigation of language and poetic form constructing and deconstructing planes of meaning, Schwab's textual odyssey furnishes the necessary first material. If, after reading Schwab, there is not always an orderly path to be seen from words to forms, or from linguistic discovery to linguistic and aesthetic performance, the difficulty is that as students of literature we have not yet mastered the relationship between language in history and language as art. Schwab argues that the relationship is crucial, but his method rests on the dramatization, presented complexly and encyclopedically, of a cultural encounter, one whose driving force originates in the love of words, the web of textuality, the society of learning and cultural appropriation. Thus, rather than reading Schwab as a failed theorist, one would do best, I think, to appreciate his great scholarly achievement as providing an occasion for theoretical orientation and self-examination.

This new translation of Schwab's major work is therefore itself a major event in the history of scholarship, and puts before the English reader for the first time one of the truly extraordinary masterworks of cultural history and interpretation.

Notes

1. The three issues of *Mercure de France* are (July 1956), no. 1115, pp. 560–61; (December 1956) no. 1120, pp. 637–91 ("Homage à Raymond Schwab"); (February 1958) no. 1134, pp. 242–309 ("inedits de Raymond Schwab").

2. André Rousseaux, "Raymond Schwab et l'humanisme integrale," *Mercure de France* (December 1956), no. 1120, pp. 663–71.

3. *Ibid.*, p. 665.

4. Schwab, "Domaine Oriental," in *Encyclopédie de la Pleiade: Histoire des littéra-tures*. Volume I: *Littératures anciennes, orientales, et orales*, ed. by Raymond Que-neau (Paris: Gallimard, 1955), p. 213.

5. Schwab, "Au moins de coincidences," *Mercure de France* (February 1958), no. 1134, p. 299.

6. Schwab, *Vie d'Anquetil-Duperron suivie des Usages Civils et religieux des Parses par Anquetil-Duperron* (Paris: E. Leroux, 1934), p. 3.

7. *Ibid.*, p. 35.

8. *Ibid.*, p. 96.

9. *Ibid.*, p. 4.

10. *Ibid.*, p. 8.

11. *Ibid.*, p. 6.

12. *Ibid.*, p. 87.

13. *Ibid.*, p. 10.

14. Schwab, *La Vie d'Elémir Bourges* (Paris: Stock, 1948).

15. Schwab, *L'Auteur des Milles et une Nuits: Vie d'Antoine Galland* (Paris: Mer-cure de France, 1964), p. 17.

16. *Ibid.*, p. 40.

17. Schwab, "Au moins des coincidences," p. 298.

18. Schwab, "Domaine Oriental," p. 108.

Translators' Note

WE hope that the presentation in English of this landmark study in the history of ideas will help the American reader gain a clearer perspective on European and American relations with the Orient, and especially with oriental religious thought (which social critics of the past thirty years have assumed sprang, without antecedents, from the Beat Generation), and that such a perspective will help foster the global awareness which is a prerequisite for the integral humanism Schwab envisioned.

Because of advances in Asian studies in the thirty-odd years since the original publication of *La Renaissance orientale* and because of Schwab's own occasional carelessness, the book includes some particulars with which specialists in the domain will quibble, but these do not weaken the validity of Schwab's general arguments on the influx, interpretation, influence, and importance of oriental texts. The only changes we have felt impelled to make in the original are tracing fuller citations for critical works which Schwab employs, arranging the bibliography alphabetically and adding references to work done subsequent to the original publication (although a full bibliography of the subject would constitute an independent volume in itself), and, we hope, increasing the usefulness of the index by adding a few subject entries.

Over the years spent at this work, we have been encouraged by Robert D. Richardson, who first proposed the project to us, by the patient support of Jerry Carter and our families and friends, by the skillful assistance of Isabelle Chopin and Raja Gharbi, and by the editorial guidance of William F. Bernhardt and Karen Mitchell. Thanks to all of them the imperfections inherent in any translation are, in this case, no more numerous than they are: but the faults that remain we must, of course, reserve for ourselves.

It is to the memory of our friend Michael Pedigo that this work is inscribed.

VICTOR REINKING
GENE PATTERSON-BLACK

Seattle–Denver, April 1984

The Reason for This Book

FEW people today seem to have heard of Anquetil-Duperron or Sir William Jones or what they set out to accomplish in India in the eighteenth century, but they have drastically altered our ways of thinking nonetheless. Why, then, is the fact generally unknown? Historians of literature and ideas have thought this a subject reserved for orientalists, while orientalists in turn have abandoned such historical generalizations. Also, an odd prejudice, the report that nothing is to be gained from oriental studies, has stopped research. The truth is that, in seizing upon the treasures of the poor Orient, critics have grasped only superficial influences that conceal the real issues, which concern the destinies of the intellect and the soul.

The ability to decipher unknown alphabets, acquired in Europe after 1750, had one incalculable effect: the discovery that there had been other Europes. Thus, in that progressive era, the West perceived it was not the sole possessor of an admirable intellectual past. This singular event occurred during a period when everything else was likewise new, unprecedented, extraordinary. The advent of oriental studies during a Romantic period abounding in geniuses and accomplishments, in great appetites and abundant nourishment, is one of history's most astonishing coincidences.

Our age, heir in its turn to that one, supposes it will recommend itself to posterity by its meditations on knowledge and its taste for encyclopedic catalogs. So many prophets of doom cry out to our age of a world near its end that it feels itself susceptible to what has never moved it before. Now is the time to present to our age a phenomenon completely interwoven with its substance—to pack it into the baggage of memory, that hurried actress racing over her lines, so proud of her accuracies, that overburdened traveler who would transform the lost living into the unknown dead.

Around 1920, in response to a question posed by the great Elémir Bourges, I began looking into an obscure luminary called Anquetil-Duperron. Thus I set out on a long path which led me to perceive the birth of an integral humanism, a crucial, unprecedented chapter in the history of civilizations.

The research to which I found myself led has filled many notebooks, and many friendships, from Sylvain Lévy to Louis Renou and Jacques Duchesne-Guillemin, have strengthened it. In this book I hope to show as clearly and as fully as possible a decisive episode in the human adventure, not forgetting that the voice of poetry must not cease to be heard.

RAYMOND SCHWAB

THE ORIENTAL RENAISSANCE

Definitions

The Orient: Word and Idea

SOMETIMES qualified by "Near" or "Far," sometimes identified with Africa or Oceania, when not identified with Russia or Spain, the concept of "the East" has come full circle.[1] As Sylvain Lévi put it, since the world is round, what can this word mean? The term originated with the Roman empire which, true to its Hellenistic heritage, placed two blocs in opposition, "our world" against some vague Asia. It appeared in Virgil's *Aeneid* in the first century before Christ: "The people of the dawn, . . . Egypt and every power of the East." During the first century of the Christian era this *res orientales* reappeared in the *Historiarum Philippicarum* of Trogus Pompeius, and *Oriens* appeared in Tacitus' *Germania*. Thus the separation of the continents became official.

The separation lasted less than eighteen centuries. The effect of oriental studies was to undermine the wall raised between the two cultures; such studies fulfilled their real purpose by transforming the exile into a companion. However, the partition was dismantled in accordance with special interests and controversies, intellectual, spiritual, or political, in the West itself. More and more the concept of the Orient was drawn into polemics, pushed toward the right or the left, the top or the bottom of the map, depending on the disposition and the stakes of those who invoked it.

Rome adopted, along with her ambition for Macedonian conquest, the bitterness toward the East engendered by the Persian Wars. As she had with everything else, she added to it her own judicial and imperial power, her aptitude for entrenched situations, and her taste for permanent institutions, in which execration was not without practical usefulness in reducing the number of beneficiaries. This left a deep impression: contrary to popular opinion, in Christian Europe religious dogmatism was less of a barrier to oriental thought than Latin education.

Already for the Greeks, "barbarian" had meant "the inferior who does not speak as we do" or "one we cannot understand." In those days one repudiated other languages rather than learn them. In the same way, the Hebrews called the Egyptians "stutterers," the old Germans called their Polish enemies "mutes," and the Teutons called the Celts "unintelligible."[2] Nevertheless, one result of the Persian Wars was that Themistocles learned Persian, and learned it well. The adventures of Alexander brought his people, who spoke but a single language, into contact with a variety of Indo-Iranian tongues. What passed between victors and vanquished through the screen of interpreters is unknown. If the Greeks knew Sanskrit, they transmitted nothing of it to us. When a return flow introduced the "barbarians" into the West, we find, to the contrary, Menander of Ephesus, to whom Phoenician was native, Berosus of Babylonia, who read cuneiform, and Manetho, who read hieroglyphics, all writing in Greek. Alexandria, the first modern capital, became interested in foreigners, the Ptolemies promoted the Septuagint translation of the Bible into Greek, and perhaps a translation of the *Avesta* as well. And it was from Alexandria that the first grammatical theory passed to Rome.

In its turn Christianity, heir to Rome as Rome had been to Athens, at first merely endorsed the separation of East and West and later, owing to the Crusades, stressed it. In Saint Paul (Romans 1:14), "Greek" and "barbarian" are symetrically expressed as *sapiens* and *insipiens*. Not to know Greek is not to know. Nevertheless, the idea of humanism was appearing even while the world of letters was breaking apart. When the eighteenth century came to reinvent humanism for itself, it was as an idea it would use against its original founders. In his *Lectures on the Science of Language* (1:128), Max Müller stated:

Humanity is a word for which you look in vain in Plato or Aristotle; the idea of mankind as one family, as the children of God, is an idea of Christian growth; and the science of mankind, and of the languages of mankind, is a science which, without Christianity, would never have sprung into life. When people had been taught to look upon all men as brethern, then, and only then, did the variety of human speech present itself as a problem that called for a solution in the eyes of thoughtful observers; and I, therefore, date the real beginning of the science of language from the first day of Pentecost.

What a revolution! a religion where a feast-day and a mystery make the gift of languages a mark of the Spirit and of love.

Actually, as knowledge and ignorance themselves cannot be absolute, neither can the ignorance of one continent about another. But at exactly what point the Greek ignorance of Asia was dispelled by Alexander's companions we will probably never know. The scarcity of information that has reached us, primarily through Arrian, is no proof of a scarcity of linguistic contact, since many of the texts have been lost, mutilated, or distorted by intermediaries. At any rate, consequences of the Macedonian expedition emerged shortly, in the third century, in the empire of Ashoka: the dialogue of King Milinda (Menander) and the ascetic Nagasena is as clear a testimony to communication as is the art of Gandhara. As Sylvain Lévi put it, "Plotinus, Porphyry, and the entire school of Neoplatonists reflect the metaphysics of Kapila and Patanjali. Mani and the Gnostics introduced the Brahman and Buddhist spirit into Christianity, while a colony of Nestorians brought the Gospels to India."[3] Festugière has demonstrated that numerous Asian doctrines were current in Rome in the second century A.D., and Filliozat has shown that the Christianity of Saint Hippolytus rediscovered the spirit of the Upanishads and has emphasized the line of ancient communication between the West and the East.[4]

No one believes any longer that such communication is of recent date. The relative regularity of sailings and caravans has been proved by the significance attached to the discovery of the monsoon and of the silk and amber roads. The great navigators of the fifteenth century did not have to undertake their Asian voyages entirely uninformed. The reality and extent of the Hindu debt to Europe and of the Western debt to India were frequently discussed, especially in the nineteenth century. The preconception of India as "schoolmistress of the human race" was replaced for a time by one of India as an insular civilization and was, in turn, refuted by the facts. Later historians acknowledge, with Grousset, that analogous problems received quasi-universal solutions, and with Masson-Oursel, that throughout antiquity Europe and Asia were trustees-in-common of a shared estate, their explanations of the world representing two scarcely divergent branches of a common immemorial tradition, probably Sumerian in origin. For his part, Foucher, who unveiled Greco-Buddhist art, concluded that aesthetic problems had posed themselves in similar terms across a diversity of climates and epochs.

In the Middle Ages, Paris and the Italian republics had sought to lay out, from the legendary landscapes of William of Ruysbroeck and Marco Polo, and from the hopes centered on the mythical Prester John, the beginnings of a new geography. Neither commercial ventures nor the disconnected embassies, though they visited fabulous sites, developed such a body of knowledge. The Arabs, being better placed geographically and linguistically, learned more, but neither for their purposes nor through them to posterity came anything like the understanding necessary to topple the old barriers.

In its connotations perhaps no single word has been so loaded with emotion, even passion, as has the term "Orient." Depending on the thinkers involved, or even the phases of their thought, the word has evoked fascination, repulsion, and dread. It has been associated with the most diverse images. Each time that portion of the world called "the Orient" has expanded or contracted, changing its fauna and flora, reason has given way to bias, antipathy, or fear. Even when the images appeared to be neutral, the ubiquity of solar myth made the concept of "the Orient" again applicable to all lands outside our own, and it became the passkey to the creations of all the heavens in turn. The Orient served as alter ego to the Occident, and sometimes its alibi, as in Racine's famous verse "Dans l'Orient désert quel devint mon ennui!" ("In the lonely East, how great my weariness grew"). When Racine wrote *Bérénice* in 1670, he had talked with Bernier, who had recently returned from Syria, Persia, and India; yet Racine characteristically spoke of the East as Limousin, Pontoise, and the Palais-Royal.

For frail decor set in a theatrical Illyria, there is Mérimée, the oriental romancer. And where was Poe's Orient located? Barrès openly called *his* orient a "Levant"—that lovely semantic monster, the "Orient-Levant" doublet, implies that the sun does not rise in the same place in French as it does in Latin. The Latin term circles the globe, the other engenders an epithet of contempt, the confusion of languages thus nourishing the life and death of nations. The excessive tendency of the term "Orient" to take on all meanings has resulted in its being branded pejorative. The strangeness it offered at small cost produced an entire Orient of sofas and erotic and satiric masques that only too often encouraged literary history to frolic in shabby exoticism. Yet one conspicuous fact is still ignored: the true impact of the Orient on a Europe sprung from Romanticism is influential in an *entirely* different way from the impact of northern literature.

The Framework of This Book

In this book I would like to explore the importance of this profound Orient. Few people remember that the world, in the sense that we understand it, dates from the period and the events of which I shall be speaking. The writings deciphered by the orientalists made the world, for the first time in human history, a whole. With the establishment of oriental studies an entirely new meaning was introduced for the word "mankind." We can hardly imagine that the acquired meaning, which we take for granted, has not always been present in humanity's consciousness. Nevertheless, it is a young idea. Anquetil's arrival in India in 1754 and that of William Jones in 1783 seem unimportant events; yet because of these events the bases for many judgments became something they had never been before. Suddenly the partial humanism of the classics became the integral humanism that today seems natural to us. For so long merely Mediterranean, humanism began to be global when the scientific reading of Avestan and Sanskrit scripts unlocked innumerable unsuspected scriptures. The workshops of the linguists generated for Europe—along with several other ideas, some fruitful, some murderous—the notion that there had existed an intelligence and a soul apart from the European. Thus the West, on inquiring into the origins of poetry and philosophy, was brought to the problems of migratory peoples and of governing races.

All the orients were revivified, but not all were equally unforeseen. The Orient of the Bible had not ceased to exist in the life of Christian nations, but its complexion and its title would change. On the one hand its imagery, which made Voltaire smile, excited the imagination as it had not done since the poets of the Reformation. This was thanks to Chateaubriand and Herder, and to new interpretations which, in England and in Germany, established the Holy Scripture as a department of great primitive poetry, serving as a model for, and a virtual challenge to, learned poetry. On the other hand, the convention by which the Hebrew vocabulary was made to include all antiquity, a law of misinterpretation generally applied by the standard authors, was abolished. In this the influence of the decipherings and excavations played an important role: up to that time, biblical antiquity had been the most ancient past known; henceforward its priority would be a matter of contention. Moreover, the question of the millennium was to be remanded to the linguists and archaeologists. A newcomer, Assyriology, seriously challenged exegesis; nothing so critical of scriptural authority had previously appeared, not even with Richard Simon or Jean Astruc. The innovators themselves had started on the trail of lost scriptures solely to nourish theological controversy. All the discoveries of scriptures issued from this battle over Scripture. But although they totally changed the notion of the world and the shape of history, biblical studies, which had been the point of departure, lost the initiative for advance. Even after Saint-Martin and Quatremère opened the field of Aramaic studies, biblical studies fell into the background for a time in France. They no longer had a home, except at Strasbourg with Reuss, nor an exemplar, except in Renan. Hebrew was eclipsed by cuneiform.

The Islamic Orient is, for us, a companion almost as ancient and familiar as the biblical, at times reteaching us Hebrew through Arabic. It is the Orient most acclimated in our literary traditions, which have, in every case, abandoned other orients whenever there has been a massive return of the picturesque Mussulman whose charm recaptures poets and storytellers through the glamour of the *Thousand and One Nights*. In this domain a very important event occurred: the teaching of Arabic and Persian had become so empirical and so disorganized by the end of the eighteenth century that it was dying in an impasse until Silvestre de Sacy, the great architect of the new linguistics, raised the blockade by the invention of a scientific method. A proliferation of studies, and imitations, resulted. Arabia's growing concern for its pre-Islamic literature extended them, while Persia, once conquered by Arabia, took over the lead, exalting its own pre-Muslim ages through Avestan, Pahlavi, and cuneiform. It was from Persia, through Anquetil, that everything began to open up: with Persia as the base, everyone from scholars and politicians to polemicists built up the East-West parallel, and the number of discoveries multiplied, as did liaisons between scholarship and creativity. In 1819 *Muallaqat* and *ghazal* passed into general circulation in Goethe's *West-Ostliche Divan*. Saadi influenced Desbordes-Valmore, Victor Hugo adopted the Firdausi of Julius von Mohl into his ideography, and the Omar Khayyam of Fitzgerald took over the customers for Marcus Aurelius.

At the same time that Sacy was establishing Persian studies, Chinese studies were being decisively inaugurated by Abel Rémusat, who was granted a chair at the Collège de France in 1814. Chinese came to exert an attraction analogous to that of Persian on the Europe of scholars, students, and literati. Nevertheless, for quite some time the China of novels and the theater would be the only one to influence thought and forms. This is only too clear from Théophile and Judith Gautier, father and daughter, down to even Mallarmé. Because of its loftiness, and its sheer size, Chinese thought remained the most difficult peak for Europe to scale. China's linguistic instrument appeared in a formidable solitude, bewildering the mental habits of the West, rendering the problem of equivalences among languages almost absurd, and refusing to allow its closed system to be drawn into the comparative school. Perhaps the most serious of civilizations, it would remain the last from which only the ceremonious could be extracted. China had had a long history in Europe, but it had been too much represented by folding screens, porcelains, and banalities. The lure of its ethics would be necessary before Confucius, Lao Tzu, the *Book of History*, and the *Book of Songs*, were included in reference books and catalogs. Western craftsmen would only slowly rework the hard porphyry figure of China. Chinese philosophy, which is essentially and historically the one most closely connected with Indian philosophy, was then hardly suspected and would be the last to be studied.

India itself had never appeared other than forbidding and inaccessible: thus the revelation of it proved overwhelming, decisive, irresistible. The prestige that India, of all the orients, enjoyed among the Romantics arose from the fact that it posed, in its totality, the great question of the Different. Unlike a unique model, India had always known the same problems as we, but had not approached them in the same ways. It presented, as had been seen only once before in the history of mankind, a past that was not dead but remained "an antiquity of today" and always. Consequently, India came to be distinguished not from Persia, China, or Judea but from Egypt and Assyria, and from the Rome and Greece of which so many emperors and revolutionaries had boasted themselves the revivers, although they were merely taxidermists.

As a complete world that can be placed alongside the Greco-Roman heritage, there is none other. A whole world that had been entirely lost became, within a few years, completely known. For the first time the image of India regally entered the configuration of the universe. Except perhaps in those times drowned in legend, when more rumor than information would have reached him, a "cultivated" man would not necessarily have included India in his considerations of the cosmos. Judea would have been included because of biblical tradition; Persia because of wars and its traditions of magic; Arabia because of its conquests and physicians, the Crusades and the schoolmen; and, for the last two hundred years, China, seemingly because of the missions. The Indic world alone remained behind its wall. And then, in a single wave, it poured forth. One came to know more and more what to think about it, and subsequently one no longer knew what to think about it.

India is an entity incomparable in its cohesion and its general level of maturity, in "the eternal in its present," and its power to embrace simultaneously several ages of humanity and to engage so many interests concurrently: metaphysics and great poetry, theology and linguistics. From the first, Sanskrit claimed the lion's share of the efforts at decipherment. It attracted qualified travelers who returned from the study of Sanskrit closer to themselves even when no closer to it. A whole picture was presented to an age to which nothing was reliable unless complete. The concerns of the countries where this picture was presented, be they concerns for sham primitivism or for the idealism and pantheism awakened by mystical doctrines or by the occult, colored all aspects of a totality that unlocked chapters to which Greek dialectics alone had been thought to have the key, and enabled a dialogue with Christianity to begin that was unprecedented and not lacking in gentleness. We never hear of any European converting to Zoroastrianism; yet Hinduism and Christianity were to exert curious attractions on each other. Gandhi's martyrdom has led spiritual men in the West to reexamine their ideas of saintliness, and it is worth knowing when and how such possibilities began.

This newly found past began to revolutionize the present in 1771 when Anquetil-Duperron published the *Zend Avesta*, the first time anyone had succeeded in breaking into one of the walled languages of Asia. Thirty years later the event bore fruit when William Jones and his companions at Calcutta founded the first Asiatic Society, in Bengal, and made the first translations of authentic Sanskrit texts. Linguistic breakthroughs then followed at an almost unbelievable tempo. The first half of the nineteenth century resounded with achievements that have today become forgotten secrets. The year 1875 seems a kind of boundary line after which few, if any important revelations occurred in the regions that concern me. The Orient's share, and particularly India's, seems fixed by then, at least in what pertains to the classification of knowledge and the consolidation of a humanistic base, by publications that summed up an era: Theodor Benfy's *Geschichte der Sprachwissenschaften Orientalischen Philogie in Deutschland* (*History of Linguistics and Oriental Philology in Germany*) appeared in Munich in 1869. In Paris a "Bibliothèque Orientale" was added in 1870 to a series entitled "Chefs-d'oeuvre de l'Esprit humain." In 1875 the Sacred Books of the East series, edited by Max Müller, began to appear in England, making the texts accessible to everyone. And in 1876 James Fergusson published in London a *History of Indian and Eastern Architecture*, the third volume of his *History of Architecture in All Countries*. On the other hand, the closing of this heroic age was marked by two opposite phenomena. In 1868 the Ecole des Hautes Etudes was founded, and permitted Indic studies to enter its curriculum in the classes of Bergaigne and Barth. Having gained general acceptance, the new humanism began to specialize more narrowly, each diverse discipline within Indic studies beginning to analyze its own acquisitions more thoroughly. The other occurrence, on which it is not necessary to dwell, was the appearance, again in 1875, of the Theosophical Society of Madame Blavatsky.[5]

Probably no demarcation can avoid being arbitrary unless it avoids the systematic; it may be that we will have to cast our line a little beyond these limits. What we cannot reproduce is the great shock with which a whole buried world arose to unsettle the foremost minds of an age, minds which knew that millennia-old cryptographies could be deciphered, how to do it, and what could be obtained through the secrets originating in these subterranean crypts. We can continue to be surprised by everything humankind may have been, but never again can we know that first surprise which came at a moment when, of all man's explorations, humanism alone had not yet had its Columbus, Copernicus, or Newton. It is no minor point that this virgin territory too was entered at the beginning of the nineteenth century when, on all sides, the physical and natural sciences were exploding.

Part One

THE PHENOMENON

CHAPTER ONE

There Is an Oriental Renaissance

A<small>N</small> Oriental Renaissance—a *second* Renaissance, in contrast to the first: the expression and the theme are familiar to the Romantic writers, for whom the term is interchangeable with Indic Renaissance. What the expression refers to is the revival of an atmosphere in the nineteenth century brought about by the arrival of Sanskrit texts in Europe, which produced an effect equal to that produced in the fifteenth century by the arrival of Greek manuscripts and Byzantine commentators after the fall of Constantinople.

"The Oriental Renaissance" is the title Edgar Quinet gives to an important chapter in his *Génie des religions* (1841) that celebrates this event. He compares the roles of Anquetil and Jones to that of Lascaris, and compares the happy discovery of the Hindu manuscripts to that of the *Iliad* and the *Odyssey.* "In the first ardor of their discoveries, the orientalists proclaimed that, in its entirety, an antiquity more profound, more philosophical, and more poetical than that of Greece and Rome was emerging from the depths of Asia." Quinet saw, like his German masters to whom the allusion here is clear, that the Oriental Renaissance marked the close of the neoclassical age just as the Classical Renaissance had marked the close of the medieval age, and that, in the same way, it promised "a new Reformation of the religious and secular world." The imagination is staggered. "This is the great subject in philosophy today." he continues. "In the Oriental Renaissance the pantheism of the Orient, transformed by Germany, corresponds to the idealism of Plato as amended by Descartes which, in the seventeenth century, crowned the Greek and Latin Renaissance."

Extending beyond the circles of specialists, here was an issue of one of the world's great agitations, and it was addressed by the literary innovators of Romanticism: "Today, for a thousand reasons, all of which foster progress, the Orient is of more concern than it has ever been before. Never before have oriental studies been explored so deeply. In the century of

Louis XIV one was a Hellenist: today one is an Orientalist. This is a great step forward. Never before have so many minds probed the great abyss of Asia at one time. Today we have a scholar assigned to every oriental idiom from China to Egypt. As a result of this, the Orient—as an image or as an idea—has become for the intellect as well as for the imagination a sort of general preoccupation, to which the author of this book has succumbed, perhaps without realizing it." Thus in the preface to *Orientales* the young Hugo creates with each word a tangible reality.

The Orient of the poems that follow is much less precise than this Orient of the preface, although there too the poet benefited from the guidance of Fouinet, who provided him with the abundant and skillful documentation on Arabic and Persian literature that Hugo scattered throughout his footnotes. But to pinpoint the developments in oriental studies between the China of Rémusat and the Egypt of Champollion so precisely, and especially to proclaim an Oriental Renaissance with such assurance, required more comprehensive information, closer to the heart of the controversy. Volney could not have been Hugo's source, as Guimbaud has suggested, because he did not carry the necessary weight; moreover, Volney had died before Champollion made his discovery. The intermediary has to have been someone especially interested in the development that unhesitatingly tied the destiny of oriental studies to the destiny of Romanticism.

Writing of himself in the preface to *Orientales,* Hugo stated: "He gave himself over to the poetry that came. . . . He seemed to see in it, shining from afar, a great poetry. It was a spring at which he had long wanted to slake his thirst. There, in effect, everything was great, rich, fruitful, as in the Middle Ages, that other sea of poetry. But since he says so implicitly, why shouldn't he say it explicitly? Until now, it seems to him, the modern age has been seen too much in terms of the century of Louis XIV and antiquity in terms of Rome and Greece. Would we not have a higher and broader view of the modern age by studying the Middle Ages, and of the ancient world by studying the Orient?"

This passage faithfully reflects several of the tenets dear to the Baron Eckstein, who was meticulous in convincing Hugo of them in the course of their conversations. It is Eckstein who invited French poets to imbibe "unexpected inspirations" from "two prolific springs"—the Orient and the Middle Ages. Two years before *Orientales,* Eckstein had written in his journal *Le Catholique*: "Oriental literature will become, for superior minds, what Greek literature was for the scholars of the sixteenth century." Eckstein also seems to have been responsible for the striking theories that in the same year sparked the preface to *Cromwell.* After 1823 he was in contact with Hugo, who was impressed by his knowledge of so-called folk poetry and who quoted Eckstein in an epigraph in *Han d'Islande.*[1]

This combination of the Orient with the Middle Ages enabled Romanticism to dismiss the centuries of Augustus and Louis XIV. Since this kind of communication explains the extraordinary success of the philological revolution, it is worth knowing that Eckstein had received his commission to promote an Oriental Renaissance from Friedrich Schlegel, his master and idol, who, after 1800, published the charter for an alliance between erudition and poetry in the *Athenaeum:* "We must seek the supreme romanticism in the Orient" (Im Orient müssen wir das höchste Romantische suchen). At the time, Schlegel did not yet know Sanskrit. After he learned it, he again formulated the program of the new Renaissance, this time in his celebrated *Uber die Sprache und Weisheit der Indier* in 1808: "May Indic studies find as many disciples and protectors as Germany and Italy saw spring up in such great numbers for Greek studies in the fifteenth and sixteenth centuries, and may they be able to do as many things in as short a time. The Renaissance of antiquity promptly transformed and rejuvenated all the sciences; we might add that it rejuvenated and transformed the world. We could even say that the effects of Indic studies, if these enterprises were taken up and introduced into learned circles with the same energy today, would be no less great or far-reaching." Completing the parallel between the two renaissances, James Darmesteter said in his *Essais orientaux* that he had scarcely ever seen, outside the manifesto of DuBellay and the Pleiade, the equivalent of Schlegel's essay in literary history.

Sanskrit was the providential answer—suddenly provided by luck on the part of the searchers—to the German Romantics' long appeals for the light of the Orient. (In the year of Schlegel's essay, Othmar Frank dedicated his *Das Licht vom Orient* to Napoleon.) Through Sanskrit came the material destined to fill in the preliminary outlines of the philosophy of history. The latter discipline had been established in 1784—the year the Asiatic Society of Calcutta was formed—by Herder's *Ideen zur Philosophie der Geschichte der Menschheit,* which acknowledged the "Orient, soil of God, rightly elected for this purpose."

In 1808 Anquetil's posthumously published commentary on *Viaggio alle Indie orientali* by Paulinus a Sancto Bartholomaeo [Johann Philipp Wesdin] also repeated the assertion: "We stand, in relation to Sanskrit, where Europe stood in relation to Greek at the time of the fall of Constantinople and to Hebrew at the time of Luther's Reformation." Ten years later Schopenhauer, acknowledging all that his ideas owed to Anquetil, wrote in the preface to *Die Welt als Wille und Vorstellung:* "Sanskrit literature will be no less influential for our time than Greek literature was in the fifteenth century for the Renaissance." It was decidedly a time for one of the great events of the mind, an event quite different from either the invention of a technical linguistics or a literary fantasy, as we so often call it today; for there is evidence that beyond the technicians and the literary men the idea of an Oriental Renaissance was an established commonplace of the time. For example, in February 1825, the director of the Imprimerie Royale, in a report supporting a request for funds, used the Oriental Renaissance as an argument.

A small selection of quotations will serve, I think, to enlighten those of our contemporaries who are still persuaded that the Orient of the Romantics was a simple game. "We are today in a period analogous to the Renaissance. In some vague way, everyone is beginning to feel this truth." This time the witness comes from a different quarter, for this passage opens an important article that Pierre Leroux published in the Saint-Simonian *Revue Encyclopédique* in April 1832, and to which he gave the significant title "De l'influence philosophique des études orientales." His "in some vague way" corresponds to the "general scope" of which Schlegel speaks, and to Hugo's "general preoccupation," and is worth all the particulars. Further, Leroux sees in the publications from Calcutta "Homer being brought to Italy at the fall of Constantinople." The consequences of this new knowledge for Christian and rationalist alike are what Leroux considers important.

Scholarly milieus and literary salons, each conscious of participating in a prodigious change that seemed to sweep all causes along in the same current, formed a single world, and spoke of the change through the artist. In 1836 the poet Jean Jacques Ampère, who was also a prophet and propagator of this Renaissance, wrote in *Revue des Deux-Mondes:* "The vast and mysterious Orient solicits and attracts more and more minds." In his *Vingts-sept ans d'histoire des études orientales* the orientalist Mohl offered this information about Ampère: "At a time when the Romantic school had seized all the young minds in France and, with incomparable ardor, promoted the study of the literatures of all peoples to find new forms there, Ampère and his friend Fauriel, who were among the founders of this movement, threw themselves into the study of oriental literatures."

Too often we forget that to approach India then seemed a prerequisite for a profound understanding of humanity. Like Schlegel, Eckstein, Ampère, and Fauriel, Barchou de Penhoën studied Sanskrit out of a love of ideas. Barchou, Balzac's classmate and friend in later life, repeated the theme in 1840. For him, fusing oriental wisdoms with our own would open "a new phase in the development of the human spirit." Since he was thoroughly acquainted with the new German historians and metaphysicians, whose works he had translated and published commentaries on, Barchou was well qualified to confirm Quinet's statement, "It is difficult to imagine any of the great German philosophical systems if one subtracts the [oriental] element."

Another of the Saint-Simonian publications, the *Encyclopédie moderne*, pointed to the wider ramifications of nascent oriental studies in all domains of thought and spirit. In 1842, in his long and thoughtful "Essai sur l'histoire de l'érudition orientale" (which Burnouf recommended to Michelet in an 1849 letter as the best work on the subject), Louis Dussieux began with the axiom "Oriental erudition is the complement of the Renaissance." Thus the humanists' long prohibition against looking beyond Greece for fear of running into barbarism, and the clerics' against looking beyond Judea for fear of running into idolatry, ends in the West. Some rather surprising events had occurred coincidentally within a short span: a spiritualist revival, the outburst of historical studies, the English conquest of Bengal, and the French expedition to Egypt. In such ways the soul of Europe was carried toward an unknown future. An acute observer such as Camille Jullian could perceive the extent of the thing: "Ancient France, Egypt, Asia, all the worlds that Greek and Latin antiquity had blotted from our memory, were at once revived. The Romanticism of 1820 was, like the Humanism of 1520, a Renaissance."

Throughout the entire century, no popularizer—whether it was the *Dictionnaire des sciences philosophiques* (1843), Emile Burnouf translating the *Nala* (1856), the Larousse *Grand Dictionnaire du XIXe siècle* (1874), or Jean Lahor concluding his *Historie de la littérature hindoue* (1888)—could refrain from repeating this article of faith: one was in the midst of a Renaissance and, like the first, it not only enriched the index of knowledge; it determined lines of thought. Many continue to think it necessary to study this major phenomenon in all its instructive detail if we would arrive at the most profound—rather than simply the most picturesque—understanding of the nineteenth century. When Pierre Martino's *L'Orient dans la littérature française au XVIIe et XVIIIe siècle* appeared in 1906 ignoring these views, Lanson's review in *Revue d'histoire littéraire de la France* called for a historical account of the successive understandings of India acquired, and Brunetière, in his "L'Orient dans la littérature française" the following year, called for "a history, sometimes anecdotal and sometimes almost heroic, of the deciphering of those sacred or mysterious writings that were, a hundred years ago, nothing but a dead letter." Brunetière confirmed the opinion of many predecessors: "The contact with oriental matters" had, in his eyes, "profoundly modified the French mind." The nineteenth century, and even the eighteenth, would not have been all they were "if the things of the East and the Far East—from India and China specifically—had not formed part of the composition of their spirit."

There is today a need to reawaken these forgotten beliefs. When the idea of an Oriental Renaissance is advanced today, there is curiosity about what is meant. People no longer know—or perhaps do not yet know—

with what consequences or by what means an unimagined mass of knowledge merged with their general view of life, disrupting it and changing the entire mental landscape within a few years. Not long ago I came across a quotation from Thibaudet that was one of those useful formulas one need only reverse in order to get at the truth: the arrival of the Orient among the Romantics had been of less importance than the discovery of Alpine scenery by Rousseau or of the American landscape by Chateaubriand. It was a serviceable masterkey: "The Orient gave nothing to Romantic thought, although it haunted everyone's imagination."

Gave nothing to Romantic thought? We shall see.

The Dimensions of the Event

Only after 1771 does the world become truly round; half the intellectual map is no longer a blank. In other words, this is not a second Renaissance but the first, belatedly reaching its logical culmination. Ficino's humanism was crippled to the extent that it was not so inclusive as Anquetil's. Thrice already had Europe discovered oriental Asia, but each time our "Mediterranean classicisms" had, according to Grousset, wanted only to find there "analogous classicisms." Here is one of the rare times when the forming of a new atmosphere can be perceived: as a result of certain repeated conjunctions of personnel and resources, a thrust in the unconscious of one or two generations, little by little a widening historical vision expanded the horizon of creative thinkers and allowed a reminting of the current coin of ideas. Henceforth the world would be one where Sanskrit and linguistics, even for those unaware of them, would have changed the images peopling time and space.

From at least the time of Herodotus to perhaps the time of Montaigne, when humanity was discussed it was a family matter inside a hermetic little Mediterranean room. Since then it has become a banality to remind Europe she is a small promontory of Asia. I say "perhaps" until Montaigne because savages were becoming an inconvenient constraint on his generalizations—but then, they were still "savages." The great question facing civilized man for three centuries would be knowing where the savage began and ended, and which of the two events was the worthier. It is a variant on the question of the "barbarian," but it reverses the terms of choice—a serious choice in that it involves questions of idolatry and the pagan, notions which themselves are soon subject to revision. These crosscurrents greatly stirred the air breathed by Voltaire, Rousseau, Diderot, and after them, Herder and the Romantics. And, dare we say, the debate is not closed yet.[2]

Although their adventures had opened perspectives primarily on war and trade, everyone knows how much we owe to the fifteenth-century navigators. We seldom remember that it was only at the end of the eighteenth century that the orientalists, making use of new channels, brought back a view of humanity different from that of the gold-hunters and the slave merchants. Formerly the only humanity had been the one reported by missionaries and already depicted. When Vasco de Gama landed at Goa, the Zamorin asked him what he was seeking; he answered, "Christians and spices." It is not quite two hundred years since the human race ceased to be divided between a center of civilization, great, like a dilated point, and the vast and contemptible unknown. This division was, moreover, contrary to the Christian ideal, which in order to function in the world, and to do so in other guises, had to unite all the unknowns to the knowns *through a common origin.* This extraordinary and decisive reconciliation was, for the first time, brought about by a wholly new work of human genius: *the deciphering of lost writings.* Until that point, humanity had lacked three-quarters of its past, and missionaries and laymen vied in the research that would determine who would plant his flag there.

The 1771 edition of the *Zend Avesta* marks the first approach to an Asian text totally independent of the biblical and classical traditions. The history *of* languages and history *through* languages both begin with this work, which is also, we could say, the beginning of world history. At first only probable, such history became certain and irrevocable when, in 1784, the first Indic scholars began the reading of Sanskrit and published, in 1785, a translation of the *Bhagavad Gita.* From the dawn of time a harvest had been ripening whose hour had come. One would think, as I have written elsewhere *[Vie d'Anquetil-Duperron],* that the ten centuries following the Gothic invasions worked exclusively to provide the elements needed for a conception of the world. The times were swarming with navigators, scholiasts, collectors, and moralists who equipped themselves with a patchwork image of men from all times and countries, and who unwittingly heralded the census of all humanity from which modern man seeks self-understanding. Now the task that had been glimpsed by Herodotus and Plutarch, and announced by Montaigne and Voltaire, could be undertaken: the comparison of us with everyone else. Here the ancient "wonders" of lotus-eaters and mermen ended: the final "fabulous" discovery would be that of human multiplicity.

The millennial multitudes exhumed by the philologists were the forerunners of all the ideas concerning "the masses." The growth in communications visibly reduced the size of the world, and would have had much less effect on international relations if the most ancient extremities of the world had not already been united in the universities. Linguistic fundamentals, mechanical invention, and political revolutions all appeared simultaneously, and the whole would have been crippled had any one of these elements been lacking. It was logically inevitable that a civilization believing itself unique would find itself drowned in the sum total of civilizations, just as personal boundaries would be swamped by overflowing mobs and dislocations of the rational. All this together was called Romanticism, and it produced, through its many re-creations of the past, the present that propels us forward. Thus in the end the unprecedented prestige of history summoned from the past the justification—whether racial struggle or class revenge—for all those changes in the poor that are called revolutions. Less than fifty years after his fellow countrymen were astonished that one could be Persian, Anquetil taught them to compare Persian works with Greek ones. Before him only the Latin, Greek, Jewish, and Arab writers spoke reliably of ancient times. The Bible was an aerolite; the whole universe of sacred writings could be held in one hand. Anquetil cast into that universe a suspicion of the untold; he said that "the common sense of the universe" could no longer be confined between the northern borders of Spain and Denmark, on the one hand, nor between England and the western edge of Turkey on the other.

Wherever oriental studies established themselves as an authentic discipline, they profited from serious and widespread curiosity, and increased it. As I have remarked in my life of Anquetil, "The Orient was no longer a fantasy of blasé cosmopolitans who turned their gaze toward faraway places; the *Thousand and One Nights* and its imitators were not sufficient to quench the thirst for the exotic, and a nature closer to the pristine was henceforth to be sought in Surat as well as in Tahiti. At the same time, antiquity ceased to be the subject of compilations of conjectures or a pantry of commonplaces. It rose from the earth in the form of restored cities where the shadow of human endeavor could be followed anew. Between the appearance of Bernard de Montfaucon's *Antiquité expliquée et representée en figures* in 1719 and that of Winckelmann's *Thoughts on the Imitation of Greek Works in Painting and Sculpture* in 1755, knowledge acquired through reading was suddenly transformed by knowledge acquired through the handling of actual objects, objects for which an active search had been made. This is the point at which the mania for excavation broke out. In 1753, Robert Wood published *The Ruins of Palmyra, otherwise Tedmor, in the Desert*. In 1757 the expanded edition of *Observations sur les antiquités d'Herculanum* by Charles Cochin and Jérôme Bellicard was published, with great fanfare. Between the two, in 1754, Anquetil left for India. Only in that same year did the Englishman James Stuart and the Frenchman Julian Leroy begin, independently, the methodical exploration of Greece. As early as 1759 Anquetil proposed extending the methods of these scientific expeditions to the other three continents, and it is through him that the mysterious dimensions encompassed by the vagueness of the term 'Orient' were repatriated from the empire of hearsay and from the wings of court theater. As the first pickax fell on lavas that Pliny had watched flow, Anquetil bounded to the other end of the ancient world, which was not termed antiquity and scarcely the world."

After examining a sample of Sanskrit characters sent from Oxford, which no scholar in Europe could read, Anquetil thought to go to India to trace the secret of this unknown writing. This inspiration, this stroke of genius, was "Columbus' egg" for linguistics. Anquetil left, convinced that he would bring back something to establish scientifically the primacy of the Chosen People and the chronology of the Bible. However, an entirely different faction also kept an eye on him with, as Quinet says, "a desire to find in the ancient Orient a society to rival the Hebraic one." What machinery Anquetil would set in motion between these well-ordered armies of the spirit! All notions concerning revelation and civilization would be reexamined. When an age of exoticism outgrows curio-collecting and the boldness of the laboratories supplements the daring of the libraries, the result is inevitable: although something is always happening, from time to time there is a "watershed" whose effect can no longer be denied. If history gives to posterity the power to restore coherence and purpose to what was only confusion in the eyes of contemporaries, rarely have the heirs been so able as then to analyze the composition of the air left for them to breathe.

The aged Chateaubriand was disturbed that he could no longer recognize the heaven of his youth. As he stated in *Mémoires d'outre-tombe*, not only had travelers' explorations changed it, but "history [has] made discoveries reaching back to the dawn of time, and sacred languages have allowed their lost vocabularies to be read." Among the upheavals created by linguistics—an invention of technicians—we should remember this one: the continent of the Hindus, the Chinese, and the Sumerians regained—with all the grandeur of its metaphysical tradition, which we had rediscovered, and with all the weight of its intellectual seniority, which we had unveiled—the power to question us. Through the authority of its age, Asia suddenly began to seem again an equal in modern controversies. For example, would there have been a Ramakrishna without William Jones or independence for India without Gandhi?

Let us delve further. Sylvain Lévi has remarked austutely: "The definitive break between the Orient and the Occident dates from the Renaissance. The ancient world is, after all, so narrow that it easily lends itself to a vision of unity." The Middle Ages still dreamed of a universal monarchy of pope and emperor. Bossuet's *Discours sur l'histoire universelle* in the seventeenth century does not exceed the boundaries of the City of God as Saint Augustine defined them, and wantonly ignores the traditions of India, of Tibet, of China, and of Japan reported by the missionaries. Not since the humanist Renaissance substituted the "mystique of progress" for that of salvation had the past so helped to mold the future. And this in itself meant nothing until 1749, when Rousseau, provoked by an academic question, discovered and proclaimed that real progress is not ahead of man but behind him. Pascal, referring to Bacon's old comparison of the human species with the human individual, had already declared that the alleged ancients were, in fact, the adolescents of history. But Pascal's inspiration was to add that as both the individual and humanity mature, they turn their backs on this fact. To them the primitive is the ideal human type. We begin by positing with Rousseau that the savage, this unknown man, is the good man. We end by not arguing with Spencer that the primitive man who is man's touchstone is also the Stone Age Man. A hundred percent or zero percent human, he is the same primitive.

These tenets, blossoming in Romanticism, assisted the spread of Indic studies incalculably. And India—this was the legendary land of naked sages! These two qualities had been united by the Greeks in a single word—gymnosophists—that through the centuries had perpetuated an image that was rediscovered intact. The second Renaissance for a large part of its history would be variations on the word "primitive." Each time someone touched buried cities and indecipherable texts, he claimed to have uncovered the cradle of humanity, the important thing being to restore its youth to a humanity overwhelmed by the notion of its advanced age *(haute-époque)*. Having done this, one can solicit from these rediscovered civilizations—whether we are, like Chateaubriand, faithful or, like Volney, skeptical—arguments to buttress or demolish faith.

CHAPTER TWO
Establishing the Texts

The First Stages of Oriental Studies

IN a paper read before the Institut de France around 1810, Lanjuinais stated: "Until the discovery of the Cape of Good Hope in 1498, Europeans knew almost nothing about India. Before that they had had only fragmentary information from Greek and Latin writers, and even after the discovery of India they had only what the Portuguese could obtain through native interpreters." Still, the first Renaissance had in Camões a great poet to proclaim the Indic conquest, as did the second Renaissance in the Walt Whitman of "Passage to India." Only a few Westerners, however, were able to approach the Indian world so long as it was rendered inaccessible by Mughal despotism. Through sheer ignorance, Felix Lacôte says in "L'Indianism," "Europeans doubted that ancient India was worth the trouble of knowing. This was a tenacious prejudice against which Warren Hastings still had to struggle in the last quarter of the eighteenth century." But by 1832, Wilhelm Schlegel was able to praise his own century for having learned more about India than "the twenty-one centuries since Alexander the Great."

Around 1700, oriental studies consisted of nothing more—or only little more—than the study of Hebrew for theologians (who were further and further removed from it) and the study of Arabic, Persian, and Turkish for interpreters bound for settlements in the Levant. Beyond that there were a few scraps of Chinese that the missionaries had collected with difficulty and, at intervals, a few rare dialects of Asia Minor that were of interest to exegetes or grammarians. Such studies themselves had declined. To find instruction in Hebrew, Arabic, or Persian, one had to go to Switzerland—or to Holland, as Anquetil was obliged to do. There, in the province of Utrecht, the schools of "the old Catholics" preserved the tradition in the course of training students for the apostolate, for Levantine consulates, or for colonial trading centers in India, Persian being at that time the commercial and diplomatic language of central Asia. Hebrew had never been taught in Paris except at the Sorbonne. The oriental languages appear to have been virtually banished from Paris, first with the Huguenots, then with the Jansenists, in whose sanctuaries they survived. A curious affinity persisted between Jansenism and orientalism, as can be seen in the nineteenth century in Sacy, Lanjuinais, Quatremère, and Garcin de Tassy. Moreover, Sacy's career demonstrated that in Holland, as in Germany, Islamic studies were dead at the end of the eighteenth century.

An important French incunabulum of orientalism is the *Bibliothèque Orientale, ou Dictionnaire universel . . . des Peuples de l'Orient* (Paris, 1697), compiled by Barthélemy d'Herbelot, who knew a remarkable number of languages for his time: Hebrew, Arabic, Persian, Turkish, and Syriac. He was singled out and patronized for this knowledge by Fouquet and later by Colbert. D'Herbelot's prodigious work, which nourished the imaginations of Hugo and Nerval, was of continuing value to his successors. It was published after his death by the first of these successors, Antoine Galland, the translator and editor of *Mille et une Nuits,* published between 1704 and 1708. The world of d'Herbelot's *Bibliothèque Orientale* was very much of a piece with the empire of the caliphs in Galland's *Thousand and One Nights.* The best information on Arabic and Persian matters and on diverse aspects of Islam could be found in d'Herbelot's book, although its field was limited in two ways: beyond Baghdad the information was no longer drawn from primary sources, and prior to Muhammad the information relied on tradition, fables, or the Western classics.

Put another way, the Orient of which this book was the "library" lacked the very aspects that especially characterize that area today in our eyes: remoteness, nobility, and a sense of the archaic. The *Bibliothèque Orientale* was similar to the books of William Postel, and d'Herbelot seems a mind of the same lineage as Postel, whom Galland mentions in his preface. For matters beyond Islam or before the Hegira, d'Herbelot had little more than second-hand references at his disposal. The few articles devoted to India or to Persia before the Arab conquest (those on *Anberkend, Beth, Brahma,* and *Abesta,* for example) were very short reviews derived from Koranic compilers, except for some information d'Herbelot was able to glean from conversations with his friend Bernier. Until the beginning of the nineteenth century, when one said "oriental languages" one meant "Semitic languages" exclusively, and the Hebrew and Arabic branches came to mind. It was this limited linguistic and intellectual landscape that would be opened up, one could really say to infinity, with the dramatic rediscovery of Sanskrit.

Both geographically and historically, what had been lacking through the

centuries and would come to dominate everything was cultural disso-
nance, a sense of *the dissident*. The known world had been wholly classical
before 1800. Or, in a sense, it had been a *classified* world. Homer was simultaneously the essential beginning and the culmination. Moreover, Ci-
ceronian standards and Horatian models were handled with greater assurance. These fruits of the classical era accorded with the wisdom that
prevailed before 1800 and culminated in a Cartesianism that had absolutely no faith in the Different: "Although there may have been as many
reasonable men among the Persians and the Chinese as among us, it seems
most useful to me to adapt myself to those among whom I am destined
to live" *(Discourse on Method)*. Both Montesquieu, although he scoffed at
his countrymen, and Voltaire, although he adapted what was useful to
his polemic, thought along the same lines. The sons of the first Renaissance needed time to extend the critical spirit into the most secure bas-
tions of universal agreement, the end of a civilization being necessary before it can develop a taste for its origins. Thus, at the moment when a
thirst for discord was spreading throughout Europe, fomenting the crises
that spawned political revolution, oriental studies, masses fundamentally
at odds with the West, began their own revolt.

It was a sign of the times that Nicolas Perron sought to revive d'Herbelot in the 1830s. Perron had gone to Egypt with the Saint-Simonians to
direct the new medical school established there by Muhammad Ali. While
there, Perron learned Arabic and Persian, steeped himself in oriental literatures, and later acted as guide for the traveler Nerval. According to
Maxime du Camp, "Perron wanted to update d'Herbelot's *Bibliothèque
Orientale*; that is, he wanted to add to it all the traditions and facts that
had been discovered in the century since its publication."[1] But Perron was
unable to locate a publisher.

What is surprising is the velocity with which this demanding, disturbing, and unique concept made its breakthrough. Its threefold mystical
prestige gained the interest of theologians, revolutionaries, and artists. For
the Romantics, the discovery of what was essentially foreign always began with the discovery of what was most primitive. In oriental matters,
the primitive was first discovered in the *Avesta* of ancient Persia, then in
the Vedas of India, and later still in the works of Egypt and Assyria.

In whatever region, the initial condition must be found before imagination can patiently reconstruct historical series. One proceeds directly to
the boundary line of the ancient, and that is the starting point for redes-
cending the ladder of time. Only at a later stage of knowledge will a reverse movement move us back up past the first glimpses of the primitive,
to arrive at a conception of its undefined predecessors. The same movement added to the admiration felt for the successes of the linguists, for

from the very beginning they had attacked the bedrock that seemed most defiant of the pick.

The case of India is always the most striking. At the end of the eighteenth century, the gracious, "baroque" India of *Shakuntala* (James Darmesteter compared Kalidasa to Marivaux in his conceits) offered an ideal footbridge for the first steps of the eighteenth century. Goethe was, along with Herder, one of the few emancipated enough to cross it. By and large, however, the builders of the bridge between East and West allowed this span to topple. There had been a good deal of expostulation against *Shakuntala*, but the reaction to the *Bhagavad Gita*, first translated at the instigation of the pandits, was quite different. In his opening lecture of 1832, Burnouf expressed the widespread hopes that sustained his studies: "It is more than India, gentlemen, it is a page from the origins of the world, from the primitive history of the human species, that we shall attempt to decipher together."

The object of our inquiry is, we could say, *a history of the process whereby the Western image of India moved from the primitive to the contemporary*, which, in some cases, means from incredulous amazement to condescending veneration. At first glance, and we shall return to this point later, literary curiosity and public taste, which followed the learned movement as best they could, and that movement itself, seemed generally marked between 1785 and 1870 by successive predilections: first for Vedism, which for a long time was as much invented as known; then for Brahmanism; and then for Buddhism, which became accessible only in the 1840s after the arrival of the Sanskrit and Pali canons. Only later would the West pass from the first hazy, heavy-handed exaltations of its Friedrich Schlegels to critical assimilation and strict comparisons.

The Prejudice for Egypt

Any attempt to retrace this history collides with three prejudices. The first, which I have already mentioned, is the assertion that the discovery of oriental thought left no serious trace on the European mind. The second is that India could not have affected European thought until after 1850. The third is that the first and the essential influence was that of Egypt. The truth is that Anquetil's translations of the *Avesta* and the Upanishads between 1771 and 1786 mark the beginning of the oriental influence. Since his translations came not from the original but from a second language (Persian), what Anquetil contributed was not a decipherment but proof that lost writings could be retrived and that closed texts could be reopened. Anquetil's achievement was a canal through the isthmus dividing the two oceans of thought and history.

Whenever anyone mentions deciphering, everyone thinks of the hieroglypics and of Champollion. And this has long been the case. Writing in the *Revue des Deux-Mondes* in June 1868, Ludovic Vitet hailed "the unparalleled discoveries" of the orientalists over the preceding fifty years. He even spoke of "the archaeological revolution for which the Orient is the theater," but calmly asserted that "the movement started with Champollion and everything began because of him. He is the point of departure for all these discoveries." Vitet's own progression following the one already established in the public mind, he then passed on to the Assyrian monuments and finally to a few words on the Vedas. Vitet did not linger. Clearly, after Napoleon's expedition to Egypt, the monuments there and the scholarly missions to Egyptian sites had already spoken to everyone. India never revived except on paper. Egypt, the only part of the ancient East already familiar to the eighteenth century, was, however, like Assyria still a gateway to the Mediterranean world and the classics.

This view of Egypt as the first and the essential oriental influence on the West is totally erroneous. In point of fact, the Egypt of the scholars was a relative latecomer, arriving only in the nineteenth century, and could be only partially revived.[2] Nonetheless, the Egyptian ideograms remained the most famous mystery, and the stroke of genius that pierced the wrappings of the mummies became the most prestigious breakthrough. Fortunately, the spectacular achievement of the deciphering of the hieroglyphics redounded afterwards to all the other decipherings. Deciphered alphabets had been accumulating for nearly forty years when Champollion, presenting his own key, became the symbolic man with the key. This is not to diminish that extraordinary figure. Beyond the dramatic effect of his discovery, the romance of a brief, flashing destiny naturally spoke in his favor, as did the ascendancy of an individual who, until Burnouf, was unique. And after all, no pasha ever sent an obelisk to Burnouf.

The recovery of Sanskrit was only half due to Western genius. The other half was due to a transmission of knowledge that still lived in local tradition. The great difference between the deciphering of the language of the Hindu and that of the Egyptian, apart from the difference in the scripts themselves, is that the hieroglyphics had not been understood by anyone for centuries. Champollion performed a unique feat: he delivered up a secret no longer kept by any living person. But that was precisely why this secret could never again become a living secret. Moreover, Champollion's was far from the first attempt to decode a thousand-year-old cipher. Thirty years earlier Sacy had begun work on unlocking Pahlavi, which would

open the way to Avestan for Burnouf. The young Champollion was fired
by the reports of these successes. When, in addressing his *Précis du système hiéroglyphique* to the king in 1824, Champollion wanted to specify what
was exceptional about his own contribution, he wrote that while ancient
Asia was known, it was still believed that Egypt would never be deciphered.

It is high time we recognize that everything depended on India, which
was our first step in repairing the damage of Babel. This was no little event
in the history of mankind, for unexpectedly it permitted the first inventory of Babel. Surveying the Hittites, the Tokharians, and all the uncovered hiding places of central Asia, man felt that the number of languages
to be tabulated bordered on the limitless, decisively altering the entire
previous intellectual landscape. The closed circle of languages, within which
the false problems, impotent intuitions, and crippled enterprises of mon-
ogeneticists such as Postel and Leibniz had always come to naught, burst
open, posing new problems, problems in reverse, on the infinity of languages.

The Background of Indic Studies

While establishing oriental studies in the full sense of the word, as an
autonomous discipline based on the direct interpretation of original texts,
Anquetil-Duperron did not immediately break with the empirical tradition. He improvised a critical tool, first by assembling the linguistic ideas
he had acquired in conversations with Parsi high priests, then by comparing various parts of a text and sifting through the interpretations brought
to him. The efficacy of these expedients, which Anquetil had employed
from the start, increased tremendously from the moment he began to
subject his native instructors to meticulous questioning about things he
read in a manuscript but about which he was not being told. His own
intelligence served him all the better when he assumed it in his authors.
To be sure, he forgot neither his purse nor his pistols in his pursuits, but
he obstinately adhered to the best course of action, which is to treat all
men as equals.

Having the temperament of an explorer, Anquetil applied pioneering
methods to his reading, questioning the man who knew only his own village in order to advance beyond the village himself. Anquetil applied these
same methods to his study of Sanskrit. He approached the new literature
by two routes. The first was indirect: he received from Gentil a Persian
version of the Upanishads, which he translated into French and Latin
successively. The second route was direct: Anquetil collected a Sanskrit

alphabet in India, independent of those which had already been partially introduced into Europe. He petitioned the office of the Propaganda Fide and obtained from Cardinal Antonelli an incomplete Sanskrit vocabulary originating with the missions. Anquetil used another dictionary and grammar which, also thanks to the missions, were in the king's library. He had, according to Filliozat, "no less ardor for Sanskrit than for Avestan," and the documents in his handwriting "which are to this day scattered throughout the Sanskrit and Indian holdings of the Bibliothèque Nationale, not to mention the collection of his own papers, attest to his considerable work in the field of Sanskrit." That Anquetil also left analogous work on Malabar and Telugu not only proves his vocation as a linguist but demonstrates his freedom from treacherous servitude to a single informant.

Anquetil had both predecessors and emulators, for during a time when Semitic studies seemed to have dried up, Indic sources were appearing on all sides. Since the 1730s, long, tentative efforts had preceded the preliminary work that laid the groundwork for the final achievement of the 1780s, an achievement that now must be seen as having been in the domain of *formal knowledge*. This is the history of the *recovery of the texts*. Later we will take up this history again in the domain of substantive knowledge in a chapter on the *recovery of the doctrines*.

The Portuguese and the Missions to India

If it is true that Vasco de Gama opened the road to India in 1498 primarily for merchants and the military, intellectual interest in India, beginning with the Portuguese, soon followed.[3] From the first half of the sixteenth century Portugal was eager to obtain information regarding the beliefs and customs of India. Spiritual considerations prompted the departure of the illustrious traveler Saint Francis Xavier, whom Max Müller thought knew Sanskrit, in 1541. A vast historical literature began when Governor João de Barros (1496–1570), often referred to as the Portuguese Livy, inaugurated a vast historical literature with *Asia; or, Of the deeds which the Portuguese performed in the discovery and conquest of the seas and lands of the Orient*. The first "decada" was published in 1552, the second in 1553, and the third in 1563. The narrative of the fourth decade of Portugal's eastward expansion, edited by João Baptista Lavanha, was published posthumously from Barros' notes in 1615. Meanwhile, Diogo do Couto had published his own *Decada quarta de Asia* in 1602, and continued the work through eight decades, publishing his final volume in 1673. Couto was a close friend of the poet Camões, who lived in Goa and Macao and whose famous *Os Lusíadas* formally annexed the Indic regions to occidental poetry in 1572. To a greater or lesser degree, all these men, as well as Joãm de Lucena, who published a life of Saint Francis Xavier in 1600, had sought information about the Vedas.

A quite useful section in Villey's *Sources d'idées* concerns the role the discovery of new lands played in the formation of the first Renaissance and the breadth of its humanist outlook: "From the corners of a world suddenly emerging from its own shadows came a torrent of narratives and accounts that nearly defied imagining. The East and West Indies had just been discovered. Returning voyagers told stories of incredible animals, gigantic plants, and monsters of every description. They had observed strange and repellant customs, religions that confounded the mind, and unbelievable laws. In imitation of each other, Italian, Spanish, and French books all repeated these disconcerting tales, and certain ancient works like Pliny's *Natural History* and a few books of Herodotus seemed to corroborate these stories and lend them authority. What fresh images for Western man to store in his brain, what ideas to assimilate, what concepts to examine and revise in the old warehouse of tradition!" There was probably nothing in these unexpected ideas that could "erode our social and individual lives," but "the ideas that had been developed about nature, about our world, and especially about mankind—morality, religion, and much more—were constantly defeated, undermined by the ever-rising tide of anomalies."[4]

In the estimation of the native populations, the Portuguese governors of the seventeenth century ruled somewhat callously. Bernier confirmed the extent to which the Portuguese penchant for heroism and martyrdom had degenerated. Louis XIV heard that the Portuguese settlements were not secure. Thus for political ends, he decided to add six young Jesuits, all members of his Académie des Sciences, to a special mission he was sending to Siam. He had them set ashore in the south of the Deccan. In this manner the "Indian missions" that eventually gained a widespread reputation for their ordeals were founded. The collection *Lettres édifiantes et curieuses* published accounts concerning them along with the outcome of their work and researches. Despite some sections that were ingenuous or partial—which Voltaire took pleasure in ridiculing, although he gained his own information with relative ease and was equally intolerant in his own way—the collection contained many extremely interesting concepts relevant to the background of Indic studies.

Communication between the Jesuits and the higher castes who provided the principal access to Sanskrit had been initiated at the beginning of the seventeenth century by the Italian Roberto de Nobili, nephew of Cardinal Bellarmin. De Nobili was an important forerunner of later Indic scholars, and even present-day travelers to India may find living traces of de Nobili's work. De Nobili composed prayers in Sanskrit and seems to have anticipated by more than a century the experience of the English school at Calcutta. However, nothing he may have written regarding his work ever appeared in Europe.

In the first years of the eighteenth century, French missionaries carried out several fruitful inquiries into Indian languages and beliefs. Unfortunately in this instance, their proselytizing ultimately brought them into contact with the lower castes, who interposed their own common vernaculars between the missionaries and Sanskrit. Their very success led the French to make concessions concerning the forms of (Christian) worship, which were called "rites malabars" or "cérémonies chinoises" (both Voltaire and Saint-Simon addressed the issue). Such concessions were denounced as scandalous in Rome, investigated as early as 1703 by Cardinal Tournon, and censured several times by the popes before the definitive condemnation in 1744. From then on, the distance between informant and inquirer became greater and greater.

In the interval, momentum was gathering in Paris: Abbé Bignon, librarian to the king and reorganizer of the Académie des Inscriptions, in 1718 invited the missionaries to seek out Indic manuscripts for an oriental library he had decided to create. By 1733 the *Lettres édifiantes* asserted that the Jesuits had succeeded in recovering a complete Veda, although the Vedas had previously been considered undiscoverable, if not irretrievably lost. Such pessimism had been long standing and can be accounted for by the fact that libraries were reluctant to make their treasures public, and further, that later travelers encountered a more reticent native population. Moreover, to the European way of thinking, a lost or guarded book was of minor importance in a country where the primary mode of literary communication was oral. Even today one wonders whether the uninterrupted oral Vedic tradition does not lie beyond the scope of the printer. Sonnerat, who returned empty-handed in 1782, and, later, Sainte-Croix, doubted the authenticity of the Vedas. In 1786, Charles Wilkins assumed that there was nothing left of them but incomprehensible fragments. Protesting against this view, Anquetil asserted that the Vedas could be found, and in 1789 Europe was astounded to learn that Colonel Polier had finally unearthed them and that they had been received at the British Museum. Polier was at the time, however, unaware of what was already in Paris. In 1791, Paulinus a Sancto Bartholomaeo again derided those Europeans who believed in the reality of the Vedas, and in 1805 Colebrooke himself expressed doubt whether the full text was worth the extreme effort that would be required to translate it.

The manuscript that had arrived in Paris in 1731 was a complete *Rig*

Veda in grantha characters. In 1733, Filliozat reports, Father Pons sent 168 items from Chandernagore in which "Vedic literature was represented only by a series of Upanishads," but which included "the principal works of grammar and classical literature" and numerous philosophical texts. This copious material, obtained at a very low cost, "attested to the importance of the relations between the Jesuits and the literate Indian community. Several years later the ease of approaching that community had largely evaporated. After 1738 the shipments from India were discontinued."

The Vedas had, from the start, been the big game of the hunt. Two targets had been sighted immediately: sacred books and the key to the sacred language. As Auguste Barth points out in *Les religions d'Inde*, the names, number, and reality of the books were known and discussed perhaps as early as the first half of the sixteenth century, when the Vedas were mentioned in the apocryphal pamphlet *De tribus impostoribus*. The quest for them was to last more than a century. Before his departure for India, Anquetil, who held an appointment in the Bibliothèque du Roi at Paris, could not have been unaware of the manuscripts the library had already received. Not only were the holdings incomplete but, above all, the key to the Vedic language was lacking. Anquetil's primary aim in going to India was to seek out the *Avesta*, but he also wanted to retrieve the complete Veda and the means of reading it. This last discovery was the most protracted. Even after the missionaries had encountered the authentic text, it remained a totally useless material possession to them, since their rudimentary knowledge of Sanskrit, so laboriously obtained, ran aground on the Vedic tongue. The one thing they knew for certain was that the Vedic language was anterior to the classical language, but their interpreters' limited knowledge remained impotent in the face of that fact. Even as late as 1771 Father Coeurdoux, relying on the opinion of Father Calmette—and they were the two principal authorities of the time—wrote to Anquetil that Vedic Sanskrit was a hopeless enigma.

For a long time Vedic literature was approached only through translations of intermediary texts. These texts themselves were suspect, and the translations, while flattering the interpreters, remained perpetually unfaithful. The translations included spurious shastras and fragments of treatises or poems that had been appended to the works of Henry Lord in 1630 and of Abraham Roger in 1651, as well as to the reports of Pons in 1740, of Tibetan missionary Marco della Tomba in 1757, of Holwell in 1764, and of the Danish missions to Tranquebar. These, plus the *Ezour-Vedam* of 1778 and the 1788 *Bagavadam* of Foucher d'Obsonville (see chapter 6), amount only to a collection of indirect versions, often distinguished by tendentious adaptations. Although a good many preliminary Indic studies had undoubtedly circulated before those of Wilkins and Jones, their primary virtue was to heighten the desire for what was not yet grasped. The first systematic and direct translations of unadulterated texts appeared between 1785 and 1789.

It was not that literal deciphering had not been attempted. Landing in an India fused with Islam since the eleventh century, where Persian and Hindustani were the principal languages, the Dutch, French, Danish, Italian and English missionaries discovered and announced the existence of an earlier language—a dead language, sacred, liturgical, and erudite, restricted to a high priestly caste, renowned for an immense and mysterious body of literature, and written in a script to which the key was missing. Formidable barriers defended this treasure from the impurity of the Europeans, who called it by various names, according to the dialect in which they first encountered it. For Abraham Roger it was *Samscortam.* Bernier employed the curious form *Hanscrit* which, with two exceptions, Voltaire also used. *Sahanscrit,* and worse, can be found in the *Lettres édifiantes.* Anquetil called it *Samscroutam* or *Samcretam* at first. Sonnerat called it *Sanscroutam, Samskret, Hanscrit,* and *Grandon* (after *Grantham*). In 1806, Adelung termed it *Samscrda.*

By 1663 *China illustrata* by the Jesuit scholar Anthanasius Kircher had provided tables of characters based on the alphabet collected by Heinrich Roth at Agra. A Sanskrit translation of the Lord's Prayer was included, along with a few ideas concerning Hindu mythology. In 1668 Bernier was in possession of these same rudiments. In 1678 the Dutch governor of Cochin, Rheede tot Drakenstein, published *Hortus malabaricus* in which he indicated the names of plants in devanagari characters. (The name *nagari,* in the form *nagher,* had been introduced to European readers in 1664 by Pietro della Valle.) In 1711, Sir John Chardin republished the Agra alphabet which had first been provided by Roth and which was later reprinted by the Saint Petersburg Academy, by the office of the Propaganda Fide, and in the *Encyclopédie.* In 1771, in his preface to the *Avesta,* Anquetil transliterated into Latin the Sanskrit alphabet he had obtained by his own means in the course of his travels. The first systematic edition of a text in Sanskrit characters was that of Kalidasa's *Ritusamhara,* brought out in Calcutta by William Jones in 1792 as *The Seasons; a descriptive poem.*

Both de Nobili and Roth had clearly grasped the rudiments of grammar. In a letter of November 23, 1740, Pons provided a preliminary analysis of indigenous handbooks of grammar, one of which he translated, along with *Amarakosha,* the best-known of the eighteen indigenous dictionaries with which he was familiar. Filliozat acknowledged Pons's importance as a precursor, and in 1739 Fourmont and Bignon prepared a noteworthy catalog of the first Indic manuscripts Pons sent to Paris. Fourmont recopied the lists the missionaries furnished, translated them into

Latin, arranged the works systematically, and incorporated the principal information in the notes accompanying Pons's list. Many of the first researchers, Chézy among them, based their studies on these works, particularly Pons's lexigraphic and grammatical studies. In his *Etudes sur l'astronomie indienne* in 1832, Biot "deplored the fact that Pons had not been allowed to initiate the instruction of Sanskrit at the Collège de France as early as 1740." Fourmont and Bignon's catalog was revised by Alexander Hamilton and Langlès between 1803 and 1807. Fauriel, one of Hamilton's students, "drafted some more detailed entries in the following years."

If the Académie des Inscriptions had not buried the documents which Coeurdoux had sent, the science of comparative grammar could have begun some fifty years earlier than it did. Be that as it may, in the second half of the eighteenth century an Austrian Carmelite, Paulinus a Sancto Bartholomaeo, collected some important materials as much linguistic as theological in nature. Earlier, in the first half of the century, the reports of the Dutch mission at Tranquebar—translated in 1745 from a German abridgment and again in 1839 by Loiseleur-Deslongchamps—had contained lists of defined words. In 1706 in *De veteri lingua indica*, Adrianus Reeland attempted to interpret, through Persian, the words preserved in Ctesias. The Jesuit Hanxleden, a resident at the Malabar mission from 1699 until his death in 1732, may have been the first European to write, in Latin, a Sanskrit grammar for his own use and to attempt a dictionary. (It is likely that Roth, who died at Agra in 1668, had compiled a Sanskrit grammar before Hanxleden; it has never been found, although it could perhaps be recovered in the Vatican archives.) Hanxleden appended to his work some Christian poetry composed in Sanskrit by catechumens. The material remained in manuscript but was useful to Sancto Bartholomaeo.

The last name to be inscribed in this abridged list of the forerunners of Indic studies is that of Nathaniel Brassey Halhed. He was the last of a series of Europeans to be taught on a one-to-one basis through a sort of local good will, about fifteen years before the group efforts of the English at Calcutta. Halhed published a Bengali grammar as well as *A Code of Gentoc Laws, or, Ordinations of the Pundits* (London, 1776). The revealing term "Gentou," which Voltaire later adopted, represented the Hindus to the eighteenth century as "gentiles" par excellence, and Bernier had previously spoken of gentiles in the wake of the Muslims. Halhed's work served as a model for Jones's *Institutes of Hindu Law,* completed by Colebrooke, and was a mine of information for Adelung's linguistic catalog *Mithridates.*[5] The first Sanskrit grammars *printed* in Europe did not come from the English Indic scholars of Calcutta; rather they are the work of Sancto Bartholomaeo printed in Rome in 1790 and 1804.

Thus, before the Asiatic Society of Bengal, there had been only tentative advances after many missteps. It was on the basis of "the data of classical antiquity" and the accounts of various voyagers that Bourguigon d'Anville and James Rennell had undertaken, in 1773 and 1781 respectively, to reshape the map of ancient India. Even Halhed's *Gentoo Laws* was based on a Persian compilation.

The Asiatic Society of Calcutta

The decisive period in Indic studies began with the arrival of English civil servants in Calcutta around 1780, who supported by the governor, Warren Hastings, began an extraordinary undertaking. Learning does not determine its own course alone, and the initial intention, conversion, yielded to or was intermingled with another intention, conquest. The aim in this period was no longer to clear a path for knowledge but for administration. For this reason, fact-finding teams were encouraged, which could produce conclusive results more quickly than individual efforts, however talented.

William Jones, following in Anquetil's footsteps, made many linguistic discoveries. While still a young man, Jones had attacked Anquetil's *Avesta*, although he later recognized his injustice. In the interim Jones had come to reconsider matters he had once thought settled. Only twelve years separated his quarrel with Anquetil from his own departure for India. During those years, Jones yearned to travel to India, but did not make the journey until he was thirty-eight. Curiosity about the Orient and its languages was seething everywhere, and Jones was already a polyglot linguist and had mastered Persian grammar, an achievement rare for his time. The English conquest gave him his opportunity. Jones wanted to administer justice in Calcutta and, from Pondicherry to Bombay, he was able to accomplish what Anquetil had first set out to achieve. The stir created by the apocryphal *Ezour-Vedam* and the false shastras of Holwell and Alexander Dow during the interval of waiting had reanimated Jones's desire to carry out research on the spot. In his preface to *Sakuntala; or, The Fatal Ring: an Indian Drama*, Jones acknowledged what his vocation owed to the *Lettres édifiantes*, although he did not hold them in high esteem.

When British authority was installed in Bengal, its first priority was to thread the labyrinth of local custom and legislation, and its representatives realized that languages would be the key to dominion. These representatives fortunately included such men as Robert Clive, Henry Vansittart, and, above all, Warren Hastings. Hastings—despotic, discredited, disputed, and legendary—was a *cause célèbre* who provoked some of the finest judicial and political oratory in English parliamentary history. Colebrooke, who began his career as a minor employee of the Exchequer in Bengal, embarked upon his own study of languages at the same time that Edmund Burke, in London, was vehemently denouncing Hastings' mistakes—with such disturbing evidence that Colebrooke considered leaving the colony because of its ill repute. Two years later Hastings was recalled to London for trial and, although exempted from corporal punishment, languished for years in public scorn.

One's judgment of Hastings becomes more complex if one cor ;iders the assessment of Thomas Babington Macaulay, who was himself a member of the Supreme Council for India from 1834 until 1838 and who served as president of the commission that created the criminal code for India. Writing in the *Edinburgh Review* (October 1841) Macaulay, who clearly did not scruple to take the side of India against its governors, writes "Our feeling towards him [Hastings] is not exactly that of the House of Commons which impeached him in 1787; neither is it that of the House of Commons which uncovered and stood up to receive him in 1813." Macaulay goes on to state simply that Hastings "had great qualities, and he rendered great services to the state." In the history of Indic studies Hastings ranks as a great benefactor. Drawn to poetry, which was his daily joy during his forced retirement, impassioned on the subject of oriental languages, and "deeply skilled in Persian and Arabic literature," Hastings had, since 1764, "conceived that the cultivation of Persian literature might with advantage be made a part of the liberal education of an English gentleman; and he drew up a plan with that view. It is said that the University of Oxford, in which oriental learning had never, since the revival of letters, been wholly neglected, was to be the seat of the institution which he contemplated. . . . Hastings called on Samuel Johnson," a man whose attainments in similar capacities were certainly no less than those of Jones, "with the hope, it would seem, of interesting in this project a man who enjoyed the highest literary reputations, and who was particularly connected with Oxford. The interview appears to have left on Johnson's mind a most favorable impression of the talents and attainments of his visitor." Moreover, as Hastings was, in spite of his excesses, the most popular of the authorities among the Hindus because of his interest in them, it was only natural that he would eventually conceive of establishing the study of their languages on the subcontinent. As Macaulay said, "The Pundits of Bengal had always looked with great jealousy on the attempts of foreigners to pry into those mysteries which were locked up in the sacred dialect. . . . That apprehension, the wisdom and moderation of Hastings removed. He was the first foreign ruler who succeeded in gaining the confidence of the hereditary priests of India, and who induced them to lay open to English scholars the secrets of the old Brahminical theology and jurisprudence."

Hence, one must acknowledge that even if Hastings proved a bit lavish with the local wealth in regard to this or that mistress, his mind also encompassed intellectual concerns. In his *Recherches*, Anquetil, who was not sparing in his criticism of British imperialism, treated Hastings with justice during his trial—in defiance of his enemies in London—and, speaking of the ingratitude that was destined for colonial conquerors, compared Hastings to the French governor Dupleix. Anquetil attested that the pandits who taught Sanskrit to the English refused any remuneration beyond the rupee a day necessary for their sustenance. If they had previously forbidden access to their books it was because, prior to Anquetil and to Hastings' employees, Europeans had approached them with a negative bias. Langlès noted: "It was in response to a direct summons from Hastings that the Brahmans versed in the Shastras . . . came to Calcutta from all parts of India. Gathering at Fort William and supplied with the most authentic texts, they drafted a comprehensive treatise on Indic law in the Hindu language. This was subsequently translated into Persian, and into English by Halhed under the title *Code of Gentoo Laws*. It was also under Hastings' auspices that Charles Wilkins studied Sanskrit and had the distinction of publishing the first translation in a European language based directly on a Sanskrit text."[6]

In fact it was Wilkins who, after Halhed had furnished the rudiments of Bengali, changed the course of linguistic history by going directly to Sanskrit, which was to reveal the structure of secondary languages although the reverse had been hoped for. Jones later asserted that he would not have learned Sanskrit without Wilkins. Within ten years—the ten years he had left to live—Jones attained a knowledge of Sanskrit that astounded his instructors. It was Hastings who had sparked the research upon which his own political success depended. Destiny's natural consent to human exigency placed in the offices of the East India Company two men who seemed only to be waiting for their cue: Charles Wilkins, who was employed there from 1770, and Henry Thomas Colebrooke, who arrived in 1783. In this same year everything came together with the arrival in Calcutta of William Jones, who had at last obtained a judgeship on the Supreme Court, where Colebrooke later sat.

These three, men of the most widely divergent character, pursued an identical vocation. One of them, a well-read jurist, affable and brilliant, enthusiastic and spontaneous, the "harmonious Jones" already well known as a gifted poet and scholar, was called by Samuel Johnson one of the most enlightened of the sons of man. Jones, the son of a professor of mathematics, had authored and published poems in Greek at the age of fifteen. At the age of sixteen, having learned Persian from a Syrian in London, Jones translated Hafiz into English verse. In 1771, at the age of twenty-five, Jones produced a remarkable Persian grammar which he translated into French. It was also in the language—and, as much as possible, in the style—of Voltaire that Jones penned his famous *Lettre* to Anquetil concerning the latter's *Avesta*. It was a witty, impudent, and ultimately unjust attack. No other orientalist, Pauthier later affirmed, had so broad a range of knowledge at his disposal as Jones did. Jones himself acknowledged that he had a thorough knowledge of thirteen of the twenty-eight languages he had studied. His open-hearted nature and his curiosity, his penetrating intuition, his ardor, and his grace can all be read in his features, preserved, fortunately, in the portrait by Joshua Reynolds and reproduced in engravings as early as 1779 and 1782. It seems fitting that his name should be given to a formerly mythical tree: *Jonesia asoka*.

Jones was interested in everything, uncovering and compiling information in many fields: Indian chronology, literature, music, fauna and flora. He discovered and guided others to the summits of poetry and philosophy, although the study of local law alone seemed entirely serious to him. But since his interests were so widely scattered, Jones, like others whose disposition it is to be easily fascinated, was not a creator of methods. His impact on the new science, which owed so much to him, was less that of the founder of a school of thought than a sower of vast fields that his successors would harvest. In 1794 he died in Calcutta at the age of forty-eight, and he was buried there. A monument was raised in his memory at Saint Paul's Cathedral by the East India Company, and a second was placed at Oxford by his widow. The bicentennial of Jones's birth in 1946 was celbrated in London, Calcutta, and New York, and by Indic scholars everywhere.[7] The nineteenth-century English poets read and frequently quoted Jones as an orientalist and admired him as a poet.

Henry Thomas Colebrooke was desended not from a mathematician but from mathematics itself. Influenced and impassioned by mathematics, or rather, impassioned by its coldness, Colebrooke carried mathematical exactitude into linguistic research, which inherited this feeling from him. Colebrooke was also a magistrate and possessed an extraordinary range of abilities and knowledge; yet he was habitually so slow in making decisions that, in whatever setting he found himself, he appeared secretive. In 1873, in his *Religions d'Inde*, Auguste Barth, analyzing the biography of Colebrooke prepared by his son, Sir Thomas Edward Colebrooke, was amazed to find the man missing—just as Colebrooke is missing from his works, and even from his personal letters. Barth wondered whether it was the subject or the narrator of the life who wished it thus.[8] As a young civil servant, Colebrooke was long reluctant to share the enthusiasm of his colleagues for Sanskrit and for the local literature, considering such enthusiasm facile and superficial. He was slowly won over by the intermediaries of algebra and astronomy; yet he revealed nothing of his interest until he had mastered the new knowledge—and he imparted it with a rigor that had, until then, hardly been attempted.

Like Jones, Colebrooke knew a number of languages by the age of fifteen, and also like Jones he had a preference for French. He was secretary of the Indian Civil Service in 1783, became a professor of Sanskrit and Hindu law at the College of Fort William in 1801, was president of the Calcutta Court in 1805, and moved on to the Council of India in 1807. In 1815 he returned to Europe, reentered private life, and subsequently produced his most important work. In 1819 he donated his priceless collection of oriental manuscripts to the East India Company library. His precision, patience, insight, and mental poise produced marvelous results in a work that has not become outdated after more than a century of admiration: the *Essays on the Religion and Philosophy of the Hindus*. Written on topics he had studied thoroughly during the first years of his stay in India, Colebrooke allowed his work to ripen thirty years before publishing it. It exerted a decisive influence in European intellectual circles. Like Anquetil, Colebrooke had a respect for human variety. His constant submission to rational truth, both as a scholar and magistrate, led him to work with positive facts, with equivalent components of a whole, with beliefs different from his own. This kind of integrity is a credit to the English school, which exhibited lofty examples of it, and compensates for the political insensitivity of certain men of action and the blindness of a certain kind of faith. Colebrooke must also be credited, again like Anquetil, with the intransigence that led him to denounce bluntly what he considered faulty or criminal in the colonial methods of his nation. As early as 1795, he did just that in a memorandum on commercial dealings in Bengal, and he continued to do so at every opportunity.

Very much in the forefront, Charles Wilkins was the first to discover and, in 1778, personally use methods of engraving, casting, and setting Bengali characters for the grammar that, before him, the company had not been able to print. Later returning to England for reasons of health, he equipped a printing press with nagari characters to publish his Sanskrit grammar, but its loss in a fire delayed publication until 1808. In 1787, soon after his return, Wilkins translated the *Hitopadesha*, a choice that would seem to betray a rather prosaic, moralistic bent had it not come from the same man who in 1784 had revealed to the West the summit of metaphysical poetry: the *Bhagavad Gita*. In 1805, when the East India Company founded Haileybury College in England for the purpose of training future employees in remote languages, Wilkins was appointed "examiner and visitor" there.

Wilkins too was interested in Indian law, and his first translation from

Sanskrit was a history of Hindu land grants. The predominant preoccupation for all the English was with legal matters—and administrative necessities. Here again the budding field of Indic studies reflected, at least partially, the circumstances of its birth, for it is clear that the linguistic conquest followed and served the political one. The work of assembling and interpreting local laws and customs stabilized British authority and facilitated further penetration. Jones declared that he would be the "Justinian of India," and in his second anniversary discourse to the Asiatic Society of Bengal on February 24, 1785, he emphasized the "immediate advantage" to be had from a knowledge of the "jurisprudence of the Hindus and Mussulmans." This immediate advantage, however, created certain injustices. Abel Rémusat, while maintaining that the Indic movement profited from being linked with the assessors and tax-collectors serving the British stockholders of the East India Company, adopted this comfortable formula: "Learning profits from all that afflicts humanity as well as from all that consoles it."[9] Michelet gives an astonishing summary (in his *Histoire du XIXe siècle*) of the mechanisms through which business, the magistracy, and more or less directly material interests extended the annexation of knowledge. We shall soon see that they also had the opposite effect.

At first the work seemed equally divided among the workers. While Wilkins was, with his *Bhagavad Gita,* extracting the kernel from the immense *Mahabharata*, Jones, more a humanist than a specialist, was unearthing the treasures of the Hindu theater and displaying an example to an admiring Europe: the baroque pearl *Shakuntala.* Jones was spirited and fired with enthusiasm. The precocious insights with which he abounded in the earliest stages of Indic studies later proved correct and fruitful. Colebrooke, on the other hand, was staid and sober, and the true philologist of the pair. The naturally compensating counterbalance between the two was another stroke of luck that enabled nascent Indic studies to make great strides forward. Jones died in 1794; Wilkins returned to Europe in 1786. Colebrooke remained in India until 1815, spending thirty-eight years there, taking part in or presiding over the whole unfolding of the heroic period. He saw the arrival in 1808 of Horace Hayman Wilson, the fourth musketeer. A new generation was taking shape out of which James Prinsep would also emerge.

The leading minds of the Calcutta society, and its publications, were by no means confined to philological research or literary interests: their original interests had been in the exact sciences, which occupied a prominent place in *Asiatic Researches.* They facilitated the rapid diffusion of the research in the same way they had always promoted the exchange of curiosities between East and West. During his twenty-seven-year tenure with the East India Company, Wilson, who had a medical background, was employed both in the medical service and in the Mint, where he was on friendly terms with Prinsep. We should note here that the first orientalists in France were scientists as well: Chézy began his career as a mineralogist and botanist, Burnouf was first attracted to the natural sciences, and the sinologist Rémusat was first a physician. Wilson, drawn to Jones through a writer's admiration of Jones' literary style, resumed his work in Indic studies with a methodological approach acquired from Colebrooke. Wilson published his *Megha Duta; or Cloud Messenger* in 1813 and in 1819 provided the first, and for a long time the only, practical Sanskrit-English dictionary. In his *Ariana antiqua* of 1841, Wilson, in tandem with Prinsep, became one of the first to sort out Indian archaeology and numismatics. Sylvain Lévi described Wilson's 1846 *Sketch of the Religious Sects of the Hindus* as one of the most plagiarized books of the century; Wilson's 1827 *Select Specimens of the Theatre of the Hindus* was no less used, and its three volumes impressed generations of European writers like Lamartine and Michelet. Scholars considered it an authoritative work, although Burnouf judged it harshly in a letter of June 2, 1828. Wilson assumed the first English chair of Sanskrit at Oxford in 1833, and published a translation of the *Vishnu Purana* in 1840. His translation of the first book of the *Rig Veda* in 1850 caused considerable stir. In European intellectual circles, he would be the most renowned Englishman in the field of oriental studies until Max Müller. Again following Colebrooke's example, Wilson was among those who struggled energetically against British colonialist prejudice and figured in the battles between "Orientalists" and "Anglicists," writing a *History of British India, 1805 to 1835* in 1846.[10]

Jones had hardly arrived in Hindustan when institutions began to arise there. During his first year an oriental college was built at Fort William and a printing press was established in Calcutta. In 1792 a Sanskrit college was begun in Banaras. The soon-to-be-famous Asiatic Society of Bengal was established on January 15, 1784 and, after Governor Hastings declined its presidency, Jones was chosen for the post. In his opening address Jones recalled that only the previous August he had been at sea, bound for a country he had "long and ardently desired to visit." The roster of the charter members of the society is impressive: among the twenty-four were Jones, Wilkins, and, among others, a certain Lieutenant Alexander Hamilton, whom we shall discuss later. In 1788 the society began publication of its *Asiatick Researches: Transactions of the Society* which were to affect Western thinking profoundly. An astonishing body of knowledge was accumulating, yet the first volume began with a modest introduction abounding in apologies: they were unable to proceed more quickly or to accomplish more in a region where pure scholarship was inconceivable,

where everyone was occupied with business, the army, or the administration—not to mention all the time a colonialist, especially a British one,
had to set aside for sports and leisure. The share of the research accorded
to astronomy and chemistry is to be expected. Moreover, the society declared in its *Transactions* that its purpose was "inquiring into the history,
civil and natural, the antiquities, arts, sciences, and literature of Asia."

The sections of the *Researches* dealing with language, literature, and art
were no less enlightening. An article by Sir William Chambers on the carved
monuments of Mahabalipuram demonstrated as much foresight or followed guides as well-informed as those who led to the discovery of the
inscriptions. A glimpse into Indian literature "communicated by Gover-
dhan Caul," whose name is clearly not European, was translated from the
Sanskrit. Jones followed Caul's oversimplified, confusing report with a
commentary that revealed the extent to which students were already in a
position to debate their teachers. The four Vedas were not only described
but distinguished according to form, antiquity, and degree of difficulty.
In his second anniversary address on February 24, 1785, Jones took pride
in having surpassed the progress of the French: neither Anquetil, nor Du-
pliex, nor Sonnerat, sent from Versailles and spending seven years in India, had been able to procure the Vedas. The twentieth, and last, volume
of the *Researches* appeared in London in 1839, though the first Calcutta
volumes enjoyed several reprintings in London. Jones's contributions to
the first four volumes—the only ones completed before his death—greatly
exceeded those of others. In 1804 a branch of the Asiatic Society, presided
over by Sir James Mackintosh, was established in Bombay. The Literary
Society, which published its *Transactions*, was begun there in 1819, and
the important *Journal of the Bombay Branch of the Asiatic Society* first appeared in 1841. When the outline of Indic literature was sketched in the
first volume of the *Researches*, Jones claimed that "The first Indian Poet
was Valmici, author of the *Ramayana*, a complete Epick Poem on one continued, interesting, and heroick action; and the next in celebrity, if it be
not superior in reputation for holiness, was the *Mahabharata* of Vyasa." As
Wilkins had already translated the *Bhagavad Gita*, Jones concluded, with
good reason, that "if one wishes to develop an accurate idea of Indian
literature and religion, one must begin by forgetting everything that has
been written on the subject, by the ancients and the moderns, before the
publication of the *Gita*."

Those who had the good fortune to encounter this *Gita*, and the ability
to understand it, realized that a new age was beginning. For eleven years
Jones commemorated the founding of the Asiatic Society with a major address. These were veritable dissertations dealing with the broadest and
most novel questions. Later addresses bore such titles as "On the Origin

and Families of Nations" (1792) and "On the Philosophy of the Asia-ticks," delivered in 1794, two years before his death. Jones's great discovery, the relationship of Sanskrit to Greek and Latin, was highlighted in a letter of September 27, 1787, but as early as his third anniversary address, entitled "On the Hindus," delivered February 2, 1786, Jones stated:

The Sanskrit language, whatever be its antiquity, is of a wonderful structure; more perfect than the Greek, more copious than the Latin, and more exquisitely refined than either, yet bearing to both of them a stronger affinity, both in the roots of the verbs and in the forms of the grammar, than could possibly have been produced by accident; so strong, indeed, that no philologer could examine them all three, without believing them to have sprung from some common source, which, perhaps, no longer exists.

In his sixth address, entitled "On the Persians" and delivered on February 19, 1789, Jones attributed a Chaldean origin to Pahlavi and assumed that Avestan was very close to Sanskrit.

Within ten years the most sublime and seductive elements of Hindu literature were, to the amazement of Europe, brought to light and translated. However, these British pioneers kept in mind objectives one might term either serious or merely utilitarian. They, even Jones, seemed to chance upon the spiritual aspects only as an added bonus, and they, even Colebrooke, saw literary value only after all else had been considered.

During the first years of the nineteenth century two men who had come to India as evangelists became involved with important grammatical work and with the publications and translations of Colebrooke, Wilkins, and Henry Pitts Forster. These two were William Carey, Professor of Sanskrit, Bengali, and Marathi at Fort William College, and Joshua Marshman. Along with the Indian historian William Ward, who was appalled by India's idolatry, they were members of the Serampore Baptist Mission. They had been obliged to transfer their proselytizing efforts to the territory of the Danish mission, since the English were not, at that time, well disposed toward them. In 1800 Carey set up a printing press which, though intended for evangelism, proved extremely useful for philology. Before long the missionary fervor had cooled, as Victor Jacquemont points out in his *Correspondance,* providing a good deal of highly instructive information on the consequences of what had begun in Serampore. Thus appeared, in characteristic alternation with political considerations, the second of the two retarding factors that were to limit England's eventual benefits from what it undertook.

The undertakings that followed no longer had the fullness of the first efforts. Although the fields of numismatics, epigraphics, and archaeology were important, they were unable to launch into general circulation the names of any great innovators. Wilkins and Colebrooke, first associated with the deciphering of inscriptions, became well known for other reasons. Prinsep was hardly known outside specialist circles, and only after his death did history, around the 1850s, harvest the fruits of his specialized studies. This situation was evident, for example, in the popular though very intelligent articles that Philarète Chasles contributed to the *Journal des Débats* in March and April 1860, in which the reading of Buddhist sculpture shed light on Alexander's expedition.

James Prinsep had left for India at the age of twenty. He was first an assayer at the Banaras mint and later succeeded Colebrooke at the Calcutta mint and as secretary of the Asiatic Society. Like Colebrooke, Prinsep had numerous interests—chemistry, architecture, natural sciences—and avidly studied coins and monuments that had already been brought partially to light in the first decade of the nineteenth century with the help of the agricultural mission. Such undertakings in this period were facilitated by the good maps that were beginning to appear; James Rennell's cartographic work was complemented by the work of Kingsbury, Parbury, and Allen that appeared in 1825. Charles Masson, a shrewd English officer stationed in the Panjab and Afghanistan, had, with a professional eye, tracked down the Indo-Grecian interchanges revealed by ancient coins. Prinsep, given these data, had in turn applied to them a brilliant insight. He had studied the Gupta inscriptions and then the bilingual coins of Bactria. In 1837 he waved his magic wand and thereafter it was possible to write the history of India: while grappling with the stone inscriptions of King Ashoka, Prinsep had succeeded in dating one of Ashoka's edicts and in establishing the relations between India and Alexander's successors. This brought to a fruitful conclusion the premature intuition of Joseph de Guignes, who in 1772 had succeeded in identifying the Hindu Chandragupta with the Greek Sandracottus.

Prinsep, who died at forty, was succeeded by Lieutenant Alexander Cunningham. In 1861, having attained the rank of general, Cunningham secured the development of archaeology in India through the establishment of the Archaeological Survey. Under his direction, thirty-three volumes were published that remain an incomparable resource. In 1845 James Fergusson began his study of subterranean temples and, in 1876, produced his *History of Indian and Eastern Architecture.* The exploration and preservation of monuments under the governments of Sir John Marshall and Lord Curzon lies beyond the scope of this study, but mention should be made of Brian Houghton Hodgson, who discovered the authentic texts of Buddhism in 1821 while living in Nepal.

Unfortunately, it is also impossible to give anything but a rough sketch of the strange mechanism by which the Oriental Renaissance—though not Indic studies themselves—had only an ephemeral career in the same England to which it owed its origin. Later the debt of several writers, especially the Lake Poets, to the Hindu revelation became clear, and the shadow of its impact on London was evident in Chateaubriand when he returned from exile. But the fire in England was soon damped. Great Britain could not, or would not, be the hearth for such a renaissance. Thereafter, even in Indic studies, the Victorians procured their best workers only by appealing to the German universities. This had already been the case with Rosen, who was born in Hanover and died a professor of Sanskrit at London. It was, above all, the case with Max Müller, who was born in Dessau in 1823 and died a professor of comparative linguistics at Oxford in 1900. Ultimately, England was to welcome many more orientalists than she gave birth to.

It was England's great disgrace to be too self-seeking in India to avoid violent reactions, after fits and starts of adaptation. Yet these fits and starts were due, as was always the case in British history, to the boldness of isolated nonconformists who would not be limited by the plans of those authorized to make decisions and who thus could compensate for the shortsightedness of those authorities. In the process they accomplished what those in the public eye were more than happy to have done without their formal consent. But in order to protect those who followed Jones from certain of those who followed Hastings, the scholars were obliged to struggle against conspiracies of narrow-mindedness. The conquerors felt obligated to defend their conquest, which meant exalting their own race and religion. This resulted in political and spiritual unrest, which spread like an epidemic. The activities at Serampore, which provided many useful publications in the early days of Indic studies, seemed to coincide with the appearance of this "missionary attitude," which wreaked havoc even though it constantly backfired everywhere. Later it will become clear how the episodes of colonial politics—the Sepoy Mutiny of 1857, the substitution of crown for company, and the proliferation of English personnel in India—came in gusts, reinforcing the English prejudice of Western superiority and minimizing, for the parent state, the phenomenon of the Oriental Renaissance.

In 1825 Guigniaut explained that he relied more on German works than English ones for information concerning the Hindu religion: "These latter are very important despite being written, for the most part, from a narrow point of view and in a rather unphilosophical spirit. The route mapped out by Jones, Robertson, and the learned Thomas Maurice was soon abandoned in England, and the Christian missionaries contributed, through their often tainted picture of the moral and religious state of these people, a great deal to the diffusion of a host of false ideas about the ancient religion of the Hindus. Abraham Roger in the seventeenth century and Sonnerat in the eighteenth demonstrated greater judgment, greater impartiality, and a more upright and elevated understanding than various authors in these later times, including the Reverend William Ward and his *A View of the History, Literature and Religion of the Hindoos* (London, 1817). (For more on this subject, one is referred to the numerous writings of the Abbé Dubois; of the Brahman Rammohan Roy, especially his article in *Monthly Magazine* for June, 1817; to the sage reflections of Auguste Wilhelm Schlegel in his *Indische Bibliothek;* and to Edward Moor's beautiful *Hindu Pantheon,* published in London in 1810.)"

Wilhelm Schlegel voiced his complaints in 1832 in his *Réflexions sur l'étude des langages asiatiques addressées à Sir James Mack Intosh et suivies d'une lettre à M. Horace Hayman Wilson.* In a letter to Wilson dated December 24, 1827, Schlegel had already reproached the English for not taking a deep enough interest in Indian culture. Having struggled for thirty years against this national hostility himself, Wilson had concluded the preface to his 1840 translation of the *Vishnu Purana* with the hope that it would interest those individuals who, in a time of utilitarian egoism and political passion, would know how to retire into meditation on the still-living images of the ancient world. As was always the case with England, there were variations—a balance of sorts between the rigidity of the officials and the liberalism of private individuals. In 1833 Wilson assumed the first British chair of Sanskrit, newly established through a sumptuous legacy from Colonel Joseph Boden, who had hoped to encourage, indirectly, the evangelization of India. In 1835 a political change in London caused the colonial government to cut off funding to the Asiatic Society of Calcutta. The society transferred all the paper stock for its publications to the government as so much wastepaper. Publications the following year were limited to those with a practical aim, and the initial work of Fort William was sacrificed. In 1868 Gustave Dugat deplored the fact that in the open competition held by the English administration for the Indian Civil Service, Italian was given the same importance as Sanskrit; Dugat saw this as a sign of the hostility that dogged Indic scholars.[11] Yet during this same period, between 1829 and 1834, the Oriental Translation Fund, created in London by Lord Munster, published 53 works. The fund's publications included Rosen's *Rig Veda Samhita* and, in 1839, Garcin de Tassy's *Histoire de la littérature hindoue et hindoustanie.* It is true that Wilhelm Schlegel, as we shall see later, expressed certain reservations about the general program and trend of the series. The costs of Müller's *Rig Veda* were borne initially by the East India Company and subsequently by Victoria's privy purse.

The Abbé Dubois was among those astonished by the excesses of proselytism. He had lived a long time among the Hindus in their villages, and his *Descriptions of the Character, Manners, and Customs of the People of India*, published first in English in 1817 and in French in 1825, was widely read. Although his treatment of the local religion was not especially favorable, Dubois openly underscored the utter failure of Christianization in India. In the unpublished correspondence of Michelet is a letter to Burnouf asking for information on this question. Bournouf recommended a work of Dubois, but added that it could not be found in any library because of the Abbé's opinions.

After the heroic period of exploration and enthusiasm, English Indic studies generally may be considered a manifestation more of British psychology than of the Oriental Renaissance. When the first European chair of Sanskrit was established in Paris in 1814, Silvestre de Sacy, who was responsible for its establishment, carefully included this brief sentence in his "observations": "No religious or commercial interest called the attention of the English government to the Hindu language and literature."[12] But there was compensation for defeat: France, ousted from India after Dupleix, was thereby outdistanced at first in the field of linguistic discovery. But owing to this misfortune, it gained a scientific passion that no ulterior political motive could alter. This same characteristic disinterestedness later distinguished France from Germany. For different reasons, and with a behavior no less militant than England's (and soon military), Germany would seek temporal well-being in the remote spiritual past of Asia. Its multiform orientalism would retain the mark of an essentially dualistic and contradictory first cause: in the shadow of the Schlegels it would be impetuous, eager, and partial; in the wake of Franz Bopp it would be methodical and blind to everything not precise, rigorous, and delimited.

The nationalistic calculations which the neighboring Germans intermingled with their science was unquestionably viewed with some malice in Paris, where such calculations blossomed less naturally. But France made better use of misfortune: the rest of Europe, in revenge for Napoleon, dissuaded France from linking intellectual concerns with pretensions of imperial grandeur. The councilors of the later French kings were wary enough of such pretensions to leave the scholars to their own business. By guarding its freedom to generalize, France created an image of open-mindedness in the eyes of Europe. French scholars working in oriental studies were not always the most numerous or the most advanced; but France was long unique in according hospitality to ideas as well as individuals and for a blend of vocations, not to be found elsewhere, that served to link scholarship to the life of society. In the first half of the nineteenth century, Paris was the hub of oriental scholarship and attracted students and researchers from all parts. The Germans came first, and as a rule those destined for London initially spent time in Paris. This was the case, for example, with Wilhelm Schlegel, Bopp, Klaproth, Christian Lassen, and Max Müller. Eckstein, Salomon Munk, Mohl, Jules Oppert, and Karl Hillebrand all came to Paris from Germany and stayed. Mary Ann Thompson Clarke wrote to Jean Jacques Ampère that Mohl was the twenty-seventh foreigner to be naturalized in order to become a professor at the Collège de France. This jest, and the fact that the Germans were admitted to Victorian England, demonstrates that the learned population exported from Germany served to balance, at least abroad, the ethnic intransigence of those who remained.

The ever-growing mass of work by Germans very often obscured the actual division of labor. Darmesteter was scandalized to see the Munich Academy of Science undertake a general census of national learning shortly before the 1870 Franco-Prussian War. He wrote: "It is a song of glory—a bit heavy at times—in twenty volumes. Each page breathes the arrogance of a conqueror. . . . The public gets the mistaken impression that orientalism is essentially a German invention. . . . The literate public's ideas on these matters are not altogether clear, nor does it always make a distinction between oriental studies and comparative grammar, the latter being indeed a science completely German in origin."[13] (It should be noted that comparative grammar came out of Bopp's stay in Paris and his exposure to the scholarship he had sought there, notably that of Silvestre de Sacy— and that Burnouf's contributions were also a positive factor.) Darmesteter alludes here to Theodor Benfey's *Geschichte der Sprachwissenschaft und orientalischen Philologie in Deutschland seit dem Anfange des 19. jahrhunderts, mit einem Rückblick auf die fruheren Zeiten,* sponsored by the king of Bavaria in 1869. Certainly, Darmesteter concludes, Germany was "the great laboratory of oriental studies." The passion for history was widespread there, and German teaching kept pace with the latest findings; at the same time, scholarship was favored by decentralization and by teams of researchers. But for Darmesteter, all the great discoveries of the 1880s seemed to be French—a phenomenon arising from heightened sensibility after a lost war and a startling intellectual invasion. In any case, in 1803, 1812, and 1816, at the time of Rémusat, Sacy, and Chézy, and until Burnouf's death in 1852, if one wanted to determine the progress in a given field of learning, one went to the Collège de France. It was through their work in Paris that Bopp and Friedrich Schlegel came to be recognized in Germany; and German orientalists came to Paris to move in a climate where a passion for culture did not activate an instinct for the systematic, to move from one field to another before settling into a specialized discipline. Around 1802, "Paris was, according to Helmina von Chézy, who hardly erred on the side of generosity, the home of all noble spirits; the worlds of intellect and art were drawn there from everywhere."[14] The three principal homes of Indian studies in Europe—England, Germany, and France—held the leading position successively. The country of Wilkins and Jones started it all and withdrew at a rather early stage; thus it has been necessary to describe England's contribution first. The real share allotted to the other two countries can be discerned only through the course of many years and by tracing many transformations. The center of major activity after Calcutta (and I stress this point not out of partiality but in order to preclude any suspicion of partiality), was in Jena, Weimar, and Heidelberg, and thereafter always in Paris.

The English primacy during the heroic period maintained after Wilson's death by Max Müller, as brilliant as it was, existed side by side with certain sometimes offensive preconceptions. Salomon Reinach wrote that "Bopp, Schlegel, Lassen, Rosen, and Burnouf studied Sanskrit in England."[15] The English studies of the first three came only after their Parisian ones, and it is the Parisian ones that were decisive. As for Burnouf, he was much more a master than a disciple of European learning. He had acquired Sanskrit from his father, from Chézy, and on his own. Still, it is only fair to note, as Louis Renou pointed out to me, that "scholarly contact with living India was secured by a small group of Anglo-Indians— Colebrooke, Wilson, and others. It is important to remember that aside from Anquetil-Duperron, and until Emile Senart in 1887, Foucher in 1895, and Sylvain Lévi in 1897, no major French Indic scholar visited India." Among the other nations, Denmark had at least two extremely valuable travelers: Rasmus Christian Rask, one of the fathers of comparative grammar, who was involved in deciphering ancient Persian inscriptions and who published an article "On the Age and Authenticity of the Zend Language and of the *Zend Avesta*" in 1826; and Niel Ludvig Westergaard, around 1840.

Part Two

INTEGRAL HUMANISM

CHAPTER THREE
Europe Learns Sanskrit

The Arrival of the First Authentic Texts

WE now have a full enough catalog to enumerate some of the major breakthroughs and their repercussions. Naturally, this is not an exhaustive list but rather a selection of convincing accomplishments, which illustrate interests that were of immediate and durable consequence at that time.

1784: On January 15, the Asiatic Society of Bengal began its meetings in Calcutta, thus marking the first year of the new era. In November the first complete translation directly from a major Sanskrit text appeared under the auspices of the society—Wilkins' *Bhagavad Gita.*

1785: Publication of Wilkins' work in London. The English version was retranslated into French by Abbé Parraud in 1787 as *La Bhaguat-Geeta, contenant un précis de la morale et de la religion des Indiens, d'après la version angluise de M. Wilkins.* (Lanjuinais's translation directly into French, based on Wilhelm Schlegel's text, was published posthumously in 1832. Schlegel's own epoch-making German translation appeared in 1823.)

1787: Wilkins' translation of the *Hitopadesha,* which Jones had also translated and which appeared posthumously in 1807. There were numerous retranslations of this work in Europe, where this text was one of the most widely circulated.

1789: Jones's English translation of Kalidasa's soon-to-be-famous *Shakuntala.* Five reprintings in England between 1790 and 1807; multitudes of retranslations, which will be discussed later.

1792: Jones's translation of the *Gita Govinda,* published in the third volume of *Asiatic Researches.* This poem of mystic love had an immediate and pronounced effect, especially on the first German Romantics.

Whether through impeccable choices or infallible odds, the local tradition so guided European inclinations that, from the beginning and in rapid succession, texts destined to make India a miracle to the West were disclosed. They represented the distinctive forms of Hindu genius at the highest stage of its development: epic grandeur and metaphysical depth, classic grace and radiant moral purity.

1794: Posthumous publication of Jones's *Institutes of Hindu Law*—not to be confused with Colebrooke's *Digest of Hindu Law*, which was published at Calcutta in 1797 and 1798. The publication of Jones's work was of major importance because it was through this primarily ethical and judicial text that Indic cosmogony became widely known. Known as *The Laws of Manu (Manava Dharmashastra)*, the work was reprinted several times in London and Calcutta. The French translation by Loiseleur-Deslongchamps appeared in 1833; the German translation by Johann Christian Hüttner appeared in Weimar in 1837. In 1825 Guigniaut wrote, "The cosmogony of the *Manava Dharmashastra* is the broadest and most comprehensive we have thus far encountered."[1]

In 1786 Anquetil published four Upanishads in his *Recherches sur l'Inde*, which was published in Berlin as part of a series edited by Jean Bernoulli that also included Father Joseph Tieffenthaler's *Description historique et géographique de l'Inde*, published in three volumes between 1786 and 1791. Anquetil translated fifty Upanishads, first into French (although the only ones in this version to be published were the four that appeared in 1786) and then into Latin. He finished this task in 1787, and the fifty Latin versions appeared in 1801–2 under the title *Oupnek'hat*. This project had no connection with the Calcutta activities; Anquetil's versions were not drawn directly from Sanskrit but rather from the seventeenth-century Persian manuscript prepared for Dara Shikoh, son of Shah Jahan—princes Bernier vividly portrayed. However, the *Oupnek'hat*, like the Calcutta movement, was exceedingly important in furthering nascent Indic studies. Not until 1897 did Paul Deussen produce Upanishads based on Sanskrit texts. He rendered sixty Upanishads, ten more than Anquetil, but he borrowed five of them from Anquetil's version because the Sanskrit originals had not yet been recovered.

Colebrooke's 1805 essay on the Veda in the eighth volume of *Asiatic Researches* and Friedrich Schlegel's 1808 essay on the language and wisdom of the Hindus set the seal on the discoveries of this initial period.

Diffusion of *Asiatic Researches*

Asiatic Researches, published by the Asiatic Society of Bengal, spread with remarkable speed and pervasiveness among scholars and writers in England, Germany, and France. Max Müller later recounted that Lord Monboddo, when informed by his friend Wilkins about the discovery of Sanskrit, dropped his idea of tracing the invention of language back to the Egyptian gods. Others, such as Dugald Stewart, were intent on crediting the invention in the traditional (biblical) way. In other words, Stewart authoritatively declared it impossible and perceived the same hoax in Jones's Sanskrit that Jones had assumed in Anquetil's Avestan.

However, the resistance of the English elite to the revelation of India did not become pronounced until the 1830s. The first generation of Indic scholars seemed on the verge of introducing a new classicism enhanced by Sanskrit. Quinet later stated, and not without reason, that each of the poets of the Lake School had begun his career with an Asian poem. The history of the connections between English poetry and India will be discussed later, but we should keep in mind here that the standard Indic masterpieces and the fundamentals of Indic thought were an important part of the London intellectual world during the first few years of the nineteenth century. Four editions of the *Asiatic Researches* sold out immediately. Jones's *Shakuntala* had five editions and gained him an international reputation. "The merits of this man are universally known and have been emphasized and detailed on numerous occasions," Goethe wrote in 1819, and forty years later Goethe recalled how the orientalist Eichorn had given him Jones's *Works*. Wilkins, Colebrooke, and Wilson did not remain far behind Jones; England prided itself on their works, and all Europe used them. Yet England remained more a place of birth than of growth. Matters there soon took an abrupt turn, and several currents of thought began to conflict. Thus while England was the native land of Indic studies, the native land of the Indic Renaissance was Germany—first at Jena, Weimar, and Heidelberg, then at Bonn, Berlin, and Tübingen. During the 1790s the impact of oriental studies in Germany was like a rapid-fire series of explosions. The *Laws of Manu*, the *Shakuntala*, the *Gita Govinda*, and *Asiatic Researches* were all soon retranslated into German, and certain texts were retranslated several times. The publications of the Indic scholars at Calcutta ignited a kind of fervid intensity in certain young Germans. In philosophy they included Schelling, Fichte, and Hegel—not to mention Schopenhauer and Schleiermacher. In poetry they included Goethe, Schiller, Novalis, Tieck, and Brentano. And among the great innovators of the new ideas that were to become Romanticism, a certain Herder passed the word to a certain Friedrich Schlegel. These various fields of endeavor were all caught up in the same excitement: the same exaltation of an original, universal religion brought back from India consumed Schlegel and Novalis; the same enthusiasm for an India regarded as the cradle of races, literatures, and histories created a profound link between the aging theoretician Herder and the young orientalists Maier and Forster. It was a happy coincidence that the year 1784 witnessed the appearance of Herder's famous *Ideen zur Philosophie der Geschichte der Menschheit,* the founding of the Asiatic Society of Bengal, and the publication of Antoine Rivarol's *Discours sur l'universalité de la langue française,* in which Rivarol had the impudence to suggest to the Berlin Academy—at precisely the same time that a youthful Germany was using every possible means to efface the very name of French civilization, and when the miraculous intervention of the Indic world was providing a basis for revising all classifications—that the moment had arrived to proclaim a "French world" comparable to the "Roman world."

Nevertheless, France once more played its role in focusing and communicating new discoveries. Within several months of its publication Anquetil had examined Wilkins' *Gita,* which he had had sent from England and which was received on June 2, 1786. Silvestre de Sacy attests to the effect it produced on his friend, on himself, and on the attentive circle composed of Lanjuinais, Langlès, and Millin which formed around them. The specialists were not the only ones to be well informed. A "Letter from London" dated December 30, 1784, before the appearance of Wilkins' translation, appeared in the *Gazette de France* on January 11, 1785. Anquetil reproduced the letter at the end of his *Recherches sur l'Inde* in 1787, adding that the Calcutta society was "taking more brilliant form each day, translating, at the prompting of William Jones, Sanskrit books relating to the arts and sciences." The letter stated:

Letters from Calcutta, dated the eleventh of last June, confirm that the new Society formed there to conduct research on the natural history, antiquities, arts, and sciences of Asia is advancing daily toward maturity. Sir William Jones has obtained for the Society several Persian manuscripts relating to the geography of this part of the world, and studies of the manufactures, agriculture, and astronomy of the inhabitants are being translated from the Indian. This learned society is currently composed of 42 members who with neither formalities nor treasury meet each week to examine the original manuscripts the Society is collecting. When all the necessary materials have been assembled, the Society will publish an Asiatic Miscellany to provide a better understanding of the subject and the kind of work being undertaken.

Nearly forty years later, in 1825, Guigniaut wrote about Hindu poetry, "The small portion of it with which we are familiar has surprised and impressed all Europe." The repercussions in Europe of the events in Calcutta can be traced from year to year and from country to country. In France the two principal scientific journals of the Directoire and the Consulat were Millin's *Magasin Encyclopédique,* which was influenced by Anquetil, and the *Décade philosophique,* which was closer to Volney; though neither failed to keep abreast of the new developments.[2] In 1788 the *Magasin* published a letter that Colonel Polier had enclosed with the Vedas he sent to the British Museum. In 1795 the *Magasin* ran an article by Langlès, who, as curator of oriental manuscripts at the Bibliothèque Nationale, was provisionally the specialist on India. Entitled "Notice sur les travaux typographiques et littéraires des Anglais dans l'Inde," it dealt mainly with Wilkins, a man whom Halhed had described as a designer, engraver, caster, and printer simultaneously. "A single man," wrote Langlès, "is carrying out an undertaking that usually requires the collaboration of a large number of artists. His first attempts are typographical masterpieces. This truly amazing man, whose name merits a distinguished place in the list of benefactors of letters, is Charles Wilkins, a scholar deeply versed in Sanskrit and known in Europe for two works he has translated from the sacred language of the Brahmans." A note tells us that these works were *The Bhagavat-Geetâ, or Dialogues of Kreeshna and Arjoon* and *The Heetopades of Veeshnoo-Sarma.* The former was an excerpt from the *Mahabarata*, of which Wilkins was preparing a complete translation that Anquetil, in 1786, believed to be already completed. Langlès noted that he himself had included an excerpt from the latter work as early as 1790 in his *Fables et contes indiens précédés d'un discours sur la religion, les antiquités et les moeurs des Hindous.* Thus in ten years, despite communications whose slowness was worsened by certain dramatic events, the essential elements of the harvest begun in Calcutta were well known in revolutionary France. Langlès's study continued in the third volume of the *Magasin encyclopédique* with a history of the Bengal society and a bibliography of its first publications. Personal ties were already beginning to form between Langlès and Polier, as they would soon after between Joseph Marie de Gerando and Sir James Mackintosh. Wilson would later correspond with the Institut de France, as Volney and Cuvier would be members of the Asiatic Society in Calcutta. For its part the *Décade philosophique* published "acounts of the life and writings of the celebrated orientalist William Jones" and "extracts from Ossian and *Shakuntala*, an oriental tale, text adapted from William Jones."[3] The association of these two poetic works in a single inquiring mind later showed up in the notes to Chateaubriand's *Génie du Christianisme.*

The principal sources of information were the *Asiatic Researches* themselves. The publisher's foreword to the French translation stated: "this collection has inspired such widespread interest in England that it is now nearly impossible to obtain a copy of the original Calcutta edition. The work has been reprinted three times in London and is almost completely sold out." In his second article for the *Magasin*, Langlès, who edited the

French translation, analyzed the first three volumes of *Asiatic Researches* that had appeared before Jones's death. He noted they "have already appeared in Europe," probably alluding to Kleuker's German translation.

It is true that the Bibliothèque de Paris possessed only the second volume of the English text: the life of nations was not, in those times, free of difficulties. For individuals the price of Sanskrit texts would always be a bit appalling. In 1814 Bopp complained that the first volume of the *Ramayana* cost him 106 francs, and in 1847 Renan was taken aback when he had to pay 90 francs for the same text for Burnouf's class. Langlès, like Anquetil, seems to have been exceptionally well supplied. He possessed the entire set of *Asiatic Researches* and Jones's *Shakuntala*, noting that "Citizen Pougens, one of our men of letters who combines good taste with erudition, has provided an excellent analysis of this Indic drama in the *Journal des théâtres.*" This is certain evidence that information, as was the case with everything related to Jones's *Shakuntala*, had passed beyond specialist circles and the readers of the *Magasin encyclopédique*. The picturesque Pougens, who was said to be the illegitimate son of the Prince de Conti and who was a pleasing storyteller later republished by Anatole France, also translated the *Voyages de Forster* and, before his death in 1833, collaborated on the *Revue Encyclopédique*, a publication we shall encounter frequently when discussing connections between Indic studies and the Saint-Simonians.

It is significant that the need for a French translation of the *Asiatic Researches* was recognized. As the linguists would have been capable, one would assume, of reading English, the publishers undoubtedly considered the work likely to appeal to a wider audience. We can further assume that this appeal grew out of the broad range of subjects *Asiatic Researches* dealt with—notably the numerous scientific articles placed side by side with the philological ones. For this same reason, the naturalists Cuvier and Lamarck and the astronomer Delambre were among Langlès's collaborators on the annotations. (Cuvier was a recruit whose importance we shall have many occasions to appreciate.) The French translation supervised by Langlès and published by Labaume in 1803 did not enjoy its expected success, as was also true of the *Asiatisches Magazin* begun at Weimar in 1802, and Lanjuinais and Joseph de Maistre later lamented the fact that it was discontinued after the second volume. Nevertheless, Jones and the *Asiatic Researches*, whether in English or French, were to be found on the writing desks of Quinet and Michelet, of Hugo and Lamartine, of Joseph de Maistre and Lamennais. On October 9, 1804, Wilhelm Schlegel wrote from Coppet requesting a copy of the *Researches* from Pictet in Geneva.[4]

There was, moreover, a duplication of Labaume's publication. It was assembled in 1803 by Ecrammeville, who did not sign his name, and was entitled *Lettres philosophiques et historiques à mylord S—— sur l'état moral et politique de l'Inde, des Indous, et de quelques autres principaux peuples de l'Asie . . . trad. en très grande partie des Asiatic Researches, des Worcks of William Jones, etc.* Ecrammeville acknowledged in the preface that Langlès had translated "the six volumes of the Transactions of the Calcutta Society," which were soon to appear. His own publication, offered at the same time, presented a selection. It was assumed that an abundant and diversified audience for Hindu materials existed. These *Lettres,* directed at the popular level, indicate the initial extent of Western interest. The second letter, based on the *Researches* and Jones's anniversary addresses, again related the history of the society. The fourth letter reconsidered the comparison between Indic cosmogony and the Book of Genesis. The doctrines were beginning to be approached accurately, but were consistently received in a rationalist spirit and with a suspicion of charlatanry characteristic of the eighteenth century. Attached to the fifth letter, which accurately recorded Sonnerat's place in the history of ideas, was an extremely curious fold-out page containing "A Genealogical Table of the Principal Divine and Renowned Figures in Indic History," including Buddha I and Buddha II, the first from the eighteenth century B.C., the second from the sixth century B.C. This was followed by a no less curious dialogue on the Buddha between a Catholic bishop and "the leader of the Rhaans, called Zaradoboura." The sixth letter translated Jones's famous 1784 essay "On the Gods of Greece, Italy, and India," in which Jones compared Hindu mythology point by point with Greek and Latin mythology. The *Lettres* thus bring into focus for us the initial phase of Western interest, which consisted of a passive repetition of the viewpoints of Jones and Wilkins.

A *Shakuntala* Era

In Germany an analogous phenomenon, though more comprehensive and immediate in its impact, arose around Herder, who as a philosopher of history had been deeply impressed in 1776 with Anquetil's translation of the *Zend Avesta* that Kleuker, who lived in nearby Riga, had given him. Herder was equally impressed with the Indic translations. In collaboration with Fick, Kleuker had translated Jones's articles from the *Asiatic Researches* into German as early as 1795. Herder himself, as the *Magasin Encyclopédique* noted in 1802, rendered excerpts from Wilkins' English *Bhagavad Gita* in verse in his *Zerstreute Blätter*. In *Ideen,* Herder had known no more of India than did Voltaire, and his understanding of it was, like Voltaire's, more imagined than real. Then, on May 17, 1791, Forster sent Herder his version of Jones's *Shakuntala*. This was of major importance, and Herder's hearty acceptance was shown by the preface he wrote for Forster's second edition. In 1798 Herder wrote another preface, this time for *Zur Kulturgeschichte der Völker* by Friedrich Maier, a disciple who was to figure prominently in German Indic studies. It is well known how Herder, in rekindling for a deciphered India the enthusiastic interest that had been felt for an imagined India, spread among the Romantics the idea of placing the cradle of the divine infancy of the human race in India—and he himself later conceived the *Gedanken einiger Brahmanen*.

Maier took up this theory. A genuine orientalist, his influence was felt as much through his retranslations as through his theories. His complete *Bhagavad Gita* and *Gita Govinda* produced a tremendous effect on Romantic circles when they were published in 1802 in the *Asiatisches Magazin* that Klaproth had begun to edit at Weimar. Thus Maier, who was a lecturer at Jena, was important in two capitals of German Romanticism. In Jena he was a personal friend of Schleiermacher and Schelling, and impressed Novalis and Friedrich Schlegel. Schiller belonged to the same groups, and his Indic readings left their imprint on his own work. In 1801 Maier contributed two essays—one on the sacred poetry and the other on the ages of India—to the *Osten Taschenbuch* edited by Seckendorf, which appeared in Weimar. Maier's audience in Weimar included two imposing adepts: Goethe and Schopenhauer. A second translation of the *Gita Govinda*, that of Dahlberg, appeared in 1802. Goethe's critical remarks on this subject in letters to Schiller on January 22 and February 19 would nourish many mystical hopes.[5] The impact of the revelation of Hindu thought on Schopenhauer is well known, and it is Maier who introduced him to the subject in 1813 when he had him read Anquetil's *Oupnek'hat*. Furthermore, in 1800 Maier had produced a study entitled *Über die mythologischen Dichtungen der Indier* that he developed in the form of a letter "To Alwina" in Tieck's *Poetisches Journal*. Through the latter, which pays tribute to the "national dreams" of his compatriots, we can ascertain Maier's link with the "Heidelberg group." Heidelberg, the home of Görres and Creuzer, was the third principal city of literary and philosophical Romanticism. Maier's *Allgemeines mythologisches Lexicon*, which Friedrich Schlegel endorsed in 1808, was a familiar reference work during this time. The nonclassical section of the work appeared in 1803, again in Weimar. In the battle of the mythologists Maier was to remain one of the champions of orientalism.

Although the *Hitopadesha* and the *Laws of Manu* spread rapidly in Germany and France, and although the two *Gitas* effected some striking conversions, as Anquetil's French and Latin versions of the Upanishads had in 1787 and 1801 respectively, the *Shakuntala* remained the great miracle. It was the first Indic work to seduce the aging Herder, and it caused the momentary love for an India glimpsed and cherished in Sonnerat to blossom in Goethe. Goethe and Herder were not the only ones to feel this effect. In 1802 Millin quoted Herder's first adaptations, and in 1825 Guigniaut exclaimed, "Who has not read the *Shakuntala?*" In 1830 Chézy, who translated the *Shakuntala* in his turn, exclaimed, "Oh most happy Forster! His simple task of reproducing Jones's English version in German was rewarded in the best way by the famous Herder's flattering remark: 'Georg Forster's name will, for us Germans, always be fondly remembered, linked with that of Shakuntala.' Oh, how I envy him!"

Forster had published his German version in 1791. He was a great explorer and with his father had accompanied Cook. Further, he was a revolutionary, a Rosicrucian, a man whose name was connected with strange and distressing love affairs. He died in 1794 at the age of forty in Paris, where he was studying oriental languages to travel, at last, to India. His beloved, the daughter of his teacher, the orientalist Michaelis, later became the wife of Wilhelm Schlegel. (This is not the last time we will glimpse the extraordinary couples created in Romantic Germany by the encounters between philology, philosophy, poetry, religion itself, and the love of women.)

Shakuntala was the first link with the authentic India and the basis on which Herder constructed an Indic fatherland for the human race in its infancy. From this sagacious work with its time-honored traditional refinement, a blasé Europe, thirsty for a golden age, could fabricate the notion of a primitive India, a concept that would prove long-lived and would obstinately seek to push back the date of Vedic poetry. There were of course in the same period and country a variety of ways to appreciate the same things: Schopenhauer's interest in India was profound, as was that of Wilhelm von Humboldt, who in 1828 thanked God for having allowed him to live long enough to become acquainted with the *Bhagavad Gita*. This was but a faithful echo of Goethe's cry in 1791 in the famous quatrain that ended "Nenn'ich *Sakontala* dich, und so ist alles gesagt" (When I mention *Shakuntala*, everything is said). Goethe's taste in these matters, however, was not unvarying during his poetic career. Goethe's discovery of the Hindu seemed to produce the shock of recognition that one hemisphere of his thought was decidedly oriental, but this was not the area of his thinking where he spent the most time. In a letter dated February 27, 1811, Goethe stated that his love for the Veda, which he had developed because of Sonnerat, was renewed by reading Jones and the new translations. He read Hindu poems in Wilson or had them translated aloud by Kosegarten, a student of Silvestre de Sacy.[6] He left notes on *Meghadula*, from which Schiller drew a passage for *Marie Stuart*, and on the *Gita Govinda*. In this same vein, but not from these books, came two poems contemporary with nascent Indic studies: "The Pariah" and "God and the Bayadere." The second poem, if not both, drew from the long-established work of Abraham Roger. Actually, Goethe was never able to put up with many-headed, many-armed gods and he made no secret of it. He hesitated at times over India—and over the Orient in general. His praise for the new humanism in the *Epigrams* had an ambiguous tone:

Whoever knows others as well as himself must also recognize that East and West are now inseparable. I admit that while dreaming between these two worlds one can waver; but such coming and going may be best done between going to bed and rising.

It was the remark of an old master who nodded his approval, bowed— and kept his distance. In his conversations, Goethe seemed to be made uneasy by the conflicts to which the lure of these two ambiences exposed nineteenth-century youth. The *Shakuntala* was a providential encounter for Goethe. The eighteenth century, with its fanatic taste for taste, was sufficiently reassured by the classical graces of the *Shakuntala*. The play did not take the author of the *East-West Divan* much out of his element, as it presented something of India that could remind him of Persian poetry. It is worth noting, moreover, that this is the same belated sensibility that characterized Jones, the first explorer in this domain, who also approached India via Persia.

Goethe had projected an adaptation of *Shakuntala* for the German stage, and it was certainly the source for the idea of a "Prologue in the Theater" in *Faust*, which according to Lichtenberger was drafted between 1797 and 1801 and finalized in 1806. The idea for the "Prologue in Heaven" was borrowed from *Job*. Heinrich Heine revealed Goethe's sources in detail. Having on numerous occasions visited Friedrich Schlegel, who was then professor of Sanskrit at Bonn, Heine himself developed a fervent interest in Indic literature after hearing Bopp in Berlin. On May 17, 1824 Heine sent three sonnets modeled after *Shakuntala* to Ernst Friedrich Ludwig Robert. Nevertheless, the same Heine wrote in *De l'Allemagne:*

It may be remarked that although Goethe sang so joyously of Persia and Arabia, he manifested a marked aversion for India. The bizarre, confusing, and obscure elements of this country repelled him, and perhaps his aversion resulted from what he guessed was a sort of Catholic ulterior motive to the Sanskrit study of the Schlegels and their friends. These gentlemen looked upon Hindustan as the cradle of the world's organization in Catholic terms. They saw in it the pattern of their hierarchy, they found in it their trinity, their incarnation, their redemption, their sins, their expiations, and all their favorite hobbies. Goethe's repugnance for India greatly offended them, and Wilhelm Schlegel bitterly called him "a pagan converted to Islam."

We can discern in Heine an aptitude for setting everyone at odds with everyone else, though, of course, he used parts of the truth. In Germany, as elsewhere, religious struggles permeated and complicated the Indic question, as can be seen later in Friedrich Schlegel's 1808 essay *Uber die Sprache und Weisheit der Indier*. This was only a temporary position for Goethe. In general the Western resistance to India seems to have stemmed more from a fidelity to its schools than to its churches.

In France *Shakuntala* determined Chézy's vocation in 1800. The young, angelic, blond-curled philologist wanted to see for himself whether the hitherto-ignored, newly discovered literature contained such hidden treasures. When he produced his French version in 1830—the first based on the original—he included Goethe's famous verses as an epigraph, and Goethe expressed his thanks in a letter in which he numbered *Shakuntala* among the stars that made his nights brighter than his days. Forty years had not dampened Goethe's passion. The appearance of *Shakuntala* was one of the literary events that formed the texture of the nineteenth century, not just by its direct influence but by introducing unexpected competition into world literature. Lamartine saw in it "the threefold genius of Homer, Theocritus, and Tasso combined in a single poem."[7] Chateaubriand, as usual, led the way. In the notes to *Génie du Christianisme*, he cited *Shakuntala* under the rubric "Sanskrit poetry" and compared it, as had Jones, with Ossian. Chateaubriand's reference indicated "Robertson's India," and in fact Robertson had dealt with *Shakuntala* in his *An Historical Disquisition concerning the Knowledge which the Ancients had of India*, published in 1791 and translated soon after into German and into French as *Recherches historiques sur l'Inde*. It was a remarkable work for its time, and Guigniaut later said that "everyone" had read it. It was one of the two factors that prompted Wilhelm Schlegel to learn Sanskrit, the other being his brother.

The works of Chateaubriand are marvelously indicative, and we can glean something of the extent of Western interest in the Orient from this statement in *Mémoires d'outre-tombe*: "Napoleon's literary career extended from 1784 to 1793—short in terms of time, long in terms of work. He occupied himself with China, India, and the Arabs." Again the fateful date 1784, the year of Herder's *Ideen* and the Asiatic Society. One wonders whether the future conqueror, like the Romantic poets, was already feeling cramped by the "molehill" of Europe and was longing for the immensity and elasticity of Asia. Chateaubriand's pen also provides firsthand evidence on the effect of the initial Indic impact in London: *Essai sur les Révolutions*, which he began in 1794, was published in 1796 and appeared in London in 1797, years of the great spread of Sanskrit. In the first chapter, while discussing India, Chateaubriand noted: "The Sanskrit, or Sacred, language has finally been revealed to the world. We already possess the translations of a number of poems written in this idiom. The strength, and philosophy, of the English in India has given the republic of letters a priceless gift." Here again Chateaubriand's principal source of information seems to have been Robertson, one of the first popularizers of the time to merit consideration. Later in the essay, Chateaubriand wished "to acquaint the readers with several fragments of oriental literature" drawn from the Sanskrit to which he frequently alluded. He felt that "a note on Sanskrit might please many readers." He referred again to Robertson while enumerating the English translations which had appeared at that time. In 1826, for the "new edition" of the *Essai*, Chateaubrand gathered together his second thoughts, which ultimately became one of the work's major attractions: his self-criticism provides us with information on the progress made by the new discipline in the course of thirty years. "This note on Sanskrit," goes the corrected version, "was rather novel at the time; nowadays Sanskrit is so well known that my quotations are no longer of interest." The quotations concerned the startling new ideas of the previous century which had borne the sensational chapter heading "Kreeshna . . . Fragment du poème Mahabarat, tiré du Sanskrit . . . Sacontala." In 1826 all of that was "so well known"!

We know that the great change that occurred between the two editions of the *Essai* was Chateaubriand's rediscovery of the Christian faith. The discovery of the domain of Sanskrit was regularly a chapter in the history of such changes. In the revision of his *Essai* Chateaubriand reproached himself for having mobilized the greater antiquity of India to oppose the chronology of Moses: "Alas! A deeper understanding of the learned language of India has succeeded in drawing these innumerable centuries back within the tight circle of the Bible. It was fortunate for me I became a believer again before having to experience this mortification." It was evident as early as Anquetil to what extent questions of biblical chronology remained a vital issue in the religious debates into which India was invariably drawn, and we shall come across frequent confirmations of this again in connection, for example, with Cuvier. Chateaubriand is an example of a great creative mind careful to revise its preliminary enthusiasm by keeping up with lingustic advances. By 1826, owing to the influence of comparative grammar, the myth of a single, primitive mother language— thought to be Sanskrit—had lost its prestige. The legendary longevity of the Vedas was toppled. Likewise, in 1796 a mania prevailed to compare Indic epic not only with the Homeric, which continues to be done, but with the "Germanic epic," a genre represented by Klopstock's *Der Messias* and even Gessner's *Der Tod Abels*. Both epics fell into oblivion, and later "Germanic epic" would mean the *Nibelungenlied*. In 1826 Chateaubriand was furious at having at first accepted the German thesis, well-established in England and disputed throughout Europe, of the similarity between ancient Persia and modern Germany.

Chateaubriand sent his *Essai* to La Harpe, Ginguené, and, notably, Delisle de Sales, and it immediately became well known in France, at least among literary men and journalists, as Sainte-Beuve later attested in the *Moniteur* (April 17, 1854). Auguste-Jacques Lemierre-D'Argy, a nephew of Antoine-Marin Lemierre, author of *La Veuve du Malabar*, which had remained well known since 1770 and which had come out at almost the same time as Anquetil's *Avesta*, wrote to Chateaubriand on July 15, 1797: "With the exception of a few criticisms concerning a few quotations that were perhaps unnecessary, and one or two comparisons that seem somewhat forced, *your Essai is enormously successful.*" It would be intriguing to know whether the criticized passages concerned the Hindu quotations and the Germanic comparisons, especially coming from the nephew of the author of *The Widow of Malabar*. In any event, by 1826 Chateaubriand had lost interst in the Sanskrit quotations, as if he were an oversensitive writer who wanted to thus eliminate the "few criticisms" leveled at his book. Ginguené and Delisle de Sales were the very men who represented the circles of the *Magasin* and *Décade*, two journals that followed the Calcutta publications closely. Chateaubriand, masking his pride as best he could with the detached tone of the artist, protested that if the book was at first well known, "it was almost as soon forgotten."

Regarding the repercussions of orientalism in its first phases, I should comment on Quinet's handwritten note among his papers in the Bibliothèque Nationale outlining his fifth lecture on *Génie des religions* at Heidelberg: "Germany: Herder, Hebraic poetry, Persian influence (Jean-Paul); Goethe, The Divan, The God, and the Bayadere;—England, Lake School, Coleridge; Shelly completely Indian;—Byron, etc." These accurate indications should be expanded upon, as there were others of significance. Throughout the first years of the century Benjamin Constant had taken up, abandoned, and then resumed a large work on religions, born in the atmosphere of Schlegel at Coppet. Sainte-Beuve wrote that Constant always "went to Fauriel to keep in touch with the latest developments of the discipline and to learn from him what had turned up concerning India and the Buddha in both Germany and England since their last meeting." Constant himself confirmed this report in his book *De la religion*.

These soundings demonstrate, contrary to popular opinion, not only that the revelation of Sanskrit was immediate and general but that it touched the most widely varied minds, each concerned with extracting from it the most serious information. In a mere decade Jones became widely known as the celebrated translator of *Shakuntala*; for Goethe he had become "the incomparable Jones," the famous Sir William Jones, and it was sufficient to quote him without explanations, as de Maistre demonstrated when he quoted Jones in his *Soirées*. The denouement of the story is that *Shakuntala* became a ballet at the Opéra de Paris in 1858, with music by Reyer and scenario by Théophile Gautier.

The Awakening of Oriental Studies in France

1793: Silvestre de Sacy, one of the fathers of oriental studies, made a breakthrough whose consequences would only later become apparent. He forged a key to Pahlavi on the basis of the copies of inscriptions of the Sassanian kings made by the Dane Karsten Niebuhr. In 1803 in Millin's *Magasin* he announced a great discovery closely related to his own: in Göttingen, Grotefend had just found the first clue to the decipherment of the cuneiform alphabets. Ever since Pietro della Valle had stumbled over the rocks of Persepolis in 1622, the efforts of the decipherers there had been frustrated. Here was one of the open questions of the pre-orientalist period. Grotefend succeeded in isolating a few symbols of the Achaemenid alphabet, but because of certain errors subsequently lost his way, and no further progress was made until Burnouf's efforts in 1836.

1795: L'école des langues orientales vivantes founded (under the law of 10 germinal, year 3). Silvestre de Sacy was named to the chair of Arabic and later, in 1806, to the chair of Persian at the Collège de France. Here it is institutions rather than discoveries that are important. The Ecole des Jeunes des langues, which went back as far as Colbert, had gone into a decline by the end of the eighteenth century. In 1790, Langlès requested its reform in the National Assembly, and reform was instigated by the *Convention nationale* based on Lakanal's report. Condorcet's famous project on public instruction included the teaching of oriental languages, to which Volney also attached a great deal of importance. Although the dead languages of Asia were generally eliminated from the educational framework, the synchronism with the research in Calcutta is striking. Although limited to living languages, the Ecole, directed first by Langlès himself and then by Sacy, played its role in heightening the general interest in the Orient that had been stimulated by the expedition to Egypt. Langlès and, to a much greater extent, Sacy, attracted many foreign students and scholars, a development that in turn affected the progress of discoveries by creating a prestige that focused interest on Paris. Sacy's debut as a professor was itself an event, almost on the level of a discovery. Luck alone, though it may play a vital role in any science at first, cannot assure success. Jones and Wilkins brought the fact of orientalism to light; Sacy provided the code upon which the exploration of the fact depended. And, like Jones and Wilkins, Sacy was a jurist.

As I mentioned earlier, instruction in Arabic was difficult to find in Europe in the eighteenth century. By the nineteenth century it had disappeared altogether. As a young man Sacy went to the Collège de France to take courses from Cardonne; the doors were closed, and the professor confessed to Sacy that there remained neither anything to teach nor students to train. Abandoned in Germany after the death of Reiske, and in Holland after the deaths of the Schultens, *père et fils*, Arabic had become an unworked lode. Progress was achieved through guesswork, and then came to a dead end. Sacy learned everything from scratch. He patiently explored the manuscripts and meticulously, with flashes of intuition, drew a method from them, as well as material for the first textbooks. As nothing outwitted him, or tired him, his inquiry extended to the limits of philosophy, developing in the process theories of general grammar and perspectives on the life of idioms. He produced a treatise on the philosophy of language, the first to be backed by rigorous experience, which became widely known and ultimately gave rise to the new linguistics. Bopp, understandably, soon hastened from Mainz to enroll in Sacy's courses, from which comparative grammar was to emerge. The entire family of great orientalists was beginning to take notice of Sacy's ideas. His classroom teaching had an even greater impact than his innumerable publications, and his most enduring contribution, like that of many of his successors, was his students, who went on to become masters because of their contact with him.

During this same period Rémusat was making progress in Chinese studies analogous to that of Sacy in Arabic and Persian studies, and the impact of the one on students, writers, and foreigners reinforced that of the other. Abel Rémusat was not so eminent a scholar as his colleague, but he found Chinese studies in the same condition as Islamic studies, and rendered them the same service. As early as 1585 Mendoza had exhibited Chinese characters, and Louis XIV had ordered Etienne Fourmont to teach Chinese. But no real success occurred until one hundred years later, in 1815. Fourmont's learning was exhausted in reading the titles of 5,000 Chinese volumes collected in the Bibliothèque du Roi. The first rough outline of Chinese grammar was that of Rémusat, which enabled a century of French sinologists to begin their studies. Rémusat had opened a new domain, as Sacy had with Arabic and Persian.

Before then there had been only a patchwork of incidental knowledge derived from the missionaries and voyagers. People came to listen to Rémusat or Sacy, or often to both of them, because they taught not only what was known but the means for learning. Sacy himself, without claiming any credit for his own involvement in the undertaking, related how legitimate sinology had been inaugurated in 1811 by Rémusat's *Essai sur la langue et la littérature chinoise*. Neither man set walls around his speciality; Rémusat produced, for his part, a serious attempt at the classification of Hindu doctrines, his *Observations sur les sectes religieuses des Hindous* (which appeared in his *Mélanges posthumes*). It had become clear that no one could break new ground in one area of Asian studies without taking India into account, particularly those whose interests were linked to China, as Pauthier later demonstrated and as the pioneer de Guignes had already shown.

It is important to understand how the intellects of the founders were cultivated, and we will later discuss the intellectual growth of Chézy and Champollion. At the age of twelve, Sacy was on friendly terms with a Benedictine Arabist who recognized the young boy's philological skills. Sacy read the Latin Vulgate and the Greek Septuagint and wished to read the original Hebrew, which he penetrated with the help of a Jewish scholar. After that, he moved on to its sister languages—Syriac, Samaritan, Ethiopian, and Arabic—and from Arabic to Persian and Turkish. (A half-century later Max Müller learned Hebrew, Arabic, and Sanskrit between the ages of eighteen and twenty, and Persian at the age of twenty-one.) Before the age of thirty Sacy let scholarly Europe know who he was. He had resolved, once and for all, to spare no effort in putting a hundred diverse, absorbing activities and duties at the service of his religious and political beliefs and of his scientific passion—all of which were one. In 1793, having taken refuge in the countryside, he had mass celebrated openly at his home. Two years later, having been appointed to the Ecole des langues and to the Institut de France, he resigned, like Anquetil, when called upon to take an oath against his convictions. In spite of his admiration and affection for Anquetil, he voted against him, out of professional conscience, in the awarding of a prize for the best translator of oriental texts. He had inflexible antipathies, and fought with equal vehemence the admission of both Burnouf and Michelet to the Collège de France.

1801: Oupnek'hat of Anquetil-Duperron, fifty Upanishads translated from Persian into Latin, based on the Dara Shikoh version. A major publication, both for its intrinsic value and for its influence on ideas. In France its forbidding form alienated it from its public, which it reached (and reached rapidly) through analyses that Lanjuinais printed four times between 1804 and 1832. Lanjuinais was, with Sacy, the last close friend of the aged Anquetil, and his own work centered on finding the oldest confirmations of biblical revelations. The *Oupnek'hat* had a decisive effect on Lanjuinais, who joined one of the first groups of enthusiasts to swell the ranks of the Société Asiatique and the Société Celtique. Like Eckstein, and yet opposed to Eckstein, he remained among those who sought spiritual sustenance in Indic studies. We should keep in mind that in Germany Schopenhauer was introduced to the India of the *Oupnek'hat* by Maier and remained profoundly influenced by it. Görres rendered in Germany a service similar to that Lanjuinais rendered in France. Anquetil's version retained its authority and was reissued around the 1850s by Albrecht Weber. Eighty years after its first publication, Mischel retranslated the *Oupnek'hat* into German, though Regnaud used Weber's edition. Max Müller produced direct translations of only twelve Upanishads, and I have already noted that even as late as 1897 Deussen had translated only ten more than Anquetil, and was unable to locate the original Sanskrit of five of them.

Hamilton in Paris and the Role of Friedrich Schlegel

1803: A milestone. The rudiments of Sanskrit reached Paris and instruction in it began. The secret had remained until then in Calcutta or had passed to London. In one fell swoop the focal point shifted and Paris then became, not without romance, the capital of nascent Indology. It happened that an officer in the British Navy, Alexander Hamilton, was staying in Paris, where he had come to collate oriental manuscripts at the Bibliothèque Nationale for an edition of the *Hitopadesha*, which had first been revealed by Wilkins' translation. Hamilton had lived for a long time in India, where he was, of course, employed by the East India Company. These two circumstances would have enabled him to meet Wilkins, a third being (as I noted earlier) that both were among the charter members of the Asiatic Society of Calcutta. Hamilton had married a young Bengali woman. While in France in 1803 he was surprised by the rupture of the Peace of Amiens between France and England. Kept as a paroled prisoner, exactly as Anquetil had been in England on his return from India, Hamilton, because of his scholarly connections, was given even more generous special treatment. At the urging of Volney, who was interested in his work, Hamilton was allowed to continue it freely. To express his gratitude, Hamilton taught what he knew of Sanskrit to his protector and a small group, at the same time undertaking to catalog the Sanskrit manuscripts at the Bibliothèque.[8] When he had completed this task, he had the generosity to inscribe next to his own name that of Langlès, who was charged with the custody of the manuscripts, although the custodian did not have the key.

Besides Volney, Hamilton's students included Langlès, Fauriel, Burnouf *père* (the Latin scholar), and a newly arrived foreigner whose presence in Paris during these years was as important to the history of Indic studies as Hamilton's own: Friedrich Schlegel. Chézy, who set out to learn Sanskrit because of his love for the *Shakuntala*, was not among Hamilton's students; he was one of Sacy's students of Persian, and very much bound to his teacher. By 1800 Chézy was eager to learn the language of India, but he dreaded arousing the jealousy of his haughty friend and professor. When Hamilton arrived, Chézy did not dare seek him out for fear of being discovered. Only in 1806, spurred on by the accumulating discoveries, and confiding only in his mother and his wife, did he immerse himself (through a procedure similar to Sacy's) in the mass of Sanskrit fragments and rudiments with which the missionaries and voyagers had enriched the Bibliothèque for more than a century. In the course of his research in the Bibliothèque he came across the skeletal grammars written by his few predecessors, and naturally availed himself of the first translations received from Calcutta, in order to elucidate the texts and formulate his own approach. He finished his work, but his personal reward for it was not great: his wife and two sons left him, and the eldest, whom he was never to see again, learned of his death in Basel in the same way Hugo learned of Léopoldine's death, by opening a newspaper. Chézy's name was on a list of the latest victims of the legendary cholera epidemic of 1832.

Friedrich Schlegel was also in Paris in 1803 and had come there looking for two things: Chézy, in order to learn Persian, and fame. He was to have more success with the one than the other, and he never forgave the country of his failure. Schlegel's wife, Dorothea, daughter of the famous Jewish philosopher Mendelssohn, had converted first to Protestantism for her marriage, then to Catholicism along with her husband, and it was she who first introduced Chézy to her countrywoman Wilhelmine Christiane von Klenke, whom he married. Wilhelmine had formerly been a governess in the household of Madame de Genlis and remained a correspondent to the German gazettes. The introduction was an unfortunate way to repay Chézy for the Persian lessons: Wilhelmine tormented the poor wretch and continued exploiting him even after his death. She left behind several volumes of memoirs, one of which was entitled *Unvergessenes*, meaning that she had forgotten nothing that could nourish a wide range of grudges. She spared Hamilton, however, and wrote that he "was not, any more than Schlegel, a withered erudite," that his science moved "in his soul, in his heart, in his imagination." Her marital rancor led to some compensating optimisms. (In 1844, in the *Zeitgedichte*, Heine wrote: "The elder Karschin is dead. Her daughter, La Klenke, is also dead. Helmine Chézy, her granddaughter, is still alive, I believe.")

Schlegel was the most zealous of Hamilton's students. He wrote to his brother Wilhelm on May 15, 1803 (the very day that war was declared between France and England): "Everything is going wonderfully. . . . I have learned a great deal. I have not only made progress in Persian, but I am sure of my Sanskrit. . . . It happened that at just the right moment an Englishman, Hamilton, the only one in Europe apart from Wilkins who knows Sanskrit and knows it thoroughly, assisted me, at the very least with his advice." Advice? At the very least? Schlegel was taking three hours of lessons every day. Judging from the indifference in his account toward the fate of his host country and toward Europe, it must have seemed to Schlegel that Hamilton had come to Paris just for him. It is true that before his lessons with Hamilton, Schlegel, availing himself of the same resources as Chézy, had worked on his own with the eighteenth-century materials in the Bibliothèque de Paris and later continued to do so. Schlegel was an enthusiast from the start. As a student of nineteen in Leipzig he announced the great discovery of the *Shakuntala* to his brother. Wilhelm, who blamed Napoleon for just about everything and seized any good opportunity to retaliate, maintained that the Continental System had delayed the arrival of Sanskrit in Europe.[9] Nevertheless, Friedrich was indebted to the Napoleonic Wars for Hamilton's presence in Paris as his Sanskrit teacher. In the final analysis, he did not grasp the language as thoroughly as Wilhelm did. Friedrich used his knowledge of Sanskrit from the spring of 1803 to the spring of 1804, translating excerpts from the epics, as well as the *Laws of Manu*, the English versions of which he was undoubtedly familiar with. He supplied excerpts from Firdausi in his journal *Europa*. He had now touched, and handled, the oriental Romanticism that his memorable proclamation in "Discourse on Mythology" in the *Athenaeum* had announced: "It is in the Orient that we must seek the highest Romanticism."

Schlegel was boarding with two young compatriots, the Boisserée brothers, who had come to Paris from Cologne to admire the works of art the sword of Napoleon had collected. They lived in the former residence of the Baron d'Holbach on the Rue de Clichy. From November 1803 until April 1804, Schlegel gave a private course on world literature there, coincidentally with his Indic studies. Thus India inevitably entered into his survey, which was published by Anstett, whom I am following here. During that same April, Friedrich's brother Wilhelm, dining with Tieck at Goethe's home, discussed Friedrich's Indic studies—at the time Friedrich wanted to undertake a translation of *Shakuntala*. Hence his projects were discussed by his countrymen; but not everyone was of the family. Arnim, who at one point was going to live with Friedrich (in the home of a woman named Polier?), wrote to Brentano on January 23, 1803, at a point when the private course was dealing with German literature: "I won't hear Schlegel until tomorrow. His lectures are likely, so it seems, to give women diarrhea."[10]

On October 9, 1804 Wilhelm, brought back to Coppet by his patroness and reunited with Friedrich, wrote to Geneva for *Asiatic Researches* so that his brother could continue his work. On December 5, Friedrich, who had returned to Paris, wrote to Madame de Staël referring to a "huge Indic manuscript" from the Bibliothèque that he was studying and comparing the *kshatriyas* to the Greek *Danaioi*. Even better than his letters as a gauge of the progress Indic ideas were making in Schlegel's mind are Benjamin Constant's recollections of his conversations with him in Coppet in 1804. Constant recorded Schlegel's attitude at the time in his *Journal intime*, while harking back to the work he himself was interminably composing, *De la religion:*

I am discovering a good reason for not discussing Indic mythology in detail in my book. It is that the subject is only now beginning to be explored and that a work dealing with the material published today would, in twenty years, be surpassed and forgotten. Moreover, the infatuation of the navigators on this uncharted sea must subside a little. For it is worth noting that whenever a man believes he has made a discovery, in whatever realm of science, he is fond of attributing everything to this discovery. The English, the masters of India, maintain that everything comes from there. Schlegel, who has devoted four years of his life to learning the Indic language, says the same thing. The French, since their return from Egypt, see the origin of everything there. Levesque, who wrote a history of Russia, locates the source of all religion in Russian Tartary. Each would have what he knows best be the source of what others know. One must be wary of adopting such a hypothesis, but it is essential to be aware of precisely what is known about a subject before beginning to write about it.[11]

Hence it is evident that India's novelty had not diminished despite twenty years of infatuation, that England remained her refuge, Germany her way station, and that each nation persisted in explaining world history through the Orient while coloring its version according to the whims of its own enthusiasms. Through a curious misreading, the first editor of Constant's *Journal intime* mistakenly included a reference to a work entitled "La religion indienne évidemment dévoyée par le sacerdoce" ("The Indic Religion Clearly Misled by the Priesthood"), whose author was allegedly a strange and unknown "M. de Shaste." In reality this was not the title of a book, but a note by Constant, and "Shaste" was not the name of a person but rather obviously designated the Hindu *shastras,* misspelled since Holwell and Voltaire. This particular incident, however, is indicative of a prevalent attitude: in this good European head the notions about India which had been substantiated were tied to the speculative ideas which had preceded them. Constant's ideas concerning a "march of the human race" progressing from fetishism to polytheism and then to theism were consistent with the dreary presumptions that spread through the entire period from Germany. It was, once again, a question of the same thing in the somewhat Saint-Martinized town of Coppet where Wilhelm Schlegel, weary of the Middle Ages, went, as Heine put it, to take refuge in the pagoda of Brahma.

Friedrich later accompanied his friends the Boisserées to Cologne, where he accepted a professorship at the *école superieure* that France had just established there. He taught a little of everything there in the summer of 1806, but he had previously resumed his private course at Paris at the request of the Boisserées, who were, along with perhaps one or two others, the only ones to attend his lectures. In the winter of 1805–6 the lectures dealt with world history, and in the spring of 1806, with philosophy. The latter were published in 1836 by Windischmann, and the former, which are particularly interesting for us, published by Anstett in 1939. Finally, in the winter of 1806–7, Schlegel gave a new course for the benefit of Madame de Staël, whose guest he was. In 1805 he spoke before friends but did not publish his lessons. However, he placed an announcement in the *Kölnische Zeitung* of April 17, 1805 (27 germinal, year 8) for the public courses he was giving "at the Collège des Jésuites."

The assertion of Hindu primacy that Constant exposed persisted with unswerving constancy in Schlegel's thinking from his discovery of *Shakuntala* in 1790, through his attribution of the supreme Romanticism to the Orient in the *Athenaeum* in 1800, to his May 1803 letter to Wilhelm announcing the progress he had made with Hamilton's help. On September 15, 1803 Friedrich wrote another letter to Tieck in which he stated, "Everything, yes, everything without exception has its origin in India." This is striking confirmation of Constant's account. A year later Schlegel declared—again to Tieck, who was among those Romanticists most immersed in the Indic sea—that he had already begun to formulate a construct of human history based on Indic history, with special consideration of India's religious importance. This was the upshot of his lectures on literature and world history—and probably no other single factor was more important in establishing an Oriental Renaissance, which is why I feel it useful to research its genesis point by point.

According to Anstett, after Schlegel "the pilgrims of wisdom no longer headed for Saïs," and the reality of India displaced the vague eighteenth-century notion of Egypt. Schlegel also studied a great deal of material concerning Iran and propagated a number of ideas on the subject that attracted widespread interest. In a letter dated September 15, 1803, he emphasized the notion of an alleged direct line from the Persian to the German language and race. During the same period, while he was studying the Apostles of the Church closely, seeking the original Christianity, he became deeply interested in the Germanic past, amassed notes on the importance of the Middle Ages, and revived Herder's thesis on the salutory nature of Germanic contributions to the Latin world. These concepts were to be widely associated with the idea of a new Renaissance. The influential *Uber die Sprache und Weisheit der Indier* took shape, was brought to completion, and was published in 1808 at Heidelberg amid this interplay of thoughts and interests, passions and labors. Immediately after its publication Schlegel wrote to Johannes von Müller on May 2, 1808 that his book was a work of "the true living science," which undoubtedly meant that it was a contribution both to an understanding of man and to an understanding of the divine. Schlegel was aware that it was surely his greatest work, the monument in which he recorded that which was not yet known, his personal imprint on the century. It could not be the imprint of a complete artist but perhaps that of a religious philosopher.

Schlegel's essay was printed in March of 1808, an extraordinary time for Schlegel, only a few days before his conversion to Catholicism, when he and his wife went to Cologne for baptism. This simultaneous advance toward a dual conversion to Calcutta and Rome was an extremely striking phenomenon, though not unique. But it was particularly conspicuous in Schlegel's case and important to this history because Schlegel was literally the inventor of the Oriental Renaissance—not because he first compared the nineteenth and the fifteenth centuries (a ready parallel, and potentially little more than an intellectual pastime), nor because, as I will discuss later, the impact of his essay was considerable and immediate, but because it was Schlegel who made what could have been no more than a pastime into a vital reality, who created a general cultural movement out of one particular field of knowledge. And he was able to do this because he, alone among all the others, saw this first and foremost as a spiritual event. The convergence of three essential factors in his mind predestined the outcome: his background as a responsible German historian, his romantic veneration for a prevenient Orient whose precedents would determine the literary future of Europe, and, above all, his faith, which led him to choose to relate everything to religious interests.

Even more important than the responsibility of the historian was the conviction that the essential work, beyond the necessary tabulation of verified facts and references, began when intuition and powerful sympathies intervened to form out of chaos a unity of events. "Not blinding himself with objectivity," as Anstett puts it, Schlegel added finishing touches that animated the immense universal landscape that came to light with the rediscovery of India. It was not the first instance of "historicity" invading European thought, but was one in which this passion was especially associated with world history. The trend from 1802 to 1830, from Fichte and Schelling to Hegel and Görres, a trend in which Schlegel stood out, marked an important stage in Western thinking about India. Schlegel's 1808 essay had its roots in his 1803 and 1805 courses, notably chapter 3 of the published version of the latter, entitled "Von der indischen Bildung," a lengthy, detailed section that referred to William Jones and quoted from the just-published French translations of *Asiatic Researches*.

It is not surprising that Schlegel's conversion coincided, within a few days, with the publication of the essay. During his final decade, 1818–28, the new courses that Schlegel had assumed in history and philosophy confirm the preeminence he accorded to religious facts—which is the source of Schlegel's originality among contemporary historians. Moreover, this attitude immediately impressed Schlegel's compatriots and contemporaries. In Schlegel's 1805 classes, the centuries already appeared to many as a march from one condition to another: in the beginning a perfect communion between men and God existed; in the final extremity this world, in harmony with divine thought, had been darkened or betrayed and had to be rebuilt. Schlegel's construct was designed to interest many of his contemporaries, and it joined the new hopeful mood that had become prevalent first in Germany but even in France (despite Schlegel's remarks on this subject). There was of course lively opposition in a Germany that saw red at the slightest suspicion of what was called the Jesuit influence; Schlegel, whom the court of Rome highly esteemed for his services right up to his death, was soon suspected of such influences. I have discussed, and will discuss further, Heine's bitter allusions to such disputes. There is other evidence as well, such as the indignation felt after reading the essay by those already irritated by the conversion of a man like Stolberg: neither Goethe, nor Schelling, nor Windischmann would accept as a positive science one whose intentions were perpetually colored by apologetics.

Their instanteous protests demonstrate that the impact of Schlegel's book was immediate and violent. The same effect was evident among many others, such as Jacobi. The learned, thinking circles in Germany were shaken; Schlegel had crystalized the Germanic need for the Orient. Schelling, setting aside his dogmatic objections, wanted to found an Oriental Academy in Munich right away, to be presided over by Schlegel. Also in 1808, while dedicating his *Das Licht vom Orient* to Napoleon, Protector of the Confederation of the Rhine and "the most powerful Avatar of all time," Othmar Frank (whose arrival along with Bopp in Paris in 1812 was, like Bopp's, a direct consequence of Schlegel's book) called for a

"Society for the Ancient Wisdom of the Orient and of the German Nation." It was Schlegel who had provided the formula for a concept of wisdom—part science and part belief—whose destiny would be linked to national destiny. Darmesteter had good reason to compare the impact of Schlegel's essay during the second Renaissance to the impact of Joachim du Bellay's *Défense et Illustration de la langue française* (1549) in the first, but it generated fewer original works, although it extended farther into the inner life.

Schlegel's career soon gave rise to a surprising number of others: those of Bopp and Frank and, a little later, Rückert, who in 1836 mirrored the famous title in his own *Die Weisheit der Brahmanen*. In 1815 the third edition of Heeren's *Ideen über Politik, den Verkehr, und den Handel der vornehmsten Völker der alten Welt* (originally published in two volumes at Göttingen, 1793–96), a major work for some years, for the first time devoted a great deal of space to India. Heeren had filled the gaps in his knowledge of this domain, which the first two editions had dealt with only cursorily, by reading Schlegel. The same year, in the *Heidelberger Jahrbücher*, Friedrich's dear brother Wilhelm asserted that nothing as important as Friedrich's essay had appeared on the subject. The essay was followed in the next two years by Görres' *Mythengeschichte der asiatischen Welt* (1810) and Creuzer's *Symbolik und Mythologie der alten Völker, besonders der Griechen* (1810–12), publications that mark the debuts of another two famous careers. There were echoes in the less illustrious works of Kanne and Rhode as well. In 1827 Friedrich Windischmann produced a systematic follow-up of the essay entitled "Fundamentals of Philosophy in the Orient," which had appeared in his father's *Die Philosophie im Fortgang der Weltgeschichte*. The Windischmanns worked near Wilhelm Schlegel in Bonn, but it was again Friedrich who was the focus for this first German school of Indic studies, and Wilhelm's adherence to India made him one of his brother's most useful conquests. Whether Heine's relentless criticism of his former professor was justified, and there is no doubt that Wilhelm had some absurd habits, it must at least be granted that Wilhelm received his impetus from Friedrich. Wilhelm surpassed his brother in application but not in intuition, and in the realm of faith he furiously opposed him.

In another connection, Heine maintained in *De l'Allemagne* that the only scientific side to Wilhelm's Indic studies was "the well-known work of his scholarly collaborator, Lassen; Franz Bopp, in Berlin, is Germany's genuine Sanskrit erudite, the most important of all." Heine was a student at Bonn in 1819 and later described the ostentatious ceremonial, confirmed by other accounts, with which Professor August Wilhelm von Schlegel officiated. Actually, after a year in Göttingen, it seems Wilhelm made a serious study of Sanskrit with Bopp in Berlin. One wonders if it was simply the common tendency to dwarf the elder brother in preference for the younger that explains Heine's passage in *De l'Allemagne*, significant on more than one point, extolling Friedrich's 1808 essay:

Since the appearance of Madame de Staël's book on Germany, Friedrich Schlegel has again presented the public with two important works, perhaps his best efforts. . . . They are *Uber die Sprache und Weisheit der Indier* and his *Vorlesungen über die Geschichte der Literatur*. With the former he has not merely introduced us to the study of Sanskrit; he has founded it. He became for Germany what William Jones had been for England. He learned Sanskrit in a most original way, and the small number of excerpts he included in his book are admirably translated. Due to his natural perceptiveness, he grasped the full significance of the epic versification of the Indians, of the *shloka*. . . . As Friedrich Schlegel's work on India is certainly translated into French, I can spare further praise. The only thing I find fault with in the book is its ulterior motive. It is written in the interests of ultramontanism. These good people had not only discovered the mysteries of the Roman priesthood in Indic poetry, but all its hierarchy and all its struggles with temporal power as well. In the *Mahabharata* and the *Ramayana* they see the Middle Ages in elephantine form. Indeed, in the *Ramayana* the struggle between the king Vishvamitra and the priest Vashishta involves all the same stakes which set emperor against pope: here in Europe the object of the dispute was called investiture; in India it was the cow Sabala.

This dispute was a theme that appealed to Heine's sense of irony, and he based a short poem on it. His debt to India was better paid by his infusion of the rhythm of Sanskrit lyricism into his two beautiful plays *Die Lotusblume* and *Auf Flügeln des Gesanges*. The truth is that Schlegel's essay was not translated into French until 1837 by Mazure, teacher of Victor and Théodore Pavie, and Théodore's career as an Indic scholar may have owed something to the event. Was it another piece of sarcasm on Heine's part to pretend that such a significant work could have been ignored so long in France? In point of fact, it was not: by 1809, within a year of the essay's publication, Manget, a professor from Lausanne, annexed the linguistic section of the essay to his translation of Adam Smith's *Considerations Concerning the First Formation of Languages*, published in Geneva and Paris as *Première formation des langues*. Smith's name was first on the title page, but Schlegel occupied more than half the book, and Manget emphasized the originality of Schlegel's contribution, its bibliographic interest, and the importance of the correspondence between Schlegel and foreign Indic scholars. As early as July 2, 1808 the *Journal de l'Empire* had given a detailed account of the German publication of Schlegel's essay. Nor did the Geneva excerpts pass unnoticed by French officials. In 1808 when Lanjuinais was chosen by the Institut to succeed Bitaubé in the *troisième classe*,

he was named to the post because he was one of the few men the members could depend on to shed light on India and Indic studies—the biography by Dacier in Lanjuinais's *Oeuvres complètes* leaves no doubt on that
score. Dacier adds that "as soon as he was admitted," and for several years
thereafter, Lanjuinais did in fact keep his colleagues current on this subject, as they had expected. In 1810 Lanjuinais pointed out the translation
by Manget, whom he called "Mauget," to the Institut and affirmed that
it had "aroused the attention of the scholarly world." In England, Henry
Crabb Robinson noted in his *Diary* that he had read Schlegel's essay, whose
author he had met in Paris in 1802, with great pleasure.

Schlegel had endowed his book with richness and allure, knowledge
and conjecture, the matter-of-fact and the hazy. Of course it sought to instruct the West about this distant revelation, but it also sought to induce
Germany to take up the Indic cause. This intent was in keeping with a
native tendency to infuse philosophy, mythology, mystical theology, and
poetry into linguistic questions. It is not at all surprising that one of Herder's disciples would, at this time, point to the origin of poetic invention
in the "inner life" of the poets and would perceive among the primitives
a fusion of the colossal with a sweetness bordering on religiosity.

According to Heine's gossip, it was because Goethe's thundering rejec-
tion had abruptly annihilated their infatuation with the Middle Ages that
the Schlegel brothers, directly named in this interdict, fell back on Indic
studies, and that Wilhelm especially supposedly sought within such studies something "to arouse a new feeling." But the link between reviving
Germany's Gothic past and claiming an ancient oriental heritage seems to
have been a basic rather than a superficial one. The awakening of German
medievalism, which was to hold an important place in the composition of
the new Renaissance, had been realized through Friedrich—and from Paris,
where he kept company only with expatriate Germans and others who
were anti-French (such as Achim d'Arnim and Charles de Villers), and
where he valued the France of Napoleon and Chateaubriand at "just about
zero."

Friedrich Schlegel made India into the cradle of all primitive purity, especially religious purity, and at the same time reanimated the idea of a
relationship between Asia and Germany. In this first decade of the nineteenth century, when the patriotism of his countrymen was transformed
into Pan-Germanism, Schlegel wrote, as Herder had already discerned and
as Hegel would later repeat, that Europe owed everything to the barbaric
invasions. From this he inferred that the Franks from France were no more
than a nation of "Frankish rascals" (*francs coquins*), and he concluded, in
the spirit of Fichte's *Addresses to the German Nation*, that Latin characters
were unworthy for printing translations of Hindu works. It was not by

chance that he fell back on the *Nibelungenlied* which he wanted to adapt, as the heavy artillery in a campaign for an Indo-Germanic epic, nor, furthermore, that Schlegel was making plans for a medieval encyclopedia.

Thus a certain conception of world history was taking shape. The history of philosophy also had to make room for oriental doctrines, and in Germany the Windischmanns and later Othmar Frank were working in that direction. In France, Degérando was one of the first and most active supporters of the exchange of ideas between nations, and it is he who introduced the name of Herder to France. In 1804 Degérando published a work with the instructive title *Histoire comparée des systèmes de philosophie considérés relativement aux principes des connaissances humaines;* it was truly the advent of comparativism. The first volume of the 1822 version devoted numerous pages to oriental systems. Degérando focused especially on Anquetil's *Avesta* and, like the contemporary occultists, he was interested in the cabala as well as an Egypt which, as he knew, Champollion was beginning to decipher. He cited Rémusat's work on China and that of Holwell and Dow on India, but also mentioned Jones and Mackintosh and "the rich collection of memoirs of the Calcutta Society."[12] He was a great admirer of Herderian Germany and drew from Creuzer's *Symbolik*, which was still quite recent and in which, according to Degérando, "a sane and vast erudition has gathered together an enumeration of all the philosophical opinions and traditions belonging to the peoples of the greatest antiquity."

Degérando had a personal relationship with Mackintosh, as did Cuvier, and demonstrated how, according to his letters, Mackintosh had "profited from his stay in Bombay, where he served as solicitor general, by studying the Brahman doctrine," and where, "as he had gained the confidence of several Brahmans, he was initiated into the most secret principles transmitted within the highest order of adepts. He was greatly surprised to discover therein an idealism similar to the one Fichte and Schelling introduced in Germany at the beginning of this century. In an extremely interesting letter which he wrote to us at the time from Bombay, and which we have conveyed to several different persons, he did his best to elucidate for us in detail this peculiar system which he himself will undoubtedly want to make public one day, and for which reason we refrain from reproducing it here." From this one can discern the immediacy of the encounters. At the very beginning of the nineteenth century a French philosopher was corresponding with English Indologists about Indic doctrines. He discussed them with a circle of friends that included not only "ideologues" but both Ballanche and Cousin, who in different ways were surely attentive to Hindu thought. In his notes to *Oupnek'hat*, Anquetil had already established a clear relationship between Hindu thought and post-Kantian metaphysics. Schopenhauer was not long in emphasizing this same relationship, and by 1841 Quinet discussed it as something which had long been understood. Having made this extraordinary preparation, Germany, whose philosophy of history had already set the stage for the advent of Indic ideas, built on this foundation new schools of idealism perfectly fitted to welcome such ideas. At this point the connection between Indology and Romanticism can most clearly be seen to be one of the watersheds in human history. The arrival of the Indic world in a Europe other than the Europe of 1800 might not have been startling enough to induce such an entirely new kind of humanism.

The Founding of the First Academic Chairs

1812: Following the news that one could contact the new realm of Indic ideas brought to Paris by Hamilton and the new methodologies inaugurated by Sacy, many had already hastened to Paris from Germany. I have mentioned Othmar Frank and Franz Bopp, and at least two others, Klaproth and Lassen, should be acknowledged. Lassen later became interested in Avestan and collaborated with Burnouf in 1826 on crucial work concering Pali. We should also note here the importance of Bopp's arrival. He came to learn Persian with Sacy and to pursue Semitic studies with Quatremère, and stayed until 1816 to probe Sanskrit with Chézy. Bopp marked, following an age of instantaneous conversions, an age of reformation, and he later definitively replaced the pandits' lessons with Western criticism. He founded the new department of comparative grammar, which Sylvain Lévi later called "one of the first conquests of oriental studies and one of the noblest of the nineteenth century." Bopp and Wilhelm Schlegel carried the spark from Paris and London to the German universities—the one, in Berlin, urged them toward scrupulous investigation of linguistic facts; the other, in Bonn, kept them within the literary and historical axis without doing much to prevent their sidelong glances toward national interests.

1814: On November 29, owing to Sacy's influence, a chair of Sanskrit was established at the Collège de France, and on January 16, 1815, his student Léonard de Chézy was the first to occupy the post. This was the first chair of Sanskrit to be established in Europe. The same royal decree (it was simply a piece of bad luck that took the honor away from Napoleon) established a Chinese chair on behalf of Abel Rémusat. In 1832 Burnouf succeeded Chézy and was to provide a great deal of momentum for the advancement of Sanskrit and linguistics. At Burnouf's death in 1852, after an interim during which Théodore Pavie occupied the position, the chair passed to Foucaux. More recently, Sylvain Lévi, who held the chair after Bergaigne, rendered the post illustrious and related the story of its beginnings.[13]

Germany, on the initiative of Wilhelm von Humboldt, followed suit in 1818. The number of chairs there rapidly surpassed the number of those in France. In the French provinces such chairs were established only belatedly: in Lyon, for instance, after the liberal but brief attempt at the Ecole de Nancy. The English universities, curiously, did not enter the competition until 1833, and then through private initiative, with the chair that Wilson held at Oxford. London followed, and the study of Sanskrit was later introduced at the universities of Cambridge and Edinburgh. It is true that as early as 1805 the East India Company, which lasted until 1857, had introduced Sanskrit into the curriculum of Haileybury College, but it was established there for the purpose of training civil servants, not for teaching pure science. There were soon chairs in the Copenhagen of Rask and Westergaard and in Helsinki, Leiden, Zurich, and Brussels as well. In Louvain, Félix Nève, a student of Burnouf, taught Sanskrit while holding the chair of ancient literature, and Adolphe Pictet, his fellow student at the Collège de France, likewise produced good results in Geneva, as did Gorresio in Turin.[14] In America, Sanskrit was taught at Yale, where William Dwight Whitney was most prominent in the field; he was succeeded by E. E. Salisbury in 1854 upon his completion of his studies at Tübingen. According to Barthold, "Even Russia was not spared the craze for Indic culture which appeared in Western Europe at the end of the eighteen century and the beginning of the nineteenth." In 1810 Uvarov's *Project d'une académie asiatique,* which would have centralized oriental studies, led Goethe to begin a correspondence with its author. In 1818 instruction in oriental languages began in Russia, but was long provided by foreigners until Petrov taught them at Kazan in 1841 and at Moscow from 1852 to 1875. Prince Saltykov's journeys to India in 1841 and 1844, accounts of which were published in Paris with numerous engravings, had but a superficial influence. Minaev's work on Buddhism was important, as Shcherbatskoi's was later. In 1855 Sanskrit was taught at Saint Petersburg, where Western scholars were imported, among whom Schmidt and Friedrich Adelung (nephew of Johann Christoph Adelung) should be mentioned, although their efforts were of varying merit. The research carried out by Roth and Böhtlingk was of unquestionable value and resulted in their great Sanskrit lexicon, which has not been surpassed. It was a German work but was published by the Russian Academy of Sciences between 1852 and 1875.

The *Journal des Savants,* reestablished in September of 1816, kept Paris current with the essential publications. The first volume of the new series, which ended in December 1817, included sixteen articles on oriental literature, two by Chézy, the others by Sacy and Rémusat. The *Journal* continued its interest in the Orient: in February 1817 Chézy gave an account of Wilson's *Meghaduta* translation, which had appeared in Calcutta in 1813. Chézy complained that Wilson had sidestepped the problem of grammar, and quoted in devanagari characters. In 1819 Dacier, Sacy, Chézy, and Rémusat were all on the editorial board of the *Journal*, along with Cuvier and Victor Cousin.

CHAPTER FOUR

The Era of Decipherings and the Expansion of the Known World

The Société Asiatique of Paris

THE year 1816, when the *Journal des Savants* was devoting a great deal of attention to oriental studies, was the same year Bopp founded the science of comparative grammar, based on Sanskrit. It was also the year the Parthenon marbles, first written off as a Roman hoax contemporary with Hadrian, were freed from Lord Elgin's warehouse and stormed the portals of the British Museum. It took a wave of young people—painters, poets, and critics—to get them there.

Since we are considering here a second Renaissance that was, as a whole, both complementary and contradictory to the first, it is edifying to consider what the first one had come to at that time. Between Julius II and Louis XVIII the Laocoön or the Apollo Belvedere embodied the Greek miracle in art, particularly during the entire reign of Bonaparte, when the Louvre, to the avid enthusiasm of everyone who saw them, displayed these two exquisite masterpieces snatched from the museums of Italy. Literature welcomed the notion of what was called primitive beauty before the plastic arts did. Herder's ideas on poetry only belatedly left their mark in the realm of ideas dominated by Winckelmann. The first time a Frenchman, the consul Fauvel, set eyes on the Aeginetan marbles in Athens, he crushed them with the epithet "hyper-antique." A term worth remembering. It reflects a disdain soon to be overturned. Sanskrit initially made its mark as another aspect of the "hyper-antique." The establishment of oriental studies signaled a higher bid for the archaic.

India's effect in this regard in the world of letters was later matched only by Assyria in the plastic arts. In 1847 the monumental sculptures of Khorsabad, the biblical Nineveh, were won for the Louvre by the valiant consul Botta; accounts by Delacroix, Baudelaire, and Leconte de Lisle attest to the impact they produced. Thereafter the strikes of the excavators' picks modified the aesthetics and credos of the schools, more or less publicly. Concepts of antiquity, nature, and art were suddenly altered and were to evolve in a direction previously closed. And here too the sudden advent of an all-embracing comparative system altered everything. At the same time a framework for Assyrian and Egyptian antiquities validated a colossal number of artworks that merged with the river of Hindu poems.

1821: Founding of the Société Asiatique de Paris, which held its first general meeting on April 1, 1822, chaired by Sacy. The London Asiatic Society was not established until two years later. Paris was, as well, the first European city to follow the example of Calcutta and to provide for the official teaching of Sanskrit. The Duc d'Orléans was honorary chairman of the Société Asiatique and opened the annual meetings in person. In 1823 he lectured on the study of languages; he acted and interceded on behalf of the Société, and once he had ascended to the throne, he subsidized it. In his presence in 1826 Sacy outlined the "guidelines for the encouragement of oriental studies." These studies were important to the state; some claim they, along with Roman history, served several of the kings who succeeded the emperor by quieting national memories. Sacy, an intrepid legitimist as well as one of the founders and leaders of the Société, had the ear of the Bourbons and of no less than Comte de Lasteyrie, who participated in his undertakings.

Dussieux, in his *Essai sur l'histoire de l'erudition orientale,* pointed out that the French institution "soon was the center of oriental philology: it provided the impulse; its journal summarized the orientalist movement; it judged what was being done; it acted as a tribunal whose decisions had final authority; its important criticism marvelously continued the tradition of French criticism which is so often felt to be in decline today [1842]. Moreover, it is to this same institution that the English sent from Asia the sacred books of Tibet and Nepal." Dussieux failed to specify whether Paris at that time was receiving only part of an allotment ordinarily sent to Calcutta, Oxford, and London as well. His reference is to the famous dispatch, an event in itself, of the Buddhist canon—100 volumes in Tibetan, 80 in Sanskrit—discovered at last by Hodgson. Foucaux immediately set to work translating the first of these and, on the basis of the others, Burnouf produced the first real account of Indian Buddhism, which had until then been conjectural for Europe. Burnouf's work marked an important turning point in 1844. Also in 1821 the publication of the second volume of Langlès's *Monuments anciens et modernes de l'Hindoustan* was completed. The first volume had appeared in 1812. I will discuss this work further in the chapter on the arts.

Among the foreign associates of the Société were Wilkins, Wilson, and Colebrooke from England and Kosegarten, Klaproth, the Humboldts, Bopp, and Wilhelm Schlegel from Germany. Also included, along with the Parisian masters Sacy, Chézy, Rémusat, and Champollion, were a number of newcomers to the field who were not, or were not to remain, unknown: the two Burnoufs, Jean-Louis the Latin scholar and his son Eugène; the two Littrés, François the Indic scholar and Emile the positivist philosopher; Degérando, Langlois, Lanjuinais, Fauriel, Bruguière de Sorsum; and then Cousin and Villemain, who as extremely popular professors launched or supported the first attempts at comparative literature and as politicians distributed the academic chairs or supervised instruction. It would seem that everyone of importance in the gathering battle of ideas had been touched by the Orient. The imposing name of Chateaubriand was clearly among those included on the membership list to add prestige; yet it signified a bit more. In his shadow, and in the wake of Ossian, an already existing penchant for certain antiquities of the old world was to benefit the new sciences and enthusiasms; many scholars were members of both the Société Celtique and the Société Asiatique. The two causes at first seemed linked by mutual concerns, just as Jones had already claimed they were linked in their origins. In 1856 the Institut de France awarded a prize to Pictet for his *De l'affinité des langues celtiques avec le sanscrit*, and in the following year Bopp expounded some of its basic ideas.

Since the beginning of the century, moreover, the question of oriental languages, both living and dead, had become increasingly vital. Volney worked unceasingly at devising a common alphabet for the languages of Europe and Asia, pasigraphy being an issue that was a popular concern at the time. His publications were spread over twenty-five years. The first, *Simplification des langues Orientales, ou méthode nouvelle et facile d'apprende les langues Arabe, Persane et Turque, avec des caractères Européens*, dating back to 1795, had met with objections from Langlès and Sacy but was rewarded with Volney's admission into the Asiatic Society of Calcutta. The last was published shortly after his death in 1820. In his will Volney commissioned the Institut to award an annual gold medal to the scholar who devised the best system for the transliteration of all the oriental forms of writing, including Sanskrit, into Latin characters. (A similar concern had already been expressed in the first volume of *Asiatic Researches*.) The laureates were frequently to be eminent orientalists, including Burnouf in 1831.

1823: The Société Asiatique began publication of its *Journal Asiatique*, which too became the first of a series.[1] There were, of course, several English periodicals, but the familiar complaint remained valid: "New policies and details of interest solely to the East India Company take up so much space that scientific or literary concerns are far from being given the necessary exposition." A better instrument had to be considered "as the study of Asian languages becomes more widespread." These comments, included in the "Announcements of the Société," are instructive: there was a desire to fill a need felt by all scholarly Europe. No doubt any prospectus is bound to be written optimistically, but the effect for Europe, if only for France, was commensurate with the announcements. In 1839, after having received Buddhist manuscripts from Hodgson and the *Bhagavata Purana* from Duvaucel, the Société received a copy of the Vedas from Prinsep. The Société was soon to be involved in publishing scholarly papers, underwriting publications, equipping expeditions, and supplying maps to travelers. It was the Société that provided Duvaucel with his resources and financed Botta's trip. 1823 brought another satisfaction: an Asiatic Society was formed in London on the Parisian model. The first meeting was held March 15, and Colebrooke, as chairman, delivered the opening address.

Yet another important event for the Société occurred in 1823: the arrival in Paris of Julius Mohl, a German from Stuttgart. Mohl had been learning Hebrew in order to become a pastor, had lost his faith along the path of exegesis and branched off into Asian languages. His professor at Tübingen directed him to Sacy, and Mohl later became a naturalized citizen in order to teach Persian at the Collège de France. By 1828 he had produced an admirable French translation of Firdausi's *Shah Namah,* an undertaking sponsored by the government. In 1829 he published *Fragments relatifs à Zoroastre.* His further work dealt with Pahlavi and Avestan.

Because of his close contacts with several well-known authors, and later the salon of his wife, Mary Clarke, who received a variety of celebrities, Mohl contributed actively to the spread of philological advances in literary circles. For a period of twenty-seven years, beginning in 1840, he was charged with the task of presenting an annual report to the Société, which proved to be a brilliant contribution. During these twenty-seven years the world of orientalists gave a great deal of attention to his remarkable reports, and their publication sustained his reputation.

Egyptology—Champollion

1822 marked the opening of another gateway in the wall of languages. Champollion's famous *Letter to M. Dacier* provided a key to the hieroglyphic alphabet, based on the trilingual Rosetta Stone inscription brought back by the expedition to Egypt. That expedition was just then concluding its publications. In October the *Journal des Savants* published a concise table of the first results drawn up by Champollion. On the morning of September 14, 1822, Champollion ran across the Rue Mazarine on which he lived, into the library of the Institut, where he knew he would find his brother, Champollion-Figeac, at work. He cried out to him, "I've got it," went home, and fell unconscious. Coming out of a five-day coma, he immediately picked up the sequence of a waking dream that was almost as old as he was, and asked for his notes. On the 21st he dictated a letter to his brother, dated the next day, which he read to the Académie des Inscriptions on the 27th.

Like Sacy and Jones, Champollion had been a child prodigy, obsessed almost from infancy with the desire to be the one to resolve the problem of the hieroglyphics. He made charcoal drawings of them on the walls of his room when he was a child and trained himself to draw them from memory, thus making them into a second life, a presence in his unconscious by which he was to be thunderstruck. At the age of twelve he wrote to his brother that he could put up with Latin only by considering it a tactic that would lead him to oriental languages. His early years were those in which the echoes of the expedition to Egypt and the conquest of Sanskrit and cuneiform were reverberating throughout Europe. But an entire century haunted by the enigma of languages had already been preparing the children born to solve that enigma. Champollion learned Hebrew on his own and moved on to Chaldean, Syriac, and Arabic, making his way through the biblical languages like the other sons of the eighteenth century. At the age of thirteen he read the Hebraic *Genesis* fluently to the prefect of his *département*, a feat reminiscent of Sacy's in the presence of his Benedictine tutor. At the age of seventeen he was appointed to the Bibliothèque Imperiale, which gave him an opportunity to learn Persian and Turkish. The Sanskrit studies brought to Paris by Hamilton had already attracted a number of followers, and young Champollion assimilated the basics of Sanskrit. By the following year he was wearing on his person a sort of talisman which he preserved and later entitled "My First Steps." It consisted of several lines from the Rosetta inscription, along with their phonetic transliteration, to which no one had discovered the secret. Champollion was eighteen years old.

The portrait of Champollion—"a spirited colt that needs triple rations," as Carré quotes the mathematician Fourier as saying—painted by Léon Cogniet reveals an extraordinary face: a fire burning within a disarray of tangled, bushy hair, an asymmetry in which all the lines of the face seem in opposition, producing the impression of turbulent, flashing thought, the image of a whole life incapable of inaction. Yet fourteen years of advancing his thought still lay ahead of him. When his discovery was finally proclaimed at the conclusion of the long dream that ended with the half-loss of life, he was welcomed with open arms. But of course Champollion's discovery, like Anquetil's Avestan and Jones's Sanskrit, was contested—notably by the unavoidable Klaproth. Champollion, a professor of archaeology at the Collège de France in 1831, died of exhaustion after his third lecture, yet not without perfecting his Egyptian grammar, his "calling card for posterity."

After a lapse of several years Champollion's work found people to continue it. From Rougé to Mariette at the end of the line, they were again explorers with isolated careers who learned everything on their own. The detective genius of the European teams, successively competing since the seventeenth century, had finally perfected, from first intuition to final verification, a method of deciphering. For the first writings tackled, inscriptions rather than manuscripts, the method was more or less the same: amid the confusion of unknown characters, a small number, repeated several times between the same symbols, were recognized, and these were called vowels. According to the origin and assumed purpose of the inscriptions, the names of persons who must have been mentioned in them were considered next. For example, the texts on the Persepolis monuments were known to have been engraved for the Persian kings, who very likely demanded that their names and titles be included, and it could be relied on that the workers did not fail to repeat them. Thus it was concluded that a certain ideogram signified "king." This "word" being found several times between two others, the immediate deduction was that the two others designated two kings, the father being mentioned after the son. As there was no doubt as to the approximate age of the inscriptions, a preliminary elimination of impossibilities made certain the reading of the names Xerxes, Darius, and Hystaspes.

For hieroglyphics the problem was at once easier and more difficult. There was an inscription in three languages, one of which, Greek, was known. However, the inscription had been written out on the basis of two systems: the one ideogrammatic, the figuration of ideas in the manner of the rebus, and the other alphabetical, the representation of spoken sounds. It was at first thought that the ideography was total and an impasse had been reached. Sacy was the first to hit upon the idea of the two systems, but his inspired hypothesis ran up against the difficulty of discerning the points at which one passed from one system to the other. Then came the correct supposition that the cartouches surrounding certain groups of symbols had to be a solemnity reserved for kings. Champollion's breakthrough, which at last and alone cleared up the enigma, was, first, that the alphabetical script, referred to as demotic, was a transliteration of Greek proper names; and second, given the fact that the texts were presented in three different scripts, the first could be found again as a sort of successive shorthand in the following two. The indispensible pivotal theory, which evolved slowly, was that all of the Egyptian form of writing was based on a phonetic system, similar to ours and not, as had been believed, on an integral ideographic system such as Chinese. It was a table of phonetic symbols valid for both the hieroglyphic and the demotic scripts that Champollion revealed in his *Letter to M. Dacier.*

One could establish a sort of psychology of the great orientalists. In addition to their capacities, the founders shared a striking kind of moral purity and uncompromising minds. Anquetil and Sacy could be reproached for their asperities, but they alone resigned their appointments during the First Empire rather than take the required oath. Philarète Chasles, who came into contact with several spheres of knowledge without self-indulgence, contrasted the garrulous levity, the haughty pedantry of the bourgeoisie with the republican resoluteness of Lanjuinais and "Professor Desgranges," whom he honored, a bit hastily, for having created Sanskrit studies in France "before Burnouf." These qualities at least to some extent would counterbalance the many tales of altercations among touchy, jealous, and irascible orientalists like Julien and Pauthier, Oppert and Halévy, and Chézy himself. Asceticism, with its Jansenist overtones, could be discerned in more than one of them, including Lanjuinais, Quatremère, Garcin de Tassy, and even Anquetil. Chézy, so as not to offend his formidable friend Sacy, did not allow himself the easier alternative of attending Hamilton's courses, while Burnouf gave up work on major texts in order to leave them for various foreign colleagues, thus providing careers for many European pilgrims to India. The moral character of the first English Indic scholars was discernible in their open struggle against colonial policies. And their generosity with manuscripts extended, through those provided by Hodgson, to all of Europe. Moreover, there was a universalism that permitted the many nineteenth-century German orientalists who were admitted without discrimination into France and England to become permanently integrated in the scholarly elites of their adopted countries.

The Level of Indic Learning around 1830

Even the most cantakerous served a useful purpose, and it is owing to this trait in Wilhelm Schlegel that we have an exact picture of the level of Indic learning at that time, for in 1832 he published in Bonn and Paris his *Réflexions sur l'étude des langues asiatiques.* (The Bibliothèque Nationale has one copy of the work inscribed to Klaproth and one inscribed to Loiseleur-Deslongchamps.) Schlegel wrote the *Réflexions* in a generally rather deft, if not flawless, French. He wrote directly in French on several occasions, including a prospectus in 1824 for an eight-volume Sanskrit-Latin *Ramayana* and his *Essai sur l'origine des Hindous*, written in 1834 and reprinted several times. Between 1820 and 1830 he published the *Indische Bibliothek*, which was intended to popularize the new learning and for which he was showered with praise by, among many others, Littré *père*, who wrote to Schlegel on behalf of his son.

By 1806 Wilhelm had rejoined his brother Friedrich in Paris; he made frequent visits to Chézy, who at that time was in the first flush of his enthusiasm, and Langlès who was hard at work himself. At the beginning of 1815 he was in Paris again, perfecting his ideas about Sanskrit with the first of those continuing Hamilton's work and carrying on technical conversations with Bopp. In 1825 Wilhelm returned to Paris to obtain the fonts of nagari characters for his editions of the *Hitopedesha* and *Bhagavad Gita*. He took the patterns from the Imprimerie Royale to Germany; thus after 1825 Bonn and Berlin had fonts at their disposal for Sanskrit. London and Oxford had typefaces that were closer to devanagari script. This solved an entirely material question that had impeded the debut of Indic studies.

If Schlegel addressed his English rivals in French (*Réflexions* was dedicated to Mackintosh and Wilson) it was because—and he did not conceal his resentment over this—the British public, not to mention the general European audience, was much more familiar with French than with German. It was not the last time one would have to wonder whether nineteenth-century Germany had gotten up in arms because its philologists could not bear to find, when Latin was abandoned, that their language had so little currency in the lettered world. All its efforts since Lessing had been focused on persuading the world that French was not worthy of being written.[2]

Schlegel's first grievance against London was that he did not find a publisher there, from which he deduced that the English were interested in India only for political and commercial reasons, as if India were England's milch cow ("une vache d'abondance," as he phrased it). Schlegel was not the only one to come to this conclusion, and he stated it without hedging. Moreover, Schlegel was relying on significant excerpts drawn from the *Report of the First General Meeting of the Subscribers to the Oriental Translation Fund, with the Prospectus, Report of the Committee, and Regulations*. This committee had been formed in 1828 by the Asiatic Society of London and had soon won the support of scientific and even social circles. The list of the British subscribers carried "the most illustrious names." It was a sign of the oriental vogue, and it had its price. On the business side, intellectual endeavor needs supporters who buy more than they read and read more than they understand. Unfortunately, these people sometimes try to dictate the choice of what they are paying for.

In his appendix, Schlegel reproduced the English prospectus *in extenso*, and it more than justified his position. Two items were prominent as the principal concerns, not purely scientific objectives but rather concerns of local theology and colonial occupation. It may have been generous of the fund to share the abundant English manuscript collections, but to venture the reminder that in oriental studies England had long ranked first offended the professor from Bonn. Schlegel wound up with an entourage of impatient students anxious to take vengeance for him on the British professors.

The first article of the prospectus concerned biblical studies. A straightforward acknowledgment. A well-established custom. Yet ten years earlier the Société Asiatique de Paris had begun by asserting that the major task of oriental scholars was to break out of "the narrow framework of biblical criticism," and we know that the Société was not in the hands of heretics. India did not appear in the prospectus until the ninth paragraph, and was immediately qualified as "British India" and was followed by the justification that seeking information about the history, geography, economics, and customs in these possessions would profit both the governors and the governed. They were founding an institution and seeking new recruits. Arguments suited to the occasion had to be taken into account. The Parisian prospectus had also made an appeal to practical interests, though more subtly. People who are not asking for money for themselves are obliged to be doubly careful to avoid scaring off those from whom they request it. As Max Müller later pointed out, "no science and no art have long prospered and flourished among us, unless they were in some way subservient to the practical interests of society." But Schlegel prided himself on his own good fortune in serving the King of Prussia, who "encourages all scientific progress, however far removed it may be from any immediate application." Bitterly, he wished similar luck to the English researchers.

In the process of demolishing English research, Schlegel did not leave much of Hamilton, to whom he and his brother were indebted for not a little of their own knowledge of Sanskrit. For Schlegel the great tragedy remained that the Germans were everywhere unrecognized and ignored. "We have," said Schlegel, "enough to console ourselves with." Yet one wonders why, historically, Germans so rarely seem like a people who are consoling themselves.

Literature had by then benefited from the important translations and the wide esteem of the "rightly celebrated English authors." The plans of the Oriental Translation Fund had included the *Mahabharata* and the *Shah Namah* from the outset. Schlegel, with the sagacity that made complete collections and the classification of vast ensembles possible, accorded Hindu and Chinese literature the highest esteem, placing them above Arabic and Persian literature; he had unreserved praise for the Upanishads and the

Bhagavad Gita in particular. Here the gravity of the Germanic mind is a good guide: "If the study of Sanskrit had brought nothing more than the satisfaction of being able to read this superb poem in the original, I would have been amply compensated for all my labors. It is a sublime reunion of poetic and philosophical genius." In these words we recognize the man of the *Athenaeum*, the brother of the Schlegel seeking in the Orient the sustenance of the new Germany, a poetry that would be a belief. He was not the first to give the *Bhagavad Gita* top ranking, but he was among those who did so most fervently. In his 1832 essay his admiration, which was then more reserved, extended to Hindu monuments, for which he claimed a prestige at least equal to those of Egypt.

When Schlegel derided the "vogue of having new and original ideas about ancient India" that was current in a public eager to "welcome the hollow dreams, false theories, and arbitrary hypotheses which are appearing in large quantities," he had Jones in mind. But doesn't his enumeration of "arbitrary hypotheses" also refer to his brother Friedrich, not long dead but unforgiven, and to his disciple Eckstein? We know that Wilhelm had no liking for anyone he thought might be involved with Indo-Christianity.

The problem with the malcontents is that they were right on several counts. Too many translations, complained Schlegel, and too soon, given the available tools. Thus each country accused the others of forgetting that they had scarcely gone beyond the first word of Sanskrit grammar. It is true that the tools remained few and primitive: each scholar could make headway into a new text only by returning, at least partially, to the linguistic stage prepared by his predecessors. In hacking his way through the underbrush, the pioneer had to stop at each step to reinvent the ax. In his introduction to Bopp's *Comparative Grammar*, Bréal confirmed "everything that touched on religious doctrines, literary works, and Indian legislation attracted the lively interest of these writers and thinkers, but they held strictly grammatical works in only moderate esteem. The study of Sanskrit, which, it must be admitted, was at the time dull and bristling with difficulties, was regarded as a painful though necessary initiation to lofty speculations."

Another work which complemented Schlegel's *Réflexions*, written at exactly the same time, was Pauthier's article in the *Revue Encyclopédique* of November 1832, "Coup d'oeil sur la langue et littérature sanscrites, principalement sur les ouvrages sanscrits publiés jusqu'à ce jour" ("A Glance at the Sanskrit Language and Literature, through Recently Published Works"). According to the article, in 1827 Rosen in Berlin had furnished "the best collection" of the grammars and lexicons produced by Hindus that the missionaries had, since the eighteenth century, provided to the

Bibliothèque de Paris. Pauthier further enumerated seven Sanskrit text-books of Western origin which had been written since Colebrooke's 1805 grammar, notably those of Wilkins and Bopp. But most of them were in-complete or depended largely on indigenous methods. Wilson's dictio-nary, published in Calcutta in 1813, was the only dictionary available at that time, and Bopp's vocabulary, published between 1828 and 1831, the only vocabulary. In 1842, the only work Dussieux could add to the list was the first Sanskrit grammar in French, which had been produced by Desgranges, a student of Chézy and a protégé of Vigny. Dussieux ob-served there was "still no elementary work dealing with the real basics, for the use of tradespeople." Such a work was provided in 1859 (the same year Oppert's Sanskrit grammar appeared) by Emile Burnouf and Leupol of the Ecole de Nancy, who also provided a *Dictionnaire classique sanscrit-français* in 1866.

During the 1830s, the years when the first definitive attainments were being evaluated, Abel Rémusat also took stock in his "Discours sur le gé-nie des peuples orientaux," which appeared in his *Mélanges posthumes*. He found that Europe had precise information about "twenty different peo-ples during forty centuries." The true place of this new store of knowl-edge between the fastidious studies of the grammarians and the facile imaginations "of all those who would rather dream than devote them-selves to study" was yet to be determined. The fantasy "that there exists somewhere a vast region, an immense country called *the Orient*" where all the inhabitants were supposedly "cast from the same mold," whereas they had nothing in common "except being born in Asia," was yet to be dispelled. Finally, it was essential that translators opt for different meth-ods from those of a literalness bristling with scholarly notes for the set purpose of embellishing the *Koran*. Within the order of the mind, all is interlinked. While orientalism was revitalizing conceptions of antiquity and philology, it was also posing in a new way the insoluble problem of trans-lation. In this field no language was at a greater disadvantage than French, for no other language is fashioned so exclusively for the analytical mind and a certain literary canon. The Hindu texts first gained renown for their poetic merit, which was frequently appraised according to the dictates of an outmoded sense of poetic taste. It is only too true that among the first translators, from Chézy to Fauche, a great deal was sacrificed for the sake of floweriness. Sacy's theories on the art of translation are a perfect text-book of elegant infidelity. Mohl later called him the king of the "florists" among the founders of the Société Asiatique.

Everyone—scholars, popularizers, and writers—bemoaned the small number of texts available to the ordinary reader. Taking stock of what texts were available, one encounters the astounding fact that as late as 1830 the infatuation for Hindu literature in France was nourished by but a *single* important text, which had been fully and directly translated only *that same year:* Chézy's *Shakuntala.* The rest were only fragments, analyses, retranslations, or commentary. Even the *Panchatantra* of the Abbé Dubois, a work long celebrated in the West for its closeness to Western fables, and previously included by Pétis de la Croix in his collection of oriental tales, was incomplete and was not drawn directly from the Sanskrit. The stories were better known through Wilkins' *Hitopadesha,* but only a small portion of this work was available in French until 1855, when Lancereau also translated it.

In Germany the situation was not much different. Wilhelm Schlegel listed *Bhagavad Gita* (his own translation was the first in German based on the original), *Shakuntala,* the *Hitopadesha,* Bhartrihari, and Manu. Amaru's amorous verse translated by Chézy (under the pseudonym Apudy) appeared in both France and Germany in 1831 (Rückert's German translation was not published until recently). England was better placed to be the initiator, yet there, as in all the European countries, what was called primitive poetry seemed to become less available the more it was admired. The Vedas were still everywhere a mystery, and the two principal epics were available only in a few passages in the anthologies. Carey and Marshman in India made a translation of the first two books of the *Ramayana* between 1806 and 1810. These were printed in three volumes, and volume 2 was lost in a shipwreck. Another, still partial attempt to publish the *Ramayana* was Wilhelm Schlegel's edition with a Latin translation published in three volumes in Bonn between 1829 and 1838. But the complete work did not appear until Gorresio's full edition with an Italian translation was printed between 1843 and 1845 in Paris. Some of the best passages were excerpted, notably by Bopp and Wilhelm Schlegel in Germany, by Chézy in France ("Dasharatha" in 1814, other episodes in 1814 and 1818, and in 1826 an edition of the "Yajnadatta" with both a French and a Latin translation by Burnouf *père*). The size of the *Mahabharata* scared off translators even longer. The publication of the complete text was not attended to by the Asiatic Society of Bengal until 1834–39. Several soon-to-be-famous excerpts—"Shakuntala," "Nala," "The Flood," and "The Abduction of Draupadi"—were noted in France by Chézy and Pauthier in the *Revue de Paris* in September 1832 and by Théodore Pavie in the *Journal Asiatique* between 1839 and 1841. In Germany the Latin translation *Nalus, carmen sanscritum,* produced by Bopp in London in 1819 and reissued in 1832, was an important event. A German translation by Kosegarten appeared at Jena in 1820. The original Sanskrit text of the *Bhagavad Gita,* which was not to be found in the 1809 Calcutta edition, did not appear until Wilhelm Schlegel's 1823 edition. The first worthwhile European *Gita Govinda* to follow

Jones's was Rückert's in 1837. After Anquetil's Upanishads, Pauthier produced only two excerpts in 1832, again drawn from the Persian version of Dara Shikoh, and Poley produced five Upanishads in 1844.

As for the Vedas, which had been the first texts sought by the enthusiasts and the object of general anticipation since the seventeenth century, the original of the *Rig Veda* was not available until 1830 in a 27-page specimen furnished by Rosen. The study of Vedic Sanskrit, heraldings of which had so greatly perplexed the missionaries and the interpreters of the eighteenth century, dates from this publication. Yet study in this area did not get its bearings until the work of the German Roth in the 1840s. He continued the work of his mentor Burnouf in the field after Burnouf had clarified the question of Avestan. In 1838 the first part of the *Rig*, prepared by Rosen, appeared posthumously in an edition that included a Latin translation. Wilson's English translation did not appear until 1848; Langlois's French version appeared in 1851. Max Müller's definitive edition, in German, was published in 1869.

An article signed by Jean Reynaud in the *Revue Encyclopédique* for 1832 urged Pauthier to lose no time in translating Colebrooke's essay on the Vedas into French. Dating from 1805, the essay is an admirable work, but according to specialists Colebrooke had not studied the entirety of the Vedic collection closely. In his notes to *Shakuntala* in 1830 Chézy felt it necessary to explain the meaning of the term "Vedas" to his readers. In 1830 Hegel observed in his *Philosophy of History*, "Several manuscripts of these Vedas have reached Europe, but they are very rarely complete. . . . Colebrooke alone has translated a part of them. Two great poems have also reached Europe: *Ramayana* and *Mahabharata*. Three quarto volumes of the first have been printed, and the second is extremely rare." In the *Globe* in 1829 Pauthier had given the opening chapters of the *Laws of Manu*, on the creation, which were reproduced in the *Encyclopédie des gens du monde*. The English version by Jones had been in widespread use since 1794; reprinted in London in 1796, translated into German in 1797, it was cited by de Maistre, Lamennais, and Benjamin Constant, and recommended to Michelet by an insistent Jacob Grimm. But it was through Loiseleur-Deslongchamps's French translation, after 1833 and again through Pauthier's mediation, that the book gained widespread currency in France. Hence Hugo's line in the *Contemplations*, "Quand un livre jaillit d'Eschyle ou de Manou" (When a book wells up from Aeschylus or Manu).

Given such a persistent dearth of texts fifty years after the discovery of Sanskrit, although forty years later Max Müller would estimate the number of independent Hindu texts at 20,000, it is astounding that such a disorganized body of literature would yet become famous, and all but popular, so quickly. "What we know from hearsay," Jean Reynaud noted, "is

vast and pervades our imagination. What we know from our own experience, what we know from having felt and savored it ourselves, is so small
that it seems as if this privilege has been granted to us not to calm our
desire but to provoke it even more." He does not intend sarcasm. One
might ask whether the capricious scarcity of information about the real
image of India did not under the circumstances create an image of an India such as the Romantics liked to picture. "Two sections of the *Mahabharata* and the *Ramayana* are known in France: the delightful story of
Shakuntala and the funeral speech of King Dasharatha; of the Puranas and
the Vedas France is only slightly familiar with a sort of cursory outline of
a few broken fragments." For the rest, the French public had to rely on
"pale imitations of the English versions," in which the double filter let
through little of the original color. "India is summed up in a few odd,
incomplete volumes. For several years almost all the progress made in
France toward an understanding of the Sanskrit language and its treasures has resulted from the work of a single man: Chézy." Reynaud's
statement was not completely accurate, but it was almost fair. After Burnouf's publications it was, however, no longer true.

At the end of 1832, just as Reynaud's article appeared, Burnouf took
over the position vacated by Chézy, who had been a victim, along with
Rémusat and Saint-Martin, of the legendary cholera epidemic. Shortly after
Chézy's death, Burnouf's first lecture at the Collège de France was published, on February 1, 1833 in the newly established *Revue des Deux-Mondes*.
Darmesteter later wrote that "with this treatise Indic studies entered their
practical period." Burnouf's personal charisma, the radiance of his genius, and the enthusiasm of his students were to influence a wider public, and his books were to reach artists and literary figures.

The Influence of Colebrooke

Burnouf, who at the age of twenty-five in 1826 had already solved the
riddle of Pali with Lassen, began in 1836 to publish his *Commentaire sur le
Yaçna*, which provided the first real key to Avestan. 1832 seems a climactic year if we also consider the Indic reflections cast on science by literature and opinion. We will soon discuss further evidence of this same phenomenon in the domains of the novel and fashion. Pauthier was again
one of the principal media, especially in his translation of Colebrooke's
"Essay on the Philosophy of the Hindus." In fact, the translation did not
appear until 1833, but it attracted considerable attention in intellectual circles beforehand. In his introduction, Pauthier reconsidered Jouffroy's observations to him concerning Colebrooke's treatise on Sankhya. Pauthier

was in correspondence with Colebrooke, and during the printing received the *Gymnosophia* that Lassen had published in Bonn. Alluding to "persons involved in the study of Sanskrit," Lassen noted that "the number is growing daily, and it might not be absurd to think that once its great importance is recognized the Sanskrit language will be studied like the Greek and Latin languages which are derived from it." It would not be the last time this wish was so expressed.

The impact of Pauthier's version of Colebrooke was remarkable. Even twenty years later in his article "Indic Philosophy" (in the *Dictionnaire des sciences philosophiques*, edited by Adolphe Franck), Barthélemy Saint-Hilaire affirmed that everything known in that domain issued from that publication. And I will cite two other examples of its impact. The first is the copy of Pauthier's translation, in its original binding, which I possess. It was given as a prize, and printed in gold letters on the cover is the insignia "Collège royale de Bourbon." My second piece of evidence will explain the first.

In 1829 Victor Cousin devoted the fifth and sixth lectures of his history of philosophy course at the Collège de France to Hindu doctrines. From the beginning he frankly admitted, "I would like to make it clear that for myself, and I am unable to read the originals, oriental philosophy is equivalent to Indic philosophy; and I say again that Indic philosophy for me is almost entirely represented in Colebrooke's essays included in the first volumes of the *Transactions of the Asiatic Society of London* from 1824 to 1827." The qualification "almost" was an allusion to Rémusat's excerpts from Colebrooke published in the *Journal des Savants* from December 1825 to July 1828, and to Burnouf's article of March 1825 in the *Journal Asiatique*, as well as a few references in Chézy, Wilhelm Schlegel, and Wilhelm von Humboldt. Thus Colebrooke's works had an immediate impact; they were very soon used by the philosophers Jouffroy and Cousin, and although Cousin did not wait for Pauthier's translation, he was conspicuous in spreading it.

Cousin's professorial comments, we should remember, had enormous impact. Augustin-Thierry preserved a memory of them as "nearly legendary." Stenographic transcripts posted in Parisian squares were spread all over France by zealous students and made their way abroad, where they prompted Goethe to speak about Indic philosophy with Eckermann. They were given equal attention with parliamentary debates in newspapers and were immediately translated into several languages. In short, they had a kind of triumph in which politics was obliged to walk hand in hand with literature. Cousin acknowledged with satisfaction that "there have not been this many lecture-goers in the Latin Quarter since the scholastics." One can gauge from this the prestige he secured for new and remote doctrines in two hours. His course had been suspended by royal edict in 1820. When it was reinstated on April 17, 1828 by the minister Martignac, one can imagine the rapture of the youth around the professor's chair. Echoes reached even Caro.[3]

Cousin's destiny in this affair was closely linked with that of his political friend and colleague Guizot. After 1830 the two moved from the opposition into the government, Guizot as minister of public instruction and Cousin as principal educational advisor. It is doubtful Cousin would have allowed Guizot to neglect a field of knowledge so close to his heart and to which he had won so many adherents. Moreover, Guizot himself was interested in orientalism, through other friends and through his second wife, Elisa Dillon, whom he had married in 1828.[4] And when was Guizot in power? Amid the changes following the "ministry of three days," he again took up, in November 1834, the ministry of public instruction, which he had held since October 1832. These were highly significant dates. The period around 1832 not only marked India's literary and worldly conquests; it was when Pauthier's work would appear. In 1834 this work received one of the prizes distributed by the royal colleges. One can imagine to which two powerful friends Pauthier owed this honor, and it is not surprising that he took care to recall Cousin's 1829 course.

This connection takes us a rather long way; Indic philosophy unexpectedly benefited from its political involvement with both the judiciary and Parliament, but matters did not stop there. On December 1, 1834 an article by Sainte-Beuve called attention to a *Précis de l'histoire de la philosophie* attributed to Salinis and Scorbiac, who had just revived the celebrated Collège de Juilly. Four major "historical periods," Sainte-Beuve noted, "are dealt with at length." First is "the period of oriental philosophy, in which the speculations of Brahman and Chinese philosophy are set forth by a writer very well informed on the most recent advances." Clearly "the most recent advances" are those of Pauthier and Cousin, both of whom Sainte-Beuve knew well personally. These advances had an important follower at Juilly in the person of Lamennais, who was appointed there about this time. As André Billy pointed out in *Figaro littéraire* (September 8, 1948), "When Lamennais lived in Juilly, the school had not yet returned to the Oratory. Since the end of the Restoration it had been headed by two secular priests, Scorbiac and Salinis, who had been joined by the Abbé Gerbet, the editor of the *Mémorial Catholique*, in opposition to which Pierre Leroux had founded the *Globe*. These excellent priests were, naturally, legitimists. The 1830 revolution persuaded them to appeal to Lamennais, who represented the new ideas of democracy and liberty." It should not be forgotten that the *Mémorial Catholique* was one of the journals through which Eckstein, since 1823, had been circulating knowledge of India in Catholic circles. Lamennais for his part had been collecting material on oriental thought since his youth. We have two principal sources through which his teaching at Juilly can be understood. One is his *Esquisse d'une philosophie*, into books 8 and 9 of which, devoted to world art, Lamennais packed the voluminous notes he had accumulated on oriental literature. The other is Sainte-Beuve's moving portrait of the hours he spent as a visitor at Juilly listening to the prophet trying out his lectures on some of the faithful.

In April 1833, when Jean Reynaud gave an account of Pauthier's translation in the *Revue Encylopédique*, he was undoubtedly writing of a friend and collaborator. He wrote: "Most of the periodicals have already informed the public of this important translation." This piece of evidence, and several others, is sufficient to show that Hindu thought was neither an unknown nor an indifferent topic to the subjects of Louis-Philippe.[5] Cousin's enthusiasm for it was not expressed euphemistically: "When we carefully read the poetic and philosophical monuments of the Orient, especially those of India, which are beginning to spread throughout Europe, we discover so many truths within them—truths which are so profound and in such sharp contrast to the petty issues that sometimes confound European genius—we are obliged to bow before oriental philosophy and to recognize this cradle of the human race as the homeland of the highest philosophy." In these lines one can hear an echo, rather amplified, of the favorable reception given Hindu texts by the followers of Diderot and then Herder, who sought the golden age of poets among metaphysicians and mystics, and by Schopenhauer and Eckstein, who believed in India as a model of all spirituality. (In the appendix to his *Premiers Essais*, Cousin boasted of having had Ampère and Eugène Burnouf among his students.)

All these tendencies had united in Friedrich Schlegel, and his 1808 essay once again elicited Cousin's enthusiasm: "Even the highest form of European philosophy," Schlegel had written, as Cousin recorded in his *Feuilles de l'Inde*, "the idealism of reason as it is set forth by the Greek philosophers, seems, when compared to the bounteous light and force of oriental idealism, to be no more than a feeble Promethean spark within the full celestial splendor of the noonday sun, a thin flickering spark always on the point of burning out." In short, the spread of texts was for a long time blocked by two types of obstacle: empiricism and the dearth of linguistic tools (grammars and vocabularies); and, as the Société Asiatique complained on several occasions, the inadequacy of the typographic equipment. Nevertheless, Hindu thought grew as a presence in the West's awareness. This growing veneration foreshadowed a new sense of the sublime that would permeate Western thought and poetry, and hastened the advent of knowledge that such veneration leads people to seek.

The Decisive 1830s—The Diffusion of Oriental Studies

Important points to consider are the kinds of publics this knowledge was reaching and the means by which it was being transmitted. Sanskrit was not the sole influence, and its impact would be difficult to understand outside the context of the whole cluster of linguistic discoveries that grew through and influenced each other. Sanskrit in 1785, Pahlavi in 1793, the cuneiforms in 1803, the hieroglyphics in 1822, and Avestan in 1832 were all openings in the long-sealed wall of languages. The first clues to Iranian and Assyrian languages were still to be exploited productively. Burnouf and Lassen, Rawlinson and Oppert soon took up the task. The founding of Assyriology was not ratified until 1842, when Jules Mohl set Botta, who had worked on cuneiform with Burnouf, on the track of Nineveh at Mosul. However, we can safely say that the road to the ancient realms of Asia was open by 1836. Within half a century the circumambulation that people had scarcely attempted, nor perhaps even dreamt of, was complete. The world had become round, thanks to a few imperishable scribbles and the midnight lamps of a few professors: the past was becoming an infinity.

If the five major discoveries in fifty years that I have just enumerated were totally new, there were others that were only apparently less so. After Sacy and Rémusat the whole study of Islam and the Far East was demystified for the first time, and moved from anarchic conjecture and the stuff of romance to systematic investigation and deep insight. Particularly notable were Etienne Quatremère, Caussin de Percevel, Garcin de Tassy, Jaubert, and Reinaud (to mention only a few) as Sacy's successors in Islamic studies, the most active and populous field of study in the Romantic era. Moreover, many of its leaders were authorities in related fields, such as Semitic, Indic, or Chinese studies. I will focus on those aspects of Islamic studies of concern to literary people. The expedition to Egypt and the capture of Algiers played a significant role in advancing these studies. The Arabic domain was the branch of oriental studies thought to be thoroughly understood, as was also true for Chinese studies. Yet Arabic and Persian studies broadened and took on a seriousness in the nineteenth century that influenced literature: a multitude of translations, one after another, of the pre-Islamic writers and of Persian poets and mystics such as Attar, Saadi, and Omar Khayyam by Sacy, Tassy, and Defréméry, among others, and Mohl's translations of Firdausi, were major events in the history of aesthetics. Nerval got his material from Dr. Perron; Lamennais's circle got its from Eugène Boré. In Chinese studies, Stanislas Julien and Bazin, along with Rémusat and Pauthier, gave currency to a certain idea of Chinese fiction and drama, while Hervey de Saint-Denys contributed an important conception of Chinese poetry. And for all these orients accumulating in Paris there were analogous acquistions throughout Europe.

We need to consider what part of all this reached the general public, to what extent the essays on the subject were accepted, and what elements of the new science entered the prevailing patterns of thought.

Among scholars, from 1820 to 1860, oriental studies enjoyed the lion's share of the lectures given at the Académie des Inscriptions and the articles printed in the *Journal des Savants*. In 1853 oriental literature led the list, with 16 article titles as opposed to 9 for all other ancient literatures combined. Camille Jullian later wrote, of Sacy and Rémusat (in *Extraits des historiens français du XIXe siècle*): "Their articles in the *Journal des Savants*, everywhere reprinted, suggested to the learned world that the Orient was at that time absorbing all the scholarly energy of France."

In the literary field, the *Revue des Deux-Mondes*, begun at the height of the Oriental Renaissance, lived up to its name. The space it reserved for innumerable reports on oriental subjects was increasingly important. J. J. Ampère alone wrote three columns for the first volume, and he discussed the *Bhagavata Purana* in several articles in 1840 and the *Ramayana* in 1847. Théodore Pavie, who had no less to offer, also figured prominently in the *Revue*, with seven articles on Hindu literature. He was, with Ampère, a sort of special reporter to the field. Quinet also wrote frequently for the *Revue*, and there were accounts of the work of Burnouf, Pictet, Tassy, Hammer, and Hervey de Saint-Denys. Many of the articles were anonymous; some were signed by Montégut, a great spokesman for foreign literature, or by Lerminier, the head of the circle associated with the *Globe*.

Moreover, the vogue for other foreign literatures manifestly benefited oriental literature. Villemain, the most eloquent lecturer at the Université after Cousin, like Cousin a government official, and one of the originators of comparative literature, wrote about William Jones in the *Revue*, although not until 1857. In his *Memoirs*, Philarète Chasles pointed out that the editors of the Romantic journals who were themselves unacquainted with oriental languages sought out writers who had a knowledge of those languages to meet the demands of readers who "wanted something new." This same demand required works on the Orient from the book trade, which benefited greatly from the taste for anything exotic. Chasles himself had an interest in the Orient, having delved into it early in his career. Between 1851 and 1860 he had contributed a number of important, carefully written articles to the *Débats* about the latest discoveries (I will return to these in connection with travel books). From writer to writer, interest in the Orient was attracting recruits. Gustave Planche came into contact with India in 1857 through Taine; Montégut developed an interest in China in 1863 because of the influence of Hervey de Saint-Denys.

The *Revue Brittannique* is another good barometer of the climate of opinion. I note some twenty articles published in this journal between 1825 and 1869 on the religions of India and China. In 1827 two interesting titles appear: "Difficultés de l'étude des langues orientales" and "Le pali." The Indic theater was dealt with on two occasions, 1834 and 1838. In 1837 articles on pre-Islamic literature and the *Shah Namah* appeared. And I am not referring—even though all such material reveals an alerted attention and a further stimulus—either to the oriental tales that abounded in the 1840s (then a widespread phenomenon) or to the five pages of index cataloguing the historical, picturesque, and other aspects of India (another very general phenomenon) between 1825 and 1879. One could repeat this experience for each country, if such statistics were not the kind of window-dressing that spoils the best of causes.[6] Careful researchers, such as Burtin and Guillemin, have surveyed the findings. In *Correspondant*, the one was surprised to see "so many articles devoted to India, Persia, and China." The other cited the article by Louis de Carné in the August 1835 *Revue Européenne* on the Indian epics, the articles on the religious doctrines of India published in December 1833 and January 1834, the three articles in the *Globe* on Buddhism (November 1829 to January 1830), and the episode from the *Mahabharata* in the *Revue de Paris* of September 1832.

Around 1830, at a time when the concept of the foreign, at the peak of its prestige, was transforming the concept of the ancient, in journals and universities alike oriental studies was one of the most alluring branches of ancient or foreign studies. There was commercial support as well. By 1825 the oriental book trade was organizing on an international scale. We can see the beginnings of this market as early as 1786, when Anquetil sent to London for the *Bhagavad Gita,* and 1803, when Langlès obtained, also from England, the latest publications. And the Dondey-Dupré bookstore placed the following advertisement on the cover of the *Journal Asiatique:* "As the result of recently established connections, we are now in a position to obtain, in the shortest possible time and at the most reasonable prices, the works of oriental literature published in England, Holland, Italy, Germany, etc." How did all this affect the general public? No matter how much we keep in mind the deceptive nature of statistics, five columns of literature relating to India alone in Lorenz' *Catalogue de la Librairie* for the years 1840–75 are impressive. In the retrospective tallies of Brunet's *Manuel du Libraire* there were more than 30 columns for Asian languages, almost all of which referred to nineteenth-century works published before 1865. Two columns concerned Indian and Chinese poetry, 3 their theater, and 2 their fiction. For "religion of oriental peoples" 45 items were listed, and more than 500 for Asian languages, of which 164 concerned Indian languages alone. Accounts of travels to India were represented by only 52 items. However, other headings would have to be consulted to obtain a full picture; within a little more than half a century some 500 works had dealt with Indic matters.

Let us look at the reference books in everyone's hands. In 1834 the article "Philologie" in the *Encyclopédie des gens du monde* (many of whose articles on oriental subjects were later included in the *Biographie Didot*) recorded in full the discoveries in orientalism and linguistics. The article contained the term "comparative philology" and mention of Burnouf, Grimm, Bopp, Klaproth, Rask, Grotefend, Wilhelm von Humboldt, Wilhelm Schlegel, and Lassen. The article "Orient" was supplemented by a lengthy note on the oriental scholars in which the curricula of the Ecole des langues orientales and the Collège de France were set out in great detail. The article "Linguistique" occupied 27 columns; the article on Burnouf, who was still alive and had held his chair at the Collège de France for only two years at the time, occupied 2 columns. The article on Buddhism was written by Klaproth. As early as 1833 the *Dictionnaire de la conversation* had devoted 11 columns to an article by Ahrens concerning the Buddha. In 1842 the *Encyclopèdie du XIXe siècle* carried an article on the Vedas by Loiseleur-Deslongchamps and another on "Sanscrit." The article "Philology" dealt with the question of rediscovered scripts and the history of the new concept of Indo-Germanism. The article divided philology into three branches, one reserved exclusively for the Orient. It is true that this article was written by Philarète Chasles, Eckstein's former secretary; it is also true that the *Dictionnaire de la conversation* was edited by William Duckett, who had translated Friedrich Schlegel's *Geschichte der alten und neuen Literatur*. But these publications remain vivid examples that accomplices of the Orient were to be found everywhere. In 1843 the second edition of the *Dictionnaire universel d'histoire et de géographie* by Bouillet, which was to be found in even the smallest libraries for generations, contained precise information on India, notably in its articles "Rama," "Sankhya," "Sanscrit," and "Veda" (in which Jones was mentioned). There is nothing extraordinary about all this: the Orient and India were thereafter incorporated into the standard scope of cultural studies.[7] But it is important to point out that this was a solidly established fact by the 1830s.

Moreover, during these years Sanskrit too enjoyed a vogue which began early and was distinguishable by the end of the Empire. It became more and more pronounced until 1832, when it seemed to receive the accolade from literature. The first membership lists of the Société Asiatique were a virtual *Who's Who*. Sanskrit became a fashionable topic of conversation at social gatherings, and we can catch snatches of such conversations from Fauriel at Mary Clarke's salon, from Mohl at Cuvier's, and from Eckstein—for whom Sanskrit was a social passport—at Lamartine's. Of course, not everyone saw it in the same way. Barthélemy Saint-Hilaire later asserted, "Sanskrit was practically unknown to scholarly Europe until the time of the Restoration," though scholarly Europe had supposedly caught up with Sanskrit by the time of the July Monarchy. But what we have established about the effects of the Calcutta publications during the first fifteen years of Sanskrit studies, that is, from 1785 to 1800, and during the Empire around the Schlegels, is adequate proof that Saint-Hilaire lacked sufficient evidence. In 1827 Langlois, for his part, maintained that an understanding of India had not yet reached nonacademic circles. Still, they were talking about it, since, as he said, it was within such circles that he was "frequently asked what Sanskrit was." He recalled that the stir regarding Sanskrit began with Bernardin de Saint-Pierre's *Chaumière indienne* in 1794 and also included *"The Missionary* of Miss Owenson and the sublime choruses of *Le Paria* which were inspired in an excellent poet [such qualifications were obligatory for Casimir Delavigne in 1821] by the memories of Sanskrit poetry." For his own part Langlois intended to satisfy the demand of the general public by providing a "Tableau de la littérature sanscrite." Thus the least one can deduce from his regrets is that they were contradicted by his hopes.

At the beginning of 1821, when *Le Paria* was creating a furor on the Parisian stage, Chateaubriand was chargé d'affaires in Berlin. He dined one evening at the home of Wilhelm von Humboldt, the minister to the Prussian king who had provided for the creation of chairs of Sanskrit at Bonn and Berlin; Humboldt himself had been won over to India by Bopp's *Nalus*. Chateaubriand met with Humboldt just when Chateaubriand wanted to learn the noble language of India. Chateaubriand wrote in his *Mémoires d'outre-tombe*, "If one had happened on a good day, one might have chatted at table in Sanskrit." Two years passed, and then in 1823–24 who but Heine turned to the study of Sanskrit, and of Hegel: *"Sanskrit und Hegel studiert er jezunder"* (Sanskirt and Hegel he studied together). Peter von Bohlen was in Bonn in the 1820s to learn Arabic. He exclaimed, "How can one be in Bonn and not learn Sanskrit!" And Bohlen did learn it, with Wilhelm Schlegel who occupied at Bonn one of the two chairs Humboldt had wanted to establish. Heine had also studied Sanskrit under Schlegel. One can perceive from this the kind of consequences historical chance can have in the world of ideas. We have already happened upon Goethe learning Persian around 1816–17 and copying Persian manuscripts, then moving on in 1821 to Wilson's *Meghaduta* and following, as best he could, the literal translations Kosegarten improvised for him. He was seventy-two years old at the time. Lanjuinais, at the age of fifty, set to work first on English and German but turned to Sanskrit in order to obtain his knowledge of the Orient directly. Fauriel assured Mary Clarke that Sanskrit was not difficult and in conversation at her salon persuaded Barchou de Penhoën, whom Eckstein had already set to work, of the same thing. When Wilhelm Schlegel devoted himself to the study of Sanskrit in 1815 he was already nearly fifty, and his recruit Humboldt was no younger. In May 1864 in his "Franz Woepke," reprinted the following year in his *Nouveaux essais de critique et d'histoire*, Taine pointed out that his friend Woepke had, during his career as a mathematician, learned Arabic, Persian, and—ultimately—Sanskrit.

The new field of philology became alarmed with a success that was, on the whole, too widespread and too facile. In its early stages it had dragged a train of decorative benefactors and adherents: worldliness had overrun the Société Asiatique; frivolity was not foreign even to some of its researchers. Between 1826 and 1829, a great dispute split the members of the Société into two factions. The dispute came about as a result of a resolution concerning "philologer-poets" and their "erotic and romantic rubbish." The accused faction, which Mohl christened "the florists," included Chézy, Langlois, and Garcin de Tassy. Anyone who has read a bit of their works will be no more surprised to see their names on the list than to see the verbose Sacy rallying to their defense. On Mohl's side were, no less logically, Burnouf, Rémusat, and Klaproth. Sacy was obliged to withdraw from the dispute because throughout the history of oriental studies the course of compromise, where uncharacteristically he now found himself, was always harmful.

Some serious reinforcements arrived from another sector: orientalism was becoming the career in which young Protestants and Catholics who had intended to enter the clergy but had lost their faith along the way took refuge. The study of Hebrew, which deprived them of their faith, provided them some related compensation. Such was the experience of Mohl at Tübingen in 1823 and of Ackermann at Strasbourg in 1839. It would also be the experience of Renan at Paris in 1845: having broken with Saint-Sulpice and seeking a livelihood that would provide intellectual nourishment as well, he soon considered putting himself in a position to succeed Quatremère at the Collège de France. Le Hir, who had been Renan's Hebrew professor in seminary, had been a student of Quatremère in Semitics and of Sacy in Arabic. Renan later dedicated his first works to Quatremère and Sacy. Henriette Renan induced Stanislas Julien to support her brother; on December 5, 1847, according to one letter, Renan was preparing to take up the study of Sanskrit with Burnouf, along with his study of Persian. Renan's veneration of Burnouf was later shown in his *Avenir de la Science*, dedicated to Burnouf's memory.

The 1830s marked the high point of these confluences, 1832 especially. It was the year Burnouf assumed his chair at the Collège de France, and a sequence of events and publications which were as much scholarly as literary occurred: the interest of the Saint-Simonians in India and Rammohun Roy's visit to Paris; Hegel's courses on the philosophy of religions; Wilhelm Schlegel's *Réflexions*; articles by Pierre Leroux, Jean Reynaud, and Pauthier in the *Revue Encyclopédique*; Lanjuinais's posthumous articles on India; and, finally, the coinciding publications of Gautier's *Avatar* and Balzac's *Louis Lambert*. Balzac's animating genius gave shape to one of his favorite characters, Louis Lambert, who in the manner of the times "regarded the Bible as a part of the traditional history of the antediluvian peoples who had shared a universal history. For him, the mythology of the Greeks was borrowed both from the Hebrew Bible and from the sacred books of India, adapted after their own fashion by the beauty-loving Greeks."

"It is impossible," he said, "to question the precedence of the Asiatic scriptures over our own Holy Scripture. For all who recognize the historical fact in good faith, the world is strangely expanded. The anthropogony of the Bible is nothing but the genealogy of the swarm emerging from the human hive, clinging to the mountainous flanks of Tibet, between the summits of the Himalayas and those of the Caucasus. . . . The spectacle of the earth's quick reparations, the extraordinary effects of the sun first witnessed by the Hindus, inspired them with smiling images of blissful love, with the cult of fire worship, and with endless personifications of the reproductive force. These magnificent images are lacking in the works of the Hebrews."

The idea Balzac was developing of the Indic world originated primarily from texts popularized at that time, the *Shakuntala* and the *Laws of Manu*. From these came images of grace, the "smiling images of blissful love," side by side with theories which were the pure German Romanticism of Friedrich Schlegel and Creuzer: universal mythology in which the Bible and India nourished the Hellenic heritage, the unquestioned priority of the Asiatic scriptures, the theme of migrations, the adoration of light by the first Aryans. For Balzac it was necessary to provide a place in a prodigy's young mind where these floating conceptions could intermingle with all such ideas of the century concerning all sorts of sciences. From mathematics to occultism, the precociousness of the adolescent and the evaluation of the period would be incomplete without the historical reveries that seemed to be reinforced by orientalism or Swedenborgianism.

A touch of hagiography in Balzac carries all this divination back to the 1810s: Louis Lambert is, almost from infancy, enthralled by the study of the Bible, like Sacy and so many of his colleagues, as well as by other unspecified "books." In any event linguistic studies figure among his impassioned readings "of all kinds" during his tenth year (around 1807). There is an allusion to hieroglyphics (again the vogue for Champollion), commentaries on the evocative quality of words that on the whole correspond to the theories of "general grammar" that became commonplace during the Empire. "By their mere physiognomy words revive in our brains the beings they serve to clothe."

As a child Lambert meets Madame de Staël, who becomes his patroness after he discusses his readings of Swedenborg and Saint-Martin with her. Lambert becomes the fellow student of Balzac at the Collège de Vendôme. And with whom does Balzac supposedly talk about this young genius? It is a dormitory neighbor who is none other than Barchou de Penhoën, the chronicler of British India, the Sanskrit scholar won over by Fauriel, the translator of Fichte, the commentator on his friend Ballanche, and, moreover, the person to whom Balzac dedicated *Gobseck* and perhaps Balzac's informant on oriental matters. If this was the case, Barchou de Penhoën was the one responsible for a remarkable error: Balzac's astounding confusion of India with Arabia, as we will discuss later.

All these boys were twelve years old; they demonstrated early a sensitivity to the discoveries and methods of the century. Their sources are indicated in the fourth letter attributed to the hero and dated November 25, 1819: "I had returned to Swedenborg after having undertaken vast studies of religions and after convincing myself of the profound truth of my youthful perceptions of the Bible by reading all the works that had been published over the last sixty years by a patient Germany, by England, and by France." Thus at the end of ten years the intuitions of this symbolic child, in whom the characteristics of the nineteenth century appear ten years earlier than they appear in history, confirm them by reference to European oriental studies, particularly those of "a patient Germany." Like Lambert, Germany, through the voices of Schlegel and Schelling, affirmed that "humanity has never had but one religion." In the historical overview of the times, India, Persia, and China are the beginning of a chain continued by Jesus and Muhammad and ending in Swedenborg, "perhaps the Buddha of the North." This link, a bit too broad, between the revelations of the orientalists and the awakening of "magism" exposes the melange in which the precocious mystics took pleasure. From such indications one can perceive what trains of preconceived notions were dragging scholarship along behind them.

The denouement of the novel comes when Lambert, in whom the tradition of ancient Asia is revived, meets in Mademoiselle de Villenoix, the granddaughter of a Jew, a probable incarnation of the cabalistic tradition. As soon as they are married, Lambert falls prey to attacks of whose nature (as with those of Ballanche) one is not certain; they might be a nervous disorder, or a period of initiation. Lambert dies, mad in the eyes of others, yet for several friends a visionary released from his corporeal substance. There can be no doubt that this entire story, in which real events intersect with fictional marvels and in which imaginary characters come into contact with living historical personnages presented under their real names, is Balzac's most elaborate attempt to transform actual experience into symbol. Swedenborgianism filled chapter 3 of *Seraphita*, while the following chapter expressed "the thirst for India." We know what a fascination Hoene-Wroński, a disciple of Saint-Martin and Fabre d'Olivet, exerted on Balzac in his *La recherche de l'Absolu.* One could find in the works of these two occultists the source of more than one of the ideas attributed to Lambert.

In 1835, in the same decade that *Louis Lambert* and *Avatar* appeared, Nerval adapted Shudraka's drama *Mrichchhakatika (The Little Clay Cart)* for the French stage under the title *Le chariot d'enfant*. The play, one of the specimens of Indian theater provided by Wilson in 1827, was not performed at l'Odéon until 1850. Around 1840 (Brémond, who recorded the fact in *Cahiers du Mois* for February 1925, was not more specific about the date) "a holy priest, Albert Hetsch," noted in his journal, "long talk with Ballanche; we deplored together the Occident's victory over the Orient at Marathon." Lamenting the victory of Hellenism over the forebears of those Persians who had few rights even in the Paris of Montesquieu! The studious and the spiritual had had some success in advancing the classification of values. It was certainly a regret that would never have come to mind a century earlier. And what was said to the contrary? "Europe excells the other parts of the world in all things." Paul Hazard, who took this remark from Moreri, has shown that this was the general attitude: Asia symbolized "the spirit of servitude."[8] (One of the tasks of the new science of oriental studies was to uproot this prejudice.) And what was being said in 1865? "Everything we think, and all the ways we think, have their origin in Asia." This peremptory retort to Moreri was the first line of Count Gobineau's *Religions et philosophies dans l'Asie centrale.* Lamartine's remark of 1853 was even more to the point: "India is the key to everything."

It is not that there was not opposition and reluctance. Even after the refutations of Rémusat and Pauthier the idea of "oriental despotism" proved hard to kill. More important, historians (Renan, for example) continued to reproach a certain oriental mentality, clearly personified by India, as unfit for history, which was, all things considered, tantamount to a European refusal to enter into the Hindu way of thinking. The incompatibilities between the Orient and the Occident, such as they were perceived in the West, were quite clear. There were always backwaters where people thought in the old way and would never prefer Flaubert's "grand barbarians" to the worshipers of Athena. Even Sainte-Beuve's criticism of *Salammbô* can not be explained entirely by a natural aversion to all greatness; it seems to me to have been a new installment of the battle between the ancients and the moderns in which the meaning of the two terms is now reversed, the moderns making common cause with classical antiquity against the intrusion of the primordial East. Such controversy brought the realization that to be "barbarian" or to be "Asian" was no longer necessarily an insult. It looked like a good sign.

Language events: Abel Rémusat enumerated the new words borrowed from the Orient and naturalized in French usage by Romantic writers. For India he cited "rajah," "kshatriya" "sutras," and "pariahs." The first and the last, not to mention "nabob," have indeed become generic nouns. The pariahs had been known from pre-Romantic authors. The word appeared in Raynal, before its usage by Bernardin de Saint-Pierre, who nevertheless explained the term in *Chaumière indienne* (Goethe first got the term from Sonnerat). The nineteenth-century dictionaries included it. The term became very popular after Casimir Delavigne's 1821 play, which impressed Stendhal, as he records in his *Racine et Shakespeare*. Another play with the same title by Michael Beer appeared in 1826. The theater bore the mark of the new terms even more decisively than the novel; witness *The Widow of Malabar* by Lemierre in 1770 and *Bayadères* by Jouy in 1810. The word "avatar" through its belated confusion with "avaro" was favored by distortion. Othmar Frank had misunderstood the term when rendering homage to Napoleon; yet the word was not to be found in a single dictionary until 1878, neither in Boiste's, nor Landais's, nor that of the Académie.

Rémusat's indignation with oriental neologisms was made public in 1843 in *Mélanges posthumes*, which Sainte-Beuve recommended to Juste Oliver. Unquestionably oriental studies had contributed notably to the verbal acclimation undertaken by the Romantics. Thereafter the sheer quantity of untranslatable terms discredited the pretended "equivalences" so dear to translators; the "florist" dispute itself was a sign of the times. It became necessary to resign oneself to crude transliterations of local terms to designate places, customs, titles, and offices strictly peculiar to certain distant countries (and also, by contagion, to the less distant countries). To a cer-

tain extent, a taste for things foreign fostered indulgence and then complacence toward the foreign vocabulary. Furthermore, the poets reveled
in it as well as in other exoticisms.

The noted sinologist Rémusat, although in the camp of the "anti-flo-
rists," exposed one of the common interests between orientalism and Romanticism when he deplored the fact that both "margrave" and "caliph"
were coming into common use; this amounted to reprimanding the use of
words that had been assimilated in the West for centuries ("caliph" was
commonly used in the twelfth century), but it also recognized that for Hugo
and Gauthier such words had sufficient poetic value in themselves. Rémusat could not understand that these words themselves aroused certain
visual images, possessed certain sonorous qualities and certain constructs
of the past, certain landscapes. Of course, the use of such words could
also be found in cheap poetry; that comes under the heading of damnable
exoticism, but then fashion and conformity never are anything but the
forfeiture of salvation. What blindness, strange in a scholar trained in
working with particularized fields of knowledge, to assume that one could
substitute "penitent" or "monk" for "yogi." It would mean renouncing
not only evocative powers but the inherent nature of the concept, a whole
outline of history, an entire irreplaceable domain of the spirit. It would be
interesting to draw up a list of the innovations introduced into our vocabularies by orientalism. For my part, the only one I have seen is Rémusat's, and it is unsympathetic.

One cannot gather a great deal from the criticisms and parodies produced in such numbers by Dupuis and Cotonet. In Mérimée's "Vase
Etrusque," published in *Revue des Deux-Mondes* in 1830, Théodore, a traveler, is overwhelmed with questions from his circle of friends because he
has just returned from Egypt. The age of Champollion has begun. He declares that the antiquities are "coming out of his ears." "Just the sight of
a hieroglyphic" can cause him to swoon. Whereupon the clever storyteller (Mérimée is poking fun at himself here, since he was very susceptible to single hieroglyphs) fills his character's mouth with "djerid," "ya-
taghan" and "khandjar." "You must see my metchla and bournous and
khaick."

"Is the pasha romantic?" asked Thémines.
"He doesn't pay much attention to literature. But you know quite well that all
Arabic literature is romantic."

Mérimée is always cautious. Otherwise he would have said "oriental
literature."

CHAPTER FIVE

The Progress of Oriental Studies

The New Prestige of Buddhism

1836: Burnouf, whose influence henceforward is paramount, revived Grotefend's discovery in his *Mémoire sur deux inscriptions cunéiformes.* Within ten years the cipher of the Achaemenid kings would be clearly understood.

1838: The first publication of Firdausi's *Shah Namah,* edited and translated by Mohl. It was first printed in sumptuous quarto format with polychrome ornaments by the Imprimerie nationale as part of its oriental series. Forty years later the smaller common edition ran to seven volumes. It was an important acquisition not only for the specialist but for the poetic repertoire, which it enriched from Hugo to Judith Gautier's *Iskender.* It represented a stage in the expansion of the long-closed circle of immortal poets: it was one more poetic work so national that it became universal. From then on, who could claim that the concept of the classics excluded Firdausi?

1840–41: About the time Viollet-le-Duc was installed at Vézelay, Pauthier provided a portable Asia for the curious, the *Livres sacrés de l'Orient,* where the *Koran* and Loiseleur-Deslongchamps's 1833 translation of the *Laws of Manu* appeared side by side, and where some of the Upanishads (summarized after Colebrooke) and fragments of the Vedas were linked with Firdausi's Persia. Pauthier's work was an important channel through which works exhumed by the philologists were to enter the larger sphere of living values. I shall discuss later how Hugo learned of all these unknown splendors from this anthology. And its title no doubt gave rise to that of Max Müller's Sacred Books of the East. By 1841 the "Savitri" episode, taken from Pauthier, was to appear in *La Pléiade,* one of Curmer's keepsake volumes.

In 1840 Eugène Burnouf began to publish his immense translation of the *Bhagavata Purana,* the fiftieth and final volume of which would not be printed until 1884 by Hauvette-Besnault and Roussel. Also in 1840 Wilson's translation of the *Vishnu Purana* appeared in London. It was from a sense of duty that Burnouf applied himself to a secondary text, as his student Barthèlemy Saint-Hilaire revealed after his death. He left the *Ramayana* to Wilhelm Schlegel, who was at work on it, the *Rig Veda* to Rosen, who was preparing its first book, and the *Mahabharata* to Bopp, who at the time was making plans for it. It was again Burnouf who in 1844 urged Max Müller, a student after his own heart, to take up work on the *Rig Veda*, a task at which Rosen had died in his thirty-second year.

The *Bhagavata Purana* sets Burnouf's era in relief; its influence was felt among poets, such as Leconte de Lisle. In 1844 a new publication appeared whose influence was even more decisive: *Introduction à l'histoire du Buddhisme indien*. Michelet, and even Wagner, was influenced by it. It was complemented in 1852 by Burnouf's posthumous *Lotus Sutra (Lotus de la bonne loi)* and Foucaux's *Lalita Vistara*. The latter was a fruit of understanding gained from Hodgson's dispatch of the canonical books of Buddhism; both Sanskrit and Tibetan versions, Pali and Prakrit, were brought together in Paris in 1837. Also, between 1834 and 1837, Prinsep deciphered the inscriptions of Ashoka. On March 1, 1860, Alfred Jacobs wrote in the *Revue des Deux-Mondes*, "thirty years ago Hodgson, a man who above all others deserves to be well-regarded by history, a resident of the East India Company in Nepal, gave us the first glimpse of the treasures of Buddhist literature and succeeded in obtaining 400 Sanskrit and Tibetan volumes, which he distributed to the Asiatic Societies of Calcutta, London, and Paris." Ten years previously a young Hungarian, Csoma de Koros, had entered the monastic life in Tibet, and his works supplemented and verified Hodgson's discoveries. On his arrival in India in 1829, Jacquemont attended a meeting of the society in Calcutta at which a subsidy was voted for Csoma; and the following year Jacquemont paid him an extended visit at Kanum. He had heard in Europe of this linguistic pilgrim who had come to Asia "like a rocket launched into adventure." At the time Jacobs was writing on the Hodgson manuscripts, Philarète Chasles was contributing to the *Débats* (March–April 1860) a series of reports no less informative for the French reader about the Indic epigraphy begun by Prinsep and its far-reaching consequences. Through these two remarkable innovations the study of Buddhism was at last unlocked. Conjecture and inference had reigned in the realm of Buddhist studies, where, since the tentative efforts of the eighteenth century, the principal contribution had been Guignes's work with Chinese sources. In 1823 Klaproth wrote a *Leben des Budd'a* which attempted to systematize the chronology of Buddha's life. Klaproth included this outline in his *Asia polyglotta*, and the *Journal Asiatique* reprinted it in the following year. It should be emphasized that progress, even through the channels opened by Hodgson, only became possible because of Burnouf, who, in 1826 in his *Essai sur le pâli*, written in collaboration with Lassen, had given access to the language of the oldest Buddhist canon (in Ceylon). Moreover, he maintained uninterrupted correspondence with Hodgson. From that time Buddhist informational tools multiplied. In 1853 R. Spence Hardy published *A Manual of Buddhism, In Its Modern Development; Translated from Singhalese Manuscripts;* a Russian-handbook by Vassilief, translated into French by La Comme in 1865, was published in 1860; in 1858 Barthélemy Saint-Hilaire produced a popularization entitled *Le Bouddha*. The figure of Buddha was growing larger in the Western world.

Vedic and post-Vedic India no longer held the foremost position; this was not only a turning point in the general history of Indic studies but a time after which, because of Burnouf, French schools created a special degree in Buddhist studies.[1] However, French schools were not alone in recognizing the usefulness of auxiliary documents. In 1820, during travels in India following those in Persia, Rask gathered Pali and Sanskrit manuscripts for the libraries of Copenhagen. Moreover, his essay *Om Zendsprogets og Zendavestas Aelde og Aegthed (On the Age and Authenticity of Avestan and of the Zend Avesta)*, translated into German in 1826, and his efforts at deciphering inscriptions written in Old Persian have an important role in the history of linguistics.

Garcin de Tassy in his turn broadened perspectives with his monumental *Histoire de la littérature hindoue et hindoustanie*. The first edition, in two volumes, appeared in 1839 and 1847. An enlarged second edition, in three volumes, appeared in 1870–71. In 1829 the Imprimerie royale published *Rudiments de la langue hindoustanie à l'usage des élèves de l'Ecole royale et speciale des langues orientales vivantes*, with an appendix "containing, in addition to the grammar, the original Hindustani texts accompanied by a translation and facsimile." In 1849 the printing house, now the Imprimerie nationale, published his *Chrestomathie hindie et hindouie à l'usage des élèves de l'Ecole speciale des langues orientales vivantes*. A student of Sacy and professor at the Ecole des langues orientales, Garcin de Tassy later taught Lancereau, the translator of the *Hitopadesha*, a work that reached the readers of Ronsard and Rutebeuf through its inclusion in Jannet's *Bibliothèque Elzévirienne*. Tassy's magnum opus was first published under the aegis of the Asiatic Society of London. Hindustani had been taught in England since the beginning of the century, along with Sanskrit and Persian, at Haileybury College for colonial civil servants. The East India Company conducted these classes there for practical reasons.

Although less important in the diffusion of ideas, other subject areas should be mentioned. The teaching of Armenian, the oldest language in

Europe, was exemplified by Saint-Martin, who, in another connection, defined the value of Aramaic for biblical studies. Ethiopian studies, intermingled with these, took on luster with the Abbadie brothers in 1839 and with Dillmann in 1846. In 1843 Dulaurier furnished several excerpts in French from fragments of Malaysian literature, and *pantoum (pantun)* became an enormously popular verse form among the French Parnassians.

Indic Studies in India, 1830

We have at our disposal a valuable account of the 1830s, the decisive nature of which I do not believe I am overemphasizing. Jacquemont's letters from India are doubly interesting for noting the state of Indic studies undertaken at the time by the English in India and also how European studies, particularly among the French, followed the English lead.

Jacquemont, who did not probe the depths of Hindu thought himself, was moved by seeing a few individuals, such as Rammohun Roy and Csoma, dedicating their lives to activities beyond the scope of his understanding. From 1829 to 1830 he attended some of the meetings of the Asiatic Society of Calcutta, while Wilson was secretary of the Committee on Literature, and offered his lively and objective impressions: "Like the Royal Society of London, and all the scientific and literary societies of Great Britain, it is composed of a small number of able men who command little respect and of wealthy or powerful but incompetent men who enjoy all the honors." Meetings were held every two months, one of which "they considered quite well attended: there were about twenty of us." It was at this meeting that Jacquemont listened to a letter sent from the Himalayas about Csoma, who was wintering in Tibet in a room whose temperature was zero and who was voted 100 rupees a month "so he would be altogether well off."

Five or six Hindus who were accorded the title "native gentlemen" because they were wealthy and lived in the European style attended the meeting. "The Asiatic Society, as a learned body, is completely worthless. No research is done jointly, and there is no coordination of the members' work toward a common goal." But then, wasn't this the lot of similar societies in Europe, apart from the rejuvenated Institut de France? Furthermore, the English were unindustrious and fond of leisure and comfort (Jones, it will be remembered, had already complained of this trait). Although "there is little science" at the society, it had few pretensions: the importance of Sacy, Rémusat, and Champollion was recognized there, and the *Journal* of the Société in Paris was highly esteemed. "They seemed to look upon the Société as the one most active and effective in advancing philological and historical knowledge about Asia. The printings of the oriental works done in Paris are also considered the most beautiful.

"Neither at the Asiatic Society of Calcutta nor the Royal Society of London are there the sort of intimate and familiar discussions transformed into conversations which often make the meetings of the Institut so instructive. A slightly stiff dignity always prevails, and respect for form causes substance to be neglected.

"I was the least dignified of those attending, but I also feel I was the one who learned the most."

On October 16, 1829 Jacquemont went to see Carey, whom he found reading the Bible, his daily habit "for fifty or sixty years." The Catholics "roam the world over on foot and barefoot to convert the faithful, and they have converted many. They go about it like the Apostles, and like them they have frequently succeeded. The English missionaries, and the Protestant missionaries in general, wait at home for the unfaithful to present themselves. Mr. Carey, a missionary, doesn't leave his home to convert the Hindus; what good would that do? Yet, despite his age, he goes every week to Calcutta to give lessons in Bengali at Fort William to wards of the Company, which pays him handsomely." Jacquemont felt that these men were forgetting their mission. Carey, he recalled, was originally a lowly country primary schoolteacher who distinguished himself by learning classical and oriental languages, and by preaching. It was on the basis of his initiative in these matters that he had been sent to convert India. At Serampore he established "his useless college," which was beautifully situated nonetheless. At Banaras, Jacquemont saw Prinsep, a Renaissance man who began his days by "some superb drawing" of a local monument and ended them by playing "new music from Italy" on his violin. With Captain Thoresby Jacquemont also visited the city's Sanskrit college, where the most renowned pandits taught 200 students, all of whom were ignorant of English.

India and Archaeology

As we have seen, Wilson and Prinsep represented the second generation of English Indic scholars, one shaped by archaeology. The study of numismatics, followed by the study of monuments, especially Prinsep's studies, unshackled Indic chronology at the same time Buddhist studies emerged from the mists. In deciphering the bilingual coins of Bactria, Prinsep was preparing, and the decipherment of the Buddhist inscriptions assured, the first authentic history of India's past prior to the Muslim conquest.

This synchronism was apparent in other activities besides those of the personnel working in India. The appearance of Burnouf's *Buddhisme indien* in Paris in 1844 coincided with a symptomatic manifestation: April marked the beginning of the *Revue Archéologique*, whose objectives were defined in an inaugural article by Charles Lenormant entitled "Archéologie," which had appeared in a preliminary form two years earlier in the *Encyclopédie du XIXe siècle*. Lenormant confessed that in his first version he had considered Indic studies of secondary importance, keeping himself "on guard against the arguments which might come from the camp of the self-important Indo-Germanists." This comment was aimed at the debates in Bonn and Heidelberg which had stirred up the orientalists of the Görres-Creuzer school. But since the works of Prinsep, Rosen, Burnouf, and Lassen on India and Persia had opened unforeseen paths, Lenormant retracted his views in a long supplementary note to the revised article: "What unprecedented progress and, consequently, how many more problems these few years have brought!"

In 1860, through Jacobs and Chasles, the literary milieu belatedly echoed what the antiquarians had voiced immediately in 1844. Lenormant affirmed (and it was his justification for the new journal), that the realm of plastic architecture was, from then on, firmly attached to that of philology. He was supported by a prospectus signed by Guilhabaud: "We feel the time has come to give wide circulation to a study that already includes, after only a few years, many hard-working supporters." It "spread little by little, then suddenly expanded in an astonishing way." This was written in the decade preceding the first works of the authors of *Poèmes antiques* and *Salammbô*. And, during the time the young science of archaeology was being tested and was calling for clarification, the editor announced he felt "that European, Egyptian, and Asian antiquities must all be included." Yet only nine years previously in his *Handbook of Archaeology*, Otfried Müller had allowed Asia only the position of a poor relative. It is true that he was an adamant opponent of the Görres-Creuzer school of oriental studies. Lenormant declared, "I do not believe that, from this time forward, a subject of any value can take shape without drawing from oriental philology."

Lenormant also stated: "The half-formed embryo of oriental archaeology which Winckelmann tacked on to his history of Greek art was sufficient for Visconti, who reduced it further when dealing with Egyptian or Asian monuments. The subject of origins was, at that time, as obscure as that of oriental archaeology. Today these two branches of knowledge are leading scientific concerns, attracting interest and requiring the solution to, or at least the examination of, the most serious problems from those who undertake them as a career. Archaeology has become, in a way, what it was in the time of Denys d'Halicarnasse: the study of origins." At this point a division of studies was required: "Thus we now have a Chinese and Japanese archaeology, an Indian archaeology, and an American archaeology. Regarding the Indics, philology has steadfastly provided the foundations for comparative grammar and the vocabulary for an aggregate of peoples who trace an enormous arc from the mouth of the Ganges to the Atlantic Ocean. But the kinds of assistance that Indian archaeology itself can provide for this admirable study are, whatever has been said, weak and uncertain." They did not provide the means "to establish or verify the dates of written monuments of literature. It is thus to be feared that this branch of archaeology will remain perpetually secondary and subordinate."

Can we be more explicit? We can discern the precise point at which European sang-froid registered the eminent interest in Indian archaeology generated by Prinsep's studies, but we cannot yet understand what was definitive about his attainments. What had changed in 1860 when Jacobs and Chasles returned to the question to declare it settled was simply that in 1858 Prinsep's contributions had been brought together in a single place, his posthumous *Essays on Indian Antiquities*. The fact remained that the art and architecture of India were not to receive anything like the same serious consideration repeatedly given to its literature. This requires some explanation: the first reason is the delay in the discovery and study of Indian art.

"As for the monuments," wrote Lenormant, "they have not yet been studied in a really profitable way. Heeren gives incomplete and frequently inaccurate descriptions. The drawings of Indian monuments were done by tourists who sacrificed everything for the sake of the picturesque. The only books on Indian monuments we can recommend are *Hindoo Excavations in the Mountain of Ellora* by Daniel (London, 1803): *Monuments de l'Hindoustan*, a work based on the preceeding one; *The Wonders of Ellora* by Seeley (1825); the essay on Indian architecture by Ram-Raz (in English, London, 1834); and a few papers in the Asiatic publications from Calcutta, Bombay, and London." All these works contained a similar and very limited stock of knowledge. What various authors gave on Ellora generally comes from the single description made as early as 1794 by Charles Malet, and the reference was sometimes confused with information in the sixth volume of the *Asiatic Researches* of Calcutta. Lenormant's citation of *Monuments de l'Hindoustan* must refer to the two-volume work published under this title by Langlès in 1811 and 1821. Finally, Heeren, who was so frequently quoted at the beginning of the nineteenth century, and who was a very useful secondary source, had drawn his archaeological knowledge in large part from Daniel, Malet, and Langlès. Lenormant's bibliography did not add anything of significance to the little included in Guigniaut's summary in 1825.[2]

"For a long time the British governors gave much less attention to the study of physical monuments than to the study of literary monuments. In the course of constructing new buildings there were cases of destruction of ancient monuments as barbaric as in the noncivilized countries of the Orient," according to Barthold's *La découverte de l'Asie*. Undoubtedly Fergusson, whose work was responsible, especially after 1875, for getting the study of monuments under way, had had predecessors as early as the end of the eighteenth century. I have mentioned several of them in the English school, Charles Mason among them. Nevertheless, whether through prejudice or incompatibility, the figure art of India ran aground on Western sensibilities. Whatever is subject to sense perception has stronger defenses against the foreign than what is experienced only by intellect and can yield to reasoning; when experience becomes tactile an obscure instinct for preservation comes into play to guard against any dislocation of habit. It was one thing to be ill-informed about Indic aesthetics when the whole experience of Indic art was absent; the reaction this art provoked when it became accessible was quite another matter. Naturally, as the interest, the attraction, of objects brought back from Asia became more marked, it especially favored those objects that arrived in quantity. Chinoiseries were already familiar in the eighteenth century. And here another factor that did not wait for philology, and that depended on it only slightly, came into play: the need to taste the exotic but at small cost, which provided the broad market for tales of voyages.

In his study Vivant-Denon caressed with his eyes a statue of Vishnu whose "finish and softness of design" he "rightly admired." Wilhelm Schlegel, who saw the two of them together (and speaks of it in his *Réflexions*), unfortunately does not record the date. We know for a fact that Schlegel was in Paris in 1816 to study Sanskrit and that Denon died in 1825. A croney of Louis XV before becoming curator of museums under Napoleon, author of the light and pleasant *Point de lendemain*, Vivant-Denon had made drawings of the Egyptian monuments and escorted the famous Rosetta Stone to France. The changes in his taste were a barometer of fashion. He had been hospitable toward the conventional works of David at a time when Raphael was also Mengs's first name.

His collection made for a sensational sale. Charles Blanc, in *Trésor de la Curiosité*, records only that portion of the sale dealing with paintings, which were primarily Bolognese; but in her diary for April 2, 1826 Mary Clarke notes, "I then went to Denon's apartments"—probably for the pre-sale exposition, Denon having died the year before—"where there were a great many things, but the only things which caught my eye were some statues of Indian gods, which stirred my imagination as everything does which comes from there." Thus the Vishnu Schlegel mentioned was not solitary. This says a great deal about the investments collectors were making during the first quarter of the nineteenth century, just as Mary Clarke's ostentation speaks for the oriental snobbery of the intellectual salons. But all this may not demonstrate any more than the Indian ivory statuette recently unearthed at Pompeii. How many intermediaries had there been? Such objects may have been no more than knick-knacks for the home, a sampling of techniques, of ornamental imports forced into an atmosphere where such a pastime gave rise to no human interest at all.

There is another anecdote, recalled by the Comtesse de Pange, which, again, I do not wish to overstress: In September 1810, Madame de Staël, who had become lost in the country near Blois with Mathieu de Montmorency, was given shelter at an isolated chateau. (This time we know the date but the place remains vague.) She wrote, "We accepted this invitation, which was a great favor, and suddenly found ourselves in the midst of Asian luxury and French elegance. The masters of the house had spent a good deal of time in India, and the chateau was decorated with all they had brought back with them from their voyages. The stay in the chateau aroused my curiosity, and I felt wonderful." To relieve the impatience she felt while waiting to learn whether the authorities would finally allow the publication of her book *De l'Allemagne,* she spent her time "examining the rareties from India."

Here is a clear link with the popularity of voyages; the great number of Frenchmen who passed through India eventually corresponded with a certain number of objects capable of representing India materially to those who stayed at home. Slowly, on a small scale and primarily through fabrics, the same thing happened to Indian objects that had previously happened through porcelains to Chinese objects. The first stage was amazement, an astonishment provoked by such encounters, the response of habit and sensibility to such remote arts. Transportable specimens of such commercial and decorative goods did create an initial stir, but never went much beyond the market of collectors or the astonishment of the ignorant.

We find objects again in the same surroundings as travel books and fashionable cashmirs; and at the international expositions as well, which is to say, only after the 1850s. The period in the antechamber was long—supposing that it is over. First the dividing line between historical periods and geographical distances had to be crossed. The prejudice for the primitive that worked in favor of Hindu literature worked against Hindu art; this prejudice faded or was overturned as the history of artistic taste was permeated with a concept, connected with the notion of authenticity, of some arts as precursors of others.

The Final Philological Stages of the Oriental Renaissance

While the figured monuments remained disputed or veiled, the translations began to move at a rapid pace toward being accurate representations. In 1844 Théodore Pavie published excerpts from *Mahabharata*, and in 1853 Valentin Parisot published a volume of the *Ramayana* that remained the only one available for some time.

1848–51: Langlois's translation of the *Rig Veda* was the first in Europe, and for a long time the only one in France, although it was undisputedly deficient: "Simple, clear, intelligible—these were its greatest shortcomings," Lacôte remarked. The reality was not obtained until Louis Renou's masterful translations in 1937 and 1947. Nevertheless, Langlois's version impressed a number of thinkers. Lamartine borrowed the Vedic quotations for his *Cours familier de littérature* in 1856 from it. The *Revue des Deux-Mondes* referred to the publication five different times before 1854. There is nothing from the other Vedas until 1870 except for quotations from secondary sources provided by Pauthier and Barthélemy Saint-Hilaire. In 1853 Saint-Hillaire analyzed Langlois's work in extensive articles in the *Journal des Savants* and then popularized him in a volume entitled *Le Veda* to which Vigny, Lamartine, and Michelet later referred. In this volume he included, with the *Rig*, excerpts from and commentaries on other Vedas, based on the work of Wilson, Benfey, and Max Müller. In 1858 he likewise rendered to Buddhism what must, in spite of everything, be called a service: his *Le Bouddha et sa religion*. But the only one of his works that still interests Indic scholars is his *Samkhya*, which appeared in 1852 in the *Mémoires de l'Académie des Sciences morales et politiques*.[3]

1854: The first volume of the *Ramayana* marked the beginning of a flood of Hindu translations by Hippolyte Fauche. He was a lackluster student of Burnouf, but his inexhaustible enthusiasm made him a fecund worker. In 1859–60 he had produced a notable translation of Kalidasa complete in two volumes, and he included in the miscellaneous collection *Une Tétrade*, which appeared in three volumes in 1861–63, the *Little Clay Cart* which Nerval and Méry had adapted for the Odéon.

Fauche's epics poured out until 1870. The last, which marked the close of an era, was the thirteenth volume, published posthumously, of the unfinished *Mahabharata*. We have to admire Fauche's dedication, even if his qualities were more those of pluck and generosity than of taste or depth of learning. His dedication reaped him no more reward from the specialists than from the educated public. His work was the kind that promised an obscure grave—precisely his destiny. And no one ever came forward to take over where Fauche had left off. Nonetheless, the sublime epilogue to the *Mahabharata* in which the hero Yudhishthira refuses to enter the

Hindu paradise unless his dog is allowed to enter with him was translated, along with other fragments, by Foucaux in *Onze épisodes du Mahâbhârata* in 1862. (Foucaux's episodes had previously appeared separately in various journals since 1842.) Fauche was responsible not only for the enthusiastic interest of Lamartine, whom his works nourished, but also for that of Michelet, who justly said of Fauche in *Bible de l'Humanité*, "Poor, in the depths of silences, unable to find a publisher, he printed *with his own hands* and published *at his own cost* the nine volumes" of the *Ramayana* and began to translate the *Mahabharata*. "He is outside time; more active, but no less Indic, than the Brahmans and the Maharishis." Each of these statements owes its preciseness to the personal relations Michelet had been eager to establish with the heroic translator; I will return to this in discussing Michelet and his connections with India. Fauche's *Ramayana* appeared shortly after the first complete edition produced in Paris, the Italian translation of Abbé Gorresio, also a student of Burnouf. (The poem was translated into Dutch by Roorda van Eysinga at Amsterdam in 1843.)

Although translation in England may have lacked great names during these years between Wilson and Max Müller, Germany seemed as active as France. After the contributions of Wilhelm Schlegel, Kosegarten, and Wilhelm von Humboldt in the 1820s, those of Peter von Bohlen, who died in 1840 at the age of forty-four, were especially valuable during the 1830s for the spread of Bhartrihari and Kalidasa. Rückert, a professor at Erlangen since 1826 and at first a specialist in Islamic studies, developed a strong interest in Sanskrit and became the most admirable of the Sanskrit translators. In 1828 he produced a *Nala and Damayanti* and in 1837 a *Gita Govinda*. There were also numerous posthumous publications, including the *Atharva Veda*, as well as the texts included in the famous *Weisheit der Brahmanen* in 1836–39 and in the *Brahmanischen Erzählungen* in 1839.

In the 1840s Poley translated, first into French and then into German, a number of Vedic texts, notably the Upanishads. Holtzmann produced his *Bruchstücke aus Walmiki's Râmâyana* in 1841 and his *Indische Sagen*, in three parts, between 1845 and 1847. The latter included translations from the *Mahabharata*. (In 1847 the Belgian Nève translated hymns from the *Rig Veda* into French.) Important dates in Indology were marked by Albrecht Weber's *Vorlesungen über indische Literaturgeschichte* (1852), Lassen's *Indische Alterthumskünde* (1847–61), Max Müller's *History of Ancient Sanskrit Literature*, dealing only with Vedism (1859), Benfey's *Panchatantra* (1859) and Adolphe Pictet's *Origines Indo-européennes ou les Aryas primitifs* (also 1859).

It was also in 1859 that the Vicomte de Rougé deciphered Phoenician. In 1857 in the *Journal Asiatique* Oppert presented a method for reading cuneiform, and he proved his method at a meeting of Assyriologists in London. His crotchety disposition laid him open to polemical debates in which

Renan was among his adversaries. In 1874 he held the first chair of Assyriology at the Collège de France. In 1850 both pre-Columbian America,
with the work of Brasseur de Bourbourg, and prehistoric America, with
the work of Boucher de Perthes, came into view. Important veins had now
been located and tapped, and revealing them became specialities.

How often do we see such a lightening conquest? Never had mankind
devoted itself to an activity so vast in time and space: amassing, laboring
over, and setting abroad the wealth of excavations. It was intoxicating.
The discipline of history, although still young, was becoming an extraordinary domain, and it is understandable that it dazzled poet-historians such
as Michelet and historian-poets such as Hugo. The birth of composite categories in itself was characteristic of the times. A confusion of two titles,
two empires, clearly indicates the force so many new pasts were exerting
on all the disciplines involved. All these separate activities were haunted
by an immemorial unity.

It was a fluke, but very meaningful, that the prestige of Greece at this
time fell behind that of Asia; Schliemann's Mycenae did not come to light
until 1875, when Fergusson was publishing his work on Hindu architecture. "Primitive" Greece arrived last, after the importance of the Hindu
sphere had already diminished. The word "antique" again had a new location on the map.

The great theoreticians who threw human aggregates together in their
thinking could content themselves from then on with elliptical allusions;
everyone understood and located in the world catalog Schopenhauer's citations of the Vedas or the *Gulistan,* or the Asian books and sages whose
names Hugo used like common nouns. As early as Musset's *Espoir en Dieu*
a unity of religions spanning the ages and climes was commonplace:

> De quelque façon qu'on t'appelle,
> Brahma, Jupiter ou Jésus,
> Vérité, justice éternelle,
> Vers toi tous les bras sont tendus.

> Whatever name you are given—
> Brahma, Jupiter or Jesus,
> Truth or Eternal Justice—
> All arms reach out to you.

The ultimate consecration that Valentin Parisot's *Ramayana* gained for Indian poetry, for India herself, and for pantheism was an inordinately savage attack by Barbey d'Aurevilly, who in blaming them for all the evils of
the century succeeded in proving their great influence on the century.

But before recording the effects of Indic studies on the theories, meditations, and works of Europe, it would be worthwhile to return to our first overview in order to distinguish the phases through which the disciplines passed.

Roughly speaking, a period of philological and literary Romanticism occurred between 1785 and 1825 and included the names of Jones, a poet; Chézy, a gentleman; and Friedrich Schlegel, a systematic dreamer. It was an ebullient time, during which a unique fountain sprang up under the rod of the pandits to nourish Calcutta (the waters thereafter portioned out by London and filtered and generalized by Paris). It was also an era of approximations; the data retained an arbitrary quality. Misunderstandings and even dubious documents antedating the discovery persisted as if they were thought to be confirmed. Primitive poetry continued to be discussed on the basis of very partial glimpses of the Vedas and the epics, while the idea of a mother language continued to be based on the mysticisms of the linguists.

The period from approximately the 1830s to the 1850s was one of linguistic organization, presided over by Bopp and Burnouf. There was a new generation of Indic scholars and orientalists; the British primacy faded and the German established itself in other capitals. The frameworks and processes became those of a science that enumerated its responsibilities and gave them profound consideration. The primitive returned to normal, while the archaic grew even older. The very rigor that replaced complacency showed the self-satisfaction of a new field no longer in its infancy.

The maturation became more pronounced around 1855. The Ecole des hautes études was soon to become influential. Bergaigne completed the break with the fetishism that regarded the Vedas as "the Bible of the Aryan peoples." Barth was ultimately to replace the concept of the Vedas as folk writings and spontaneous poetry with the notion of the Vedas as the ritual poetry of a small priestly circle. Scholarship extended its attention to all the ancient peoples, and became more colorless in the process. Now the exception would have been not being aware of India; but those for whom it was more than a vague term came to divide themselves more and more into two parallel sects that did not mix. The one included scholars, who became ever more aloof from the public at large; the other was composed of esotericists who struggled for their share of public attention by constantly deriding the scholars.

In France the long and fairly miraculous agreement that had linked this difficult science to the cycle of fashion was falling apart. The coups of genius were past, and the luster of newness could no longer be relied on. Ultimately Sanskrit came to be taught only to those who were considering teaching it; the speciality became cloistered. Literary history made it pay for this by unjustly forgetting the many years they had shared together. "Renan, who owned his general views on the contrast between the Aryan and the Semitic genius to his contact with India, believed that Sanskrit still had something to teach us," Lacôte wrote in his essay "L'Indianisme." In 1884 Bergaigne, on the contrary, in his preface to *Shakuntala* said that Sanskrit literature was of no further interest to learned society. In the *Histoire de la Nation française* (edited by Hanotaux), one could later read in the article by Strowski that the "efforts to introduce all that had been omitted—Indians, Chinese, etc.—into our curricula and our books have been in vain, and we continue to omit them."

Indic studies, and oriental studies in general, had gone through the three major phases which Max Müller assigned to all science in his *Lectures on the Science of Language:* the empirical, the classificatory, and the theoretical. Moreover, as overlapping is not excluded, premature theories, even those that prove erroneous, usefully precede the first precise analyses, and the theories ultimately accepted came to limit perspectives rather than broaden them. This is normal in the history of a science: in the beginning the hypothesis is the medium for advancement; in its maturity a theory of synthesis arises. Meanwhile, a general phenomenon of schism, which restricts the focus of each discipline, multiplies the total number of disciplines and of the authority localized in each of them. The principle of comparison, which the immensity of history greatly fosters, is employed to open these specializations to the study of everything human: languages, religions, societies, and arts. As the distant pasts of all continents are incorporated into our sense of culture, all hierarchies of the mind are completely upset; one sets about examining, as Anquetil had prophesied, the archives of the entire human race.

The New Universal History: Syntheses and Textbooks

Works encyclopedic in form were multiplying: composite anthologies of texts, textbooks, and catalogs of world history. Asia seemed on the verge of entering decisively into the sphere of classical humanism. It was a revealing phenomenon that on two separate occasions in the 1840s French translators of German works recognized that it had become necessary to add from then on sections concerning the Orient, which the author ten years earlier had not thought about. Otfried Müller's *Handbook of Archaeology*, mentioned above among the foes of orientalist excess, and Jacobi's *Mythological Dictionary* are cases in point.

Otfried Müller was adapted for the wide market of the *Manuels-Roret* by a certain Nicard, who wrote in his preface that the author had "accorded the right to be called an artistic people in the full sense of the word only to the Greeks. Consequently, he only cursorily discusses the art of all other peoples not directly related to the Greek tradition." The translator's attempt to redress this imbalance did not, as we have seen, lack precedents. Müller had included a brief chapter on India, but his discussions of Elephanta and Ellora as epics now seem weak and obsolete. The work of Jacobi dates from 1830–35; in 1846 his translator, Théodore Bernard, declared: "We would especially beg the reader's indulgence for the mythologies presented in addition to the two classical mythologies. The articles relating to them belong entirely to us, as Jacobi dealt exclusively with Greco-Roman polytheism." The articles had clearly been added for those interested in the Orient and were based on "the fine work of modern scholars," a reference to Jean Reynaud, among others, whose article "Zoroastre" in the *Encyclopédie nouvelle* had attracted considerable attention. This does not necessarily imply impeccable scholarship on Reynaud's part, as his article "Joghis" attests.

The scholarly collections spoke primarily to other scholars. The increasing number of them in each country demonstrates more intensive activity, but still a group activity. A more representative venture in popularization appearing at the end of this period in 1870 carried the title *Bibliothèque Internationale Universelle, Collection des chefs-d'oeuvre de l'espirit humain*. Two years later the publication was reissued with a restricted title that indicates the inclination of its editors even more clearly: *Bibliothèque Orientale publiée sous la direction d'un Comité scientifique international*. Indeed, respected orientalists figured among its collaborators and contributors. The change in title was warranted by the appearance of two new volumes. The first, devoted entirely to a republication of Langlois's *Rig Veda*, thus enabled that work to reach a wider audience. The second reprinted, in addition to basic Assyrian, Chinese, and Egyptian texts, selections from other Vedas by Barthélemy Saint-Hilaire, Pauthier's adaptation of Colebrooke, Foucaux's *Lalita Vistara*, and a variety of miscellaneous Hindu poems. The work represented a broad attempt to record the results of the new philologies and to provide the public with a world anthology.

The historical encyclopedias were the third proof of a generalized awareness. We can distinguish here two sets of syntheses.

On the one hand were constructs, based on the Herder-Creuzer-Görres model, in which the systematic approach and the "Philosophistorie" that had become the scholasticism of the Romantic movement were applied to historical materials. First of all there was Guigniaut's translation of Creuzer, so extensively altered as to be a new work. The four volumes published in German in 1810–12 became ten volumes published in French between 1825 and 1851. And as for the translations of Müller and Jacobi, and as

Heeren himself would do for new editions of his own works, the translator would add material on some of the significant developments pertaining to India and shift or reverse priorities. No less significant, if only
for dates and phases, was Benjamin Constant's *De la religion considérée dans
sa source, ses formes et ses développements*. As early as 1804 Constant was
discussing his work, first with the Schlegels, then for many years with
Fauriel. From 1824 to 1831 he published it in installments, confirming Sainte-
Beuve's statement on the reasons for his slowness. Constant wanted to
make successive use of the advances of orientalists in all countries that
served his own scholarship. The resulting book was a hybrid, a laggard
that brought itself up to date. The classification of various religions, which
was the point of departure, foreshadowed the end of the eighteenth-century outlook. The idea of "sacerdotal religions" tied to the existence of
secret doctrines, dear to the German mythologists, allowed for the pos-
tulation of a single belief and a universal pantheon. However, there was
not the least complacency, either for Lamennais's position, which substituted assent for sentiment, or for Eckstein's universal revelation and "lifeless gibberish." A modified rationalism undertook to revise the very idea
of religion in light of the discoveries of sacred texts. To no longer consider
the Vedas a primitive work but rather the product of "liturgical thought"
was to anticipate Barth's theory by half a century. William Jones and the
Asiatic Researches, the *Bhagavad Gita* (following Wilson's translation), and
the work of Creuzer (after Guigniaut's translation) were widely known and
profusely invoked. It was a rather good point that Barbey d'Aurevilly
conceded to the semirationalist in his squabble with the false friends of
Christ. In this category of broad generalizations, I will confine myself for
the moment to the observation that there will be a great many descendant
works to organize, including those of Quinet, Michelet, Jean Reynaud, and
Pelletan, all of whom attempted to write the *Summa* of history and of their
own times. In literature the prototype for them is undoubtedly Chateaubriand's *Génie du Christianisme*, but their abundance is explained by the
pressure of scholarly information and the influence of intellectual Romanticism which France took over from Germany.

Contrasting with this was another series of works embodying the techniques of a new universal history in which the oriental peoples were no
longer regarded as challenging *le droit de cité*. Here Golbéry's 1828 translation of Schlosser serves as a counterpoint to Guigniaut's translation of
Creuzer. I will return to this in dealing with the historians themselves. I
have had occasion to point out Hegel's contribution. His *Lectures on the
Philosophy of History*, based on material presented in 1830–31, were edited
from his notes and published posthumously by Gans. Gibelin assures us
that it was Hegel's only book that "became truly popular." The *Storia*

universale comparata e documentata published by Cesare Cantú after 1838 also dealt with oriental subjects. It was translated into French in 1843 by Eugène Aroux, the Dante commentator, who had revived Rosetti *père*'s theory of *The Divine Comedy* as a secret book of the Cathers. We should remember too that one of the first cultural histories based on the fledgling science of orientalism was the set of notes Goethe appended to the 1819 edition of his *East-West Divan*. Following trails Herder had only recently broken, he proved to be a master historian despite the fact he did not see his vast project through to the very end.

In 1869 François Lenormant, son of the Egyptologist who wrote the preface to the *Revue Archéologique,* produced a *Manuel d'histoire de l'Orient jusqu'aux guerres médiques* in the form of a syllabus. The second volume dealt with the Assyrians, Babylonians, Medes, and Persians; the third with the Phoenicians, Arabs, and Indians. The copious bibliographies, which included references up to the work of Eckstein, drew upon eighty years of Indic studies. Lenormant called primarily upon mythic or poetic texts. The *Bhagavad Gita, Bhagavata Purana, Lalita Vistara*, and *Laws of Manu* were offered as a documentation for the essays on Brahmanism and Buddhism. Fifty pages concerning Ayran societies were written as a running commentary on the *Ramayana* and *Mahabharata*. Victor Duruy greatly helped the assimilation of this new knowledge by including Indic studies in his own textbooks and in the curricula of his courses at the Université whenever possible.

Indeed, the inclusion of India in the repertoire of contemporary ideas depended on two vehicles: books and oral exposition. After making major contributions to the diffusion of Indic ideas, the first arrived at a certain limit, which it seldom exceeded. In 1875 Maspéro produced his mammoth *Histoire ancienne des peuples de l'Orient,* which was later abridged for classroom use and through which the notion of "a classical Orient" was reestablished—that is to say, was walled up again in the Mediterranean. There were decidedly two Orients: only the one consisting of Egypt, Iran, and Mesopotamia was admitted to the Université, as if any contact with the other might contaminate Hellenism. India remained pigeonholed with what was called the Far East, although Persia, its twin sister, slipped in on Herodotus' coattails. Although Mediterranean, Palestine was, for other no less sacred reasons, a plague quarantined from the curricula. The strange thing is that such relics persisted not only in the endowed chairs that looked out for the health of young minds but in the best scholarly works (Glotz's *General History*, for instance, but not that of Cavaignac). After having given way to world histories that forgot to exclude three-quarters of the world, Europe slipped back. Soon a French historian was taking satisfaction in the fact that Europe had returned to the confines of Bossuet. It is true that this was a literary historian, a field in which by middle age one's inflexibility can come to be an admired trait. Our schoolchildren were encouraged to comment on the biblical revelation or on the orientalism of Lamartine or Hugo, but the Psalms, the Vedas, Li Po, and Firdausi were interdicted. The poetic traditions of India, China, and the Bible, all of which together were considered of less importance than Pentadius, became the untouchables of literary instruction.

By 1819 Burnouf *père*'s famous syllabus of Greek grammar had placed within the reach of the secondary schools some of the concepts of the comparative grammar that Bopp had devised some three years earlier. These ideas worked wonders. In November 1829 Eugène Burnouf created a course in comparative grammar at the Ecole normale which he taught until February 1833. According to Barthélemy Saint-Hilaire, "Although Burnouf did not publish any part of his lectures, they were so vividly remembered not only by his students but by all the generations of students who attended the Ecole normale for twenty years, down to 1852, that the inadequate notes of the lectures are still today very much in demand by undergraduate and graduate candidates alike. They have been lithographed to provide for their wider use, and the notebooks are passed religiously from hand to hand from one class to another."[4] This parallels the episode and behavior shown toward the Indic studies diffused by Cousin's lectures.

In his turn in 1839 Emile Egger, a fervent disciple of Eckstein, adopted the comparative method in his own courses at the Ecole normale. And Bréal emphasized the importance of this development in his preface to Bopp: over a hundred years previously Sanskrit began to be included in the standard reference books placed in the hands of future professors, and their enthusiasm for the new field is borne out by numerous accounts. One of the results of the founding of the Ecole des hautes études in 1868 was the creation of the second chair of Sanskrit in Paris, which Bergaigne held after Hauvett-Besnault and before moving on to the Sorbonne.

In his treatise *Sur les rapports de l'Inde et de l'Europe* (read at the Institut historique on February 21, 1835), Eckstein gave an indication of the penetration of Sanskrit into the schools. "Since Sanskrit has been introduced into the schools and universities, all the studies of classical antiquity, far from being abandoned, have spontaneously revived." In his preface to *Notions de grammaire comparée* in 1854, designed for grammar classes in the secondary schools, Emile Egger remarked that regular instruction in comparative grammar, which involved some rudiments of Sanskrit, had been introduced into the academic curricula of the Second Empire. It soon became an elective and was rarely mentioned thereafter. The foundation of a school of Indic studies at Nancy in the 1850s by Emile Burnouf, Leupol, and Guerrier de Dumast, one of the first members of the Société Asia-tique, is rather conclusive evidence of the interest accorded to these mat-ters during this period, a time when Amiel was wondering whether Eu-ropean corruption might not be redeemed in such studies. Guerrier de Dumast ventured to produce a manifesto with the explicit title *L'Oriental-isme rendu classique dans les limites de l'utile et du possible* and later, with the backing of friends in Paris, defended his ideas at the Sorbonne. Condor-cet's plan for public education already included a chair of oriental lan-guages, by which he probably meant living languages. In 1818 Ballanche, like Bonald, in an "Essay on Social Institutions" pointed to language the-ory as the basis of any political structure and according to Sainte-Beuve wanted to replace Latin instruction with instruction in "oriental lan-guages." When in 1848 the Collège de France was temporarily trans-formed, on paper, into a school of public administration, future civil ser-vants were to have been required to take courses in Sanskrit as well as in Persian and Hebrew.[5]

Nevertheless, France saw no swarming-time comparable to the one in Germany that encouraged political division and particularism among its states. According to Nève in 1868, "There is probably not a single well-known university in this country that has not established a Sanskrit course as one of its newly created courses." This had been true for a number of years, if we can credit a letter on the subject in the *Revue Germanique* in 1858. And indeed in 1833 in the *Revue Encyclopédique* Jean Reynaud had made a bitter comparison between German schoolchildren, all of whom were hard at work on Sanskrit, and French schoolchildren, who were still confined within the Greco-Roman order. "It's unbelievable!" cried the scandalized Reynaud. It is equally shocking that a complete set of the Cal-cutta publications was not found in a single Paris library. Whether such gaps reveal negligence or hostility, the vigor of the protest shows an in-dignation corresponding to a new need. Whether scholarly or popular, literal or creative, disputed between the enthusiastic and the disquieted, the subject matter of a new kind of knowledge was now present, and the instruction by which it could be understood was likewise there. An al-most infinite mass of texts had been sought out and a staggering number of lost writings that led to dizzying heights of thought had been re-covered. The existence of this new knowledge weighed heavily on the spirit of Romantic Europe. The knowledge of India, the Orient, was certainly felt, but more than that, its presence was felt.

"If I were asked," said Max Müller, "what I considered the most im-portant discovery of the nineteenth century with respect to the ancient history of mankind, I should answer by the following short line: Sanskrit *Dyaus Pitar* = Greek Ζεὺς Πατηρ = Latin Juppiter = Old Norse Tyr."

Rawlinson, quoting Müller's comment, adds, "This work was carried on by Burnouf, Roth, and Max Müller, and from their patient researches sprang the study of Comparative Religion, which has had an affect upon modern thought only comparable to that of Darwin's *Origin of Species*. Max Müller said that the two great formative influences in his life were the *Rig-Veda* and the *Critique of Pure Reason*."[6] Had this been the equation drawn only in Müller's mind, we could easily solve its significence; but Müller's case was, as we shall see, far from exceptional.

Part Three
THE ORIENTAL RENAISSANCE
IN OPERATION

CHAPTER SIX

The Doctrinal Stages

We need to know how the religions of India were portrayed, at what point Buddhism was first glimpsed, and what was first sought in the books of the Brahmins, or in what were thought to be the books of the Brahmins.

—Gustave Lanson, 1906

THE full meaning of the literal stage of the Oriental Renaissance—the quest for texts, decipherings, linguistic foundations—cannot be grasped until we consider the doctrinal stages that resulted from and justified them. The Western estimate of Hindu thought depended primarily on philological activity, although there were other factors. The rational had, since the first spasmodic, conjectural contacts over the broken course of centuries, remained attracted by the pull of the supernatural. The few episodes that we know of, probably because they drew attention to the more marked points of similarity, concern rare moments occurring between the confused age of Pythagoras and the composite atmosphere of Plotinus.

From the dearth of documents we can infer that what pagan Greece defended from Indo-Iranianism was less a body of vital doctrines than a framework of mental habits. One can easily imagine what common origins were revived. The opposition of the Christian West, on the contrary, appears to have been based more on fundamentals than on formulations. But here again there are a good many nuances to consider. In following the chronology, one discovers that as a broader understanding of the forms developed, formal considerations bothered thinkers less. Ultimately, weren't the most tenacious resistances, as in pagan times, those of mental habit?

Because India first appeared to Europe as a land for colonization and a field for missionaries, it was inevitable that India's difficult teachings would be inquired into less as the colonizers became more certain of the necessity of inspiring respect for matters they wished to place beyond dispute. Thus the means of grasping the complexity of the problem were delayed by more than two centuries, and prolonged, rigorous efforts were necessary before the common good could be disentangled from the complexity. This mutual advantage lay in the fact that although the two worlds differed totally in their methods of acquiring knowledge and in their sets of solutions, they both pursued the same spiritual and intellectual goals. This pursuit required a great deal of generally conscientious effort that was frequently based on false information and, in the end, simultaneous loyalties to the spiritual and the philological.

The First Attitudes and Reactions

There was no knowledge to speak of until after the Portuguese settlements. Buddha was mentioned by Clement of Alexandria; the Vedas appeared in the work of Saint Hippolytus and again conspicuously in the sixteenth century. Europe began its discussion of essential doctrinal points two hundred years before it gained access to complete texts. Not only were most of the first European students of these doctrines evangelizers but, as we have seen, and this is much more disturbing, most of the first indigenous instructors were converts. Consequently, works acquired before Indic studies were themselves adaptations. Obtained from genuine sources, but through inaccurate interpreters, they aimed at reconciliation if not complaisance. The Western customers for such works were not about to dispute their validity. Even during the period inaugurated by the Calcutta school, there was an abundance of works whose authors seemed to have acquired their information firsthand, but had not. They may well have been capable of discussing their beliefs with the faithful, but in languages other than the Sanskrit of their scriptures.

Abridgments and adaptations preceded translations, which themselves preceded definitive editions. The Vedas, the epics, and the Puranas were long discussed on the basis of excerpts or commentaries. For half a century the acquired knowledge remained what it had been in the first decade: the *Bhagavad Gita*, the *Laws of Manu*, and the *Oupnek'hat*. The lightning revelation was followed by very little headway. To begin with, for two centuries what was believed to be known had passed through a series of screens. More than once it was the most dubious representatives of the local cults whom Western apologists questioned. The Brahmans, the caste generally the least accessible to them, were generally the most knowledgeable. In other castes as well they were destined to reach those whose faith, and perhaps thought, was the least reliable. And I am not even mentioning moral quality, as more than one traveler did. In India the ancient faith was not a barrier to welcoming a new faith. The difficulty was that introducing foreigners to a faith considered inseparable from its native land gave them the discouraging suspicion that everything they did, no matter what, would remain only an approximation. Did they know enough about Christianity otherwise to calculate its influence? We can discern a penchant for manufacturing a Brahmanism more amenable to export, for translating remote beliefs into familiar language for the benefit of Europeans, in the information the Protestant and Catholic missionaries of the seventeenth and eighteenth centuries relied on. What is more, although the spiritual geography of the new continent remained vague, these same missionaries, through a more or less general impulse, seem to have rejoiced each time the opportunity arose to glimpse an expected affirmation of the ancient world revelation in the new continent. Most of the spurious texts intended to hasten understanding, and doomed to delay it, were compiled or commissioned by them.

The first to disembark had no doubt that they were in heathen lands, and they anticipated only the fabulous. It was precisely that which the intermediaries were most ready to give them. The profusion of myths, the odd practices, increased substantially in their eyes through a prevalence of popular sects which reinforced their expectation of barbarism. At the same time the persistent yearning for doctrinal purity that they encountered in their students added to their impatience to equate all sorts of spiritual principles with biblical monotheism. These two opposing tendencies worked together to make superficial similarities of terms, dogmas, and rituals convincing and effaced the sharpness of distinctions in the minds of each of the two interlocutors.

Undoubtedly, the different beliefs of the one appeared to be credulities to the other, a further reason to imagine that the lost souls could easily be separated from their errant faith, to the benefit of essential truths. The Hindus saw as symbolic what the Europeans took for magical; the Hindu in turn retained from the images of Christianity parceled out to him those elements that *disoriented* him the least. Thus the Hindu was close to encouraging the Western penchant for trying to translate "Ishvara" as "Eternal" and drawing the Trimurti toward the Trinity. At its beginning the Indo-European dialogue was something like one between two well-intentioned deaf people. As it happened, the way for the true explanation was prepared by an initial misunderstanding connected with two barriers. The one was intolerance, which caused the Westerners to lash out against some huge shocks: the widow's funeral pyre, child marriages, the taboo regarding cows, the perpetuity of castes, and so forth. The other was complaisance, which caused them to gloss over rigorous dogmatic distinctions. Perhaps these errors provided the necessary stimulants. One must return to this point as one becomes able to judge it better.[1] Thus in the preface of his 1840 *Bhagavata Purana,* Burnouf stated, "I don't need to point out that I found here absolutely no trace of Greek or Christian ideas; where are the Indian works in which up to now such ideas have supposedly been positively identified?" Thus in his 1898 *Cosmologie hindoue* the Abbé Roussel concluded that "many similarities of words" had been retrieved, "but few similarities of ideas." The Hindu monotheism had "only a name in common" with ours. For the Creation, the Trinity, the Incarnation, the Redemption, all the fundamental tenets, there was still no possibility of comparison. Naturally, this is only another way of looking at it; it represents one side of a tug-of-war. It is striking to observe, during the first period, both the faithful and the *philosophes* zealously competing, on the contrary, to efface distances and nuances.

We should not forget that oriental doctrines straightway became subjects and arguments of controversy for these two camps. To the extent that the policeman of the mind named science was not there to keep order, each gang grabbed from what looked to it like a construction site whatever seemed to it to be the handle of a weapon. This was done with few qualms, since India itself seemed to be setting the example for such freedom with a swarm of texts that treated its sacred authorities like an open field where its genius for interpolation could ignore all bounds. However, Western reason did not delay seeking an order among these intricacies, whereby mental stability triumphed over juxtaposition. It attempted an analysis that had not been made previously, or that had been made only in the manner of the country. The Western mind soon felt it could make a better determination of the relative merits of successive contributions to the history of sects than local indifference had made. The fact remained that the original stock of concepts, for want of direct contact with the texts, produced a kind of commonplace language that was most likely to be deficient in those very distinctions whereby truths could be found.

Principal Dates: Truncated Shastras and False Vedas

Between 1630 and 1790 reports and fragments reached Europe in three or four principal waves. During the period of incunabula, which lasted until around 1660, the major figures—Henry Lord and Abraham Roger— were connected with the Protestant missions; around 1720–40 the Jesuits intervened with their contribution of the *Lettres édifiantes;* the period between 1760 and 1780 saw the commentaries of Holwell and Dow, the *Ezour-Vedam* and the appearance of the *philosophes;* and between 1780 and 1800 the conscientious research of Anquetil and Sancto Bartholomaeo coincided with the scientific foundations being laid at Calcutta.

During the first two stages, all original information clearly resulted from dogmatic inquiry. The missionaries were the first to have recourse to the learning of the pandits. Two concerns came into play here, at times in alternation, at others simultaneously: the conviction of refuting superstition and the hope of liberating an oppressed truth. Voltaire, as was his habit, simplified. Snatching the lead from the theologians, Voltaire posed no questions about authenticity. Never was a mind less concerned with the critical; never was a critic more expeditious. If a text did not prove to be Semitic in origin, Voltaire saw absolutely no reason to discuss its value. Voltaire's behavior is understandable if his motives are explained as those of a political journalist; the sometimes clumsy enthusiasm of the missionaries and their possibly naïve biases were followed by the tricks of the polemicist. And polemics is, by definition, a genre that produces only an *effect*.

Certainly there was excess on both sides. Voltaire found material in Bouchet with which to amuse his public. Ward (and how many others?) long believed they owed "the idolators" nothing but undisguised scorn. But if the defenders of a church are motivated by an overwhelming impetus to exclude the beliefs of others, this is mere child's play compared with the dauntlessness of skeptics who lump all beliefs together. Diderot himself, in the *Encycllopédie*, referring openly to the missionaries, observed that their ardor had frequently altered things, "sometimes for the better, sometimes for the worse." We can follow the progress of the principal articles by studying the informants who shaped them. With the first of these appeared the reasonable practice of transmitting a tradition obtained from indigenous scholars. This is what the English chaplain Henry Lord, the German Jesuits Kircher and Roth, and the Dutch missionary Abraham Roger did. The same practice was later carried on by such travelers as Bernier. It required a great many detours before the lesson they drew from such an approach could be distilled.

Henry Lord

Lord's *A Display of Two Forraign Sects in the East Indies, viz; The Sect of the Banians the Ancient Natives of India and the Sect of the Persees the Ancient Inhabitants of Persia, together with the Religion and Manners of each Sect* (1630) was translated into French by Briot and appeared in Paris in 1667 under two different titles, the one announcing a history of the religion of the "anciens Persans," the other that of the "Banians." The first title specified it was dealing with the Persians "who are presently in East India," in other words, the Parsis. The book also provided the first excerpt from the *Zend Avesta* to appear in Europe. But more than half the work was reserved for a discussion of the beliefs of India itself under the rubric "the religion of the Banians." (The entire population is identified with its tradespeople who placed their stalls in the shade of the banyan trees.) Fifteen chapters deal with the Banians, eight with the Parsis, and the book was subtitled "Histoire de la religion des Banians."

Lord's outline of the doctrines, drawn from local documents, became a sort of Decalogue that had reportedly been handed down to "Bremaw," god during the second age of the world. Lord calls this code "the *Shaster*," as if it were unique and the Indic counterpart of the Persian *Avesta*. We know that *shastra*, of which this was the first European spelling, is a generic name that applies to a great number of didactic treatises. What the mind and language of the translators grasped created a fabulous biblical novel: God creates the world by blowing on the waters through "some great cane or like instrument" and thus separates the elements. We see the first man and woman, Pourous and Parcoutee (Purusha and Prakriti), "feeding on the fruites of the earth, without the destruction of any living creature." A page such as the one where Moses implicitly appears as a watermark allows one to savor what the collaboration between a compatriot of Charles Perrault and a British chaplain returned from Surat can yield. It concerns four brother gods among whom the primitive world is divided.

"And because Brammon was of a melancholy constitution, and ingenious, God indued him with knowledge, and appointed him to impart his Precepts and Laws unto the people, his grave and serious looke, best befitting him for such a purpose: for which cause hee gave him a Booke, containing the forme of divine Worshippe and Religion." The Hindu myth is adapted in a well-bred style, like the Greek myth of Psyche in La Fontaine. The sudden appearance of a character with a "serious looke" who we are told is a God who "wanted to be served" (like the god of *Athalie*) is a theatrical touch. The bounds of language led to a shrinking of the mental landscape. The cosmogony is reduced to a sort of Arabic *Amadis*: merchants and diamonds, mountains, castles, talismans—one is taken down paths that lead above all to the *Thousand and One Nights*. The history of the ages of the world and of successive creations includes a good many views on the distribution of divine attributes, but confusions of vocabulary interpose themselves at each step. The "bosom of the Almighty" and the "Last Judgment" propagate dubious equivalences.

Of immediate interest in such simplifications is the topic of reincarnation; it touches the core of man's chief interests and bluntly delineates two climates of thought. It had always been India's best recruiter in Europe; it impressed the Greeks, and it later fascinated Voltaire and his successors.

Lord broaches the subject in a way that later became common, through one of its conspicuous results: the prohibition against eating meat is taken as a sign of the claim that animals are "endued with the same soule that man is." How can India be unaware, Lord wondered, that according to the "philosophers" plants have a vegetative soul, animals have a sensible soul, and only man has a rational soul, which alone is immortal? We can recognize here a classification appearing in the *Timaeus* which, endorsed by the official education of the Middle Ages, proved hard to kill until Descartes. Moreover, Lord continued, the Book of Genesis categorically denies this point: God allowed Noah to eat meat. Probably the poor Banians had taken their bizarre ideas from Pythagoras, who was venerated among them. Abstinence from wine is no more defensible: had not God made wine to gladden men's hearts, even if it entailed maintaining a reasonable forbearance? Galen called it "the nurse of old age" and Plato himself, who was also not without links to "those people," considered wine "God's remedy against old age."

Neither Pythagoras nor Plato, strictly speaking, invented metempsychosis. It goes without saying that it was they who taught it to India; had they not learned it themselves from Egypt? Could anyone doubt this chain of events? Lord had what was for him the only clear guarantee, the same he had for the sensible soul and wine: the authority of Greek and Latin writers. The notion of rebirths was a monstrosity, long since filed away and disposed of. After samsara, karma made its first appearance on the horizon of European curiosity. The usefulness of reincarnations was that "the soule was impure by the sinnes and corruptions of the body, therefore it was needfull it should bee sublimed from this corruption, by such transmeation out of one body into another, as Chymicall spirits gaine a purer essence by passing through the Still or Limbecke, divers times; every Distillation taking away some of his grosse part, and leaving it more refined." The theme of rewards leads to images of the Christian paradise. There was no need to refute the "supposall of a metempsychosis" for the simple reason that "the immortality of the soule wee evince without this Chymera of the Fancy." Far from purifying itself by passing through successive bodies, the soul could only become further tainted, "as water becommeth defiled by infusion into an uncleane vessell," which is not to say that one is unaware of the role of labor and of contemplation.

The chaplain contrasted all these idolatries not only with the arbitration of the Bible, but with the common sense of an enlightened time—as if the age of Voltaire had already dawned. All the same, there was less fanaticism in the West from the church than from the universities. Certain Indian practices seemed to make Europe jumpy. Actually it was just reliving some schoolboy memories. Lord is a good example of this: suttee was explained for him by quotations from Strabo and Propertius. He was quite willing to allow, contrary to Postel's supposition, that "Braham" was not a descendant of Abraham. Classical education offered no contradiction on the point. The great obstacle between the two hemispheres was not to be the Roman faith but rather Roman literature.

Abraham Roger

Abraham Roger's influence on thought regarding oriental matters was much different from Lord's, and more memorable. His maxims from Bhartrihari were, for the first time, more of a translation than an adaptation. A Dutch missionary at Coromandel and Batavia from 1630 (the date of Lord's book) until 1647, he died in 1649. His work on the religion of the Brahmans, originally published in Latin, was not published in Leiden until 1651; it was translated into German by 1663 and into French in 1670 in Amsterdam. In this last instance, the Flemish title *(De Open-Deure tot het verborgen Heydendom . . .)* became the following, which is worth reproducing in full: *The Open Door to obtaining a knowledge of hitherto-undisclosed Paganism, or A True Representation of the Life, Manners, Religion and of the Divine Service of the Brahmans who dwell on the Coromandel coast and the surrounding country, by the said Abraham Roger who resided many years on these shores and who very exactingly researched all that he found most curious, with remarks on the names and things of greatest importance. Translated into French by the said Thomas La Grue, master of arts and doctor of medicine.*

Roger's investigation figured among the undertakings of several European countries that sent informants to India in the interval between *Discourse on Method* and the death of Descartes. The title underscores the identification made between the traditions of India and "hidden paganism," which is to say, the non-Christian mysteries. It was to be the obsession of the eighteenth century, during which the Hindus definitively became the "Gentoos," the pagans par excellence. On the other hand, the ancient prestige of the country of the gymnosophists was rekindled by the hope that its magic tradition would prove to be a corruption of the universal primitive revelation. This was an obsession that persisted from Creuzer to Eckstein and Lamennais.

While expressing satisfaction that a great deal was already known about the peoples of India, La Grue, the French translator, declared in his preface "To the reader" that he was surprised that "until now there has been no one who has propounded what constitutes their religion and the ceremonies they observe in their holy services." In particular, no one "has been able to convey the true bases of their religion, their particular feelings, and the opinions they hold concerning God and holy matters." Of course, the goal was to enlighten "these poor benighted peoples." Through "their transgressions" they had "easily managed to discover the true invisible God through visible things and their causes." It became a question of premeditated exploration, from which they expected not only information but edification. On neither ground did their confidence swerve. In chapter 10 Roger maintained that the Brahmans were "extremely ignorant regarding philosophy." Like Lord, he meant that they had not read Plato et al. One of them in particular, Padmanaba, gave Roger instruction in his faith while Roger was a minister at Palikat, La Grue informs us. The missionary wanted to be able to preach with full knowledge of the local beliefs. The pandits continually welcomed his questionnaires without surprise or apprehension. How far did the encounters go? The book begins its "second part dealing with the belief and religion of the Brahmans" with this lively sentence: "No one should think that they are entirely similar to animals, nor that they recognize neither God or religion." Roger went so far as to add, "On the contrary, we should have altogether different feelings about them." He who had seen and heard ascertained a vague sense of the presence of God among the "idolators," though not without precautions. Unfortunately Thomas La Grue pointed out at the bottom of the page that these precautions were necessary, and was disturbed that they were not more severe.

Nonetheless, the progress over Lord was considerable. Roger's account remained in the realm of the fabulous, its attention fixed on rites, superstitions, the whole outer shell of the Hindu faith. The usual objections were brought up again, and the objection against child marriages appeared. But while confused notions were beginning to be sorted out, some fundamental ideas were beginning to appear. Roger was right in proclaiming that he was opening some doors. First of all he discerned the "diversity of sects." Thus he mentioned Shaivites and Vaishnavites, La Grue supposing Vishnu was "a common noun" equivalent to God, which seems to be a hasty translation, though perhaps not an ill-considered one. Better still, "Ramanuja Weistnouwa" was distinguished among the Vaishnavites. It was rather advanced to be able to mention in Cartesian Europe one of the greatest Vedantic scholars, even if it was from the traditional point of view that he was one of the incarnations of Vishnu. On the other hand, yogis and sannyasis were depicted as recluses living in the forests. Roger had conferred a great deal both with Padmanaba and with four other

Brahmans on the various systems and their essential points. In more than one passage, a thread of understanding was grasped. The avatars of Vishnu are mentioned, although their names are not recorded. This leads to the story of Rama and Sita. Buddha is mentioned in his turn, but, it is true, as one of the avatars of Vishnu.

Roger provided Europe with a great number of important concepts concerning India. He admitted that despite their disputes concerning "the sovereign God," all sects recognized "a sovereign God who is absolute and unique." The profound monotheism was extricated from the visible polytheism. Another crucial subject was the soul. "It is the shared opinion of the Brahmans that the soul is immortal and that it will be eternal." But Roger remembers from his discussions with the Brahmans that there are two doctrines: according to the one, the soul had always been in God and "is composed of his essence." According to the other, the soul was outside God and "was sleeping until the world was created." Roger presented the question of monism to the West with the same seriousness with which it had been presented to India. On the other hand, Roger's final chapter, on eschatology, seems extremely clipped.

Roger was also the first westerner to describe the Vedas and define the prerogatives of the Brahmans. The main prerogative was reading the sacred book "which is the pagans' book of the law, which includes, in itself, all they must believe and all the rituals they must observe. This book is written in the *samscortam* language: all the mysteries of paganism are written in this language, and the Brahmans, who have no intention of involving themselves in commerce, learn it. This Vedam is divided into four parts: the first is designated as *Rogowedam*, the second as *Issourwedam*, the third as *Samawedam*, and the fourth as *Adderawanawedam*." We can discern through the double falsification of Tamil and Flemish the appelations that would later become familiar: the *Rig*, the *Yajur*, the *Sama*, and the *Atharva Veda*. A hasty analysis of the Vedas is also given. One can better appreciate Roger if one considers how scanty and false d'Herbelot's scholarship is in the articles "Beth" and "Anberkend" in the *Bibliothèque Orientale*, which appeared nearly half a century after Roger's work. Roger also marked, finally, the first evidence of Indian sensitivity on the subject of the fourth Veda. According to Padmanaba it no longer existed (as was to be frequently repeated), and with its loss the Brahmans had lost the omnipotence that formerly, thanks to this magical code, made them the superiors even of kings. Roger himself appears to have been familiar with no more of the Vedas than the Vaishnavite hymns in the Tamil language. Although Bhartrihari belonged to the Sanskrit domain, Padmanaba had obtained a translation of his work; it occupied twenty-five pages in the French edition.

Athanasius Kircher

This French edition was enriched by an addition: an excerpt entitled "Des décrets et opinions des Brachmanes" from *China monumentis qua sacris qua profanis illustrata* (1663) by Athanasius Kircher. Thomas La Grue, a strict Protestant, with complacence if not with malice, added to the work of his coreligionist a complement from a Jesuit who had been less open-minded than Roberto de Nobili. As a sinologist, Kircher judged the religions of India with suspicion and heaped invectives against them. Roth, who had collected the first specimens of the Sanskrit alphabet at Agra, was his informant. Kircher was particularly fond of joining the epithet "ridiculous" to anything touching on transmigration and was not sparing in suspicions of deceit or reproaches of absurdity. He saw in the avatars an offense against the dogma of the Incarnation. It is understandable that a Christian conscience would prove sensitive on this point, but given the sequel, does it not seem that it was precisely here that the West became vitally attached to the principle of identity?

The excerpt from Kircher includes six pages of an "Abridgment of the Natives who inhabit the Coromandel coasts" which offers us a glimpse of Kircher's method of inquiry. We are told that this abridgment was composed by a local scholar and sent to the Dutch governor Arnold Heussen. One feels in the work the effort of a Hindu seeking to make himself understood to foreigners unfamiliar with his country, its language, or its beliefs. There is a God "living eternally whose corporeal being is never known and can never be known. . . . His shadow has no eye and yet nonetheless He sees everything in the world, has no ear and yet hears everything, and although we maintain that He is not here and there alike, yet He is always everywhere in the world." Such definitions seem typical to me: they cannot be disavowed by a Brahman, yet they are not foreign to the Christian nor even, perhaps, to the deist. This particular definition precludes neither the spirit of the Psalms nor that of Spinoza and yet does not betray that of the Upanishads. Its pantheism is not irreconcilable with its transcendence.

Abraham Roger and his theological curiosity left their mark on libraries and literatures, notably through Goethe, a faithful reader who later borrowed subjects for his poetry from Roger. He also avowed he was struck at an early age by the 1681 German translation of the physician Olfert Dapper's *Asia, of Naukeurige beschryving van het rijk des grooten Mogols, en een groot gedeelte van Indiën (Asia, a detailed description of the realm of the Great Moguls, together with a large section concerning India.)* This was an account of Dapper's voyages to the Great Mogul published in Holland in 1672 and filled with Brahmanical imagery. The Protestant missions had other representatives important in the history of Indic studies. Among the Dutch are Baldaeus and Melchior Valentijn, "whose learned collections are rich mines which have not been adequately explored," as Lanjuinais wrote at the beginning of the nineteenth century when the new science of Indic studies was also benefiting from documents collected some hundred years earlier by the Danish mission established in 1706 at Tranquebar on the same Coromandel coast. Anquetil mentions them frequently, and Max Müller rated Bartholomew Ziegenbalg (1683–1719) highly. It should be noted that if the doctrinal canvassing nourished by the missions (some of which were established in the north, others in the south) brought forward divergent traditions, the greatest number of canvassers were dependent on Tamil-speaking respondents. This fact was not without influence on the condition of the texts used, as we have seen with certain shastras and, above all, the *Bagavadam*. In the *Encyclopédie*, Diderot gathered what he knew of Vedic and Brahmanic beliefs under the heading "Malabares."

Bernier and the Curiosity About India

François Bernier left for Syria in 1654, moved to Egypt, and then lived in India until 1668. He had predecessors there, notably Pierre Malherbe and Tavernier, but unquestionably no one did more than he to render India familiar and desirable to educated society in the seventeenth century. He was a physician by trade and a philosopher. He had studied the one discipline at Montpellier and the other under Gassendi, whom he greatly admired; he was a fellow student of Chapelle and Molière and, perhaps, of Cyrano. Bernier was widely known and lionized both before his departure and after his return. Saint-Evremond spoke of him as a "joli philosophe" to their friend Ninon de Lenclos, with whom Saint-Lambert later paired Bernier in his dialogue *Analyse de la femme*. In his *Eloge de Gassendi*, Bernier admitted it was "not displeasing to hear it said, 'There he is, the great traveler!' "

Bernier was one of those who contributed to the establishment of the "Great Mogul" as a character in European literature. Physician to Aurangzeb for eight years, intimate friend of a high court official, Bernier exchanged lessons in biology and Western metaphysics for the concepts of Brahmanic theology, for he had an avid curiosity that sought the real India behind the conquered India. He was encouraged in his research by his Parisian correspondents and also by his encounters with other travelers, religious and lay, starting off at the time on the same trails. Thus through Bernier we can verify and fill the gaps in the general ideas Kircher borrowed from Roth, whom Bernier had seen a great deal in Agra. Unfortunately, Roth did not feel he had anything to add on these subjects. In a letter dated November 13, 1661, reminding Bernier that he was following the route of Apollonius of Tyre, Chapelain adjured him to inquire about books and doctrines. In November 1661, Chapelain entrusted some letters and packages to Tavernier, who was returning to the court of Aurangzeb and who was Bernier's companion during the entire month of December 1665. Bernier's lengthy and important response to Chapelain was dated "from Shiraz in Persia, June 10, 1668." Another letter from Chapelain was entrusted to Chardin, who had met Bernier in Surat on his way to Paris in 1667. On February 11, 1669 Chapelain received the letter from Shiraz, which said:

First of all, do not be surprised if, although I do not know *hanscrit*, the language of the scholars, which I will discuss further on, and perhaps the very language of the ancient Brahmans of India, as will be seen presently, I nevertheless tell you many things drawn from books written in this language, and you will learn that my Aga Danishmand Khan, partly at my request, partly from his own curiosity, took into his employ one of the most well-known pandits in all India, who had earlier had a pension from Dara, the eldest son of the king Shah Jahan, and that this pandit, besides having drawn to us all the most learned pandits, was by my side for more than three years. When I was weary of explaining to my Aga the latest discoveries of Harvey and Pecquet on anatomy and of arguing with him the philosophies of Gassendi and Descartes, which I translated for him into Persian (for that was my major occupation for five or six years), the pandit was our refuge, and it was for him to argue and to relate to us the fables that he recited seriously and without ever laughing; it is true that we grew so thoroughly disgusted at the end of his churlish lines of argument that we were almost unable to listen to him further.

One relishes this picturesque instruction. But from this time on, it was a question of fundamental interests between the two intellectual hemispheres. It is regrettable, though not surprising, that Western stomachs manifested signs of indigestion. It should be mentioned that the pandit of Dara Shikoh, the brother and victim of Aurangzeb, was the famous translator who provided the Persian version of the Upanishads which Bernier was to bring back to Paris and which Anquetil was to translate.

"They say that God, whom they call Achar, which is to say unmovable or unalterable, sent them four books which they call Beths, a word meaning learning, because they claim that these books contain all wisdom. The first of these books is called Atherbabed, the second Zagerbed, the third Rakbed, and the fourth Samabed." Following the Tamil transcript provided by Roth and Kircher, we have a transcript based on Persian. We should note that these related spellings (*Beth* and *Bed*) later appeared in the *Bibliothèque Orientale* of d'Herbelot, a friend of Bernier who, there can be no doubt, received his information from him.

The pandits did not claim that their law applied to everyone, but on the contrary, that God had made their religion only for them. Nor did they claim that Christianity was false; it was good for the Christians. God might "have made several paths leading to heaven; but they could not understand that our path was, generally speaking, for all the world while theirs was only fable and invention." Bernier had heard missionaries identify the Indian trinity with the Christian one, but he was not convinced and does not seem to have favored this tendency. "Moreover, I have seen the Reverend Father Roth, a Jesuit, a German by nationality and a missionary at Agra, who has applied himself to the study of *hanscrit* and who has had a great deal of access to it, and he asserted that not only was it borne out in the books of the gentiles that there was a God in three persons, but that the second person of their trinity had been incarnated nine times."

He developed this point in the very terms one of his instructors used, adding, to our disappointment: "I have written many things about it throughout my memoirs . . . and I had had the characters of their *hanscrit* language provided for me; but having found on my return that all of that, or at least the better part of it, was printed in the *China illustrata* of Father Kircher, who had learned it in Rome from the same Father Roth, I shall content myself with pointing out his book to you. . . . I shall add these words so you know I am no less obliged to Henry Lord and Abraham Roger than I am to these reverend fathers Kircher and Roth: I have compiled a hundred things concerning the gentiles that I have found in the books of these gentlemen that would have given me a great deal of labor to arrange as they did." Bernier assures us at least that not only was there a certain contemporary manner of approaching Hindu doctrines, there was a certain Hindu steadfastness in the manner of laying these doctrines open to foreigners. It is interesting to see an eyewitness confirm the accuracy these other documents achieved for their time.

Bernier's letters were read by Chapelain at the home of the chancellor Séguier, the house where the Académie held its meetings; copies of some of this assiduous and voluminous correspondence later passed through the hands of Sainte-Beuve and Victor Pavie. Bernier's interest in distant doctrines, stimulated by a great scholar like Chapelain and a keen mind like Chapelle, to whom Bernier had addressed another significant letter in 1661, was united with an unswerving faith and a passion for the most recent breakthroughs in learning and science. Bernier, moreover, is the first example of those active intermediaries between Indic studies and literature whose number later swelled during the Romantic period. Bernier was on familiar terms with Racine and Boileau, having collaborated with them in 1671 on the famous *Arrêt burlesque* "in which," according to Caullery, "the court ordered the chile to go straight to the liver without any longer passing through the heart . . . on penalty of being turned over entirely to the Medical School." Bernier later provided Molière with "particulars which," according to Picavet, "helped him ridicule in *Malade imaginaire* physicians who were attached to outdated practices and were enemies of the theory of circulation." Indeed, Diafoirus speaks the language of Riolan, head of the long opposition that set the Faculté de médecine de Paris against the still-recent discoveries of Harvey (1628) and Pecquet (1651).

Most important, Bernier was to become the dinner companion and daily interlocutor of La Fontaine at the home of Madame de la Sablière, where, after an assiduous youth spent with Ninon and the Duchesse de Bouillion, he first came into contact with his intimate friend and future executor of his will, the d'Herbelot of the *Bibliothèque Orientale*. This provides a perspective on the relationships established during the reign of Louis XIV between literary creation and curiosity about the Orient. His contact with Bernier renewed La Fontaine's wellsprings. Louis Roche noted in his life of La Fontaine: "Bernier is one of the men to whom La Fontaine is most indebted. I find frequent signs of this in his *Second Recueil*. We should remember that the traveler Bernier had spent a long period in the states of the Great Mogul. It was after his return that the fabulist La Fontaine availed himself of oriental sources, in any case in the *Livre des lumières*. Simple coincidence? I think not. He seems to have been influenced by Bernier's travel books, which appeared in 1670–71, as well as by his conversations. The story of Aurangzeb, filled with strange and moving accounts, must have carried the mind of the poet toward the fabulous Orient. Why does the Great Mogul continually creep into the book—for example, in the fable of the Hermit and the Vizier, or the tale of the Wishes with which, moreover, only Bernier could have familiarized him?" (The only other account he could have used could be found only in the yet-untranslated Hebrew text—which had prompted La Fontaine to exclaim, "If only I had learned Hebrew!" Here is an echo of his conversations with Bernier or d'Herbelot.) "And who had told him the story of Bassa and the Merchant? Or again, how can one not recognize Bernier, despite all the differences in situation and character, in this man who runs after adventure, who goes to see the Great Mogul, who, like Bernier, passes on to Surat, and who on his return home finds his friend fast asleep? Bernier! Certainly one can perceive his memory, his influence, on every page, in everything touching science or philosophy."

In 1670 Bernier published *Histoire de la dernière révolution des Etats du Grand Mogol*; in 1688 he published "Memoire sur le quiétisme des Indes" in *His-*

toire des Savants and "Introduction à la lecture de Confucius" in *Journal des Savants*. In 1699 the complete edition of the *Voyages* was published posthumously, reprinting the two great philosophical letters on India—to Chapelle in 1661 and Chapelain in 1668—previously published as "Suite des Mémoires" in 1671. In the interim, the *Voyages* of Tavernier had appeared in 1677, those of Thévenot in 1684, and the Persian travels of Chardin in 1686. Tavernier, with the full flair of the century, struck the imagination with his sumptuous and eventful adventures of a merchant made fabulously wealthy by, and then abruptly ruined by, the jewels of India. More favorable in his description than in his attitude, Tavernier repeated, after conversations with the Brahmans, matters regarding caste, suttee, the life of the soul, and the nature of God, but without shedding much light on them. Bernier had heard about the Puranas and, like Abraham Roger, had an inkling of the six classical schools *(darshanas)*. Anquetil referred to his information frequently. In his discussions of India, Buffon consistently cited the naturalist Thévenot and Tavernier; the only thing he took from Bernier was a passage on Kashmir.

The *Lettres édifiantes*

The Jesuits gave the early eighteenth century the most extensive, best classified, and most penetrating store of oriental knowledge. The *Lettres édifiantes* do not begin well in respect to India. In the very first letter, June 1, 1700, Father Pierre Martin explained the caste system, openly acknowledging that the first converts had become Christians in order to protect themselves against the Muslims or to conciliate the Portuguese conquerors, or were pariahs or from the lowest castes. Next came letters from Madras from Father Bouchet to Huet, who had become bishop of Avranches; these were the letters that Voltaire later found so amusing. The two correspondents were eminently Greco-Latin westerners: in their eyes it was India who was indebted to the West for all its knowledge. By his mania for agreement, Bouchet deformed everything he reported. He did provide a general idea of the fourfold Vedas, but had no doubts but that they had been copied "from the law of Moses." When the missionary conversed with Huet between two voyages, the subject they found most fascinating was metempsychosis.

A development that followed Father de la Lane's letter of January 30, 1709 seems significant: having allowed that Indic polytheism was a misrepresentation of the original religion, one could detect in it nonetheless, as a paramount term, union with God. From then on the history of the soul was concerned profoundly with the fact that so little was known about

India. Of course, not all minds were so open, but from 1730 to 1740 two informants of the first order, Fathers Calmette and Pons, were. The missions were able, contrary to all expectations, to gain access to the Vedas, although, as I have pointed out, they could not extend their Sanskrit studies back to the Vedic language. They had to resign themselves to excerpts from commentaries obtained, like the manuscripts themselves, from Christianized Brahmans. On these fragile foundations Calmette, in his letter of September 17, 1735, based his scheme to prove to the Hindus that their belief was not different, "for the unity of God, the characteristics of the true God, of salvation, and of the judgment, are all in the Vedas," but "like flecks of gold dust in piles of sand."

Pons himself was as well versed in doctrines as he was in language, in which regard he anticipated the English scholarship by nearly half a century. His letter of November 23, 1740 is remarkable; Pons was often both broad-minded and accurate in his perceptions. Of course, he also ventured some rather dubious parallels: for example, upon discovering the formula "Om, Shanti, Shanti, Shanti, Hari," he wrote, "You are no doubt aware that the letter or syllable *Om* contains the Trinity of God, and the rest is a literal translation of *Sanctus, sanctus, sanctus, dominus*. Hari is a name for God, which means ravisher." Nevertheless, one is amazed at the perspicacity with which Pons analyzed the authentic essence of Hindu systems and applied fundamental distinctions: he was the first to discriminate "two theologies, Brahmanic and popular," the former containing the Vedas, the latter drawn from the Puranas. In addition to defining moral doctrine, which he treated with remarkable respect, Pons described the esoteric value of the Shastras: "Their unique purpose, the aim of all the philosophical pursuits of the Brahmans, is to deliver the soul from the captivity and miseries of this life by means of a perfect bliss, which is essentially either the deliverance of the soul or its immediate effect." Here Pons reached a valid coupling of the spiritualities, the hopes, of the two religions, which marked a definite advance.

Other important distinctions followed: Pons was familiar with the names and chief characteristics of the six schools of the Vedantists. He was the first to have accurate information about Buddhism (which he called *Bauddamatham*), and he identified, before de Guignes, the Buddhism of China and Tibet with that of ancient India; he also mentions Jainism. Pons elucidated a number of concepts that was remarkably large for 1740. The work of Bernier and Roger is mere child's play by comparison. The dogmas of emanation from or union with God are analyzed in the interpretation accompanying each of the schools *(darshanas)*; among these, the Vedanta according to Shankara, which all the sannyasis mentioned, was acknowledged as the most important, and the significance of *maya* to it was pointed out. What distinguishes this school from the others is its view of the simple unity of a living being that is, quite clearly, the self or the soul. Nothing exists but this self. "The concepts provided by the disciples of this Being are admirable. In its natural oneness, it is, in a way, triune through its existence, its infinite light, and its supreme joy; everything there is eternal, non-material, infinite. But because the personal experience of the Self is not consistent with this very beautiful idea, they admit of another principle, which is purely negative and which consequently has no real being, the Maya of the Self; that is to say, illusion. For example, I believe I am now actually writing to you about the system of Vedanta, but I am mistaken. In truth, I am *self*, but you do not exist; I am not writing to you at all. No one has ever conceived of Vedanta, nor of a system; I am mistaken, that is all, but my delusion has no existence. That is what they explain through the analogy they always repeat of a rope on the ground which one might think to be a snake." If one reflects how the missionary Pons had access only to still-partial and frequently secondary texts, and that he was blazing a trail through unprecedented ideas, one can appreciate his accomplishment in putting Shankara's integral idealism within the reach of readers who had, at that time, studied neither Berkeley nor Kant.

Naturally, more than one reflex caused him to recoil. "A pride more disgusting than Lucifer's" was his assessment of the formula "I am the supreme being, *aham evam param Brahma*," by which the created being deduces maya. Pons was also the first Christian to fear that superficial likenesses might pose a danger of conversion to his brothers: "The new missionaries must be on guard when they hear the Brahmans speaking so emphatically of the natural oneness of God, *Addvitam* [Advaita], and of the falsity, *Maya*, of the wealth and pleasures of this world." Pons provided an exceptionally interesting exposition of the development of the "School of Sankiam" (Sankhya) founded "by Kapil" (Kapila) and of the "School of Mimamsa"; only Colebrooke, eighty years later, would carry the analysis further. Pons concluded modestly, "I am not very well acquainted with the facts of the other schools; even what I am pointing out to you here should be regarded only as a rough sketch that needs to have many lines added to it, and perhaps several erased, by a hand more skillful than mine. It is enough for me to make you aware that India is a country where many new discoveries can still be made." Much respect is due the author of such words writing at such a time. The effect of Pons's work is less impressive. Having assembled the collection in which this letter was included, Father du Halde sent it "to the Jesuits of France." He drew attention to only two letters, neither by Pons, and declared that the rest were "of no particular interest." Pons's letter had come too soon.

Holwell, Dow, and de Guignes

The third stage: the contributions of Holwell and Dow, the *Ezour-Vedam* and the *Bagavadam*, showed no really remarkable advances, although they were much remarked. They rendered concepts that were no longer new familiar.

During the same time the monks' research was being carried on quietly. In 1742 the Danish mission at Malabar, mentioned above, which had been publishing transactions at Halle since 1718, included in them a supposed analysis of the *Yajur Veda* which, in fact, was a statement of modern Hinduism. The confusion arose when the mission had received the account orally from a Brahman of Tranquebar, a region where a nominal attachment to the Yajur school especially prevailed. It also points to the predominance of documents gathered in Dravidian regions. However, it seems that almost no one except, of course, Anquetil, paid any attention to this important study until Albrecht Weber in 1853. The sixteen-volume *Historiarum Indicarum* of 1752 by the Italian Jesuit Maffei was new only in appearance. In 1757 Marco della Tomba, attached to the mission to Tibet, extended the inquiry to some of the northern regions that had scarcely been investigated. He mentioned that he had no insight into the Vedas, Shastras, or Puranas; but his work was impressive, for with the help of a Brahman from Banaras, he was the first to translate something of those two primordial monuments the *Ramayana* and the *Bhagavad Gita*.

John Zephaniah Holwell, a surgeon in the British navy, was among those travelers who were early fascinated by oriental spirituality. Unfortunately, his knowledge seems to have been limited to the vernacular languages of India. He related that he had obtained a sacred code, translated it with a pandit, and then lost all of it in the fall of Calcutta except for a fragment included in *A Narrative of the Black Hole, Interesting Historical Events relating to the Province of Bengale and the Empire of Hindostan*, a book of military adventures whose publication in 1764 created a great stir.

The two volumes of the French translation of 1768 retained the title *Événements historiques intéressants relatifs aux provinces du Bengale et à l'Empire de l'Indoustan* and added these particulars in its subtitle: "The mythology, cosmogony, festivals, and fasts of the Gentoos who follow the Shastah, and a dissertation on metempsychosis, a dogma falsely attributed to Pythagoras." It was an eloquent subtitle, and the contents of the book were equal to it. The preliminary introduction, like so many others unveiling India, maintained that all preceding works on the subject were in error. For the moderns, who followed the lead of the ancients in this, the Hindus were nothing but dull-witted idolators; the Catholics knew nothing of the Hindus except for those quotations a few natives fished out of their memories and translated poorly. Like Lord, as his title demonstrated, Holwell took "The Shastah" to be the name of a single work covering all dogma, which later led Benjamin Constant's editor to think it was the name of a man. This "Shastah," we are told, is simply the Bengali equivalent of "the Viedam" and the pure model of the gross falsification peculiar to Coromandel. The notion that Sanskrit texts had been corrupted in the Tamil tradition was correct; but the distinction between Vedic substance, commentaries in the Shastras, and readings of the Puranas was never made.

Once again the information had been derived wholly from conversations with Brahmans. The volume devoted to doctrines, where rituals and cosmogony tiresomely prevailed, included only a small number of articles. The endless myths of "angels," their struggle and their "fall," which later showed up in Voltaire's work, passed for essential teachings. Metempsychosis was given the same stress. Schlosser later maintained, "The best essay on the religion of Brahma is to be found in Holwell's work published in Leipzig in 1778."[2] Translations into several languages were quick to follow, and the book became widely known. Guigniaut provided a more sober estimate in 1825: he found no authenticity in Holwell's documents, only "an Indianism recent and miscellaneous," and he denounced "the same trait" in the canoness Marie-Elizabeth Polier, who had used them extensively in *Mythologie des Indous, travaillée sur des manuscrits authentiques rapportés de l'Inde par le colonel Polier.* Indian beliefs were too often known on the basis of such compilations.

Major Alexander Dow's *The History of Hindostan,* translated from the Persian of Firishta, appeared in the same year as the French translation of Holwell, 1768, and was rendered into many languages and widely diffused in its turn. French translations appeared in 1769 and 1771 and, through the intermediary of a Swiss librarian named Sinner, another translation appeared in 1776 under the title *Fragment de l'histoire de l'Indostan, avec une Relation de la religion ancienne de ses peuples et des Bramines, tiré de l'anglais.*[3] It was a curious work. Having discovered a manuscript of the *Purgatory of Saint Patrick* in the library at Berne, Sinner began his publication with this text because he was struck by the similarities he perceived between its philosophy and samsara. Metempsychosis was again in the limelight.

In the process of translating a Persian history of India attributed to Muhammad Kasim Firishta into English, Dow had associated himself with some confused notions on the idealistic interpretation of the world according to the Vedas. Sinner, who was better informed than Dow, and a better historian, took the European works on India into account. He was familiar with, and assessed, Lord, Roger, Kircher, Bernier, the *Lettres éd-*

ifiantes, La Croze, and the Abbé Mignot. According to Sinner's *Essai sur les dogmes de la metempsychose et du purgatoire enseignés par les Bramins de l'Indostan* (Berne, 1771), Holwell and Dow "have both vindicated the Brahmans of the charges of idolatry, of polytheism, and of the absurd doctrines which have been imputed to them up to today. They have shown especially that the three divine beings, or the three persons, Birmah, Bistnov, Sieb [Brahma, Vishnu, Shiva] simply signify to the scholars of Indostan the three attributes of the divine Being, creation, continuance of the universe, and punishment, or God as Creator, Preserver, and Avenger, or rather Reformer."

This supposed progress seems to me extremely dubious when compared to Pons. The distinction between sure doctrine and popular superstition was becoming more marked, but the obstacle of vocabulary remained. Holwell had not succeeded in assimilating Sanskrit; Dow had attempted it with the help of a Brahman, became annoyed with it, and fell back on Persian. He too identified the Shastras with the Vedas; Holwell maintained they were much more recent. Nevertheless, there was some improvement between Holwell and Dow. The latter knew that Brahma was not a prophet, that "Shastra" was simply a generic designation, and that four Vedas existed, although he was unable to gain insight into them. His intelligence and humility simply enabled him to draw more from conversations with the pandits than had been the case before him. Sinner notes that Dow was particularly interested in mysteries. It was characteristic of the time that mysteries were the perpetual lure of India. It can be seen especially in the studies of Mignot and Sainte-Croix, who sought to bring the Indian mysteries closer to those of Eleusis and to the writings of Iamblichus; this tendency had a particular resonance for the century of Lavater and in a period wrought by Illuminism.

Sinner recognized the mediocre quality of the interpreters whom the European investigators frequently employed. His conclusions, meritorious for the year 1776, give us a precise idea of knowledge before Jones: "Along with the missionaries, the English authors, and the Parisian scholar, we can conclude from all this that no one will have satisfactory insights into the theology of the Brahmans until someone has learned the idiom called *hanscrit,* or *sanscrit* or *samscret.* Let us put all our hopes on the English." Thus Sinner underscores the fact that the valuable collecting endeavors of the missions had come to a standstill while the officers and civil servants of the conquering English proved that only their own crews could get things under way. (Here is the value of Holwell and Dow.) As for "the Parisian scholar," the allusion clearly calls to mind the studies pursued at the Académie des Inscriptions, which proved that a genius for conjecture was no substitute for an apprenticeship in Sanskrit. The Abbé

Etienne Mignot, a great collector of manuscripts, had published five papers on the history of doctrines in which the original stock of knowledge was put to the best possible use. On the basis of his speciality, Chinese, de Guignes provided his *Recherches historiques sur la religion indienne et sur les livres fondamentaux de cette religion* in 1776, the year of Sinner's prediction. De Guignes's undertaking is greatly valued today; Filliozat has remarked that thanks to his work, "the civilization of India was no longer an enigma that one had no means of deciphering. It took its place among the world's other civilizations, and the science of Indic antiquity found its methodology." The Shastras of Holwell and Dow, the *Bagavadam,* and the four Upanishads translated by Anquetil in 1787 were in an anthology entitled *Indische Schrifte,* the first volume of which was published in Zurich in 1791.

Voltaire Launches India

Voltaire's views and opinions regarding India were first presented in the *Essai sur les moeurs* and were modifed and elaborated during the 1750s as subsequent publications, such as those of Holwell and Dow and the *Ezour-Vedam,* appeared. These works became widely known in France because of their usefulness in Voltaire's polemics. Voltaire acknowledged in the foreword to the *Essai* that, first of all, India had arrived at the right moment to enable him to correct Bossuet, according to whose world history "everything in the world was done for the sake of the Jewish nation." Henceforward the balance in favor of India and China, the true elders of the family of mankind, would be restored. It was from them that everything came to Europe, from them that the idea of the revolt of the Titans came to the Greeks, from them that the Book of Enoch, from which Christian doctrine devolved, came to the Jews. And, moreover, "the Jews took everything from other nations," a theory that was to enjoy quite a success, like all those that reduce the number asked to dine at the family table. Those who applied this theory did not know, perhaps, that it came from Voltaire.

At one point, Voltaire allows, without batting an eyelash, the progression "Bram, Brama, Abraham, Ibrahim." At another he blasts Father Bouchet for having allowed it. Sometimes only the Hindu and Chinese religions are innocent of barbarism, and the beginning of Holwell's Shastra is "truly sublime." Sometimes the Brahmanic rites reveal the mind "in all its misery," and these ridiculous superstitions tend only to the tyranny of an Asian priesthood, elsewhere contrasted with Western priests. In all sincerity Voltaire consistently finds in the India of Holwell concepts familiar to Christianity. He admires metempsychosis for the valuable moral and political restraint reincarnation imposes, and traces its origins to diet. In this he was a true founder of the sociology which, with Salomon Reinach, would later refer to metampsychosis as "a product of the overstatement of the social instinct," declare it "less scientific" than "the idea of evolution," and see the boarding school as a "druidic relic."

In the same way that he ignored the clerical Anquetil and referred to the *Avesta* only through Hyde, Voltaire continued to interpret Holwell through Strabon, from whom he concluded that the Hindus worshiped a creating, rewarding, and avenging god. Voltaire was fond of repeating, as he did in *De l'âme*, that "our religion was hidden deep in India" and "incontestably comes to us from the Brahmans," a conclusion that churchmen, given similar information, had not arrived at. Even though its traditions and practices cart along "a most tedious rubbish," the *Ezour-Vedam* remains "the work of a true sage" reacting against the stupidities of the priests: "It is an argument of philosophy against Indic theology," he maintained, since its apparent contradictions revolve around the fixed points of execration of the Indic clergy. Very perspicacious! This false "Vedam" was a transcription made to order for the *Western* clergy.

India's great glory was that it had professed a Voltairean deism. The Hindus "were unable to establish a religion except on the basis of universal reason," Voltaire states in the fourth chapter of the *Essai*. It is odd that this is what Lacordaire reproached Lamennais for teaching. What is more, the Hindus "pronounced the word 'soul' vaguely and at random, as we all refer to it." To stress the missionaries' incapacity to see anything in India but the devil, Voltaire magnifies Holwell and Dow, revealers of "sublime secrets." He was right to congratulate himself in the *Lettres chinoises, indiennes et tartares par un Bénédictin* that the texts would not have attracted so much attention without him. Voltaire had a profound enthusiasm for this new field of learning, and felt a vital need to exert himself on behalf of whatever would open new perspectives and upset habit.

The *Ezour-Vedam:* A Moral Tale

Voltaire refers to the *Ezour-Vedam* incessantly; it was not only one of the greatest weapons in his arsenal, it was one of his most cherished discoveries. He had personally received the manuscript in 1760 from the hands of the gallant chevalier Modave (or Maudave) on that knight's return from India. Voltaire ceremoniously presented the manuscript to the Bibliothèque du Roi the following year. He maintained that it was definitely anterior to Alexander's expedition, written by the Brahmans, and perhaps identical to Pons's "Ajour-Veidam." He presented it to the librarian Caperonnier on July 23, 1761 as a translation from Sanskrit "by a highly intelligent man who was a correspondent with our Compagnie des Indes, and who has an excellent command of French; he gave the manuscript to Maudave, the commander in the service of the king of a small fort on the Coromandel coast."

The same work appears in Anquetil's papers in the Bibliothèque nationale under the heading "ancient commentary on the Veda, translated from Samskretam by a brame of Benares," with a note by Anquetil dated August 27, 1766. According to this note, "a Swiss, M. Court de Gebelin, from Geneva," who was actually from Nîmes, although he had studied at Lausanne, had entrusted Anquetil with another copy, brought from Pondicherry, by "Barthélemy, an alderman of that city" (Geneva). The manuscript had been found among the papers of Barthélemy, who had had other Indic works translated. "It is conceivable that Modave had drawn his copy from this source. This Swiss has since affirmed to me that it is the same work, and that Tessier's copy contained an additional chapter at the end." Or perhaps Modave had received the manuscript from his father-in-law, a commanding officer at Karikal. In his edition of Sancto Bartholomaeo's *Voyage aux Indes orientales* Anquetil cites a letter from a Jesuit written in 1771 saying that it was, in that instance, not a question of a Veda, but of Vedanta. Father Mosac, superior of the Jesuits at Chandernagore in 1756, supposedly prepared a translation of the *Ezour-Vedam* with local Brahmans that was reportedly brought to France. It was published in 1778 at Yverdon in two volumes and entitled *l'Ezour-Vedam ou ancien commentaire du Vedam, contenant l'exposition des opinions religieuses et philosophiques des Indiens.* The editor, annotator, and writer of the preface, who remained anonymous, had used the two copies that came from Voltaire and Anquetil. He attributed them to "an arch-Brahman from the Cheringham temple" who knew French. He had also availed himself of the *Bagavadam,* which had not yet been published. The *Ezour-Vedam* was translated into German at Berne in 1794 by Ith; this edition gave the name of the French editor, his friend Sainte-Croix.

Voltaire saw in this manuscript the most precious, and perhaps the oldest, book of the Orient and gave its title the sense "Explication of the true, pure Veda," by which we can trace how the Western refutation of the idolatries reported by the missionaries became the *indo*latries of the pamphleteers. After having submitted the book to a Brahman, Sonnerat had considered it a controversial document invented by some missionary to prepare an Indian clientele for Christianity; Father Paulin in his turn detected Christian influences in the work. In 1810 Lanjuinais thought it the work of a Coromandel sectarian combating popular Vedism "in order to maintain pure theism or the quietism of the illuminated."

The answer to the riddle was given in 1822 in *Asiatic Researches* by Francis Ellis. Some English civil servants found the original of the *Ezour-Vedam* at the Catholic Mission at Pondicherry, together with similar compositions concering the other Vedas, all written on a paper that came from Europe and juxtaposing the Sanskrit text, written in Latin characters, with a French translation. They found themselves faced with a major undertaking the intentions of which were becoming apparent. A study of the handwriting, which betrayed a Bengali copyist, clarified these intentions further. Moreover, one of the manuscripts mischievously bore the unequivocal dates of 1732 and 1751 rather than the pre-Alexandrian dates that Voltaire had stubbornly upheld. One tradition maintained that the writings were all the work of Roberto de Nobili, which would have made them about a hundred years old. But their general tone contradicts this notion: Nobili, who had founded the mission at Madura in 1620, had adopted the dress of the Brahmans and took the name "Romaca Brahmana." But the *Ezour-Vedam* reflects the ordinary learning of the missionary circles rather than Brahmanic sources. Louis Renou states, "The original Sanskrit, which came from a Bengali Hindu, was translated by a native interpreter at the Pondicherry missions. . . . The text skillfully attempts to criticize 'the idolatry' and polytheism of the Puranas in the name of the older and purer doctrines of the Vedas." The Jesuits had isolated this element of primitive purity, which had become apparent to them in their talks with the natives, in order to find an Indic spirit amenable to their teachings.

Thus the overly celebrated treatise, from which Voltaire had drawn his comparisons to bludgeon the Christian religion and priesthood, had been invented by this very priesthood for its own propaganda! It is one of the most delightful chapters in the history of polemics. Voltaire, on the strength of the infallible Holwell, and with his same calmness, had invoked "the Shasta" with no doubt it was "anterior to the Veidam by 1500 years." And that was not the end of the moral tale of the *Ezour-Vedam:* one is astonished to see how often at the beginning of the nineteenth century a text so clearly discredited was still cited. When it was cited by Lamennais it can at least be said that the material intended for missionary work returned to its natural use. After all, why should a usurped reputation give up its own existence? Reputation is always a question of external relationships.

Polier and the *Bagavadam*

Originating in the missions, but conveyed by travelers (Polier is as notorious in this regard as Holwell), the *Ezour-Vedam* carried a dangerous cargo. We know about Polier's life in India through a biography written by his cousin, a canoness, from his dictation. His family was originally French and emigrated to the Swiss canon of Vaud. As a child he suddenly became obsessed with the idea of joining an amazing uncle employed in the English civil service who had an important position in Calcutta. Arriving in India in June 1758, at the age of seventeen, he found himself, like Anquetil, in the midst of a war among the Europeans. His uncle had already been killed, and the young man enlisted as a cadet with the English. Having been trained in mathematics, he was made an engineer. Since competitors were scarce, he was commissioned to superintend the fortifications of Calcutta at the age of twenty-one. This position led to important command posts over both British and native troops, to high office among the nawabs after he had adopted local customs and dress, to numerous intrigues, honors, and disappointments, intimacy with the Great Mogul, and ultimately the rank of lieutenant colonel, which the English had difficulty in granting to this Swiss citizen. Returning to Switzerland shortly after the Revolution, Polier made a tender and late marriage there, and soon after, on an estate near Avignon, his throat was slit by brigands, operating under the cover of the Reign of Terror, who had been attracted by the legend of the treasures of Golconda.

Polier, during a period of exceptional stability in Lucknow made possible by his patron Warren Hastings, had wanted to write a history of the Sikhs. This led him to seek information about the Hindu religion, and he was surprised to find that so little was known about it among travelers, including himself; there had been no effort made to separate fact from fiction, and, moreover, it was difficult to meet highly educated natives. A knowledge of Sanskrit was essential to a clear understanding of the native informants, who laced their conversations with a good many untranslatable terms. Polier undertook a serious apprenticeship, and he had the good fortune to be in India at the right time, the very moment when the studious English of Calcutta had won the sympathy of the Indians. He was also fortunate in having a good teacher, the same one who had just taught Sanskrit to William Jones: Polier struck up a friendship with this man, Ramlochan, who, having roamed the entire subcontinent, had settled near Lahore. As a Sikh, Ramlochan took an interest in Polier's research, and since he was a Kshatriya he was authorized to hear readings of sacred books.

In addition, Ramlochan was as conversant with poetry as with mythology; he was always accompanied by two advisors who belonged to the Brahman caste and consequently could recite Veda. Polier kept close to this scholarly trio and made them dictate summaries of the epics, the avatars of Vishnu, the story of Krishna, and as he put it, "the whole system." He submitted his work to them and, attaining their approval, brought it back with him to Europe. Moreover, he attached a letter to the copy of the Vedas he delivered to Jones in 1784 describing how he had obtained it. He was aware that his predecessors had never published anything but fragments of Shastras. Having decided to clear up the question of the supposed destruction of the Vedic books, he learned in 1779 that they were extant in Jaipur. Because of his connections in the lesser Indian courts, he obtained from a rajah the permission necessary to receive a copy of them. Another rajah took the trouble to collate the copy and arrange it in eleven folio volumes, entrusting them to Polier on his solemn promise, which Polier was to keep, that in Europe the sacred books would never be polluted by contact with an animal skin but would be bound, rather, in silk or velvet. When transmitting the books to the British, Polier later added a further condition to that of the rajah: that Jones and Wilkins each be authorized to keep one of the eleven precious volumes in his possession during his lifetime.These items were not so complete as their donor believed; other Vedic texts were found later, notably by Jones and Colebrooke.

One wonders whether Polier's indifference to his own writings was the indifference of a man of action, one of the rarest kinds, or the indifference of a disciple of the Brahmans. He left writing, on all matters, to his cousin, who "fashioned" the *Mythologie des Indous* published in 1809 from papers that included résumés of poems, Puranas, and doctrines. Polier confined himself to talking about his studies to the canoness, a process which unfortunately inspired her to present the whole work in the form of a more or less fictionalized dialogue between Polier and Ramlochan. She thus imitated a sort of oriental catechism for which the *Ezour-Vedam* was the model. Herself erudite to the point of pedantry, and filled with unction, she seemed more obsessed with a concern for similarities (which had wreaked so much havoc) than moved by a critical spirit.

The story of the *Bagavadam*, a work at first accorded great importance, as we have already seen, is not unlike the story of the *Ezour-Vedam*. Father Calmette, one of the precursors of Indic studies in the *Lettres édifiantes*, had been among those who had sought the Vedas around 1730. He had, as Filliozat has said, "recourse to the offices of a capable young Tamil scholar who knew Latin well and French perfectly, Maridas Poullé, the interpreter for the Compagnie des Indes at Pondicherry. Equally at home in the two cultures, Maridas Poullé was an unrivaled thinker and quite exceptional for his time. He lost no time in perceiving the necessity of establishing scientific exchanges between India and France." He communicated with French scholars, notably the astronomer Le Gentil, who "hailed the Tamil scholar and one of his colleagues as his teachers." In the linguistic field, Poullé advised Coeurdoux, a pioneer in comparative grammar, aiding his discovery of "the linguistic relations of Greek and Latin to Sanskrit." Indirectly he aided Joseph de Guignes, who in 1772 would discover that *Sandragouten* (Chandragupta) was identical with *Sandracottus;* de Guignes published his findings in 1777.

Poullé provided analogous services for Anquetil and Sonnerat. Foucher d'Obsonville, a sailor and naturalist who led an eventful life, returned from India in 1771 after an absence of twenty years and in 1785 furnished a supplement to Sonnerat's *Voyage.* It was Foucher who was to publish the *Bagavadam* which Maridas Poullé had translated. In 1783 Foucher had already authored a book whose title is too delectable to be overlooked: *Essais philosophiques sur les moeurs de divers animaux étrangers, avec des observations relatives aux principes et usages de plusieurs peuples.* The hierarchy presented in this work would prejudice a mind open to samsara. He did not do much to overcome that prejudice with the publication in 1788 of *Bagavadam ou Doctrine Indienne, ouvrage Indien canonique, sur l'Etre Suprême, les Dieux, les Géants, les Hommes, les diverses parties de l'Univers, etc.*—another significant title, revealing a classical education. The epigraph "Juvat integros accedere fontes," borrowed from Lucretius, underscored the same ambition as Polier, to reach at last the original sources. But this ambition was no more realized by the sailor than it had been by the canoness.

The skeletal adaptation of the immense *Bhagavata Purana* was the most striking example of what Vedic texts lost by passing through Tamil versions. In his "Discours préliminaire," Foucher seems to question the ability of the French translator, whose previous record refutes such a charge. De Guignes, who had received the manuscript in 1769 from the minister Bertin, with whom Poullé was corresponding, had no high opinion of it. Sancto Bartholomaeo possessed a Sanskrit copy which he declared in his 1804 grammar *Vyakarana* to be a worthless apocrypha. And in his catalog of Parisian manuscripts published in 1813, Hamilton did not hold it in any high esteem. The earnestness, dedication, and sympathetic efforts of Foucher d'Obsonville are worthy of respect. He kept himself well informed about contemporary works. His commentaries, however, never got off the ground, nor did they provide any keys. Tradition attributes to him the possession of other materials that were lost after him: but should it be considered a great loss? What counts is the impression of the man, and the numerous uses made of the *Bagavadam,* concurrent with the *Ezour-Vedam,* up to the Romantic age.

Real Access to the Doctrines: Anquetil-Duperron, Disciple of Indian Sages

The new age had now begun. In 1787, one year before the *Bagavadam,* Anquetil-Duperron provided the first authentic version of four Upanishads in the second volume of his *Recherches historiques et chronologiques sur l'Inde,* based on methods which in 1784 still surpassed those of the Calcutta society. Anquetil had partially conquered Sanskrit on his own, but perhaps not well enough, in the end, to translate from the original. The fact is that he had no original version at his disposal at all, and even today's translations from the Sanskrit have not entirely recouped their debt to him.

Anquetil's collection of the Upanishads was the famous Persian translation made at Delhi in 1656 by pandits summoned from Banaras by Dara Shikoh, the son of the Mughal emperor who was anxious to compare all religions. Bernier, who had known the leading translator well, had brought back a copy of this work. According to Anquetil's working notes for *Oupnek'hat,* the manuscript he used at the Bibliothèque du Roi to check Bernier's had been received from Gentil; the *Législation Orientale* in 1778 was more specific: "from the north of Bengal in 1776, from M. Gentil, knight of Saint-Louis and a captain of cavalry in the service of France." Also in 1778 Anquetil announced the French translation and three dictionaries: Malabar-French, Telugu-French and "Samskretam"-French. In reality the only part to be published in French was the four Upanishads in 1787; after completing his work, Anquetil revised it totally in 1801–2, substituting a Latin translation.

Anquetil's was the most decisive step that had been taken regarding doctrines. It is only right that he remain as celebrated for his revelation of the Upanishads as for his revelation of the *Avesta.* A leaf glued into those rough drafts declared, after quotations from Saint-Cyran, Le Maitre, Arnaud, and Saint Augustine: "The Zend books and the *Oupnek'hat* present the same truths as the works of the Platonic philosophers, and perhaps these philosophers received them from the oriental philosophers." According to Anquetil, publishing proof of a universal belief (even if whole truth had been known only to the Christians) could only be useful to religion. Roger and Pons had already expressed this idea; what changed everything in Anquetil's case was his experience of this relationship of spiritual universality which he affirmed.

By the time of the "Discours préliminaire" to the *Zend Avesta* in 1771, Anquetil had already undertaken the other work and had rightly perceived how Vedanta dealt with the eternality of matter and with emanation. In 1776 he published excerpts from the Upanishads in the *Journal des Savants,* and referred back to them in *Législation Orientale* in 1778. These studies were not so widely noticed as Voltaire's on the *Ezour-Vedam.* In his *Recherches historique et géographiques sur l'Inde,* Anquetil has a paragraph on the methods employed by all the inquirers before Indic studies so lucid in its simplicity it bears reproducing: "Most of the travelers are

satisfied to ask the Brahmans (and it is the same process with the ministers of religion in all countries) about the basis of their doctrines, what
they believe on this and that; some of them go so far as to procure excerpts from their theological books. The answers, the excerpts, may be
accurate, but they might also be analogues of the circumstances, the mind,
or even the views of the one asking the questions. The only way to know
the truth is to learn the language well, to translate the fundamental works
for oneself, and to then confer, book in hand, with the scholars of the
country which the materials treat." Nothing more sensible has been said.
Here is the whole secret in a few words. Here is the reason for the relative failure of Anquetil's precursors and for his own success.

At the last minute, Anquetil added an appendix to his *Recherches.* He
had just obtained a copy of Wilkins' *Bhagavad Gita,* published the preceding year. He admired those aspects of Wilkins' work which made it an
important event, and later in his "Observations on Sancto Bartholomaeo"
he gave fresh praise to Wilkins for the *Hitopadesha* and reproached him for
publishing the work only in driblets. He denounced the remaining prejudice: Wilkins had condemned the casuists of India. Anquetil assumed an
opposing position unprecedented in its impartiality: "Each nation, each
theological or philosophical school anywhere, has its own way of explaining its ideas and of understanding them. The universality of these abstract distinctions demonstrates that in fundamental ethics, as compared
with theological precepts, the results are not so obvious as one imagines.
Let us study the Indians as we do the Greeks and the Latins: when we understand them well it will be permissible for us, if we are better than they,
to criticize their course, but without arrogance, without rancor, and without ridicule." This admirable liberality of judgment was then to be found
in but a single man, and undoubtedly it would have been difficult to find
it outside a single nation. Anquetil's emphasis compensates for Voltaire's
tone. In the name of the same humanity, however, both claimed for India
the same "égalité": but for one of them, a master polemicist, freedom was
at the same time both a principle and a commodity.

Anquetil was also alone in perceiving the problem of inducing Europeans who viewed the Indian world to stop setting the primacy of a Greco-
Latin education against other types of education, which was considered
cultural heresy. It was Anquetil above all who created in his mind this
second Renaissance. It was because he had given up opposing cultures
that, from that time onward unswervingly faithful to his Church, he later
assumed that the Church could not forbid his becoming a disciple of "the
sages of Asia." His thinking never ceased to be worldwide in scope; in
this Anquetil was in agreement with the concept of universal revelation
found in the letter in which Wilkins, sending his *Bhagavad Gita* to Has-

tings, demonstrated, probably prematurely, its exceptional correspondence with Christian dogma.

The *Bhagavad Gita*'s impact on Europe must be kept in mind. No text could, by its profound metaphysics and by the prestige of its poetic casting, more irresistibly shake the hold of the tradition of a superior race. "It was a great surprise," wrote Lanjuinais, "to find among these fragments of an extremely ancient epic poem from India, along with the system of metempsychosis, a brilliant theory on the existence of God and the immortality of the soul, all the sublime doctrines of the Stoics, the pure love which bewildered Fénelon, a completely spiritual pantheism, and finally the vision of all-in-God upheld by Malebranche." Elsewhere Lanjuinais found Illuminism, Spinoza, and Berkeley in India. These revelations were soon confirmed, and extended, by the Upanishads. Here precisely was the beginning of the fervor later felt for Indic studies by the German spiritualists and idealists, by Eckstein and Schelling. Friedrich Schlegel called the *Bhagavad Gita* "the handbook of Hindu mysticism."

At the same time the lure of Hindu morality was felt through the extraordinary success of the *Hitopadesha*, translated by Wilkins in 1787 and retranslated into French by Langlès in 1791. "Only the sacred books of the Jews and Christians," according to Lanjuinais, "had been translated more frequently and into more languages than this original anthology of Hindustan." The simultaneously mythical and moral effect of the *Laws of Manu* should also be noted.

The invocations repeated in the frontmatter of the books in which Anquetil propagated Indic thought were not theatrical touches: the first page of the *Recherches*, a semimystical page itself, reads "A la Vérité [To Truth]." The dedication of the second volume of the *Oupnek'hat* reads "Anquetil-Duperron Indiae Sapientibus S. D." (Anquetil-Duperron sends greetings to the wise men of India). This volume was completed on October 9, 1795, and the translator, while imploring the Hindu sages not to look with disdain on the work of one of their disciples (such subordination had rarely been proclaimed in this way), referred to the life he was leading, following their example in the Paris of the Revolution. The existence of important ascetic schools outside Europe had already been suspected, but this was the first time that the textbooks of such schools were in evidence, and especially that the teachers in them were courted.

Such a stone tossed into the Mediterranean basin created some ripples. While studying the *Oupnek'hat* in order to make it accessible for those interested in it, Lanjuinais wrote to Anquetil in 1802 that he was puzzled not so much by the textual difficulties but rather by "the basis of this doctrine of unification" which "surprised" and "engrossed" him, without making him "a proselyte." He was undoubtedly responding to his correspondent's zeal as a way of excusing himself for not having gone further. Later he reproached Eckstein for going too far. In other letters written the same year, Lanjuinais came back to the idea of seeking, through Brahmanism and Zoroastrianism alike, a common source of traditions anterior to Abraham; these hypotheses, deep-rooted in the West, might seem arbitrary if they were not being rehabilitated today by the idea of a "Euroasiatic" tradition originating in Sumer.

Lanjuinais reworked his analysis of the *Oupnek'hat*, which ultimately took the form of a comparison between excerpts from Anquetil and from the English translations of the Upanishads provided by Rammohun Roy in 1817–18. On the basis of Anquetil's "Dissertation préliminaire," Lanjuinais isolated four principal tenets of post-Vedic doctrine: affirmation of the supreme being, the origin of the world through emanation, the existence of a superior spiritual world, and the influence of the stars on terrestial bodies. These ideas were debated as early as the first years of the Empire in circles where we know Anquetil found support from Sacy, Lanjuinais, Millin, and Langlès; in the opposing camp were Volney, a certain Schnürrer from Tübingen, and the young Hagemann, a student of Hamilton at Paris, whose early death was a loss to oriental studies.

It was not merely the amount of interest and the accuracy of information that later changed: questions of doctrine came to be posed on a level and in terms which were to remain almost invariable. Anquetil sought the essential, and he achieved a remarkable synthesis on any given point, *maya* for example. The copious notes to the *Oupnek'hat* (his solitary table-talk), while touching on a wide variety of subjects in some cases, decisively linked the concerns of Western philosophy with those of Hindu learning. Lacking certain tools, Anquetil made some mistakes concerning specific details, such as maintaining that the *Bhagavad Gita* was "not a part" of the *Mahabharata*. But he at least established, in contrast to Wilkins, that the *Gita* itself did not contradict the spirit of the Vedas, and that the Vedas did not express popular superstition, as had been repeated since Holwell. He discerned, both in the still inaccessible Vedas and in the Upanishads, the same high "doctrine of the unity of God," including, in a hierarchy of actions and works, "the sublimity of the state of pure contemplation, without action," and "as the principal object of faith," "the presence of the universal spirit in all that exists," along with "the identification of man with that spirit." Before insisting on the three necessary stages of purification, Anquetil, summarizing Pons's research and revising it according to data provided by Wilkins, concluded: "God is all-in-all, above imperfection and perfection both universally and in each particular principle, being and nonbeing alike. This is the doctrine of the Vedas and of the *Bhagvat guita.*" In passing, with a single line, he traces an explanation of castes which long remained unequaled: "The *Bhagvat guita* prescribes the duties peculiar to each of the four castes . . . and these details were necessary since in the doctrines of the *sankhiah* these works were an obligation. . . . The specific duties of each person, according to his state, even if not faultlessly performed, are greatly preferable to the duties of another state, no matter how flawlessly these duties might be performed." Anquetil's last sentence concluded a study and a life: "Soon the chill of age will ice the blood in my veins. I will have, at least, the satisfaction of carrying to my grave the hope of seeing India linked to Europe through the rapport, the communication of minds and ideas, more worthy of man than the vile objects of commerce—gold, silver, gems, fabrics, spices—which have until now united the two continents. I will die happy in saying: the Indians may love us."

For the Romantic era, the *Oupnek'hat* remained, in the words of Lanjuinais, "the most useful book one can study in a European language to gain an understanding of the ancient systems of religion and philosophy of the Brahmans." The orientalist Saint-Martin reaffirmed this in the *Journal Asiatique* in 1823. The link reestablished at that time between Hindu doctrine and Western occultism also appeared with Lanjuinais, who expanded the connection and launched parallels that carried as far as the other Saint-Martin, the Unknown Philosopher, via the naturalist Bonnet. Lanjuinais's sense of orthodoxy was shocked by such comparisons; it was also disturbed by a doctrine of salvation which ignored grace, by an absolute spiritualism or an absolute materialism, and by a contemplative method conditioned by physical processes.

Yet Lanjuinais rendered no less justice to a way of thinking he regarded as unrivaled: "This system, apart from the abuses made of it, has a character of sublimity that the Greek and Roman imagination was unable to attain: a single being, and this being an eternal mind." There was, in such a reclassification, an intellectual courage which marked an important change. Europeans regarded the coexistence of plurality and unity, Lanjuinais continues, as a contradiction. India resolved this seeming paradox by speculating on two distinct planes: "The moral, religious, and political order belonged to the first faculty of reasoning; ineffable union with God belonged to the second." At last the necessary distinctions between orthodoxy and popular cults were made and the line from Brahmanism to Buddhism to Hinduism traced. We should remember that before being printed Lanjuinais's accounts were read before the Institut in 1808 and subsequent years. Dacier's academic account of Lanjuinais, in its turn, reiterated that Indic spiritualism "preceded and surpassed" other philosophies in the pursuit of its great plan of unification. Victor Cousin was soon to sanction such views on the basis of the English works. Coinciding with Anquetil's work were the works of Sancto Bartholomaeo, notably the *Systema Brahmanicum Liturgicum, Mythologicum, Civile, ex monumentis Indicus Musei Borgiani Velitris dissertationibus historico-criticis* (Rome, 1791), which are important to the history of orientalism perhaps primarily for their philosophical progress, for their influence did not significantly extend beyond specialist circles.

Friedrich Schlegel: Welcoming Hindu Philosophy as an Equal

Friedrich Schlegel pursued his activities at precisely the same time as Lanjuinais; his *Uber die Sprache und Weisheit der Indier* appeared in 1808, and he had been staying in Paris just at the time the publication of the *Oupnek'hat* was being completed. Could he have been unaware of it or ignored its contents? That would have been as unlike him as acknowledging his sources. In his *Geschichte der alten und neuen Literatur* he confined himself to pointing out the extraordinary doctrinal richness of the Upanishads and, like Colebrooke, made a point of brushing the *Oupnek'hat* aside as "useless." Useless? Certainly not to his fellow countryman Schopenhauer. In compensation, Schlegel retained a great respect for the impoverished *Bagavadam*.

Uber die Sprache und Weisheit der Indier contains two clearly distinct parts, one on linguistics, the other on doctrine. The turning points that allowed the metaphysical tradition of India to be discussed on an equal footing with the Greek tradition were Anquetil's work of 1787 and 1801, Schlegel's and Lanjuinais's works of 1808, and Colebrooke's and Cousin's works of 1824–29. The acceptance was accentuated by the French translation of Schlegel, which did not appear until 1837; in it Mazure argued against the author, basing his position on information acquired in the interval, as if the question of equality were no longer an issue.

Schlegel had to content himself with a general introduction of "oriental thought" and with making distinctions more among various periods than among diverse systems. His interpretations of Manu on transmigration and emanation were not entirely free of disparities; it is understandable that the circle of Goethe and Schiller and that of Schelling were alarmed by the forced tendency to discover a Credo, a Church. However meritorious it may have been of Schlegel to set aside the excessive charges of "a sinister, frightening, degrading superstition, poisoning everything," in order to maintain that one could not "deny that the ancient inhabitants of India had knowledge of the true God," he neglected a certain prudence by pointing to "belief in the immortality of the soul as a certainty so solid and clear that the thought of another life is the governing motif which dominates all the actions of the Indians." Is the meaning of "another life" the same in the Indian and Christian religions? This basic ambiguity is again accentuated in *Geschichte der alten und neuen Literatur*. Hence the religion of India could be seen as "an altered or a misunderstood revelation," a revelation not at all direct and literal, of course, but one obtained through "the manifestation of inner feeling." These ideas, this language of the period, indicate the ultra-sensitive points at which India touched the Romantics.

Schlegel ultimately went so far as to attribute to India a long and vain aspiration for "a concept of a God distinct from and superior to the world"—in short, an aspiration for transcendence. Although he later reaffirmed the unique privilege of the Chosen People, he did so only after ascribing "a striking affinity with the orthodoxy of reason and religion" to the India of the Puranas and to the Persia of the *Videvdat*. He made no secret of interpreting in all antiquity, including Greece, "external revelations" in the manner of the symbolists. The idea of an external Christianity was one which Creuzer held dear, and it would be found again in Eckstein's "anterior Christianity." And would Lamennais himself later be exempt from it? A rehabilitation of pantheism was taking place in the margin of the poetic. An *Allergötterei* united India and Greece. Schlegel derived from this "the deification of great men and saintly persons," a euhemeristic (or Voltairean) derivation: the "patriarchs" of India had supposedly been only "divinized men." It is clear what "the apotheosis of extraordinary men," among whom Schlegel did not hesitate to set Buddha and Ganesha, was to mean for the times of Quinet, Carlyle, and Emerson. Perhaps it is not too difficult to imagine the use in still later times of certain images set in motion by Schlegel's interpretation of emanation as a "doctrine of return" and a theme of "a circular cursus."

India is indebted to Schlegel for proclaiming it, with Greece and Germany, the most philosophical of nations. In the religious domain, meticulous distinctions often gave way to the temptation for comparison. But a formula such as the following took on a meaning which subsequent controversies have not exhausted: "All truths relating to God are, in a higher realm, in immediate contact with each other." This could serve as a motto for the history of tolerance. These seeds may have germinated at a distance in an enterprise such as the one in 1833 of Pastor Bochinger who studied Indian monasticism and Hindu contemplation as parallels of Christian ideas. But the 1808 *Uber die Sprache und Weisheit der Indier* especially affected two other undertakings that were nearly contemporary and that were mounted in the same spirit which had animated Schlegel's work: they were Görres' *Mythengeschichte der Asiatischen Welt* (1801) and Creuzer's famous *Symbolik und Mythologie der alten Völker, besonders der Griechen*

(1810–12). Questions of anteriority counted for little among researchers who were in constant communication. There was little interest in knowing who, whether from Jena or Heidelberg, whether Schelling, Schlegel, or Creuzer, had launched the speculation about religion. Schlegel at least started young and went back to the sources. Görres exploited the first conquests of orientalism to bolster general theories on the origins of religion and universal revelation. Then in the twinkling of an eye, Creuzer made himself the authority on these subjects and became an oracle for a while. However, despite the extraordinary success of Creuzer's system, India would not have had its true place except for the efforts of the French adapter Guigniaut, a student of Sanskrit under Chézy and the elder Burnouf, who totally rewrote the section on India that thereafter, with Creuzer's consent, formed the beginning of the first volume, which Guigniaut augmented with extremely important notes. Nothing is more edifying than this 1825 publication, for in it one can grasp both the level of knowledge and the intellectual climate of the time.

Guigniaut, following Schlegel in this respect, extended the comparisons between Brahmanism and Christianity.[4] Moreover, in the foreword he frankly explained his scheme of "religious philosophy," again with Creuzer's approval. On the other hand, the account of Hindu religion showed evidence of a very searching and an always scrupulous inquiry. Nevertheless, it teemed with premature statements—at times Guigniaut was aware of them and warned his readers of them. The scarcity of available materials, especially on Buddhism, inevitably became apparent: "The history of the religion of the Hindus, at least for the period preceding our age, or at most for the vague period of reformation attributed to Buddha, is actually as yet unknown to us."[5] There was a need to increase the number of translations of complete texts—we are by now familiar with this appeal: "There is a great divergence of opinion among the scholars regarding these books, and in general we are not in a position either to determine the respective dates of these books or to recognize and trace with any certainty the progression of ideas that developed out of Hindu literature."[6]

A prolonged rush to know somehow, after a fashion, and the use of partial knowledge had established some bad habits; basing opinion on real scholarship was to be a long and exacting task. And can one say the task is completed even today? It got thoroughly under way only after the 1830s. Combined with the enthusiasm out of which the mob of Romantics was born was the relic of a charitability eager to end in brotherhood. Moreover, it is unfair to paint a West peopled exclusively by contemptuous missionaries and stiff philologists through whom together India had supposedly been entirely misunderstood. The names of Nobili and Pons, Jones and Wilson, Anquetil and Bochinger, Bopp, Burnouf, and Müller, among others, are sufficient to show that in many encounters Europeans, regardless of category, did not allow themselves to be blinded or confined by prejudice or selfish interests.

CHAPTER SEVEN

The Birth of Linguistics

Language as a Religious Problem in the Age of Postel and Leibniz

"Hebrew for the holy writings and likewise Chaldean and Arabic."
—*Pantagruel*, 2:8

THE history of languages and their philosophy ceased to be a matter of religion. This was the immediate characteristic result of orientalism. It is all the more striking as the position arrived at appears diametrically opposed to the original intention. The new position is associated with the name of Franz Bopp, the original position with the name of Guillaume Postel.

The fathers of the Church, whom the scholars of the Renaissance followed docilely, had already persisted in seeking the origin of all languages in Hebrew. The study of biblical languages kept linguistics an adjunct of theology, which considered origins the main problem and which furthermore presumed there had been a common origin that would explain everything. Consequently, another deduction imposed itself: it was taken for granted that there had been a primitive group of languages springing from a group of peoples and that in recovering the one the other was bound to be restored. This dual hope was seen as a means of taking revenge against Babel. Thus the pioneers of language followed two ideas derived from religious faith and political messianism: to confirm the revealed nature of the Scriptures and to restore a universal society.

Therefore "the primitive" was viewed as an El Dorado. With Sanskrit, people imagined that the original language had been grasped. In his notes of 1838, Quinet reflected the persistent illusion which Heidelberg had transferred from the theological to the ethnic sphere when he expressed the desire to trace the primitive language to "la race Japhétienne." In his

Uber die Sprache und Wesiheit in 1808 Schlegel discerned "a primitive cloth of striking uniformity," "an incontestable relationship," "some truly marvelous concordances which cannot be attributed to pure chance" in mythology and language.

At the beginning of the sixteenth century after a linguistic quest in the Levant, Postel, a professor of Hebrew, Greek, and Arabic at the Collège Royal, sought the universality of religion along with that of language and outlined a prospectus of comparative grammar. "This man," said Dussieux, "had almost predicted the nineteenth century."

Although his orthodoxy was highly suspect, the spirit of his time nonetheless propelled him into the service of faith. The work of translating the Lord's Prayer into all available languages had already begun—fifty languages by 1593. Moreover, this work would prove priceless to future linguists. Confirming the anteriority and university of Hebrew were also important considerations. Sixteenth-century education had done little more than introduce the chairs of Arabic, Hebrew, and Chaldean settled upon by the ecclesiastical authority of the Council of Vienna two centuries earlier. These languages had commonly been included in the curriculum since before the Renaissance. Given this fact, we should remember this was a manifestation of a humanism impatient to take a census of all knowledge. From that time forward the newborn science of linguistics was tied to the newborn scientific spirit: the physicians of Montpellier were unstinting in their pursuit of Arabic and Hebrew, which remained, until Silvestre de Sacy, the substance of oriental studies. Naturalists, such as Pierre Belon, made scientific expeditions to the Asian shores of the Mediterranean, and their catalogs of plants and animals evoked all the exoticisms, including the American. Relationships between science and linguistics, in keeping with the tradition of European astronomers and physicians celebrated in Asian courts, are found again in the seventeenth century with Thévenot and Tournefort and in the eighteenth century with Sonnerat and Foucher d'Obsonville. The continuity culminated with the first English Indianists and presaged the parallelism between linguistics and the natural sciences.

Within this encyclopedic tidiness, and within the narrow circle where certain scholars thought everything could be dated on the basis of Jewish history, Postel registered the relationship of the different languages in his *De originibus seu de Hebraicae Linguae et Gentis antiquitate deque variarum linguarum affinitate liber* (Paris, 1538), published at the same time as a comparative alphabet of twelve languages. It was not until 1861 that Max Müller pointed out in his *Lectures on the Science of Language* that confusing the history of languages with the history of races falsified everything: the facts stated in the Bible by no means necessitated a community of primitive languages; the Old Testament genealogies are irrelevant, the terminology they use does not coincide with ours. "It is well to bear this in mind, in order to prevent not only those who are forever attacking the Bible with arrows that cannot reach it, but likewise those who defend it with weapons they know not how to wield, from disturbing in any way the quiet progress of the science of language."

Then there was the hope of world peace. In Postel's work the link between the two causes is clear: six years after the first work, he published another which was the logical conclusion of the first, *De orbis terrae concordia libri quatuor* (1544). The curious but normal thing was that the same connection reappeared with the Saint-Simonians, who transferred many religious biases to science, and with Proudhon. Moreover, Postel, a man brimming with visions, foreshadowed Father Enfantin with his cult of "the new Eve," the "mère Jeanne." The marriage of linguistic and humanitarian goals also commanded the attention of Leibniz. We know what a major role, noted especially by Renan and Max Müller, Leibniz played in the study and solution of linguistic problems with his *Dissertation sur l'origine des langues* (1710), a subject which had obsessed him since childhood. Thanks to Jean Baruzi we are equally familiar with his plans for "a global religious organization." Since his childhood he had associated his dreams about alphabets with those about numbers. In order to proceed from the known to the unknown, rather than from the assumed to the dubious, he asked that the principles of the exact sciences be observed in linguistics, and he gathered information on distant idioms through missionary reports himself. In 1670 he took a stand against the fixed prejudice that regarded Hebrew as the universal preestablished idiom. True he admitted, "I began as a philosopher and ended as a theologian," a general acknowledgment that can be seen here in an unexpected application: he certainly wanted to oust Hebrew, but for the benefit of German (a language which he refrained from publishing anything in, however), which had even more "traces of something primordial." Leibniz was, like many others, convinced of an original group of nations and languages, and it seemed to him "Teutonic has preserved more of the natural and (to speak in the language of Jakob Boehme) of the Adamic." Consequently, this language "closest to God" was also the one which gave expression to the world "in the richest way."[1]

For the first time, but not the last, one could see sprouts of the national vindication that was to infest linguistics. This vindictiveness was born at the time Louis XIV's irruptions were exasperating the German sensibility, which later became enraged when the Napoleonic invasions confounded a Germany which had reassured itself with two novelties—Pan-Germanism and comparative grammar.

Language as a Philosophical Problem:
The Age of Court de Gébelin

"How surprised Leibniz would have been—who, with the instinct of genius, predicted the common parentage of European languages 120 years ago and sought to discover their birthplace in Asia—if it had been pointed out to him that a language with an admirable structure, rich in literary production in all genres, and with striking similarities to Greek and Latin and to the Germanic and Slavic dialects had been preserved beyond the Indus." This statement, with which Burnouf opened his class on Sanskrit at the Collège de France in 1832, is a good dividing line between eras.

Postel remained the prototype of the orientalist until the Calcutta publications. In another respect, the ideas of Leibniz, insofar as they were consistent with those of Locke, were to influence the Rationalists. Impassioned by language, the eighteenth century did not dwell on the philosophical ground of the problem but concerned itself with the quest for origins—a concern repeated from Maupertuis to Condillac, Condorcet, and Volney himself. Turgot made his debut as an etymologist, and nearly made a career of it, for his lucidity was unrivaled in the field (the *Lettres sur l'origine des sciences et sur celle des peuples de l'Asie addressées à M. de Voltaire* in 1777 by Bailly underscores the fashionability of origins). An immense stir continued around the publications of Court de Gébelin; his *Monde primitif analysé et comparé avec le monde moderne* (1773–84) fascinated generations until Nerval; he was also the author of *Histoire naturelle de la parole ou origine du language, de l'écriture et de la parole universelle, à l'usage des jeunes gens* (1776) which was reprinted 40 years after its original publication.

We need to take the temperature of this linguistic, and especially etymological, fever which rose as the eighteenth century advanced, although it did not suspect what prayer a new Asia promised to answer next.[2] Suddenly it seemed that after all mankind's secrets had been reconsidered, the common bond would be found in the languages which diversified humanity. The origin of languages was the first thing which Herder discussed with Goethe when he met him at Strasbourg. His first published essay, published in a journal at Riga in 1764, had examined "the learned languages." He was discussing the subject at that time for an academic examination; he treated it jumbled together with Hebraic poetry and the sybilline writings of Hamann. According to Lévy-Bruhl, for Hamann and Jacobi "to philosophize was always simply to deepen the discovery of language." An entire age that tended to make all other problems dependent on verbal ones had dawned; the problems of languages had never, perhaps, been discussed so widely or with so much veneration as in this period of the Revolution and the First Empire, which appears to us to have been an age of action.

We are familiar with the eighteenth century's infatuation with general grammar. Brunot, who stressed it, considered it protracted by the revolutionaries "Tallyrand, Brissot, Daunou, Deleyre, and Masuyer." All these generations had fixed their attention on the secrets of language, upon which, in their view, the secret of the world depended. This attitude is obvious among the rationalists: consider the entire second chapter of Chénier's *Tableau de la littérature*, the lectures by Sicard *(L'art de la parole)* and by Garat *(Analyse de l'entendement)*. In plain language, the competence of the last-named caused this curiosity, this contagion, on behalf of the new oriental philology, to operate very precisely: "When one sees the great number of divinities before which the human race has, for centuries, lived trembling and prostrate, arise from hieroglyphic writings, one becomes frightened by the power of *symbols.*"

The linguistic fascination was certainly no smaller in the opposing camp; one encounters numerous examples of it, notably in Lanjuinais, who perhaps, Brunot wrote, "provided the best example of a believer for whom this study was the essential mode of intellectual training." Garat recalled that Rousseau was long stymied by the origin of language and despaired of ever explaining it. One can see that oriental thought and the origin of language together were suddenly regarded as the keys to the ontological problem, and as the arbiters that would decide between the dogma of creation and the mechanistic hypothesis. These linguistic presuppositions had a greater effect than is generally known, even on the long-protracted confusions regarding the imagined points of interdependence between Hinduism and Christianity. As late as 1791 Volney, in *The Ruins,* believed to have proved the identity of Christ and Krishna by etymologies, equally spurious, of the two names.

Only in 1806, the last year of his life, did Adelung succeed in publishing the first volume of the long-famous *Mithridates* (the title was drawn from the legend of the king of Pontus, who owed his successes to a memory that enabled him to speak 22 languages). The volumes that followed were published by Adelung's nephew and his disciple Vater; the work concluded with a consideration of contributions to Sanskrit scholarship. In 1823 the young Adelung became director of the Oriental Institute at Saint Petersburg, which was attached to the Ministry of Foreign Relations. He was much interested in linguistics and authored papers (in German) on the relationship between Sanskrit and Russian (1811) and on the *Glossarium comparativum* of Catherine the Great (1816). He also compiled the first Indic bibliography, *Bibliotheca Sanscrita* (a title adopted only in 1837 with the second edition), in which numerous inaccuracies have been noted, as Adelung was no great scholar and relied more on Ward than on Wilson; but it was a work that paved the way for the priceless *Bibliothecae sanskritae sive recensus librorum sanskritorum hucusque typis vel lapide exscriptorum critici specimen* of Gildemeister (1847).

Catherine the Great closeted herself for a year to compare the entries in a monstrous universal dictionary that had mobilized German scholars, Russian ambassadors, and even George Washington as canvassing agents. The first volume appeared in 1787 with a list of words translated into 51 European languages and 149 Asian languages. This *Linguarum totius Orbis vocabularia comparativa* was certainly a remote descendant of Postel's work. In 1790–91 a second edition contained lists in 280 languages. The empress was far from being the principal author of the work, having left the basic labor to the German naturalist and traveler Pallas. Pallas died in 1811, and on January 5, 1813 Cuvier delivered an "Eloge historique" in which he said in reference to another of Pallas' publications, the *Samlungen historischer Nachrichten über die Mongolischen Völkerschaften*, which appeared in two volumes between 1776 and 1801:

> An essential part of the history of peoples, one which takes us back further even than their written documents, is the knowledge of their languages. . . . No government encourages this important study more than that of Russia, whose subjects speak more than 60 different tongues. The Empress Catherine II had the ingenious plan of drawing up a comparative vocabulary of all the tribes under her rule. She worked on the project herself for some time and charged Pallas, who of all her scholars had seen the most peoples and learned the most languages, to gather the Asian vocabularies, but with the exacting demand of following the list of words which she had drawn up.

The original title of the work was lovely: *The Comparative Vocabularies of All the Dialects and Languages United by the Right Hand of Our August Personage.*

One wonders whether luck caused so many things to interest naturalists in linguistics at the time the two fields of knowledge were expanding and drew Werner, whom Cuvier also eulogized, into proximity with Pallas. The mineralogist Werner, the famous "master of Freiberg," the author of some rather astounding explanations of the world, the idol of the engineer Hardenberg-Novalis, had also set his mind on constructing a universal etymological dictionary. Jean-Paul Richter, a mythic figure in European Romanticism, could in turn be seen burying himself under as many alphabets and grammars as he could find.

Certain details concerning these rivalries and the atmosphere surrounding them appeared in the work of a well-meaning writer who had been steeped in it: Lanjuinais collected several articles on Indic studies dealing with these events in his *Oeuvres*. One article in the *Magasin Encylcopédique* of June 1807 analyzed the first volume of *Mithridates*. The account revealed that Volney, one of the ideologues most enamoured of oriental linguistics, had prepared a report in 1806 on Catherine's *Glossarium comparativum* for the Académie Celtique (which had been founded in 1800 in connection with the Institut and which later became the Société royale des antiquaires de France). In January 1805, on the occasion of his visit to its workshops, the Imprimerie Impériale presented Pope Pius VII, who was staying in Paris at the time, with a sumptuous *Oratio Dominica* in 150 languages. Several Asian idioms, notably Sanskrit, were included, but in Latin characters, since the devanagari script was not added to the type fonts until 1815. As a precedent for *Mithridates*, Lanjuinais cited the work of Conrad Gesner in 1555, who had also been one of the forerunners of zoology. Lanjuinais expressed the hope that the Abbé Hervas would complete his *Catalogo delle lingue conosciute* (part of which had been published as a *Vocabolario poliglotto* of 140 languages) and that de Murr would complete the *Bibliotheca glottica universalis* "on which he has been working for fifty years."[3]

Lanjuinais followed this with accounts of the systems of oriental spelling and transcription for which Volney expressed enthusiasm from 1795 until his celebrated testament and with a "Discours" on Court de Gébelin destined to preface the republication in 1816 of the *Histoire naturelle de la parole*. The "general grammar" that Bacon had previously called for now fired the minds of Daunou and Garat, rationalist and ideologue alike (as did pasigraphy, which occupied even Volney) and produced such works as *Hermes* by James Harris (1751), translated into French by Thurot, and *Formation mécanique des langues* by de Brosses (1765, reprinted 1801). In 1799 the *Principes de la grammaire générale* of Silvestre de Sacy appeared and was immediately translated into Danish by Lang Nissen; it was reprinted in 1803, translated into German by Vater in 1804, and reprinted again in 1815. In 1800 Degérando published *Des signes et de l'art de penser considérés dans leurs rapports mutuels;* in 1803 a "Traité" by Destutt de Tracy appeared in the second volume of *Idéologie*. Goethe too at the conclusion of his notes to the *Divan* took an interest in the question of oriental languages, including such details as proposed systems of alphabetical transliteration; he referred to the old d'Herbelot, and it seems improbable that he would have ignored Volney.

Lanjuinais's evaluation stops at 1815: comparative grammar appeared with Bopp the following year. In a later review of Klaproth's *Asia Polyglotta* (1823), Lanjuinais demonstrated that the full significance of the event had been felt: "In the eighteenth century, scholars still said there were four mother-languages in the world and 72 dialects. Linguistics, as a general science of languages, has formed rather recently, and Adelung's *Mithridates,* which Vater completed, informed us a few years ago that more than two thousand dialects, which share words to a greater or lesser degree, exist among mankind."

Mazure, another good witness, specified that the revolution of ideas was due primarily to "the introduction of knowledge concerning India which has operated in Europe since about the middle of the last century." Prefacing his 1837 translation of Schlegel's *Uber die Sprache und Weisheit der Indier* he also reviewed the illusions that preceded the arrival of Sanskrit and lasted until Pezron and La Tour d'Auvergne. The first wave of enthusiasm sought to derive everything from the rediscovered world. Although in 1808 Schlegel was not entirely free of etymological excesses, he ruled out the hypothesis of a single original language and even gave up the idea that Sanskrit was "the most ancient of derived languages," discerning that the earliest was by no means the simplest, although certainly the most intelligent. He was led to these ideas on the religious perfection of the earliest ages through Creuzer. He credited these new views to William Jones, although he reproached Jones, not without cause, for a residue of systematic unitarianism. Indeed Jones, if he suspected the Indo-Germanic kinship, had not yet come to the idea that Hebrew and Arabic might be outside the family. Adelung in his turn compared Sanskrit and Semitic words, believing them to be brothers. Schlegel was definitely the first to establish the bifurcation which Bopp was later to analyze scientifically and definitively.

The questions of origins had come alive again and was the grand prize of the game in which Bonald, La Maistre, and Lamennais were, for different reasons, betting on orientalism. In 1796 Bonald founded his *Théorie du pouvoir politique et religieux* on the assumed divine origin of language, the orthodoxy of which was later disputed. Henceforth language, the vehicle by which social forms were transmitted from one age to another, was to demonstrate, Rousseau to the contrary, that human society is not a voluntary convention but a primitive *donné.* It should be noted that although in his chapter "Empires de l'Asie" Bonald was still ignorant of India, confining himself to a conventional Egypt, he seemed one of those most affected by the etymological mania (in *Le catholicisme chez les romantiques* Viatte cites examples from Bonald that bring to mind Brisset, "the prince of thinkers"). Maine de Biran, who for his part responded to Leibniz' *Commendatio charasterica linguae universalis* and to the systems of Maupertuis and Turgot, took up the problem of language in opposition to his friend Bonald and to Lamennais in his critical "Essai sur l'indifférence." He refuted the argument for "universal reason" dear to the latter and that for "revealed language" dear to the former, and these matters were of great concern to Biran himself.

Such an obsession among the philosophers of the period, which was exceptional for the great number of child prodigies who wanted to read all languages by the age of twelve, was followed by the arrival on the scene of a privileged language which gave rise to linguistics and then to cries of joy with which Herder, Goethe, the Schlegels, the Humboldts and Chézy greeted it and which Quinet and Michelet echoed—is this not the place to speak of marvelous coincidences? All of them were waiting, and some even refused to go on waiting, for a discovery: when it happened it was because Sanskrit, this America of languages, had been discovered in the search for Cathay. Max Müller wrote that all its predecessors were doomed to failure, but that a happy accident, like an electric spark, crystallized all the floating elements. That electric spark was the discovery of Sanskrit.

At first the mystical side of the question seemed revived by the revolution which would come to efface it: this can be seen in the works of Bonald and later in those of Lamennais. In discussing the 1818 *Essai sur les institutions sociales* in which Ballanche sought to substitute Sanskrit for Latin, Sainte-Beuve said in 1834, "The question of the origin of society may be directly reduced to the question of the origin of language." This idea had been prevalent since Rousseau, and especially since Bonald. Everyone came face to face with this basic question. Some explained the entire social order and organized the entire political order on the dogma of revealed language; others based their explanations on the idea that "language was invented by mankind." A footnote made it clear that by supplanting Latin with "the languages of the Orient," Ballanche wished to thereby pave the way for "new intellectual forms." Sainte-Beuve emphasized other important ramifications, which we will discuss later: Ballanche's numerous contacts were of varying intensity, but he maintained constant affinity for the theosophists on the one hand, such as Saint-Martin and Fabre d'Olivet, as well as the messianic Hoene-Wroński, and with Fourier on the other, and later had a strong influence on the Saint-Simonians. Saint-Martin was the moving spirit of Ballanche's interests in linguistics. Even the traditionalists themselves, especially Joseph de Maistre, paid regular attention to esotericism. And for esotericists like Fabre d'Olivet, language was the great key. Thus precisely at the time that linguistics, which by its very nature involved all the mysteriousness of the human spirit, was freeing itself from theology it fell under the spell of a sub-religious form of thought. Furthermore, as soon as the question of India was posed, a hope, which was not the hope of a scientific discipline, began to ferment again.

Language as a Scientific Question from Schlegel to Bopp

The investigation begun by Friedrich Schlegel of this small and belated discovery that the primitive was not so simple as the contemporaries of Rousseau or Herder believed, but was, on the contrary, complicated, multiform, and synthetic, touched on a principle which was to come to characterize the modern age. This idea, that "The first day of creation saw the greatest synthesis," became explicit in the works of writers ranging from Jakob Grimm to Renan, whereas the eighteenth-century *philosophes* had entertained the mistaken and sterile hypothesis that languages began in poverty and gradually grew richer. Renan recorded the reversal and perceived signs of it in Fauriel and Ozanam, who were trained by the first Sanskritists.[4] Corollary: there are questions of evolution, there is no problem of origins. This statement by Vendryes later became typical: "One always creates surprise by saying that the problem of the origin of language is not a linguistic problem. . . . The idea that a comparison of existing languages might lead to the reconstruction of a primitive idiom is a chimera."[5] Even the idea of the anteriority of Sanskrit, after having improperly served the initial progress of Indic studies, was to lose its supporters. Romantic acuity, through its imagination, had foreshadowed the truth: Renan credited such intuitions to Schlegel, as they emerged in his final course on the philosophy of language, where he pointed out that the most ancient languages to which we have access are no more the first human language than the deepest layer of rock we can reach really constitutes the earth's core.

According to Bréal, Schlegel's famous essay of 1808 "opening the era of Sanskrit studies in Europe . . . had one great merit above all its others, which was to foreshadow the importance of these studies and to summon critical effort to them without delay." But "after the first chapters," Schlegel lost his way "in a thick fog of hypotheses." We have seen that his reading of the essay convinced the young Bopp to go to Paris. Now at last, worn out by the theological or poetic era, an independent linguistics and comparativism would be sciences cultivated in their own right. Bopp "created a striking contrast to the scholars who represent the age of faith and enthusiasm in the history of Sanskrit studies. The future author of the *Comparative Grammar* was to inaugurate a new phase: he brought with him the spirit of scientific analysis." It was to be the end of the old dream, re-expressed from Postel to Herder, which spoke of the original to the Postelians and of the primitive to the Herderians.

Nevertheless, there was not a total rupture: Bopp himself, as Meillet showed, was a man of the eighteenth century who "claimed to go back to the beginning of matters which could be known, as the progress of the science he created made clear to his successors, only through historical development." He imparted a new direction to deep-rooted ideas. In the wake of Leibniz, Herder had not only shown that languages contained, as Bréal says, "the oldest and most authentic evidence of the way peoples thought and felt," a concept which was to fascinate French ideologues; along with Hamann, he also acquired, while promising an illusory primitive simplicity, correct views on what Renan called "the interior unity of languages." This path cleared the way for Bopp. Herder had started with the presupposition of an *Ursprache* expressive of the *Urvolk*, but this postulate led him, as Meillet has pointed out, to a strict study of "historical antecedents . . . of which the last century has furnished the freshest and most original examples. Comparative grammar is part of a totality of systematic research on the historical development of natural and social events originated by the nineteenth century and established when it set about to systematically compare Sanskrit to Greek, Latin, and German."

Like Jakob Grimm and so many other rivals, at the beginning of his career Bopp was subject to the passion of the time; he had already learned the principal European languages by the time he arrived from Aschaffenburg, where he had been like a son to his teacher Windischmann, who sought to derive all philosophy from the Orient. Seconded by his real son Friedrich, it was Windischmann, a great admirer of Herder and a backer of the ideas spread as much by Friedrich Schlegel as by Creuzer, who urged Bopp toward India. As a young student Bopp decided to seek the new learning in Paris, at the time represented by the methods Sacy had developed for Arabic and Persian and the traditions with which Hamilton had endowed a few adepts, of whom Friedrich Schlegel was the most distinguished. Bopp arrived in 1812 and began work on Sanskrit, little by little substituting the methods of Western criticism for the imperfect tools that had come from Calcutta. He left France four years later at the age of twenty-five to publish his first work at Frankfurt, the definitive *Uber das Conjugationssystem der Sanskritsprache in Vergleichung mit jenem der griechischen, lateinischen, persischen und germanischen Sprache*, the first work in which William Jones's lucky intuition became a method.

Bopp's publications, notably his Sanskrit grammar and lexicon, continued between 1824 and 1833, the date of the first edition, at Berlin, of the monumental *Vergleichende Grammatik des Sanskrit, Zend, Griechischen, Lateinischen, Gothischen und Deutschen*. During this period Burnouf, for his part, returned to the language of the *Zend Avesta* and the authentic decipherment of Avestan, which, along with the discovery of Sanskrit, was another piece of good fortune that gave Bopp verification of his method and a chance to extend its application. Concurrently, as in the history of rival explorers of uncharted seas, the Dane Rask carried his expedition forward by recognizing the relationship between the Germanic languages and Greek, Latin and Balto-Slavic, although he was unaware of the Sanskrit trail. His *Undersogelse om det gamie nordiske eller islandske sprogs oprindelse (Investigation on the Origin of the Old Norse or Icelandic Language)*, in which the Nordic route intersected the oriental (which he had, moreover, personally taken), was completed in 1814, but was not published until 1818. Bopp's first work was situated midway between these two dates. The two expeditions owe nothing to each other, which demonstrates the inevitability of the discovery at that time. And what is more, in 1819 Jakob Grimm published his *Deutsche Grammatik*, another comparative grammar. One imagines oneself reading the voyages of Cook or La Pérouse, of Stanley or Livingstone. From at least the same time as Burnouf (after his interest in the Achaemenid inscriptions) Rask played an increasingly recognized role in the work on Avestan. The date, 1826, is marked by the German translation of his monograph *Om Zendsprogets og Zendavestas Aelde og Aegthed (On the Age and Authenticity of the Zend Language and of the Zend Avesta)*.

Bopp's great innovation was not discovering analogies between families of languages, which Postel and Leibniz—and perhaps Origen—already knew, which Coeurdoux had emphasized in 1767 before Jones did so in 1786; rather it was showing, as Bréal says, that "there is, alongside history per se, a history of languages which can be studied in itself and which carries its own precepts and philosophy." Max Müller later said that the linguist had no more need of being a polyglot than the botanist did of being a gardener: he had to study language, not languages. Bopp's debut was greeted in proper German style: the king of Baveria granted him a subsidy which allowed him to perfect what he had learned from Chézy with what he might hope to learn from Wilkins and Colebrooke in London. There he discovered Wilhelm von Humboldt, ambassador to London from the king of Prussia, a great political figure and a great figure in several sciences. Bopp taught Humboldt Sanskrit and enthusiasm for Sanskrit, a task at which he was assisted by Wilhelm Schlegel, who also came over from Paris where he too had acquired both learning and ardor. Humboldt was not only the man who later uttered a resounding shout about the *Bhagavad Gita* and with whom Chateaubriand nearly spoke Sanskrit at the dinner table; Humboldt was the minister who brought about the creation of the first chairs of Sanskrit in Germany in 1818, one created especially for Bopp at Berlin, the other for Wilhelm Schlegel at Bonn.

Humboldt was not free of the psychological interest in discovering in each language "the very nature of the psychic activity of each people." Bopp, on the contrary, contemplated language per se, excluding any parasitic considerations in order to isolate its autonomous modes of life, laws of structure, and internal evolution. He founded the new world of language, clearing away residual ideas concerning Indic languages as well as European ones. India was extraordinarily blessed with grammatical genius, but endless points of form were but one chapter in a ritual book encompassing all human activities; Bopp broke away from all external liturgy. European theologians and philosophers believed that language underwent only degenerative transformations. As the successor to Hebrew for the former, or to the state of nature for the latter, Sanskrit could be no more than a primitive *donné* which had become bastardized and fractured. Bopp succeeded in proving that language in its most ancient state was also language at its most complex.

Through its scholarly and literary journals, such as the *Annals of Oriental Literature,* the *Journal Asiatique,* the *Edinburgh Review,* and others, Europe kept abreast of linguistic publications that no longer focused predominantly on pleading the cases of individual nations; families of words were treated like living beings with distinct existences, equipped with behaviors to which changes of climate brought nothing but changes of costume. The epochs of general history no longer determined their fortunes and the values placed on them, for the diverse elements of human speech became groups animated by the rhythms of their own peculiar epochs. This is a good occasion to stress a point that will bear repeating: linguistics, parallel with natural history, sprang into existence to discover and demonstrate that it is essential to forgo reasoning along preestablished lines in order to admit the infinite and unexpected character of the human species.

Cournot took a great interest in the contribution of linguistics to the history of ideas, notably in chapters 3–5 of his *Traité de l'enchaînement des idées fondamentales dans les sciences et dans l'histoire,* chapters 14–16 of his *Essai sur les fondements de nos connaissances et sur les caractères de la critique philosophique,* and in two sections of his *Considérations sur la marche des idées et des événements dans les temps modernes.* In this last he clearly diserns that the new ideas "on linguistics, and the very name linguistics itself, belong to the nineteenth century. Only grammar and grammarians were known previously. In the absence of fixed principles, etymology was a discredited science; and in the absence of precise notions about the true relationship of languages, the quest for a supposed primitive language was a concern that discredited it even more. In the eighteenth century especially, philosophers set less store in the study of languages than in the study of language in a rational and abstract sense. Instead of attending to comparative grammar, that is to say, the comparative anatomy and natural classification of languages, they studied general grammar, without probing deeply enough to determine whether it was anything other than the logical pattern that we have a tendency to create under the influence of habits provided for us by the grammatical structure common to those languages with which we are familiar. Again, light came to us from the Orient; it dawned on the day that European thinkers learned that the sacred language of the Brahmans had astounding affinities with the venerable idiom of Latium, that German and Avestan greatly resembled each other; the day when finally the existence of a great family of languages, which we generally refer to today as the Aryan, was recognized." And here is the correlation Cournot makes with the natural sciences: "As a result of this coincidence of investigations, at the present time no science partakes more of the physiognomy of a natural science such as botany than linguistics does, because indeed nothing bears a greater resemblance to the organic structure, to the growth and development of a plant, than the organic structure and development of a language." The normal references to Max Müller follow, with a mention of the reservations with which this "metaphor" was received.

Proudhon, an Anachronistic Linguist

The distance that had been covered can be gauged by an isolated man who had not budged. In 1837, at Besançon, Proudhon, who was twenty-eight, happened to reprint *Eléments primitifs des langues, découverts par la comparison des racines du grec, du latin, et de l'hébreu*. The title seems to belong to the new age, but the work, long famous and attributed to the Abbé Bergier, was of the old school. It dated from 1767, four years before Anquetil's book on Avestan. Proudhon added to the printed work an anonymous "Essay on General Grammar" in which he adopted the worn-out theory without suspecting what it was. Sainte-Beuve, his first biographer, pointed out that because he was unfamiliar with the role of Sanskrit, he placed the cornerstone of our Babel "on the plains of Sannar or Chaldea." He was unaware of the "whole headwaters from which Indo-Germanic flowed," not having ascended "the Greek and Latin branches" or "the Semitic stem." "Why did he not speak to Eugène Burnouf, who was already a master in France?" The young Proudhon remained a humanist of the first Renaissance in the very heart of the second. His great reference work was the Old Testament; a precocious bookworm, he had, like so many others, taught himself Hebrew, but his reasons were those of a printing-house foreman faced with an edition of the Vulgate. It was then that he retraveled the old route of Postel toward a universal fraternity; twenty years after having outlined, and then abandoned, his dream, he acknowledged in a letter to Bergmann dated January 19, 1845 that he had imagined "the possibility of demonstrating the unity of the human race through the unity of its language."

It seems that something of this illusion of the old believers stayed with Proudhon. The monoglot man promotes the monotypic man. When his political adversaries republished his youthful "Essay" without his consent in 1850, it seemed like proof of his anticlericism—a fact worth mentioning. Proudhon instituted proceedings against them, and lost. Sainte-Beuve acknowledged that Proudhon, who "continued and completed the work of Abbé Bergier, inevitably assumed the same point of view, that of Moses and the biblical tradition." Linguistic studies were later surprisingly evident in the spirit of Proudhon the reformer. Coming to Paris, he enrolled in Burnouf's course. Sainte-Beuve stresses this fact and, as Proudhon's biographer, sought information about him immediately after his death in 1865, by addressing himself to those who knew him best, three or four professional linguists, and dedicated the biography to the closest of these friends, who was the most specialized, Bergmann.

Bergmann was a student of Burnouf who retraced the road leading from the oriental languages to the Scandinavian. Sacy and Fauriel were among his friends. He considered his translations and commentaries, which began in 1838 with the *Poèmes islandais tirés de l'Edda de Saemund*, as "a tool for important discoveries in comparative philology." The benefits of the comparative approach had already appeared through a perception which the schools of Schlegel and Creuzer lacked: citing Hindu epics in his outline of general mythology, Bergmann meant to mark not only the absolute unity of myths but "the origin and distinctive character of non-revealed religions." He was a believer, and hence some controversy with Proudhon arose. But Proudhon undoubtedly influenced Bergmann. One year after Proudhon's "Essay," Bergmann defended his theses before the Faculté des Lettres at Strasbourg,[6] one of which bore the title, of interest to us, *De linguarum origine et natura*, translated into French in 1842. In 1861 another major work appeared, the *Prose Edda* of Snorri, translated under the title *La Fascination de Gulfi, traité de mythologie scandinave*, which again mentioned Burnouf and Sacy in its dedication. In 1864 Bergmann published *L'unité de l'espèce humaine et la Pluralité des langues primitives*, which had been the sphere that preoccupied Proudhon in 1837.

Bergmann was not the only orientalist or linguist on familiar terms with Proudhon. Foremost, and among the best known, was Pauthier, a compatriot of Proudhon and also a student of Burnouf. At the outset there was another compatriot, Fallot, who confined himself, it is true, to studies of Old French and died young without publishing anything. Around 1829 at Besançon, forced to take any job in order to live, Fallot annotated a Latin edition of *The Lives of the Saints*. His Latin was unsure; Proudhon, a proofreader at the printing house, caught his mistakes for him, and they straightway became fast friends. Such intimate acquaintances are significant, and all the more so since they multiplied. It was a *fourth* linguist, again a close friend of Proudhon, who in 1839 published the sole posthumous work of Fallot. His name was Ackermann.

At first headed for the ministry, Ackermann, like Mohl, lost his faith when he launched into exegesis and found himself again through linguistics. Burnouf was his guide, as he had been for Bergmann, and sent Ackermann to Berlin in 1840 to his correspondent Alexander von Humboldt. Ackermann was twenty-eight years old; he lived in Berlin another sixteen years, involved in studies of French language and poetry. But he had a better way to extend his name to our time: he gave it to a better student than himself. Madame Ackermann's nihilism, cultivated in Berlin circles, is a reminder of how much the tributaries of German metaphysics mingled with the current of Hindu pantheism. A true child of the Oriental Renaissance, she was successively influenced by the French Romantics, headed by Hugo, and then by the orientalists Stanislas Julien and Eichhoff. In Berlin she was a frequent visitor at the home of Schubert, a friend of Rückert, where she met Varnhagen and Alexander von Humboldt; it was there too that she made the acquaintance of Ackermann, himself a friend of Eichhoff. As a solitary widow at Nice, she recalled that the reading of the Hindu poets was a major event in her life.

Such confidants attested to a tendency that persisted in Proudhon, who, on November 15, 1840, became annoyed because Ackermann wanted to publish a collection of poems instead of "some linguistic or psychological study." To Proudhon it was all one, and he continued to seek the imagery of human societies within comparative grammar. He endlessly repeated the advice "work hard at grammar, study comparative psychology." At this point he was over thirty, and the imprint of printing-house foreman, grammarian, and dreamer of ecumenical concord endured. One cannot discern whether his imperious organizational logic was the cause or the effect of his taste for grammar. During the same decade, in 1842, he again became excited by a Postelian dream: *De la création de l'ordre dans l'humanité*, which he dedicated to Bergmann. Thus it seems there was a consistent link in his mind between political organization and the proper administration of language, a conviction that only a single kind of order existed, and that the order of words conditioned that of cities. Proudhon's protracted need for order had earlier struck Sainte-Beuve, who perhaps colored it with a bit of malice; that the subject of language infallibly aroused him is an indication of the depths at which the linguistic fever burned among the generations.

Language as a Weapon of War from Klaproth to Gobineau

The purity of knowledge which Bopp at last attained did not endure for long without exceptions and contaminations. When Salomon Reinach stated, with unreserved admiration, that "the concept of Indo-Germanic unity dates from this work of genius," Bopp's *Comparative Grammar*, he put his finger on the source of the trouble. Bopp was not representative of all German learning; the explosive element inherent in a certain manipulation of linguistics was ignited when Germany came into contact with Avestan and Sanskrit. In 1823 Klaproth calmly awarded his Indo-European fatherland the appellation Indo-Germanic. This was the beginning of a singular adventure which was to lead Europe and civilization far astray. In 1813, while Goethe was studying Persian in an effort to forget the French invasion, the Englishman Thomas Young, a physicist who had won fame in the field of optics and a philologist who had participated in the deciphering of the hieroglyphics, ventured the term "Indo-European." The German orientalists had previously drawn a great deal of satisfaction from the relationships, which they considered obvious, between the languages, and consequently the peoples, of Asia and Germania; they lost no time in persuading the rest of the world that they represented, in modern times, the pure continuation of the superior race, having inherited their language directly, notably from the Persians.

Klaproth's audacity was a stroke of genius in a domain where everything depended on words. Born in Berlin in 1783, Klaproth, who died in Paris in 1835, badly repaid the hospitality he received there. He left the Société Asiatique the memory of his intolerable behavior and questionable actions. By displacing the new sovereignty of a nobility composed of newly rediscovered languages through verbal legerdemain, he insured Germania birthrights and race-rights for the very near future. The politicians of historical studies, always a plentiful species, sought their revenge by means of historical precedents. It was quite clear that Germania could not forgive Racine and Maupertuis for Napoleon. The imperial administration had heard Fichte verbally annihilate Rivarol's notion of "a universal French language." A new development in the linguistic arsenal was commonplace by 1859 when Adolphe Pictet, in the foreword to a well-known book, linked the term Indo-European to "Arya," taken from the Vedic vocabulary where it means, simply, "noble."[7] Gobineau had previously demonstrated how a dangerous ethnic innuendo could arise from a misused linguistic graph.

Thus an unforeseen aspect of the Oriental Renaissance appeared: the German reaction against the Latin and French coloration of the first Renaissance. The two principal paths of the inroads were linguistic and pro-

Germanic in the one direction and metaphysical and pro-Aryan in the other. The later popularity of Schopenhauer in the 1850s sanctioned a fundamental dispute between a spirituality born of India and carried on through a long Aryan tradition which was allegedly pure and wholesome, and a corrupting Semitic exploitation of this spirituality which was the cause of all evil. This aspect of Gobineau and Schopenhauer was continued in Wagner, Houston Chamberlin, and Nietzsche.

In vain had Bopp written, in the preface to the second edition of his *Vergleichende Grammatik*, "I use the term Indo-European for that family of languages whose most important members are grouped together in the present book. . . . I cannot sanction the term Indo-Germanic, since I do not see why one should consider the Germanians to be representative of all the peoples of our continent. . . . I would prefer the term Indo-Classical." In vain he reiterated that, for his part, Wilhelm von Humboldt "avoids the appellation Indo-Germanic" and concluded, "As for the present, in order to be more generally understood, I will use the term Indo-European, the use of which has already received a certain sanction in France and England." Nonetheless Germany, and frequently scholarly Germany, inflexibly revived and exploited a pretension of a resemblance to Persian, the primogeniture of a chosen people, which Leibniz himself had allowed to pass. Doubtless this tendency was no less continuously disowned in its own country; I have just cited Bopp and Humboldt. Although a personal foe of French classicism, Wilhelm Schlegel declared himself violently opposed to the theories Klaproth set forth in his *Asia Polyglotta*; and Schopenhauer for his part said, in *The Art of Literature*, "Nothing revolts me more than the term Indo-Germanic languages, that is to say, the language of the Vedas put into the same bag with the eventual jargon of the aforesaid savages [the Goths]." This stratagem of false labels was employed rather frequently, sometimes with comic effect. In the chapter on the Hindus in *Manuel d'histoire des religions*, Chantepie de la Saussaye's French translation of *Lehrbuch der Religiongeschichte*, the titles and subtitles speak only of Indo-Europeans, but the text, conforming to the German, obstinately refers to the Indo-Germanics—that Germania embracing, inter alia, Greece and Italy. We will see that Hegel, for one, had previously made such an annexation.

The "primitive" set forth by Herder calls to mind what Belaval has pointed to in the works of Leibniz: the languages "which can lay claim to the highest rank are the Germanic languages, and among them the purest is German." German most richly expresses the world, which "in a sense represents God (*Mundus ipse quodammodo representat Deum*). And the moral world? Here too German surpasses all other languages by virtue of its inaptitude for falsehood and untruth." As many of his compatriots of the time confirmed, Leibniz expressed similar ideas between 1670 and 1714. Why then did he himself shun the unique German language, superior to all others, as a vehicle for his writings? Evidently because a universal injustice, which his fellow countrymen were later to redress, caused it to be disdained by the scholars of other countries.

When Leibniz showed that the ancient Germanic civilizations "to a large extent" controlled "the origins of the affairs of a Europe inundated by Germanic peoples since the decline of the Roman empire," the element of truth in this assessment seems to us compromised by the use we have seen Wilhelm Schlegel and Hegel make of all too similar propositions. When Leibniz celebrates "a naturalness" in the Germanic language that unites it with the origins of the world, with God himself, it reminds us of another quotation: "The Germans have continued to speak a language whose natural and original life has always been intact." Here "life" signifies "the type of existence which has its origins in the very source of all spiritual life, in God." But this is from Fichte at the time of Schlegel and Hegel, a century after Leibniz, off to war against the language of French classicism. One can see clearly the chain by which linguistic propaganda dragged spirituality into a political intrigue whose objective was to recapture the first Renaissance from the Latins by undisputedly possessing oneself of the Orient. The sarcasm of Fichte's *Fourth Discourse to the German Nation* naively gave the game away: the idea was to do away with the primacy of the languages derived from Latin, especially French. How was it even possible to speak of French? "One does not compare what is dead to what is living. . . . Any comparison of the Germanic language with the neo-Latin languages is thus useless." Moreover, Fichte, in 1807–8 invoked only Greek: what a godsend for philologists in making Avestan and Sanskrit accessible. Fichte had no need of neo-Latin. French literature, since its vehicle was a dead language, was itself dead: there might be "a time when something will take the place of poetry. . . . That people will then celebrate their golden age, and the source will be exhausted." Thus Corneille and Louis XIV were disposed of ten years before the appearance of Lamartine and at about the same time that Schlegel's essay on the language of the Hindus appeared. Thus the roles of a conspiracy which had no other object than the verification of history and the salvation of humanity were quite naturally distributed among the various parties.[8]

The consequences of the invasion of the Palatinate states had already given rise to an argument that became tedious after the Napoleonic Wars: the *Codeus argenteus sacon*, written in Eastern Gothic, was the most primitive text in all the languages of Europe. "The source of the European languages is Old Scythian, from which Old German and Old Gothic arose; from which in turn Greek and Latin derived their origin." And through

Scythian the origins of Germanic were plunged deep into Asia: in short, it was the beginning of the Word. The final solution of the Indo-Germanic myth was, it must be said, very fitting: it had been born under the sky of Klaproth, it was to be killed under the sky of Bopp! "The thesis of German ethnographers that the Indo-Europeans are the Germanians . . . has been destroyed by Siegmund Feist. . . . The Indo-Europeans are not the Germanians, the Germanians are not the Europeans." But the dangerous confusion of linguistic facts and ethnic theories perpetuated for more than half a century after Max Müller exposed the fallacy had enough time to produce, through national conflicts, more ravages than those previously produced by the wars of faith. It is now one of the consequences of the second Renaissance that is still most alive, and it lives on without being mentioned. During the nineteenth century the dominant influence over linguistics passed from theology to politics: this twist, which has so shaped our destinies, was wrought by the arrival of oriental studies. Through them the eternal mystery of mankind's unity claimed a new chance. For one thing, the unity was no longer enjoined as an undertaking of fellowship but was based on a hierarchy concocted by those who would benefit from it the most. This was where philosophy, so proud of turning the profits of faith over to the faculty of reason, led.

The Liberation of Linguistics and Mythology

After linguistic technique had been separated from the ontology of language, mythology in its turn was established as an autonomous science; this was not possible until the Vedic cycle allowed the early history of myth to be pushed back beyond classical Hellenism, while comparative studies shed light on that history through the history of words, those "dead myths."

In France the excesses of euhemeristic rationalism had come to a standstill; in Germany the excesses of symbolism were in a like state. For the former the advent of oriental studies, for the latter their progress, was an impetus that can be gauged by the importance Renan attached to Guigniaut's *Religions de l'antiquité*. The work, in ten volumes, was published at intervals between 1825 and 1851; it was a complete recasting of Creuzer's famous *Symbolik*. While completing his own very loose adaptation nearly forty years after the publication of the original, the French scholar appended the works of his foreign colleagues which had appeared in the interval. Renan takes advantage of this fact, in his *Etudes d'histoire religieuse*, to retrace the history of mythic studies and to measure the distance traveled. We should note that in Germany the discussion of such studies awoke an interest comparable to that which was later to split British politics between Orientalists and Anglicists.

In 1825 Guigniaut's first volume benefited from "the curiosity which animated the minds of that time and moved them to seek the solution to problems that intrigued the well-informed part of public opinion by a better understanding of history." Renan's unction here calls attention to several facts: undoubtedly the interest in historical studies by Augustin Thierry's contemporaries was similar to the interest the compatriots of Creuzer or Chateaubriand had in the mythic or the mystic viewpoints. These considerations seemed hackneyed in the 1850s. The passion which had been lost left room for the discipline in which Max Müller so rigorously specialized.

It was in Germany, in the first decade of the century, that, as Ricarda Huch has pointed out in *Les romantiques allemands*, "an onslaught of philologists and antiquarians sought to restore, through the written and figurative monuments of antiquity, the meaning of the great enigma which the primitive world left to learning." The school of Creuzer dovetailed with those of local metaphysics, which were also warmed by the fumes of Schellingesque unitarianism: "The neo-Platonic spirit of Plotinus, Porphyry, and Proclus seemed to revive in this grand and philosophical manner of explaining ancient symbols. . . . This mystical enthusiasm, the first transport of the natural philosophy then budding in Germany, had its excesses and its own kind of intoxication. Creuzer has all the shortcomings of the Alexandrian masters: symbolic exaggeration, a highly pronounced tendency to look high and low for the most mysterious, and at times the most intemperate, syncreticism." One has "difficulty imagining" the fascination with which Schelling, in his campaign for "the unity of knowledge, faith, and will . . . the ultimate and supreme aim of humanity," monopolized "young minds."

These excesses of the symbolic school, which also championed oriental influences, provoked the rise of the historical school, and of the advocates of Hellenism. Several accounts make clear the extent to which the debate preoccupied two or three generations. For example, Karl Hillebrand's account in *Littérature grecque*, his French translation of Otfried Müller, follows very closely the account by Renan which I quote here: "Convinced that the Greek religion, like other religions, must have had a hieratic stage, and not encountering this characteristic in the spontaneous work of the Greek genius, Creuzer fell back on the colonizations and influences from the Orient. This twofold exaggeration was at odds with two schools of thought within mythic studies in Germany: the excess of symbolism was opposed by a faction represented by Voss, Hermann, and Lobeck, totally negative and antisymbolic; and the misuse of oriental influence was opposed by the purely Hellenic school of Otfried Müller, Welcker, and others."

It was a controversy which the rediscovery of India at first made inevitable, and then vain. I can give only a fragmentary view of it here. It is another aspect of religious controversy. Voss singled out Creuzer and attacked him as "an agent of the Jesuits" for his theological interpretations. The characterization and the accusation were to be seen again in the closely related quarrels arising from the conversions of a Stolberg or a Schlegel, when Calcutta was discovered to lie on the road to Rome. The disputes eventually ended in the irruption of a massive, impassioned, authoritarian materialism, with Feuerbach defining Christianity for Prussian Germany as "a perversion of human nature" while developing, according to Renan, "a haughty and exclusive Germanism." Here we rejoin the paths that have come down from Schopenhauer and Klaproth.

Later, when the time for the necessary retreat came, Barth summed up events from the scientific point of view: at the outset, "the *Zend Avesta*, very imperfectly understood, and the theology of the Puranas, accepted as a revelation from the primitive world, came to be mixed up with even more suspect pieces of information concerning a bogus oriental antiquity—Chaldean, Phoenician, Egyptian—handed down to us via a decadent Hellenism. From all these elements elaborated on with a vast but confused erudition, under the sway of a romanticism eager for mystery and a philosophy inclined to abstract formulas, the symbolism of the Görres and Creuzer school emerged." A corresponding tendency in France was a faithfulness to a rationalism enamoured of the mysterious: "From the same elements, combined with anti-Christian tendencies and the slightly dry spirit of the French eighteenth century, emerged in France the school of Volney and Dupuis." The difference was that while in France everything was ascribed to the sacerdotal domains in order to reproach them for their exploitation of credulity, in Germany this was done in order to venerate them as the preservers of the great secret of the universe. "To destroy the foundation of this imposing edifice" it was essential to rediscover "the true Egypt, the real Phoenicia, the actual Hindu prehistory." Since that time comparative mythology has been established by Grimm, Kuhn, Roth, and Benfey in Germany, by Max Müller in England, and by Burnouf and Bréal in France.

Thus, one and the same phenomenon: linguistics and mythology existed frenziedly a priori until an encounter with an authentic antiquity of *language* dictated to them a truth whose form and substance were identical: this antiquity could only have been Indo-Iranian.

CHAPTER EIGHT

Repercussions in Literature

Unblocking the logjam of linguistic problems was the logical effect of a series of decipherings; discovering an entire mental world was the natural fruit of a gathering of texts. I have discussed the textual and doctrinal stages; it can well be imagined that literary creation was not the least of the areas to be affected by so many new ideas, yet no one seems to believe it. The question awaits us at numerous turns; it has many faces, changing according to country and period. Romantic France of the 1820s and 30s, and then of the 1850s and 60s, if the principal field of scholarly activity only at certain times, was generally a field for lively exchanges of ideas. We will discuss this period in France at length further on; but France received these themes, or theses, from abroad, and it is important to perceive the Indic coloration in the literature of England, where the new philology had been born, and Germany, where it responded to the appeals of the writers.

The India of the English and American Poets

Before Indic Studies

At the end of the eighteenth century, the France of Voltaire and Rousseau and the Germany of Herder anticipated the Calcutta discoveries; seventeenth-century Europe had already clamored for them: Leibniz was one of the first in whose head "the oriental lobe" seems to have developed. For Descartes, the choice between Orient and Occident was justified only by utility and convenience, which have nothing of the lofty. It is with some amazement that one discovers, thirty years later, the wake left by the news Bernier brought of Brahmanic India in the Parisian intellectual world.

There was at the same time an exactly corresponding phenomenon in

England. The wake Bernier left in the circle of La Fontaine, Chapelain, Boileau, and Molière was also left by the English voyagers in the circles of Milton and Dryden. There was nothing new about this fascination; such deference to travelers is characteristic of stay-at-homes. There were English translations of Bernier and Tavernier in 1684; a French translation of Thomas Roe made in 1663 was frequently reprinted, notably in 1696 through the efforts of the elder Thévenot (the Bibliothèque nationale possesses one of these printings, annotated in the hand of Huet; Ovington had to wait until 1725 for a translator).[1]

Before Bernier, but after Pierre Malherbe, who returned in 1609, Sir Thomas Roe had resided at the Mughal court from 1615 to 1619, and his *A Voyage to East-India* was published in 1665. It was England which had opened this realm, with Lord, a chaplain at Surat. His stories of marvels there were later echoed in Ovington's *Voyage to Surat in the Year 1689*. A whole body of literature in which the wonders of India and Persia were joined spread the magic of "the silken East," which Milton termed "the gorgeous East," in London. Milton had read Sir Thomas' account and perhaps met and conversed with him: *Paradise Lost* came two years after Roe's *Voyage*. Milton was too much of a poet not to have been charmed, first of all, by the names, creatures, places, and things that contained all the unknown—or rather, all the excesses of the known. Milton welcomed this extraordinary geography and naturally gathered, avidly, an entire harvest of new, vague, and symbolic landscapes: to Babel and Baca, to Memphis and Oeta, was added "the Indian mount," and the Ganges to the Hydaspes. The traditional Eden was quite naturally enriched by the paradisiacal images localized by the navigators. Thus when, after the fall, Adam and Eve are seeking a way to cover their nakedness, it is not a grape leaf that they choose; given the broader images of climate, they need the immense leaf of the Banyan fig tree "such as at this day to Indians known/In Malabar or Decan spreads her Arms/Branching so broad and long, that in the ground/The bended Twigs take root, and Daughters grow/Around the Mother Tree"—the same Banyan that, in an indirect way, had provided Lord with the name "Banians" some thirty years earlier. One can imagine that Milton himself, like his Satan, while seeking "with wandering quest a place foretold . . ./ere now created, vast and round," frequently gazed toward "the eastern gate" and thought with fondness of those "who sail/Beyond the Cape of Hope." The place devolving upon oriental lands was symbolic; it is said they appealed solely to the restless imagination of the poets, but we shall see the consequences of the things which began with *Paradise Lost* in 1667.

At the least and without delay, and with an atmosphere very close to Bernier, was Dryden's *Aureng-Zebe* in 1675, a drama which enjoyed a great

popular success. It is the cycle of images—history overlaid with enchantment, dynasties, battles, intrigues of the seraglio, treasures and fakirs—
which, thanks to Bernier, Roe, and Tavernier, to Galland and Pétis de la
Croix, peopled an entire side of the poetic imagination of the time. And
there had been quite illustrious precedents: it should be remembered that
one of the first glimpses of the Buddhist repertoire in modern literature
comes in Shakespeare. The theme of "a pound of flesh" upon which *The
Merchant of Venice* is constructed and the fable of the "three coffers" have
no other origin. In *Macbeth* one of the witches cried, "Her husband's to
Aleppo gone, master o' the Tyger," an allusion to the ship *Tiger* which in
1583 carried "a party of English merchants, armed with a letter from Queen
Elizabeth to the Emperor Akbar" to Tripoli and from there to Aleppo. "From
Aleppo they followed the old caravan route to the Euphrates, and made
their way down-stream to Basra. From here they went to Ormuz, where
they were arrested by the Portuguese and sent to Goa. Eventually, however, they escaped and, after many adventures, three of them reached the
Imperial Court at Agra in 1585."[2] A similar interest was shown a century
later in sojourns at the very same place, the palace of Aurangzeb, the
grandson of Akbar.

The Lake School and Politics

The great period of India in English poetry naturally coincides with the
revelations of Calcutta, or followed them soon after. The first British administrators had found out everything they could concerning the local
civilizations, disentangling Indic thought from its Islamic overlay; the Indic scholars who rose to answer their call were doubtless hoping for a real
universality of culture.[3] This attitude was unable to win over any large
number of the isolationists for whom the exchanges between civilizations
had to be made in a single direction; the small number who succeeded in
fathoming the reality only collided with the bustling mass that trembled
at the prospect of losing its beliefs or power.

Until the Great Mutiny of 1857, the East India Company was the principal organ of government. At first the company was favorably inclined
toward the local religions; but in the nineteenth century it was to increasingly avoid contact with them. In 1817 Sir Thomas Munro protested racial
prejudice. The breach widened to the point of hostilities in the 1830s, an
extremely decisive period for English economics and politics, in which industrial vertigo, evangelical revivalism, and social disputes were inter-
twined. The civil servants imbued with the Victorian spirit, to whom Macaulay must have seemed a dazzling precursor, no longer went to India

to gain knowledge of a new world or its mode of existence but to maintain British prestige or complete a useful phase in their careers. The literature written by company employees or their relatives prior to Rudyard Kipling created a new view of India. This phenomenon occurred precisely at the time that the fashion for orientalism which invaded European salons and intellectual reviews was taking shape: this explains why Great Britain was not the home of the Oriental Renaissance. One would have expected to find it there, since India was under British dominion, but that was precisely why it was not.

Indeed, a dispute about colonial administration was emerging, and growing acrimonious, between the Anglicists and the Orientalists, in which the latter term took on a very specific meaning: the debate centered on whether European or Indian education should obtain in the colony. The corollary question of jobs for the natives was also raised. The attention paid to Indic literatures was to be dependent on these mundane disputes. The dispute began over the issue of an annual subsidy of ten thousand pounds which the company, in reviewing its 1813 charter, had seen fit to allot to public instruction. The question was how to provide for the best return on these funds. A little-discussed "filtration theory" prevailed at the time, but this trickle was drying up. The critical issue was how to establish a system of higher education, since Indic traditions and methods could not be adapted and it was not believed that European ones could be imposed. The two sides clashed primarily in Bengal, stirring up small groups of educated natives who besieged the government. This was certainly most unfortunate for the Orientalists, for they had but a fragile foothold and were without the moral qualities that would enable them to sustain the contest. British historians have gone so far as to hold the movement of Rammohun Roy responsible for the Indian hostility to Hinduism which, between 1820 and 1830, had supposedly encouraged the young English administrators to imagine that they were dealing with "a decayed society." In addition, the funeral pyre of widows, the sacrifice of daughters, the marriage of children, the untouchables, the "regrettable aberrations of Hinduism" came to form the established litany of execrations that soothed the consciences of so many colonialists. It should be noted that Wilson, the intrepid leader of the Orientalists himself, had defended his clients more with ardor than with tenable arguments.

It is important to recognize that native education, religious as well as literary, had degenerated severely. Keshab Chandra Sen, writing about his childhood, described how "the ancient scriptures, the famous records of numerous Hindu sects, had long been discredited. The Vedas and Upanishads were sealed books. All we knew of the immortal *Mahabharata*, *Ramayana* or *Bhagavad-Gita* was from execrable translations into popular

Bengali, which no respectable young man was supposed to read."[4] In this period of decline the vernacular literature itself had had nothing for two centuries worthy of the tradition of Tulsi Das or Tukaram. Finally we have seen from Jacquemont's account that a certain indolence prevailed among the British philologists at Calcutta.

The defeat of the Orientalists was achieved through the ill-informed but energetic talents of Macaulay, who could be called the patron saint of English Indophobia, with Kipling as his successor. Even those among their compatriots who did not share in their prejudice admired the zest with which they shouldered it.

The question before us now is simply whether . . . we shall teach languages in which, by universal confession, there are no books on any subject which deserve to be compared to our own; whether, when we can teach European science, we shall teach systems which, by universal confession, whenever they differ from those of Europe, differ for the worse; and whether, when we can patronise sound Philosophy and true History, we shall countenance, at the public expense, medical doctrines, which would disgrace an English farrier,—Astronomy, which would move laughter in girls at an English boarding school,—History, abounding with kings thirty feet high, and reigns thirty thousand years long,—and Geography, made up of seas of treacle and seas of butter.

In all of English literature, perhaps nothing more cavalier, more Pickwickian, has ever been written. This resounding "Minute of the 2nd of February 1835, on Indian Education" by Macaulay cut short the eagerness of young people for Indian languages. It lightened the burden of governors set on fortifying the subcontinent without cutting into the budget at home. Bentinck "as Governor-General should have seriously considered the demolition of the Taj Mahal and the sale of its marble. He 'was only diverted because the test auction of materials from the Agra Palace proved unsatisfactory.' "[5]

Macaulay was counting on nature to replace Hinduism with Christianity. He suffered some disappointment in this respect—even the Hindus who accepted Anglican culture kept their own religion. As for language, the conqueror declared his own to be official in 1835. Twenty years later it was, nevertheless, necessary to allow education in the native dialect in certain provinces. Outside Bengal, contact with less passive people revived an interest in or indulgence of other ways of being and thinking. But soon the Great Mutiny, and the merciless repression that followed it, destroyed all the pacts and left only malice and misunderstanding.

These various phases are reflected in literary history. The first English poet whom India profoundly inspired was William Jones himself, and it should never be forgotten that he had only slightly acclimatized oriental poetry in adapting it for his compatriots. Goethe clearly pointed this out in his notes to the *Divan:* "As a far-seeing man, he seeks to connect the unknown to the known, true values to recognized values. . . . And it was not only from the archaeological side but also from the patriotic side that he had to endure a good many annoyances: it vexed him to see oriental poetry debased; this is clearly shown in the harshly ironic article *Arabs, Sive de Poësi, Anglorum Dialogues,* condensed into only two pages, which he inserted at the end of his work on the poetry of Asia." Jones was as famous in England for his original poetry as for his introduction of India. The two aspects of his reputation reinforced one another, and both are present in the hymns he addressed to Hindu divinities celebrating a religion "Wrapt in eternal solitary shade." The first German Romantics, Schelling and Novalis among them, were very much taken by these hymns, before they became popular in England. In 1857 Villemain cited and translated another verse from Jones's "Hymn to Surya" in the *Revue des Deux-Mondes.* In 1828 Quinet stated that this work was remarkable in promoting a passion for Asia among the poets of the Lake School: "Lake School, Coleridge, Shelley completely Indic, Byron, etc." How accurate is this?

After reading the copious scholarly notes in which they comment on their own work, one cannot doubt that the poets of the Lake School had read the *Asiatic Researches.* Byron himself, who did much to interest the political opposition and moral nonconformists in the Orient, seems to have read at least the poetical works of Jones. Southey, the author of an "Indian epic," *The Curse of Kehama* (1810), referred to Jones by name, displaying a knowledge of the Hindu religion which he drew from the *Bhagavad Gita,* the *Gita Govinda,* the Vedas, and the *Laws of Manu.* He celebrated the descent of the Ganges in the manner of the *Ramayana,* fifteen pages from which he quoted in full. In his first volume of collected poems in 1827 Tennyson was scarcely less explicit.

In 1811 Shelley, who knew Southey's Indic epic and its Persian counterpart, *Thalaba,* plunged into pantheistic visions which were in evidence ten years later. It is true that in his "Queen Mab" (1813) Shelley could be thought closer to Volney, and that he gathered some lovely oriental names from the old d'Herbelot; furthermore Shelley was more impressed by Jones's poetic side, frequently the Persian poetry, the *Thousand and One Nights* triumphing over the Vedas—a development with which, after Beckford and Morier, we are quite familiar. But it is Shelley's "Adonais" (1821) with its open-hearted pantheism which is important to us here. It was no longer a matter of exploiting a setting or extending a vocabulary; a doctrine was sought within a new spiritual climate beyond the games of the imagination. In such writers, as we will see in Wordsworth, the influence was far

more than skin deep. It was not just a passing fancy in the history of poetry, as we will see with the Americans. "Adonais" had spoken with the
depth of a soul: "He hath awakened from the dream of life . . . The One
remains, the many change and pass." "He is made one with Nature . . .
He is a portion of the loveliness / Which once he made more lovely." One
can not believe that the echo of Vedanta has not infused new life into a
certain concept taken from German metaphysics.

It is exactly the same with Wordsworth:

> And I have felt
> A presence that disturbs me with the joy
> Of elevated thoughts; a sense sublime
> Of something far more deeply interfused . . .
> A motion and a spirit, that impels
> All thinking things, all objects of all thought,
> And rolls through all things.
>
> ("Tintern Abbey")

> To every natural form, rock, fruit or flower,
> Even the loose stones that cover the highway,
> I gave a mortal life: I saw them feel,
> Or linked them to some feeling; the great mass
> Lay bedded in a quickening soul, and all
> That I beheld respired with inward meaning.
>
> (*The Prelude*, Book 3)

> Our birth is but a sleep and a forgetting;
> The Soul that rises with us, our life's Star,
> Hath had elsewhere its setting,
> And cometh from afar.
>
> ("Ode: Intimations of Immortality")

> Brook! whose society the Poet seeks . . .
> It seems the Eternal Soul is clothed in thee
> With purer robes than those of flesh and blood,
> And hath bestowed on thee a safer good;
> Unwearied joy, and life without its cares.
>
> ("Brook! whose society")

Wordsworth was "a pantheistic idealist" in the German manner, according to Sarrazin, and like Goethe's and Shelley's his pantheism remained
"essentially moral and providential." Hindu dogma was slightly distorted
by this limitation, but at least it was not merely a plaything.

With Blake, a solitary visionary, we again encounter affinities between occultism, Neoplatonism, and pantheism extending toward fellowship with animals and objects, as well as toward the annihilation of the self. I have not seen any definite contacts with Hindu texts pointed out; yet the accumulation of coincidences among the intellectual fashions which promoted Boehme, Schelling, and the Upanishads simultaneously is striking. The same observations hold true for Coleridge, and the same mixture appears in the work of his brother-in-law Southey. Coleridge's poetry is doubtless one of the great innovations of England, which was not impoverished in this domain. From Byron to Edgar Allan Poe, Coleridge's poetry was wonderfully contagious; and it was no small secret, this bizarre Orient without a country which this poetry brought them. But Coleridge's influence as a religious philosopher was even more widespread and durable. The *Biographia Literaria* is full of instances of the author's contacts with all the mysticisms turned up by the wake of the German Romantics; Boehme and Schelling were again foremost, along with the *Naturphilosophie* born with the new Indic studies. Other names, which at the time shone brilliantly, have faded. India had its place in the works of the Scotsmen Campbell and Thomas Moore. Moore's widely famous *Lallah Rookh*, written in 1817, gave him an international reputation. It was translated into French by Pichot in 1820 and adopted for the opera by the Saint-Simonian Felicien David. In it the India of Bernier reemerged in the figure of Aurangzeb.

Another tradition took form at the beginning of the nineteenth century among certain English poets, and its hostility toward Indic themes became pronounced:

John Leyden and Bishop Heber, at the beginning of the nineteenth century, wrote verses of some merit, but they both viewed India as a land of ancient decaying pomp and of dark mysteries. Leyden, like Wellesley, saw and was shocked by the infant sacrifices at Sagur. His verse has an undercurrent of hostility against all Hinduism.

> On sea-girt Sagur's desert isle
> Mantled with thickets dark and dun,
> May never morn nor starlight smile,
> Nor ever beam the summer sun.

From about 1836 this tradition had become firmly established. India was the "Land of Regrets" in which Englishmen spent years of exile amongst a people half savage, half decadent. This idea runs through Leyden's *Ode to an Indian Gold Coin*, and the works of a number of Anglo-Indian poets, of whom Sir Alfred Lyall is probably the best remembered. His *Meditations of a Hindu Prince* and *Siva* show an attempt to appreciate the Indian point of view, but Lyall was always a stranger in a strange land, looking with contemptuous pity upon a people over whose heads

> the deities hover and swarm
> Like wild bees in the tree-tops, or gusts of a gathering storm.[6]

Sir Edwin Arnold was by far the most important of this Victorian group. From 1857 to 1861 he was headmaster of the Sanskrit college at Poona, where he became interested in Hindu poetry. His merit (which Vivekananda took pleasure in recognizing) was to spread Indian themes and images among the general public; unfortunately his zeal had a certain expeditious quality, and his tastes inclined toward the level of those he addressed. In 1861 he drew his *Book of Good Counsels* from the *Hitopadesha* and his *Indian Song of Songs* from the *Gita Govinda* in 1875. Above all, in 1879 he compressed Buddhist legend and doctrine into his *The Light of Asia*, which was to enjoy a boundless success in English-speaking countries: "The scripture of the Saviour of the world / Lord Buddha, Prince Siddartha styled in earth."

Carlyle

Arnold's work was one of the later channels through which Buddhism reached a good many American hearts. There had been others before. As Régis Michaud points out, "Happily for the Americans, an English philosopher, hazy but original, had set the Kantian ideal in seductive formulae. An impulsive and inspired pamphleteer had exalted it in a bas-relief of the Apocalypse. Coleridge and Carlyle translated Kant for Anglo-Saxon minds." Carlyle was the link with the origins, for he was close to the German Romantics, and at the same time as the English orientalists he seized on the importance of the Hindu discoveries. He set forth his ideas on them in a notable discussion of Novalis, and we shall soon see the importance Novalis has in this history. When Carlyle commented in 1829 on his mysticism in the essay entitled "Novalis," he considered the idealism which Kant, Berkeley, and Reid expressed in his own time and drew a parallel between German and Scottish metaphysics and those of India: "Of the ancient Pyrrho, or the modern Hume, we do not speak; but in the opposite end of the Earth, as Sir W. Jones informs us, a similar theory, of immemorial age, prevails among the theologians of Hindostan."

He had read Friedrich Schlegel thoroughly. In the 1830s, in the essay entitled "Characteristics," he included an enthusiastic three pages on the famous *Uber die Sprache und Weisheit der Indier* of 1808 and its "philosophical speech." Although very much of the English gentry, Carlyle boldly, passionately, sided with Schlegel's conversion to Catholicism and pleaded on his behalf for "the sacred mystery of a Person" against all the wrathful voices which had branded Schlegel a renegade. Thus we have one more echo among the diverse reactions that Schlegel's essay provoked. They were hardly less diverse in America, where one critic wrote that Schlegel's essay "forms nothing short of an epoch in the history of European learning, and even of letters and philosophy."[7] In another connection Carlyle threw light upon a passage in *Die Lehrlinge zu Saïs* by pointing out in it a path that, through Schopenhauer, would recover the sad meaning of Hinduism. Carlyle concluded concerning Novalis, "With his stillness, with his deep love of Nature, his mild, lofty, spiritual tone of contemplation, he comes before us in a sort of Asiatic character, almost like our ideal of some antique Gymnosophist, and with the weakness as well as the strength of an Oriental."

A good indicator of the inroads which the new image of India was making into the English soul, and evidence of how India's mythological landscape obsessed the subconscious of Romantic Europe, can be elicited from the nightmares of Thomas De Quincey: it was in 1816–18 (the period of Chézy and Wilson in Indic studies) that the morbid creative visions related to "the pains of opium" became exacerbated. The mysterious Malaysian visitor of De Quincey "becomes Asia itself; ancient Asia, solemn, monstrous and complicated, like its temples and religions; everything from the most ordinary aspects of life to the classic and grandiose memories that she comprises, conspires to confuse and stupefy the European mind. It was not only China, bizarre and artifical, prodigious and wizened like a fairy tale, which crushed his mind. This image naturally evoked the neighbouring image of India, so mysterious and disquieting to the western spirit, and then China and India soon formed a menacing triad with Egypt, a complex nightmare with varigated agonies. In short, the Malay had evoked the whole immense and fabulous Orient."

In 1860 Baudelaire took it upon himself to translate these passages from De Quincey:

I ran into pagodas: and was fixed, for centuries, at the summit, or in secret rooms; I was the idol; I was the priest; I was worshipped; I was sacrificed. I fled from the wrath of Brahma through all the forests of Asia: Vishnu hated me: Seeva laid wait for me. I came suddenly upon Isis and Osiris: I had done a deed, they said, which the ibis and the crocodile trembled at. . . . I thus give the reader some slight abstraction of my Oriental dreams, which always filled me with such amazement at the monstrous scenery, that horror seemed absorbed, for a while, in sheer astonishment. . . . Over every form, and threat, and punishment, and dim sightless incarceration, brooded a sense of eternity and infinity that drove me into an oppression as of madness.

From Novalis and Jean-Paul to De Quincey, to Nerval, and to Baudelaire himself, cannot one see the artificial paradises which a sort of shared dream of Western poetry added to the Asia of the scholars?

Transcendentalism, Emerson, and Whitman

Comparable mixtures colored the complex melange of Transcendentalism in the United States, where Swedenborg, along with Plato and Plotinus, mixed with German Romanticism and recollections of the Lake School. Emerson was familiar with translations of Sanskrit, Persian, and Pali texts; his attested reading between 1836 and 1861 includes English versions of Anquetil's *Zend Avesta*, the *Rig Veda*, the *Shah Namah*, and the Upanishads, and the *Bibliotheca Indica* of the Asiatic Society of Calcutta, in addition to several histories of India, its literature, and its doctrines.

Neither for Emerson, born in the New England of whalers and traders in opium and tea, nor for Thoreau, is it fair to assume, according to William Leonard Schwartz, that European Romanticism directed the thinking of an entire generation exclusively to the Near East. Both Emerson and Thoreau had been steeped in Buddhism. It is true that for a significant group Transcendentalism was, on the whole, the American form of Romanticism; what had come from Germany, up to the time of the Homeric scholar Wolf, had been brought between 1817 and 1824 by three of the men who founded the Transcendental Club in 1836. "Transcendentalism," Emerson wrote, "is God communicating himself to man," a definition in which one can see how a word which jars so completely with Indic spirituality could have been compared to it by the heirs of Pietism. Neoplatonism, idealism, quietism, a religion of inner meaning, innundated the new continent in the wake of Schleiermacher, Herder, and Schelling (undoubtedly through Coleridge as well). Moreover, French Romanticism itself was reflected here: Herder was widely perused in Quinet's translation, and Emerson borrowed *Histoire comparée des systèmes philosophiques*, in which Degérando made room for India, from the Boston Athenaeum in 1831.

In Emerson's very first works, those of a poet, written before he became primarily a moralist, a pantheism drawn essentially from Vedism appeared. Twenty years later the pantheism of the great poems in *Nature* (1836) found a more perfect expression in the poem "Brahma," whose lines

> If the red slayer think he slays,
> Or if the slain think he is slain,
> They know not well the subtle ways
> I keep, and pass, and turn again,

were inspired by Edwin Arnold's translation of the *Bhagavad Gita:* "He who shall say, 'Lo! I have slain a man.'" "Brahma" appeared in the first issue of the *Atlantic Monthly* (November 1857), edited by James Russell Lowell, and caused a curious sensation of stupor and mirth. Lowell wrote to Emerson in a letter dated November 19, 1857: "You have seen, no doubt, how the Philistines have been parodying your 'Brahma,' and showing how they still believe in their special god Baal, and are unable to arrive at a conception of an omnipresent Deity. . . . Let me thank you in especial for one line in 'Brahma,' which abides with me as an intimate—'When me they fly I am the wings.' You have crammed meaning there with a hydraulic press." Perhaps so much astonishment, even laudatory, before this image proves that India, which had become so banal in Europe, was not yet so in America. While serious people were bogged down in wondering about the explication of such a subversive philosophy, "somewhat wiser was the little school-girl in the story vouched for by Mr. E. W. Emerson," who was "bidden by her teacher to learn some verses of Emerson. Next day she recited 'Brahma.' The astonished teacher asked her why she chose that poem. The child answered that she had tried several, but couldn't understand them at all, so learned this one, 'for it was so easy. It just means "God everywhere." ' "[8]

Under the influence of a Carlyle, whose ideas he had modified, Emerson at Concord devoted himself to "The Oversoul." He had been born twenty years after the publication of the *Asiatic Researches;* his era was one which believed in the Universal Mind. In Emerson's *Journals* there are numerous references to Zoroaster, Confucius, and the Vedas, and to the Sybils and the Hindus, who provided new keys to the secret of the spirit. On October 27, 1845 Emerson wrote in his journal: "Trace these colossal conceptions of Buddhism and of Vedantism home, and they are always the necessary or structural action of the human mind." And on October 1, 1848: "I owed . . . a magnificent day to the *Bhagavat Geeta.* It was the first of books; it was as if an empire spake to us, nothing small or unworthy, but large, serene, consistent, the voice of an old intelligence which in another age and climate had pondered and thus disposed of the same questions which exercise us. Let us not now go back and apply a minute criticism to it, but cherish the venerable oracle." It is no accident that Thoreau left his friend Emerson his collection of oriental books. Today the reader of Emerson's essays is struck by their fusion, to all appearances completely natural, of Indic pantheism and laicized gospel morality. There is little doubt that it was one of the most effective vehicles through which Indic teaching, even if distorted, became familiar to the Occidental.

The poet, drawn from Emerson's own experiences for his essay "The Poet," was embodied neither by himself, as he recognized, nor by friends among other poets who were more or less Indianists—Thoreau, Lowell, and Whittier—but by Walt Whitman, as Emerson realized and as Whitman knew. When *Leaves of Grass* appeared in its original form in 1855, *the poet of the times was Longfellow.* Then came Emerson's letter of July 21, 1855, to Whitman, anointing him with Longfellow's title: "I greet you at the beginning of a great career."

Here, once again, as Gabriel Sarrazin points out, are the same relationships: "His doctrine is German and his teachers are English." And, further, no critic approached Whitman without finding "the great oriental mysteries" in him. Thoreau, a good judge, had been struck by this as early as 1856; but when he remarked on it, Whitman reacted like a man who had never heard of such things. Yet Whitman confessed that he had read Hindu poetry in preparation for his own; when he was quite young he had soaked himself in it, along with Greek tragedies and the *Nibelungenlied.* Here is the beautiful gluttony of a self-educated man who, having calculated his destiny and being bent on making exceptional progress toward it, devoured everything in order to nourish his image of the universe. India came to him from two sides: through German idealism, which nourished itself on India, and through Transcendentalism, which might be termed, as Gay Wilson Allen calls it in his *Walt Whitman Handbook,* "the offspring of a German father and a Hindu mother." The great professions of faith were later to be those of pantheism and syncretism, the belief of "Song of Myself," "embracing the ancient cults and the modern cults . . . I admire the Shastas and the Vedas." And in "To Think of Time," "I swear I think now that every thing without exception has an eternal soul." Or the same conception in "Chanting the Square Deific": "Old Brahm I, and I Saturnius am . . . I, the general soul, / Here the square finishing, the solid, I the most solid." And above all these lines from "Passage to India" come to mind: "Passage indeed O soul to primal thought / . . . / To realms of budding Bibles. / . . . / Passage to more than India! / . . . / O soul, voyagest thou indeed on voyages like those? / . . . / Soundest below the Sanscrit and the Vedas?"

It is not surprising that Edward Carpenter, who was among the first enthusiasts, followed his chapter "Whitman as Prophet" in *Days with Walt Whitman* with "a selection of pieces drawn from the Gospels and the sacred literatures of India and China, and compared to passages from *Leaves of Grass,*[9] including this one from "Passage to India":

Eclaircise the myths Asiatic, the primitive fables.

Not you alone proud truths of the world,
Nor you alone ye facts of modern science,
But myths and fables of eld, Asia's, Africa's fables,

The far-darting beams of the spirit, the unloos'd dreams,
The deep diving bibles and legends,
The daring plots of the poets, the elder religions . . .

Passage to India!
Lo, soul, seest thou not God's purpose from the first?
The earth to be spann'd, connected by network,
The races, neighbors, to marry and be given in marriage,
The oceans to be cross'd, the distant brought near,
The lands to be welded together.

This recalled and fulfilled all the unitarian hopes which had nourished Romanticism, especially in the hearts of the German theoreticians. Before singing of the "Old occult Brahma interminably far back, the tender and junior Buddha" that he clearly saw, Whitman seemed to remember the other poet, Camões, who had first felt the significance, "For purpose vast, man's long probation fill'd," of the confrontation of all philosophies: "Again Vasco de Gama sails forth." And I myself did not anticipate, when at the beginning of my research I was admiring the humanism of an earth which had become completely round, that I would discover Whitman's line "Thou rondure of the world at last accomplished."

Indic Studies and German Romanticism

I have discussed the kind of enthusiasm that greeted *Asiatic Researches* in Germany and prepared the way for Friedrich Schlegel's *Uber die Sprache und Weisheit der Indier*, which reflected this enthusiasm in 1808. But my main concern has been the points scored by the instantaneous diffusion of Indic studies. I must now show how deep and how lasting this permeation of German thought and literature was. This will serve to fill in the gaps in the above discussion on the diffusion of *Asiatic Researches*.

On the whole the situation in Germany was comparable to that in England; but it seems that Germany took things to heart in a different way, and probably with good reason. England was wondering what to do with India, this foreign body. Germany's only question was whether it would become absorbed in the India revealed by England or whether it would, rather, transform India into a national interest. Moreover, the repercussions were uncommonly animated and prolonged. Perhaps it is in poetry that these repercussions were most conspicuous. In metaphysics and spirituality there were vast consequences with no comparable examples elsewhere but with aftereffects everywhere. Local Germanic inventions, notably the philosophy of history and the philosophy of religions, moved on to other capitals, where they were usually diluted into literary genres.

Jean-Paul Richter and Novalis

The French Romantics have been greatly criticized, and not without reason, for having reduced the weighty Orient of the Germans to picturesque exoticism. Nevertheless, one cannot ignore the fact that the powdered-wig Orient advanced through the successes of the *Persian Letters*, of *Zedig*, and of the whole corpus of erotic or satiric travesties, and could whet the appetites of Gauthier or Nerval by incorporating adaptations of Tieck, Wieland, Hoffmann, and others. On these frontiers of fiction, halfway to the vocation of philosophy, the Indic musings of two temperaments as original as those of Novalis and Jean-Paul Richter seem to me to be placed. I also note that the blend of fiction and system in these two writers, and their hesitation between the two—they were the first occupants of the house—can be explained by dates. As early as 1790 Novalis had become enraptured by Herder's *Ideen;* as early as 1792 Jean-Paul created a Hindu protagonist in a novel, in a role remotely allied to those Vigny sketched forty years later. Herder and Maier, the humanists of Jena and Weimar, were the principal reference points; we are already familiar with their activities in translation, prefaces, and studies, and it was not only Novalis and Richter who were influenced by such work. The *Gita Govinda* marked a turning point in Schelling's thinking; *samsara* haunted Novalis. Herder drew on his own experience for the "Gedanken einiger Bramanen" which appeared in the fourth collection of *Zerstreute Blätter* and which Rückert later used as a model. That which concerned "primitive poetry" and "universal revelation," two fundamental chapters in this history, will be discussed below.

Jean-Paul Richter's *Hesperus,* written between 1792 and 1794, appeared in 1795, the same year as *Wilhelm Meister*. Emmanuel, who is also Dahore, one of the protagonists of this mystical and sarcastic composite, incarnates an India behind which one can perceive the *Chaumière indien* of Bernardin, the talismans of Balzac, and *Les Fleurs* of Guerrier de Dumast and Leupol. "Emmanuel's soul seemed to live, like a Brahman, on the flowers of poetry, and his language was, like his manners, often poetic." This kind of equivalence is characteristic of the times. Thirty years later one finds this same thing in the works of Nodier, whose imagination had been fired by reading Friedrich Schlegel. In his *Mélanges tirés d'une petite bibliothèque*, Nodier wrote that India was not better known because "it is not a *classical* land but only a *romantic* land, a land poetic and marvelous." Indeed, this is how India appeared to those who continued to see it as a "happy country of enchanters and fairies, a kingdom of adventures and wonders, so ancient in the order of time, so new in the order of societies." We will return to this latter theme of India as the childhood of mankind. It was an idea common to all the German Romantics and came to others from them.

Jean-Paul was among the first to apply the theory; his Emmanuel is "the most gentle and the greatest of the men who came here from East India" (here the ideas of Rousseau were dressed in motifs provided by Jones). Emmanuel describes himself: "Look, in Asia this hand has closed the eyes of eight noble beings—no friend has survived me. I am hiding in Europe—my turbid story lies in the flow of the Ganges with the ashes of my parents." But this is followed by praise of Indian spirituality, which is explained by the abstinence from meat.

The imprint of Herder also marked Novalis' first works.[10] Novalis often returned to this model to nourish his own scheme of universal religion. As a very young man he had gathered outlines for a philosophy of history and later sought a revelation of the primeval world in the symbolism of pagan myths. This activity, still based on Herder, led him to place the Garden of Eden, which he considered recoverable, somewhere in the Himalayas. The works of all these German precursors introduced and amplified a belief in the ultimate reunion of the soul, after its fall and its wanderings, with its divine origins. Jones himself had immediately compared Indic and Pythagorean metempsychosis and Platonic myth and had translated the *Gita Govinda*, which captivated Germany in the 1790s, to illustrate his thesis. Jones had also connected Krishna, Pan, and Isis as an example for his contemporaries, who until then had been preoccupied with the mysteries of Greece and Egypt. Before Novalis, Jones had composed "A Hymn to the Night" inspired by the Vedic hymn book.

Asiatic Researches was well known in Novalis' circle. This was true of Schelling and, above all, Friedrich Schlegel. And among Novalis' frequent reading was the *Zerstreute Blätter*, in which Herder showed himself transformed by the first Hindu texts to reach him: *Shakuntala,* the *Bhagavad Gita,* and the *Laws of Manu.* He had successfully translated into verse the passage from Wilkins' *Bhagvat-Geeta* that contained Arjuna's pantheistic vision ("Ich bin der Schöpfung Geist, ihr Anfang, Mittel und Ende"). The translator's commentary linked the Hindu doctrine of the universal soul with the pietism of an intimate God and the mystery of union, associations destined for a long life. The translator concluded the dialogues on metempsychosis with a "Hymn to the Night-Mother," which Novalis probably did not forget. As a young poet Novalis was further affected by the Indic writings of Maier, whose influence on Herder we have seen, as well as on the Weimar circle, from Goethe to Schopenhauer, and on those at Jena who were to play an important role in Schleiermacher's education. It seems that Novalis' reading of Maier was what led him to Jones. A profound interest in the pagan mysteries developed in these surroundings, as we have seen in many thinkers in eighteenth-century Germany and France alike. Meiners, in a treatise popular at the time, gave the "secret writings" of the Hindus as the key to these mysteries.

Novalis was most directly influenced by the strong personality of Schelling. Jones's *Gita Govinda* had fired Goethe's imagination even before it was retranslated into German by Dahlberg, and his enthusiasm spread to Jena. For Schelling this poem of mystical love became an important event; he interpreted it as laying open the essential mystery of the human spirit, a mystery which then supposedly passed from India to Egypt, to Eleusis, and finally to an esoteric gospel known to Saint John and Saint Paul. The system that Schelling developed in his writings in 1802 and 1803 bordered significantly on the themes of Novalis' essays and *Hymns to the Night:* a new universal religion destined to restore the knowledge of forgotten mysteries and fulfill the message of esoteric Christianity. This was the point of departure for constructs and hopes which were to go a long way, and to undergo a good many metamorphoses from the Illuminati to the Saint-Simonians, from the Neo-Christians to the Transcendentalists. Schelling himself extended such theories in a poem to Ceres, the mother goddess, who founded the mysteries at Eleusis after the loss of her daughter Kore. Schelling's letters, notably those to Wilhelm Schlegel, demonstrate the link which for him ties these ideas to the *Gita Govinda.* All of that, it is true, came after *Hymns to the Night* but must have been a treasure shared between Schelling and Novalis in 1798, a year of intense exchange between the two thinkers, the year also of *Die Lehrling zu Saïs.* (In an 1825 lecture published in his *Einleitung in die Philosophie der Mythologie,* Schelling again celebrated the "imperishable valor" of William Jones and later made a point of noting the importance he attached to Burnouf's work.)

It could be said that since then all German idealism had an Indian tint. Anquetil was right to compare, in the notes to *Oupnek'hat,* the Upanishads to Kant's system which, in attributing all things to the thing-in-itself, became the father of his idealism. When the day comes that a philosopher studies in technical detail the influence exerted by Hindu thought on those who shaped nineteenth-century philosophy, he will be surprised that such influence was not recognized earlier.

The same grand illusion of a unique primitive religion, discovered in paganism and, in a purer form, in India, an illusion Herder and Maier supported, was in the air; in other words, in many of the more or less creative minds of the times. A strange episode made this illusion personally dear to Novalis. In 1797, out of the memory of his dead fiancée, he created a cosmic mystery that explained existence and identified Sophie von Kühn with the universal *sophia* that is also Christ. On June 29, Novalis wrote in his journal: "Christ und Sophie." The consequence was to equate absolute love with religion ("Absolute Liebe . . . ist Religion"), and the term "mystery" became commonplace in the group, especially between Novalis and his close friend Friedrich Schlegel. Now as Novalis in his turn became fired by the *Shakuntala*, which was dazzling all the poets, he created from it a new name for death, and gave as its country the homeland of a seraphic vision of a Sophie manifesting the divine Cosmos. In addition the poet had another reason for linking Sophie's death as a child at the age of fifteen and the India which his milieu considered the childhood of humanity: India united the values of the childhood of the vanished young soul with those of humanity's original religions. "Morgenträume unseres Geschlechtes," the childhood dreams of our species, had been Maier's definition of Sanskrit poems.

What was referred to as magical idealism established links between a system of clairvoyance and a mystique of history, poetry, and human love. The two *Gitas* arrived in the West to sanction this link. The themes of India as the home of art and the soul, the fountain of wisdom, the ocean of metamorphoses, and—above all—the universal soul, spread among Herder, Maier, Schelling, Novalis, and Friedrich Schlegel. They are especially noticeable in certain of the *Spiritual Songs (Geistliche Lieder)* and the *Hymns to the Night*. Hymn 5 stages the adventure of the universal soul: "The night had become the mighty womb of revelations" and then "a son of the first Virgin Mother" is born, with whom "the prophetic richness of the East" begins. Thus the episode of the Wise Men ends with a singer who first came to Palestine from Greece, departing "with joy, toward Hindustan, his heart intoxicated with sweet love poured out in flaming poetry under the merciful sky." This represents Orpheus-Christ-Krishna. "He ascended newborn to the summit of the world," sings Novalis of Christ. Here was another image from the vocabulary for initiates. The summit of the world represents, in Herder's construct of universal religion, an India original and paradisiacal. The *Spiritual Songs* contain an explicit prophecy: "The East is lighting up in the distance, the past is being restored, and India shall, even in the very North, flower with joy for the Beloved."

All this is significant to the extent that Novalis is important to the history of poetry and intellectual adventure. And everything Indic studies owed to Schlegel's *Über die Sprache und Weisheit* remained under the sway of emotions shared by Schlegel and Novalis. They became friends toward the end of 1791, and as Novalis wrote to Schlegel, "You have been the High Priest of Eleusis for me. Through you I have learned of heaven and hell." Through these words their joint reading of Meiners on the Orphic mysteries lived on. We now have before us the links of the chain that allow us to appraise the role the Hindu discovery played in the Romantic diffusion of a myth of universal religion, views which were ended, in the Görres-Creuzer stage, by the intervention of philological specialists and, in the Eckstein chapter, by the headstrong interpretation of dogma. However, at the same time Novalis, and more than one of his followers, was no less enthusiastic about gnosis, ancient Germanic mysteries, and according to what he wrote to Schlegel, theosophy and alchemy. In that respect too there were lines of descent which cannot be ignored.

The Divan, Heine, Rückert

One could not expect that Goethe would have been interested in Hindu matters to the point where they would vie with the Greek, nor that he would be the most steadfast of his countrymen toward them. And yet even Goethe, hesitating even in the *West-Ostliche Divan* between sensuality and profundity, transmitted and endorsed the very lessons of oriental wisdom that rejected and dissolved the limits of life. Certain poems—"Wiederfinden," for example—strangely approach the themes of *Hymns to the Night:* a belief in a seesawing of the universal soul between dispersal among transient forms and a return to essential Unity. It was the famous "Sterb und Werde" of the "Seelige Sehnsucht."

After having seriously explored the field of oriental studies with the specialists Jones and Hammer, Maier and Klaproth, Sacy and Kosegarten, simply as a reader of some and an interlocutor of others, Goethe championed the oriental cause to the point of planning an encyclopedic *Divan* and a series of poems in honor of the great orientalists. In the end all that remained of so vast a plan was a set of extraordinarily interesting notes added to the *Divan.* Later Goethe unquestionably detached himself from the science they represented, but this was as he was growing old and to the extent that "all that is passionate" in him was, as he remarked, dying out. Indeed, these two forms of enthusiasm which Goethe had had for Asia—sometimes a simple quest for an "opium" to ease the pain of the world, at other times a philosophical passion—were the very kinds of ardor which made the introduction of India an event of incomparable magnitude in the West.

And then there were, particularly in the Indic realm, literary consequences of the *Divan;* a few words here will suffice to call them to mind. Broadly speaking, these consequences carried the names Heine, Rückert, and Platen. Especially for Rückert such consequences affected an entire destiny; the contact with India furnished Rückert with a kind of genius whereby he entered the great tradition of German translators which the Schlegels had rendered illustrious. Heine noted that the *Divan,* appearing immediately after *Faust* and ushering in Goethe's final period, was a crucial example for the new literature: "Our lyrics are aimed at singing the Orient." Moreover, this was what he himself did, this poet who was a student of Sanskrit under Wilhelm Schlegel at Bonn and under Bopp at Berlin. I have already quoted Heine in this regard when discussing the prodigous impact of Friedrich Schlegel's *Uber die Sprache und Weisheit der Indier.* Schlegel's essay and Goethe's *Divan* were the two literary poles of attraction. What this magnetism produced in Heine's poetic works can be seen in the many serious or amusing allusions his collections contain, and in a few of his important prose pieces.

Friedrich Rückert became a student of his friend Bopp even though he was Bopp's elder and already had a knowledge of Sanskrit. Rückert is, I believe, the only example of a true poet, famous for his own work—the overrated "Song of the Breastplate" which appeared in his *Deutsche Gedichte* (1814)—and a fine professor of oriental languages who was a better poet as a translator than as an original creator.[11] His translations, notably that of the *Atharva Veda,* were worthy of being considered original works. I have already called attention to this fact with his celebrated translations of *Nala and Damayanti* (1828) and of the *Gita Govinda* (1837), a work dear to Herderian Germany. In 1836 Rückert produced *Die Weisheit des Bramanen* and in 1839 *Brahmanische Erzählungen,* titles that call to mind Herder's "Gedanken einiger Bramanen" and the Schlegel essay responsible for Rückert's first enthusiasm. These were works in which Rückert accepted responsibility for doctrinal content.

Herder and "Primitive Poetry"

The time has come to deal with two matters which I have broached on several occasions and which dominate our approaches to the Oriental Renaissance: the myth of "primitive poetry" launched by Herder and the theme of "universal revelation" the expansion of which Friedrich Schlegel above all recommended. These problems are well enough known, however, that I need present only a summary of their more interesting aspects with regard to the Indic domain.

All the cherished preconceptions on which, even today, our idolatry of the infantile and the primitive rests can, from a bird's-eye view, be traced to Herder. To the extent that there are beginnings to anything, it was Herder who hit on the idea (although Thomas Percy's *Reliques of Ancient*

English Poetry in 1765 antedated Herder's *Volkslieder* by thirteen years) of opposing the most exotic types of poetry to the stale poetic tradition common to academic classicism. Herder was still timid in his first demonstrations and lackluster in his examples, like all those who, attacking a prevailing opinion, cannot predict to what extent it will turn in their favor.

Herder too had precursors: in 1758 Diderot had written, "Poetry needs something enormous, something barbaric and wild." This formula was frequently invoked: one of the first to do so was Barbey d'Aurevilly, who showed precisely how this idea served the new prestige of Indic poetry. Herder's notion of the primitive answered Rousseau's naturalistic teachings. But the decisive impact seems to have been his reading of *De sacra poesi Hebraeorum*. Here the English bishop Robert Lowth maintained that the Scripture had not been inspired by God except internally; this allowed biblical texts to be compared with the poems of Homer and Ossian, at that time believed to be the most ancient texts accessible. Herder went further with this kind of laicizing. A third factor was the ideas he had received from Hamann, his first idol. Hamann, one of the tumultuous personalities who had such a great effect in the Germanic climate, maintained that poetry is the natural language, the "mother tongue" of humanity, a dogma which was to blossom in all of Europe's Romantic movements.

In 1762, in *Aesthetica in nuce*, Hamann had stated explicitly, "How then will we revive the dead language of nature? Through pilgrimages to Arabia Felix, through crusades to the Orient and the restoration of its magic." And Novalis, thirty-six years later, seems to have written *Die Lehrlinge zu Saïs* to illustrate this principle, while Friedrich Schlegel helped him to divert the pilgrims to Egypt toward the Ganges. The great preoccupation with human origins which had grown to fever pitch in the eighteenth century called for, and made inevitable, frequenting the Orient which was at the same time on the verge of being reached through an encounter of historical chance and human genius: its mark remains the symbolic date 1784, when Herder's *Ideen* coincided with the founding of the first Asiatic Society, in Calcutta.

Naturpoesie, which corresponded with *Naturphilosophie*, soon broke out in Germany and was expressed in the *Naturgeist*. Archaicisms going back to the four corners of the earth buttressed it: Gaelic bards, the Eddas, the *Nibelungenlied*—inevitably the Vedas were soon to fill the empty place that awaited them. Perhaps nothing worked more in favor of the rediscovery of the Orient, and especially of the Vedas, this nebulosity of an Indic studies in the process of forming, than the clarion calls to the skill of an infallible Nature as against the artifice of the classics. Goethe, a belated classicist who thought in Greek and often wrote in Gothic, found himself a faithful student of Herder when he came to his study of the Orient; this accounts for his explicit statement prefacing the *Divan:* "Here I want to penetrate to the first origin of human races, when they still received celestial mandates from God in terrestial languages." It was all there, the divine origin of language and of poetry, which was also the origin of societies, into which the modern bard plunged for rejuvenation *(Verjüngen).* When Herder had begun to explore this question in the *Abhandlung über den Ursprung der Sprache* which, as we have seen, impassioned his century, he gave a lovely definition: "Man is an animal who sings," very similar to Blake's notion of poetics as "warbling birds." These conceptions gave rise to a reign of poetic absolutism interchangeably referred to as primitive, spontaneous, or popular, which remained uncontested among the young until Villemain and Sainte-Beuve. It was in this way that Friedrich Schlegel's maxim, "Romantic poetry is a progressive poetry of the universal," was best accomplished. Here the universe to be rediscovered was one of primitive poetry, Homeric or Edenic. And indeed this universe was peopled with anonymous writers recruited from everywhere and animated by an entire movement which, sparked first by Vico, then by Wolf's success, disowned the individual Homer for the benefit of nameless heirs. Here again we can see the beginning of an idea which is still with us today: the distrust of Great Men in history. In biblical matters, the dissertation of the physician Astruc, which appeared in the same year as Lowth's, dissected the Book of Genesis into the work of several unknown writers. What was to become an era of integral analysis, and a revenge of Plurality on Unity, was initiated by a good many simultaneous approaches, to which we should add all the preparations for the empires of the Irrational and the Unconscious.

Into this great intellectual adventure the bundle of Sanskrit texts abruptly dropped. One can imagine the massive reinforcements supplied by the arrival of hundreds of thousands of verses, myriads either without authors' names or attributed to poets so legendary that their names were assumed to be collective. The Vedas were the triumph and the confirmation of anonymous genius; the *Ramayana* was proof that everyone and no one was named Homer. One can now understand by what additional means a friend of Herder, and his guide in Hindu wisdom, had been able to teach him to see in this literature previously undreamt of the "childhood dreams of our species."

And finally, everyone at Jena, especially with the advent of the French Revolution and subsequently Napoleon, had local reasons, specific and substantial reasons for ennobling the "primitive." It was that much more recaptured from Louis XIV. It was at last the revenge of the "barbarian" who had been cursed and degraded too long. Homer then, less cherished in himself, was called upon, along with the Scandinavians and soon India, to rehabilitate the Germany of the *Nibelungenlied*. The Gothic cause and that of the Middle Ages had first enlisted Herder along with *Sturm und Drang*, and now it drafted the Orient. From this time forward, through the negation of the term Renaissance, long applied to the disciples of the Latins, the way was truly open for a separate Renaissance, oriental and barbarian. The assault on French sensibilities accused of all manner of poetic and ideological ills, an attack often personified in Wilhelm Schlegel, naturally laid the blame on the most vulnerable, everyday forms, a rationalism known throughout Germany as *Aufklärung*. An important maneuver in this campaign, according to Comtesse de Pange, was Herder's attempt "to humiliate the pride of an autonomous and sovereign faculty of reason faced with the omnipotence of a hidden God." To achieve this end Herder exalted "the primitive periods when irrational elements predominated, barbarian and heroic ages, ages long distant in which language was elaborated and in which legends and myths were formed."

It is worthwhile, I believe, to consider how the diffusion of Hindu poetry was facilitated by its service to nationalistic causes. In 1774 in *Auch eine Philosophie der Geschichte der Menschheit*, Herder avenged the Middle Ages, then considered a corruption of Romanism or the first stammerings of modernity. For Herder they became "the youth of the Christo-Germanic civilization whose senility was represented by the eighteenth century." [12] In 1808 Friedrich Schlegel showed in his *Uber die Sprache und Weisheit der Indier* how "the Germanic races," that is to say the Aryans, were attracted by "the elevated dignity, the magnificence of the North." In other words, they settled in lands where they would be the ancestors of the Schlegel brothers. In his 1830 *Lectures on the Philosophy of History*, Hegel allowed only four great historical periods: the oriental world, the Greek world, the Roman world, and the Germanic world, identified with the entire history of Christian Europe—the Aryans, Alexander, Caesar, Charlemagne. Always us.

The famous theory of the ages of humanity central to Herder's system made great headway. The theory was new only in its adaptation of a well-known theme, the Golden Age, and in its reversal of the old textbook rule of the great centuries. It was to provide essential articulation both for literary manifestos, such as the preface to *Cromwell*, and for philosophical or social constructs. The most memorable use of this theory was that of Auguste Comte, who skillfully turned the childhood arguments against the theologians, its inventors. Jean Reynaud went so far as to term "paleontological" the age his teacher termed "theological." The "three ages" or the "four ages" are the passport to the thought of an entire epoch. Can one imagine that this was done during the period of the discovery of India without any remembrance of the colossal Indic chronologies that had such an immense impact on Occidentals? The division of four *yugas* within the immensity of each *kalpa* had been among the first revelations of Lord and Abraham Roger. After the *Lettres édifiantes*, Holwell and Dow had revived the grandiose vision of the "year of Brahma." All this was particularly apparent in *Génie du Christianisme*, although Chateaubriand did not take the four yugas "seriously." Bailly's *Astronomie indienne* had already established a broad audience for such notions.

Even though special interests crept into the great historical classifications Herder inaugurated, it was primarily a passion for standardization which was at work. This blend of method and chaos, this amalgam of the scholarly and the chimeric which had so frequently tempted the German soul, found one of its best moments at the turn of the century when a furor for rethinking the world insinuated itself everywhere. Three or four blocs of civilization came to be considered unique, the only ones that were imperial, adult, and divine. Beyond that the conviction began to emerge that a single race had dominated throughout, the only race to be truly received in the palace of the spirit, the tall blonds who were also the true youths of eternal history. Moreover, beyond its various appearances in time and place, beyond mythologies and revelations, great natural poetry, itself divine, also had to have been *one*. In the ensemble of Romanticism, "the poetry of the universal" was linked with universal religion.

Tieck, whose *Poetisches Journal* in 1800 included Maier's letter extolling Hindu poetry, announced three years later it was essential to be familiar with the troubadours, the sagas, and Sanskrit poetry. A standard nomenclature for the higher poetries, those nationalistic and archaic, was established: in 1812 in *Geschichte der alten und neuen Literatur*, Friedrich Schlegel, one of those who worked on such a nomenclature, referred to an idea of great poetry as primitive and unique. Homer, Firdausi, the Romanceros, the Eddas, and the *Ramayana* were, to Schlegel's way of thinking, the honor guard of the *Nibelungenlied:* the sagas served as introductions to Germania, Homer as a reference, the *Ramayana* as the family tree, and Latin poetry as the foreground. "The fables," Eckstein wrote, "upon which the Indic, Persian, and Hellenic epics rest are the same as those which form the basis of the *Nibelungenlied*." And thus the broad historical classification discussed above appeared along the trail blazed by Klaproth and marked with the linguistic label "Indo-Germanic." It was still the same campaign to prove that everything—language, habitat, epic—that sprang from the true chosen people, the Aryans, belonged to Germany.

The *Nibelungenlied* was one of the sledgehammer arguments in the strategy. Its Homericism was a refrain heard constantly at the universities: in 1838, Quinet picked it up at Heidelberg and faithfully jotted it down in his working notes. "The Hindu epics are for the Indians what the Homeric poems are for the Greeks; they correspond to the age of the Nibelungen for the Germans." The Indic vein intersected that of the German Middle Ages in the works of Wagner as late as the 1850s, and the choice momentarily wavered. Gervinus had decidedly baptised the elements of the future *Ring* cycle "a Germanic Odyssey."

In 1846 Salvandy, the French Minister of Public Education, sent a professor, Nicolas Martin, to Germany to research contemporary poetry. Martin happened to be the nephew of Karl Simrock, an orientalizing poet best known for his poems attacking Napoleonic France and as editor of the *Nibelungenlied*. Moreover, Martin's *Poètes contemporains en Allemagne* published in 1860 contained copious chapters on "Germanic Epic" and the *Nibelungenlied* and all that Simrock, Gervinus, and Grimm had done for them. "These epics," wrote the French emissary, "claimed their rightful place alongside the *Iliad* and the *Odyssey*."

It must be acknowledged that some of the best minds in Germany were indignant over this confusion. Goethe told Eckermann that the mania of their countrymen in trying to equate the *Nibelungenlied* with the *Iliad* had tainted all their literature. In 1805, amid the lover's quarrels of the "Heidelberg group," Voss, an old classicist, declared to Brentano that "to compare the *Nibelungenlied* to Homer, as Arnim has done, is to confuse a pigsty with a palace." The fact remained that the active names in Romanticism—Arnim, Brentano, the Schlegels, Tieck—were determined not to separate the destinies of the Homeric heroes, beginning with Vyasa and ending with Siegfried. Heine wrote, "For a long time there was nothing more important, in our country, than the book of the Nibelungen; and the classical philologists were more than slightly outraged to hear this epic being compared to the *Iliad* and, even worse, to witness an increasing debate over which of the two works was the greater. The public, in this instance, rather resembled the children whom one asks in all seriousness, 'Which do you prefer, a horse or jam?' " The German epic, discovered too soon, had first been scorned by the Aufklärung, led by Frederick the Great; it was revived, along with nationalism, against the invading French. Martin said that in 1813 the *Nibelungenlied* had become almost a sacred text.

It is not without interest that the most vehement disciples of the Indian epic, Schlegel and Eckstein, were equally enamoured of the epics of the Middle Ages. It is significant that the knowledge of epics, the taste for them, the interest in them, was so lively in an atmosphere charged with the discovery of India. Homer and the Bible, two inexhaustible questions in the realm of the mind and the spirit, again became intensely vital matters and quickly permeated the Indian question.

The Heidelberg Group

I return briefly to what was termed the "Heidelberg group," which was characteristic of the Romantic alliance between philologists and poets, between primitive poetry and oriental studies.[13] The first encounters took place in 1803–4. The jurist Savigny was the occasion for it. He had married Cunegonde Brentano, whose brother Clemens was named professor at Heidelberg by Marburg at the same time as Creuzer. Tieck was to have joined them at the university, but came only in 1806. Arnim was in Heidelberg from May to September, 1805. Görres arrived October 30, 1806, also without having obtained his professorship. The dean of the collaborators, Creuzer, was about thirty years old. The youngest, Arnim, was about twenty. The average age was one of boldness and accomplishment. Tieck, who as early as 1802 had dreamed of editing the *Nibelungenlied*, which he considered a collective work on the Homeric model, pursued the Middle Ages. Brentano moved in the direction of popular poetry and induced Görres to publish his *Die teutschen Volksbücher*, the manifesto of the group. For their part Görres and Creuzer steered poets toward the Hindu epic. All the members of the group were multi-talented, and many were eccentric. Görres, a professor of physics, discovered the little-known genius of Hölderlin. Creuzer, a theologian at the beginning of his career, belonged to the astounding class of German romantic lovers. He was smitten in the summer of 1804 by the famous Karoline von Günderode, of whom Brentano had been enamoured. Brentano became jealous and, in the end, Creuzer left her and she stabbed herself to death on the banks of the Rhine, July 26, 1806. The irritable Voss, who passed through the group, quarreled with Creuzer and accused him of having secretly taken up with the Bavarian Jesuits.

There were other crossings of paths where we meet again some old familiar faces: the Schlegels. Friedrich had recently published his *Uber die Sprache und Weisheit* with the group's publisher. When it came out in 1808 Arnim called attention to it in the group's journal, and reproduced excerpts of Hindu poetry borrowed from Schlegel, along with some of Schlegel's original poetry. Wilhelm Schlegel picked up Tieck's idea of editing the *Nibelungenlied*, and one of his students, Friedrich von Hagen, provided the first complete translation in 1807. *Das Knabens Wunderhorn* by Arnim and Brentano, in which the love for folk poetry crystallized, appeared in 1805. Soon Creuzer proclaimed that the old mythic symbols had to be sought in India. He developed this idea primarily in his major work *Symbolik und Mythologie der alten Volker* (1810–12). At this point the Heidelberg picnic, to which each person had brought personal provisions to feed a common hunger for the Orient, folk poetry, and the mystique of history, broke up.

"Universal Revelation" from Schelling to Friedrich Schlegel

The revival of poetry along with the religious awakening was not, then, a simple coincidence: the fundamental principle that Herder discovered in Lowth authorized him to consider Christianity a "continuous revelation," from which many concluded that it was only about to begin.[14] There was no lack of evidence that Christianity had already taken a variety of forms in history, a notion to which the privileged case of Brahmanic India brilliantly attested. Moreover, the brand new field of philosophy of religion hankered from the beginning to undertake such unification, resulting in a program that adapted itself to Quinet's formula "the genealogy of the Eternal within the limits of time." We should keep two essential points in mind: for the Neo-Christians on the one hand the age of dogma had not ended but had barely begun; for others the universal religion of the period before Babel remained visible, if not intact, in the supposed paganism of India.

In his maturity Friedrich Schlegel very much embodied this notion of renewing living religion alongside timeless religion. We should keep in mind the common date of his dual conversion to Rome and Calcutta: since 1800 he had moved toward both Catholicism and Sanskrit. In 1808 his baptism at Cologne coincided, within a week, with the publication in Paris of his *Uber die Sprache und Weisheit*. It is no surprise that the apologetic zeal of his work hit a sensitive nerve in Lutheran Germany and, above all, in its poets. The simultaneous experience of Catholic spirituality and Vedantic metaphysics merged in the neophyte Schlegel with the ideas he had drawn from his teacher Herder: having at first learned through poetry, a poetry that gave nourishment to the soul, Schlegel sensed in himself the important link between these two major concerns—natural poetry and universal, uninterrupted, revelation. His essay insisted that "the ancient inhabitants of India not be denied the knowledge of the true God." This was orthodoxy itself, to maintain that, until Babel, the truth was one and the same for all mankind. The point at which German Romanticism, soon followed by the rest of Europe, made serious changes was in asserting that the universal revelation virtually unrecognized in India provided fresh proof of the dogma, and that this revelation would help build a more vast Church. This was the position of Eckstein and even Lamennais.

German Romanticism—Romantic because its leaders undertook all human matters with the illusion, the purpose, of placing all in one—also undertook to trace everything back to its origins. In the convenient vocabulary of short German particles it would seem that "Ur" was the key to "sym," which intruded itself everywhere. The application of these principles developed around ancient paganisms: all at once their myths and

mysteries were assumed to hold secrets common to the faithful of all nations. It was the advent of what was called Symbolism: the single truth,
now clear for the Christians, had been known and preserved even among
remote or unbelieving peoples by the sacerdotal families who allowed this
truth to be perceived by the masses only through the veil of legends.
However, one had only to lift the veil to discover in all the legends the
same unique lesson.

Such was the work of Creuzer and Görres at the beginning of the nineteenth century. It had a consequence very dear to Friedrich Schlegel: it
was to reconstruct, by means of an opposite approach, a mythology common to the whole world of his day. Synthesis would follow analysis, effect would flow from study. Here an interest as much literary as religious
came into play. Well aware of the mainspring that had propelled great
ancient poetry, and that had not been replaced (this was, from another
angle, the perpetual question of "the marvelous"), Schlegel wrote: "Our
poetry lacks a central point, such as mythology was for the ancients."
Precisely. A faith strong enough and young enough to unite the world
would secure this lost community among poets.

The groundwork for this thesis, or hope, had been prepared by one of
"a single God for all mankind" which Schelling had developed in 1799 in
his fourth lecture on the *Philosophie der Mythologie*. The theories, new at
that time, which stated there had always been but one mythology in the
world shared by all peoples, can be accounted for only by the discovery
of Sanskrit. As was so often the case in Germany, historical studies, even
of the most ancient past, offered immediate applications: the discovery,
in the furthest reaches of the ages, of a world mythology had to be of use
to the living. Germany was to create for modern Europe "a fusion of the
mythological traditions of all humanity." All the legends of India and
Greece, of the Scandinavians and the Persians "had to be" accepted as
components of a new universal religion that would regenerate a world
distracted by rationalism. The strange account written by Karl Hillebrand,
one of the most lucid philologists to cross to France from Germany, is worth
reading.[15] Also worth reading are the curious studies in which Leo Joubert,
in 1863, showed how Creuzer, following Voss, extracted the pagan myth
system from a garbled biblical tradition, and how Gladstone fearlessly
placed Homer himself in this sacred tradition. This is an entirely different
matter from the dogma of the Universal Revelation; it is the affirmation
of a direct, unbroken line, a set of equivalences, between Homer and
Moses.[16] Tocqueville, with a better balanced judgment, wrote to Gobineau in 1843: "There is certainly a mass of maxims and ideas which, before being collected and bound together within a single cover as the Gospel, was scattered and consequently inert in the books of Greece and the

Orient. In fact I came across a great number of them the other day in the laws of Manu." More imperious deductions were being drawn from Schelling.

They were fermenting in the animated group through which Novalis, Schleiermacher, Schiller, Hegel, and Fichte passed, along with Schelling and the Schlegels of the *Athenaeum*. By the age of fifteen Schelling knew Arabic as well as Hebrew; his father, a pastor, was a specialist in Hebrew and already a comparatist. Hegel was one of Schelling's fellow students of philosophy and theology at the seminary at Tübingen. At the age of seventeen, then a student of Herder, Schelling lectured on the philosophy of mythology, and in 1798 Goethe arranged for his appointment at Jena, where Schiller and Fichte were teaching. At Munich, where he taught the philosophy of mythologies and the philosophy of revelation, Platen was among his enthusiastic students around 1825. Schelling, along with Schopenhauer, was at that time, according to Winternitz, the philosopher most influenced by the *Oupnek'hat*. He shared Creuzer's belief that, thanks to research which had extended to the Vedas comparisons until then restricted to Greek mythology, the primitive unity of the human race was becoming a historical truth rather than a theological hypothesis. Subsequently, that science acquired the idea of "an original monotheism that, after the dispersion, supposedly became polytheism." Here again are the three ages: Schelling places the second, the age of progress in which he felt spirituality had taken precedence over the worship of natural forces, in India. "The content of revelation was not different from that of mythology nor from that of the religion to come. The natural gods were not made of a different substance from the supernatural God. . . . Christ already existed before the revelation, but he was a cosmic force 'in the world.' "[17]

This was the outcome, both logical and fantastic, of the entreaty that had been made for more than a century by both Christian and Hindu spirituality. Since the first contacts, westerners had been struck by the similarities of doctrines and legends; now in addition there were not only moral congruences but similar poetic conventions, a powerful lever on souls accustomed to a personal God. It was in a Germany literarily awakened by Rousseau and Diderot and philosophically attached to its mystics via Neoplatonism that "personal feeling" became the highest authority. A powerful "league of faith" operated against the Aufklärung: "In the name of philosophy and history, Hamann, Herder, the poet of history, Jacobi, the philosopher of feeling, challenged the conclusions of a negative science." Out of this came Brentano, "this half madman and half poet, and Hoffmann," the creator of a popular mysticism of terror and presentiment.[18]

As for myths, even Otfried Müller, who offered such resistance to the oriental and the subjective, wrote in 1825, having by then become steeped in Herder, that "what is primitive in religion is not its speculation on dogma but its imprecise feeling of the divine." This calls to mind that statement of Georg Brandes, "The religion of the romantic is the aspiration for religion." Until Goethe's *Divan* one could, according to Lichtenberger, detect "the conviction that a principle common to all religions existed and that it was this principle which was the truly sacred element in religion."[19]

For Schleiermacher, as for the entire circle around Novalis, the source of all religion "can be found," according to Ricarda Huch, "in the unconscious or in the Orient, from whence all religions came." We should note the association: the Orient of these dreamers was very much the home of dreams, the two concerns being linked. Yet in Schleiermacher's 1799 *Uber die Religion*, oriental religions appeared only furtively, an unaccustomed sign of discretion for this group. Nevertheless, Schleiermacher wrote, "The Holy Scriptures have become the Bible through their own force, and they do not prohibit any other book from also becoming a Bible." When we remember that the Veda was to be christened "the Bible of the Aryans," everything becomes clear, and the expression takes on a concrete meaning. The books that had just been discovered in India demonstrated that the area of revelation was not confined solely to the past, and the Schelling-Schlegel circle, for whom the time of revelation was still open, accepted them as proof. Schelling retained Creuzer's idea that the pure primitive religion had fragmented into shining stars. Like Schelling, Schlegel thought it remained to reconstruct the primitive holy unity. It was from such bases, as well as those of Fichte and Hegel, that the young science of orientalism was to promote unitarian ideas.

For a time it seemed as if Friedrich Schlegel would be the one to formulate the new religion. He followed cautiously in the footsteps of Herder and Maier at a time when "Orient was becoming a magic word for the German spirit. Hölderlin dreamed of a 'Dionysian' Asia as the source of all regeneration. Novalis, one of the initiates of whom Friedrich Schlegel spoke, raised his eyes toward the Orient, from whence the light would come. . . . It was in the Orient," that is to say, India, "where the true treasures of romantic poetry lay, an 'esoteric' poetry which seemed to grasp, beyond the human sphere, the nature of the universe."[20] Insofar as oriental specialization and religious belief became explicit in the works of the most active representatives of the group, one sees more clearly how spiritual concerns were applied to literary interests.[21] Before his conversion in 1808, Schlegel displayed an almost occult prescience and was tempted by the pantheism that Heine later said was "the open secret of Germany." Heine, who in April 1823 announced that he had spent the entire winter studying "the non-Semitic portion of Asia" and reading Schelling and Hegel, implied that through their Catholicism his friends were reawakening the pantheism of the ancient Germans. Schelling's theory on "the spirituality of the material" was significant in relation to occultism, and to magic itself, and was not very far removed from Baader or the memory of a tradition embracing Paracelsus, Boehme, and Hamann.

Naturally, enough confusion existed over Schlegel's work that the pure Indic scholars would style him a "hierophant," but his zeal in 1808 was that of a sincerely orthodox man. Thus after his example had demonstrated incongruities in the hopes that had first been raised in the wake of the new oriental studies, he showed how certain of those hopes held promise of interesting the Church itself. "The enthusiastic hope of a general Christian restoration," of which he wrote in the foreword to *The Philosophy of History* in 1825, was later repeated in the works of his disciple Eckstein, along with the theme of universal revelation. And Schegel carefully specified where he had gotten his idea: he listed the names of Champollion, Rémusat, Colebrooke, "my brother A. W. Schlegel, and the two Barons von Humboldt," a definitive confirmation of his 1808 essay. Madame de Staël had already written, "The philosophy of the Indians can only be thoroughly understood through the German idealists, whose similar opinions aid them in conceiving it."[22] If it was not Friedrich who convinced them, it would have been "my brother A. W."

For Friedrich Schlegel the revelation was "an altered or misunderstood revelation" arising from "a manifestation of interior feeling." According to Eckstein, who sought "an anterior Christianity" in "the antiquities of paganism," it was "the primitive revelation, the foundation of natural religion." These views were widely held at the time and soon took their place in Lamennais's great scheme of unification. On August 15, 1823, Maine de Biran noted in his journal, "The philosophers of the most distant antiquity taught, with a marvelous accord that seems to give proof of the origin of a shared tradition, the unity of a reason supreme, universal, and creative." And he referred to Rémusat's memoir on Lao Tzu, a philosopher whose "reason" was very close to the "universal consent" of Mencius. We should understand that the idea of the primitive was becoming the mainspring of spiritual hope. Just as India gave assurance that there had been a body of poetry before that of the schools, it was believed that a religion had been discovered there which predated that of the churches.

Ozanam was one of the young people through whom, while the century was still young, we can measure the impact of the first oriental discoveries. Lamennais had annotated Anquetil and Jones in 1807 at the age of twenty-five; Ozanam was not yet seventeen in 1831 when, while inaugurating a similar scheme to demonstrate the truth of Catholicism through historical studies, he sought a primitive revelation "across regions and centuries . . . exhuming all the myths, from the savages of Cook to the Egypt of Sesostris, from the Indians of Vishnu to the Scandinavians of Odin." For this adolescent, "a question of obligation, *What is the religious future of humanity?* developed, became clear, and gave way to a question of fact, *What was the primitive religion?"* And he indicated his instructors explicitly: on September 4, 1831 he wrote, "The *Mithridates* of Adelung, the symbolism of Creuzer, the works of Champollion, of Abel Rémusat, of Eckstein, of Schlegel and Görres, give us rich mines to exploit." Three months later on December 18, he enlarged his list with significant references, setting the rationalist school against the school called the *traditional,* "not because it has broken away from reason, but because history is its base, and tradition is the point of departure for its methodology. In its ranks appear Chateaubriand, Lamennais, Eckstein, Ballanche, de Bonald and, from Germany, Schlegel, Baader, Stolberg, and Görres." Again the hope of regenerating society through a sound interpretation of primitive religions. Finally, on January 7, 1834, he announced that he had just completed two articles on India for the *Revue Européenne.* Then, on February 5, 1835: "I am now rather seriously studying Hebrew and Sanskrit." At that point he was in Paris and had met Eckstein.[23]

The period between 1780 and 1830 should be viewed as half a century of young people, all ready to give the world a new beginning: the past that was emerging could not be considered dead, for it advanced under the banner of the future. Fulfillment of the desires of artists and believers was anticipated from it. One of the principal reasons for India's success was that India was not regarded as something to look back on, but rather as something in which to seek the future. The discoveries the specialists were making became the growing tip of a new, extraordinary life: it was felt that poetry, and perhaps even religion, would take on entirely new aspects. The prestige they drew from the memory of their origins merged with the intriguing romance of deciphered scripts and rediscovered worlds. This exhilaration was also felt by the generations which understood, better than ever before, that no one had ever resembled them. This produced an excitement about ideas that can only be compared to the excitement of our contemporaries for the world of technology.

Part Four

THE PERSONNEL

CHAPTER NINE

Well-Prepared Ground

W E have already glimpsed, at more than one crossroads, the avenues connecting Germany and France. Everyone knows how many charms, and then how many misdeeds, the children of the century saw in a neighbor they discovered only belatedly. Compared with a Germany bent on changing the climate of Europe, India had a faraway beauty to recommend it; for France the recommendation was at least twofold, since the Indic world that came to France from Germany had come to Germany via England at a time when, all at once, the German mind represented a new realm of ideas. Literary appetites were particularly whetted by the dissimilar and the foreign, and the appetite for mystery was completely revived after a spiritual fast lasting for more than a century that had ended in a series of deaths. It was a stroke of good fortune that the arrival of India in Europe coincided with the birth of Romanticism—India, which so resembled the romantic half of the human spirit.

The Generations of Sensibility

In nineteenth-century France the generations of the first three decades judged, yearned for, took inspiration from, and especially dreamed through the memories of Madame de Staël and Chateaubriand, two great figures of the Romantic *avant garde*. Now, between 1800 and 1820, the same years that marked the first steps of French Romanticism, oriental studies made decisive headway in Parisian opinion. Apart from the two protagonists, another current also preceded Lamartine—that of Chénier and of Constant's autobiographical novel *Adolphe*. Thus the two movements—the one scholarly, the other creative—were associated from their beginnings. In France the scholarly movement had indeed preceded the other, and had probably cleared the way somewhat; by contrast, the initiatives of Indic studies and Romanticism were reversed in Germany. What laid the groundwork for it all was eighteenth-century intuition, à la Rousseau, which came more and more to efface eighteenth-century rationalism. At a time in France when the seeds of a new literature and belief were beginning to germinate, two voices, each enchanting in its own way, two geniuses at adaptation to circumstances, advocated the "vague des passions" and the life of the feelings, the one giving assurance that beauty would awaken belief, the other that the human species would bring itself to perfection. These two augurers, the one shaking off the Ossianic West, the other the Wertherian East, vigorously encouraged the intermingling of the primitive and the natural with the foreign. According to Nodier, Madame de Staël established for many minds that "Germany still has all the poetry and the greatness of a primitive people," while the Comtesse de Pange stated, "For more than thirty years *De l'Allemagne* was the Bible of the Romantics."[1] Silvestre de Sacy's son gave another account: "Madame de Staël's book, proscribed by the Empire, and read with enthusiasm by the naive youths of the Restoration, familiarized us with Germany."

There are a thousand indications confirming how faithfully Germanic lessons were repeated in the oriental domain. One example will suffice: in his review in the *Revue Encyclopédique* of April 1832, in the midst of the Indian vogue in France, Pierre Leroux invoked the Asian origins and the Aryan migrations in terms that seem completely uncharacteristic of a French writer. Yet the confusion is easily cleared up when one realizes that Leroux took the passage almost verbatim from Schlegel: "We, the men of the North" (the opening is significant), "we have forgotten our Ossianic lays and our old epics, based on those traditions which themselves were borrowed from the Orient but transformed by our ancestors in the long pilgrimage that led them from the steppes of Asia to the northern fjords, who later spread them, like fertile seed, in Germany, England, Spain, and France." The meaning is clear: the epics alluded to are the Eddas and the *Nibelungenlied* as well as the *Chanson de Roland* (discovered in 1832), whose brothers were being rediscovered in the works of Valmiki and Firdausi. The ancestors referred to are the barbarians wronged too long by a false Renaissance.

In this way the strokes that modified and shaped the soul of the country and the times accumulated so that that soul would embrace everything that arrived in France: the French Soul of 1820–40 became Romantic, and that opened it to everything Indianism meant and conveyed. In his *Mélanges posthumes*, the sinologist Abel Rémusat denounced the collusion between Romanticism, orientalism, and Germanism with open irony: many people would take an interest in oriental literature even though "so many find our own literature old and exhausted. Many writers are trying to break trail far from the routes traced by Corneille, Pascal, and Fénelon, far from those tread by Racine, Bossuet, and Voltaire. Assuredly the Northern route is the quickest one by which to avoid their tracks, but the Oriental one might lead even further, and it would be a great misfortune to remain classical after visiting Chinese, Tartar, Arabic, and Hindu ways for a few years. A good many people have already gone on ahead, despite the fact the models have scarcely been glimpsed." Further on he exclaims, "Then let us seek, even if it be at the furthest ends of Asia, a mine that is rich and untouched . . . let us endeavor to be allowed to gather what we may in the vast fields of the oriental imagination, to take anything that strikes our fancy, to leave behind everything considered unreasonable, and especially everything that seems too reasonable. . . . In this way there will be complete satisfaction: we will sail ahead on the ocean of romanticism." With that word he lets the cat out of the bag: the oriental scholar Rémusat feared that the goal itself might provide the basis for literary modernism. "We will have something new, something bold, something extraordinary . . . and it is impossible that we will not have, out of the jumble of so many varied hues, an abundance of mutually incomprehensible words, and associations of ideas that by their nature are incompatible." It will be remembered that William Jones had already compared *Shakuntala* with Ossian, a relationship quickly repeated in the *Essai sur les Révolutions* and the *Génie du Christianisme*.

Chateaubriand

Chateaubriand should be praised first of all for having definitively discredited the prestige of rationalism, which went hand in hand with classicism. "He was the first," wrote Sainte-Beuve in his *Portraits Contemporains*, "to round on the eighteenth century, and he held up to it an unexpected shield dazzling with light." And Taine wrote in *Nouveaux essais de critique et d'histoire*, "The effect was enormous. . . . Truth became obliged to be poetic rather than literal." Renascent literature would become associated with several requests that originated in Chateaubriand's 1802 *Génie du Christianisme* and that logically furthered the scholarly renaissance: anticipation of a great religious tide, veneration of a distant past in which historical understanding expanded, and an invitation to a cultural uprooting that was seen or expressed as a kind of emancipation. One wonders whether the oriental mode would have so quickly and so forcibly affected Hugo, Lamartine, and Quinet if it had not come to them during the 1820s, when the influence of Chateaubriand was freshest and most active. Two major inducements were offered: the revival of religious belief and a poetry reinvigorated by sources far removed in time and space.

There was the promise of an Orient that approached the miraculous. It might, according to one's experience, come also from America or Asia Minor. For his part Chateaubriand struggled between India and Canada. The Orient that now appeared exceeded all expectation: oriental studies truthfully fulfilled a need that had given rise to a dubious Orient. It satisfied still another need that was not, at the time, inevitable in French literature nor common in any other: a craving for the grand. Without thinking or intending that it should benefit the pagans, Chateaubriand to a very large degree awakened this craving; and it was this craving, satisfied with incredible speed and fullness, that was fulfilled in a poetry of grandeur. In his critique of *Génie* Ginguené remarked that Chateaubriand had merely salvaged "the poetry of the prophets, the psalmist, and the hymnographers." This amounted to hollowing out, in the desert of *Henriades* and *Coras*, the place which the arrival of Hindu and Persian poetry would fill.

However, Chateaubriand accomplished something more specific: I have pointed out that in his first book, the *Essai sur les Révolutions,* and as early as 1797, he had introduced to France the new field of Sanskrit studies, then centered in London. Five years later in *Génie du Christianisme* his enthusiasm seemed somewhat refocused, precisely because it *was* the genius of *Christianity.* Here India only appeared to serve as a stepping stone, and *Asiatic Researches* served only to bear out that the *Lettres édifiantes* had uncovered everything worth finding. It would be difficult to imagine that Chateaubriand knew nothing of Friedrich Schlegel, if only through British intermediaries or through German symbolists, when he wrote in his chapter "De la redemption": "The secret was of such a divine nature that the first men of Asia spoke only through symbols. . . . Thus it is not at all surprising, given man's propensity for mysteries, that the religions of all peoples have their unfathomable secrets." He concluded by showing the essential elements of mystery in all religion, but not without stipulating that he did not intend to compare them "with the mysteries of the true religion." Here, as in all things, he played the role of herald; it would have been uncharacteristic of him to go back to the sources. He had blind confidence in Bouchet—the butt of Voltaire's jokes—who affirmed that "The Trinity is known" in India. He readily referred to the Asiatic Society of Calcutta, but seems to have gotten all his information from Robertson, as he had done in the *Essai sur les Révolutions.* Thus India could not be admired for herself; she served to verify the Gospels, and to make the "only Bible" stand out as "a monument apart from the others" and "completely unique." So much for a Bible of the Aryans. But this line of argument assumed the Indic event to be something already achieved, and it thus served to complete its installation.

Madame de Staël, Transmigrations and Palingenesis, Nodier

Madame de Staël in turn plumbed the well of desire in the decade following *Génie du Christianisme*. It was no accident she became a specialist in the coming and going between nations and passed on elaborate German passwords. She was a born genius of transition; she was Germanic at heart in her preference for the indeterminate, but above all in her passion to make a place for the unsuspected. However worthy of the great classics her personal art may have been, it is she who succeeded in destroying the classic formulary in France.

De l'Allemagne, her book on Germany, was the vehicle of the aesthetic launched forty years earlier in the manifestos of the *Sturm und Drang* movement: the supremacy of spontaneity, war against "the whigs," and the exaltation of the Gothic. A shared sense of the infinite brought about a lasting marriage between German religiosity and the *vague des passions* that remained one of the most captious things about *Génie du Christianisme*. The scattered allusions in *De l'Allemagne* are evidence of de Staël's grasp of Germany's poetic and mystic new wave, very close to the point where these innovations lapped upon those of orientalism. Recommendations of "the nocturnal side of nature" became commonplace and were repeated word for word by Hugo, who although he did not mention de Staël by name obliquely referred to "the German theosophist" to whom she had attributed this domain, and thus all the more clearly betrayed his source. De Staël represented Herder as bringing about "a rebirth of faith in poetry" in this way: "Deeply versed in oriental languages, he had a kind of admiration for the Bible similar to what might be inspired by a sanctified Homer." An apt phrase: nothing better describes Herder as a corrector of Lowth, and it was precisely this "kind of admiration" that French poets were to have for the holy books—and, to an extent, for all such books that came from Asia. It was the poets' adoration for a body of poetry that sanctified their own.

De Staël was the first to shed light on the role of Count Stolberg for French readers; Stolberg had, said de Staël, published a history of Christianity that brought into play "some extremely interesting research on the different religions of Asia." It was the first manifestation of a syncretism whose counterpart appeared in Stolberg's striking conversion—the Orient had led him to Catholicism. We will frequently encounter the tumult de Staël provoked: *tolle* among the Protestants, contagion in Eckstein and in Friedrich Schlegel and his wife, indignation in Goethe, and irony in Heine.

In the following chapter de Staël, logically, deals with "mysticité." She draws together Jacobi's interior sentiment, Herder's revealed poetry, Stolberg's oriental Christianity, and the theosophical revival then centered on

Jakob Boehme in Germany and taken up in France by Claude de Saint-Martin. In her discussion of the system of Schubert, one of Hamann's most conspicuous successors, de Staël stresses the theme that all the Romantics promoted and that came to characterize, as in Germany, their understanding of Indic studies: "It conceives nature as an ascendant metempsychosis in which, from the stone to human existence, there is a continual progression that advances the vital principle degree by degree until the fullest perfection is achieved." This then banal road of pantheism was also present in Friedrich Schlegel's *Allergötterei:* "All that exists is an outflowing from the divine; every being is a god, more limited, more wavering than the supreme god; all is inspired, living; everything is filled with gods." Thus in the 1808 essay Hindu thought was placed side by side with Platonism and Neoplatonism.

After 1804 Schelling, unlike Schubert, was tempted by a theory of descending and expiatory reincarnations. In the year of Schlegel's essay, Otto Heinrich, Graf von Loeben, an eccentric successor of Novalis, published a novel, *Guido,* under the pseudonym Isidorus Orientalis; Loeben identified himself with his hero, who was reincarnated as a stone, a spring, and a flower successively.

This calls to mind the verses

> Chaque fleur est une âme à la nature éclose,
> Un mystère d'amour dans le métal repose
> . . . Un pur esprit s'accroît sous l'écorce des pierres.

> Each flower is a soul budding in nature,
> A mystery of love lies in metal
> . . . A pure spirit grows within the husks of stones.

These *Chimères* by Nerval are dated 1845: by this time the theme of successive existences was already well worn among French Romantics. Lamartine had based his extensive cycle *Visions* on the idea of infinite return. He brought out this theme in episodes of *Chute d'un Ange,* which follows *Jocelyn* where we read:

> . . . Car dans l'isolement, mon âme qui déborde
> . . . Au monde végétal s'unit par sentiment,
> Et, si Dieu réduisait les plantes en poussière,
> J'embrasserais le sol et j'aimerais la pierre.

> . . . For, in isolation, my overflowing soul unites in
> . . . Feeling with the vegetable world,
> And if God reduced the plants to dust
> I would kiss the soil and love the stone.

I will return to cases of creative writers "oriented" by the scholars, notably that of Lamartine, who announced a "History of the human soul and its transmigrations from successive existences and trials, from nothingness to its reunion with the universal center, God." This is practically a repetition of the phrase that de Staël attributed to Schubert. And in the following lines in *Contemplations* Hugo came just as close to Schlegel's formula:

> La bête, le rocher, l'épi d'or, l'aile peinte,
> Tout cet ensemble obscur, végétation sainte,
> Compose en se croisant ce chiffre énorme: Dieu.

> The beast, the rock, the golden grain, the painted wing,
> All this obscure collection, sacred vegetation,
> Fuse to compose this enormous cipher: God.

But, contrary to prevailing opinion, the theme of reincarnation was, at the time of *Contemplations*, an old habit with Hugo and other poets; it was only revived in the 1850s by the popularization of Buddhism as elucidated by Hodgson and Prinsep. Straightway Indianism made its way in the West along the same route as pantheism. This is not surprising. But if it is a significant fact that the former rekindled an interest in the latter, it is even more important, contrariwise, that a ready-made pantheism awaited the arrival of Hindu "wisdom."

It must be remembered that the lucid editors of the *Lettres édifiantes*, to say nothing of Bernier the follower of Gassendi, were quick to point out the relationship of Vedanta not only to Platonic idealism but to Christian spiritualism. ("For my soul to see the great soul of the world" was already the final wish of the masterpiece of the Reformation, *Les Tragiques* of Agrippa d'Aubigné.) In 1777, seven years before the Asiatic Society of Calcutta, Bailly wrote in his *Lettres sur l'origine des sciences, et sur celle des peuples de l'Asie*, "we are indebted to the Brahmans for the idea of the universal soul," adding that "Malebranche, who taught us that we see everything in God, was, without suspecting it, merely a seventeenth-century Hindu." Such assertions were quite common in Bailly's contemporaries, in the work of Anquetil, and among Anquetil's readers. Madame Quinet portrayed her husband in this way: "Immersed in the study of German philosophy and of oriental antiquity, he was soon swamped by the torrents of pantheism. The pantheist doctrine, which gave a soul to every inorganic creation—stone, flower, star—is poetry itself. During that time everyone drank from that spring to the point of giddiness." She also quoted one of her husband's statements: "The exterior forms of the universe are simply the product of this creative force, the world-soul, which exists eternally, while its fleeting manifestations vanish like individuals or species," and she made no secret of the fact that everything that passed through Quinet's mind regarding "the dogma of pantheism" was in "the German style."

The case of Nodier is interesting for several reasons. He was the host at whose home poets like Hugo met orientalists like Pavie and Fouinet; he was also accused by Barbey d'Aurevilly of having disseminated and supported in France an idolatry handed down by the Schlegels. When Parisot's *Ramayana* was published, Barbey maintained that the Indic vogue was over and complained that it had been blinded by naïveté. He considered himself left in possession of the field and blasted the Schlegels and their French imitators for having propagated a mirage. As for Hindu poetry, he concluded icily, "There is none."[2] Sensitive to Indianism, Nodier was connected, through his meditations on naturalism, with the Cuvier cycle, which will be discussed later (Meyranx, on the occasion of the famous Balzacian debate between Cuvier and Saint-Hilaire, was under Nodier's command at the Arsenal). In Nodier's writings we see the effects of Volney, with his taste for universal alphabets, and of Gébelin, with the history of speech, of German idealism, and of secret societies.[3] The traces of metempsychosis, more or less evident as Nodier's work progressed (notably in *Adèle,* 1820), led to the frantic profession of faith in *Palingénésie humaine* in 1832. Before being combined with *Rêveries,* this strange piece had been published by the *Revue de Paris* in the summer of 1832, at the height of the terrible cholera epidemic that so greatly influenced both literature and the imagination. Obsessed by the plague and himself ill and alone, long believing himself at death's door, Nodier forged a system which he did not doubt resulted from a sudden enlightenment and a perception of "the obvious nature of truth." He wrote about it with the joy of a "child soul" to his old friend Charles Weiss on July 21, 1832, stating that this thought had become for him more certain and "clearer than the sense of [his] own existence."

Here Indian reincarnation was amalgamated with or substituted for theories of physics found in the research of Werner, Schelling, and Baader on the unique principle of materialized spirit. The answer to the universal riddle was that creation did not end with man, that man was the precursor of a superior kind of being which man was merely the preliminary step toward. Nodier drew a child's conclusion from metempsychosis: universal life, which began as a mineral, did not end with the mammal that was, up to that point, the most complete; the prolongation of the series was no longer sought by a spiritual man in a world beyond, but was rather maintained to be within nature by a pupil of the naturalists. In addition, Nodier could say that in providing the explanation for "the whole of creation, with its beginning and its end," he was "committed to follow, in the footsteps of Cuvier, an intelligent idea embodied in the mysteries of the ancient world." He especially kept alive the work of Charles Bonnet, one of the first to have introduced the term "palingénésie" in the eighteenth-century and a brilliant natural philosopher whom Cuvier himself admired; Bonnet pursued great schemes at Geneva analogous to those of the mineralogist Werner. Here, explicitly, Nodier gave the whole line: "The sages of India, and after them Pythagoras, Charles Bonnet, and Kant, who are the three greatest geniuses of all time, all perceived something of it; Cuvier did too, but the chain broke in his hands and he dared not repair it. I am holding the chain, I am sure of it, and not a single link is missing." Here, in the end, one detects the tone of a reader of the Illuminati.

Nodier's allusion to Cuvier is precise: the founder of paleontology had become interested in reopened chronologies through his knowledge of India; but here again the strong convictions of the pastor made him unshakable on the authority of Moses and the biblical genealogies. In welcoming him into the Académie française in 1818, the Comte de Sèze celebrated him as the author of "the admirable discourse" on the revolutions of the globe, in which he "demonstrated that immense chain that ties together in a world-system the evidence of nature, historical documents, folk traditions, and our religious monuments" and "proved to what a great extent this system agrees with the inspired narratives of Moses." On the other hand, Cuvier's scientific temperament caused him to oppose the enthusiasms that supported the notion of the primitive; he held with the Greek idea of an infancy of humanity that had poetry as its mode of expression. Thus, without intending to, he preceded the Positivists, who considered the theological age the age of stammering. In his speech answering Sèze's welcome, Cuvier cited "these people on the banks of the Ganges whom the same principle causes to revolve in the circle of eternal childhood," and stated as proof of this notion that he believed they were not "disencumbered from the restraint of poetic meter." Nodier's bizarre hypothesis concerning the man of the future certainly did not pass unnoticed, and it must have been spread about even before the publication of *Palingénésie humaine,* since as early as January 1831 Frédéric Ozanam, a student at Lyons, adopted it, modifying it to conform with his own beliefs.[4]

With Bonnet in 1769 it had been *Palingénésie philosophique;* with Ballanche in 1827 it was *Palingénésie sociale,* and with Nodier in 1832 it was *Palingénésie humaine,* not to mention others (Restif de la Bretonne, for example), which demonstrates how solid the chain was. The first link was in "philogistic" and other systems that, especially in the German atmosphere, inflamed the minds of good calculators. The last link can be found in other consequences determined by the revival of similar ideas in Fourier's *Théorie de l'unité universelle*. These were all themes similar to those we will see in nineteenth-century speculation, if only in certain pages of Michelet's diary (Bonnet also influenced Vigny and Balzac).

The three or four great names mentioned by Nodier are a perfect indication of what was both possible and confirmed at that time with regard to confluences among three currents whose force it would be difficult to exaggerate: the awakening of a pantheist mystique, the vigor of the new physical sciences, and the humanism newly completed by India. The mechanisms of such phenomena of collective psychology begin to be glimpsed today. According to Béguin, in certain climactic ages, "the same rhythm recalls to the surface of human consciousness . . . three tendencies joined together by affinities which are, in general, unsuspected. The tendency is for irrational knowledge to find its expression in cosmogonic myths, in doctrines of universal correspondence, and in all that the occult tradition develops under the name of alchemy, numerology, and so forth. The next tendency, derived from the above, is toward a decipherment of nature from which the individual sciences are born. The final tendency, by another derivation from the same source, is to assume that poetic imagination is capable of revealing the true and hidden structures of the universe.

"These perspectives, however reckless they may be, singularly alter the modern outlook, according to which we are in the habit of allowing, for example, that the various occult 'mystiques' of the eighteenth-century developed merely as an irrational reaction against the dominant philosophy of the Encyclopedists or, to take another example, that in the nineteenth century the belief in the indefinite progress of science and the religious orientation of the poets were in total opposition."[5] Nothing applies more appropriately to the state of mind at the turn of the eighteenth and nineteenth-centuries: a keen appetite, followed by a scientific gluttony during and after the merry feast of the Directoire; esoteric or poetic explanations of the world in which the flames of occultism are reflected or in which the temptations of magic appear unexpectedly to lie behind science and faith.

The theme of transmigrations was such a commonplace of Romanticism that it became a mark of originality to take the opposite view. Baudelaire did not miss his chance: "We know very well," he wrote in 1852 to Fernand Desnoyers when sending him four poems, "that I am incapable of becoming emotional about plants, and that my soul is rebellious over this odd new religion which will always have, it seems to me, something shocking about it to all *spiritual* beings. I can never believe that the *soul of the gods lives in plants*, and even if it did live there, I would not worry much about it, and I would consider my own soul of a much higher value than sanctified vegetables."[6]

India and the Occult: Joseph de Maistre and Lamennais

It was not surprising that the sentient God of the German pietists found favor in a France born of Rousseau and Diderot, since the origin was in part common to them both. Since the religious revival was accompanied by pseudo-mystical dilations, Hindu spirituality, as soon as its terms became clear to European eyes, was drawn into compromises with Neoplatonism, mysticism, and occultism. In the eleventh and final interview in the incomplete *Soirées de Saint-Petersbourg* of Joseph de Maistre (1821), the Senator, one of the participants, links the issue of Illuminism to that of the pagan oracles and biblical prophecy. He recognizes the importance of the movement and the seriousness of its intention; Maistre himself, of course, would probably have grave reservations, since the sect was outside the Church; yet he would neither forget nor deny the connections there had been and the memories he retained of them. One feels that the conversation is taking place between two lobes of the same mind. The name of "the chevalier Jones" appears in the first conversation, and he is mentioned again in the last. At every step of Maistre's *Correspondence*, William Jones, the *Asiatic Researches*, and the *Laws of Manu* are bound up with the hope of a Christian awakening, and the whole work breathes a call for global unity.

Masonic lodges, to which Maistre had belonged, were very active at the time and took an interest in the philosophical and esoteric aspects of the Indic discovery. Millin slips this curious regret into one of the first articles which popularized Indic studies, that in the *Magasin Encyclopédique* in 1803: "All the secrets of ancient Hindu Freemasonry have disappeared in the face of the constant tenacity of the Calcutta Society." Theosophy gained ground in Masonic circles, which were hostile to materialism and interested in a magic to which animal magnetism seemed to contribute a scientific base. A large number of German orientalists were affiliated with such secret societies: Herder with the Order of the Illuminati at Weishaupt, Klaproth and Forster with the Rosicrucians. In France the initiations affected writers such as Cazotte and Senancour. The latter's attraction to themes of the period was shown by his *Rêveries sur la nature primitive de l'homme*, which began to appear in 1799 (they did not reach final form until 1823), and he discussed oriental doctrines in his *Libres méditations* in 1819.

An instructive case in point is that of Starck at the end of the eighteenth-century. He began by learning, among other things, oriental languages from Michaelis, who was also Forster's teacher and, later, Wilhelm Schlegel's father-in-law. Starck himself taught oriental languages at Saint Petersburg in 1763 and was, in addition, a very active Freemason.

In 1766, he converted to Catholicism at Paris in the Church of Saint-Sul-pice; at the time he was interpreter of oriental manuscripts at the Biblio-thèque du Roi. In his *Hephestion* in 1775 he asserted that true paganism was "the esoteric religion of the mysteries" whose origin he placed "in Egypt, in Tibet, in India, everywhere there was a strongly organized priestly caste." All this served as a basis for Schelling, Schlegel, and Creuzer. Starck recommended to Duke Karl von Mecklenburg that he read, as a body, Porphyry, Iamblicus, the *Zend Avesta* of Anquetil, and Holwell on India. Starck meant to link the Masonic investiture with "the learning of Egypt and India."[7] These kinds of connections were becoming commonplace. Consequently, Starck excluded Judaism from the spiritual domain on the grounds that it had "nothing hidden or interior, nothing that could be the secret of the priests and the prophets."[8] And this sort of preemptory judgment certainly bore no less fruit in Germany, down to the time of Schopenhauer.

Lanjuinais is another very edifying witness. He gives us, notably, the connection between the Bonnet school and that of Saint-Martin—the nat-uralists and the supernaturalists. As part of one of the papers he gave at the Institut de France between 1810 and 1812 on Indic discoveries, he as-sociated the two prophets, when discussing *maya*, in order to comment on transmigration. Moreover, when following the commentaries that An-quetil himself had appended to the *Oupnek'hat* in 1801, he pointed out, "In the singular doctrine of modern theosophy, there are ideas strongly analagous to the Indian system of the *Oupnek'hat*." Anquetil, like many of his contemporaries, thought that these ideas had passed from India to Persia and then to Europe, and that they contained a single, albeit composite, truth. Lanjuinais stated this explicitly in regard to the Upanishads: "This system is really a blend of Spinoza and pantheism, theosophism or Illu-minism, quietism, and even idealism in the manner of Berkeley." He demonstrated each of these assimilations point by point.

What was the attitude of the theosophists themselves, who were faced with the simultaneous rediscovery of India and of Boehme and theoso-phy? In the eleventh year of the Republican calendar, 1803 in the Grego-rian, the year of Hamilton's arrival in Paris and the year after *Génie du Christianisme*, Saint-Martin, in *Le ministère de l'homme-esprit*, was enthusias-tic about "the numerous treasures that the literature of India is beginning to offer to us"—the *Asiatic Researches* (the editors of the time were often unaware that this title was that of a journal), the "Mahabarat," one hundred thousand stanzas, and the *Oupnek'hat* of Anquetil with excerpts from the Vedas. In fact, the idealistic pantheism of Saint-Martin corresponded with Vedic dualism. A piece written by a friendly hand and entitled "Re-cherches sur la doctrine des théosophes" was appended to the *Oeuvres*

Posthumes of the "unknown philosopher" in 1807 and meant to rank this doctrine in the great traditional lineage: here it was associated with not only Pythagoras but with "the Magi" and "the Brames," and with new quotations from the *Mahabharata* and the *Oupnek'hat*. This was not to insist on a provenance but to demonstrate, like the faithful Christian, truth through universality. "Europeans, in seeing the relations and striking similarities between the dogmas of India and those published by diverse European theosophists, will not suppose these theosophists have been in India to learn these things. The time is perhaps not far off when these Europeans" will plunge into these ideas, which were now guaranteed and clarified for them by the ideas in which they could see the origin of the Egyptian and Greco-Roman theogony. Thus at the beginning of the century, after twenty years of Sanskrit, there was clearly, in each domain, a promise of global unification.

In addition, since Saint-Martin always claimed to be orthodox, his "pensées" in the *Oeuvres* alluded to the universal revelation: "The fruits fall in the West, as to the foot of the tree, when they are ripe. The root has always been in Asia, and it is in Asia that, like a great river, this source has spread its waters over all the earth, so that all things could come and quench their thirst" (#201). A source, the Orient (above all "Aryan," the Orient of the Magi and the Brahmans), a river, the Tradition (and not the Church). Here theosophy agreed with an entire philosophy of history and religion that culminated in Schopenhauer and Gobineau. Saint-Martin's extraordinary influence provides a means of determining how much theosophy contributed to the furtherance of such ideas, and even to the prestige of Sanskrit.

Fabre d'Olivet wrote *Sage de l'Hindostan* and saw two divine envoys, "Ram and Krisnen" rise into view. They "penetrated [his] thoughts, foretold the future, and cured illnesses; everything, all nature, seemed submissive to them." Fabre enrolled them in the universal catalog of visionaries; his waking dreams of Indian metaphysics had a nostalgia similar to what had been felt for the lost tribes of Israel. Fabre traveled in Germany, where he met the philosophers of the day and where he was invested with the heritage of Jakob Boehme. In *La langue hébraïque restituée* in 1815 he took up the esoteric question again from a linguistic point of view. He established "three mother tongues, three oriental languages: Hebrew, Sanskrit, and Chinese." Viatte is right in stating that Fabre "shifted the center of human history and wisdom toward Asia," but it is an exaggeration to say that he was "the first." Friedrich Schlegel himself and his colleagues at Jena had at least Anquetil as their predecessor. In any event, Fabre "particularly indicated the fundamental tendency common to all initiates." His value for us is that his deduction that he was born in a period which had been made for him marks the coincidence of Illuminism with the decipherment of Sanskrit.

Most of the writers of the time had been influenced, one way or another, either by Fabre or, more probably, Saint-Martin. Between 1830 and 1834 the young Sainte-Beuve, an apprentice physician, crossed the domains of Saint-Martin, Lamarck, and Saint-Simon. These associations were proclaimed emphatically in *Volupté*, where he called Saint-Martin "the modern Solomon" and recalled that Lamarck's lectures were inspired but that he himself did not "embrace such overly simplified hypotheses." At Juilly, Sainte-Beuve heard Lamennais develop an extensive survey of modern knowledge. He noted, "The most exact logic, joined to the most rigorous orthodox base, opens a path between Saint-Martin and Baader." I have already briefly discussed Lamennais's position à propos Cousin's lectures on India. By 1807 Lamennais had accumulated pages of notes on the *Avesta*, the *Laws of Manu*, and *Asiatic Researches* with a view to a book that would lead to a reconciliation of all differences at Rome. In 1830–31, he returned to his study of these works in order to add fresh materials to his lectures, which later, in 1841, the year of *Génie des Religions*, became *Esquisse d'une philosophie*. It was in the flush of preparation for this that Sainte-Beuve drew the picture of an enthusiast extemporizing in the company of friends "A great work of religious philosophy . . . which by means of a completely rational approach promises to embrace the entire order of human knowledge on the basis of a simple notion of being." In this role of eager enticer, at which he excelled, Sainte-Beuve gives us some curious side glances at the Oriental Renaissance and its environs. It was Sainte-Beuve who later shed light on India's new adventures among the Saint-Simonians after it had passed from the foyers of the Martinists to those of the Fourierists.

Ballanche and the Saint-Simonian Orient: Leroux and Reynaud

Written in September 1834, Sainte-Beuve's account was close to the time of the events: it was around 1828 that the *Prolégomènes* of Ballanche brought "religious inspiration to the still materialistic Saint-Simonian school. As a witness to the effect this work produced on some of the more vigorous minds of the school, I can affirm the extent to which the effect was direct and immediate." Saint-Simon had at times taken an interest in the still-vague Orient; under the influence of the Illuminati, his successors modified his inspiration. Our splendid auricular witness took care to explain the origins of the new trend through Ballanche: "He is a Christian, that is to say, he believes in the revelation brought to the world once and for all by Jesus. . . . But he is a Neo-Christian in that he believes in successive interpretations of this dogma and in the increasingly far-reaching discoveries that human insight, progressively transfigured by ancient literature, must make." In his *Orphée* he contemplated "a kind of Genesis of high paganism," in which he "included all humanity outside the Judaic tradition and before history." Among those who echoed Saint-Simon's ideas I have mentioned, along with Chateaubriand, believers like Eckstein who later propagated these ideas of exterior and anterior revelation in conformity with the lessons of their German masters. And among these inspiring influences we find, once again, Saint-Martin: Ballanche, despite his reservations, made use of "expressions that must have been borrowed from the mysterious theosophist": the *Magianism of the word* and the *Magianism of man* in nature. And here again Charles Bonnet appears: Ballanche was indebted to him for "the very name and concept of palingenesis, the endless and ascending ladder of progressive existences."

Ballanche is wedged in a burl of the history of souls, like a workman behind the scenes. Long unknown to the general public, he was brought to fame in the 1830s specifically by the Saint-Simonian and Mennaisian upsurge. The general characteristics of his career make him a rather symbolic figure in the new Renaissance. Like Michelet, he was the son of a printer, a man from the provinces who became acclimated to the ways of Paris late. In 1816, according to A. Rastoul, he wanted to praise "the epic anterior to history," and took an interest in the Lowth of Herder. In the company of a group of friends, including Madame Récamier and Lacordaire, he went to the cemetery at Dieppe to read his *Vision d'Hébal* in which he proposed to give an outline of the history of the world; when this became an academic subject, he planned "a theodicy of history," the notes for which are still extant in the stack of his unpublished works. He was in a direct line with what Erdan called "historiosophy." Now, "early on," wrote Sainte-Beuve, he knew Fourier in his native Lyon. By 1809 he had read *Neuf livres* by the recondite and famous Coëssin, whom he later saw in Paris, where he also met Hoéne-Wroński, "who, in his *Prodrome* claims the honor of being the first to express, in 1818, a political view which the *Essai sur les Institutions* stated at the same time as he." Ballanche also had personal ties with Saint-Martin and Fabre d'Olivet, "whose ideas attracted him too" and from which "he profited." He had many descendants at Lyon: Jean-Jacques Ampère, Victor de Laprade, Blanc de Saint-Bonnet and, above all, Ozanam. Before lecturing on *Génie des religions* Quinet saw a good deal of Ballanche between 1829 and 1836.

Ballanche was the crossroads man *par excellence*. He continued the idealism of Novalis when he wrote in *Ville des expiations*, "The poetry of life is its true reality." He founded his utopia on a revelation similar to that of Schlegel and Creuzer: "One of our tenets . . . is that a single revelation, forever the same, has been modified according to the languages of the peoples, but that these are only surface alterations." Two themes were blended to produce a major undertaking, the production of a "Christian epic" entitled *La foi promise aux gentils* in which he linked up with the Christian missions to India. Moreover, the many ramparts of the mystical city were there as a reminder that "the general traditions are diverse expressions of the same idea." *Palingénésie sociale* established "the identity of the metaphysical ideas that lie at the root of Indic doctrines with those contained in the writings of our modern theosophists." Another junction: "Certain Germans, such as Görres, are seeking to reconstruct the myths of Asia, veracious dreams, in which nature was revealed to sleeping humanity." However, nothing in this period planted the idea of perpetual unity, of human identity, more deeply than the dream by which Ballanche influenced the utopians. He achieved little, and badly; he abounded in plans, but had only meager creative force. But many streams flowed from this ingenuous chemist of societies, soaked in mixtures of historical philosophy and mystical sociology. Heine, whose own afflictions enabled him to put his finger on the source of other people's troubles, maintained that Ballanche was much more loved than read, but to be read is not the only kind of luck, and probably not the best.

After a phase of "nervous accidents," which according to Sainte-Beuve brought on "the great climactic period in his life, the actual moment of *initiation*," Ballanche, who had been immersed until then in reading French mystic writers and Greek mythology, was affected by other "initiations"—Egyptian ones (Egypt was for a long time the popular initiatory climate, as witnessed by Cagliostro, *Die Lehrlinge zu Saïs*, and *The Magic Flute*). Relations with occultists followed. *Antigone* appeared in 1814; "One of his friends said to him, 'Do you know you have written a Martinist poem?' " Joseph de Maistre, an authority on the genre, wrote to the author interpreting the book "in a theosophical sense." Then the Orient took hold of him again, as it had his friend Fabre d'Olivet, through linguistics. In 1818 the *Essai sur les Institutions* plunged Ballanche into "the fundament theory of language." Sainte-Beuve said that this theory was "of major importance in his work" (as it was in the work of Bonald, who was also allied with the Illuminists at this time). According to Vialle, for Ballanche in *Palingénésie sociale*, "orientalism obtained legitimacy in the French mind: it is no longer an isolated theosophist but an Academician who proclaims the Orient to be 'our cosmogonic and intellectual birthplace,' who saw a pale reflection of India in Egypt, and the reign of immobility, the eternal source of dogma, in India." Ballanche asked that "the languages of the Orient" should replace Latin in "primary education."

"Shouldn't Sanskrit be taught in the schools, like Greek and Latin?" His *Essai sur les Institutions* stated, "The human mind must be capable of contemplating both the magnificent cosmogony of Moses and the elevated metaphysics of the Indic gymnosophists." His *Vision d'Hébal* (1831) stated, "Moreover, we will also include a commentary on the *Bhagavad Gita* in our synthesizing chart of humanity." Fabre d'Olivet's attitude toward India was also discussed at this point, as well as that of Eckstein. According to Viatte, "The Neoplatonics, the Sanskrit enthusiasts, profoundly modified his thinking. They helped crystallize the hazy Platonism of his early writings into a system."

Ballanche's attitude was a perfect indication of the link established at that time between the recent lessons of revolutions and wars and the philological revelations that fueled the philosophy of history. Barchou de Penhoën, in his article devoted to Ballanche in the *Revue des Deux-Mondes* in 1831, underscored the extent to which these two diverse events had become superimposed on each other: "New social worlds are clearly to be seen in our future, and those who walk at the head of nations have the mission to lead their peoples toward these new regions; at the same time, new worlds seem to be emerging hither and thither from the night of the ages, and are visible to the eyes of the Schellings, the Müllers, and the Hegels. . . . [Hegel's *Vorslungen über die Philosophie der Geschichte* was published that same year, and Barchou himself translated the German philosophers, all of whom were interested in India.] Thus, amid this multitude of events which in previous times would have filled centuries but which we have seen crammed into such a short timespan, some aspect of this accumulated history, some aspect unperceived by ordinary opinion, insignificant to it, was perhaps an immense and sudden illumination for Ballanche."

Hippolyte Carnot, one of the leaders of the reformed Saint-Simonian movement, explicitly confirms Sainte-Beuve regarding Ballanche's prophetic influence: "We were on the watch for any philosophical manifestation that had a religious bent. We held Ballanche's *Palingénésie sociale* in high esteem and extended our research to the works of the Unknown Philosopher and as far as the *Neuf livres* of Coëssin." There is yet another quarter in which occultism prepared the ground for India, which was soon to receive its best support from the Saint-Simonian journals and through articles written by the movement's most active adherents. "Saint-Martin . . . had died in 1803; Coëssin (1779–1843), an impassioned, impoverished man who had gone by the name Mucius Scaevola during the Revolution, had published *Neuf livres* in 1809. He followed this with a theory of social forms, and in 1810 he founded the Christian House, an organization intended to raise man to Christian perfection." In 1829 Carnot, who wrote the above, wrote, at least in part, the *Exposition complète de la foi* of the Saint-Simonians, in which one finds this article of a pantheism almost certainly influenced by the Upanishads: "God is one, God is all that is, all is in Him, all is through Him, all is Him."

Hippolyte Carnot was one of the many recruits the sect was enlisting at the Ecole Polytechnique; Michel Chevalier and Jean Reynaud were two others. Carnot and Pierre Leroux, an ex–printer's devil who joined the group under the patronage of Sainte-Beuve, were the orientalists of the set. Michel Chevalier was involved in 1832 with the plans for the *Système Méditerranéen*, whose goal was to reconcile, through a policy in the spirit of Enfantin, "the old dualism of spirit and flesh known as *Orient* and *Occident*."[9] Othello or steadfastness symbolized the one, Don Juan or fickleness symbolized the other; the one was the absolutist of morality, the other the anarchist of morality. Although a preposterous comparison, this was still a profound and ingenious outlook. When we have considered all sides of the Orient-Occident problem, we will be able to reconsider this one, an image, frivolous on the surface, containing a truth whose contrary had generally been accepted. The Orient rigid and faithful, the Occident fickle, nomadic; yes, this would be a proposition worth studying.

For the friends of Enfantin, the Orient was "an aspect of God," the Mediterranean "the nuptial bed of the Orient and the Occident." It was not only "old Judea" and "mysterious Egypt" that were dear to the hearts of the faithful, but India and China as well: "The Father had spoken to the West and the West had not understood. The East, the ancient land of the prophets, had, beyond doubt, heard. Enfantin felt an attraction toward the way of thought and speech of the great orientals. Among them, at least, one does not reason—one knows." Despicable logic and contemptible common sense were quite out of place in the Orient. "There," as Maistre stated, "science flies more than it walks and preserves, in all its aspects, something airy and supernatural." After the Saint-Simonians split into two groups headed by Enfantin and Bazard, the former sought "the Mother" in the Levant and then in Egypt, where they found Nerval's oriental instructor, Dr. Perron. Appointed by Muhammad Ali to direct the medical college he had created in Egypt, Perron learned Arabic and Persian and thereafter immersed himself in oriental literature: it was Perron who wanted to rewrite d'Herbelot. Maxime du Camp, the source for this information, was introduced to the group on his return from Egypt by Charles Lambert-Bey, whom he had met in Cairo. Perron also benefited from seeing the old Chevalier Jaubert, who had been drawn to Egypt principally by Enfantin's belief in successive existences and in "the diffusion of the soul throughout humanity." This was, decidedly, the major oriental attraction at the time. Gautier will provide us with further evidence of it among the Romantic writers.

But the second faction interests me more. Here, no sooner had Reynaud and Leroux served out their prison terms, which had terminated the trial of the Saint-Simonians, than they founded the *Encyclopédie Nouvelle*. Reynaud contributed articles on "Zoroaster" and, the usual association, "Druidism," which attracted considerable attention. In 1854 in a highly successful book, *Terre et Ciel*, he placed the ideas of stellar transmigration within the grasp of everyone; he had introduced these ideas in the *Encyclopédie nouvelle* in 1837 in the article "Ciel," which was reprinted in 1847 in *Considérations sur l'esprit de la Gaule*. On behalf of the Saint-Simonians the other, Leroux, had taken over the *Globe*, which had been founded in 1824 by Paul Dubois, the professor of Sainte-Beuve, and had supported the Romantic movement, especially by disseminating foreign literature. The *Globe* frequently had echoed Eckstein's articles in *Catholique*. It was in the *Globe* that Pauthier had made Hodgson's discoveries known in 1829. Leroux had become familiar with the ideas of Saint-Martin and Fabre d'Olivet through their followers. At the time of the schism, he and Carnot launched the *Revue Encyclopédique*, whose extremely important effect on the diffusion of Indic studies has been discussed. Leroux himself had published his own work in the *Revue* as well as that of several authoritative writers; one of his articles bore the significant title "De l'influence philosophique des études orientales." Again in this article one encounters the treaty concluded between historical and natural sciences after the French Revolution: Leroux held that oriental studies served humanity no less than the discoveries of physics and chemistry. This was an important statement, and one that would be repeated. As could be expected, ideological controversy was immediately aroused: to take up biblical studies again, as was being done, was all very well, but what was particularly required was "to familarize the disciples of the Bible with all the bibles of the Orient." It was the same old song: the Vedas were "the Aryan Bible." "When that is done, a new era will begin, for the human spirit will have changed its horizon and Christianity will have taken its place in history. It will have yielded the governance of human life to a more comprehensive religion." Here once again is the nineteenth-century persuaded that the world was on the verge of recommencing its religious life and, as always, thanks to the discovery of Sanskrit.

Something of this grand illusion was to remain in *Génie des religions:* before writing the book, Quinet had seen a great deal of Reynaud and Leroux. The same notion was even more pronounced in Michelet's *Bible de l'Humanité* and in his many religious outpourings. It was a basic theme of the Oriental Renaissance, and of a certain political circle: a Reformation tending toward laicizing Christianity. Leroux noted with regret that, before oriental studies, the Bible "had no analogues." The debate came to center on how far the analogies could be carried. In the end, Renan, as a man of letters and as a man of the Greek Renaissance rather than as a believer, asserted that the Bible and its unique prerogative of universality had not been undermined. According to Leroux, "the study of the Orient has, as it were, dispersed the Bible, as a prism disperses light. Each part of this marvelous anthology has at last found models to which it can be compared." The second Renaissance, announced Leroux, would produce the same effect as the first, a schism between two classes of mind: "On the one hand it will bring religious minds back to Catholicism; on the other it will complete the destruction of Christianity in favor of a new religion." Here, well informed, he noted that this had already happened in Germany and he stated categorically that the tendencies represented by Eckstein and his associates were the cause: "It is from this doctrine of a Christianity anterior to Christianity, which the German school has advanced, and from the use which the school of Lamennais has made of it, that logical weapons are being prepared today." This was confirmation by a lucid contemporary of genealogies that have become obvious to us.

More articles followed in the *Revue Encyclopédique*, showing the extent of the group's interest. To make this interest felt, Jean Reynaud, in the same issue of April 1832, seized a slender opportunity—the recent translation of Amaru by Antoine-Léonard de Chézy under the pseudonym A.-L. Apudy. In the following issue, for June, the *Revue* explained its philosophical program, à propos Fourier whose "epochs" were compared with the Indian "kalpas." In November there was a major article by Pauthier on the state of Indic knowledge which had come "to upset our historical and religious beliefs." His conclusion was, "We are taking part in the discovery of a new oriental world, the ancestor and precursor of our own." Finally, in May 1833, Reynaud published an account of Colebrooke's famous *Essays* which Pauthier had translated. Pauthier did a great deal; he was one of the first to sanction the Indo-Christian response which Rammohun Roy had given to Schlegel and Eckstein's Christo-Hindu endeavors.

The Hindu Response: Unitarianism and Rammohun Roy

At the other end of this reopened world an unfamiliar voice was rising that was to sound uncommonly loud. To this day, behind the patient work of scholars, the dialogue started then between the souls of two civilizations continues. It quickly caught the attention of scholars: Rammohun Roy was quoted by Lanjuinais as well as by Langlois. In 1832, the same year as his stay in England, Burnouf paid Roy an extensive tribute in the *Journal des Savants*, as Pauthier did in the article mentioned above and in his presentation of Colebrooke. The occasion for doing so arose from the publication of Roy's fragmentary and annotated translation of the Vedic texts in London. Before 1820 this high-born Hindu, who at a very early age had set out to learn Latin, English, and the language of the Bible, boldly sought to reconcile Vedism with the Gospels. Here is an astonishing symmetry with a certain Romantic Christianity! In the early part of 1831, Roy's initiative prompted the emperor of Delhi to send the reformer on a mission to Europe; there he made long-lasting contacts in theological and learned circles.

The following year, 1832, the year of numerous articles in the French journals, Roy went to Paris. His visit attracted a great deal of attention; even Jules Bloch's suggestion that he was received by Louis-Philippe seems plausible. He undoubtedly spoke French badly and resolved to return after having learned it better, but death at Bristol in November 1833 intervened. Yet one cannot imagine that his English would pose any problem to educated Parisians interested in India. Burnouf, notably, who had English friends, would certainly have taken advantage of such an Indian contact since he had not been able to travel there. And in the ordinary course of things, Roy must have taken an interest in the Saint-Simonians—at least in Pauthier, who belonged to both groups. According to Romain Rolland, Roy's "journals were enthusiastic" about the revolutionary cause in various European countries, particularly "in revolutionary France in the days of July 1830." Hippolyte Carnot, one of the founders of the *Revue Encyclopédique*, had fought during the Three Glorious Days (July 27–29, 1830). In an article by Pauthier, the *Revue Encyclopédique* proclaimed the significance of Roy and the movement he represented. Here was an extraordinary undertaking which, above all, could not have been conceived during any other age of the world, and which spoke of a new age to the innovators. It is well worth seeing how, and from where, this movement arose.

Europe's knowledge of the Upanishads through Anquetil has as its origins a Hindu unitarian attempt that foreshadowed and made possible Roy's efforts. In 1665 the Mughal prince of Delhi, Muhammad Dara Shikoh, eldest son and heir apparent of Shah Jahan (r. 1628–58), wanted to compare the sacred books of all peoples in order to attain and adopt the ultimate truth. Such a desire went back as far as Milinda and continued through Tolstoy. Dara had Moses, the Psalms, and the Gospels explained to him. Not satisfied with that and having heard of the Vedas, he summoned the ascetics of Banaras to instruct him in Brahmanical doctrine. For this occasion he ordered a remarkable version of the Upanishads made in Persian, the lingua franca of Asia at that time. It is this text that, in the following century, found its way to Anquetil through the efforts of Gentil and that Anquetil retranslated between 1776 and 1796, first into French and then into Latin, and published in 1801–2. As good historical fortune would have it, the same pandit-scholar who had been Dara's principal translator also became Bernier's most valuable instructor, and Bernier, as I have mentioned above, brought a separate manuscript of the *Oupnek'hat* to France. Two years after beginning his daring religious comparisons, Dara was assassinated by his brother Aurangzeb. Dara's liberties with the law of the Prophet came at a perfect time to serve Aurangzeb's calling as a usurper. But, once again, the work that Dara had initiated impressed an important adept: it was this text which a century and a half later fell into the hands of Rammohun Roy, and which he, in turn, translated and annotated in local dialects and English. It must be said that shortly after his birth the example of such parallels had been established by William Jones, who himself had become a student of the Brahmans Radhakanta Sarman and Sarvoru Trivedi: the Hindus were moved by Jones's sincere desire to know their true beliefs. They soon became the pupils of their disciples, whose processes they adopted, beginning with the printing press, an instrument whose diffusion always rendered a critical spirit inevitable within a short time.

Born in Bengal into a family of Brahmans around 1772 but receiving his first education from Sufis, Roy learned Persian and Sanskrit, Hebrew and Greek at an early age and wrote English with facility. In 1804 he inherited a considerable fortune from his father. His first book, *"Tuhfatu'l-Muwah-hidin,* or *A Gift to Monotheists,* was a theological tract in Persian, the main contention of which was that people attach too much importance to particular forms of religion and forget that falsehood is common to all faiths, since all are dependent on fallible human teachers for interpretation."[10] Spurned as much by Hindus as by Muslims, he withdrew to Calcutta in 1814, held a job for a time in the Bengali administration, and resolutely devoted himself to the monotheistic reformation of the local religion. Contemplating a fusion, he founded the Atmiya Sabha in 1815 and from that time forward propagated the belief in, according to Burnouf, "a single God, eternal, infinite, who demanded no other form of worship from his adherents than the practice of a strict morality." In the Vedic excerpts translated into Bengali, Hindi, and English, Roy wanted to show "the purest deism," as Burnouf would say, or "a Hindu theism," as Pauthier expressed it. Taking up his message from the other end, in 1820 Roy published, at the Baptist Mission Press in Calcutta, *The Precepts of Jesus, the guide to Peace and Happiness: extracted from the Books of the New Testament ascribed to the four evangelists. With translations into Sungscrit and Bengalee.* Attacked by Marshman, an English missionary from Serampore, he issued three *Appeals to the Christian Public* "on behalf of the independence of morality" in which he maintained that the dogma of the Trinity was not to be found in either testament and that it amounted to a form of polytheism. His *Translation of an Abridgment of the Vedant, or the Resolution of all the Veds* appeared in Calcutta in 1816, and two Upanishad translations (the *Mandogya* and the *Katha*) in 1819. All these works were soon known in Europe, not only in England, where Roy arrived in 1831, but in France as well. (My source here is the important pages Burnouf devoted to him in the *Journal des Savants* for December 1832, prior to Pauthier's reference to them the following year in his appendix to his translation of Colebrooke; Guigniaut had already noted the importance of Roy's work in 1825.) Roy appealed to a purity of "primitive worship" against its later distortions, especially in *A Defense of Hindoo Theism in Reply to the Attack of an Advocate for Idolatry at Madras* (1817), *A Second Defense of the Monotheistical System of the Vedas in reply to An Apology for the Present State of Hindoo Worship* (1817), and *An Apology for the Pursuit of Final Beatitude, independently of Brahmunical Observances* (1820). The celebrated Brahmo Samaj (Church of the Supreme Being) was created in 1828. Like the Romantics, Roy denied any suggestion of syncretism; he wanted to go to the universal root of faith. Burnouf acknowledged Roy's sincerity, but was still waiting to see if Roy had not "allowed himself to be preoccupied with a systematic hidebound idea." It is not surprising that a linguist paid particular attention to nuances of vocabulary: he doubted whether the word "God" corresponded exactly with the sense of "Brahma," whether "a Christian would accept the definition the Hindus give to their god as *soul of the world.*" This distinction concerning the true extent of the concept of unity was one it would be necessary to return to frequently: "If *Brahma* is termed *unique,* it is in the sense of a single soul, into which all individual souls return, animating and supporting nature. *The unity attributed to him is more a notion of totality than one of true unity.*" I emphasize Burnouf's brilliant formula for to me it seems to dispell most of the confusions concerning pantheism in which so many Romantics took pleasure.

In Pauthier's articles in the *Revue Encyclopédique*, the hope was for a simply human event, the advent of a unified humanity; this, he wrote, was "the first link that ties the oriental world to the occidental world." Five months before in the same revue Leroux had declared: we are seeking "a broader Pantheon, a Pantheon commensurate with the word *Humanity,* so recently invented, with this notion which men confined within the limits of family, caste, or nation in times past never knew." He concludes: "The present must be reconnected not to a portion of the past but to all the past if it is to be catapulted into the future." An outstanding characteristic of the enthusiasm for Hindu thought in the Romantic period and one that cannot be overstressed, contrary to prevailing opinion, is this interest taken in the things of life: India was embraced as a reservoir of facts that were not outworn but perpetual, of forces that held out a possible future for each sect and school in the West. The importance of India to the Saint-Simonians was confirmed by their opponent Louis Reybaud. He pointed out the influence of Pauthier's translation of Colebrooke on them; he attacked the Vendantist accent of the formula, mentioned above, which Carnot had included in his *Exposition de la foi*. According to this hostile witness, a Hindu "hodge-podge" had supposedly given the Saint-Simonians the means of dispelling what they termed "the Catholic dualism," that is to say, the means of reconciling spirit and flesh. In this they linked themselves to ancient chimeras being revived in Germany. Reybaud, who had been a merchant in India, wrote the following outburst under the pseudonym Jérôme Paturot in 1842: "Wherever one goes, one steps on a messiah."

Taine and Barbey D'Aurevilly

Max Müller himself later saw a current of living water and a dream of a new religion in India, and perhaps the whole world, in the kind of effort that Roy represented. In his *Nouveaux essais de critique et d'histoire* (1865), Taine hailed the efforts of the Saint-Simonians presented in Reynaud's *Terre et Ciel*: "A few Christians are taking a step toward philosophy, and several philosophers are taking six steps toward Christianity. Among all the schemes being exchanged, that of Reynaud seems to us the most worthy of attention. He gives voice to a tendency in public feeling and in this respect deserves full study. . . . Reynaud is a mathamatician, formerly a Saint-Simonian, who, after having begun a sort of encyclopedia with Pierre Leroux, has recently collected and developed his philosophical views in a formal body of doctrines." Reynaud creates a dialogue between theologian and philosopher. "He holds out one hand to Saint Augustine, the other to Herschel." Taine, like others, saw evidence for nothing more than "conciliatory and unfruitful overtures." But he ascertained, "Everywhere one sees extended hands and offers of marriage"—a phenomenon reminiscent, in its two essential causes, of a hellenistic prefiguring of orientalized Romanticism: "The vogue of oriental prophets, especially since the second century," wrote Filliozat, "was linked to a decline of rationalism.

We can say further that this vogue is not to be explained solely as a phenomenon within the evolution of hellenic culture. It was also due to the fact that, at the very time traditional ideas were no longer sufficient, a real influx of data regarding the Orient took place."[11]

The collection of essays that included Taine's article on Reynaud in 1865 (very close to the *Vie de Jésus*, 1863, and the *Bible de l'Humanité*, 1864) also contained an essay on Buddhism and another on Franz Woepke: the Orient in fact occupied a considerable portion of the *Nouveaux Essais*. Buddhism was brought up again by the publication of Köppen's *Die Religion des Buddha und ihre Entstehung;* the critic referred not only to Wilson and Colebrooke but to Burnouf and Spence Hardy's *Manual of Buddhism.* It was, as we know, the Buddhist vogue brought about by Hodgson and Prinsep that revived the interest in Indic matters at this time. This allure alarmed a great number of minds then as well. In 1858 in his study *Le Bouddha et sa religion,* the unmoved Barthélemy Saint-Hilaire deplored the fact that India was exciting the passions of too varied a clientele. "It is unfortunate that at this point in time the doctrines which are the basis of Buddhism meet with such high esteem among us, an esteem of which they are unworthy. For some years we have seen the rise of systems in which we are told of the glories of metempsychosis and transmigration." Here Saint-Hilaire hesitates: this was an allusion to Reynaud among others, and also, later on, to Schopenhauer, for whom the vogue began at the same time.

Another thundering objection was voiced by Barbey d'Aurevilly when he attacked the translation of Valmiki published by Victor Parisot in 1853 and criticized Reynaud in 1854: "The distinguished author could find nothing more forceful to do than gather together from the dust of humanity's dreams which are the most corroded by the centuries and the most transparently deluded, the system ruminated by India—this philosophical cow—of a progressive metempsychosis that sentences man to the galleys in perpetuity and makes mincemeat of his immortality!" And again: "This laughable system of metempsychosis is worthy, at the most, of inspiring a song from the Marquis de Boufflers or Béranger." According to Barbey, Reynaud's book "cribbed most of its material" from Maistre's *Soirées de Saint-Petersbourg* in which we have seen memories of India and of the Illuminati. Under the heading "Writers and Religious Philosophers" in Barbey's *Les Oeuvres et les Hommes* are also significant articles attacking Saint-René Taillandier for undermining religion by means of hypocritical syncretisms, attacking Caro for his *Saint-Martin,* and Renan for *L'origine du langage.* Barbey denounced all of them for circumventing the truth and swamping it with external doctrines and teachings. He found the same fault in many others (for example, Michelet, Ampère, Quinet, and Fauriel) when he congratulated Gorini for having defended the Church in 1853 when it was attacked by its enemies, the worst of whom were, for Barbey, those who prided themselves on "eclecticism and impartiality."

As for Taine, he seized the opportunity to take a new look at the entire history of Indian thought, beginning with its Vedic origins, and to enlarge on Brahmanic society and religion. His work is remarkable for its stylistic grace and power of classification. Soberly absorbed in his analytical spirit and his faith in measurement, this most Western of philosophers relaxed when dealing with Buddhist charity, to which he devoted some moving pages. He noted its similarities with Christian charity, and made a statement that I underscore as recording one of the most lasting significances of the Oriental Renaissance: *Of all the events in history, this concordance is the greatest.* In the end he distinguished between these two kinds of love by means of a judgment wherein the rigor of the critique is curiously married to the *petitio principii:* the Christian sentiment "is more limited, for it does not extend to animals, as in India; it is less metaphysical and does not lay emphasis on the idea of universal nothingness, as in India." So concedes the Western mind. He frankly acknowledged, moreover, that for him the great difference could be stated in this way: "It is European and not Asian," a notion in striking agreement with the stance Descartes assumed regarding the Chinese. But Taine lost no time in moving from the language of reason to a vocabulary of passion, taking as the distinguishing mark between the two worlds, by which one could be considered "healthier," that the one addressed itself "to souls which are less ill." Hence he concluded that this world by itself "does not lead to passive quietism." The European reader might expect this conclusion, but an oriental reader might see it as a lion painted by a man. The last phrase of the chapter carried the stamp of the period, and the mark of the sectarian can be detected in it as well: the two traditions were confounded in the same praise for having initiated the worship of moral powers and for having conceived "the brotherhood of the human race."

This was followed by an admirably written study dealing with Indic speculation and its practice as a separate subject. And here again an important finding of the Oriental Renaissance is endorsed: "A perspicacity that carries a basic idea to its conclusion is characteristic of Indian thought; strictly speaking, it is the Indians alone who, with the Germans, possess the genius for metaphysics. The Greeks, though very subtle, are timid and measured in comparison, and one can state without exaggeration that only on the banks of the Ganges and the Spree has the human spirit grappled with the basis and substance of ideas." Finally, Taine's penchant for biology fortunately intervened to make him attentive to the evolution of Hindu belief in the course of time: "It has developed and blended in the course of centuries, and the story of its legendary and metaphysical transformation, of its pagan and Brahmanic mutations would make for a long theological history." Here a differentation of schools and periods is for the most part an established fact.

The Positivists

The intransigence of the Positivists has often been blamed for blocking the penetration of Hindu spirituality in France. Auguste Comte had no feeling for India. In his *Système de politique positive* he cast India in a utilitarian role: "The uncommon persistence of the theocratic regime in India will not prevent Positivism from finding, with the natural assistance of Persia, the real points of contact. This is a necessary prerogative of a doctrine that, always attentive to the whole of human evolution, is capable of appreciating the most ancient systems of sociability." Thus Brahma and Buddha were assimilated as forerunners of Comte. Was the religion of "the Great Being" not an adaptation of dogmatics to the new science of universal history?

It is the *Cours de philosophie positive* that evolved the discovery of a "great fundamental law" according to which "each of our principal ideas, each branch of our knowledge, passes successively through three theoretical stages: the theologic or fictive stage; the metaphysical or abstract stage; and the scientific or positive stage." How many times, for more than half a century (including Herder and Hugo's Preface to *Cromwell*), had one heard about the three stages! German Romanticism had infected *historiosophes* with this tertian fever. For Comte, Hindu thought, whether one approached it from a philosophical or a religious point of view, crumbled under the blow of the fatal rule declaring anything that did not deal solely with "reality" or "utility" old-fashioned. These two exclusive values were proclaimed in the *Catéchisme positiviste* and were later combined to produce a Religion of Humanity which was, at last, free from all theology and metaphysics. This left little room for India. In the Positivist Calendar, in the first month, entitled "Moses, the first theocracy" (each of these terms is here invidious), we find Manu on the 10th day, Zoroaster on the 12th, Buddha on the 14th, and "the theocracies of Tibet" on the 18th. India was truly in bad company. The first section of the "Positivist Library of the nineteenth century" allots 30 volumes to poetry, from which Hindu poetry is totally absent, although one can find "the seven masterpieces of Walter Scott" there. India is only dimly present, thanks to a textbook by Heeren, in the section on history. In the section on synthesis, the door opens for the Bible and the Koran, but not for the Veda.

In Littré's edition of *Cours de philosophie positive*, and in the second of the two prefaces he wrote for it, Littré the Indianizer, the fellow student (as he recalled) of the two Burnoufs, did not feel he could defend the domain of his teacher Chézy against the law of his teacher Comte. He merely attempted to preserve for the former a purely historical importance, in compliance with the commandments of the latter. "Is it possible to arrest the decadence of theological opinions, however attentuated, which have governed and continue to govern the moral world in their Judaic, Christian, Musulman, Brahmanic, or Buddhist forms? It is in the Christian form that the diminution is most marked; but it is important to consider the problem as a whole, and whether we like it or not, distant beliefs are dependent on the fortune of Western belief, in whose province the guiding concepts of human affairs are formulated. Islam, Brahmanism, and Buddhism are affected, however strange it may seem, by the blows to Christian theology in Christian countries."

Nevertheless, Littré had no intention of underestimating the results of the new historical sciences: "Auguste Comte's book has provided for the long-term development of the positive spirit among Western peoples. There is no need to annotate it or, as the common phrase goes, to update it. In the preface that precedes this study I have warned against falling into the misgivings that may have been born with such great and varied innovations as have arisen within our time in the sphere of science: stellar astronomy, spectroscopy, the strange study of cosmic corpuscles, the equivalence of forces, the deciphering of the Egyptian hieroglyphics and of the Assyrian cuneiform writings, the deepened understanding of the Vedas and the sacred Buddhist texts, and finally the unexpected resurrection of prehistoric man." He concluded that the Positivist philosophy, unlike theology, had no need to resort to "caviling in order to come to an agreement with all that." Thus once again the arrival of Sanskrit supported Romantic hopes for a global religion; but here it was, thanks to Sanskrit, thanks to the classification of all oriental studies in the new realm of science, an antireligious religion.

Pantheism and Orthodoxy

The element of spiritual temptation in the Sanskrit revelation suggested by Saint-Simonianism was clearly alarming to the orthodox outlook. We have already seen this à propos Brahmanism in Lanjuinais's reactions to reading Eckstein, and again in Barbey d'Aurevilly's outbursts against Hindu epics and against Jean Reynaud, and even in Lacordaire's reservations about aspects of Lamennais's universalism. There is no question that this had been one of the great sensitive questions of the first part of the nineteenth century. The question was strangely revived at the time Buddhism was elucidated; the proof lies in the dogmatism with which a Barthélemy Saint-Hilaire spurned the spirit of the same texts whose literal meaning had so engrossed him. Another authority on Sanskrit literature, a remarkable comparativist and one of the most uncompromising defenders of the faith was Ozanam, the student of Quinet and Fauriel, a favorite child of the Ampères, a man familiar with Eckstein and Lammenais, who took a stand in his turn.

Ozanam's critical writings are perhaps the best evidence of his profound connections with Saint-Simonianism. And his two volumes of *Mélanges*, which bring together articles on Ballanche and Fauriel, on Romantic pantheism and Buddhism, allow us to take stock of the various trends that have held our attention. The historical utterances of Saint-Simonianism claimed it stood on the philosophy of history "in order to announce the fall of the Christian God." And it is on this ground that Ozanam too insists on battling Saint-Simonianism, concluding the controversy in this way: "All the historical works concur in demonstrating that mankind's original religion was emphatically not a coarse fetishism, but rather an undefiled monotheism, a sort of primitive Christianity." (This was what Indic studies had provided in opposition to the eighteenth-century rationalists, and was now advancing against the theoreticians of the three ages.) Ozanam's phrase "a sort of primitive Christianity" invokes a striking parallel with Eckstein's "anterior Christianity." In criticizing the famous *Exposition de la doctrine*, Ozanam accuses its authors of wanting "to eliminate the research of the orientalists that contradicts their own views." He gives as evidence their allegation that European civilization alone offered an unbroken and well-known history. India had indeed first been accepted as an argument in favor of a religion of mankind, but was then cast back into the darkness of the theological age.

It will be remembered that, clearly, from that time forward no ancient doctrine could remain firm, nor could any new doctrine be justified, without relying on Indic attainments or without taking India's contribution into account. This is verified by Ozanam's second article, on the naturalists, where Ozanam once more invokes Cuvier's name, along with Humboldt's, as having proved "the agreement of scholarly research with the books of Moses." A whole previously encountered group reappears: "Benjamin Constant rendered a striking homage to the Christian religion in a work undertaken on an aesthetic impulse." He was followed by "the Creuzers, the Schlegels, the Hallers, the Stolbergs, and the Ecksteins," all those who had "returned to the bosom of the Church," and, with one exception, through orientalism.

Thus we arrive at the heart of the matter: the revival of pantheism, which was the basis for the whole Saint-Simonian metaphysics. In the unity of substance, "the new apostles seem at one time to renew the ancient doctrine of metempsychosis [an allusion to Jean Reynaud], at another time to renew the glory introduced by the faraway, such as the immortality of great men." (We will see this again, notably in the works of Michelet and Emerson.) And at still other times it seemed only a question of material progress. These "Réflexions sur la doctrine de Saint-Simon" are dated 1831, a period of Indic diffusion through the efforts of Reynaud, Pauthier, and Leroux. Ozanam's article "Sur le Bouddhisme" dated 1842, intended for Catholic readers, followed, as would be expected, not only Colebrooke but also Hodgson's "Sketch of Buddhism" published in the second volume of the *Transactions* of the Royal Asiatic Society. The newly acquired understanding of Buddhist beliefs brought to light a danger which, until then, only Anglicanism had feared. In France, where it was particularly studied, positions on Buddhism were hardening in a way they had not hardened regarding Hinduism. And it was not only in France: Ozanam quotes Friedrich Schlegel as stating in his *Philosophie der Geschichte* in 1828 at the end of his career what he had not said in his 1808 essay. Not only "is the would-be similarity between the two religions Christianity and Buddhism not real, . . . it is like that between man and ape." Ozanam stresses that beneath identical expressions "lies the endless difference of things," and there are some expressions "that cannot be aped: these are faith, hope, and charity. When these are missing, the illusion of similarity cannot endure."

Strengthening the defense of Christianity along these lines and recalling the false arguments drawn from the comparison of the Bible with the Koran, he concluded by demonstrating how general the alert and the campaign were at the time: "The explanations that Abel Rémusat gives, and that Wiseman develops in his eleventh lecture, have destroyed Volney's impious hypotheses, which no one has since dared to reproduce." (Needless to say, although the three theological virtues denied India were not mentioned, the anteriority of Christianity later formed the subject of more complex discussions.) Ozanam points out in detail that the Buddhist threat was but the last salient of the old pantheist offensives that German Romanticism had recently launched again: "They have reappeared through the metaphysical systems of Germany." We have already been enlightened as to these connections, but perhaps we will not have measured the full extent, the full consequence, before reading this: "They [the pantheist offensives] for some time threatened to invade science, arts, and morals. They continue to be halted by what remains of good sense and morality in European society. But eloquent voices have pointed them out as the greatest religious peril of our time." After this it is strange to hear historians stubbornly maintain that India was, for the nineteenth century, only a fantasy for the dilettante. Speaking of Ballanche, whom he was intent on exonerating, Ozanam claimed that Ballanche had not participated in the propaganda of "a third revelation, which the Saint-Simonians had so abused," which came, as we know, from the Herderians, among others, a presentiment of which must be forgiven "even in Maistre." The 1830 revolution was to dictate to Ballanche in his *Vision d'Hébal* the affirmation, as much opposed to Michelet-Quinet as to Schleiermacher-Schopenhauer, that "the human race is definitely not developing a new religion." Ballanche's writings had, nonetheless, encouraged this hypothesis in many of his readers.

Finally, in his essay on Fauriel, Ozanam confirms once again the final link between Indic studies and the *idées-forces* of Romanticism. Ozanam begins with the very idea of a new Renaissance: Fauriel had concentrated on the epic and the primitive "with the distinction of a mind made for universality. It was at the time that the sacred language of India, its scholarly, poetic idiom whose study would provide Europe with the treasures of an immense body of literature and revive the marvels of the Renaissance of Greek letters in the sixteenth-century, were beginning to be spoken of. Fauriel thus had no rest until he had learned Sanskrit." This knowledge in fact was to overtake his previous research: "Nowhere did the bases of Fauriel's vast learning become more visible than in the 1836 course in which he intended to clarify the Homeric poems through the study of the general history of the epic.[12] He plunged himself into the furthest depths of the Orient in order to consider its prodigious epics, hollowed out, as it were, from the mythological traditions of India, like the subterranean pagodas of Ellora and Elephanta." This is followed by two eloquent pages on the *Mahabharata* and the *Ramayana*, ending naturally with the *Nibelungenlied*. Ozanam had been personally attached, at first, to the Indic epics but later became much more attached to the Germanic—a relapse into the same old succession. Two facts remained: the progression would become a familiar one in France, and it revivified the epic according to prescriptions Germany drew from India.

From "An Appetite for Miracles" to a Critical Age

The great innovation of Romanticism, an old hope of the first Renaissance and a characteristic upshot of the second, was this tenet: nothing is as important as the universal. Throughout the entire period, in all learning, from genius to genius, a requirement for emotion, beauty, and faith triumphed, set an almost limitless bound which took on a totality. There were few events in political or social history that were not propelled in this direction; not a country, not an individual, for whom the issue was not raised. Some expressed it with force or at personal risk. It was Germany, needless to say, which placed it within the most obvious system.

The vocabulary of the stars of the *Athenaeum* was shot through with *sympoésie, symphilosopher, symphysique*, and *symbibliser*. An entirely spontaneous sense of the fabulous lay in wait there, ready to exploit scientific advances. It was further inflamed by a new or revived feeling, that of the flight of time, which prompted a desire to live several existences simultaneously and unite the contrasts. Another consequence was that the present had value only as a promise of a future whose past guaranteed that it would be extraordinary. The final result was that these conquests of the historical spirit postulated the abdication of the critical spirit. This paradox had a logical base. At the same time the former limits of knowledge were being stretched on all sides, people came to test their elasticity, and to admit their uncertainty more and more. Henri Brunschwig, whose fascinating conclusions I am following here, throws light upon pre-Romantic Germany with his expression "the appetite for miracles." He exposed a regression there whereby an organizing rationality became an instinct for confusion. One must concede that Romantic France, on the contrary, recognized a great many nuances. (Moreover, we should be very suspicious of the so-called "primitive mentality." Isn't this, after all, what poets call the poetic state? Doesn't the "pre-logical state" of savages afford civilized people the convenience of not having to explain logic?)

The passage from the first to the second Romantic and orientalist period resembles the last stage of childhood. The editions themselves, the material aspects of the books, their density, their spelling, passed beyond the vacillating, nonchalant, and prodigal stages. Toward 1840 everything became tighter, confident, and legitimate. Between the period of Chézy and that of Burnouf Indic studies lengthened their stride alongside a Romanticism that was moving past the age of incunabula. Then came one of those rare pauses of history in which a meteor seems to harden.

At first it had been an exclamatory and invocatory era; a spirit of the time was called forth, significantly reinforced by rites and excavations. Then it occurred and the page was turned. The vacation of the critical spirit was to end. The reveries that several intermediaries, overexcited by the opening up of so many worlds, conveyed were to encounter barriers. Naturally, French Romanticism had its share of fools, some of whom continue to be dear to the French. But there was this difference between French and German Romanticism: in France the fools and the sages were not the same person.

The Literature of Panoramas

Throughout the Occident those impassioned by synthesis attempted a fresh elucidation of history, the world, and religion by utilizing the panoramic view of all things that humanism's annexation of the vast Orient provided. In 1852 Eugène Pelletan, whom Viatte calls "part-Fourierist, part-student of Jean Reynaud," advanced a modern logic for the Creation in his edifying *Profession de foi du XIXe siècle*. In this historical and philosophical collection (two chapters of which are practically lifted from Quinet, as Erdan pointed out in 1855), India held an important place. This ambitious work, another apocryphal "Bible," was too vast and too tainted with the topical to achieve durability. In any event, it remains an interesting and cogent monument of the Oriental Renaissance.

In 1854 Jean Reynaud's *Terre et Ciel*, an exegesis of this new time, appeared. Not surprisingly, many traditions, from Pythagoras, Neoplatonism, and Druidism to intuitions living "in the secret depths of our souls," met in this work. The moving conviction that sustained the whole book, the hope for a total explication of humanity, was one that, as we have seen, animated the close of the eighteenth century. Here was a hypothesis at once historical, philosophical, and theological of a "fifth age" in which the problems of the soul, human origins, and otherworldly destinies would become clear. The first three ages were geological or paleontological, the fourth the age of the human species. Here again we encounter the mania for "ages" that was stimulated by the Hindu concept of *kalpas* and ended in something akin to Positivism. Reynaud revived de Staël's dogma of an indefinite progress which held that nineteenth-century humanity was entering a final era (one thinks again of Nodier) in which it would inevitably find the solutions, previously sought in vain, to the serious questions that tormented it. With this continuity Reynaud pursued his eschatology in parallel with an analysis of historical fact. History, the great recent conquest, was, page after page, the support, the verification, of metaphysical and visionary conjecture. More seriously than in Nodier's work, the rational hope for perfectability was amalgamated with the mystical hope of a new faith.

Saint-Simonianism believed itself to be the religion the century proclaimed it could no longer be without. After the last revolution of 1848 caused messianism to move from the spiritual to the political realm, religious hope kept its feet on the ground. The heaven over which it kept guard was that of astronomy; with Reynaud and Hugo metempsychosis became stellar migration. The impressive number of works—not only those of writers like Pelletan and Reynaud but Bunsen and Pressensé, which we will discuss again in their own context, or the *Bible de l'Humanité* or

Dieu, which had corresponding works elsewhere in writers like, for example, Emerson and Carlyle—is a characteristic phenomenon of the century. For everyone, oriental studies and to a great degree Hindu thought played a decisive role. Invoked on numerous occasions in the general enterprise of global explication, such thought was present in the subconscious of the time.

The following passage from Reynaud's *Terre et Ciel* gives us an example of these messianic enthusiasms: "A new period will succeed the present one, but it will be the first age of a new human species. While waiting for these events, which the march of the world has caused us to judge henceforward inevitable, let us fervently apply ourselves to the service of the age in which we were born. Do you not feel that it is drawing us to the love of God and of our fellow beings with more energy than there has ever been in any of the ages that preceded it?" This was the deeper justification of Romanticism. Before smiling at it, we should remember that our century has invented no other justification. With equal seriousness it in its turn proclaims a dawn that all the millenarians together supposedly could not have foretold. The last invention is that the love of one's fellow beings runs counter to the love of God. The conception the present world has of itself, which was probably born among the many transformations since 1789 and even since the first Renaissance, could only be what it is in the wake of a past that has finally become whole. This conception began the day the philosophy of history exploded the biblical horizon of Bossuet: the earth's map cannot change without changing the map of the heavens.

CHAPTER TEN

The Moving Spirits

HOW, and by whom, were these discoveries, whose existence we have ascertained, disseminated? To answer this we must study the particulars of certain figures and their actions. First two representative men, Eckstein and Quinet, appear. It is not without reason that these two men supported the Oriental Renaissance: the one gave it its initial articulation within German Romanticism and its final adjustment within French Romanticism; the other provided the transition from enthusiasm to lucidity, or, one might say, from a ravenous appetite to an ordered diet.

The Eckstein File

In 1836 the recovery of lost languages and the foundation of linguistics were a matter of common knowledge: so many marvels in less than half a century were enough to affect the public, but were they enough? The personal influence of a few leaders was important; so was the crowd of foreigners around the university chairs. But so was the ringing of the bells and the activities of the bell-ringers; brilliant minds require many obscure ones. The scholars provided the treasures of oriental studies; the semi-intellectuals, the semi-writers, created the atmosphere of orientalism. Throughout the books that give us our documentation for the phenomenon of orientalism, whether written during the period or retrospectively, we encounter an officious character whose repute is so great that those who attest to it seem to forgive his personal insignificance. He was at home everywhere, with scholars as well as with poets and spiritualists, perhaps because each of these categories took him to be from the other. The man who styled himself "Baron" Eckstein will prove to be no less effective a guide for us than he was for those of his own time.

His biographer, P. N. Burtin, had good grounds for stating that, in the journals of the time, the oriental domains were "approached from a point of view precisely analogous to Eckstein's," and to conclude that "the Baron contributed no small amount to the awakening of this taste."[1] The Baron flattered himself that he had always held aloof from the cliques of scholars and writers, but this reserve of his memory was equaled only by his own lack of reservation. He was a born go-between, as others are born creators. Chasles, his former secretary, believed he perceived in him only the ideas of others, but the case is rather that Eckstein needed them in order to give birth to his own.[2] His specific genius seems to have been a gift for combining, and indefatigable high spirits. Although a personality *for* his times, he was, as such celebrities sometimes are, not altogether someone for history. But to ignore him is impossible; he is a channel. Thus, the first question is, where did he come from, and with what?

The Origins and Antecedents of the Personage

Born in 1789 of German-Danish extraction, in his earliest youth at Altona he was admitted to the circle of the aging Klaproth, who as Goethe said had no doubts of having "something sacred in himself." There Eckstein also saw Jacobi, who, at the time vainly, invited de Staël to this principal hearth of the spirit, and whom she later portrayed as head of those "who took religious feeling and innate conscience as their guides." All this left its mark, and Eckstein forgot nothing. He began to make contacts with the French. There were numerous exiles around Hamburg, one of whom had, as early as 1800, converted Count Friedrich Stolberg and his wife to Catholicism. This conversion, as we have seen, caused quite a disturbance in the German countries and later led to the conversion of Friedrich Schlegel and his wife, which led in turn to Eckstein's conversion. Eckstein also passed through the groups of occultists from Holstein who had favored Duke Peter von Oldenburg, whom Eckstein later called "an old fool," but who also influenced him. At Heidelberg he again came into contact with secret societies, the Rosicrucians and the Tugendbund. He returned to the conspiracy a little later on the side of the border police. These shifts of allegiance colored his initial activities in France, and a new influence was later added to these: Creuzer was then in his prime at Heidelberg, and he engaged Eckstein, the perpetual schoolboy, in the study of myth and oriental languages, especially Sanskrit, the great novelty. It was a decisive period for the man whom Heine later nicknamed "Baron Buddha." It was, Eckstein later said, his Indic studies that converted him first to Lutheranism (his father was of Jewish descent) and then to Catholicism. It must be granted that his imitation of Friedrich Schlegel was, for him, a form of sincerity.

A police officer under the employ of Louis XVIII at Gand and Brussels and later at Marseille—after having been in the service of the emperor of Austria, an envoy for the Foreign Office with no known mission and received everywhere with no trace of suspicion—he was probably only slightly particular about his enthusiasms. He was armed with various abilities, even though none of them can be called talents, except for his powers of influence and persuasion. He remained a stout porter of ideas who honestly thought himself a creator of great ideas. His life was easily set in motion on several levels simultaneously, as is witnessed by his frantic, vague participation in politics, his conscientious and disordered linguistic studies, and his constant and long-lived Christian faith, from which, however, the heterodox temptation did not seem permanently uprooted. The Schlegel he knew in Vienna, who had indoctrinated him from 1808 to 1813, was then approaching the final stage of his Indic conviction while deepening his own faith at the same time. Eckstein attended Schlegel's lectures on the history of ancient and modern literature and repeated Schlegel's improvisational strides among historical landscapes. His own efforts at discipline, which succeeded with difficulty in drawing an intermittent self-control from an improviser's nature, became more marked with the years; the wrinkles of character are not erased with age, but they can be smoothed out. And one of Eckstein's significant successes was in aging well.

Eckstein recounted that from 1819 to 1822 he had buried himself in the Indic manuscripts of Langlès, again following in the Schlegels' footsteps. He wanted "to extract the primitive revelation from Langlès's fragments, to decipher the most remote mythological language of antiquity." This was the program, totally that of Creuzer and Schlegel, by which he would infuse the new German teaching, both intellectual and spiritual, into the Romantic ideology of France. "Natural religion" was extended to include the pagans and the literary sacraments of the primitive. When Eckstein gave his own definition of Romanticism as the marriage of popular mysticism, German theosophy, and exotic poetry, he was merely peddling the answer book, chapters Hamann, Novalis, Herder, and, as always, Schlegel.[3] He unpacked his stuffed bags before a generation of young people, converted by de Staël and Chateaubriand, who were discovering lessons nearly uninterrupted since Diderot. What portion of his wares did Eckstein succeed in disposing of?

One follows his path to two stock phrases that, again, were not original with him. The first is the formula "Oriental Renaissance" itself. I have not found any mention of it before those in the works of Friedrich Schlegel in 1803 and 1808. Is it possible that Schlegel, who was excited by this notion, transmitted nothing of the tradition to his student at Vienna? So far as we know, Eckstein was the only one able to instill the idea of an oriental renaissance in the poet—and prefacer—of the *Orientales*. In the period between 1823 and 1829 both Eckstein's propaganda and his contacts with poets multiplied. The second cliché, associated with the preceding one in the *Catholique* in 1826, was a result of Eckstein's contacts with Herder and Schlegel: it is the famous "nomenclature-type" designating poetries of the first rank, beginning with the Vedas, which were the work of no one individual and which were considered the property of everyone, especially the Indo-Germans. This theme would make an indelible mark on the works of Hugo, who grew angry with the idea in *William Shakespeare*, yet who nevertheless conceived *Légende des siècles* within the same community of interests as "the Eddas, the Vedas, and the Romanceros." Eckstein particularly excelled in marking the community of interests between the upsurge of orientalism and the claims of the Gothic. The two topics alternated or merged in his lectures and articles. It was certainly not Hugo who dreamed up the reunion of the two for the preface of *Orientales*, where, along with the supposed linguistic relationship, one of the two essential components of the Indo-German montage appeared: Homer was the base, India and Persia the two lateral sides of the pyramid whose peak was the German Middle Ages.

On the basis of meticulous research, his biographer concludes that Eckstein's principal activity may have been "the liquidation of the eighteenth century." This is an understandable conclusion, from a French viewpoint. The French took an interest in the troubadours; Eckstein set the *Minnesingers*, whom he considered closer to primitive purity, over them. To support his contention he called attention to the then-common insult of "barbarism" in order to turn the implied slur against the French Academicians. Praising the Schlegels for having returned the Middle Ages to its rightful eminence, Eckstein seized the opportunity to give the Germanic nations credit for Romanticism, claiming for them, by universal consent, the monopoly on "the discernment of the beautiful." Moreover, "all Europe, which was formerly Latin, is now Germanic, for the peoples of the North established all the southern empires." This racial claim made maximum use of the resources of its accomplice, so-called natural poetry. The Middle Ages and primitive poetry were the great weapons against the great enemy that Eckstein called "the abject and narrow philosophy of the eighteenth century." This was by no means an isolated outburst; the idea that eighteenth-century rationalism had been intellectual rationing was nothing new. It is significant that the expression of this view emerged from polemics: the writer of the preface to the *Soirées de Saint-Pétersbourg* in 1821 naturally wrote as Eckstein did in his *Annales de la littérature* in 1823: "the abject philosophy of the eighteenth century." It had become a cliché. A word will suffice to recall which foreign interests, while making use of Rousseau, identified this rationalist philosophy with French literature. In order to relieve French literature, which was declared worn-out if not stillborn, it was the Orient, especially India, which was given the task of providing the pedigree for the Middle Ages. The curious thing is that when this engine of war arrived in France, it found all gates open. The preface to *Orientales* joyously greeted the constellations of another hemisphere come at last to eclipse the Sun King. The preface probably carried this sense in spite of the poet; forty years later Hugo would denounce the idea that it was "the Occidental India" which Germany was advancing behind a shield of twisted history.

Eckstein's Verbal Campaign

An exuberant herald of the Oriental Renaissance, Eckstein was not simply a naïve immigrant magnifying the country he had left to the detriment of the one he had chosen; serving both nationalism and universality simply shows a lack of critical judgment. Some were amused at his dual tendency, but no one was angry about it. His impact was greater than one would imagine; even today writers have taken the generous view that the writers of yesterday took. The substance from which he was molded had something of a liquid quality to it—its natural function was to spill over. Since his personality moved itself along by the process of recharging itself in the presence of successive inspirers and discharging itself in the presence of other listeners, he operated mainly through personal contact. And what is exceptional about Eckstein's flights of words is that they left behind so many afterimages.

This is not to say that one should disregard Eckstein's innumerable articles in the literary, scholarly, political, and religious periodicals. I am thinking less here of his copious contributions to the *Journal Asiatique* or the *Revue Archéologique*, which were read by experts, but rather the flood of articles from 1825 until his death in 1861 in *Annales*, *Drapeau blanc*, *Catholique*, and *Correspondant* which won over a public that without his articles would most likely not have taken an interest in Sanskrit. With them an interest was generated akin to that surrounding the question of the soul. The *Catholique* "penetrates milieus inattentive to recent discoveries of philological science, and the young Romantic poets as a group . . . will feel their curiosity awakened by these still unexplored literatures" in such journals.[4] But most important was the impact Eckstein had in person. His genuine talent for speaking was accentuated by the additional attention given to the picturesque gaucheries of a chatty foreigner (his secretary

Chasles gave evidence of this curious prestige). Egger, Eckstein's dazzled follower, after discussing Eckstein's written work, continued: "Even more original, if it is possible, were Eckstein's speech and conversation, and they were also more instructive, especially when he allowed himself to be led by some congenial listener; but he was more the master of himself than is the impetuous thinker."[5] And then the very number of words was an essential factor in itself. Had Eckstein been less loquacious, India would have been less familiar to the France of Louis-Philippe. He symbolizes the major importance of the work accomplished by the powers of speech on behalf of orientalism.

After 1823, at the same time as his contacts with Hugo, which deserve a special section, Eckstein had access to Lamennais, who frequently published him in *Drapeau blanc*. Their relationship was not without its setbacks. At first Eckstein's Orient encountered some well-entrenched ideas in the mind of his interlocutor. During this time Eckstein also saw a great deal of Lamartine. In 1838 Valentine de Cessiat, a nephew of Lamartine, whom Eckstein had instructed in and entertained with India for fourteen years, wrote to a friend: "Eckstein delights us by his inexhaustibility; his vast learning, his brilliant and impassioned speaking, and his ability to translate from Sanskrit and German. His is a dictionary that turns its own pages and that needs no bookmark." (In 1824 Eckstein was already supporting Lamartine's candidacy for the Académie française.) Again we see the effect of Eckstein's discourse, with its weight and its rapid and warm reception. And again the yoking of India with Germany. Louis de Ronchaud, who heard Eckstein during one of his many visits to Saint-Point, confirmed that he "was amazingly spirited when he was in form."

In 1828 in the home of Madame d'Hautefeuille, Ballanche happened upon Eckstein, who had slandered him (this was not the first time he had slandered Ballanche, to the point of outraging the kindness of the Récamier salon): they left close friends, each of the two "mouths" closed by the eloquence of the other.[6] In 1831 Eckstein went to see Montalembert and spoke with him about Novalis; Montalembert straightway wrote a piece on Novalis, and Sainte-Beuve mentioned Montalembert's "fine article" to Victor Pavie. Eckstein returned, and Ozanam saw him there with Sainte-Beuve, Ampère, and Vigny. Greatly influenced by what Eckstein had to say, Ozanam took an immediate interest in the Orient; he became a new recruit to Sanskrit and for him its literature always carried Eckstein's stamp. That same year Heine encountered Eckstein overwhelming the pious dowagers of Faubourg Saint-Germain with Hindu sermons. Smiling, Heine attributed the nickname "Baron Buddha," of which he was probably the author, to "the frivolous French." In 1831 the Baron was seen leaving Mohl's home furious at Michelet for his lack of respect toward Charlemagne; he left his interlocutor, who was a bit weary of being primarily a listener, with the image of "a man completely swamped by the Vedas."[7] In 1835 he paid his first visit to the home of Madame Récamier. Chasles maintained that, thanks to his Teutonic clumsiness, "his entry to all the salons and boudoirs of the Restoration was guaranteed." Around 1840 or 1850 he was a guest in the home of Daniel Stern, where Emerson, as well as Littré, Michelet, and Mickiewicz were also received, and in the homes of Princess Belgioioso, Madame Swetchine, and Madame de Custine. He came off all the better among people of high society for being taken seriously by studious people. During the last years of his life he was in close contact with Thureau-Dangin and Egger; the latter, an enthusiastic publicizer of Bopp, considered the number "of ingenious and profound ideas" which "shone from this hearth" incalculable. In 1862 Egger dedicated his *Mémoires de littérature ancienne* "to the memory of Baron Ferdinand Eckstein, a generous and profound mind whose lively and universal curiosity singularly enlivened historical studies." Eckstein died in 1861, and Mohl, who admired the purified faith of Eckstein's last days, spent among the brothers of Saint-Jean-de-Dieu, eulogized him in his *Vingt-sept ans d'histoire des études orientales*. Renan, who always quoted him with respect, did the same in the *Débats*. Henri Martin prepared a presentation of Eckstein's work. In the Saint-Simonian milieu Eckstein had also been befriended by Augustin Thierry. Burnouf was a true friend to Eckstein, and Michelet consulted him.[8] Sainte-Beuve honored him with the words "a great knowledge," "a veritable expanse of mind." Eckstein's death was one of the rare occasions on which Sainte-Beuve was unable to keep silent about the Oriental Renaissance in which he had so many friends.

One can glimpse some of the ramifications: Egger, on account of Eckstein, left behind thirty-six copybooks of notes on India and the mark of Sanskrit on several university generations; Brunetière studied Eckstein's articles on India, which resulted in the alertness, as well as the documentation, one perceives in his critical studies. The *Dictionnaire de la conversation* in 1833 printed two articles, one after another, each entitled "Bouddha," which stressed the danger of confusing one Buddha with another. Two years earlier in his *De l'Allemagne*, Heine had called attention to his fellow countryman who was proving "with prolixity that there were two Buddhas, which the French accepted solely on his word as a gentleman." The theory of two Buddhas, at a time when Buddhism remained the most obscure zone of Indic studies, furnished a means of explaining its differences from Brahmanism; this idea appeared in Benjamin Constant's *De la religion*. In any event, Eckstein accepted responsibility for the hypothesis in the August 22, 1823 issue of *Drapeau blanc*.

The extent of Eckstein's influence on Hugo is surprising; we have seen some signs of this influence, notably that Eckstein had suggested the theme of the Oriental Renaissance to Hugo for his preface to *Orientales*. This was only natural: Hugo was easygoing enough to choose his informants badly. At first a royalist and a Catholic, Hugo was struck by the person of the baron who was editor of *Drapeau blanc*, Lamennais's right-hand man, and a representative of the mysterious German learning. There is a certain excitement in listening to people who are intoxicated by their own words; there is nothing in the sound that disturbs the sound of one's own mind; their self-anxiety meshes smoothly with one's self-confidence. Hugo was only twenty-one at the time of these encounters and correspondence with Eckstein, who was thirty-four. Hugo's output then consisted almost entirely of a number of odes, as opposed to Eckstein's bottomless stack of writings. The year Hugo completed *Han d'Islande* was the year Eckstein became editor of the *Annales:* he invited Hugo and Lamartine, who were already contributing, to entrust the first fruits of Romanticism to a periodical in which he was, according to his biographer Burtin, extending "the inheritance of the *Conservateur littéraire*" and leading the way to the *Muse française*. And in fact Hugo provided Eckstein with two important poems, "Jehovah" and "Ode sur la mort du duc de Berry."

Before *Cromwell*, Hugo went through a period of change during which his individuality took form within a great respect for the ideas, knowledge, and reactions of his colleagues, particularly those ideas that had originated in Germany. Since he did not know German, Hugo relied for his information on those who did.[9] The distinctive epigraphs in *Han d'Islande* carry Eckstein's mark, even those not taken directly from him. On November 28, 1824, mindful, no doubt, of the need for ever-attentive courtesy, and ever-careful strategy, Hugo wrote, with many deep bows: "I am still following the lead, Monsieur le baron, of the articles with which you sometimes deign to enrich *Drapeau blanc.*" To ask that all the contributors to this journal have the "high excellence" of the great savant Eckstein "is to ask the impossible." For here is a man who possessed "three qualities eminently: learning, talent, and conviction."[10] (All this would, moreover, be acceptable, if certain adjectives were added to the first two terms.) There was an exchange of writings: "Your views on popular poetry are elevated and profound." Hugo would relay them to Lamartine, "who will be charmed" by them. Here was the bond: Eckstein was the connection between Eddas, Vedas, and Romanceros. *Le Catholique*, which carried the theme of the Oriental Renaissance, had been discontinued by the time *Orientales* appeared, but it had produced and driven home its effect. It was then that the "thirst" for the Orient, whose progress can easily be followed from de Staël and Lamartine to Michelet and finally to

Barrès, began to be expressed. These images that produced lumps in the throat and lay heavy on the heart could only be lightened, and these thirsts could only be slaked, by turning to lofty Asia. This would become a commonplace of Romanticism.

In June 1826 Eckstein announced a discovery, an amalgam in Shakespeare of a genre "severe and tragic" with a genre "high-spirited, parodic, and droll." Eckstein was certainly not the first to have noticed this; but through whom, aside from the Greeks, had Eckstein been able to arrive at an understanding of the form? Through "les Indiens." In December 1827 the Preface to *Cromwell* appeared and threw open the door. Here was another sensational novelty. The preface proclaimed the three ages of poetry. We have already been edified as to the originality of this theory. Eckstein took it up again, discussing a primitive or sacerdotal age, an epic or heroic age, and a dramatic or comic age. As an application of this rule, in his journal he paternalistically counseled Hugo to give up the outmoded forms of ode and epic. For nations that had attained maturity, "dramatic poetry is . . . what poetry was for nations in the centuries of heroism." One can imagine the influence the advice from a world sage to devote himself to the theater had on the young poet, still irresolute and on the lookout for the voice of his age. Several months later Hugo cast his lot with drama, and underscored this transformation with a peculiarly significant proclamation in which he adopted the very ideas of his counselor. But the bet would be lost completely with the failure of *Burgraves*. Then at the last minute Hugo's career took a sudden conclusive turn: as a result of Hindu poems and Eckstein's influence, the epic was rehabilitated. Under Eckstein's explicit influence Lamartine led the way back to it, and that aspect of Hugo's genius had its revenge. This reversal impudently contradicted the theory of the three ages, but was in keeping with the elevation of poetry that was primitive, collective, and universal. In April 1832, ten years before *Burgraves*, the *Revue Encyclopédique* announced, through the pen of Leroux: "Today new fruits are beginning to be produced by fresh contacts with the Orient." In November 1832, Pauthier exclaimed regarding the Hindu epics: "The world's most colossal literature is a fossil literature that has had no parallel since the Flood." It was the "diluvian" aspect of these great poems that Lamartine strove to duplicate; some metaphors taken from the realm of Cuvier were in the air at the time. Pauthier recalled Jones's remark from "On the Literature of the Hindus," "Wherever we direct our attention to Hindu literature, the notion of infinity presents itself." These were magical words for the great minds of Lamartine and Hugo. Henceforth Dante and Milton, the apex of genius according to Chateaubriand, were mere child's play in comparison with the epics that ran to over a hundred thousand lines. In poetry as in religion, Romanticism would give the world the unprecedented; Hugo and Lamartine promised oceanic poems set forth in unlimited episodes.

All notions of the epic were regauged in the presence of the lengthy classics of Persia and especially India. Thus once again the leaders of French Romanticism set out toward their future, toward such climates and such dimensions as could ease the heart's heavy burden. Lamartine clearly labeled the vast construction of *Jocelyn*, *Chute d'un Ange*, and *Visions* "hindoustanique" (even though this was a linguistic misunderstanding), but they were not merely fragments. In Hugo's work the repercussions were slower in coming, delayed by his intervening experiments in the theater, but were better thought out and more lasting. Both Lamartine and Hugo would comment on their encounters with India. Lamartine did so in his 1856 *Cours de littérature*, where he verified that writers had become familiar with Hindu texts through Eckstein's translations. Hugo did so in *William Shakespeare*, where India is discussed and in the end rejected to the extent that the predeliction for "anonymous" poetic traditions, not long since received from the lips of Eckstein, ceased to be fascinating. Nevertheless, what Lamartine termed, indiscriminately, Indian or "Babylonian" was certainly no less present in the definitive works of Hugo: try as he might to call back from his Latin education the myths of Rome and Athens, he could only imagine them through a titanism inconceivable before Indology, Assyriology, and Paul de Saint-Victor.

Indo-Christianity

"Eckstein had become the focal point for a group of Catholics who believed in the man and his works, and who assisted him in them, a group of young people buried under a mountain of books—Sanskrit, German, and English. One day correcting proofs for a work on the Vedas, the next day recasting an article on Victor Hugo into more acceptable French, lost in a thicket of texts and in quotations as tangled as creepers in a virgin forest, we used to compare ourselves to the serviceable quadrupeds that smell out and unearth the truffles in the woods of Périgord." This was the account of one of the members of this group, Louis de Carné, on leaving the Eckstein laboratory.[11] The essentials are all there: Indic propaganda, Germanic propaganda, advice for Hugo. This feverish and at times collective activity went on from 1823 to 1861. Here one can see how the oriental product was implanted in the Catholic milieu. The mixture of spiritual and scholarly mass production reportedly provoked lively reactions from believers and philologists alike. I have referred to this in connection with the Saint-Simonians, whose objectives were entirely differ-ent but whose arguments were rather similar. Lanjuinais, among others, later wrote several "Letters to Baron Eckstein concerning the necessary and spontaneous belief of mankind," and "On the dangers of his Indo-Christian Catholicism."

The cliché that the Vedas were the "Aryan Bible," so in keeping with the postulates of Schleiermacher, was discredited in its turn. In the 1850s Renan—one cannot be sure whether he was a man of letters discussing religion or a man of religion discussing humanism—blocked the road the old cliché had traveled: "Israel alone among the peoples of the Orient had the privilege of writing for the entire world. The poetry of the Vedas is admirable, certainly, and yet this anthology of the first songs of the race to which we belong will never replace the Psalms, the work of a race so very different from our own, in the expression of our religious feelings. In general the literary works of the Orient can be read and appreciated only by scholars; the Hebraic literature, on the contrary, is the Bible, the book *par excellence*, the universal reading. Millions of people know no other poetry." And Renan later criticized the supposed similarities between the legend of the Buddha and the life of Christ.[12] This latter point corre-sponds to one we have seen in Ozanam, and the preceding point to one we have seen in the writings of Barbey d'Aurevilly. Vehemence of expres-sion aside, a reclassification became essential after more than half a cen-tury of illusion.

In righting the balance, things often went to the other extreme, and the orientalists often seemed to be the ones in the biggest hurry to deny that Hindu poetry might come to life again for the poets or even for the gen-eral reader. Darmesteter confirmed Renan's view of an India reserved for specialists: "An educated person who applied himself to the study of In-dia could elucidate a wealth of feelings and images for himself and float freely on the seas of Indic poetry, but he would not discover a great and beautiful body of literature to offer the European reader." In his preface to his *Shakuntala* in 1884, Bergaigne was even more discouraging: "In gen-eral the initial enthusiasm that greeted the discovery of Sanskrit has now been abandoned. . . . This literature presently attracts, almost exclu-sively, scholars, philologists, archaeologists, and religious historians. It is a generally accepted idea, which Indic scholars rarely contradict, that lit-erary interest per se is for the most part lacking in Sanskrit works." That such a monstrous statement could be issued without the slightest hint of protest from a single Indic scholar is scarcely creditable. Thus in the very year that marked the centenary of the Asiatic Society of Calcutta, the sit-uation was completely reversed. The literary disrepute completed the ob-literation of a religious temptation that had engendered a literary fervor.

There are some interesting passages in Hegel's *Philosophy of History* concerning what this temptation and Eckstein's contribution to it were: "Thus, the essential interest to be found in the study of ancient peoples is the ability to go back to the point where it is possible to find, in greater purity, fragments of the first revealed knowledge." The theme is one of a universal revelation which thereafter would not be corrupt, but on the contrary purer among the pagans. Appended to this conclusion is a long note at the bottom of the page of Gibelin's French translation which is worth quoting in full:

We are indebted to this interest for many estimable discoveries in the field of oriental literature, and for a renewed study of treasures brought to light long ago, relating to the Orient, its mythology, its religions, and its history. In cultured Catholic countries, government did not long elude the demands of these ideas and felt the need to establish an alliance with science and philosophy. Abbé Lamennais has insisted, eloquently and authoritatively, that one criterion of the true religion is that it be universal; that is, catholic and the most ancient. In France the Congrégation has worked zealously and diligently, to the end that such statements are no longer regarded—as no doubt it used to be sufficient to regard them— as tirades from the pulpit and affirmations of authority. The religon of *Buddha*, a man-god, which is quite widespread, has become particularly conspicuous. The Hindu Timurtis [*sic*] was clearer in its basics, as was the Chinese abstraction of the Trinity. Abel Rémusat and Saint-Martin have carried out the most praiseworthy research in Chinese literature and have, where possible, branched out into Mongol and Tibetan literature, like the Baron Eckstein, who for his part did so in his own way—that is, with the perceptions and methods of natural philosophy, superficial and drawn from Germany after the manner, and in imitation, of Friedrich von Schlegel, but with more feeling than Schlegel shows; in his review, the *Catholique*, Eckstein has given his support to this primitive catholicism and has, in particular, directed an equal share of government subsidies to the erudite faction of the Congrégation, with the result that even journeys to the Orient were organized to find more hidden treasures which, it was hoped, would provide further elucidation not only of the deepest doctrines but of remote antiquity and the sources of Buddhism in particular, and which would contribute to the cause of Catholicism in a manner which was certainly circuitous but interesting to scholars.

This gibberish—whether it originated for the most part with Hegel, with the publisher Gans, or with some other annotator of the time (or the translator himself, for that matter)—is instructive even in its vagaries and desultory discourse: the importance, recognized by his contemporaries, of Lamennais's notion of universality, into which India was recruited and which Lacordaire denounced, this still conjectural Buddhism that obsessed many minds and caused an increase in scholarly missions, whereby Hodgson was able to complete the work begun by Csoma de Koros; Rémusat wrongly invoked as a champion of spiritual rapprochements when, in fact, he was an adamant adversary of them; and finally, Eckstein explicitly tied, through his compatriots, to the Schelling-Schleiermacher-Schlegel tradition and, moreover, attributed with a new function, distributor of official subsidies, which would shed light on one facet of his activities at the Foreign Affairs office (where, as Burtin points out, by 1818 he had proposed excavations in the Orient to his superior Decazes).[13]

In 1827 at the height of Eckstein's activities, Benjamin Constant wrote another note in his *De la religion*, commenting on this sentence of Hegel's text: "It is a complete mistake to suppose that one can raise the religion of India above all ancient religions, like the devotees of that new eucharistic species which places it nowadays almost next to Christianity." Constant's note blames a theocratic conspiracy modeled on that of the Orient: he carefully avoids mentioning Eckstein by name (it is known how much of a *bête noir* he was for Constant), but the description leaves no doubt: "A witty man whose learning is similar to that of all the students who spend some time at the German universities" (and Constant was in a good position to speak on their behalf), a man who faked the texts and whose most important argument was the very one for which Heine reproached Eckstein, that of a grand nobleman saying "I give you my word of honor that I am right." There is no need to go on multiplying examples. During the first half of the nineteenth century, when initiates spoke of an Indo-Christianity originating in Germany, it is clear they meant Eckstein.

Was There "An Indo-Germanic Gang"?

Thus, had this peculiar man been less long-winded, the theological aspect of the East-West question would probably not have emerged so soon from the principalities of Germany, since the introducers of new ideas there complained that the world took so little interest in them. After a great many disparagements of Eckstein's intellect, which remained, despite himself, superficial, we must give him his due: he oozed vitality at every pore, his enthusiasm extended to all studies and every aspect of the past. This essential gift, which his contemporaries discerned, led them to speak of his "powerful vigor," "a thousand leaves tossed to the four winds," "a bolt of lightning flashing constantly among the clouds."

Certainly Eckstein had no monopoly on the remarks he made: for example, his classification of epics by "nomenclature-type" squared with another cliché of the period, that of universal literary families. India and Persia would still have touched the poets without Eckstein and would still have raised questions for believers. The phenomena were simply more phosphorescent in his wake. His work was a certain intellectual conquest of his adopted country, and the surrenders he caused were quick and plentiful. To what extent then did Germanism compromise his orientalism? Eckstein seems to have been unaware of any compromise. Not that his incontinence lacked malice. Just the same, Eckstein's quality of "conviction" which Hugo saw so clearly, and which either crushed or overwhelmed his listeners, eliminating the rebels in either case, was consistently the conviction of being the ambassador of the best. If characters such as Eckstein demonstrate a lack of self-doubt, it follows that the causes which adopt them as defenders are, for them, unassailable. There is nothing occult in Eckstein's fidelity to his native land. Eckstein's *Catholique* straightforwardly professed, in no uncertain terms, to be a Parisian replica of Görres' *Katholik*, on which Eckstein had collaborated, and of a number of other German periodicals. And Görres gave Eckstein his seal of approval, calling Eckstein's "the most authentic German mind to be transplanted into France. The *Catholique* is born of German schools, has studied with German teachers; it has assimilated their characteristics and treats the subjects that concern it with their mentality."[14] The same is true of its harmony with Creuzer on the interpretation of myths, about which it made the same avowals.

These connections were obvious to everyone. And many did not refrain from describing them in harsh terms. The examples I have given would be sufficient had not the complaint of Hoene-Wroński introduced a specific charge that demands an answer.[15] Through the radiant clouds of his criticism flashed the denunciation, repeated four times, of a veritable organized "gang" which he at times termed Indo-Christian, at times anti-Church, and yet another time "Indo-Christian mysticism from Germany." There can be no doubt that, as with Benjamin Constant and Lanjuinais, the term Indo-Christian was a reference to Eckstein, who here again was not mentioned by name. Moreover, here he was placed by his title, Baron, in the same bunch of reprobates as Friedrich Schlegel, Görres, and Baader. The list is not surprising, but Wroński saw it as a clear case of political and heretical conspiracy. He was willing "to refrain" from producing the evidence of the conspiracy. Besides, what good would it do? There was no accounting for any of it if one did not admit the existence of the German gang "whose mystical systems of religiosity" represented "an infernal necessity" that always pointed to Friedrich Schlegel.

To be sure, Wroński was not noted for his sang-froid. But Sainte-Beuve, in an article in 1833, two years after Wroński's accusation, attributed a truly unusual dual quality to Eckstein: on the one hand the man plowed the Germanic furrow that de Staël had cut through the literary circles of Paris;

on the other, he was an all-but-official foreign resident in French territory, such as there had always been (probably an allusion to Grimm or perhaps Wilhelm Schlegel, whom de Staël had brought in). Eckstein was not only alive at the time, but Sainte-Beuve knew him and exchanged visits with him almost excessively. Thus he would hardly want to offend or embarrass him. One can imagine that Eckstein accepted, perhaps even insisted upon, Sainte-Beuve's judgment. He agreed with Sainte-Beuve on a great many subjects and used the pretext of his friendship with Sainte-Beuve to further his own attacks. The most likely explanation can be found in remembering Eckstein's most distinctive feature: he too was a born crossroader. For this reason he was bound to unite and distort all the impulses and stimuli of his time and country. To inventory all his mind was stocked with, and all his mouth conveyed, one need only refer to the various rubrics we have already identified. The most important one was that all his entreaties were addressed directly, personally, and with irresistible liveliness, to the French Romantics. A general conspiracy may well have existed, and I am convinced that one did, but it was also a conspiracy of the period and the stars.

The Profound Sense of the Oriental Renaissance

Eckstein always moved toward what outshone him: the advent of oriental studies in Germany appeared to be a great historical opportunity, a unique good fortune to be exploited. Herder's entire system militated in favor of reassessing the long-unappreciated barbarians. Hegel managed to call all Christianity "the Germanic world." The Middle Ages were no longer to be considered one of the last resorts of historical studies, but the exemplary youth of the world that the invaders' virility had regenerated. What was beautiful and powerful could no longer be defined by a pretended order, appeasing notions tidied away in cautious or classical cadres; rather they would have to be defined in terms of effervescence. In short, for the first time the static was vigorously opposed by a principle that one day would raise a furor in the name of the dynamic.

The concept of creative genius changed directions; it was drained of its ancient conformity to set models, which sapped it with conventionality, and was filled with the assets of breakthroughs. Thereafter the sanctity of revolt was attached to it. The revolt was primarily—and this was its great motive force—against the preconception called classicism, which had to be taken by its roots and scrutinized as to its very origins; other dazzling pasts were used to break the monopoly of the prestige that the Greco-

Latin past enjoyed. Thus it was a declaration of war—a "war of myths,"
in the words of Max Rouché, a remarkable historian, who said in his
translation of Herder's *Auch eine Philosophie der Geschichte:*

The very idea of the Renaissance, which was antibarbarian and anti-Gothic, was
represented as an Italian myth. . . . Herder's rehabilitation of the Middle Ages in
1773 was an antirationalist myth and a glorification of modern Germans in their
struggle against the cultural hegemony that France enjoyed as propagator of the
"philosophy of the enlightenment." Through Herder's writings the people who
had overthrown antiquity dared at last—after a delay of more than a thousand
years—to justify themselves to history. The Renaissance, as its name alone implies, was an indication of the unpretentiousness of barbarians who were anxious
to annul their own handiwork, the Middle Ages, and to thereby repudiate themselves. . . . With Herder, on the contrary, the descendants of the ancient Germans repudiated such deferred self-reproach and such belated homage, which
constituted the Renaissance, to antiquity, their victim.

Herder's philosophy of history represents a decisive moment in a "dialectic of justification." Herder salvaged and ennobled the barbarians as such,
sanctioned their destruction of the ancient world, and condemned any attempt to restore it, as had been done in the Renaissance.

Or rather he outlined "a veritable Renaissance deferred." The war of
myths goes back further than Rouché suspected: drawn up in opposition
to classical mythology was an entire mythical world, more vast, more
original and authentic, within which classical mythology seemed no more
than a detail. This newly discovered world would be a dependency of these
fair-haired brutes who in this way would restore the true law and who
would best serve destiny by razing the Roman world. For, in the dialectics of justification, this was an all-important episode, yet one that seems
to have been overlooked: *Herder's immediate successors discovered the means
to insert their ethnic interests into the very concept of Renaissance.* From that
time onward, this interest would be preserved, and sanctified, among
themselves.

One day they planted their flag on territories that had recently been reclaimed in the Orient and named this *the* Renaissance. Unexpectedly, the
ancient world, that of the other Renaissance, the land of classicism whose
privileges were thus revoked, was generally delighted at the news. Was
not the Oriental Renaissance the true, deferred, Renaissance? It was definitely a great piece of historical luck, for ethnic interests alone would not
have been sufficient to produce the Renaissance that here was linked with
a great deal of human interest, with the cause of humanism itself. The
arrival of oriental studies in Romantic Europe may have seemed a sign of
fate: those whom the spirit of the Renaissance had always opposed found

in these studies another Renaissance which was no longer finite (in any sense of the word) but limitless (with all the incentives of the boundless) and which was their own to the full extent (or to the full excess) that they baptized themselves the Asians of the Occident. Germany, which considered herself thwarted by a Renaissance identified with papal Rome, Roman law, and the Muses, replaced it with the Renaissance of an Orient associated with invasions, a Renaissance of the violent and the indeterminate, of possibilities and paradox. And since Germany did not lack a sense of daring, she confronted the Western mind with the great question of its origins, though not without perverting the question by her desire for vindication. And although she did not lack a mania for seizing the world, Germany engaged the human mind in what is perhaps its greatest adventure.

Two young husbands were arguing. "The worst thing about women," said the first, "is that they are never faithful." "No, no," replied the other, "the problem is that they always are."

The Quinet Repossession

A Typical Adventure

The case of Edgar Quinet is as close to Eckstein's as effect is to cause. Quinet went to Germany for fulfillment in the 1830s when the reality of the situation there was beginning to differ singularly from what Germany's propagandists promised. The historical school of Niebuhr and Otfried Müller was renouncing the tyranny of orientalist theories that claimed to have traced the origin of Greek thought to India. Creuzer's excesses had provoked Voss's antisymbolic and antitheological reaction. "Asian migrations" were still turned to account, while a newly arrived and aggressive materialism simultaneously caused philosophy to lapse into politics. Examining Guigniaut's translation of Creuzer, Renan later stated that interests had changed markedly since 1825. The young Quinet, who had come to Heidelberg to examine the spirit of old Germany, witnessed the advent of a new spirit during the critical moment of its transformation. From day to day he saw the antagonisms, instabilities, seethings, and threats. His fluctuations were a topsy-turvy reflection of local nationalism. As the German insinuation became an open campaign, Quinet collected himself. At first he saw a Germany serving primarily the cause of Indic studies; one fine day he saw that Germany was serving itself in everything.

No Romantic was more clearly marked by his reading of Chateaubriand

and de Staël; from the former he inherited glowing language and a poetic conception of history, from the latter an inclination toward a Germanic ordering of thought. Quinet's mother had him read *De l'Allemagne* by the age of ten; he was already obsessed with Goethe. The seriousness of his Protestant education gave him the conscience of a missionary writer, but the object of the mission would be secularized and the spirituality would remain latent as his belief turned to faith in history. Opposition to religious orthodoxy, however, did not signify adherence to rationalism; within his anti-Jesuit politics there would appear to be a resentment of the love of God, a despondent hope that romantically took consolation in a future and churchless religion. In 1857, sixteen years after its first edition, Quinet, then in his fifties, dedicated his *Génie des religions,* in which India and Persia were magnified, to Dumesnil, who had substituted for him at the Collège de France because, as the dedication stated, both of them had sought, and found, "the elements of a new faith."

In the Shadow of Herder, In the Arms of Creuzer

Although Quinet probably got his first inkling of Herder from de Staël's book and began his reading of Herder with either *Die Vorwelt* or the *Ideen,* the revelation of Herder's thought came to him through a chance encounter. Quinet did not know a word of German at the time, and he set out to learn it by translating it. This is, perhaps, not a bad method, but it produced dubious results in the case of the *Ideen.* The twenty-two-year-old boy hurried from Charolles to Paris in January 1825 and almost immediately found a publisher. Berger, the son-in-law and colleague of Levrault, young himself, "caught fire" in turn and introduced Quinet to the influential Victor Cousin, who had recently returned from visiting philosophers in Germany. Quinet brought him a preliminary outline of the introduction and part of his translation. Cousin had discovered the advantage one could take, once one was successful, of many things, including young people. He lavished kindness on Quinet, who saw him every week for almost an entire year and swore only by this god.

At some point Quinet met Michelet at Cousin's home, and straightway recognized in him a kindred spirit. The two friends had common interests and passions that immediately sealed their mutual understanding, which was confirmed by their parallel studies of Herder and Vico and later blossomed under the great Indo-Iranian themes. Cousin flattered himself that he had promoted his "young friends" to introduce Herder and Vico, respectively, into France. But the beneficiaries left some doubt on this point. In any case, Quinet united German philosophy and orientalism before

Cousin's efforts to do the same at the Collège de France. It was the tradition of Herder that Quinet went to seek in Heidelberg. At the same time, Cousin referred him, as Berger simultaneously did, to the celebrated Creuzer who was heir to this tradition. When, according to Tronchon, whose *Le jeune Edgar Quinet* I am relying on here, Quinet dropped in on Creuzer, whom he called "perhaps the only man of genius left in this country," at the end of 1827, Quinet saw but a single portrait on the wall—Herder's. It was under this flag that the professor received the student with open arms. Creuzer "directed his studies of German subjects" and allowed Quinet to translate his work into French. They "saw each other almost every day," and "the serenity of Creuzer was a veritable blessing for Quinet." Creuzer would be embodied later, in 1860, as the sage Taliesin in Quinet's *Merlin l'Enchanteur*. For his part, Creuzer related his encounters with the young Quinet in *Aus dem Leben eines alten Professors*. Nevertheless, seeing his old teacher again in 1857 shortly before Creuzer's death, Quinet judged him harshly: it was Creuzer and his colleagues who had "scrambled the centuries," "by placing metaphysics before poetry and song in primitive times."

In the first flush of Heidelberg, Quinet had endlessly thanked the heavens for "having led him to this delightful place where everything invites one to reflect." He wrote to Michelet, "Our philosophy of history seems very young to me, young like ourselves, and I rejoice at seeing how much work remains for us to do." He immersed himself in the simultaneous study of philosophy and languages, which included Greek, but also naturally included the oriental and the German. Quinet, however, does not seem to have probed, or perhaps even attempted, the rudiments of oriental languages except through the work of Western philologists. His working notes attest to his scholarship and conscientiousness, but he primarily cites the Sanskrit texts of European translators and commentators.

Quinet's translation of Herder's *Ideen* was dedicated to Creuzer "as a token of profound gratitude" and was followed by an *Essai sur Herder*, whom he did not hesitate to call "a philosophical disciple of Jesus." Pen in hand, he read the sixty volumes of Schelling's reflections and drafted his own theory of history on the basis of them. He prided himself on his efforts to endow French thought with German models and stimuli from which, he felt at the time, he would never deviate. When the famous translation was finally about to be published in Paris, Quinet, still working within the Herder-Creuzer framework (Michelet, citing him in *Oeuvres choisies de Vico*, 1835, spells his name *Quinette*), tackled a subject vital to him—*L'Origine des Dieux*. In this work, said his wife in her *Edgar Quinet avant l'exile*, he was "pursuing the three branches of human knowledge: religion, history, and cosmogony." It was his way of becoming identified,

as he had written to his mother in 1825, "with the concept that our century must bequeath to the world." He was moving "where the universe
is headed." In 1831 he published a study, "L'Avenir des religions," in the
Revue des Deux-Mondes: thus the same seed which would later produce
Ahasvérus, his great fictional work, and *Le génie des religions,* his great critical
work, was already bearing fruit. His lectures at Lyon, which he began with
prodigious success in 1839, on the same subject, and even with the same
title as this last work, bore his characteristic mark—a mixture of indelible
impressions and original repetitions. The basis, substance, and commentary came from his German education, concerning which Cousin's venge-
ful remark aimed at Quinet, to which Sainte-Beuve gave wide circulation,
is well known: "You will never extricate yourself." Nevertheless, his organization of the Indo-Iranian domain, his structurings of the whole, are
those of a powerful and liberated mind. And the reason Quinet is such
an excellent source of information concerning a certain influence is that
he later repudiated and exposed it. Heidelberg was clearly the source of
his lectures at Lyon; but it was followed by remarkable detours and, finally, a reversal of his position.

Creuzer's influence extended even to Quinet's love life: he was indebted to Creuzer for introducing him to his future wife, Mina Moré, the
daughter of a French emigré who was for Quinet "the personification of
Prayer." They began, as was the custom of the country, by feasting together on poetry and philosophy, history and myth, music and religion.
But in September 1831 a period of intense Lutheran fanaticism set in, and
in the grips of "Teutomania" Quinet's future in-laws insisted the young
Frenchman pay the penalty for 1813. There were heated scenes, followed
by a temporary breach. In a few weeks Quinet had tacked together an
inspired revenge: *L'Allemagne et la révolution* was the work of an enlightened man, and Quinet sent it off to Michelet for publication in the
Revue des Deux-Mondes.

Quinet had hit upon the one phenomenon of civilization for which even
the Oriental Renaissance could not compensate Germany, the French
Revolution. It had been a sudden and complete realization for him. He
divulged his discovery so violently—the discovery of a Prussianized, in-
tractable Germany now stripped of all ideals and riveted on material gain
and of the blindness of the French, who were being threatened by this
"German unity"—that Michelet took alarm, called Quinet's tract a pamphlet, and advised him to be prudent. For a long time the *Revue* refused
to publish the piece, insisting that Quinet tone it down. The overly lucid
witness stood by his opinions and had his way in the end. Although the
Revue would only agree to publish excerpts, the full text was published in
book form early in 1832. Thirty-five years early Cassandra announced Sa-

dova and what followed, and did not cease to do so. Such an attitude rendered the Herderian relics that contradicted it even more salient.

Quinet's trip to Italy came just after its publication. His resentment against Germany's extreme abuse of Italy, a country of great beauty, was reinforced at every turn. He traced the advance of ancient peoples on tablets at Ostia and conceived, on the basis of the methodology of the philosophy of history, the first idea for what would become the *Génie des religions*. In an Italy both revealed and revealing to which he had come to forget Heidelberg's anti-Latin frenzy, Quinet compiled notes "on the origins of religious societies considered from the study of their poems and monuments." At the same time that he was preparing to rip up the still intact and generally unilateral contract of admiration of the French Romantics for Holy Germany in *Allemagne et Italie,* he was building a major work on the basis of the principles of German systematics.

On his return to Paris, he again became a drawing-room man, a role he always played reluctantly and yet always with a success whose sheer delight always drew him back. He was an important newcomer in the salon of Madame Récamier, who commissioned him to write the review of *Mémoires d'outre-tombe* which turned up, surprisingly, in *Allemagne et Italie.* Madame Récamier's home, l'Abbaye-aux-Bois, had two floors, the upper of which was soon rented out for the sake of economy to Mary Clarke, a favorite of the mistress because Chateaubriand, the sovereign of the salon, found her amusing. The restless Irishwoman became enamoured of Quinet at first sight "with an infatuation that she made no effort to conceal and about which she was teased by everyone."[16] This house became one of the active symposia where specialists in oriental studies, its popularizers, and celebrated and receptive writers exchanged views. Clarke was at first in love with Fauriel, and later became the wife of Julius Mohl. In these two salons, whose two floors "sometimes merged," Quinet again met, besides Sainte-Beuve and his shadow Magnin, the versatile Ampère, Mohl's intimate friend and roommate, a man who, like Fauriel, quickly became versed in all branches of oriental studies; Augustin Thierry, Saint-Simon's former secretary; and Thierry's own secretary, Armand Carrel, who had relinquished Vico to Michelet. It is worth remembering, as I have said before, that every exchange was a living influence that both the drones and the workers counted on.

To provide a few more excerpts from Quinet's engagement book: Janin's home was always open to him; he dined once a week with Lacordaire and had recourse to Lamennais during his great quarrel over French epics. In 1836–37 he sent this sample of an average weekly schedule to his mother: Sunday—Madame Récamier (Ballanche); Tuesday—Princess Belgioioso (Heine, who did not care much for him); Wednesday—the widow Hoche; Thursday—Mary Clarke; Friday—Odilon Barrot; Saturday—Lamartine. Friendship with Mickiewicz, locket from David d'Angers. In touch with Constant, Guizot, and Villemain. In autumn of 1833 he "very frequently" saw Hugo, with whom he had formed a friendship at the time *Orientales* was published and with whom he also talked a great deal about his own epic poems. By 1829, back from Morée, he had a foothold in the Cuvier salon, crossroads of the scholarly and literary worlds. When he returned to Germany in December 1834 for reconciliation and his nuptials and had settled down there for several years, he was again involved, this time in Germany, with "all the distinguished men."

It was no surprise that Quinet's mind was one of the first to give evidence of the theory of nomenclature-types. As soon as he turned to creative literature, Quinet headed straight for the epic form, which had been only a dream for French literature. *Eloa* in 1824 had been epic only in intent, a miniature version of Milton trumpeted by Chateaubriand; in French literature it was always more a matter of individual stanzas than of whole structures. Quinet was alive to the spirit of monuments. In 1833 Magnin acknowledged Quinet's "instinct *cosmogonique.*" He intervened in the Young France movement to apply certain lessons illustrative of Eckstein's scholarly propaganda. Such was the significance of *Ahasvérus:* in the thought of the Eternal the Vedas encountered the entire human adventure. The dates of composition are revealing: in 1831–32, Quinet rejected Germany, had a falling-out with Mina, and extolled Latin beauty out of spite; in 1834 he had an equally abrupt reversal of feelings and raced off to be near Mina and Heidelberg. In 1833, between these two dates, he wrote *Ahasvérus*, an attempt at French epic that was typically Germanic—even Faustian—in style. In *Ahasvérus*, Quinet's taste for Urpoesie had matured, and in it the fellowship between all poetic traditions, from the Vedas to the *Nibelungenlied*, bore fruit. Still another event during these same years was the discovery, so important for Quinet, of previously unknown epics, thanks to which the country of his birth would no longer need to envy the country of his schooling. In May 1831 Quinet announced to his mother that he had, two weeks previously, uncovered in the Bibliothèque royale "French national poems of 40–60 thousand lines, all based on the Celtic traditions." This Celtism, as one might well imagine, appeared at just the right moment to counterbalance the *Minnesingers.* We know what multiferious disputes arose from his discovery. Quinet settled the quarrel once and for all, and Paulin Paris—whose *Histoire poétique de Charlemagne* was published in 1865, followed by *Littérature française au moyen âge*—would no longer be definitive. Difficult problems were arising, several of which had not been solved. Quinet's intuition and boldness, and the very noise of the battle itself, did much to urge the still faltering study of French medievalism forward, which was certainly one of his objectives. Even Goethe appreciated the initiatives of this improvisor.

An Expansionist Undertaking

Although Quinet was one of those best qualified to appreciate what splendors were still to be seen in the new French poetry, he lacked the poetic gift needed to give France the masterpiece he predicted for her. Not that he didn't make every effort; Madame Quinet encouraged him to speak of it ardently. I cannot resist imagining his conversations with Hugo and Lamartine on the topic. No one at the time was completely sure which of them would succeed in replacing the routine of more or less isolated and ephemeral compositions with all-embracing ones. It was *Ahasvérus* in 1833 that led the march toward the epic: Lamartine did not fall in until *Jocelyn* in 1836 and *La chute d'un Ange* in 1838. In the end it was Hugo's destiny to achieve the goal. Although we now consider Quinet a failure as a poet, his poetry was a major event for his contemporaries. The impact of his works on his times was all out of proportion to their intrinsic value. For two decades Quinet was considered a major poet, called by the names of his heroes, first *Ahasvérus,* then *Merlin.* But ultimately Quinet's poetry prepared the way for the prose of Flaubert.

Quinet's true creation was the prose epic. And yet, unfortunately, its lack of verse was its greatest flaw. At the least Quinet sought and pointed out the ways to greatness; he was aware of this while composing his *Napoléon* in a style the opposite Musset's, which he called, "simply, the poetry of fops." But greatness in art is not a measurement, it is a mystery. What was great in Quinet's work was the intention; what was lacking was not the artist's inspiration, but rather the forceful stroke, the placement of accents. Quinet remained a precursor because the very inventiveness of his work occurred again and again without advancing. It was as if he saw endless couplets but never the pattern of a work, the structure of a chapter. The stagnation of diction within his own beautiful lines perpetually froze the stream of his words. One leaves these areas of arid munificence with keen disappointment: it does not seem just that destiny would not grant this man the tiny grain that would tip the scales and endow the Oriental Renaissance with its crowning work. *Ahasvérus* contains some admirable passages, but they are only bits and pieces. We are reminded of Professor Cousin's distressing remark: the student Quinet did not "extricate" himself. A hundred superior concepts remain imprisoned in a mass of words, treading on their own heels. Although a friend of Quinet, Magnin expressed his embarrassment over the poet's work in December 1833 in the *Revue des Deux-Mondes,* which had published excerpts from it three months earlier. Magnin felt that Quinet's book lacked authority, that it showed little promise of enduring beyond its initial impact; yet he understood that it marked an important beginning.

Some of the book's merits underscore a characteristic of the new Renaissance: in a century that was, more than any other, a time of openings, it *undertook an expansion,* which was possible for Quinet because he used the very substance of this new Renaissance, the pattern of a multifaceted colossus raised up from the earth. This boundless dialog between the monuments and souls of all civilizations seemed to set the stage for *a philosophy of historical poetry.* And this appeal for the gigantic, where the more learned Quinet collided with the more creative but more cautious Hugo, was eminently satisfied by the remembrance of these incentives to grandeur that remained hallmarks of nomenclature-type: from the Orient came works such as the Hindu epics and the *Shah Namah,* from the Occident came such works such as the Eddas and the *chansons de geste.* They all swirled through *Ahasvérus,* which transformed syncretism into literature. Here is one of the many songs of "the bird Vinayena" in the First Day:

"Look, it is from my beak that the grains of life fall one by one to create the plants and the forests; I drop the water lillies into the vallies. . . . The leaves quiver, the rushes cry aloud; already the stars take flight like a covey of golden-winged birds setting forth for distant countries." In the snake's reply we heard the rhythms of images and phrases, the breath of what would be Flaubert's style: "I see only mountains that coil back on their links, only rivers that glide serpentine beneath the forests, only the horse Séméhé that runs forever without rest beneath the talons of the jinns, sweating blood, his silver tail buffeted by the winds. At his breastplate, two eyes blaze; his color changes with each moment—now he is pale, now black, now blue as the heavens, ravaged like the venom that falls from my mouth. Oh, how pitiful to see him!" And again the bird's refrain: "I rose to the topmost branch of the tree of the world; I followed the flight of the swiftest star; I descended into the valleys where rain never falls; everywhere I found only the morning lark, only black-winged jinns, only the oriole hanging her nest from two silken threads, cradling her chicks on the newborn world."

This was the beginning of an aesthetic that would move through Flaubert, Baudelaire, Leconte de Lisle, and the Parnassians, a kind of museum loveliness new to French literature which has endured to our times in the works of the Symbolists, its almost exclusive votaries. Let us remember all these for the time when the lasting works of the Oriental Renaissance will be asked of us.

In the fourth section of the First Day, entitled "Human Tribes Assemble on the Summits of the Himalayas," we find a truly "Aryan" theme. The First Tribe asks the Ganges, "he who has the broadest banks and torrents deep as the sky," to carry them where he is going. The Ganges replies, "Like me, one day you, with your tribe adorned in pearl necklaces, with your fragrant centuries, your gods, your murmerings, and your cities, will vanish into your ocean and your eternity." Here is a synthesis of views on migrations and a brief statement on the Vedic spirit. India, Persia, Babylonia, and Judea, all the recovered antiquities, all the primitives, were linked, through the character of Humanity-as-the-Wandering-Jew, with the medieval and the modern. Then both the lessons remembered from Quinet's days at Heidelberg and the grudges he bore against his German masters there burst forth in unexpected confessions. On the one hand, in the sixth section of the Third Day, Mob, Death, uses the Heidelberg esplanade to symbolize "the skepticism from across the Rhine, of Voss or of Heine, or even Goethe himself."[17] On the other hand, the hero voices the full measure of unsated spirituality that Quinet brought back from Germany: "It would require a new religion to restore repose to my mind, a religion from which no one has yet drawn. This is what I seek. Only there will I be able to slake the eternal thirst that consumes me." I emphasize these points because these are misunderstood texts whose real meaning dominates my inquiry. This impossible new religion, so often appealed to by German Romantics—and Quinet with them—on the faith of philological revelations, and the thirst for it that developed among them, seems like the one in this specific passage in which what might have been hope for Schleiermacher could be only nihilism for Flaubert. Can one imagine such a hope in Quinet? Yet at the head of the first published excerpts from his poem was this declaration: "Humanity has a dull torment in her entrails as if she were going to give birth to a God."

Ahasvérus is strangely autobiographical. This becomes quite clear when, in the interlude of the Third Day, "The Poet" curses his wife's native country and contrasts it with "the sun that rises from Asia" over Morée. A deep incompatibility separated Quinet from the Germanic spirit. It was rooted in one of the fundamentals of orientalized Romanticism, upon the very principle of the famous nomenclature-types. Ever since his youth Quinet had adhered to the cult of personality: "It was through his clear understanding of the role that devolves to human personality that Edgar Quinet avoided the kind of pantheistic intoxication into which his admiration of Herder might have led him."[18] Thus in 1838, in his critique of Strauss's *Life of Jesus*, Quinet refuted the Wolffian theory applied to either Christian origins or Homeric poetry. Moreover, as the leaders of the German movement passed away, Quinet gradually became alienated from Germany itself; it was them, rather than the country, that he came to identify with the new Renaissance: "The old German genius is breaking down. . . . Goethe and Hegel have gone the way of Lessing, Klopstock, Schiller, Kant, Fichte, and Herder, the heroes of the German Renaissance." Behind this new spiritual void an increasingly menacing thing was creeping toward the motherland of the Revolution, an element that alarmed the most unshakable aspects of Quinet's character; his spiritualism was unmanned by it; the liberal in him was deeply apprehensive.

It was in 1838 at Heidelberg that Quinet prepared, along with his course at Lyon, the arguments contained in his dissertation on primitive Hindu poetry, *De Indicae poesis antiquissimae natura et indole*, which he defended at Strasbourg on January 25, 1839. Although, according to Madame Quinet, he was still dominated by Germanic influences in this "thorough study of sacred oriental texts," he voiced a strong reaction against his friend Lamennais's excessively Germanophilic *Marseillaise de la paix* in a poem that Michelet later ventured to read at the Collège de France. Karl Hillebrand corroborated Quinet's reports and misgivings: during "the ten years from 1837 to 1848" German scholarship underwent a complete transformation, becoming militant, secular, and bellicose in the process. It was the end of "the peaceable and scholarly Germany of the 1820s." The new Germany was "determined never to relinquish the battlefield, and voices from the rostrum drowned out the peaceful murmur of scholarship not involved in, and foreign to, the national way of life." Thereafter it became fashionable "to look with disdain upon this glorious past when a volume by Niebuhr or Creuzer had been of greater importance than the signing of a commercial treaty." German philologists enrolled themselves in the nationalist movement, as linguistic demands had urged them to do since Fichte and Klaproth, if not since Leibniz. We have seen how, when Europe abandoned Latin as the language of learning, German scholars rankled at the fact that they could be read by only a few. They subsequently plunged themselves even more exclusively into German modes of expression, which gave rise to specific modes of thought; then, feeling more separated than ever, they blamed the rest of the world for just about everything that went wrong and found it particularly at fault for not having become German—a favor they would have to perform for it. The universal Goethe himself found it difficult to forgive the Orient for encroaching upon the national. In a conversation with Eckermann (February 15, 1824), Goethe stated, "Germany alone has, in all the genres, attained such a high position that our eyes can scarcely take it all in, and on top of that we are obliged to be Greek, Latin, English, and French! And now there is the Orient, to which they are mad enough to send us. A young person must be absolutely bewildered."

In his lengthy introduction to *Allemagne et Italie*, Quinet, who excelled in this kind of writing, recognized, along with his contemporaries, the French mistake in accrediting only two or three "grands siècles" as worthy escorts of the century of Louis XIV; but he also demonstrated how in its turn a certain German intolerance served "the pain of national pride too long repressed. . . . One tore up the testament of the grand century with a kind of rage." In his need for liberal views, Quinet, boldly restoring the seventeenth century to its true historical place, passed from despondency to indignation when the country he had believed to be composed entirely of love and poetry became a country "of doubt and anger." The outbursts "of insults, obscenities, and cynical rage" that revealed the annihilation of an enthusiasm accentuated what was senseless and unreal throughout the entire field of history itself, an essential lack of "sympathy and charity, or rather of humanity," an "indifference fluttering between good and evil, between justice and injustice, between liberty and tyranny." All this makes a great deal of sense: the beginning of a Renaissance, of a humanism, had also been the beginning of the modern world. One does not want to speak of or announce the ultimate failure of what this humanism was going to become in Germany. We are still torn apart by that rupture; too much has resulted from this indifference, scientifically installed, toward justice and injustice, liberty and tyranny, the racial wars provoked by Schopenhauer and Gobineau and the reversal of moral values drawn from Hegel. The initial corruption undoubtedly appeared in the vindictive nature of the Herderian Renaissance; but the "Asiatic patriotism" that Quinet denounced in Görres, a follower of Herder, the author of *Mythengeschichte der asiatischen Welt*, who was nicknamed "the fourth ally" of the Holy Alliance in 1814—this was altogether another matter. "It is Görres who, discussing the unfaithfulness of Alsace, said in a fit of Asiatic patriotism, 'Burn Strasbourg and leave nothing standing but the spire of the cathedral to immortalize the revenge of the German peoples.' "

Nevertheless, later in *Génie des religions*, Quinet referred to Görres as "a sort of Occidental Purana," "based on the model of the Ganges philosophers." The German language "seems to be drawn directly from the source of oriental speech." The Germanic race continued to possess an astonishing "genius for contemplation" that made them "a sort of Christian Orient, an Asia within Europe." Rückert's popularity proved that "Persian poetry . . . moves the German heart as if through the memory of a second fatherland" in such a manner that "today the German genius seems to complete itself, to confirm itself through the genius of Persia and India." Moreover, in his letters and pamphlets Quinet condemned contemporary Germany for its despair and nihilism; yet in his book it is Germany alone that "has avoided what has been called the literature of despair." He had previously denounced the demise of spirituality in Germany, yet here "Christianity, having entered almost entirely into the theories of the German metaphysicians, has never suppressed, even for a single day, the German mind, so that Germany progressed from religion to philosophy without violence. . . . She was never for a single moment confronted with nothingness, and thus the memory of such a confrontation does not poison her present." Certainly there is a grain of truth in his observations, but could we thus say that the literature of despair did not spring from *Werther*, or that the vortex of pantheism, which from another perspective has been called "a nameless anguish," did not suck the German mentality into itself?

The Oriental Renaissance: A Nineteenth-Century Question

Be that as it may, such were the German themes of the Renaissance which Quinet circulated in France. By his different talents and influence, Quinet's effort reinforced Eckstein's. He continued to rely on German philologists for vital information in the field. He had good reason to allege in his old age that "the philologists today . . . are all bringing new facts to light, thanks to newly translated and published manuscripts, but in 1839 we possessed nothing." In the German universities he had received an education that "was passed down like a shibboleth. From Schlegel to the twentieth century a steady transmission, scrupulously maintained, provided close ties that bound all learned men together. With a more or less clear awareness of the objective, each one worked for the glorification of the Germanic genius, the only authoritative interpreter of the Aryan genius."[19] Fustel de Coulanges denounced this particular apitude of German researchers for exploiting historical materials politically.

Quinet denied having been duped, and twenty-six years after the publication of his book recalled that he had resisted the "Alexandrianism" of the Creuzers—a defense that satisfied Michelet, Jean Reynaud, and perhaps Burnouf.[20] Quinet had indeed stigmatized undertakings in which all differences of age and thought were obliterated, "in which all points of time so approximated each other as to become identical," in which the pantheism of Schelling was linked with that of Iamblicus and Julian the Apostate and in Germany attributed to primitive peoples "emerging from chaos, the accumulated learning of the philosophical schools."[21] Quinet made up for his contradictions by the constancy with which he rejected the impersonality of history in the German manner. He embodied the resistance of the French mind to the excesses of a peculiar intellectual faculty that simultaneously led to both the systematic and the vague. The *Génie des religions*, which continued in the direction pointed to by Chateaubriand, launched a series of French adaptations of the philosophy of history, as *Ahasvérus* had been a French adaptation of the Faustian epic. In books and in the salons Quinet's religious history prepared the way for the arrival of "histoire-poésie."

This composite is now out of date, but it served its purpose for its time, and it left behind it some rather beautiful remnants. Without the Oriental Renaissance that Quinet introduced, it would be difficult to imagine such poems of Hugo's as "Dieu," "L'Ane," "Religions et religion," and *William Shakespeare*, the Daphne cycle of Vigny, or the model for Flaubert's *Temptation of Saint Anthony*. Reshuffling epic nomenclature as the manuscript of his lecture notes for 1838 show, Quinet concluded, "With respect to the influence that poetry might exert, we can be sure, first of all, that it will be of some consequence to the literary forms of the future. An entire civilization [that of the Hindus] does not emerge from oblivion in this manner without affecting the human imagination in one way or another." "Oriental" poetry, as Quinet would reiterate in his lectures at Lyon the following year, is "a new metal cast into the mold of modern humanity."

In his affirmation that "The Oriental Renaissance is an important question for the nineteenth century," Quinet set forth what he had previously noted. He was by this time a nineteenth-century man, just as he had hoped he would be at the beginning of his career. A nostalgia for a lost paradise coincided with the need that Europe, unconsoled by its religion, felt for a Homeric age. Ancient Asia with the most sacerdotal of literatures seemed to suddenly hold out the promise of secret treasures. After the convoy launched by Eckstein and Quinet, one no longer wrote for the same world, because one no longer thought in terms of the same world.

Through some predestination, Quinet made his debut as a professor in a city of the Illuminati. Introducing his course at Lyon on April 10, 1839, he placed it under the patronage of Ballanche, "the most spiritualistic of the writers of our day." Moreover, he had been named to the chair at Lyon by Salvandy at the insistence of Creuzer and Madame Récamier. Among the audience crowding the spacious auditorium were Blanc Saint-Bonnet, Chenavard, Victor de Laprade, and Saint-René Taillandier. *Ahasvérus* had been a revelation for Saint-Bonnet and inspired his enormous *L'unité spirituelle*, an immediate success on its publication in 1841. Also in 1841 Quinet would find a publisher for Laprade, who idolized him; in Laprade's *Psyché* the themes of the philosophy of religions were applied to primitive times. Chenavard, a painter led astray by ideology, impatient to "encyclopedize" his ideas on walls, projected an enormous plan for a mosaic for the Pantheon in which, under the simple title "The Philosophy of History," he planned to depict Ballanche's *Palingénésie*.[22]

In 1841 Quinet's course became a book. Lèbre analyzed it at length in the April 15, 1842 issue of *Revue des Deux-Mondes,* where oriental topics were discussed with all the familiarity of topics already integrated into European thought. Nevertheless, not everything had yet been said for Egypt or Assyria or Persia, which still awaited Burnouf's decipherment of Avestan, or for India, for which only a single Veda had been translated, whose "mythological poems had been studied for only a short time," and where there was still no clear understanding of Buddhism. Lèbre reconsidered the question of a Hinduized Christianity, but his study revealed more rigidity than new information. As might be expected from this sort of article, Lèbre did justice to the major role Quinet played in the service of these ideas: "This universal understanding of all that is beautiful is one of the blessings of our times, and something that is especially new in France, where not long ago only the Greeks and the Latins were appreciated. The opinions of La Harpe on Aeschylus have about the same merit as those of Schlegel on our French theater. Today we know how to greet the geniuses of all times, and no one has fêted them better than Quinet."

CHAPTER ELEVEN

Founders and Intermediaries

HUGO'S adherence to the Oriental Renaissance in the preface to *Orientales* is all the more significant when we consider that three years earlier in the preface to *Odes et ballades* his poetic standards were still those of Chateaubriand: Homer and the biblical prophets. In 1826 he lacked patriarchs with whom to overthrow Boileau, but the *Musenalmanak* journal of primitive poetry imported from Germany soon provided the necessary reinforcements. In the interval between Hugo's two collections, Chézy and Dubois had published one episode from the *Ramayana* and another from *Panchatantra* (1826), Langlois had published *Théâtre indien* and *Monuments littéraires de l'Inde* (1827), and Mohl's translation of the *Shah Namah* had begun to appear (1828). Hugo's allusion in 1829 to scholars confined "to one of the idioms of the Orient, from China to Egypt" was an obvious reference to Rémusat and Champollion and left the middle ground to Chézy and Sacy. Although it was not Hugo's lot in life to keep abreast of scholarly publications, he did not always deprive himself of them; more frequently, however, he only heard about them and had the best parts summarized. We will see how, to a large extent, the views writers held on the discoveries depended on a few reliable informants, and I will discuss the first and last sets of such informants.

Eugène Burnouf

Eugène Burnouf was the great Burnouf.[1] It was he who taught Littré, Fauche, Théodore Pavie, and Barthélemy Saint-Hilaire, those marvelous agents for the Orient. They all developed a veneration for Burnouf, along with a fondness for the studies to which he introduced them. Jean-Jacques Ampère was also a student of Burnouf, although he, along with Fauriel, belonged to the generation already initiated into oriental studies by Hamilton and Chézy. It is often said that Burnouf's students included many more foreigners than Frenchmen; yet in addition to those mentioned above we may list, among the more illustrious, Langlois, Adolphe Régnier, de Saulcy, Lancereau, Baudry, and Renan. It is true that his influence spread far and wide through those who carried his teachings.[2] Each country, including Russia, contained former students of Burnouf who had become masters, all of them—Max Müller, Roth, Gorresio, Nève, Pictet—deeply affected by his memory. Schelling was surprised that in spite of all its upheavals, France was still able to produce "men such as Eugène Burnouf," whose activities he considered no less important than those of a philosopher. Saint-Hilaire attested that at Burnouf's death the German school bowed before this royal personage. At the same time Villemain honored Burnouf as "a philologist of genius," a brevet that everyone endorsed. Burnouf's works bore, above all, the mark of a creator. Rosen wrote of "A truly human heart with the mind and the spirit of a scholar."[3] In Burnouf human virtues achieved intellectual grandeur. In his obituary of Burnouf on July 2, 1852, Mohl exclaimed there had never been a scholar "less covetous of all that tempts men's ambitions. I do not believe that he ever knew the full extent of his fame in Europe and Asia." Burnouf had obtained his great repute "without the least effort by either himself or his friends, but solely through the irresistible impact of his scientific discoveries." Naudet's account shows Burnouf killing himself with work, refusing all invitations in order to be at his desk by three in the morning, seeing only a few friends, and leaving his work only to go to the Collège de France, the Institut, and the Imprimerie royale.

Burnouf was praised from all sides (admiration likes to flock around a worthy object). Saint-Hilaire himself, who had been a classmate of Burnouf, began to warm toward him and pointed out that Burnouf's lectures were passed from hand to hand among generations of students at the Ecole normale supérieur, who lithographed them, as Mohl confirmed. Naudet recalled this young professor who was barely older than his students. This lithograph can be added to the stenography of Cousin's course in the records of oral influence. Mohl described Burnouf's course on the Veda at the Collège de France as "an enchantment." A striking page from Michelet remains the most important statement on Burnouf. It figures in the epilogue to Michelet's 1855 volume on the Reformation in his *Histoire de France*, where it is strangely tacked on to a note concerning the Turks and the Jews. Michelet needed to find an outlet for a grief that could contain itself no longer. With heartfelt eloquence one genius treated another's capacity for genius as an equal. In stressing the extent to which Burnouf's authority accredited the idea of the Oriental Renaissance, Michelet put his finger on the decisive influence personal prestige and contacts carried. For Michelet, who was, in another connection, receiving the same message from Quinet, such contact was clearly important. Michelet began his portrait of Burnouf by crediting him with the concept of a common bond between Buddhism and Christianity—a common theme of the times:

The result of his scholarship fully reflected the dictates of his heart and common sense. How many times during this felicitous friendship of some thirty years I benefited from my talks with Eugène Burnouf, who was always kind and endearing, however serious. Yes, dear and forever missed. [Burnouf had been dead three years.] Every day, my heart filled with great sorrow, I passed the house where everything taught us the value of the *lotus de la bonne loi,* passed by this scholar's chambers, so well-lit, so sun-filled, where on wintry days we used to warm our pallid Western learning in his Indian sun. The emanation of languages, exactly the same in Europe as in Asia, and the corresponding formation of religions, which was no less symmetrical, was his favorite topic, and my delight.

This is what I have carried away from that house: his light, which still warms me, and the clarity of his words, in which I so plainly saw the unique miracle of two Gospels, the one arising from the Orient, the other from the Occident. What a moving identity. Two worlds long separated by their mutual ignorance met suddenly again and became aware of their oneness, like two lungs within the same chest or two chambers of the same heart.

How well I sensed there the sacred watchword of the Renaissance: *the unity of the soul of humanity,* the peace of religions, the reconciliation of one man with another and their fraternal embrace.

One can perceive the connection, the passage from religious unity to human universality. Michelet drew from the example of his dearest friend the stimulus for his own development. At the same time he calls for a popular version of the "Buddhist Gospel," drawn primarily from Burnouf's writings (would this be an overinterpretation?), he also calls for a popular version of the *Avesta* and of the Cabbala which was connected to "the ancient traditions of Persia from which the Jews drew so extensively during their Captivity. Sublime metaphysics! so ancient and so modern! which, from one side, is the echo of the word of Ormuzd and, from the other, the stunning precursor of Hegel's doctrine." The historian enthusiastically hailed, as Reuchlin and Postel had done, "the venerable pioneers who opened the door of the sanctuary to us," and Michelet could not "restrain [his] gratitude to those who carried us into the sanctuary. A hero opened Persia to us; a great critical genius revealed Indian Christianity to us. The hero is Anquetil-Duperron; the genius is Burnouf." Was Indian Christianity, then, derived as much from Burnouf's work as from Eckstein's? In any event, here was the announcement of the *Bible de l'Humanité,* the breviary, after *Génie des religions,* of the Oriental Renaissance—and Burnouf was responsible for it. After an interval of ten years, during which his feeling for Burnouf grew deeper, Michelet wrote to him when he lost his father, "Who is dearer to me than you?" The 1864 edition of the *Bible de l'Humanité* provided two references: one is to *Génie des religions*, a "sparkling book" that "expresses in fiery strokes the profound intimacy of religion and nature." The other was a reference to Burnouf: "I adhere most closely to Burnouf, to his *Yasna* and *Etudes* where he frequently amends Anquetil. His recent conversations have also sustained me. I do not believe I have deviated in the slightest from the spirit of his work." Once again, the oral tradition.

A simple example of how Burnouf's lofty reputation as a scholar affected Romantic circles can be seen in how David d'Angers approached him and asked to add a medallion of him to his series of famous contemporaries: "It is not only," Angers wrote Burnouf, "to the man of genius that I dedicate this medallion, which I have had great pleasure in making; it is also to the man whose character I deeply value. . . . I would be very happy if this opportunity should allow me to become permanently acquainted with you." (David was famous himself and twenty years older than his model.) On October 22, 1840 Burnouf extended his friendship by sending the sculptor his translation of the *Bhagavata Purana*. He included a letter in which he stated his regret at not being able to send the *Mahabharata* or the Vedas but that he had left this task to Théodore Pavie, who in fact published excerpts from the Indian epic the following year. Pavie, the friend and compatriot of the one and disciple of the other, had probably put the two correspondents in touch with each other. To obtain an idea of other literary connections, we should remember that Angers's small circle was linked with that of the Arsenal; moreover, Mérimée, with whom Burnouf fraternized at the Académie des Inscriptions, used his influence with Cormenin in 1852 to provide a pension for his colleague's widow.[4]

After Michelet's eloquent voice that of Renan, although less rich in overtones, provided several apt phrases.[5] Burnouf's biography was only the history of his works, and yet "he was superior to his works" because he opposed glossiness and aimed only at scientific and moral truth. "The history of the human spirit was the supreme goal he set for positive science, history founded on the most painstaking and searching study of detail." Wary of whatever might not guarantee a certain austerity, and wary even of his own eloquence, he wanted only to be an editor and translator—an admirable decision for a philologist, both rarer and more difficult than it may seem. This produced "the seeming disproportion between his reputation as a superior man and the nature of his works." It should be noted that, in Darmesteter's opinion, Burnouf marked the end of the mystical generation of orientalists and began "the positive period of Indic studies." "We have frequently heard him state that his only guide in his work was the most abstract view of duty, and he felt that he had no need to expect any reward from public opinion."

Renan, like Michelet, could not refrain from continually referring to this unforgettable man. When in 1862 he defended his own teaching at the Collège de France, Renan took cover in Burnouf's example and quoted the passage I have quoted from Burnouf's opening lecture in 1832: "It is more than India, gentlemen, it is a page from the origins of the world, from the history of the human spirit, that we shall attempt to decipher together." At the age of twenty-five Renan, who had just completed his *agrégation* in philosophy, was fully immersed in the orientalist milieu. He had related that it was Augustin Thierry, one of the intellectual sovereigns of that time and an intimate friend of the Indic scholar Fauriel, who had advised him "with fatherly benevolence" to write the studies for the *Revue des Deux-Mondes* and the *Débats* which later formed the basis of *Avenir de la science;* Sacy, "the old Jansenist," also encouraged his work on this book. Renan dedicated the book to Burnouf, professed himself to have been his respectful student (in 1849), and recalled his lectures of the previous year at the Collège de France: "It is your image that I have constantly before my eyes. . . . In listening to your lectures on the most beautiful of languages and literatures of the primitive world, I came to realize what previously had been only a dream: science becoming philosophy, and the loftiest results emerging from the most meticulous analysis of details."

Here was a characteristic to which they all referred: the more strictly Burnouf adhered to the letter of the text, the more the extent of the general views he refused to rush into became perceptible to his audience. A short phrase like "science becoming philosophy" illuminates the kind of revolution the Oriental Renaissance was and seems to portend what Leconte de Lisle would later draw for poetry from the "science" that he also identified with the knowledge of a multiple antiquity.

Again returning to the panegyric, Renan later said of the exhumed texts, "There is not a single one of these works from which I have not drawn more philosophical substance than from the entire collection of Descartes and his school." Such bold affirmation of a new era of thought naturally introduced, now in the work of Renan, the very subject of the new Renaissance: "India has almost as much right to furnish themes for our arts as Greece." Friedrich Schlegel spoke along these same lines when he proposed that the journey to Rome for young artists be replaced with a journey to India. Yet there was still this "almost." It was not expected that anyone would abandon the Acropolis; it was a reclassification of values that burst forth from all intelligent minds. Sainte-Beuve, although he did not see fit to offer a full-length portrait of Burnouf (personal relations aside,

Burnouf deserved one as much as Mohl), nevertheless seized every opportunity to commend his work.

Eugène Burnouf (1801–52) at first fancied himself a lawyer, but not for
long. At the age of twenty-two he was instead attracted by the courses ot
Chézy and Rémusat, and by the Ecole des Chartes that was just being
formed. He chose oriental languages as his field of study. His father, who
had studied oriental languages since around 1815, became his teacher; but
to a greater extent the student was self-taught. At the age of twenty-six
Burnouf knew enough Sanskrit to teach it to his former classmate Saint-
Hilaire and to Littré—Sainte-Beuve says "around 1822–24," which would
mean at the age of twenty two. In any event, Guigniaut cited the young
Burnouf in 1825 in a note to his translation of Creuzer for "an extremely
literal Latin version" of the *Manava Dharmashastra* "written for a class given
by the celebrated professor Chézy." (One finds Burnouf's first exercises,
with comments by his professors, in Feer's catalog.)[6] By 1826 Burnouf had
published, in collaboration with Lassen, an *Essai sur le pâli*, a linguistic
field he inaugujated, a riddle he solved at the first try. And it is through
his extraordinary progress in the field of Pali that Burnouf opened an essential avenue of approach to a genuine understanding of Buddhism. In
November 1829 a comparative grammar course at the Ecole normale was
established for Burnouf that he taught until February 1833, when he succeeded to the chair of Sanskrit at the Collège de France vacated by Chézy,
who had died in the cholera epidemic of 1832. Burnouf also made his decisive contribution to the decipherment of Avestan, which had remained
an insoluble question since Anquetil's partial successes, in 1833. Burnouf's brainstorm was to point out that Avestan was a language contemporary with Vedic Sanskrit, and that both of them had to have originated
from the same source. While the *Commentaire sur le Yaçna*, published in
two volumes in 1835, proved its particular point, it also established a general method in such a brilliant manner that, according to Darmesteter, it
was called "a textbook for discovery."

Since the *Avesta* was already unintelligible at the time of the Sassanians,
it had been translated at that time from Avestan into Pahlavi. The most
ancient parts of it were not understood, although the recent parts still were;
thus the Pahlavi translation of those portions was a valid one (it could
have been noted in Burnouf's time that the Parsis in India knew enough
Pahlavi to act as guides in that language). It was known that in the Middle Ages one of them had retranslated a part of the translation into poor
Sanskrit, with commentary—the *Yasna*. It was in this retranslation that
Burnouf, with what Meillet has called "inspired good sense," tackled only
the most recent portion of the *Avesta*, "in which native tradition served as
a good guide and which is clear itself." In this way, Meillet adds, Burnouf

discovered an ancient Iranian dialect very close to Sanskrit: "Eugène Burnouf noticed that the forms of the Avestan language, while containing certain particular Iranian features, fell within the framework of Sanskrit grammar. The indigenous translation that he had at his disposal provided the meaning of words and sentences; the Sanskrit grammar allowed an almost immediate classification of each of the forms." Bopp kept close watch on the decipherment and helped Burnouf on it from time to time.

Burnouf's works on Buddhism belong to a later series: *Introduction à l'histoire du buddhisme indien* in 1844 and the author's last testament, the *Lotus de la bonne loi*, in 1852. The first publication especially influenced the European mind. We will later see how an opera by Wagner nearly followed from the composer's enthusiastic reading of Burnouf's work, which was, as Mohl put it, "a flood of light falling on the chaos of Buddhist doctrines and restoring order." For the second volume, which was to be published posthumously by Foucaux, Burnouf had compiled a Burmese dictionary. Yet he felt the work was incomplete, so he took it up again and added twenty *Mémoires* explicating particular points in the history of Buddhism. He never for a moment "paid attention to the delicate nature of his health." Here, both through an indifference to fame and through a profound sense of humanity, were truly all the signs of the distinguished pedigree of the orientalist for whom, as for Anquetil, being sick at every port of call was simply another reason to forge ahead. "Burnouf's ardent love of learning blinded him to the wasting away of his vitality." At the age of fifty-one "he died, truly a martyr to the cause of learning." Julius Mohl, who wrote these words, spoke further of Burnouf's "marvelous sagacity," "bold concepts," "nearly infallible soundness of judgment," and then laid down his pen, unable to continue his work in a world deprived of such a man.

Silvestre de Sacy

Silvestre de Sacy (1755–1838) was also a master, but more like the kind one encounters in school. His talent for organization was equal to Burnouf's, but his vision was not of the same caliber. His, even more than Burnouf's, was the great name in oriental studies throughout Europe. It was to Sacy that Germany sent its Bopps and Mohls, and it is Sacy who laid the foundations for all branches of oriental studies.

Sacy had a strong personality—and was more generous with his projects and undertakings than with his sympathies. He was one of the last admitted Jansenists, and Anquetil, both in grateful memory of the sect he had known intimately as a young man and because Sacy was his last friend,

left Sacy his oriental manuscripts and personal papers. Gazier, the historian of his coreligionists, wrote that Sacy "had been secretly affiliated with
the 'Oeuvre des Convulsions,' which was still in existence, where he was
called 'l'Angéli, petit pontife de l'Oeuvre,' and that Sister Angelique had
a high opinion of him" (again another example of orientalism's ramifications among secret societies). Sacy was not in any way descended from
Lemaistre de Saci but, out of admiration, had just the same adopted an
anagram of his Christian name Isaac.[7] (I have already pointed to Garcin
de Tassy, Quatremère, and Lanjuinais among the ranks of orientalists with
Jansenist sympathies.)

Either because of the vehemence of his convictions or because of his
somber temperament, Sacy often seemed difficult to approach. He was a
severe man, particularly with himself. In the first part of this book we saw
his childhood avidity for learning unknown languages and his tenacity in
acquiring them and going beyond the entirely empirical knowledge there
was of them at the time. He was often up in arms over one issue or another, such as when he quarreled with Klaproth, or during the battle of
the "florists" in the Société Asiatique, when, with a natural illogic, since
he had always held to eighteenth-century ideas of the liberties French taste
allowed to translators, he sided with the hidebound opponents of the
"beautiful infidels." It was also Sacy, obstinate and in defiance of merit,
who blocked the admission first of Burnouf and then of Michelet to the
Collège de France. He stated that his objections concerned scholarship and
literature, although other dogmas were undoubtedly at issue as well.

In *L'Avenir de la Science*, Renan follows his warm description of Burnouf
with a contrasting description of Sacy: "Silvestre de Sacy is, to my mind,
the typical orthodox scholar." Is there an element of irony here, coming
from the pen of an adversary irritated by someone who conceived of science and faith in a manner other than his own? "If one were seeking only
exactitude of critical detail one could certainly not ask for a science with
higher standards. But if one looks further, one sees the strange spectacle
of a man who, though he possesses one of the vastest eruditions of modern times, has never had an important critical insight. When I was re-
searching the works of this highly respected man, I was always tempted
to ask him, what is the point? What is the point of knowing Hebrew, Arabic, Samaritan, Syrian, Chaldean, Ethiopian, Persian, what is the point
of being Europe's leading expert on oriental literature, if one has not reached
the idea of humanity, if such learning is not directed toward a higher,
religious aim?" Given what we know of Sacy's interest in religion, the final remark is surprising. The real objection turns on the limits that personal character may impose on intellectual talents; but one may wonder
whether the objection reflects as much Renan's mind as Sacy's. Wouldn't

Renan's great reproach be that Sacy did not pose theological questions in the same terms he did? Other accounts insist on the steadfastness and harshness of Sacy's Jansenist and legitimist positions and that he was, above all, an example of a mind in which the broadening of his knowledge had not breached the zone of beliefs. It would seem that Renan was certainly objecting on behalf of a new humanism.

A forceful presence in all fields, Sacy is among those who cannot be overlooked. Although his writing style may well be dull, it nonetheless regained some kind of vigor through the knowledge, opinions, and actions that it firmly implanted across a century. Young people drawn to the study of oriental languages thought first not of Chézy or Langlès but of Sacy. Like Bopp, Jean-Jacques Ampère, a representative of such generations, felt Sacy's magnetic attraction and called him "the patriarch of the orientalists." Sacy fascinated Germans, and not only because each chair of oriental studies in Germany was held by one of his students before Bopp's students held them, but because Goethe, with whom Kosegarten frequently spoke, kept current with Sacy's work and saw the Orient in and through him. The list of Sacy's disciples was long—in France they were, notably, Chézy himself, Quatremère, Jaubert, Garcin de Tassy, and Reinaud. Of equal benefit to the Oriental Renaisance was Sacy's importance as a public figure, which made him the incarnation of oriental studies in Paris during the Empire and the Restoration. In 1795 he was professor of Arabic at the Ecole des Langues orientales, where he was director after 1824 and which owed everything to his encouragement. In 1806 he moved to the Collège de France and became its administrator in 1823. In 1814 he successfully promoted the establishment of chairs of Sanskrit and Chinese at the Collège and, at the same time, a chair of Hindustani at the Ecole and had two of his students named to the Sanskrit and Hindustani posts. In 1816 he became director of the Académie de Paris. In 1822 he presided over the newly formed Société Asiatique. In 1833 he became permanent secretary of the Académie des Inscriptions. He had a seat in the Corps législatif from 1808 to 1815 and was made a peer by Louis-Philippe in 1832. For fifty-eight years, from 1780 to 1838, he was a tireless worker, contributing to countless publications, not all of which were reserved for specialists. It was Sacy who wrote the section on oriental languages and literatures for the "General Survey of the State and Progress of the Sciences and the Arts and Letters from 1789 to 1801." And this austere man frequented the salons; he was one of those to be found at the home of Cuvier, along with Ampère, Mérimée, and Stendhal, where his knowledge and fanaticism fell on the ears of educated society. Nerval took the story of the caliph Hakim from Sacy's *Exposé de la religion des Druses* for his own *Voyage en Orient*. Sacy also crossed Sainte-Beuve's path, although he spoke primarily of Sacy's son, an important journalist for the *Débats* and, with Philarète Chasles, librarian at the Mazarine.

Antoine-Léonard de Chézy

A student of Sacy and Langlès, Antoine-Léonard de Chézy (1774–1832), whose health prevented him from taking part in the expedition to Egypt, had only two things going for him: his faith in work and the intellectual means of accomplishing it. He remained a professor whose talents were known only to his students, since he published very little—for which they reproached him. Even worse, Chézy imbued the small part of his work that did reach the public with an amateurish tone. Chézy is important for the rigor with which he edited texts, but when he set about writing commentaries his style fell into the most affected eighteenth-century swoonings. A sentimentalist with blond curls, he entered into married life with Helmina von Klenke, the most vindicative of German women. She was the Schlegels' gift to French scholarship, recompense for lessons that Friedrich preferred to forget. It was she who recounted Chézy's life, with a liberal dose of malice, for the biography by Michaud upon which Chézy's successors drew; his obituary notice, following his death in the cholera epidemic, was written so heinously by the inescapable Klaproth that Sacy fulminated against it. As early as 1819 the wretched scholar all too lucidly prophesied to Bopp that he would leave only "a very slight mark that time will soon efface." In 1825 Bopp wrote bluntly in a letter to Wilhelm Schlegel that he could not expect much of Chézy or his followers; and Burnouf wrote to Bopp in the same year that Chézy promised that he would publish everything and in fact published nothing. Wilhelm Schlegel, who detested Chézy, was forever harping on Chézy's indolence in his letters and referred to him as the remora of the Sanskrit ship.

All the same, Chézy had the good fortune to hold the first European chair of Sanskrit. But whom can one name among his students, aside from Burnouf, who was more a student of his own father? There was Langlois, who was no luminary, and there was Desgranges, a grammarian whose influence was minor. And there were others, of course, but they contributed even less to his reputation, although they respected his kindness. In the war of the florists Chézy was inevitably on the wrong side—the one that opposed Burnouf and Rémusat. "Chézy, sweet and melancholy by nature, elegant and classical in his imagination, became particularly attached to the forms and poetry of the language that seemed to him an emanation from the Garden of Eden. And, either through obstinate adherence to the established system, or through a desire to attract an audience for this unknown literature more easily, he veiled its beauty in a great deal of embroidery. He set to work bringing its strange and gigantic figures within the proportion and pattern of French physiognomy by substituting an artificial ideal for a real one." Naudet drew these conclusions, which all too often hold true in the general history of translation, in his *Notice sur Burnouf*. There is no doubt but that while wanting to adapt India's originality to the Académie française, certain overly obliging paraphrasers in fact long rendered its true beauty inaccessible. Scholarship did not always protect the best-intentioned translators from committing this fundamental error: in 1884 the approximation of *Shakuntala* by Bergaigne and Lehugeur would again join with the methods of Chézy and Sacy.[8]

Chézy's most valid works were the publication of an episode from the *Ramayana*, with a Latin appendix by Burnouf *père*, in 1826 and the first, definitive edition of the text of *Shakuntala* in 1830, with a translation and notes that served many writers, especially Gautier. Chézy had used a Bengali version, and it is this book that prompted Goethe to write to Chézy that *Shakuntala* was "a star that makes the night more agreeable than the day." We have already seen how, after reading Jones's version, Chézy exclaimed, "I shall never forget the impression it made on me." Chézy expressed his enthusiasm for the *Bhagavad Gita* in a similarly animated way in the *Journal des Savants* of January 1825. Their successors may have regretted that the new scientific rigor was slow in cooling off the minds of the pioneers, but it was such excitement that aroused the enthusiasm of others. I will not recount the spartan episode in which Chézy hid from his friends Sacy and Langlès in order to learn Sanskrit by himself through struggling with the *Hitopadesha* and materials amassed by eighteen-century missionaries, nor will I recount the episode with Rémusat. It is sufficient to recall, in reference to Rémusat, that for a good many adepts—Stanislas Julien, Saint-Hilaire, Pauthier, and Rémusat himself—Chinese was inseparable from Sanskrit.

The Transmitters

Among the Renaissance agents who plied between scientific and literary production, Julius Mohl, a genuine scholar, and Jean-Jacques Ampère, an eccentric informant, should be listed, since through their contacts and activities they both belong to what was, from our perspective, the realm of action. This realm included personnel from both the Université and the salons who played leading roles in intellectual Paris at the beginning of the nineteenth century. Nodier's salon at the Arsenal was

where poets came into contact with orientalists such as Pavie and Fouinet, and Nodier, as we have seen, had diverse ideas on Schlegel's views
on India and palingenesis. At Duras's salon Rémusat met Cuvier in an
atmosphere created by Chateaubriand. The salon of the painter Baron
Gérard near Saint-Germain-des-Prés discussed the topics of all the other
salons. Ampère, Quinet, Cousin, Mérimée, Stapfer, Sainte-Beuve, Delécluze, and Hugo gathered at all these hearths. It was a single circle. Writing to Ampère in September 1825, Mohl said that he had met Burnouf
and Sainte-Beuve, Ballanche and Fauriel, and Humboldt, "an inconceivable man" (and a student of Sacy) at the same time. He had heard Ampère read at Cuvier's salon and Quinet read at the home of Madame Récamier. Jal later remembered having met Fouinet at the home of Nodier
and Rémusat and Cuvier at the home of Gérard. In the salon of Millin, a
crossroads for the real aristocracy and the aristocracy of the scholars during the first years of the century, the young Champollion had observed
both realms.

The Cuvier Salon

Cuvier received guests at the Museum of Natural History, sometimes
in a suite of rooms that formed the library, sometimes in the small round
salon called "the Tent," which was lit from the ceiling and littered with
books. A great number of visitors to this room left descriptions of it behind. Young people came there under the influence of two attractions,
the young ladies of the house: Clémentine, whom Ampère loved (though
the feeling was not altogether mutual), and her half-sister Sophie Duvaucel, whom Stendhal fluttered around. At least equally important for Cuvier's guests was the certainty of being introduced to all the leading figures of scholarly and literary Europe.

Attending one of these soirées, Madame Ancelot found herself, as she
recorded in her *Les salons de Paris*, face to face with Cuvier, who, sur-
rounded by a large circle of guests, was speaking of "Asia and the ancient
peoples of that beautiful region, their laws, their writing, and their imagination. He was assessing the pettiness and the greatness of our present
society as well as the splendors and vices of past civilizations. It was at
once an admirably instructive and witty chat." Sarah Lee depicts Cuvier
on another occasion, this one in 1828, tracing Champollion's trip to Egypt
on the map for his guests. Everything that originated with Cuvier carried
a prestige that was underscored in April 1830 by the stir caused in Paris
by the session of the Académie française at which he welcomed Lamartine as a member. Politics was the principal preoccupation of the day;

nevertheless, the press gave full coverage. Sainte-Beuve wrote a review of it, and could find nothing but d'Alembert to compare with it.

It is not only in Cuvier's conversation that India appeared. When Nodier returned to the idea of reincarnation, he stubbornly referred to Cuvier as one who had sought and found the key to the "mysteries of the ancient world," which all the circles of Romanticism at Jena located in India. And above all Cuvier's writings across the years show a certain coherence. In 1803 Cuvier was associated with the translation of the *Asiatic Researches* for which Langlès asked him to provide scientific notes. In 1812 the famous *Recherches sur les ossements fossiles* appeared, and Cuvier's theories on questions of remote antiquity in it attracted attention, as in the *Journal de l'Empire,* December 23, 1812. Beginning with the second edition in 1817 this work was prefaced with a "Discours sur les révolutions du Globe," which held a place in the first half of the nineteenth-century comparable to that held by "Introduction à la médecine expérimentale" in the second. In 1816, shortly after the establishment of the chairs of Sanskrit and Chinese, *Le règne animal* referred to linguistic classification, notably that of Sanskrit. The foreword added to the "Discours" in 1821 emphasized strongly how linguistics had opened up the history of the human race: "The history of ancient peoples—an essential foundation for any positive opinion on the history of the world itself—has not failed also to provide a number of important insights over the last years through the studies of several German and French scholars, and through excerpts from the sacred books of the Hindus that the English scholars have given us."

In this passage Cuvier strikingly confirmed and complemented the conversation Madame Ancelot had overheard; even certain terms are identical. I notice the preciseness of the information of Cuvier the naturalist concerning the respective shares of the various nations in the progress of Indic studies. And during this same decade allusions no less localized would be sprinkled through the preface to *Orientales*. It is interesting to observe a biologist's attentiveness to philology at a time when the reverse was greatly in evidence. Another example can be seen in the revised and expanded edition of 1825, where Cuvier, who calls attention on the title page to his admission to the Asiatic Society of Bombay, takes the discoveries of orientalism into account on several points. Corroborating Sarah Lee this time, he invoked the discoveries of Champollion, which were on everyone's mind at the time. However, the discoveries of the Indic scholars command a more important place in his conclusions.

Like his friends the Humboldts, he respected oriental studies for their place within the mingling of new sciences competing against and reinforcing one another. He maintained that since the most ancient authentic historical documents were relatively recent, in order to delve deeper into the past it was essential to turn to the poetic and sacred books of the Hindus, Egyptians, and Chaldeans, particularly the first. One could not expect chronological exactness: Cuvier, who had unshakable confidence in the texts, defended the biblical calendar. On the basis of a reading of Jones and the *Asiatic Researches,* which he knew well, he discussed Bentley and Colebrooke: "After the Vedas, the first revealed works and the foundation of all Hindu belief, the literature of this people, like that of the Greeks, begins with two epics—the 'Ramaian' and the 'Mahabarat,' a thousand times more colossal in their marvels than the *Iliad* and the *Odyssey,* even though one recognizes in them traces of metaphysical doctrine of the kind that has generally been termed sublime. The other poems, which comprise, along with the first two, the great corpus of the Puranas, are no more than legends or versified novels written at different times by different authors and are no less extravagant in their fictions than the great poems."

It is clear that the naturalist's opinion on a domain far removed from his own and on contributions that contradicted religious tradition was not altogether favorable. Nonetheless, his interest counted for something in an age when no one could forget the man who could be credited with reconstructing an animal species on the basis of an unearthed bone. Inevitably, a man appeared to reconstruct a prototype of the human species by identical methods: with the linguistic bones dug out of Asia, which had already been referred to as fossils (Reynaud speaks of an "âge paléontologique" and Pauthier of a "littérature fossile"), one could retrace the outline of the first human adventure. Undoubtedly Cuvier himself would have assented to generalizing his system of historical anatomy into a philosophy of history, a universal law. Assuming he was not displeased to see collections of linguistic bones accumlating, his system would dovetail perfectly with systems wherein philologies led to sociologies that became linked with evolutionary theories. One notes an extraordinary coincidence between the new ideas in biology and the new ideas in history; one day it may be possible to write that Gobineau did for human races what Lamarck did for living species.

The Parallels Between Linguistics and Biology

The collaborators brought together in 1803 for the translation of *Asiatic Researches* into French had more than a quick encounter. The French text was interspersed with two series of annotations, a philological series by Langlès and a series on the natural and exact sciences entrusted to Cuvier, Lamarck, and Delambre. From the beginning, as we have seen, the

Indic scholars at Calcutta, for the most part biologists or mathematicians themselves, linked the different branches of knowledge closely. The harmonious progress of linguistic and biological knowledge toward a true view of evolution was an event of major importance. It seems likely that the very word "evolution" owes its initial prestige to the use made of it at the close of the eighteenth-century by Charles Bonnet, who also launched the term "palingenesis," which was destined for such a Romantic fortune. It was Lamarck who was to clarify this latter idea and establish its definitive usage.

In the Paris of the First Empire there was, first of all, a great interest in the affairs of the Museum of Natural History, previously called the King's Garden, which Jussieu salvaged in 1793. This interest is clearly reflected in the recollections of Michelet, who made the museum one of the two poles of intellectual life (the other being the Museum of French Monuments under Lenoir). It was at the museum that Lamarck, known as early as 1778 for his *Flore française,* created a new science whose name need only be written in order to make all its repercussions resound: biology. The name appeared in 1802 in his *Recherches sur l'organization des corps vivants.* Lamarck gave the term this definition: "It embraces all that relates to living bodies" (a more general meaning than has remained, but which is preserved here). In the same year the German scholar Gottfried Reinhold Treviranus published *Biologie, oder Philosophie der lebenden Natur für Naturforscher und Aerzte.* In his turn in 1809 Lamarck published a book with a similar title that bore a striking resemblance to books of the historical genre and that was to open a new intellectual era: *Philosophie zoologique.* This was the beginning of *transformism.* It came only three years before the foundation of comparative linguistics by Bopp in 1812, just as Darwin, a continuator of Lamarck, was to do work that paralleled that of Max Müller, a continuator of Bopp.

Such parallelism seems rather striking to me. Breaking with Linneaus' theories, which assumed species independent of one another, Lamarck's discovery particularly pointed out the broad spectrum of "individuals who, undergoing the effects of circumstances, seem through the millennia to have evolved to the point of being transformed."[9] Wasn't this what comparative grammar and the science of language were, for the first time, to point out? Seeing this, can't one understand better the gathering of orientalists in Cuvier's salon and of linguistic ideas in Cuvier's mind? The similarities extend to another point: Lamarck's theories immediately collided with theological arguments and with questions of exegesis, just as the rediscovered writings begat controversies over biblical chronologies. It was precisely these controversies that alarmed Cuvier the believer and that he began to combat. By 1793 Lamarck had received an important reinforcement. At the age of twenty-one, Geoffroy Saint-Hilaire had been named by Daubenton, a collaborator and successor of Buffon, to inaugurate zoology at the Museum of Natural History. What further perspectives Saint-Hilaire was to open can be measured by his establishment of the still-unprecedented disciplines of comparative anatomy and embryology. To discover the unity of organic composition and to simultaneously extend comparativism to the structure of living bodies were further rapprochements that bespeak the spirit of the period, a period of human thought about humanity.

Lamarck and Saint-Hilaire shortly became a camp, the camp of the new doctrine—since facing them another camp inevitably arose to safeguard the dogma of the Creation, a Genesis arisen once and for all. The antagonism was so keen, and of such great consequence at the time, that, in the presence of Arago, Napoleon, worried about his efforts on behalf of religious restoration, subjected Lamarck to the utmost abuse. Within the scientific and imperial establishment, Cuvier was the champion of the traditionalist camp. He himself had given up the ministry in favor first of geology and then of zoology. The odd part was that in the same way that Saint-Hilaire had been named to the Museum of Natural History by Daubenton, Saint-Hilaire sent Cuvier there to play "the role of a new Linnaeus." In 1796, at the age of twenty-seven, the newcomer Cuvier was an important official personage, a widely recognized master. A member of the scientific branch of the Institut, he was not only soon to hold a seat at the Académie française but even at the Académie des Inscriptions. He was also a professor at the Collège de France. Thus he had many opportunities to meet linguists. We should again remember that, like their English predecessors in India, the continental Indic scholars were frequently naturalists like the Humboldts and Ampère or physicians like Rémusat, and that Burnouf and Théodore Pavie were also first interested in the natural sciences.

In 1804 a piece of good luck occurred that was of service to the naturalists and that galvanized them as the conquest of India had the linguists: some surprising bones were discovered near Paris and immediately declared "antediluvian." The effect was to revive, in another field, the question of the Flood that had fascinated Anquetil and generated the first controversies over the Orient. The Protestant Cuvier always placed the Flood foremost among his arguments for the defense, just as Anquetil, whose polemics were slightly Jansenist, had done. And here was the foundation for yet another science, paleontology, whose agreement with other sciences, all of which at that time were obsessed with the problem of origins, it is unnecessary to underline. (Geology, which du Luc had named such as early as 1778, took on a distinct existence only little by little.)

The parallel progress of comparativisms? From 1800 to 1805 Cuvier delivered lectures at the museum, soon collected and published, that aroused enormous interest. According to Madelin's *La nation sous L'Empereur*, in these lectures Cuvier established *a law of the correlation of forms*, "according to which, since all parts of an organized body are in harmony with each other, it is sufficient to know one organ in order to infer positively all other components from it." If such concepts, which generated like methods, were truly absent from the mind of a Bopp or a Burnouf, the least one can say is that there are some miraculous patterns and conjunctions in historical happenstance. No doubt Cuvier departed from this law in savaging the evolutionist hypothesis, for from the Empire to the Restoration the dogma of the fixity of the species was decreed to be in the public interest. But this in itself animated the mental landscape and made the debates of the specialists into a general passion that obsessed the minds of men of letters like Hugo, Balzac, Sainte-Beuve, and Michelet. In a new age where, through the technique of its verbal instrument, literature was considered to be consolidated with the sciences, the arrangements and disarrangements of the scientists engaged the attention of literary figures. This is an extremely important fact because at the same time, from Lavoisier and de Monge onward, sciences based on numbers had snatched the supreme authority away from those based on letters. It is clear that textual knowledge began to lean toward the disciplines of calculation; it also seems evident that the great scientific systems were magnetized by the historians, who, sympathetic to orientalism and linguistics themselves, were the new definers of the human domain.

One can glimpse such connections not only in Cuvier's writings and conversations but also in his salon and his relationships, such as those with Albert Stapfer, Degérando, and Eckstein, important figures who were making an era that would be forgotten by those who followed in their wake. These were members of the small group that laid the scheme for a *Revue Germanique* which would be prevented from materializing during the Empire by the master's veto. Cuvier was involved in a great many other committees, foundations, and journals (he was on the editorial board of the *Journal des Savants*, among others) in which a number of categories of inquiry and research coalesced. His contemporaries, both fellow actors and witnesses, were aware of this community of interests and nourished it with some species of the vast hope that foretold a new age. In his *Geschichte der alten und neuen Literatur*, Friedrich Schlegel wrote: "It could be said that, in the same way that the history of peoples has had its heroic times and in the same way that the present stage of nature was preceded by another more ancient, as both the vestiges of so many revolutions and the remains of so many gigantic animals that have perished still bear witness to, so also intellectual development and the imaginative poetic force have had their marvelous and gigantic times." Mazure, in his preface to the French translation of *Uber die Sprache und Weisheit der Indier*, stated in 1837: "It is in this way, after having cleared the interior field, that the virtues of analogy will become great enough to enable one to reconstruct an entire language with the aid of a few component parts, just as, having discovered that many hitherto unknown species have been wiped from the face of the earth, the great Cuvier was able to specify the species to which an individual belonged after being shown only the most simple and commonplace fragments." Eckstein had written the same kinds of comparisons in the 1820s: "Just as men like Cuvier and Humboldt are discovering the mysteries of structure in the bowels of the earth, so men like Rémusat, Saint-Martin, Sacy, Bopp, the Grimms, and Wilhelm Schlegel are pursuing the recognition of the inmost structure and the original grounds of human thought in the words of language."[10] Could one ask for a more explicit statement? A striking application of these views was provided in 1826 by Schlosser's *Universalhistorische*, to which we shall return later, in which he elucidated primitive times as a disciple of both Bopp and Cuvier. Linck, from whom Schlosser draws, had also based his accounts of early times on a conjunction of geology and linguistics.

Balzac, Geology, and Sanskrit

Balzac cherished few ideas, few associations, more than these: "Cuvier and Geoffroy Saint-Hilaire appealed to him as much as a Lavater or a Gall did; Balzac described human society in the same manner that naturalists describe animal species."[11] Balzac's dreams of such syntheses carried the names of Louis Lambert and Arthez; moreover, these same groups were to be found in Balzac's writings in the two circles—that of the cipher and that of the letter. Between 1817 and 1820 Louis Lambert "saw a great deal of Meyranx" (who was trained by Cuvier to become Nodier's principal assistant at the Arsenal) and "became a cherished and admired member of the coterie on the Rue des Quatre-Vents over which Arthez presided."[12]

The coterie was pictured in this way in *Illusions perdues:*

Arthez admitted no outstanding talent who did not also possess deep metaphysical knowledge. He was undertaking at this time an examination of all the philosophical riches of ancient and modern times in order to assimilate them. . . . He was studying *the written world and the living world* [my emphasis], thought and deed. His friends included knowledgeable naturalists, young doctors, political writers, and artists. . . . Then came Léon Giraud, a profound philosopher, a bold theoretician who had investigated all the systems, assessed them, expressed them, and drew them to the feet of his idol, Humanity. . . . Foremost among his friends was Meyranx, who died after having set in motion the celebrated debate between Cuvier and Saint-Hilaire on the great issue that was to divide the scientific world between these two equal geniuses, a few months before the death of the man who supported strict science . . . and who opposed the pantheist who was still alive and revered in Germany.[13] Meyranx was the friend of this Louis who was soon to be torn away from the intellectual world by an anticipated death.

Now I have pointed out the exchanges orientalism had with occultism in the head of "this Louis" Lambert; here they also share common interests in the natural sciences. There is, alongside Lambert and Arthez, a third mysterious hero in Balzac's work who, like Lambert, learned "oriental languages" in order to construct "a theory of volition." This is Raphael, the hero of *Peau de Chagrin*. The curious sort of messianism that the simultaneous discoveries in history and in biology inspired in Balzac can best be seen in this novel, written in 1831. The amplitude of his view calls for lengthy quotation:

Have you ever thrust yourself into the vastness of time and space by reading Cuvier's geological works? Have you, swept away by his genius, hovered over the limitless abyss of the past, held by the magician's hand? The soul—discovering slab by slab, layer by layer, beneath the quarries of Montmartre or the shale of the Urals, those animals whose fossilized remains belong to antediluvian civilizations—is appalled to glimpse the billions of years and millions of people that feeble human memory and the indestructible divine tradition have now forgotten, whose ashes have piled up on the surface of our planet in the two feet of dirt that give us bread and flowers. Is Cuvier not the greatest poet of our century? Certainly the words of Lord Byron have bred a number of moral flurries, but our immortal naturalist has reconstructed worlds out of bleached bones; like Cadmus he has rebuilt cities with teeth, repopulated the forests with all the mysteries of zoology with only a few fragments of coal, and rediscovered populations of giants in the foot of the mammoth. . . . After countless dynasties of gigantic creatures, after races of fish and clans of mollusks, the human race finally appears. . . . Warmed by Cuvier's retrospective gaze, these puny men, born yesterday, cross chaos, intone an endless hymn, and configure the past of the universe into a sort of retrograde apocalypse. Their appalling resurrection in the present is due to the voice of a single man which grants to us the usufruct of this scrap within a nameless infinity that all spheres share and that we have named Time; this minute of life makes us pitiable.

Into this collection of visions and hypotheses, this indefinitely extend-
ible framework, the great Romantic minds projected the aggrandizements
that the revelations of the linguists and the naturalists contributed to history. Balzac's allusion here to fish and mollusks shows that he was just
as well informed about the scientific controversy as the poet who had referred to the various "cantons" of oriental studies was. Balzac's 1830 phrase
"a sort of retrograde apocalypse" could serve as a definition of Hugo's
epic poems or Michelet's grand syntheses thirty or forty years later. What
Balzac the curator venerated in the lectures of Cuvier is what Hugo, Sainte-
Beuve, and Michelet, members of the opposing camp, would ascribe to
Lamarck or Saint-Hilaire. And here is how linguistics was seen in the novel:
in *Peau de Chagrin*, an elderly antique dealer shows the hero the skin of
an ass which bears a magical inscription so deeply ingrained that no effort
can rub it out. The beauty is that Balzac gives the text of the inscription
in Arabic and has the antiquarian coolly say to the young Raphael, "Ah!
You read Sanskrit readily. Have you perhaps traveled in Persia or Bengal?"

One might wonder whether Balzac did not deliberately place this confusion of an unlearned man in the mouth of the merchant, but there is
not the slightest chance. The antique dealer is presented as a well-trav-
eled man of great learning: "I have seen the whole world. My feet have
tread the highest mountains of Asia and America." He is also presented
as a linguist: "I have learned all the languages." A dubious point. The
man has received the talisman from a "bramine." Balzac, clearly fooled
by his Arabic text, takes it for Sanskrit. Had he never seen devanagari
characters, or did he imagine that the Orient, conceived as a whole, had
but a single form of writing? A meeting enabled me to obtain the opinion
of Professor Abel of the University of Brussels on this misadventure. He
was inclined to think that Balzac's Arabic text had been concocted by some
ill-intentioned acquaintance, a little conspiracy hatched around Balzac to
poke fun at his hastily acquired learning. But even so, what can be said
of the hundreds of thousands of readers who, for more than a century,
have passed over the dazzling blunder without a question? Is it possible
that not a single orientalist, not a single Arabist, has ever read the book?
And what became of the passage in translation?[14] The mistake might be
attenuated by attributing it to a confusion with Urdu, a language in which
the vocabulary includes some Sanskrit words and which is written in Persian script, but was Balzac concerned with precision to that extent? He
joins a learned view of India, which is new, to the India of the romances,
which is anterior, by the linchpin of cabalism, which is a passport to
everything.

To complete the picture of the links between the history of literary and of scientific invention, it will suffice, until we return to the topic with Michelet, to recall the fervor that Lamarck's courses excited in the young Sainte-Beuve, an ex–medical student. In *Volupté,* Sainte-Beuve dwells on them emotionally and at length as a decisive phase in his intellectual development: it was one of a multitude of impressions that would remain with him, along with those of Saint-Martin, Ballanche, Saint-Simon, and Lamennais.

Jean-Jacques Ampère

Cuvier's home became a trade fair for the ideas of Romantic Europe where students and mentors alike were welcome. There Julius Mohl, just arrived in Paris, observed the young Ampère (1800–64), who, with his back to the fireplace, was reading a poem of his own composition. Mohl had not, in his native Tübingen, imagined a philologist giving such a performance before an audience of naturalists.

Ampère's mind could serve as a map of the interchanges that the vortex of novelty swung from southern Asia to the northern Baltic. The son of a great physicist, he exerted an influence that his friend Sainte-Beuve seemed almost to overestimate. With his aptitude for adding to the semi-talented what he detracted from the fully talented, Sainte-Beuve was rather fond of righting the balance that Providence had tilted in distributing her gifts. He did not miss any of Ampère's courses at the Collège de France (it is true that he had worked to get him his post there). After substituting for Fauriel and Villemain, whose very names recall the introduction of foreign literature into higher education in France, Ampère succeeded Andrieux. What is significant is that the widening concern for universality left its mark on generations of students. In uniting ancient heroic Sanskrit poetry with that of Europe Fauriel did what Quinet and Ozanam would later do, and taught Ampère how to do it as well. Ampère's mind in particular signaled the bifurcation of orientalism and Germanism. In 1820 he learned "the language of Ossian" and translated him in 1828 in collaboration with Mérimée. In the August 1832 issue of *Revue des Deux-Mondes* he considered "Sigurd an epic tradition common to India and the Nibelungens." In the December 1836 issue he discussed Burnouf's decipherment of Avestan. Traveling in Germany, he wrote to Charles Lenormant on November 6, 1828, "While you penetrate into Coptic and the hieroglyphics, I plunge further and further into the North and by so doing will finally catch up with your Orient, for one can arrive at it from any direction."

His father, a multifaceted genius, had first given him a taste for botany and geology, fields which at that time offered the most promising careers for the young. But literature carried him away. Those born with the century had good reason for hesitating between the two domains. By the age of twenty-five Ampère had written seven tragedies; all of them had been accepted at the Théâtre français, but not one reached the stage, and the author soon lost interest in drama in favor of philology. It was at this point that in *Vingt ans d'histoire des études orientales* Mohl described Ampère plunging *through Romanticism*, with "his friend Fauriel, one of the first authors of the movement, into the study of oriental literatures." Mohl clearly indicates that this inclination was caused by "the incomparable zeal" with which young people were rushing headlong into "the study of the literatures of all peoples in the search for new forms." This establishes one point: the vogue for foreign, essentially Romantic, literature benefited Indic studies, and in another connection the taste for India passed in the ordinary course of things from the philologists to the poets. In the 1820s and 1830s a novice who perceived that poetic composition was decidedly not to be his lot fell back for compensation on the poetic delights offered him by the world repertoire; it was Fauriel, then a student of Hamilton, who urged Ampère to learn Sanskrit.

Sainte-Beuve would later write, "Ampère's mind and imagination seem to have been torn at an early age between two principal inclinations: the poetic and the historical." One sees the same thing with Pauthier. It is not uncommon for a professor to write verse or for a poet to engage in scholarship, but the adventure of the orientalists and the Romantics makes this more noticeable. Around 1818, at an age when his poetry was developing, Ampère, along with the unfortunate Sautelet and Stapfer, made up part of a group that was preoccupied with Obermann, Byron, Jean-Paul, myth, and all the fashions of the day. During Ampère's second stage he took all the courses: Chinese, Sanskrit, hieroglyphics. His knowledge of such subjects was better and more extensive than one would think in view of how little he drew on them. The flaw that Mohl termed "an insatiable curiosity" prevented him from extracting anything enduring from "patiently accumulated material." "On behalf of oriental literature one can only regret that he did not remain more faithful, for he was perfectly suited to win friends for it." This fact is established beyond doubt, but it was to a large extent due to oriental literature that young Ampère was so generally well liked. It was a shame for him that his interests were spread too thinly: "He lacked nothing but the ability to limit himself and to concentrate." On that score we can take the word of someone who lived with him for a long time; Sainte-Beuve confirms Ampère's "successive magnetizations," notably through Fauriel and his "taste for origins." Ampère was among the first militants to emancipate art and stretch historical thinking by multiplying points of comparison. In his 1836 article on Persia and oriental studies, he spread the Schlegel-Eckstein formula: "Oriental studies have a particular attraction at this time," much as Greek studies did in the fifteenth century. A born go-between. In 1865 a collection of his articles in the field of oriental studies was published posthumously, thanks to Barthélemy Saint-Hilaire, Ampère's equal in mediation. Most of the articles had appeared in *Revue des Deux-Mondes* between 1833 and 1847 and provide a tableau of the works of Rémusat, Burnouf, and Mohl on China, Persia, and India. Ampère tolerated commonplaces concerning the great, so-called spontaneous world epics; he showed a lack of critical spirit and of independence from Germanism in affirming the myth of collective or anonymous poetry smack in the middle of a discussion of Firdausi, whose personal genius clearly indicated the impotence of a "national tradition" to produce, by itself, a genuine epic.

In 1826, having hightailed it to Germany to avoid marrying Clementine Cuvier, he met Wilhelm Schlegel in Bonn, the brothers Grimm at Kassel in 1827, and Goethe at Weimar, who "greatly admired" Ampère's friend Cousin. In Berlin, Ampère visited Wilhelm von Humboldt, who inflamed his interest in pre-Columbian languages—and then resolutely branched off into the study of Scandinavian ones. In 1829 at Hyères he struck up a friendship with Syon, a correspondent of Maistre and Mérimée, who "adores Sanskrit and geology" (an example of the association of the sciences even in the provinces) and who "is a great enthusiast of palingenesis," a doctrine for which he had inherited the Lyonnese weakness of his father, an intimate friend of Ballanche (we are now coming round full circle). In March 1830 he began his lectures at the Athénée de Marseille with a "Discourse on the History of Poetry" that Thiers published in the *National*. In 1841 he visited Asia Minor with Lenormant. He knew everyone and everything, and one suspects that his influence was felt especially through personal contacts and conversation, which, once again, was the destiny and until now the secret of the Oriental Renaissance. Ampère's teaching attracted more curiosity than it satisfied. Sainte-Beuve, who declared himself "in some respects a student of Ampère" in his letters, depicts him in *Mes poisons* as incapable of communicating his enthusiasm: "It is literature on donkey back. . . . All Ampère's ardor is so consumed by doing research that he has none left for applying it." Yet no one was listened to more; in the salons this was certainly the case. Ampère was the great man in Madame Récamier's salon, and straightway a great suitor, no less regaled, at the neighboring Clarke-Mohl home. Between Fauriel and Xavier Marmier, it was Ampère to whom the glamor of unknown literatures clung. Mérimée, another friend, welcomed him as a member of the Académie française and established Ampère's importance, which an entire period recognized.

It would have been a sufficiently significant contribution to gain accreditation for comparative literature, which Villemain had already invented, but Ampère did more within the field our inquiry covers. From oriental research he went back, again like Fauriel, to medieval research, which he associated with the oriental, and there his personal mark was more outstanding. Celtic, which had received only cursory attention in England after Buchanan (1589), hardly ever received systematic treatment except for Pictet's in a study of an Indo-European cycle that Bopp took up in 1837. Medieval studies did not get their bearings until Pastoret's classes at the Collège de France in 1804 and Daunou's in 1819. After around 1820 museums and committees were established and publication projects began. The movement received a shot in the arm with the first volume of Michelet's *Histoire de France* in 1833, the same year Ampère began his course at the Collège de France, where he tackled medieval Latin literature and then passed on to vernacular texts. Faral, Ampère's successor, advances an opinion that enhances his contribution, citing "the perspicacity of a mind which missed nothing, for which the smallest detail was filled with significance, and which knew how to discern unerringly the dominant characteristics of periods and individuals." The articles following Ampère's return from Egypt in 1839 "are written in an admirably confident style. But what should not be overlooked in the work of a man who was dominated by the literary spirit are the fine qualities of his scholarship." He was, notably, the only person in France at the time to accord Diez' work on the romance languages the recognition it deserved, which even Littré did not do.

The Salon of Mary Clarke and Julius Mohl

It was in 1824 that Ampère, lionized on his return from Italy, made the acquaintance of Mohl at Cuvier's home. And it was Mohl, who had come from Germany to study oriental languages, who took Ampère to Rémusat's lectures. From April 1831 until his marriage to Mary Clarke in 1847, Mohl and Ampère lived and worked together. Mohl is described by Louis de Launay as "a singular German, a little English and vaguely gallicized . . . who taught successively at the Académie des Inscriptions, the Société Asiatique, and the Collège de France. . . . Ironic, cynical, and a stranger to any sentimentality," he nevertheless worked himself to death on his translation of Firdausi and, whether sentimental or not, succeeded

Fauriel as a suitor to Mary Clarke. They were married three years after Fauriel's death; the love letters between Clarke and Fauriel were published by one of Mohl's descendants who had piously preserved them. Fauriel was fifty when he had first experienced this passion for the twenty-nine-year-old Scotswoman; he was seventy-two when he died in 1844. She was fifty-four when she married Mohl in 1847. He was seven years younger than she, but died in 1876; she lived to the age of ninety. The Clarke-Mohl salon at Abbaye-aux-Bois functioned from 1830 to 1880, and great numbers of European literary, scientific, and political celebrities flowed through it unceasingly.

The Clarke women, mother and daughter, had taken over one floor in the home of Madame Récamier, who, "when Chateaubriand seemed altogether bored, was very happy that Miss Clarke was there." In 1838 she took up residence in the house of the master: "Ampère said that she 'was the delight' of René and that the great man on several occasions made use in his works of expressions that he had heard her use and that were characteristic of her."[15] The literary world debated her charms. For Stendhal, who loathed her, she looked "like a question mark." Quinet, whom she idolized, stated, "she is fortunate that she gives no thought to her face." According to Guizot, "she had the same hair style as her Scottish terrier." Chateaubriand described her in a phrase suspectible to several interpretations: "The young Englishwoman resembles no one." On one point at least she resembled the contintinental legend of her countrymen: she took an extraordinary interest in people in whom everyone was already interested. A brief, stormy affair with Amédée Thierry (she was slightly off the mark, since he was only a brother of the great Thierry) had preceded the one with Fauriel, who called her "my angel." Her letters show that one of her passions was to observe at close range what made a professor at the Collège de France tick. Mistress of a house that entertained prominent members of the Université and the Parlement, she was equally attracted by the anatomy of such great minds as Hugo, Chateaubriand, Dickens, Longfellow, and Turgenev, as well as Montalembert, Renan, Prévost-Paradol, Jules Simon, and Guizot. A gourmand of the aroma of fame.

In love with one of the first French Sanskrit scholars, wife of its foremost Persian scholar, she discussed their fields with them and with those around her. In 1827 she wrote Fauriel, "I am very eager to talk with you about India and Greece, and I would like you to beat me into learning Sanskrit." Beneath her Bettina simper, this mischievous thirty-four-year-old had latched on to the vogue. She brought up the topic of India several times during the same summer. In August Fauriel replied to her that Sanskrit was no more difficult than Greek: "I have persuaded Barchoux [Barchou de Penhoën], whom I meet from time to time, to learn Sanskrit."

The Clarke salon was certainly one of those in which Sainte-Beuve drew nearest the Oriental Renaissance. He was a regular visitor there—indulgent to the wife, friendly to the husband. In 1844 he obtained Fauriel's papers from them, which he used to document his voluminous analysis, one of his best. He later devoted an extensive study to the *Shah Namah*, the only one of such poems brought back from Asia to have the benefit of his attention. Sainte-Beuve declared that Mohl's teaching was listless; more touched by his friend's work and conversation than he wished to appear, he once wrote that a piece by Scribe appeared "thin and less than trifling . . . to one who dwells amid the *Shah Namah* and epics from the Orient." This was an unusual emotion for Sainte-Beuve. It was rare that he said so much about oriental poetry and its effects.

For Julius Mohl, three or four descriptions, drawn by masters, will suffice: the portrait Sainte-Beuve included in *Nouveaux lundis*, those by Renan and Max Müller in the preface to *Twenty-seven Years of Oriental Studies*, and a few traits from Augustin Thierry, who was in a doubly good position to have reliable information—through the confidences of his brother and from the throne of the blind Homer whom the Récamier salon adored. Born in Stuttgart in 1800, Mohl was sent on March 5, 1823 by his master and uncle, chancellor of the university of Tübingen, to Cuvier and Sacy, who along with Rémusat, Fauriel, and Burnouf welcomed him. He added Arabic and Persian to Hebrew, which had been for him, as for so many others, the path from theology to oriental studies, according to Max Müller. Mohl wanted to learn what ideas had governed humanity, especially during the primitive periods of oriental history.

In 1826 Mohl turned down the offer for a German chair of oriental languages, preferring to edit and translate, at the expense of the king of France, the imense *Shah Namah*, the printing of which under the title *Livre des Rois* began in 1833. Mohl was to remain a Parisian; certainly the quality of the scholarship he found in Paris accounted a great deal for his choice, and his friendships there and the atmosphere perhaps weighed as heavily. It was in another Parisian salon that he made the acquaintance of his compatriot Humboldt, and he held the attention of such powerful personages as Villemain, Guizot, Cousin, and Thiers. His translation of Firdausi was completed in 1878 and was a princely repayment for the hospitality he had received. Naturalized in 1838, Mohl was named to the Institut in 1844 and to a professorship at the Collège de France in 1847; he became inspector of oriental publications in 1852, the same year in which he succeeded Burnouf as secretary of the Société Asiatique. The reports he gave there spread his influence as year after year he called attention to important publications in oriental studies. Attached no less to India than to Persia, after 1840 he called for the publication of the Vedas, while Burnouf, thanks to funds that Guizot had allocated, was having Prinsep transcribe the Vedic manuscripts. "In daily contact with Eugène Burnouf, and always in accord with that rare intellect," writes Renan, "Mohl was like the center of a vast inquiry in which nothing that might contribute to increasing our understanding of several of the most important chapters of human history was neglected." Renan briefly summarized the immensity of the discoveries made during those years and concluded, "This was the golden age of oriental studies." Assyriology also originated with Mohl; his intuition, perhaps also certain reminiscences of the failed pastor, led him to point out the necessity of excavating Mesopotamia. In 1843 he sent Botta in search of Nineveh and supported his digs at Khorsabad. By 1845 Botta and his 200 Nestorian workers had cleared "two thousand cubic meters of walls covered with inscriptions and bas-reliefs," the best of which were sent to Paris. Botta was recalled to Paris in 1849, but Mohl continued to lobby for extending the French expedition: Oppert went to excavate in Mesopotamia in 1851 with Fulgence Fresnel, a cousin of Mérimée and a student of Rémusat, who lived next door to Ampère.

Mohl was known for his modesty and reserve and, according to his fellow countryman Max Müller, "a certain brusqueness of which he could never rid himself and which more than one observer charitably attributed to his German blood." Although he was completely acclimated to Paris, he did not forget his origins, "German by nature, French by taste, English by his fondest affections," and "with true friends in each of the three countries." In the international salon of his wife, he dreamed of an accord among these countries, but he came to despair of such agreement, and the advent of the Second Empire spelled "the final ruin of his dream." The salon at least remained to him "a sort of free port, open to all those who came to Paris to see whatever was most deserving of being seen there." Renan, who wrote these descriptions, enumerates not only all the distinguished Europeans but "all the opinions" that "joined hands" there. But we should not imagine that the stiffness which the word salon implies is the case here. At the home of Mary Clarke's mother one sees a small group of intimates waiting for their guests after dinner, shedding their coats, putting on their slippers, and snoring on the couch until the first ring of the bell.

The publication of the *Shah Namah* "was much more important to the literary history of the century than the bruited appearance of a host of works destined to die," as Ampère immediately declared in the *Revue des Deux-Mondes* in a striking 1839 article that Massé quotes; this notion seems to have been, for Ampère, a requital for abandoning creative literature. Sainte-Beuve's two articles on Firdausi in 1850 shaped public opinion by developing Ampère's favorable opinion; thus the great name passed from master to master. Lamartine introduced the story of Rustam, "one of the most epic and most dramatic of the old Orient, which embodies the Orient completely and very vividly," in *Le Civilisateur; Histoire de l'humanité par les grands hommes*. For Hugo, Firdausi would enlarge the repertoire of key names that were the equivalent of arguments in his poetic dialectic. In several vehment pages of *Bible de l'Humanité* Michelet asks Mohl for the secret of "the sacred soul of Persia," "living water that flows fresh and pure in the murky depths of forgotten canals." And as if to mark the character of the Oriental Renaissance with his enthusiasm, he applies the term "sagas" to the folk heritage from which the national poet of Persia drew.

Fauriel

Fauriel can also be considered within the context of Romanticism, the university, the circle of Chateaubriand and Madame Récamier, and the tradition of Schlegel and Hamilton; he was one more link in the Renaissance chain. Sainte-Beuve, who knew him best, found in him "the eighteenth-century becoming the nineteenth naturally" (Fauriel was sixty years old in 1832) and described him as concluding the action by which Madame de Staël (he had been her first reader) and Benjamin Constant "ingeniously transformed the century which was finished, disseminating its insights and extending its discoveries in a good many directions and along a good many paths." Sainte-Beuve himself called Fauriel "a hyphen." Sainte-Beuve's portrait was firsthand, based on direct confidences from Mohl and Cousin and on Fauriel's personal papers. Fauriel was an exceptional figure with an eventful life and an immense reputation, but in the final analysis (and he was not the only example of this), all the acclaim he received from his contemporaries dissipated like smoke in posterity. Ampère and Fauriel are two vivid examples of that favorite of the gods: the *irresistible failure*. An extraordinary seductiveness was held in reserve for gifts of intellect that would never be spent in written works, a marvelous balance left to install wonder in audiences and capture their hearts. The best part of themselves remained their deeds, the delights of their speech, and lit up their faces with all the need to be loved that was not channeled into written works and that, in spite of themselves, continually chose the present moment over the lasting. Their power to arouse interest had to bring subjects to life for their contemporaries, for that power would die with them. Was it even a choice on their part? A somewhat admirable, somewhat dreadful case of the man who *could* create a work, but who is not utterly compelled to do so. The man who is not consumed by the work, whose work never springs completely to life because it is constantly over-whelmed by life itself. It is not that the inner life is denied to such people, but that it has too many competitors. In this respect a man like Quinet was a borderline case, more and more won over by action. "A man who spent almost his entire life in spreading his understanding and pouring out his ideas within the bosom of friendship": beneath the Louis-Philippe style of Sainte-Beuve's description one can see in Fauriel an honorable man who spoke his life.

The young Fauriel (1772–1844), ex-secretary of Fouché and a regular frequenter of the homes of the ideologues (in 1802 he began an affair of twenty years' duration with the beautiful widow of Condorcet), was equally at home with the first Romantic fashions: Ossian, the Germany of Charles de Villiers and Manzoni, as well as Herder and Vico, from whom he learned to love "poetry, particularly at its first stage of growth when it is almost identical with history." This led him as much toward the Greek lyrics and those of the troubadors in *langue d'oc* as toward the nomenclature-types of Eckstein: "If, on his way to the poetry of Provence, he could find the longest way round, through the *Nibelungenlied* or the Eddas, he took the greatest care not to miss it." It was Fauriel who reinforced the German ideas in Ampère: "His influence on Ampère at the beginning of his career was considerable; he contributed to the development of the instinct in this lively temperament that turned it toward literary origins." It was on this basis that Sainte-Beuve, elsewhere so opposed to the proposition of cut-ting the person of Homer into pieces, endorsed Ampère's idea by listing, directly after the first Homer to have the name, "the three Homers of whom we were long unaware . . . the Hindu poets Valmiki and Vyasa and the Persian Firdausi." Ampère, Fauriel, and Mohl: is it not now clear to what extent personal relations could achieve what book-learning could not?

Although he was well placed and well qualified to do so, Sainte-Beuve denied us a comprehensive study of the orientalist movement, a lacuna for which there has been no compensation. Perhaps his heart did not have room for such great things, or perhaps if he had pumped his blood into the second Renaissance he would not have had enough left for the first. He touched lightly on our Renaissance à propos Mohl, Eckstein, Ampère, and Fauriel, the only figures to whom, as a friend, he devoted full-length portraits. Burnouf, Sacy, Chézy, Pauthier, and Barthélemy Saint-Hilaire appear only occasionally. Moreover, in his judgmental *Mes Poisons*, Sainte-Beuve chided himself for the public attention he gave to such figures as Pauthier and Ampère. He had a taste for pivotal people, providential fig-ures for historians, test-tube cases for the chemists of literature.

In 1803 Fauriel was a fellow student of Friedrich Schlegel in Sanskrit; in 1821 he became the confidant of Augustin Thierry, whom he had first met at the home of the Tracys and afterwards at the home of Mrs. Clarke. He was "a no less fervent or essential recipient of Wilhelm Schlegel's confidences on India and his scholarly Asiatic project." Here, thanks to Sainte-Beuve, we happen upon one more significant conversation on Sanskrit between two important speakers, Fauriel and Thierry. At this time Wilhelm Schlegel had been forced to leave Paris before he could complete his font of devanagari characters, which had been his mission in coming to Paris, and he asked Fauriel to take care of the matter for him. Schlegel subsequently entrusted Fauriel with collating the Persian manuscripts of the *Bhagavad Gita* for the Latin translation that he was preparing. In 1823 Fauriel, who had contributed to the establishment of the Société Asiatique, published a study of Wilhelm Schlegel's *Indische Bibliothek* in the Société's *Journal* (Chézy published a similar article in the *Journal des Savants*).

At Chézy's death, Fauriel wrote to Mary Clarke, "I cannot forget the zeal and the pleasure with which he gave me my first Sanskrit lessons. It is a relationship that had its duties and its closeness just like any other, and I will respect it all my life." His first Sanskrit lessons? Were those from Hamilton so negligible? The same year he was receiving them, along with Friedrich Schlegel, Volney, Langlès, and Hagemann, Fauriel nonetheless felt himself competent to write about Indic philosophy in the *Décade philosophique*. In the *Archives philosophiques* in 1818 and in the *Revue encyclopédique* in 1819 he examined Bopp's system. In his classes at the Sorbonne during 1833 and 1834 he focused a great deal on Sanskrit literature and language. It was only after his political friends were brought to power in 1830 and created a chair of foreign literature for him that he specialized in the poetry of southern France.

What he carried over to his study of a field of poetry that was postulated to be primitive and alleged to be sponanteous was of great significance. Edmund Faral points out the great delay of the *Chanson de Roland* in restoring to ancient French poetry a position equal to that which had, until then, been occupied solely by the *Nibelungenlied*. It was only in the 1850s that the cumulative efforts of Monin, Francisque Michel, Saint-Marc Girardin, Genin, and Vitet succeeded in accomplishing this. The theory of epics "overflowing" from popular genius continued to impose the notion of "cantilenas"on the medieval scholars, which did not finally collapse until the theory was exploded in 1884 by the Italian Pio Rajna. By then it had been exactly sixty years since Fauriel had revived the Germanic error of the superiority of "natural poetry" and applied it to popular Greek lyrics. Having listened to Professor Fauriel and his successor Ozanam, Renan endorsed the idea in 1845 in *Cahiers de jeunesse,* where he applied it to the *Chanson de Roland*. It was not until 1912 that Bédier ruled out the hypothesis that there had been previous versions of the poem;

Bédier assigned the blame for this notion particularly to the prejudices of Herder, the Grimms, and Fauriel. After Bédier, the *Chanson* would no longer be considered the final state of an enigmatic Carolingian cycle but the consecration of a local legend by the genius of an individual. How could a poet worthy of the name have ever doubted this law? That is precisely what Hugo had never done.

Fauriel had ideas, information, and advice for everyone, as we have just seen in regard to Ampère and Thierry. We have also discussed his concern for Constant; Fauriel discussed Constant's magnum opus, *De la religion*, with him for years and provided him with documentation for it. "But, for the most part," Durry writes, in *La vieillesse de Chateaubriand*, "he never managed to write down his ideas, and when he did write them down it was in the style that Henri Brulard considered an example of bourgeois baseness." (Brulard and Fauriel hated each other because of their conflicting suits for Mary Clarke.) But Fauriel also supplied the ungrateful Stendhal with material, Arabic anecdotes, for his book *De l'amour*, a logical counterpart to Constant's book. Fauriel had fuel for all fires.

Delécluze, Ozanam, and Lamennais

On a great many of the paths that Fauriel encouraged Ampère to travel, we encounter another person who also had a great many contacts. Etienne Delécluze (1781–1863) was a frequent resident of Fontenay, where he saw a good deal of Latouche, the patron of letters, and traveled by diligence with Burnouf, father and son, who lived at Chatillion. Delécluze haunted a salon in the countryside that Jean Reynaud and Pierre Leroux frequented assiduously during the years they were working on their *Encyclopédie nouvelle* and where Quinet came to read his *Prométhée* to his two friends. Delécluze respected several individual Saint-Simonians, but as a rationalist he balked at their doctrine almost as violently as his friend Stendhal; the latter, who witnessed the raucous and lively reunions of the young at Delécluze's home, stated, "I have never encountered anything comparable, and I do not mean to say superior."

In 1830 in the *Revue française*, Delécluze revealed the Arabic romance *Sirat Antar* and translated portions of it from the English version; the French version of 1819 had passed unnoticed.[16] Delécluze later added excerpts from Firdausi, based either on Mohl's translation or on the 1832 English version. These were gathered in the course of his study of chivalry, to which he would return in 1838 in *Revue des Deux-Mondes*. It was by chance that he had laid his hands on the English *Antar* in the Bibliothèque nationale: the upshot of this event was that after 1831 the orientalists Chézy, Fresnel, Loisleur-Deslongchamps, Pauthier, Garcin de Tassy, Burnouf, and Stanislas Julien sent Delécluze their translations so he might review them in *Journal des Débats,* which he did until 1837. At the *Débats* he again encountered Sacy's son, who held an important position. Struck by the effect of his first columns and by the fact that in 1824 Rémusat had translated a Chinese novel (Chang Yün's *Yü Chiao Li*) under the title *Deux Cousins,* which had been read as avidly as any French novel, Delécluze broadened his ambitions: he wanted, as he said in his *Souvenirs,* to "give the public," although he himself could not read the originals, "a general idea of oriental philosophy, law, and manners, based on the works" of the specialists and, through this undertaking, to provide access to the journals for the oriental scholars themselves, thereby completing the mission. It was in this way that an orientalist column came to be established in the *Journal des Débats.* Doesn't such a plan indicate a real trend? The journalist Delécluze set forth the plan in earnest to his editor Bertin and advised him to assign the column to Julien, since China seemed to him to have aroused the greatest interest. China was, for Delécluze as well as for the period, the area where oriental romance was located. Bertin found Delécluze's arguments convincing. Perhaps overly convincing, for, faced with the prospect of an Asian contamination, Bertin, terrified "of awakening the barbarians," became frightened for Europe, and there the matter came to a dead end.

For Bertin, but not for Delécluze. He would, in the course of his most outstanding undertaking, remember this Orient through which he had passed. Delécluze next set out to restore the cult of the Renaissance, the first Renaissance this time. He devoted numerous studies to the Renaissance that were intended to form a coherent whole. In these articles he reacted against the passion for the second Renaissance, but in spite of everything he ended up applying certain ideas of the Oriental Renaissance in the process. This occurred in two ways, and in each of them we again find the skeptic. On the one hand, at the outset he expressed the opinion that oriental chivalry was anterior to European chivalry and accounted for it in part. Ampère challenged the article on this point, denouncing the innuendo he found there, which he considered hostile to Christian spirituality. As a matter of fact, the ideologue Ginguené had already advanced this notion in 1813; interestingly enough, Villemain took up the same idea in order to checkmate Schlegel's redistribution of Mediterranean spoils among the Nordics, and it is also curious that in his *Etudes historiques* Chateaubriand reported the idea, along with a tribute to the splendors of *Antar* (perhaps from fidelity to Abencerrages). Fauriel supported Delécluze; the two of them also agreed on the subject of the Middle Ages, where they again encountered Villemain, who was opposed to the vogue for German Gothicism and its ally, so-called popular poetry, to the point of calling the infatuation with old French epics "a literary paradox." Delécluze, in no uncertain terms, turned in favor of the Italian Renaissance the movement begun in Germany to repudiate and replace it.

It was for this that he was numbered among the adversaries of the Orient; yet it was Delécluze who in *Dante ou la poésie amoureuse* (1854) collected all the foreign traditions, particularly the oriental, which would serve as suitable verification of the Dantean concept of symbolic love. He again discussed *Antar,* alluded to Firdausi, Nizami, al-Muqaddasi, and Wali ("The Petrarch of India"), and referred to Chézy, Sacy, and d'Herbelot, as was commonplace for the educated society of the time. The necessity for universal evidence was very much a nineteenth-century idea; even a "history of renaissances" that was hostile to Germanism furthered the encyclopedic research that the philosophy of history promoted. During this time oriental studies had a prestige that everyone used for his own purposes. Delécluze, a rationalist, drew material from oriental studies to annotate the idea of love that had most resembled a religion—and likewise material to enlarge Stendhal's views on this topic. India supplied other arguments for the spiritualist camp, and Delécluze was well aware of this, for his studies of Dante and Saint Francis of Assisi employed information gathered by Ozanam, who had traveled the same routes.

Frédéric Ozanam (1813–1853), as we have seen on two previous occasions, passed through all the significant groups. He was almost part of the family at the Ampère home and hardly less close to Ballanche, another native of Lyon; the *Vision d'Hébal* prompted him to say in 1831 that "the fulfillment of Christianity" was "the goal of all historical evolution." He met Vigny and Sainte-Beuve at Montalembert's home about this time and was influenced by Eckstein. At the age of seventeen he wrote to his friend Fortoul that he wanted "to know about a dozen languages in order to consult the sources and the documents . . . to study . . . the history of religious belief in all its complexity." This had been exactly the same method and objective of the young Lamennais some thirty years earlier. As an adult, Ozanam urged his friends to "establish the truth of the Catholic religion through the antiquity and universality of the beliefs and traditions of the human race." In all such traditions and beliefs, "leaving aside the mythological elements, he isolated . . . the unique, primitive, universal element and named this the Christian element. The traditionalism of Lamennais and the researches of Görres and Baron Eckstein were on the lookout for points of contact with the Christian revelation in all religious conceptions, however rudimentary. Such studies excited Ozanam, who expected to find new proof for his *credo* in a comparative history of religions."[17]

In January 1832 Ozanam heard Abbé Gerbert, a close friend of Lamennais and a collaborator of Eckstein's, "open his lectures on the philosophy of history." We can imagine the spirit of this opening lecture by recalling that Gerbert had devoted four chapters in his *Considérations sur le dogme* to "primitive traditions." By the following summer, Ozanam was planning a Conference on History for Young People, "where the various systems would be summoned to appear, and where Christianity would consider and judge them." The event was scheduled for December. "The mythology of India, the poetry and its influence and oriental literature," wrote Goyau, were among "the topics that Ozanam dealt with personally during the year 1833." And Sainte-Beuve made a friendly allusion to the enthusiastic young people "in the self-confident movement for the restoration of Christianity through learning." These latter words should be underscored, for "learning" *(la science)* meant the history of origins, including the Orient. A few words will suffice to show the impact that the ideas of this eloquent apostle made: they were, of course, highly influential in Catholic circles, where they had had predecessors. His admission to the faculty of the Université was acclaimed, and his thesis on Dante, which had not attracted much attention, became an important event. On his jury, along with Villemain and Guigniaut, had been Fauriel, who would invite him to serve as his substitute, and Cousin, who the following year offered him his choice of this replacement post or Quinet's chair at Lyon. No sooner had Ozanam opted for the Sorbonne than his teaching gained renown. Caro and Sarcey were among those attending his lectures, Renan was enthusiastic about them, and Lamartine wrote of them, "Each time he breathed, he took your heart away and gave you his." He died before the age of forty, after having been a professor only some dozen years. Ozanam always retained his interest in "barbaric times" through his Italian and German studies.

Another indication of the position oriental studies occupied in spiritual controversies at that time: in 1844 in the opening pages of his *Manuel de philosophie ancienne*, Renouvier felt compelled to spell out what he meant by the term Orient, which was then used indiscriminately. He specified India, Persia, Egypt, Phoenicia, and China as especially significant for philosophy. All the same, "in such a remote past, the Indians alone impress us as a truly philosophical nation. In the course of a period barely ended today they traveled all the great paths of intellectual research." In his *Manuel* Renouvier assumed a position between the two camps of Hindu primacy and Greek supremacy; he was more inclined toward the latter, for the reason that Indic philosophy "was never independent of the supernatural and divine revelation of truth." This argument was readily repeated by all the rationalists. Even though Renouvier was one of the first to perceive clearly the profound quasi-theological unity of all Indic thought, and even of all expressions of it, he attacked the extremist propagandists and criticized both the classifications that Friedrich Schlegel prematurely established among the systems and Schlegel's linguistic theories. Renouvier had harsh words for the indiscretion with which Pauthier, in translating Colebrooke, ruled against Greece on the question of the exchange of influences. It was, in short, a rejoinder to Victor Cousin's course fifteen years after the fact.

We must now bring our discussion around to Lamennais (1782–1851), as we already know how so many of the ideas which concern us passed through him, and I shall discuss him further when we come to "the question of the soul." Lamennais notes that "on November 13, 1807, between 4 and 5:30 A.M.," while working on an article about dissenting sects, he feverishly recorded "a torrent of vague ideas that overflowed onto paper." It was a blueprint for the reconciliation of all the churches, which Christian Maréchal published.[18] Among the paragraphs that poured forth, the eighth mentions the need for "a knowledge of the oriental languages." The need "to place oneself in rapport with the literary spokesmen for these languages," namely Sacy, followed. Thus as early as 1807 we find a young Catholic militant who considered the new field of learning indispensable. What was more, if Lamennais had ascertained the need for it, it was due to the influence of the Hebrew professor at Saint-Sulpice. Paragraph 18 makes this clear: "One should obtain the *Bibliothèque Orientale* of Assemani and that of d'Herbelot, the preface to the *Zend Avesta* by Anquetil, and the papers of the Calcutta Society." Such was the bibliography that the seminarian drew up for himself during the Empire. He then proceeded to carry out this project: 29 pages of notes on the *Avesta* were found in his papers. With his brother, pen in hand, he also read Manu in Jones's translation, which produced another 34 manuscript pages. He annotated d'Herbelot and even Pastoret. All of this later reappeared in his writings and his actions. In *L'Avenir* Lamennais presented the various branches of learning, including languages and history, as a collection "filled with God." "Languages . . . are even more the monuments of God than they are of the nations that spoke them; they are God himself, for as it is written, the Word is God."[19] But it was in his *Essai sur l'indifférence en matière de religion* (1817), a crucial book, that the memory of his initial readings produced results: Jones and the *Asiatic Researches*, Anquetil and the *Avesta* were quoted profusely (so too, alas, were Maurice and the *Ezour-Vedam*, for which Lanjuinais reproached him). The *Essai* seems to have achieved Lamennais's youthful wish: to recreate the religious unity of the earth by proving, through universal consent, the truth of Christianity. Here Lamennais joins Friedrich Schlegel, whose intuition in 1807 perhaps only slightly preceded his own. His faith in the universality of the revelation was strikingly apparent on page after page; his deductions would later provoke the condemnation of Lacordaire, which we will discuss in its proper place. "It is particularly from the Orient, the cradle of religion, the arts and the sciences, that this primitive tradition that we insist upon must be drawn. It is from there that it has passed to all peoples. No single historical truth is as rigorously demonstrated as the existence of this tradition, confirmed by all the monuments of antiquity." And, "With the Indians, as with all other peoples of the earth, one can recognize, underneath the most bizarre fiction and fable, *a cult that was orginally pure* and that became corrupted only through the course of time." The emphasis was Lamennais's.

We have a photographic image of Lamennais's work as it was developing during the 1830s; it comes from Sainte-Beuve, who was one of the lecture-goers at Juilly, as from time to time were Hugo, Lamartine, and the future orientalist Eugène Boré. Sainte-Beuve depicts the reformer in the process of thinking through the reconciliation of orthodoxy and political freedom, and also tending "to extend himself into the scientific disciplines and place them in harmony with religious faith." The program had not changed: "A great work of religious philosophy which . . . promises to embrace, through a completely rational method, the entire order of human knowledge, beginning with the simplest notion of being." This "completely rational" method was precisely what was to give rise to controversy. Sainte-Beuve insisted on the risk: "The most exact logic, joined to a rigorously orthodox foundation, clears a place between Saint-Martin and Baader." Sainte-Beuve was strangely moved: "While the author was reading, my attention was very frequently diverted from his words and I heard only his voice, and was entirely taken up with his unusual accent and with his face that seemed lit from within. I experienced soul-to-soul revelations arising from the depths of his being, so that I saw clearly a very pure essence." And with uneasy admiration, he watched this "eagle of intelligence" gamboling in the depths of space and time, deprived of "his Saint John to bring him back and guide him."

Mérimée

On the side of the skeptics we may list—along with Delécluze, who became only slightly orientalized, Stendhal, who had no mercy on either Fauriel or Mary Mohl, and even Sainte-Beuve, whose effusions were often superficial—Mérimée, whose resistance serves as a good test metal. Mérimée was in contact with all aspects of the new Renaissance and those involved with it: a habitual guest of the Cuviers, a close friend of Fauriel and of the Mohl-Clarkes, to whom he introduced Hugo, he also belonged to the Ampère-David-Pavie group. He wrote about Champollion and the hieroglyphics, and in 1831, at the home of Gérard, he became friends with Charles Lenormant, first the disciple and then the successor of the Egyptologist and a nephew by marriage to Madame Récamier; Lenormant held a chair of history at the Sorbonne, thanks to Mérimée ancient history, and he began his lectures there with an exposition of western Asia. He died during a trip to Greece, where Mérimée had been his traveling companion. Mérimée was no less acquainted with Jacquemont and published accounts of his work as well. He interceded for Mohl, procured documents for the Société Asiatique, was responsible for Burnouf's appointment as inspector of oriental typography at the Imprimerie royale and, twenty years later, had a pension granted Burnouf's widow. In addition, Mérimée was the first cousin of Fulgence Fresnel and met many orientalists through his various functions and his involvement with committees and learned societies.

One of the rare occasions Mérimée expounded on such subjects was at Ampère's reception into the Académie, at which he was designated to give the welcoming address. There were brief allusions to his friend's work "on the literary tradition of the Orient, on Indic and Persian epics and the Chinese theater" that linked them with "the general studies" of Villemain "on poetic imagination and *comparative criticism*," which was widely considered a contribution of the new humanism. Praising the omniscient Ampère for having introduced "all classes of readers to the recent discoveries of oriental philology," Mérimée also commended him for having compared Orient and Occident "sagaciously" and for giving "an attractive form" to the "sometimes gruesome apparatus" of scholarship. Could a well-bred man, in the midst of an address to the Académie, have taken fewer precautions? With the drapery of pomp, which did not detract from his official image, Mérimée adorned "this noble inquisitiveness which is, nowadays, taking the place of a perhaps overly proud indifference." A Romantic by nature, was he congratulating himself that the old temple of literary taste was getting a bit of fresh air? A goldsmith who knew real gold, Mérimée found, as Rémusat had, that the preferences of the homebodies were "excusable in a people that boasts such names as Bossuet, Corneille, and Molière." Did some sort of reticence prevent the name of Racine, against whom Stendhal and his friends had carried out their first campaigns, from being added to the list? What gratitude did Mérimée hold for Ampère for having begun his career by translating Ossian with him? In the style suited to the occasion, Mérimée acknowledged "the sublime discoveries" secured "for an age of the world in which human intelli-

gence has made marvelous advances," and coldly welcomed "the astonishing facility with which they manage to be spread and propagated today."

The perfumes of Asia seem to have done little to soften the test metal
in Mérimée. One is surprised to see certain small groups that were so obsessed with physical love were so resistant to the mystique of the Orient.
The fact remains that sometimes we encounter someone for whom the
Oriental Renaissance was important only as one element of the period,
and sometimes we encounter someone styling himself a *diviniste*, to some
extent like Saint-Martin, who thought, "It is not enough to have spirit; it
is essential to have spirituality."

Stanislas Julien, Pauthier, and Fouinet

A multitude of capacities, temptations, fits and starts—these are the
marks of renaissances in most of their men. They leave a great many of
them abandoned along the road of personality beside those who do not
"disengage" themselves, as Cousin put it. Pauthier (1801–1873) who started
out to be a poet, then a linguist, in the end was important as a popularizer. A good Indic scholar and an even better sinologist, he was widely
challenged; the squabbles with which Stanislas Julien dogged him remain
legendary. Even Oppert's disputes with Léon Halévy did not lend so much
credence to the stereotype of the cranky philologist, which Heine especially highlighted: "These erudite antagonists have enriched learning with
two important discoveries: Julien, the noted sinologist, has discovered that
Pauthier does not know Chinese, and Pauthier, the great Indianist, has
discovered that Julien does not know Sanskrit." Stanislas Julien (1799–1873)
had been another of those child prodigies whose linguistic feats characterize the beginning of the nineteenth century. After a precocious period
as a Hellenist, which enabled him to be named to the Collège de France
at the age of twenty-four, he went on to learn Sanskrit, Persian, Arabic,
and Hebrew; that is to say, he followed in the footsteps of Chézy, Sacy,
and Rémusat. Having opted to specialize in Chinese, Julien succeeded
Rémusat in 1832 and subsequently brought the jealous fury of a proprietor to bear on the preserve of Chinese studies.

Pauthier's influence on poets through his *Livres sacrés de l'Orient*, a work
compiled from second-hand information, sprang from the fact that he had
originally set out to be a poet himself. In 1822, as chance would have it,
he was a corporal, then a sergeant in the 55th line regiment at Strasbourg,
where Vigny, a captain, arrived after leaving the *gardes rouges*. Sainte-Beuve
determined the details of their first meeting from a letter he obtained from

Pauthier himself and which he appended to his article on Vigny in *Nouveaux lundis*. In July 1823, when the regiment was passing through Nancy on its way to Bordeaux, the captain had the sergeant assigned officers' quarters. "As of that day we were friends. In our garrisons at Bordeaux, l'Ile de Ré, and Pau, we were frequently together." Both of them kept clear of the café life, that is, from the rest of the troops. Vigny's first poems had appeared in 1823, and he was not discharged from the service until 1827. In the interval he worked on *Cinq Mars*, which appeared in 1826 and brought him into fashion. During its composition he discussed the work a great deal with Pauthier, who attested to the exactness of the landscapes and the authenticity of the documents. Pauthier had traveled the former with the novelist; the latter he "had seen when attending the removal of the seals which took place after Vigny's death and at which [he was] present as executor." The intimacy and trust the two men shared was uninterrupted to the end. In designating his old friend to ensure that his last wishes were respected, Vigny marked the place he kept for Pauthier in his thoughts. In 1827 after their great talks on the work-in-progress, Pauthier, who was also discharged at that time, had decisively shunted himself to the Orient through the *China* of Rémusat. Thereafter he guided Vigny's curiosity about this domain.

Like Ampère, Pauthier first believed himself to be a poet. In 1825, amid the excitement over pan-Hellenism, he had published *Helléniennes ou elégies sur la Grèce*, which was preceded by a "Letter in Verse" to Lamartine. In 1826 his *Mélodies poétiques et chants d'amour* appeared with a concluding "Letter in Verse" to Nodier. There were few flashes of genius in Pauthier's verse. Following the general paradox, its romanticism was expressed in the style of the old school. But many of the allusions in his poetry at least marked out the other path that would lead the young man to better renown. Here, alternatively, were Germanism and Asiaticism: an imitation of Friedrich Schlegel, epigraphs from Goethe and de Staël, patronage of Zoroaster, Mithra, Odin; here were Arabia, India, Persia, and Kashmir; here were the evocative and scholarly names of Cathay, Kandahar, Krishna; and here was a taste for a blend of philosophy and poetry. In 1838, by which time he was immersed in scholarship, Pauthier produced a translation of *Childe Harold's Pilgrimage* as well.

In his diary, Sainte-Beuve chided himself for the attention he granted his "scholarly friend" in *Nouveaux lundis*: in *Cahiers* he viewed Pauthier as a poet, but in *Mes poisons* he expressed an opinion on the value of the poems. "*Liris* began with bad poetry, which, highly overrated by highly obliging friends, found its way to and were the ruin of a novice publisher. . . . *Liris* himself, not particularly disturbed by this, had volume after volume of his poems printed. And always with the same success. At last, for the sake of peace and quiet, he settled down to study; he knows languages and even goes beyond Europe to explore India and to travel, from time to time, to China—through books, that is. One thinks he has returned from his chimera, one respects him and is about to congratulate him . . . but better not. After he has conversed with you at length one evening about his work, his projects, about Upanishads, Puranas, and the *Book of Documents,* and after he is already on his feet and is shaking your hand as he is taking his leave, he tells you in great confidence that one day he must transform all of that into a great composition in verse which will enrich our poetry, a single unique bouquet of all the flowers of the Orient at once. Unable to hold himself back, at the last minute he lets his cherished secret out of the bag. The inmate of an asylum whose madness consisted in thinking himself a multimillionaire seems cured after years of treatment; his doctor, pen in hand to sign the man's release, is explaining to his assistants and to the director of the asylum that the patient has been cured. The patient, smiling most graciously, waiting for the doctor to finish, leans over toward him and whispers in his ear that as soon as he leaves the hospital, he will put a million at the doctor's disposal by way of thanking him for his trouble. That is our poet!'

A charming story for conversation on a slow train. During the Romantic period William Jones was constantly considered as good a poet as he was a linguist. What is disturbing are the strange titles that interlace the list of scurrilous pamphlets Pauthier and Julien exchanged: "The Sacrifice of Desère, a lyric poem," awarded a prize by the Académie de Besançon; "The Comet and the Eclipse of 1832, a letter in verse"; "Discourse addressed to the Mayor and the Municipal Council and to the National Guard of Neuilly-sur-Marne on the occasion of presenting them a flag and the sword of General Douzelot" (1843). (Nevertheless the poet of *Destinées* retained some warm feelings for this childhood companion with whom he had then discussed his art.) Was there some connection between the very positive source of inspiration of Pauthier's poems and his simultaneous entry into the ranks of the Saint-Simonians? We have seen his contributions to the *Revue Encyclopédique.* Or were the Saint-Simonians still a sore point with Sainte-Beuve? In any event, such inclinations caused Pauthier to be numbered among the militants of anti-Christianity.[20]

Ernest Fouinet, another good example, underscores the new fluctuations of interest and ambition among so many attractions for the intellect: Hugo, who well knew, called him "a young writer of learning and imagination." Hugo had met Fouinet at Nodier's home; Hugo was working on *Orientales* at the time and read a few pieces from it there. He was also asking his friends for a translator who could familiarize him with "the loveliest oriental poems."

That Fouinet provided Hugo with accounts of the Orient, just as Fauriel had done for Stendhal, was still probably no more than a result of the time-honored indulgence in exoticism. Only now the knowledge was exact: it had passed from the fantastic to the actual, and thereafter the poets approached these fairytale regions with a submission to its reality, from which the storytellers of the preceding century would simply have shielded themselves. Formerly the vague entity known as the Orient had furnished a cheap source of stylishness for polemical fancy dress. Now its exactness aligned it with a new concept of the poetic closely connected with the documentary. Under the name of Hugo—almost a generic term—when the writer of the new age came into contact with this poetics, inseparable from scholarship, he felt pressed to adhere to what he would, at first, call a Renaissance, as Hugo did in the preface to *Orientales*.

Hugo thought he would inform himself about a few Arabic beauties, the "loveliness" of an indistinct Orient. Instead Fouinet revealed horizons to him that were unexpected even after Eckstein's promises. A nearly forty-year-old specialist was instructing a twenty-six-year-old poet, and giving him justifications for the stance Hugo had at last taken on behalf of a liberated poetics against the classical relics. The poet makes use of those who know, while retaining the attitudes of those who imagine.

At the age of seventeen in 1807, Fouinet had enrolled in the Ecole des Langues orientales and became a member of the Société Asiatique as soon as it was founded in 1821. He contributed to the *Annales Romantiques* between 1826 and 1834 and then to the *Livre des Cent-en-Un*, and published a novel in 1832. Sainte-Beuve had called attention to Fouinet's poetry in 1824 in the *Globe*. In 1830, in *Choix de poésies orientales traduites en vers et en prose*, Fouinet turned again to several texts that Hugo had borrowed from him the year before. Using the weight of Hugo's name, Fouinet had advanced pre-Islamic poetry into the literary mainstream, and in this way *Orientales* played a role in France corresponding to the role that the *Divan* played in Germany. Owing to Fouinet's papers, which Hugo sent directly to the printers to be added to the notes to *Orientales*, great names such as Amru al-Kais, Rumi, Attar, and Firdausi became widely known.

After this brief luck, Fouinet faded from the Romantic scene, but he did not disappear. Sainte-Beuve mentioned him and his work on more than one occasion in his letters to Victor Pavie. From 1828 to 1833, when he traveled, Sainte-Beuve never failed to send his greetings to Fouinet through Hugo or Pavie; it was the same group in which Ulric Guttinguer and the brothers Deschamps were to be found. On July 13, 1833, Sainte-Beuve wrote that he had been at Fouinet's home: "Married, his wife a bourgeoise artist: albums, love songs, paintings jumbled together in tiny rooms, on the beds; she is a glib talker and very spoiled by her music teachers, so that

Fouinet is led around by the nose." It may have been that way; but it is certainly odd that, in the descriptions of certain good friends, the chief figures of an age are reduced to an assortment of jumping jacks. The author of *Mes poisons*, unmarried in spite of himself, was rather inclined, when he visited a married couple, to envy the husband his wife, or else to envy the woman's friendship with her husband. In 1837 a new novel by Fouinet was honored by the Académie, and praised publicly by Villemain on that occasion for its naïveté. Whether or not Sainte-Beuve's view of things was any clearer then, he did, correctly, thank Villemain for his attention. In 1845 Fouinet's last novel appeared and seemed to be a success, but its author died the same year.

Another example comes from Guttinguer who, writing to Fouinet on July 3, 1836, saw in him "the most immutable of beings, always the same poet, fashioning verse in bulk and better than ever—in a word, the most constant of us all." This was a decidedly characteristic trait in one poet among the followers of the second Renaissance who did not want to die young (even as those of the first had probably said in Latin verse), a phenomenon well recognized in Germany in the correspondence between Friedrich Schlegel, Rückert, and Platen. The pattern appears again in the context of Fontaney's journal, which in 1831 recounts meeting at Nodier's "the simple, out-of-place Fouinet," welcoming his visit, meeting him again several times at the Arsenal, along with Hugo, Emile Deschamps, Musset, and Astolphe de Custine. Another feminine image: a fleeting glimpse of Fouinet, "always out of step," dancing with the poet Mélanie Waldor. The same year, at Gérard's house, it was Fontaney who encountered Wilhelm Schlegel "chatting about Persian painting, looking at Chinese drawings." Thus did Asia circulate among the conversations in the home of Gérard, as well as in the homes of Cuvier and Nodier, where, we know through their correspondence, Fouinet's talk supplemented the dossiers he sent to Hugo.

Valentin Parisot

We cannot omit the appearance of Valentin Parisot, however episodic it may have been, among those who shared a deep interest in the languages and poetry of the Orient. Strangely, his appearance was doubly fortunate: it attracted all the lightning that had been gathering in Barbey d'Aurevilly against Indic studies, and it personified the heroism of orientalists for Théodore de Banville. In *Mes souvenirs*, Banville reserved for Parisot one of the most moving portraits, which he placed after the one of Philoxène Boyer, a fanatic of scholarship who had introduced Parisot to Banville. It was Boyer who, having all the libraries in his head, had educated Henry Houssaye in Hellenism. Parisot liked Banville's poetry, and when he arrived from the provinces went to see him. Banville wrote:

Parisot was almost unknown to the public at that time and remains so today. But we knew that this extraordinary scholar, this encyclopedic mind, was another Pico della Mirandola even more astounding than the first. He knew, without exception, all modern and ancient languages, including Sanskrit, and he wrote epic lyric verse in all of them. He had translated the *Mahabharata* and had put 200,000 stanzas of Vyasa into French prose. . . . No sphere of human knowledge was foreign to him. As for myself, I have always been identical on a very small scale to "Lamartine, who knew only his own soul," with this one exception—I do not know my soul.

Valentin Parisot came to see me, and I found him to be . . . the most Parisian of men, coherent and decent beyond expression. . . . Although his days and nights were consumed with study . . . he knew the exterior life . . . as well as a professional boulevardier. . . . Like the great intuitives such as Cuvier, a great introducer of new ideas, this collector of words reconstructed the entire beast with the slightest fragmentary remains. . . .

He was a university professor, having obtained a chair of foreign literature in the provinces, at Grenoble. He had written his application in Italian verses that were so beautiful, so pure, and infused with such great inspiration that they dared not refuse him. . . . He knew the complete works of all the poets by heart and recited them with the rhythmic music proper to them.

Banville's portrait is not without its naïveté, which was more or less deliberate. In any event, this kind of linguistic voracity combined with a hypertrophy of the poetic organs and with talents for several forms of vitality was a novelty that must have left its impression on the attention and imagination of nineteenth-century educated society. One notes in passing the return of comparisons to Cuvier.

In 1853 Valentin Parisot published the first complete French translation of the first book of the *Ramayana*, prior to which Chézy had rendered only two epiodes, and Eckstein a third; Fauche did not begin his translation until 1854. The text itself had been published only in part at that time, and Parisot went no further than it did. He dedicated his work to Eugène Burnouf with a long poem originally written in Sanskrit, the feat that gave rise to Banville's hyperbole. The book included a French translation of the dedication, based on Parisot's Latin translation, by Auguste Vitu, a journalist who was executive secretary to the prefect of Isère. In his introduction Parisot did not fail to compare Valmiki with Homer, the *Shah Namah*, the Edda, and the *Nibelungenlied*, and even to introduce comparisons with Coleridge—all in Sanskrit, in which Burnouf was proclaimed "moon of the sea of vicissitudes of the cult of Buddha."

Théodore Pavie

Our information concerning Théodore Pavie (1812–1896) is, in a way, privileged. Here before our eyes Romanticism and Indianism finish blending. Théodore spent his childhood in Angers with his brother Victor, listening to witches' tales, searching for rare plants, and watching sailboats on the Loire. Their father, connected through Chevreul with the school there, was David's patron, and when he became a famous sculptor, David returned the father's kindness to the children.

The elder Pavie came up with the idea of adding a column to the paper on local events that he published. The names of the first contributors to the column are worth noting: Cyprien Robert, a Russian-style bohemian who later succeeded Mickiewicz in the chair of Slavic studies at the Collège de France; Adolphe Mazure, who translated Schlegel's *Uber die Sprache und Weisheit der Indier* in 1837, who became the veritable educator of the two sons, who would later put him in touch with Hugo; Eloi Jourdain (Charles de Sainte-Foi) and the two Boré brothers, the three of whom would become the youth brigade of Lamennais, and of whom Eugene Boré subsequently became a distinguished orientalist. In 1824, the first year the column appeared, Victor, who was eighteen, published some poems in it that were modeled on the new school, particularly Lamartine. More than a little surprised, Victor's father sent the poems, along with others and a carefully written letter, to Hugo. The great man sent back an enthusiastic response, such as only he knew how to write, and in 1827 at Paris, Victor straightway became a regular guest in Hugo's home. There he met Lamartine, who remained impressed with him, and Sainte-Beuve, still at the beginning of his career, in whom he inspired an affection that would not be betrayed.

While Victor was following David to visit Walter Scott and Goethe, Théodore, at the age of seventeen, sailed on a commercial ship bound for Louisiana to visit a cousin who was a settler there. He traveled over the entire continent, and ten months later he wrote to his father that he was going to return to France. His father wrote back, "What for?" Hence Théodore again set out to intoxicate himself with the open spaces of America. He did return fourteen months later, in July 1830, having assimilated a remarkable amount of English, Spanish, and Portuguese. In 1832 he left again, this time on an old tub of a ship, and landed in Buenos Aires after a crossing that lasted a hundred days, during which he did his part as a deckhand. South America offered another vastness, the sweep of the pampas, the heights of the Andes crossed in the dead of winter with a caravan headed for Chile. During the exhausting ordeal of the journey, Pavie read Lamartine or sketched.

On his return he wrote travel pieces that the *Revue des Deux-Mondes* published in 1835. He set to work learning German, then Hebrew, Arabic, and Sanskrit, followed by Garcin de Tassy's course on Hindustani and Stanislas Julien's courses in Chinese and Manchu. He was probably dreaming about a voyage to India, much as he had in times past. In 1837 he seemed immersed in oriental studies to the point of making himself ill. Julien advised him to translate a selection of Chinese short stories; Burnouf asked him to translate excerpts from the *Mahabharata* for the *Journal Asiatique*. This was the origin of Pavie's 1844 volume, the first to present a more generous selection of texts of Hindu poetry other than the *Bhagavad Gita* to the French reader.[21] Sainte-Beuve acknowledged receipt of the volume in a friendly way but said nothing about the work. Burnouf later said Pavie was his best student and designated him as his successor. Yet when Théodore Pavie became his replacement in 1853 it was for only four years. He was later nominated for the Académie. It was largely because he had failed to attain either a chair at the Collège de France or admission to the Académie, and because he saw what strings were being pulled to oppose him, that in 1857 Pavie chose to return to his travels, toward which the vocation of his inner life inclined him. Until his death his craving for a world open before him seemed unsated.

His extreme old age bore the nostalgic stamp of "a voyager who has given up voyaging but who cannot console himself."[22] His compulsion for movement became a compulsion for staying put. Yet in September 1839 he at last fulfilled his vow; he accompanied an English officer to India. They soon parted company, however, and, like Anquetil, Pavie went vagabonding on his own from port to port and then returned by the longest route, around the Cape.

It was only after his return from this last voyage that he specialized in Indic studies. When he was preparing himself for this voyage in 1837, Mazure's translation of Schlegel appeared, and one can only assume that Mazure influenced Pavie's vocation. Mazure had added 130 pages to the work, including a preface, appendix, commentaries, and discussion. Remarkably well-informed on, and impassioned by, linguistics, oriental studies, and philosophy, Mazure deeply regretted not having been able to learn the recovered languages: there can be no doubt that he sought compensation for his own ignorance in the learning of his student. Indeed, I discern a likely allusion to Théodore Pavie in the following sentence, written at the time the young man was making himself ill by his excessive study of Sanskrit and Chinese: "Our century has known many orientalists. We cannot cite them all here; some have passed away in recent years [Sacy, Champollon, Rémusat, and Saint-Martin], others are alive and give light to learning [Burnouf], and yet others are younger but growing and moving toward fame!" (This was meant for Théodore Pavie.)

Before Pavie served as Burnouf's replacement at the Collège de France, the Société Asiatique created a preparatory course in oriental languages and literatures for him to teach. Buloz, whom Pavie met again at Sainte-Beuve's home, urged him to begin to contribute articles again, thus prompting the series in *Revue des Deux-Mondes* between 1843 and 1857 that, along with those of Ampère, did much to make humanism universal. But to call Théodore a specialist would be an injustice; his brother Victor said, "I know only two things, dogma and fantasy." An admirable statement, which applies eminently to both brothers. In 1857 Théodore wrote to his father that, before lecturing at the Collège de France, he felt like asking his audience: "What do you want from me? Grammar, words, phrases? Have pity on me, I beg you and let me set sail again, or let me dream." His impending departure would be final: for months he thrashed out the question of retirement, which would divide his life into two nearly equal parts, some forty years spent traveling through countries and pasts and another forty-odd years that would be spent encouraging recollections of things in preparation for something different.

A country proprietor who was generous rather than possessive, channeling his interest into all that was human around him, Pavie continued to send accounts to the *Revue* for another eight years, but put nothing into them except the landscapes and figures he had before his eyes. Still he would return to his old vocation on one occasion, which aroused a great deal of interest, to lecture on Indic poetry at the Faculté catholique at Angers. Occasionally he would go to Saint-Servan to watch those who were still sailing and all the preparations for departure. "Let me set sail again or let me dream." His ingenious charity was another way of getting outside himself. In conversation, literature cropped up again and again, and regrets. Never anything confined or weighty, it was, on the contrary, always an extraordinary life force: a marvelous actor, Pavie could bring his distant adventures back to life as well as he could mime the characters and ways of speech of his province. He retained the gift of observation that, along with his brother, he had first focused on plants and insects and that he later focused on languages. How true it is that linguistic activity belonged to the realm of biology.

And then Théodore Pavie would open his sketchbooks, spread his maps, and "dream" about dates and itineraries. And during meals he would have his guests sample strange fruits from trees that came from other climes.

Victor Pavie, Sainte-Beuve, and Magnin

While Théodore set sail, Victor followed the overland route. In spite of the shyness which a contempt for worldly pretensions instills in dreamers,

Victor was an important figure in intellectual Paris. Although only a transient Parisian, he was in the front lines of the battles over Romanticism. His most important achievement was editing, in 1842, *Gaspard de la nuit*, a project that Renduel had abandoned and that Sainte-Beuve perhaps urged him successfully to complete. Retiring ten years before his brother in 1835, he became the kind of fair-minded provincial man who gives strangers food for thought. Since he was no longer anybody, he was more of a somebody. One peculiarity was that he liked the visits he paid elsewhere to be brief and those he received to be long. Ultimately, his importance to us here was his influence on Sainte-Beuve; he was someone whose self-effacement prevailed over Sainte-Beuve's boastfulness.

Hugo told him repeatedly, "It is you I love best," and repeatedly asked, "What better friend do I have than you?" It was in him, and in him alone, that Sainte-Beuve confided both that Hugo's friendship was a "sanctuary" for him and that his maliciousness resulted from "a repressed poetry" and "unrequited love." Sainte-Beuve took refuge in this priviliged friendship in which he grieved for and judged himself, and rediscovered his better half, which he lost whenever he entered into dialogue with the faithful, whose interior life he envied yet did not want for himself. Isn't this a rather common attitude in Sainte-Beuve that could explain his silences concerning movements, such as the Oriental Renaissance, in which he would involve himself only indirectly? The delight in omission of the great critic: "I do not systematically elude all the important subjects that pass by."

One can discern a curious relentlessness in *Mes poisons:* after the barb aimed at Pauthier is another, addressed to "Francisque Michel and Stanislas Julien, the philological animals, *Bestiae linguaces.*" Nor was *Mes poisons* sparing of the librarian Charles Magnin (1793–1862), who appeared under the name "Salin." Magnin's job won him the honor of preparing the weekly bibliographies and book parcels from which Sainte-Beuve drew his articles. Yet Magnin's importance in this function went beyond that of having his friend accepted as a contributor to the *Globe*, where he was an important figure. Magnin, a hunter and skinner, trapped many different kinds of game for the taster, and Sainte-Beuve's letters show how much he enjoyed having such rich foods laid out before him to tantalize his appetite without engaging his digestion. In *Causeries et méditations* (1843) Magnin brought together articles that had influenced the times. One can frequently conclude from them that it was Magnin who brought the key subject of so-called popular or anonymous poetic works to Sainte-Beuve's attention. Magnin referred to this idea several times; in 1830 he wrote a long study for the *Globe* on the Homeric methods of Vico and Wolf, which Michelet and Quinet infused with contemporary relevance. (Magnin was one of the first to praise *Ahasvérus.*) The columnist Magnin readily enthused over "the great Indic epics, the Sagas, the *Nibelungenlied.*" The *Globe* did a great deal for the diffusion of the Germanic theses. Magnin saw at close range the philologists who mingled with literature and the medievalists who mingled with oriental studies. A great friend of Ampère, Magnin failed to succeed him at the Collège de France in 1834, but, along with Fauriel, he substituted for him between 1834 and 1836, and in 1838 he replaced Sacy at the Académie des Inscriptions.

In all these circles, tastes for the foreign were a dime a dozen. What was less common was to liken this fever for the universal, this entire trend toward a critical history of humanity, to Astruc's bold inquiry, in days gone by, into the multiple authorship of the Book of Genesis. This comparison shone like a beam of light from Magnin's pen, and he concluded: "It is clear that, owing to a host of superb works, the darkness that has but lately enveloped the origin of the popular epic in all societies is at the point of dissipating. Light is coming from every country, from Greece, Scandinavia, India, France, and even Judea." Such thoughts acquire serious import when one considers Magnin in 1853, alone and suffering, seeking the one true religion and carefully sifting through all of them, including Brahmanism and Buddhism, before returning to Christianity—paths along which Vigny and Amiel were also seeking at about the same time.[23]

In the midst of these controversies and agitations was a man who brought the full weight of his influence to bear, especially upon literary people: one feels there was a gap between the importance of the role thus played by Barthélemy Saint-Hilaire and the significance of the concept that he personally formulated. Faithful to his teachers Cousin and Burnouf in his capacity for a full career, Saint-Hilaire bore a stronger resemblance to Cousin. At first a progressive journalist, he became a professor at the Collège de France in 1838 and executive secretary to the director in 1840. He subsequently served in the Chamber of Deputies, became a member of the Académie and a minister; he even was a member of the opposition. All in all he was an important figure in major affairs of state who left behind him both a reputation as a translator of Aristotle and a portrait in Larousse. As administrator of the Collège de France in 1848, he agreed with the police on the manner in which Michelet should give his lectures; two years later he had them suspended. He was an advocate of orderly affairs. His work on Sankhya was of a scope that is still unequaled. Concerning this doctrine, he concluded, "We condemn it without reservation."

CHAPTER TWELVE

Chroniclers and Novelists

The Historians

EVEN before her soul was known through her works, India secured a vast number of supporters in the Occident. In the respect shown for the Indic world, business and political interests, military exploits and setbacks, and the magic of oriental lands of faery were the first important elements. Subsequently, the Renaissance movement turned out to be both beneficiary and promoter of such haphazard preparations. The effect successive colonial struggles, especially those of the latter eighteenth-century, had was to increase the publication of studies on Indian history substantially, and as the Sanskrit texts were approached, many such publications included brief insights into philosophy and religion. Since it was essentially England that was interested in the subcontinent, works in this category were primarily British. Soon translated, they attracted attention to the sacred books and the methods of reading them. This was true even in France, since the French contribution at this time consisted mostly of travel books.

If the name of Sir William Jones soon became well known to any well-read person and the *Asiatic Researches* moved directly into the public domain, it was doubtless because, as I have shown, *Shakuntala*, the *Bhagavad Gita*, and the *Laws of Manu* struck the mind in rapid succession. But if the idea of an Asian revelation, either massive or diffuse, reached the general public, it was also because certain excerpts, analyses, and considerations drawn from the Calcutta research also found their way into the writings of historians, voyagers, and geographers. Whatever touched on the manners and customs of distant regions was eagerly read, but none of this material was as eagerly read as the Abbé Raynal's *Histoire philosophique et politique des Européens dans les deux Indes*, which contained no philosophy except what residue might remain in the context of political economy, and which was remarkably blind to religious beliefs. Moreover, it was ill-timed.

Published in 1780, it preceded the reading of Sanskrit by four years. Similarly, in 1762 the Académie des Inscriptions had heard the copious reports from Abbé Foucher concerning ancient Persia at the very time that Anquetil was retrieving the *Zend Avesta,* which would reduce Foucher's work to nothing. But still nineteenth-century writers continued to refer to out-of-date eighteenth-century documents. Lamennais based arguments on the *Ezour-Vedam* and its annotators, as if he were unaware that the work he was citing was apocryphal. Writers retained incongruous and premature images that had arisen in the two centuries during which India had only been presumed. And wasn't there also an endless *journalism about India?*

Robert Orme, who was among the most important English informants, was read widely in France between 1765 and 1791. His *History of the British Nation in Hindustan* prompted Anquetil, a personal friend of the author, to call it "a masterpiece of common sense and impartiality." After 1750, the repute of Holwell and Dow was based on the glory and romance of military adventures. For the following generation the great authority was Robertson, who never left Europe. He did not concern himself with India until the very end of a successful career, when he turned his enormous reputation, acquired through his works on Scotland and America, to the advantage of the Indic world. As late as 1873 the *Biographie Didot,* in its article by Rathery, affirmed that Robertson's work on India needed little change. Robertson's only travels to India were undertaken through his reading of Rennell's *Memoir of a Map of Hindustan* (1783–93). He was as ignorant of Sanskrit as anyone else. Nevertheless, the appendix of his *Historical Disquisition on the Knowledge which the Ancients Had of India* (1791) amply disseminated the notions he had concerning the immense body of Sanskrit literature and the first translations to reach Europe. The book went through several printings and was soon translated into French (1792–1821) and into German in 1792 by Georg Forster. It was partly through his reading of Robertson that Wilhelm Schlegel developed his desire to learn Sanskrit.

Another work that appeared at almost the same time and that was widely cited at the beginning of the nineteenth century was A. H. L. Heeren's *Ideen,* published in two volumes at Göttingen in 1791 and 1796. The second volume dealt with Asian peoples, but India was considered only as a Persian satrapy, as in the accounts of classical authors. In the 1804 edition, Asia was advanced to the first volume: the balance was reversed. But it was only in 1815, in the third edition of the first two parts, that an important section dealing with Indian history was added. In other words, the priorities had shifted within the framework of Asian history itself, which was, as I have said, due to the influence of Friedrich Schlegel. Furthermore, Heeren, who likewise had no personal knowledge of Sanskrit, used Robertson and Madame de Polier as well as Schlegel and Colebrooke. He dwelt on the poems and doctrines and was one of the first to stress Indian art.

The audience obtained by Thomas Maurice (1754–1824) and William Ward might seem surprising; both were pastors alarmed by the seductiveness of Hindu doctrines and symbolize the missionary outlook. Maurice believed he had rediscovered the Christian trinity throughout the Orient; his *History of Hindustan* (1795) was still considered authoritative by Schlosser in 1826. Ward was apparently terrified of "idolatry."[1] Colebrooke, tactfully hinting he was inclined to discuss them as politely as possible, called attention to the numerous deceptions about the history, literature, and religion of India in Ward's book, which had been published at the Serampore mission in 1811 and reprinted several times in London. In an unpublished letter dated August 21, 1837, Burnouf wrote to Michelet that Ward's was "A dry book, a kind of table of contents . . . written, furthermore, from the most narrow and bigoted Protestant viewpoint." In his translation of Colebrooke, Pauthier too exposed some of Ward's blunders, such as assuming that the title of a book was the name of its author.

Francis Wilford, less known outside scholarly circles, had a different emphasis. A Hanoverian who in 1771 arrived in India, where he entered the British service, he died at Banaras in 1822. He was among the first Europeans to work on India's legendary geography and history. He knew a great deal, although he was sometimes a bit lax about his sources and his likings. After relying on works of fiction that the pandits had obtained for him, he later frankly acknowledged that they had lied to him. His essays, notably that "On the Chronology of the Hindus," continued to be of use after his death. He collected manuscripts and learned Sanskrit; his principal authorities, the *Vishnu Purana* and the *Bhagavata Purana*, were exploited only by those, such as Wilson and Burnouf, who came after him. William Jones, at first wary, came to accept Wilford's conclusions, publishing his early work in the *Asiatic Researches;* later Jones reacted violently against Wilford's etymological excesses.[2]

The contributions of the French historians, momentarily effaced by the English conquest, reappeared in the nineteenth century with the histories of ancient and modern India by Collin de Bar (1814) and Lacroix de Marlès (1828); the picture-postcard descriptions of French India by Chabrelie and Jacquet (1835), which Burnouf reviewed; and the Abbé Dubois's *Description of the Character, Manners and Customs of the People of India* (East India Company, 1816; French edition 1825).[3] There were also many "Descriptions" whose only interest, whether they be military, geographical, or anecdotal works, lies in their great number. The Danish-French geographer and publicist Malte-Brun inaugurated this phase in 1803 which soon encompassed *Magasin Pittoresque* (1833), *Univers Pittoresque*, and travel journals, including *Annales des Voyages*, which he founded in 1808. Books by naturalists, geographers, and philologists, such as Humboldt's *Kosmos*, had a prodigious readership.

In the works of the historian Schlosser (1776–1861) one sees how geographic and geologic thought joined history in exploiting linguistics. Hence when Schlosser applied himself to the question of migrations, the debate on which drew from all these diverse disciplines, he explained them by both "the nature of the soil and the affinity of the languages of the Semitic branch." As early as 1808 Friedrich Schlegel pointed out that the history of migrations could be clarified through the history of languages, metal working, domestic fauna. In 1826 Schlosser provided a prototype with his *Universalhistorische Übersicht der Geschichte der alten Welt und ihrer Kultur (Universal History of Antiquity and Its Culture)*. The book was translated in 1828 by de Golbéry, who considered that its author and the authorities he cited (Herder, Heeren, and Creuzer) "henceforth [belong] to the French public no less than to the nation for which they were destined." Also in 1828, while visiting the masters at Heidelberg, Michelet greatly regretted the absence of Schlosser, who was in Italy at the time. Schlosser reconstructed primitive times through the use of Cuvier, Humboldt, Lacépède, Sacy, and Rémusat. He referred to Cuvier's famous "Discours sur les revolutions du globe," stating that Cuvier would always be his "foremost guide." And he emphasized the importance of another work whose title is quite vivid: Linck's *Die Urwelt und das Alterthum, erläutert durch die Naturkunde (The Primitive World and Antiquity Explained by the Natural Sciences; Berlin, 1821)*. Linck too based his arguments on the comparison of languages, including Sanskrit. Schlosser's work is remarkable for the comprehensiveness of his information and views and for his careful attempts at prudent interpretation that check the inclination toward generalization. And although he based his work in the Indic domain on the most reliable authorities in literature and linguistics—Jones, Wilkins, and Colebrooke—he still concluded by asserting that Holwell's 1764 contribution was the last, and best, authority. He prolonged the error that insisted that the occidental notion of history could not be applied to the Orient.

The Voyagers

Among the travelers themselves, scientific vocation took precedence over the lure of adventure. There was the intrepid self-control and sacrificed youth of the naturalists such as Jacquemont and Duvaucel who followed Foucher d'Obsonville. The emotional element persisted alongside the scientific element in the composition of the ambience which promoted Indian matters. (Sonnerat merits more than one reference, but his *Voyage aux Indes Orientales et à la Chine*, published in 1782, produced a sensation that the Calcutta publications would soon absorb.) Even those expatriots who died early and who had made up their minds at the outset to travel to India for some reason besides linguistic curiosity contributed to spreading the kind of interest that encouraged the study of languages. In 1818 the young Duvaucel, brother of the engaging Sophie, broke loose from the Cuvier household and headed for India, which was one reason India was frequently mentioned in correspondence and conversation. From India Duvaucel sent the Société Asiatique de Paris the manuscript of the *Bhagavata Purana* that Burnouf later used.[4] (As Langlois had, moreover, in his *Monuments littéraires;* see Chezy's article in the *Journal des Savants,* April 1827.)

The most striking expedition of all was that of Victor Jacquemont, who lived in India from 1828 until his death in 1832. A naturalist, Jacquemont was a polyglot, and I do not mean a linguist, only reluctantly and because of circumstance. Passing through England in preparation for his depature for Asia, he was welcomed in London by the Royal Asiatic Society and was given complete access to its library; yet he left no trace of having consulted Hindu texts or of having made any contacts with oriental scholars there. His motives for learning Persian, and through Persian Hindustani, were completely practical ones, and he did not begin to study them until he was on the boat for India. When he arrived he feigned a scornful indifference to both the temples and what they contained. It was the impassivity of a skeptical dandy. His excellent biographer Maes quotes Baudelaire's remark that Jacquemont had "a banter as apt to mystify the ministers of Brahma as those of Jesus Christ." Jacquemont wrote to Destutt de Tracy from India: "My father might be a little cross with me for not bringing him back any truly profound Indian metaphysical system, but I have a boat on the Ganges which is now en route down to Calcutta from Delhi loaded with things which are much more real than his *Essences of Reality:* records of the physical and natural history of the regions I have visited so far." Quoting this letter in his *Idéoloques,* Picavet added, "Sanskrit seems to have had only a philological interest for him, since it had served only to fabricate theology, metaphysics, and other similar bits of nonsense." We have already discussed Jacquemont's reception at the Calcutta Society, his visits to Carey, Prinsep, and Csoma, and his lively portrayals of them; yet Michelet was justified in writing, "When I read the letters from this witty, worldy minded Jacquemont, I think of the wretched, virile, heroic voyage of our Anquetil-Duperron." This is not the only case where it seems to me that the Oriental Renaissance necessitated a certain élan from its agents. This man who did not like drama stirred the literary world by the drama of his death—and who can say to what extent Baudelaire's precocious dreams of India might have been the result of the legend of India that Jacquemont transmitted to him?

There was something prophetic about the sudden departures and returns that Mérimée's "Vase étrusque" depicted in 1830. This kind of dashing in and out of scholarly expeditions spanned the century in relays, which thereafter became uninterrupted. After the flamboyant household names and the din of a few martial expeditions, men like Fresnel, Saulcy, Lenormant, Taylor, and Renan drew continuous attention; Asian soil occupied minds with digs and inscriptions. Familiarity with accounts of archaeological ventures served as a counterpoise to the abstractions of "philosophistoire."

There were many historians of India, both those who became so because they found themselves in India and those who were already Indic historians and went to do research in the field. At the end of the period that concerns us, the accounts of Jacolliot (1868), Lamairesse, and Louis Rousselet's *L'Inde des rajahs* (1864–68) would broaden the audience for Indic studies.[5] Between 1840 and 1860, Théodore Pavie, a genuine Indic scholar, alternately published scholarly works and oriental tales, the latter doubtless causing the former to be more widely read. An aura of the romance of adventure continued to cling to actual scholarship concerned with Hindu matters. The adventure of Demetrios Galanos, born in Athens in 1760, was closer to those of Anquetil and de Nobili than to those of Polier or Foucher d'Obsonville. Galanos landed in Calcutta in 1786 to be a private tutor in the home of a merchant; in 1792 at Banaras he took up the Brahman way of life, in which he continued for the remaining forty years of his life. Passionately interested in ancient Hindu literature and religion, Galanos published nothing during his lifetime, but his manuscripts, bequeathed to the University of Athens, were published in seven volumes between 1845 and 1853. In 1823 he had entrusted a translation of Kautilya to a compatriot who published it in 1825 at Rome under his own name. Galanos' posthumous works included Greek translations of the principal literary works of India, and he compiled several dictionaries.

Similar kinds of experiences included those of Csoma, as we have outlined above, and the Russian musician Lebedev, who lived in India from 1785 to 1797 where he devoted himself to music, Sanskrit, and modern languages. Lebedev returned to publish a grammar of these languages in England: *A grammar of the pure and mixed East Indian dialects, with dialogues affixed . . . arranged . . . according to the Brahmenian system, of the Shamscrit language . . . with a recitation of the assertions of Sir William Jones, respecting the Shamscrit alphabet . . . calculated for the use of Europeans.* Lebedev then went on to Saint Petersburg, where he set up the imperial Sanskrit printing house, publishing his *Contemplation impassible des systèmes des Brahmanes de l'Inde orientale* in 1805.

Etienne Jouy and Philarète Chasles

Toward the end of the eighteenth century and the beginning of the nineteenth, fantasies based on travels established, to a greater extent than the scholarly discoveries did, a certain number of literary themes that, strictly speaking, were especially akin to fairy-tale drama and melodrama if not to ballet. Still, frequently their point of departure was personal contact with India, and their outcome was often an access to accurate knowledge. Such, following the case of Etienne de Jouy (1764–1846), was the case with Philarète Chasles.

The stories of pariahs, popularized by Bernardin de Saint-Pierre's *La Chaumière indienne*, led to two plays, one by Casimir Delavigne in 1821 (a great success according to Stendhal in *Racine et Shakespeare*) and the other by Michael Beer in 1825. Military or fantastic episodes illustrated the adventures of the rajahs, and revived the drama of burned widows or the romance of Indian dancing girls.[6] Such categories appeared in company with each other, or almost, in the works of Jouy, the author of the opera *Les Bayadères* (1810), which Napoleon attended, and of a tragedy, *Tippo-Sahib*, produced at the Théâtre français in 1813. These were but masques, which belong primarily to the history of theatrical costuming and staging, and Jouy's work was nothing new. Lemierre had already presented his epoch-making *Veuve du Malabar* in 1770. But Jouy was scornful of the play, having had personal experience of the things Lemierre had depicted on the stage. He stated in the preface to *Tippo-Sahib:* "I spent the first years of my youth in East India, in the beautiful regions through which the Ganges and the Indus flow, in the midst of the most ancient, gentle, kind people on earth; I lived under the influence, or rather under the charm, of those immutable customs of this poetic religion in which the most knowledgeable of orientalists, Sir William Jones, discovered the origin of all the fables of Greece."

Jouy had pursued a military career in India just before the French Revolution. However superficial his information may have remained, it is nonetheless interesting to see the oral influence, clearly revealed by Philarète Chasles, which passed through Jouy's home: "I sought colors in the most accurate travelers, in your bayadères, who offer a comprehensive

portrait of the customs of these women, and in your conversations in which
the habits of a people interesting for their antiquity and simplicity, for the
pleasure and the austerity of their customs, were recalled with such precision." In 1825, three years before becoming Eckstein's secretary, Chasles,
who was Jouy's secretary (doesn't the transition from one to the other seem
like a logical progression?) began his career with a small volume of prose
and verse that he entitled *La fiancée de Bénarès: Nuits indiennes,* dedicated
to Jouy. (We should not forget that the extreme social importance of this
picturesque member of the Académie was an acknowledged fact among
his contemporaries; in 1830 Jouy became mayor of Paris and curator of the
Bibliothèque du Louvre.) There was an exchange of the finest courtesies
between the veteran and the novice: Jouy praised Chasles for his "Essai
sur l'Opéra français," which he appended to his own collected works
where, in the chapter entitled "Observations on French Mores at the Beginning of the Nineteenth Century" we note a certain "History of a Shawl,"
which bears out how well cashmeres had advertised the image of India.
Jouy mentions the Baron d'Orvilliers, a famous collector of oriental objects, and related his adventurers in Kashmir, giving fully informed evidence concerning the notorious suttees.

All Jouy's writings are sprinkled with allusions to India and to the time
he spent there. At times these are superficial and regrettable, like *Mes
Voyages,* a letter in verse written on his return:

> Partout l'Indien imbécile
> Sert la cause de ses tyrans
> . . . Les atrocités d'un lord Clive,
> Les brigandages d'un Hastings.

> Everywhere the idiotic Indian
> Serves the cause of his tyrants
> . . . The atrocities of a Lord Clive,
> The banditry of a Hastings.

The preface to *Tippo-Sahib* affirms: "The idea of India is present in all my
memories." Jouy cited not only William Jones and the *Laws of Manu* among
his references, but Maurice and Michaud's *Histoire de Mysore,* a book well
known in its time. In his "Historical Preamble" to his *Bayadères,* Jouy presented "one of the Puranas" and analyzed the "Bayadere" of his predecessor Goethe, whom he called "the Voltaire of the North." He recalled
with satisfaction that the costumes for his opera had been designed in the
style of the wardrobe provided by "a young lady of Chandernagore" who
happened to be in Paris at the time.

In the dedication to his *Fiancée de Bénarès*, Philarète Chasles (1798–1873) clearly explained in what respects this subject appealed to him: "The blend of the interests of a novel with the color and rhythm of a poem; the alliance of a prose fable and verse hymns connected to the fable itself; the portrayal of Indian customs accurately recounted; and the union of a philosophical design with the most indefinite realms of faery that the imagination can create." This was in 1825 when Chasles was twenty-seven years old, and his comments are representative of how the marvels of India appeared to young people seeking literary careers during the initial period of Indic studies. For his part Chasles rejected the term Romanticism, being unable "to comprehend a word that contains no idea." Returning from a long stay in England before Jouy's campaign on behalf of India, Chasles had probably encountered in London the interest in Hindu matters that had impressed the exiled Chateaubriand there some twenty years earlier. And we find that the notes of Chasles's first collection speak more clearly on this matter than the poems they annotate. The poems represent the Orient of Shaktas, minus the spirit and somewhat more up-to-date, although the customary "shastras" are cited more than once. But a documentary interest appears in the references that augurs the turning point of his career.

Chasles declared that he had taken as a subject "an Indian tradition" provided by Thomas Moore's *Lallah Rookh*, whose novelty still seduced him, as had "Paradise and the Peri," which continued to obsess him; but before long it was Edward Moor's *Hindoo Pantheon* (1810) that Chasles was citing. Chasles's references also included, omitting the travelers, the first specialists, Haafner, *Oriental Researches*, William Jones and *Asiatic Researches* and the *Laws of Manu*. It is revealing that Chasles cited such references by copying from the English; indeed, Chasles was so Anglicized, so persuaded that India could be approached only via England, that he inadvertently naturalized the Dutchman Abraham Roger as "l'Anglais Roger." All these authorities, however, left Chasles more unsure than ever: "The poetry, the love songs, the tales that can be sung in the Hindu language are referred to by the word *giet*. Such is the *bhaguat-giet*, or song of the tiger, an epithet sometimes applied to Krischna. This song has been translated into French and other European languages." Such blunders are characteristic of the first stage; the same man who fell into such inaccuracies would, in a few years, be the one to provide one of the best popular accounts of the advances in Indic studies. I have already mentioned his article "Philologie" in the *Encyclopédie du XIXᵉ siècle*, where he set forth the issue of rediscovered scripts. In 1825 he used Jouy's narratives to fill the gaps in the fragments he had brought back from England and displayed these embryos of disparate knowledge in 1828 in conversations with his employer Eckstein. Always the oral influence; always the transition from fiction to understanding.

In 1865 a number of important chronicles of oriental civilizations appeared in the first volume of *Voyages d'un critique à travers le vie et les livres* (*A Critic's Travels Through Life and Books*), "by Philarète Chasles, professor of the Collège de France, curator of the Bibliothèque Mazarine." One chronicle in particular, some forty pages long, contained what its title promised: "Alexander's Expedition and Greek Relations with Hindustan, as Verified by Buddhist Monuments" (first published in the *Journal des Débats,* March 25–April 22, 1860). It was immediately clear that the object of Chasles's enthusiasm had changed; the readings that Chasles cites in his footnotes include works by Lassen, Weber, Barthélemy Saint-Hilaire, Wilson, Julien, and "above all, Prinsep." Indeed his primary objective is to record and comment on, for the use of general readers, the recent attainments of Indic epigraphy initiated by Prinsep, whose work had made it possible to verify and amplify the fecund intuition that had led Jones to identify the Sandracottus of Arrian with the founder of the Gupta dynasty.

It was an opportunity for Chasles—which he seized vigorously—to recall, with a suitable economy of words, the entire recent history of Indic studies. He accurately dated it from Anquetil-Duperron, followed by Jones; he gave each his due, put every thing and every man in place with a gift for both critical discrimination and rapid synthesis that enabled him to omit nothing essential. His work was, perhaps, no more than an echo from scholarly circles, but it was straightforward, consistent, and useful. Referring to the work of Albrecht Weber, and doing it justice, Chasles carefully called attention to Weber's failure (which also infuriated Darmesteter later) to recognize the French contribution. Chasles named everything that was, for him, of consequence. He clearly was not aspiring to the poetic rehabilitation of such writers as Quinet and Michelet in the tabulation of the successive Indias he was endeavoring to record, but he was perhaps at least as effective as they and closer to the professionals in other matters. Chasles focused on heroic figures and underscored the importance of the inscriptions that had led to the discovery of Ashoka behind Prayadesi (Piyadasi) and of Chandragupta behind Sandracottus; he called attention to the problem of interchanges between Hellenism and Buddhism. It was in his analysis of Buddhist doctrine that he reached his inevitable limit: "Buddhism has been able to give birth only to a foolish body of literature." "Buddhism only lulls populations into sleep." As usual, a devotion to Greco-Latin culture excluded rival wisdoms. All the same, an inquisitive mind that had first been attracted to Asia by her old clothes reached a valid meditation on history through the stimulating vicissitudes of scholarship. Such was, in part, the adventure of the occidental mind.

Fiction

India was something that the Occident began to seek again. Next to the influence of adventure, and overtaking it, was the influence of an inexhaustible fairy-tale Orient. The popularity of Prester John and Marco Polo and the great navigations had advanced the glamor of travel, an attraction which the *Thousand and One Nights* had inherited and substantially increased. It was above all the *Arabian Nights* that had moved Balzac. In what direction we have seen. Balzac's appetite for mystery, even if it was merely verbal, was gluttonous. Mystery, the Orient, treasures—it was a kind of lavish windfall at the wave of a wand. In him the mysterious led to the magical, the magical to the fabulous, as in Fortunatus. His India was primarily the India of Golconda, the personification of the Orient-as-alibi, an Orient of talismans and jewels, of liberties with no foundation and power with a false bottom, where fortune and good fortune were the conjurations of conspirators and sorcerers who could overturn all sense of walls by reupholstering a few of the furnishings. We will encounter these daydreams pushed to the limits of the fantastic in the Orient of Théophile Gautier, and in the *Bibliothèque bleue*, a collection of fairy tales on the fringe of the Oriental Renaissance where there was also a clientèle for occultism. This is not to say that the announcements of texts flushed from the bushes, of linguistic imbroglios, and of keys fitted to ciphers did not themselves provide a congenial rendezvous for trappers with their stories of trails and savannahs. We will see how Edgar Allan Poe, the same author who covered his poetic landscape with an oriental atmosphere, also invented the cryptographic tale.

The Indian short stories of Joseph Méry were also significant in advancing orientalism. From 1846 to 1869 his exotic narratives became more and more widely circulated. Six editions of his *Damnés de l'Inde* and eighteen editions of his *Guerre du Nizam* had been published by 1868. It was also Méry who, in collaboration with Nerval, had translated Shudraka's *The Little Clay Cart*, which was performed at the Odéon on May 13, 1850 as *Le Chariot d'enfant*, drawing an extraordinary crowd that besieged the theater on opening night. The legend of Méry as the custodian of the most authentic India has survived to the present day: "If India had not existed, Méry would have had to create it." His contemporaries voiced such praise with hardly any irony: "Not only does he have a perfect knowledge of it from a distance, but there is only one man in the world who can make his way through this formidable theogony . . . it is Méry. . . . There is not one line from Kalidasa or Bavabhuti he can not complete when someone says the first word of it." Such was Gautier's assessment. Dugat, himself a historian of orientalism, spoke of "Méry and Gérard de Nerval, two poets, the one the most Hindu who ever existed, the other the most oriental in the world."

A good many products fattened the growing idea: since 1804 the shawls of India, poised on the shoulders of three generations and dear to Jouy, had mingled names and images of living India with the life of salons and families, and it was this commercial India that amazed the first chroniclers of the international expositions. Aren't we straying far afield from Indic studies here? I'm not so sure. The India of the expositions impressed Gautier and Maxime du Camp, and Rimbaud never forgot the exposition of 1867. In his *Histoire de XIXe siècle*, Michelet was delighted that the value of Hindu civilization was finally done justice to "in the Reports of the Great Exposition," probably that of 1867. It also seems that through Michelet a given anecdote could be crossed with a given fancy to produce an awareness in the thoughts of his contemporaries: while Méry's writings were establishing the character of the "nabob," the procession of the last king of Oudh was passing beneath the Parisian sky, and in January 1856 Michelet noted, "Parading by in the rain and mud . . . this Indian luxury, these pink and yellow colors mixed with gold and silver [was] shamefully spoiled by our pitiless winter."

Finally, there remained some singular links between the attraction of Indian objects and a certain mythic aspect of learning; I am not referring here to initiations. At the time of the first contacts, Europeans remembered all that mathematics owed to the Hindu genius; nabobs and "moguls" had, from their side, opened their mysterious palaces to Westerners who brought them astronomical or medical secrets. These kinds of interests had characterized the Asiatic Society of Calcutta from its creation. I note a symbolic indication of how public imagination and opinion could link such activities to the romance of quests and voyages: in 1827 Peter Dillon, an English navigator, began an investigation into the disappearance of La Pérouse. Whom did he ask to fund the expedition? The Asiatic Society of Calcutta. And who recorded the fact for us? Jules Verne in *20,000 Leagues under the Sea*. In passing he revived the ghost of the great astronomical observer Jean-Sylvain Bailly, whose metier had led him into a dialogue, running to several volumes, with Voltaire (both while he lived and after his death) on the shastras of Holwell and Dow. According to Bailly, at the source of human intelligence there must have been a people whose descendants had all deteriorated. In this way Bailly came to locate

Plato's Atlantis in the place where, ever since Sanskrit had become truly known, there had supposedly been a continual, compassionate Indo-Iranian people, as he argued in his *Lettres sur l'Atlantide de Platon et sur l'ancienne histoire de l'Asie* (1779). In 1777 in his *Lettres sur l'origine des sciences, et sur des peuples de l'Asie,* Bailly, who had read Gébelin's work thoroughly, had located the origin of universal myths, which supposedly indicated "the successive habitations of the human race and its advance toward the equator from the pole," "at the north of the earth."

It must be added that the lure of the Islamic Orient continued to predominate in all quarters and frequently increased the lure of India. Thus we can see how the *Arabian Nights* and Marco Polo influenced Thackeray, Matthew Arnold, and James Thompson. The year 1824 marks the appearance of James Morier's astonishing novel *The Adventures of Hajji Baba of Ispahan,* which left deep impressions. Fitzgerald's famous translation of the *Rubaiyat* of Omar Khayyam had an even greater impact. The lure of international expositions was also important in England, where the first was held in 1851. Sprawled over the counters, an entire Orient delivered itself to England's very doorstep, and the industrial possibilities of India were of lively interest to the City. One of the most exasperating questions that England's presence in India raised throughout the period of conquest was the death blow it may have dealt to the traditional activity of artisans. Politics remained the most active intermediary between India and England; hence the Great Mutiny of 1857, whose noisy echoes resounded throughout all Europe from England, became for Villemain a reason to give a new, extremely glowing portrait of William Jones, judge, scholar, and poet.[7]

Part Five

ERUDITION MEETS CREATIVITY

CHAPTER THIRTEEN

India and the Blossoming of Lamartine

Advisors in Oriental Studies

THE profound Orient, especially India, was of greater concern to the French Romantics than it has been to their biographers. Joseph de Maistre, Lamennais, Ballanche, Benjamin Constant, Michelet and Quinet, Lamartine, Hugo and Vigny, the Saint-Simonians, and more than one naturalist-turned-biologist pursued studies related to these regions. Behind each poet I believe I can glimpse one or more advisors in oriental studies, not unlike the small, nude inspirers on the ceiling of the Sistine Chapel who lean over the shoulders of the prophets and whisper into their ears about a hidden science. The fact that many such advisors had set out to become poets themselves made them all the better as deputies for the impatience of genius (which is no less important than patience). Besides Eckstein and Fouinet, those in close contact with Hugo included Pauthier and Théodore Pavie, all of whom Hugo had met personally a few times before becoming familiar with their publications. Foremost and most diligent among those close to Lamartine were Eckstein, Quinet, and later Barthélemy Saint-Hilaire. Vigny seems to have been approached alternatively by his kinsman Bruguière de Sorsum and his sergeant Pauthier, to have been influenced by Saint-Hilaire, and to have conversed with Adolphe Franck. Most of these minds were won over only to the extent they chose to be, and never to the point where they knew they would cease to be themselves.

After 1813, in Weimar, where Indic studies had one of its first homes with Maier, Klaproth, and Kosegarten, Goethe similarly availed himself of such advisors. It was only natural that the poets had themselves provided with some passwords to a world of eternally new ideas which, as a whole, concerned and was beyond them. It was characteristic of France and consistent with her tradition of sociable art and scholarship that the writers' informants were not only scholars and not only temperaments who blended the two together, but individuals who were important in society. In Germany the stylist Goethe opened a general and circumspect view of the universal, and Rückert masterfully combined the practice of philology with the practice of poetry. In France there was less of the systematic and the studied and more of the directly human. This might be one of the reasons why the Oriental Renaissance, a hypothesis in Germany, was actually experienced only in France. There was no single intellectual capital elsewhere where people filled with enthusiasm and grounded in the critical spirit, interested in information and in imagination that was always brought back to a discriminating tradition, could meet several times a week in a small number of pleasant houses. Between 1820 and 1830, from the Jardin des Plantes to Abbaye-aux-Bois and to Saint-Germain-des-Prés, interchanges on oriental matters seemed to be a neighborhood business.

Lamartine

Lamartine's case is illustrated through his own testimony. By 1823 or 1824, Aymon de Virieu had introduced him to Eckstein. Their relations covered the period between *Méditations* and *Jocelyn,* during which Lamartine stated that the project that busied his brain was a vast epic in multiple episodes. We know, from a letter cited by Valentine de Cessiat, that by 1838, the year of *Chute d'un Ange,* Eckstein had been seeing Lamartine for fourteen years. One could therefore expect that Lamartine's India would not be a scholar's; instead, thanks to a virtuoso of oral expansiveness, it was one of those obsessions vital to creators, and thanks to a specialist in the universal, it was also one of those airy constructs that serve as a launchpad for reveries. Lamartine "leafed through" his visitor, an inexhaustible improviser who came to sight-translate passages from German and Sanskrit texts for him. For his *Cours familier de littérature* in 1856, Lamartine tackled the texts, pen in hand; but, as an avid reader of Bernardin de Saint-Pierre, he had been living with the essential themes of mystical union, of fraternity with animals, and of expiatory reincarnation for a long time.

As for the sincerity with which he assigned himself an oriental soul, this is one of those matters where it seems advisable to apply the standard of the poets to the poet. Lamartine's Orient is, of course, difficult to locate on the map; undoubtedly the excitement he showed when embarking for Palestine in 1832, a "great undertaking" in "the inner life," and his constant shivers of pleasure when faced with the Asiatic world sprang from his sense of values as a poet. But what kind of person was he? Perhaps he was akin to the sage Plotinus who in A.D. 242, a period scarcely less disquieting, dropped everything to follow the Emperor Gordian's expedition against Persia in hopes of contacting gymnosophists.

In 1827–28 Eckstein adapted fragments of the *Mahabharata* for the *Catholique;* at the same time he advised Lamartine to broaden his poetic horizon by delving into the ancient poetry of the Orient, a charge similar to the one he addressed to Hugo. At a time when apologizing for the absence of the epic in France was a prevailing theme, these two renowned young poets were still relying on the successes of their odes and verse letters. (The prospectus for the *Orientales* in 1829 again praised Hugo's accomplishments in these genres at length.) To poets with a Latin education India brought the temptation, as against the routine of fragments, to write rivers of poems. As early as 1814 in his translation of "The Death of Yajnadatta," Chézy emphasized that the *Ramayana* was at least four times as vast as all of Homer. But Béranger himself—Béranger! the prototype of a great poet for his contemporaries—Béranger, dazzled by *Jocelyn,* later asked Fortoul whether Lamartine "wants to compete with the Indic epics." Thus the rumor that one could possess a template for unprecedented poetry descended all the way to those zones. What Lamartine would call "the sea of poetry" had now been glimpsed in remote Asia; now the very architecture erected by Dante and Milton, long the Pillars of Hercules in the West, seemed like nursery blocks. Lamartine resolved to devote ten volumes of sustained poetry to his "epic of the soul."

We have seen in the *Génie du Christianisme* how the new models had, until then, failed to reassure French poets and return them to the old epic style, as was also evident in Quinet's hesitation between epic and philosophical dialogue which caused him to cast sidelong glances at *Faust.* Vigny verified this uncertainty when in 1825 he noted explicitly in his journal that he was renouncing poetry since he was unable to believe in poetry on the grand scale, even recognizing the failure of *Eloa* in this respect: "I have always had a feeling for the epic spirit; *Moïse* and *Eloa* have epic characteristics as, in my opinion, does most of my poetry, but since length is one of the conditions for such vast conceptions, and since length is intolerable in French verse, I was obliged to attempt it in prose, which resulted in *Cinq-Mars.*" When, looking back on a past of poets in 1856, Lamartine attempted to situate his poetic works within the whole historical context, wasn't he doing that same thing done by Eckstein, his advisor of thirty years earlier? Here Lamartine set "the gigantic character of primitive poetry" against "the degeneration of poetry in more recent periods," the "virility" of the one opposing the "affectation" of the other.

Art is not a matter of quantity, but questions of size pose those of hierarchies: there are levels to which the short-winded and weak-hearted simply have no access. India struck medallion-makers through its monuments—and not India alone, it is true. A great many manifestations combined in the 1830s: collections of foreign epics, studies of epics, exhumed *chansons de geste* and lectures of the first comparativists. Even writers like Ozanam and Delécluze linked Dante with Firdausi or Valmiki. Lamartine subsequently characterized his own vast projects as "antediluvian, primitive, oriental" poetry, and as "a Hindustani epic." "Which means that the cyclic poem he conceived in 1821 would have the breadth of works written by Brahman poets, of the Vedas or the *Ramayana* which the Baron Eckstein, one of his new friends of the time, discussed with him regularly."[1] In 1824, following their meetings, Lamartine outlined a draft, worked and reworked indefinitely, of a vast, all-embracing metaphysical poem, an ambition that was to shimmer before this genius of not yet thirty who was first intoxicated by the resounding success of isolated poems, an ambition that he perhaps took pleasure in setting too high. It was for, and through, the writing of his "epic of the soul" that he lived. He sought religion in the manner of his century, and he performed an act of worship before an Indic poetry that was almost inseparable from a religion.

Jocelyn, published in 1836, was a success, but *Chute d'un Ange* two years later was a failure. Did this mean he had been mistaken about the act of poetry or about his own genius? Subsequently he fell back an another tactic, progressively deluding himself into believing that he wrote poetry only out of nonchalance. Was he not humiliating the poet in himself that he had not managed to be? Interior vicissitudes are frequently less simple than observers—and perhaps the subject himself—think. A writer like Lamartine is not unaware of how fragile his personal sense of perfection is. It is essential not to stop revising too soon and even more essential not to lose the benefit of a certain rapidity and volume of outpouring—and it is this sense of one's own *flow* that is a difficult thing for true-born poets to learn. And it was precisely the fluvial that the example of Indic poetry fostered. Lamartine had good enough ears, and good enough critics, to suspect, at least during his darker moments, that there was something frozen in certain overworked passages, something premature in other passages, and something in the whole that defied human power. He again became the author of admirable improvisations, the kind of works one tosses off to one's readers in order to clear one's mind of them; these addresses, to Hugo for a wedding anniversary, or to the Comte d'Orsay, were no longer the kind of writing that is a reason for an existence, but rather the small change of a belief, as if the Indic-style epic had been an essential wager that had been lost, so that now one changed one's bets.

Yet bits of the sunken treasure floated back to the surface. Formerly when bringing a vital undertaking to a head—the thousands of verses of *Jocelyn* or *La chute d'un Ange*—Lamartine introduced them in installments comparable to those already published from the works of Valmiki or Vyasa. He provisionally detached them from the work as a whole, but with the firm resolution of rejoining them to it. This conception of a "successive epic" can also be found in the works of Hugo, in *Légende des siècles, Dieu,* and *La fin de Satan.* Until the end there emerged in Lamartine's work the flotsam of a great, sunken project: he and his spokesmen never ceased advancing the great title he believed he would obtain in the eyes of men. This desire to influence mankind takes several forms in overly gifted minds that are hardly ever content with any single one of them and thus pass back and forth from one to the other. In 1853 Lamartine published a set of four meager episodes that bore the title which was to have been that of the immense whole: *Les Visions.* Lamartine attached some importance to the work, having already publshed it in 1851 in *Nouvelles confidences.* In 1873 some new fragments, dated 1823 and 1824 (the Eckstein period) appeared, along with a full chronology and analysis of the entire poem. Moreover, the pocm was represented as having been intended to include 48 songs. In his preface to this posthumous edition Laprade emphasizes the central place the work held in the inner life of the poet.

It is true that when the remainder of his poem burst over his head like, as he put it, a soap bubble, leaving him with only "a few drops of water, or rather a few drops on ink, on my fingers," Lamartine acknowledged only Dante as his model and authority. These drops included *Jocelyn, La chute d'un Ange, Le poème des Pêcheurs* (lost in his travels) and "a few other rough drafts of epics I worked on and then suspended work on." According to Citoleux it was apparently not until 1836 that the model for the innumerable, until then obtained from Dante, was obtained from the Indic epic; from then on Lamartine always qualified the scale of his own epic-in-progress with the term "Hindoustanique." But it was more than a matter of scale—it was also a matter of the pantheism awakened by the Romantic Orient, as the few words set as the frontispiece of *Les visions* proclaimed in 1853: "This was to be the story of the human soul and its transmigrations through successive existences and ordeals, from nothingness to reunion with the universal center, God." The prefatory note included in the "new editions" of *La chute d'un Ange* showed clearly the subject of the work as a whole: "It is the metempsychosis *of the spirit,* the human phases through which the human *spirit* passes in order to fulfill its perfectable destinies and achieve its purpose through the ways of Providence and through its ordeals on earth." In this mixture one seems to discern Hindu *samsara* used as a vehicle for Madame de Staël's idea of infinite perfectability (which Lamartine nonetheless denied to India), followed by all the notions of palingenesis in the air at the time and even Saint-Simonian ideas, with the whole lot ultimately rectified by the memory of Christian dogma. One hardly knows whether the subject was the terrestial improvement of humanity or the progressive purification of the soul. In the prefatory note to the first edition the wording seems decidedly religious: "the human *soul* and the successive phases through which God causes it to achieve its perfectible destinies—isn't this the most beautiful theme of lyric poetry?" Why was the term "spirit" later substituted for the term "soul"? From one period to the next the spiritual mission seems to have evolved in the direction of a political mission—and social messianism seems to have become heir to the hope for a religious revival.

That specific recollections from readings or discussions about India left their mark throughout the published "episodes" is demonstrated by a number of details: the name "Lakmi" is given to a character in *La chute d'un Ange,* where there is also a similarity between the flight of Cédar and Daïdha and the story of Nala and Damayanti. The idea of Nirvana seems implicit in several passages:

> Il n'eut plus qu'une soif, un but, une pensée,
> Anéantir son âme et la jeter au vent . . .

> He had only one thirst, one goal, one thought—
> To annihilate his soul and cast it to the wind.

The transposed theme of a wheel of existences appears:

> Tu ne remonteras au ciel qui te vit naître
> Que par les cent degrés de l'échelle des êtres . . .

> You can rise again to the heaven which witnessed your birth
> Only by the hundred steps of the ladder of being.

Although "Le Désert," a poem through which oriental antiquities file, contains lines that term pantheism a "second chaos," transcendence seems to admit of several interpretations:

> Si je n'étais pas tout je ne serais plus rien . . .
> Mais ce tout, centre-Dieu de l'âme universelle,
> Subsistant dans son œuvre et subsistant sans elle . . .

> If I were not everything, I would no longer be anything . . .
> Except this everything, God-Center of the universal soul,
> Subsisting in its work and subsisting without it . . .

The twelfth lecture of the *Cours familier* sets forth a doctrine that appears to culminate definitely in a syncretism born of the philosophy of history. In addition to the information he acquired from Eckstein, Lamartine read Wilson and Ward in English and heard Cousin and Barthélemy Saint-Hilaire lecture on doctrine. In *Histoire de la Restauration,* Cousin is described in exceptionally enthusiastic terms for the eloquence of his philosophy lectures, and there were regular dinners at the Rue de l'Université with Quinet, Michelet, Lamennais, and Eckstein. On July 28, 1838, ten years after the Eckstein period, Lamartine wrote to Virieu that he had been living "in philosophy. But Indian philosophy eclipses all others for me: it is the ocean, and we are only clouds." He had read part of the Vedas in Eckstein's translation: "I read, reread, and read again . . . I cried out, I closed my eyes, I was overwhelmed with admiration in my silence. . . . I felt as if a heavy hand had hurled me out of bed with physical force. I leapt out of bed, barefoot, book in hand, my knees shaking. I had an unconsidered urge to read this page in the posture of worship and prayer, as if the book were too holy and too beautiful to be read standing up, seated, or lying down. I knelt in front of the window in the rising sun. I did not weep, for I seldom shed tears, either in rapture or in suffering, but as I rose to my feet I thanked God aloud that I belonged to a race of created beings capable of conceiving such explicit notions of His divinity and of giving them such sublime expression." Lamartine attached enough importance to this account of being thunderstruck that he revised it from an earlier version. Originally he had depicted himself, without dating the event, in a room of an uninhabited country house, gathering up, by sheer chance, "a few half eaten away pages of translations of Indic hymns." It was the first time, he said, that he had laid eyes on them. He invested the translator with the qualities of a philosopher, poet, and Orientalist, "a Brahman of the West, unappreciated by his own people, living in one century, thinking in another." Lamartine may have complimented Eckstein so lavishly as a way of consoling him for the long time he had had to cool his heels in the waiting room before Lamartine would gather up pages gnawned by rats in an abandoned summer house: thirty-two years is a long time to make a prophet one regularly receives wait before reading his work. I notice that Lamartine included a letter Eckstein had written him on "the mystical poetry of India" in his text, but the letter contains no indication that their exchange of ideas on the subject had been recent.

In all likelihood, on the eve of writing his *Cours familier,* Lamartine was assailed with scruples that led him to round out his previous reading with more literal and more extensive knowledge, for he wished to take successive Indic experiences into account. At another time he had "carried a volume of English translations from Sanskrit hunting" with him. This time, at least, his reading was intentional. He no longer concerned himself with the Vedas, but with excerpts from the *Mahabharata* in Hastings' and Wilkins' translations, particularly the *Bhagavad Gita*. Since he cites Barthélemy Saint-Hilaire's edition of the Vedas in another passage (and takes Saint-Hilaire down a peg or two for his half-heartedness), Lamartine's preparation of the "Talks on India" could be no earlier than 1854. Nevertheless, on several other occasions Lamartine indicated, still without giving any specific chronology, that his initiation into India was a fluctuating process spread over a good many years. It was only in the fifth talk, the third on India, that Lamartine recalled his initial impressions, which were of Chézy's translations *Brahmane infortuné* and *Sacountala*. In this connection he quoted the preface in which Chézy related his own first encounter with Sanskrit poetry—and I am certain that is where Lamartine found his own reading list, for Chézy mentions both Wilson and Wilkins in his preface, along with *Asiatic Researches*.

Several stages seem to emerge: Lamartine's reading of Chézy, his reading of the *Bhagavad Gita* and Wilkins, and his reading of Eckstein's texts and Saint-Hilaire's Vedas. On November 11, 1855 Renan wrote to Max Müller, "As you know, the Académie des Inscriptions et Belles-Lettres is offering a prize for the best work on a certain number of the hymns from the *Rig Veda*, and Eckstein wants to compete or urge his friend Haug to." Also in 1855 Baudry and Régnier had provided studies of the Vedas, and Saint-Hilaire's edition had been published in the preceding year (Langlois's translation of the *Rig Veda* dated from 1848–51). Müller, who published a critical edition of the Sanskrit text of the *Rig Veda* between 1849 and 1855, was interested in this piece of news. It was also in 1854 that Fauche's *Ramayana* had first appeared. Thus between 1851 and 1855 there had been an attentiveness to, and movement toward, Indic poetry that must have inspired Lamartine's ideas for his *Cours familier* in 1856. However, this was the period in which Prinsep's Buddhist discoveries were being mated to Schopenhauer's popularizations.

Lamartine devoted an entire volume to India containing an analysis of the *Bhagavad Gita* and expositions of masterpieces of the epic and the theater—talks 3 through 6 of the *Cours familier*, more than 300 pages. Thanks to his knowledge of the English translations, Lamartine was able to reveal an episode, missing from Fauche's translations, which he was perhaps the first in France to discuss: the sublime epilogue to the *Mahabharata* in which Yudhishthira refuses to enter paradise unless his dog is also admitted. One wonders when Lamartine became familiar with this passage, whether he was anticipating or remembering it when, in the ninth epoch of *Jocelyn*, he cried out in praise of the dog Fido, "Ne crains pas que de toi devant Dieu je rougisse!" ("Do not fear that I will be ashamed of you in God's presence!").

Beyond these specific homages, the effusions of these pages overflowed in the presence of the Hindu effusion. Here, during the interval
between Michelet and Quinet, was one of the three great voices that spoke
in France for the soul of India, for the tone and dimensions of India: "The
greatness, sanctity, and divinity of the human spirit are the dominant
characteristics of the philosophy contained in the sacred and primitive literature of India. From it one inhales a breath at once holy, tender, and
sad, which seems to me to have recently passed from an Eden closed to
mankind. This poetry, like the opium that grows on the plains of the
Ganges, produces ecstasy. I always remember the sacred vertigo which
seized me the first time my eyes fell on excerpts from *Sanskrit* poetry."

Again we touch the chord with which the Romantic West, whether from
the poetic realm of Goethe, Lamartine, and Michelet, or from the learned
realm of Chézy and Humboldt, hailed the discovery of this totally unexpected literature. It was not merely a new wing to be added to old libraries; it was a new land to be hailed in the cheers of shipwrecked men. In
a poetic text profound evidence can be traced through the timbre of the
images. Here there are two unforgettable series of images: the image of
the circumstances of Lamartine's new encounter with India, and its relation to kindness to animals. He had just shot a buck and, like Vigny in
his *Mort du loup* (written in 1838 but not published until 1843) in the decade following *Jocelyn*, he felt like an assassin. After shooting the buck,
Lamartine took from the pocket of his hunting jacket an English translation of the *Mahabharata* and, he said, read from it the episode in which
Yudhisthira demands his dog be admitted to paradise. Prevailing opinion
has it that *Jocelyn* did not pay attention to the lessons of Buddhist charity;[3] yet I note that after the incident of the buck and Yudhishthira Lamartine wrote, "From that day on I have not killed. In its moving commentary on nature, the book had convinced me of my crime. India had
revealed to me a broader charity of the human spirit, charity toward all
nature." This is not the only example of India shaming Western butchery;
I shall point to another, at least as striking, in Richard Wagner.

The second series of images is composed of the dual theme of easier
breathing and slaked thirst, which at the time was inseparable from the
discovery of Asia. Michelet's orchestration of the theme is the most masterful: "Greece is small, I suffocate; Judea is dry, I pant." Approaching
the habitual reservations of a West faced with a supposed quietism, Lamartine touched lightly on similar sensations of relaxation and dissolution, at times evoking the sleep of opium and at others mystical ecstasy.

Between his praise of Indic philosophy in the third talk and his lengthy
encomium on Indic poetry, Lamartine inserted at the beginning of the
fourth talk eighteen chapters devoted entirely to seeking a general defi-

nition of poetry. Or rather an *indefinition* of poetry. Poetry-as-mystery. A given, a universal, guaranteed by what was thought of at the time as the primitive. Such notions washed over whatever was said concerning wisdom, truth, and history and bathed the whole in a sort of general bias so characteristic of the period that one quite naturally finds the Herderian theory on human epochs there in a new form. Circulating in the background is the essential lesson of the second Renaissance that inspired Lamartine in his twelfth talk and in *Le Désert:* that all spiritual inventions, all the moral creations of humanity, form a basso continuo. By 1824 Michelet was reveling in variations on this theme. For Herder history, viewed in its totality, was the conscience of humanity through which the Absolute, the Divine, was sought. The very design of *Les Visions*, and even Lamartine's publications on the lives of great legislators and heroes, correspond in his work to this need for, this worship of synthesis. By reliving everything that mankind had ever experienced, whether it was a heroic or a wretched act, whether it concerned philosophical systems or religious ideas, Lamartine, like Michelet, assigned himself the task of becoming the geometric center of all the adventures of the centuries, a position common to the sons of those who had discovered at one bound the boundlessness of the past. And the Romantics were confident that by assuming this position they could determine forever the nature of the modern.

CHAPTER FOURTEEN

Hugo Troubled by India

Iran, Egypt, and India were profound places.
—*Toute la lyre*, 3:3

O NE day at Hugo's home, Victor Pavie showed David d'Angers some books tucked away and remarked, "He doesn't like them, but he makes use of them."[1] Hugo's times directed his attention to the fruits of the spirit. His preying eyes scanned without being noticed, and he had an aptitude for grabbing in full flight, like a foraging eagle. Another royal prerogative was that of amalgamation, which produced a superabundance of passionate images, organic disorder. Amid the medley of references, his radiant memory operated with the perfect instincts of a virtuoso. His classifications became part of an impalpable plan for a unique destiny. Spread out on Hugo's music stand, oriental thought was the score that would argue with the conductor.

From 1828 on, the Orient nourished the cipher code that the poet used for his interior soliloquy. The Orient would become one of the cabinets of commonplaces that genius needs in order to secrete its original thought. Hugo wrote only two long general commentaries on the Orient, one in the preface to *Orientales* in 1829, the other in *William Shakespeare* in 1864. These are works from two different periods and reflect two different attitudes. However oriental Hugo may have seemed, he proved to be reticent on the topic. He had reason to bring up his Latinness repeatedly. Sometimes he stopped at the surface; at other times he revealed himself to be in touch with the depths of Asian thought, but then only as if he had reached them through his own region of terror.

Speaking of the Oriental Renaissance in 1829, he said it was developing and needed to be developed. He was taking part: "He offered no resistance to the poetry that came to him." Fouinet placed the Orient in his hands; Hugo gathered the majority of the Fouinet materials together in the end-notes to *Orientales* and kept a good number of them in his files. He bestrode the treasure imposingly: "It is a handful of precious stones that we are taking, haphazardly, from the oriental mine." Didn't this amount to washing his hands of the perfumes of Arabia? Yet he had already noted the names of Jones and Sacy in *Orientales*. Such splendid learning had remained theoretical in the preface and conventional in the poems. As long as the Orient was no more than skin deep, he yielded to the lure of fashion and his own nature in order to splash his novels and poems with oriental colors. Beyond that the Orient gave frequent stimulus to his inner syllogisms, but its presence was bound to remain one that was watched: what is striking is that Hugo, faced with the Asian immensities, did not experience the feeling of well-being, the free breathing that Lamartine, Michelet, Balzac, Quinet, and even Goethe spoke of. Hugo generally saw in them not images of liberating plains nor images of exalting summits, but rather images of a dark and vertiginous abyss. He did not raise his eyes to an Asia that was the roof of the world, but lowered them to an India that was the depths of mystery.

Hugo's *Orientales* and Goethe's *Divan*

Doesn't Goethe's shadow move behind Hugo's *Orientales?* Hugo was most attentive to the effect he was producing on his German colleagues. And who, at that time, who had any pretensions to poetic greatness would not have kept a watchful eye on such powers as Goethe and Lord Byron? Moreover, the attention was reciprocal. All the time Goethe was speaking with Eckermann, his had his eye turned toward France. Knowledgeable readers have long been mindful of the comparison between the *Orientales* and the *Divan.* The comparison reached its culmination in 1851 with *Les poètes de l'Allemagne* by Henri Blaze. Blaze praised the Germans' recourse to authentic sources, their search for the profound Orient; for them "the central concern" was "the human soul" in all climes. In *Orientales*, on the contrary, what held the attention were mummeries and "cast-offs," "dilettantism" and "splendid lyric qualities." As usual, meditation and awareness were recognized in German art, leaving the French artist only the "passion" for "examining costume" and the mania for "color." Even if that were accurate, pitting a twenty-year-old Hugo against a sixty-year-old Goethe would remain questionable. But it is doubtful whether metaphysical density is always where one assumes it to be. Undoubtedly the seriousness of the old Germanic student nourished his "Walpurgisnacht"—but shouldn't it also be acknowledged that the author of *Faust,*

Part Two had thumbed mythological dictionaries with a no more authoritative hand than the one with which Hugo flipped through Moreri? They were different dictionaries and used for different reasons; one can say no more.

Hugo's whole Orient has something sparkling about it, but doesn't all of Goethe's antiquity, including Asia, have something chalky about it? Which of the two was the greater egoist? The German poet turned Asia into a screen in 1813 so he could avoid watching the national catastrophe. He took refuge in a Persia of small walled gardens and beds of love. On October 23, 1823, Goethe spoke to Soret about the pastiches of August Platen-Hallermund and admired in them "an amiability that makes us overlook the fact that the moral is a bit frivolous. One recognizes a touch of the *Divan* in them." The Orient of the German Romantics had all the great ceremonies of the residence of a petty prince. Merx, a professional, considered Goethe's Orient—rightly, Lichtenberger confesses in his translation of the *Divan*—"a nonexistent phantasmagoria," because "he does not want to portray either the Orient or the Occident . . . but *mankind* which, by intuition, he uncovers in the one as well as in the other." The difference between Goethe's Orient and that of the *Orientales* is that with Goethe the picturesque element is interior. But even in the most haunted parts of *Faust*, pageantry—which plays an important role—is quite unlike that of Hugo. In lieu of the ibis, the boa, and the hippopotamus which Blaze perceived in Hugo, there are telchines, lamias, and centaurs—again the "cast-off." Probably not the costumer's cast-offs, but at least the antique dealer's. In literature there are no Last Judgments. Anything that might be ventured concerning the pureness of intention and the acuteness of thought, so as to decide between Hugo's and Goethe's maturity, even if it were limited to the oriental domain, would not be long-lived.

Hugo and the Hindu Poems

In *William Shakespeare*, a monument that would necessitate endless commentary, Hugo convened around his hero the supreme geniuses whom he called "les Egaux," the Equals.[2] In manuscript, the work had no representative from India. Only when the book was in galley proof, and at the entreaty of his publisher Lacroix, did Hugo include the Hindu epics. Sending the proofs to Hugo on February 2, 1864, Lacroix, amidst a great deal of praise, slipped in a regret. He had just read the *Ramayana* and the *Mahabharata*. "I am," he wrote, "enchanted. It is a whole poetic world." He was surprised that Hugo did not "make mention of it in the enumeration of great works of the human spirit." Probably it was "because they have no given names." Hugo was indeed setting up an avenue of co-lossi—how could he place headless geniuses in it?

The following day the diligent editor pointed out another gap: Germany was not adequately represented by Beethoven; Hugo ought to replace him with Goethe, or "at least Schiller." Lacroix did not stop after such a good start: he proposed a whole string of candidates, long since taken for granted, a nomenclature-type that was by then sixty years old: Homeric and Hindu epics, Eddas, Romanceros, the *Nibelungenlied*. On February 11 Hugo responded about Germany—not, however, without balking over so much interference. Goethe was out of the question, he was "overrated." An overly bourgeois Olympianism? Perhaps, it was implied, two Jupiters in the same Olympus would be one too many.

In the end, Germany would be called "the India of the Occident." Wasn't this association clearly a continuation of the dialogue with Lacroix, and a bit spiteful? This was not, in Hugo's frame of reference, a very good mark for Germany. Schiller was clearly upgraded, but Goethe could thank Lacroix only for securing for him this dreadful and customary attribute: "indifference." Zealous editors notwithstanding, the fact would remain that "the great German is Beethoven." The comparison of Germany with India was widespread; Germany itself took pride in it. It is intriguing to see Hugo revive the comparison as a means of flattery on the important date of September 1870, when he launched his address "To the Germans" to convince them to spare Paris: "Germany is to the West what India is to the East, a sort of great forebear. Let us venerate her."

On February 14, Hugo sent Lacroix his reply on India, another defeat for the editor. The poet claimed to have at his disposal *all* the "anonymous poems." Poets sometimes tell the truth like women who lie, by endowing numbers with the value of feelings. Hugo had thoroughly studied, as Berret has pointed out, the *Livres sacrés de l'Orient* (1840), whose author he knew; but it is also true that, aside from the *Laws of Manu*, Pauthier was very brief with India, generally confining himself to summarizing Colebrooke and including nothing on the epics. For them, Hugo was grudgingly obliged to swallow the tepid water of Barthélemy Saint-Hilaire, whose principal works date from 1850 to 1860. Specialists grant that "for a very long time he provided the bases of knowledge, on the whole accurate, that the general French public had of Buddhism." For the exiled Hugo, Saint-Hilaire faded as a person, but his name became a generic term, a shorthand symbol, for all those against whom Hugo continued to direct fiery diatribes. Yet while working on *William Shakespeare*, Hugo acknowledged having at hand the *Journal des Savants* in which, in 1853, Saint-Hilaire's study on the Vedas had appeared. The library of Hauteville House also contained the *Revue des Deux-Mondes*, which also included a good deal of Saint-Hilaire's work. And we know Hugo read the journal carefully because he took a quotation from the *Hitopadesha* from Théodore Pavie's article in the August 15, 1855 issue and transformed it into a verse for "Aigle du Casque."

Pavie, for his part, had analyzed the *Ramayana* in the same revue and had discussed the Vedas, while Ampère had contributed articles on the *Ramayana* and the *Bhagavata Purana*, and both these writers were, for Hugo, familiar and dear names. A further evidence of Hugo's good scholarly reading was "Bouche d'ombre" (1855), which stated:

> L'ange laisse passer à travers lui l'aurore,
> Nul simulacre obscur ne suit l'être aromal;
> Homme, tout ce qui fait de l'ombre a fait le mal;

> The angel lets the dawn pass through him,
> No obscure semblance follows this fragrant being;
> Man, all that casts a shadow has caused evil.

Foucher has pointed out in these lines a very probable reference to the Indian Damayanti's singling out her true husband from among the gods who had taken on human shape, since only the human casts a shadow (the "Nala" episode was translated and famous before this poem appeared in *Contemplations*). In July 1870, Hugo lifted Mesha, King of Moab, from Oppert who, through an article in the *Journal des Savants*, had made him a topic of conversation. Likewise, while writing *Le Rhin*, Hugo used a volume written by Chézy's widow as a reference, and he must have been aware of *Shakuntala*, translated by her husband in the year following *Orientales* and which Lacroix spoke to him about as if speaking of a work in the public domain. The "Reliquat" of *William Shakespeare* listed, among Hugo's working references, Philarète Chasles (clearly the volume *Orient*), the brothers Grimm, and the *Journal des Savants*. We know that Hugo, encumbered by academic monographs, periodically instructed Meurice to clear them away for him.

From his very first working notes for *William Shakespeare*, Hugo had ideas about the Hindu epic that would crop up again, sometimes word for word, in the additions he finally consented to at Lacroix's prompting. Why, then, did he at first refuse? Lacroix, he said, had guessed the reason: aside from the fact that there was "a great deal of rubbish" in the Hindu collections, repugnant to his love of "the sun," they lacked the presence of the creative self that was, for Hugo, a requisite mark in all that he worshipped ("Le moi latent de l'infini patent, voilà Dieu"; "The self latent in the manifest infinite, that is God"). The correspondence with the editor stopped there. Lacroix, having been dressed down, did not labor the point. Perhaps Hugo, having rejected the suggestion, felt more comfortable about letting it gain some ground, for here he added a striking page on India. The theme his advisor had suggested seemed to return there, amplified by the very objections of the one he advised. Hugo compared all the epics to one another; those of India, attached by a thread to the altar of personality, expressed "a multiple self." The principle was saved, even sanctified, by reference to the "inscription of Ash-Nagar": "These books were not written by man alone."

Nonetheless, the hierarchy was maintained. The poet confined the anonymous rhapsodies "at the summit of art" within an inferior class of summits: "The composite works in countless stanzas, particularly the great Hindu testaments, which are expanses of poetry rather than poems, are an expression at once sidereal and brutish of humanities past, and derive a vaguely supernatural air from their very deformity. The multiple selves that these myrialogies express make them polyps of poetry, prolix and surprising enormities." He concludes, "We prefer the works that carry names. . . . The self of a man is vaster and more profound than the self of a people." This was altogether the last word, as far as the public was concerned, of the dialogue with Lacroix. There, in short, was the answer that seemed to be missing from the series of letters.

Hugo was not the first to react against the fanaticism for popular anonymous poetry. But he did so with a straightforwardness of assertion, with flashes of illumination and felicitous definition, that demonstrated how much seriousness there was in the attitude of individualistic French romanticism that opposed collectivistic German romanticism. Hugo was not only in agreement with Villemain and Sainte-Beuve, but also with Renan, who focused on the question in his *Origines du Langage* in 1858, stating plainly that "there was a Homer" and that "the popular poetries themselves, so fundamentally anonymous, always had an author," so as to finally confer on India herself the privilege of signatures: "We know the authors, or at least the families, to which each of the hymns of the *Rig Veda* belong, and nonetheless those hymns can be counted among the number of the most impersonal creations that exist."

But why did Hugo assume such a position regarding India at this time? The precise reason and date are easily understood: If Lacroix, in 1864, thrust the Hindu epics on Hugo it was because, as he said, he had recently read them, since they had "just been" translated. Yet Hippolyte Fauche had published his *Ramayana* in nine volumes between 1854 and 1858 and had begun the publication of the *Mahabharata* in 1863. What had "just" happened was that in 1864 Fauche had provided a two-volume abridgment of the *Ramayana*. The scaled-down work was both more accessible to the nonspecialist and published by none other than Lacroix, the publisher of *William Shakespeare*. Lacroix would have first seen Fauche's abridgment in manuscript and it was perhaps through meetings with Fauche that he was able to give evidence of being so accurately informed on the state of Indic studies. But, in this connection, didn't Lacroix's humanistic emphasis dovetail with his interests as a publisher when he argued so obstinately to obtain a blast on the bugle from Guernesey that would benefit Fauche's publication?

For his part, Michelet celebrated the year 1863 as the first in which he was able to read the *Ramayana;* he does not state by reason of what circumstances. His correspondence with Fauche, among his unpublished papers, leads one to think that he had started on it by the spring of 1863, perhaps spurred on by the appearance in French of the *Mahabharata,* which he eagerly became one of the subscribers for (he had already, in 1842, read, pen in hand, the English version by Wilkins). An outgrowth of the contact with Fauche, which Michelet initiated in July 1863, allows us to complete the chain of events: at that time Michelet hit upon the idea, to which Fauche immediately agreed, of publishing an abridged *Ramayana* in two volumes intended for the general public. Michelet failed to interest his own publisher, Hachette, whom he approached first, but a few months later, Lacroix, Hugo's publisher, undertook the project. Hence Michelet was the source of the change of interest which, via Lacroix, suddenly commanded the poet's attention and burst into the entryway, or at least the threshold, of his Equals.

Hugo's relations with the Orient had always been checkered. After the act of adherence of the *Orientales,* there had been the public withdrawal recorded in 1835 in the "Prélude" to *Chants du Crépuscule:* "The Orient, the Orient—what do you see there, poets?" And the Orient was reduced to "a mysterious day in a taciturn sky." Hugo was taking stock of the sphere of interests that the dawning century had created by weaving together oriental discoveries and a spiritual revival. And he was probably inclined to despair of the two together. But wasn't this clearly complementary to the preface to *Orientales?* After the Renaissance declined intellectually, a spiritual decline followed. If, in 1835, the poet sighed, "C'est peut-être le soir qu'on prend pour une aurore! / . . . Ce soleil qu'on espère est un soleil couché" ("It is perhaps the evening that we mistake for a dawn / . . . The sun we had hoped for is a sun that has set") it was because, once more, he was becoming the voice of his century, a century now suffering a doubt proportional to its initial exaltation. The 1830s were the years in which Lamennais, at first followed by the poets, lost hope; Hugo's *Chants du Crépuscule* not only reflected the political turmoil of France and Europe,

it was the first collection in which the loss of religious faith was confessed.

Eight years later there was another swing of the poetic pendulum: a
surprising piece written in July 1843 (later included in *Contemplations*) depicted the poet climbing "the ladder of existences," first the mountain,
then the oak, the lion and, finally, man—and the poet in question was
Dante, who was in this way linked with India, as he was in the work of
Ozanam and Delécluze *(Ecrit sur un exemplaire de la Divina Commedia)*. The
themes of reincarnation, pantheism, and the universal soul grew in Hugo's mind and blossomed in his *Contemplations*, the final stage of a multiple impact, for everything suggested such ideas to him. Not a single poet
at that time omitted using them, and their very proximity thrust them toward him in a continual wave. Amid the spiritual instability of the generations between 1830 and 1850, the belief in transmigration was a passkey that each individual used in his own way: Buddhist doctrine entered
into widespread use through Burnouf and Schopenhauer. Moreover, after
1840, and particularly during his exile, when he was bound to listen more
attentively to the remarks of certain fugitives from Saint-Simonianism (and,
we should add, from occultist contaminations), Hugo, like Michelet, linked
the cycle of Renaissances with the cycle of revolutions. The mention of
Hindu names and texts increased, and flakes of Asian wisdom, until then
suspended in the unconscious, snowballed.

The "Successive Epic"

1854 marked an important turning point: the poet buried himself in his
"Apocalypses." In October he believed he had found "the universal solution." He established the ladder of existences in "Ce que dit la bouche
d'ombre" the penultimate poem in *Contemplations*. He had remembered
Fourier's ideas on the unity of nature, the sensitivity of the stars, and me-
tempsychosis, and had culled more ideas from Boucher de Perthes, Jean
Reynaud, and Pierre Leroux. He had a copy of Delisle de Sales's *Philoso-
phie de la nature* with him at Guernesey and must have been familiar with
Anquetil's *Avesta*, if only through Lamennais, and even, according to Caro,
Saint-Martin. Everything was accumulating and would culminate in a ri-
valry with Lamartine, which we will return to presently. Hugo had let
Lamartine blaze the trail (we should bear in mind that Hugo had known
Eckstein as early as Lamartine had). We are familiar with the progressive
flowering of the "Petites Epopées" in *Légende des siècles*, the arising and
enlarging of the epic spirit in the evolution of the poet. Having failed to
lay on the tragic genre its full charge of mystery in *Les Burgraves* (1843),

Hugo carried his hope forward with an expansion of the epic genre. Moreover, the 1840s, when the two greatest poets were no longer satisfied with short compositions, were the years in which the new school looked as if it had given all it could—a literary mode that had lasted twenty years, which is a great deal. Invention no longer seemed to be renewed, and the innovators found themselves rendered obsolete by their own repetitions and those of countless apprentices.

Writing in *Revue des Deux-Mondes,* June 15, 1842, a few months before the publication of *Les Burgraves,* Charles Louandre reproached the Romantics for having set their sights too high: if poetry "has remained powerless it is because it has overestimated its strength and its impact; it is because it has, in a skeptical century, believed itself, without reason, transported into primitive epochs." Here was the heart of the Romantic battle, clarified by one of the governing ideas of the Oriental Renaissance. Just as *Burgraves* was about to appear, Louandre was preaching reason; shortly after its failure, the ovation given to Ponsard's *Lucrèce* resounded with the din of antiromantic vespers in which the murmers of twenty years were relieved. But the true masters, so vulnerable to public opinion, construed in their own way the lessons they drew from such outcries: they revived themselves by accentuating what they were being challenged for: in their eyes the only error was in not having seen far enough or spoken loudly enough.

Never, perhaps, had "primitive epochs" and "a skeptical century" entered into such an intoxicating alliance as during those years when Quinet was offering his widely anticipated historical constructs and poetry was being assigned the mission of extracting the meaning of millennial history for the masses. In a decade when archeological literature, such as *Poèmes antiques* and *The Temptation of Saint Anthony,* was brewing, Victor Hugo, the most sensitive barometer of the intellectual climate, was being roused by these great shifts in the wind. Decidedly then, in 1854 the poet, according to Berret, "was devoting himself entirely . . . to what he called his *Apocalypses."* Around 1854 to 1856 the passage from deism to polytheism was completed; no one any longer doubts that the primary agent of this transformation was the example of India. The most explicit acknowledgment of this was "Suprématie," which was part of the 1877 *Légende des siècles.* It is known that this poem was based rather closely on a dialogue from the Upanishad that Pauthier had quoted throughout his long introduction to his *Livres sacrés.* Previously, in *Dieu,* the core of which dated from 1855 to 1856, the place assigned to India among the principal religious systems was singularly limited. Hugo had not allotted India a single one of the eight divisions, of the eight figures, that encompassed the great periods in the history of the soul. Manichaeism, although dealt with rather brusquely, at least secured a symbol—"Le corbeau," "The Raven." An equal honor was denied Brahmanism and Buddhism despite the fact that the preeminence of Manichaeism over them might seem debatable (the same subordination was reproduced in *William Shakespeare*). A poet always states his true motives, even if he has other motives he does not state: there was something in the Hindu expansiveness that would inevitably appeal to and slake Hugo's thirst for the immense, yet that collided, in fact, with a vital need to adjust the disproportionate, to prune the forest into shape. In all cases, for Hugo, the opposite pole was named Legion.

In the poem Hugo left it to the Angel to make his own pantheism known. Accordingly, India is in evidence, yet scattered. She has her revenge by imposing on Hugo such miraculous verses as these, which imply, whatever else, a familiarity with the essentials:

> Dans les grottes de l'Inde ou dans les rocs d'Eubée,
> Lieux où l'on croit toujours être à la nuit tombée,
> A Claris où la fleur mandragore chanta,
> A Delphe, à Sunium, dans l'île Elephanta,
> Ou dans la Bactriane ou dans la Sogdiane . . .

> In the caves of India or in the rocks of Euboea
> Places where one always feels in the depths of night
> At Claros where the Mandragora sang,
> At Delphi, at Sunim, on the isle of Elephanta,
> Or in Bactria or in Sogdiana . . .

Or again:

> O voûtes d'Ellora, croupes du mont Mérou
> D'où s'échappe le Gange aux grandes eaux sacrées . . .

> O, vaults of Ellora, ridges of Mount Meru
> From which the great sacred waters of the Ganges flow . . .

And:

> O prodigieux cerf aux rameaux noirs qui brames
> Dans la forêt des djinns, des pandits et des brahmes . . .

> O prodigious, black-antlered stag which bugles
> In the forest of jinns, pandits, and brahmans . . .

"The gloomy gods of India" would remain a reprimand in Hugo's language. Pejorative epithet, guarded emplacements—the homage to India is at once a veneration and a reticence. Hugo's Orient definitely expanded after *Orientales*, but it was in the direction of those regions toward which Fouinet had guided him—the Islamic. In *Légende*, Islam took the lion's share of what was allotted to Asia; the collection of ascetics and tyrants was, as a rule, borrowed from Arabia, Turkey, and Persia. It had been Fouinet who revealed to Hugo, in 1828, Farid ad-Din Attar's extraordinary "poem of religious philosophy," *Mantiq ut-Tair (The Conference of the Birds)*. I am convinced, as was Elémir Bourges, that it was here that Hugo found, quite exactly, his prototype for the magical birds in *Dieu*. In its turn the French Middle Ages, which Hugo's publisher recommended as being more accessible to the general public, injured the cause of the Orient and eclipsed the "Apocalypses." Owing to many of its features, Islam disoriented the Greco-Latin tradition, which Hugo defended like his own skin, less than India did. A kind of vertigo, a recoil, was evident in the works of the ex-Virgilian when faced with an entire hemisphere of apparently inorganic art and thought. An entire history without dates, an entire civilization without individuals, an entire pantheon with shifting branches could only confound his need for categories, for framed images.

Like his rivals, Hugo certainly succumbed, as a verse artisan, to the desire to vie with the Vedic immensities. But the spirit of India occupied his subconscious very little. We have proof of this that is as irrefutable as a mental photograph: the records of the table-rappings at Jersey (we should not forget that Hugo was bent on including an entire argument in *William Shakespeare* in defense of the tables). Some of the records that Gustave Simon published, those for September 1853 to July 1854, overlap the gestation of *Légende* and the first drafts of *Fin de Satan* (mss of 1854) and *Dieu* (ms of 1855) fairly exactly. Muhammad readily responded to the poet's summons, but there was total absence on the part of Brahma, Buddha, and Vishnu; they were too lacking in human qualities, in personality, in fixed attributes, to nourish apparitions. The sign of a cancelled sale, I believe, for Hugo: a diverse plentitude, incapable of confinement to a given group of portable images and thus not susceptible of being entered into an ordinary code. Apart from the fact that this pantheism would confuse that of the master of the house, it disconcerted him in that it vacillated, historically and ideologically, between two classifications, animism and monotheism.

Moreover, it so happened that, except for "Suprématie," Hugo had nothing further to do with India after the years 1850–60 unless it was to borrow some rhymes in general use, terms for his vocabulary of images. Nevertheless, a thought such as the following will always retain an Indian accent:

Les flocons des vivants tombent en neige immense;
La vie est une roue éternelle, et résout
La naissance de tout par le meurtre de tout.

The flakes of the living fall in an immense snow;
Life is an eternal wheel, and dissolves
The birth of everything through the murder of everything.

These admirable lines from "Mangeront-ils," spoken by Zineb, Hugo's spokesman in the presence of death, are imbued with a Hindu resonance.

The Accord with Michelet

When in 1864 Hugo only grudgingly admitted the Indian rhapsodists among his Equals, he nevertheless found himself strangely in accord with Michelet, who at precisely the same time was becoming the most zealous partisan of things Hindu. And they professed their agreement gladly. The one wanted to "fashion the Bible of the Peoples," the other to write the *Bible of Humanity*. Their accord was profound. When he received a copy of *Sorcière* in 1862, Hugo declared he "loved all" of it. In 1860, as if in response to *Origines du droit français*, he had synthesized, in the philosophical preface to *Les Misérables*, Herderian theses on "the identity of legends."

"In every being the universal spectacle slowly constructs the image of God." From that formula he would construct his epic trilogy. This preface, especially in the section invoking India, indeed seems a prose commentary on the "Voices" of the poem *Dieu*. There, rushing beneath his pen were Brahma, Manu, the Vedas, as in Lamennais's "Man's involuntary God," and as in Lamartine's "Brahmanism of Providence."

Poetry constructed of history was one of the major innovations of the new Renaissance. And nothing was closer to Hugo's very nature, nothing better suited to fulfill his riskiest desire—to encounter the Absolute at the end of a historical series. It was a method that he dissembled remarkably well: "How can we disregard what happens when we have been given the task to eternalize it, when the relative is nothing other than the absolute awaiting thought?" Indeed, Joseph Baruzi asks, "What is the absolute if not infinite diversity becoming absorbed in unity?" From this came the idolatry of nomenclatures—an insatiable need for reference: for the deists, salient facts and illustrious agents in world history took the place of "authorities," who had, for the faithful, been the apostles and the doctors of the Church. But by entrusting to the great representative heroes, to those selves of time, the prerogative of embodying the absolute in the human, one was contradicting not only the Germany of anonymous poetry but the lessons of Hindu wisdom as well—which is precisely what, with inevitable energy, *William Shakespeare* recorded.

The parallelism with the visions of Michelet and Quinet would become more marked in Paul de Saint-Victor, who romanticized their themes and brought them forth in a more usable state of preparation. It was from Saint-Victor that Hugo gathered the myths upon which he constructed his outline for the immense trilogy. Berret states, "He did not overlook a single line" of Saint-Victor's *Hommes et Dieux*, one of his "brevaries." The article "Ceres and Proserpine" in that anthology, which dates from 1867, was an important source for "Between Giants and Gods" in *Légende des siècles*. Saint-Victor characterized his role well when, later, in the preface to *Deux masques*, alluding to the propheticism that had been the vehicle for the idea of Indo-Iranian primacy, he took pride in having brought it, "in part, from erudition to the life of art." And Saint-Victor spread the ideas that Michelet had put forth as early as his 1848 course.

The *Bible de l'Humanité* appeared in 1864, a few months after *William Shakespeare*. A complete record of the exchange of letters between 1834 and 1869 has been left to us.[3] They show that Hugo and Michelet were surprised that they had so often worked unwittingly along such parallel lines, and as the poet wrote to the historian, "at times" dipped their "pens in the same inkwell." They also had a good many informants in common, whom they shared with Lamartine as well. But Hugo dissociated himself from this triad in no uncertain terms by granting India nothing in the end beyond an admiring reservation: a line in *Littérature et Philosophie*, a few strokes in *Dieu*, a single poem in *Légende*, three sumptuous and aloof paragraphs in *William Shakespeare*. Scattered references from which dread and terror are seldom absent—such would be India's portion.

The Race with Lamartine

When he had bowed toward Hindu grandeur in his *Cours familier*, and this had long been the case, Lamartine himself had not yet contacted it except through prose. His own prose testimony would constrict Hugo's— it was, once again, competition with the most equal of the Equals. Hugo kept an eye on his rival's publications: we have already seen echoes of *La Chute d'un Ange* in *Légende*. And Hugo had good cause not to fail to read the third through the sixth sections of Lamartine's *Cours familier* and not to forget them. Lamartine ended the volume with an extraordinary poem addressed to Madame Hugo, "in memory of her wedding," in which her husband was boldly termed "a drunken vinter."

If one imagines that the prospect of reviving a subject recently dealt with by Lamartine was enough to make Hugo recoil, one would merely be applying to the Hindu domain a reaction which, à propos this same *William Shakespeare*, Hugo had already admitted in the domain of English literature. While the book was being printed, Lacroix suddenly confessed to Hugo that he had accepted a study on Shakespeare from Lamartine prior to Hugo's and that he would issue Lamartine's volume first. Hugo became immediately and violently angry at the competition: "That makes it a closed race," he wrote to Lacroix on Feburary 28. "We are becoming, Lamartine and I, like two young students competing for first prize on a given topic." The situation worried him so much that he dashed off a note to himself, as if to confirm his determination: "Monsieur de L—— is publishing a work on Shakespeare. I believe it would be proper to postpone the publication of my book bearing the same title." Once he had thought the matter over more carefully, however, he reversed his conclusions. In fact, what he would demand of the publisher was, on the contrary, that he not publish Lamartine's work until six months after his own.

But Shakespeare was less than ever a restricted domain: both Hugo and Lamartine had been anticipated there by that perpetual predecessor Chateaubriand. It was in Chateaubriand's *Essai sur la littérature anglaise* in fact that Hugo had found the term *Egaux* that became central to his own work. Chateaubriand, in 1836, had been the first to think of grouping the most sublime poets of the other nations around the English poet, and the first to term this gathering "a society of illustrious *equals*." The expression was repeated *and underscored* in the dithyrambic preamble for the *Revue des Deux-Mondes*, where Hugo had the opportunity to read the passage on Shakespeare that was among the "choice pages" excerpted in that publication. Moreover, the *Revue* added, Chateaubriand "belongs to that society himself." Hugo twice in his turn stated that "supreme art is the religion of the Equals" and concluded that it was "not at all a closed society," thus reserving his own place in it. Hugo did not decline competition on Shakespeare with Chateaubriand, who had christened him an "enfant sublime," but he did refuse it with Lamartine. And the idea of taking second place on the matter of India could not have appealed to him either. Who knows whether it was not Lamartine's unrestrained enthusiasm for the Hindu epics that may have restrained Hugo's own enthusiasm, making it clear to him that such an art could not at once fit in with two poetic appetites that it was impossible to merge.

Hugo defended himself from the poetic religiosity suited to German Romanticism, and widespread for more than half a century, in which, according to him, the notion of mystery bordered on the vice of disorder. There was always in Hugo something of the rock, which was lacking in the femininity of Lamartine and Michelet; an elemental instinct made him wary of such female forces. Consequently, he distrusted all such notions (even while he availed himself, in his own eyes, of the "popular" or "primitive" quality) which not only exceeded individual faculties but submerged the limits of the person as well. He said exactly what he meant to say when he styled Germany an India: he suspected in both the same danger for the spirit. Was it to play a trick on Goethe that he called Beethoven the great German? Here was the real mental reservation: "Music is the speech of Germany. Music is the vapor of art." The real worry emerged elsewhere: "These two geniuses, Homer and Shakespeare, closed the first two doors of barbarism." In another place one sees India fluctuating between Aeschylus, who was disproportionate (and there was still something of Asia in him), and Germany, which was vaporous.

It was through its wish for engulfment that the Germany of Herder and Schopenhauer plunged into the great oriental tides. It was this call for the deluge that Michelet and Lamartine unknowingly repeated in their outcry against Western narrowness. And this was precisely what Hugo's instinct for self-preservation refused to sanction. He neither accepted nor delighted in losing himself in the tide, precisely because the rock in him was not confident of its incompatability with submersion. It was not really Lamartine that Hugo was jealous of when Lacroix brought him to book about India: he was jealous of Hugo. India was one of those numerous poet's secrets that he had no need to overaccount for.

In fact, however, the opinion he expressed was overshadowed by the influence he came under. After *Burgraves* he planned a major poem on India and foreign continents. Perhaps after the flight of his daughter the India that took her became, in the animism of the poet, a hostile woman. If he was obliged to give an opinion he was relatively sincere in offering a guarded one. In fact, when he tallied up the ledger of his waking dream he did not find that the Hindu page amounted to much at all.

In Hugo India remained something largely nameless; yet he was a person in whom many essential things inevitably continued to move beyond the pale of inventories and catalogs. India occupied broad expanses of a sort of ultra-nomenclature through which the legacies of gnosis and the Cabbala voyaged. A poet—and in this respect Michelet in his insomnias was one in the same way that Hugo was—is filled with buried cities, interrupted origins, and primitive clans that must be reborn. It was from such a fantastic interior growth that Hugo himself borrowed his "composite mythologies." Although the only thing that rose to the surface was, from time to time, an occasional scaly torso, a shadow on an island, a nod in a certain direction, or twelve or two syllables such as *yogi, fakir,* or *Brahma,* this verdure cloaked his consciousness like a nutrient seaweed from the depths.

He could, or would, give no more than an obscure testimony to it. Did he know to what extent the presence of India would inevitably be linked to the whole century he breathed and yearned for? Hugo functioned without difficulty as an "alembic" (the word is his own) in which the fruits of the imagination and the dreams of the ages of mankind fermented into essences. What is important is not this or that borrowing from this or that reading, but rather the porousness of genius that produced that prodigious compound we call Hugo's thought. The proliferation of poems in infinite forms, similar to planetary systems, would probably not have grown in that Latin mind if the full complicity of the period had not aided it through the experiences of those who took their own experience expressly from India. Ultimately Hugo not only gave a decisive form to the India of Romantic Europe; his inner mechanism extracted from India, without giving him a complete account of how it did so, the active elements of a composite metaphysics, a theology in suspension.

CHAPTER FIFTEEN
Vigny Tempted by India

WHETHER by chance or by choice, Vigny spent a good many hours with orientalists early in his career. The first two came his way through his regiment. Pauthier, who carried Vigny's Bible in his pack, served under him in 1823. In 1818 Bruguière de Sorsum married Vigny's cousin, the sister of the Comte de Montlivault, the colonel of Vigny's regiment. Sorsum seems to have met Vigny the following year—his climactic year, the year of maturity when he discovered Chénier and became fond of Byron.

Bruguière, whom Baldensperger characterizes as "a well-read administrator and former advisor to Jerome in Westphalia," turned to literature after some disappointment in his career and lived part-time in Touraine and part-time in Paris. A mutual passion for English poetry drew him and Vigny together. He had translated *Shakuntala* in 1803, after William Jones's English version, adding an index of notions borrowed from Forster's German translation, which he had discovered through Anquetil's French edition of the travels of Paulinus a Sancto Bartholomaeo. Thus he was on the path to India. In addition, he reproduced a list of works used by Forster that show him to have been well informed about recent publications. Furthermore, the history of the new field of Indic studies was recounted by William Jones's preface, which also prefaced Bruguière's French edition (a prospectus for a French translation of the *Asiatic Researches* appeared opposite the title page). Bruguière later set to work learning Sanskrit as well as Chinese and was among the founders of the Société Asiatique in 1822.

According to Hugo, Bruguière was supposedly a well-known figure around the time Vigny met him. Book 3 of the first part of *Les Misérables* begins with an extraordinary chapter entitled "The Year 1817" in which, among a good many untraced allusions, is this brief sentence: "1817 is the year Bruguière de Sorsum was famous." Biré required no less than a thick volume, also entitled *The Year 1817*, to contradict, point by point, this single chapter from Hugo's novel. According to Biré, Bruguière was neither celebrated nor claimed to be. The Académie had singled out one of his poems for praise in 1807, and later, in 1821, he produced a verse translation of one of Southey's poems as well as a few of Shakespeare's plays. Why then did Hugo pen this ironic hyperbole? Bruguière was a great admirer of Hugo, and Vigny recommended him to Hugo in a letter dated October 3, 1823 that implored Hugo to love Bruguière for Vigny's sake (Vigny had already commended Bruguière to Emile Deschamps with the same warmth). It is clear that Vigny's affection for Bruguière was not negligent or superficial. We see the same feeling in Vigny's letter of October 7, 1823 to Montlivault, but Bruguière died four days after the letter was written—thus it was too late to do any good. Why had this memory disappeared or soured in Hugo's mind in the 1860s?

Vigny lost no time in commemorating Bruguière in a very careful, important article in *Muse française* in January 1824 (another question arises: published in such a prominent place, was it possible that Hugo had not noticed it?). It is true that although Vigny praised Bruguière's translations of Shakespeare, he made no reference at all to the translation of *Shakuntala,* but we know that, having taken it upon himself to publish his friend's works posthumously, he felt he could defer "the outline of a more detailed study." Yet in the 1850s Vigny cited *Shakuntala*—in either Bruguière's translation or Chézy's—to his correspondents as a text he knew well. As a novelist, he also drew material from picturesque works such as those by the Abbé Dubois and Michaud.

Vigny's friendship with Pauthier began just at the time of Bruguière's death. The depth of this friendship is borne out, this time, by a reverse devotion: Pauthier, whom Vigny named his executor, would perform for Vigny the same service that Vigny had assumed for Bruguière. There seems a symbolic constancy in such death-denying attentions among men who, together, were haunted by Indic thought. And it is hardly imaginable that Bruguière did not discuss Indic poetry, or Pauthier Indic philosophy, with such a faithful companion and such a meditative poet as Vigny. In 1842 Vigny revealed his knowledge of Manu—translated, it is true, by Loiseleur-Deslongchamps, but popularized by Pauthier.

His interest extended to the cause of philological progress: through his mediation the two volumes of Desgranges's grammar, the first Sanskrit grammar published in France, were composed at the Imprimerie Royale between 1845 and 1847. At one point Vigny briefly attempted to learn Sanskrit himself. His contacts with India were almost uninterrupted, and grew deeper steadily.

As with so many Romantic writers, Vigny's essential thoughts are to be found at least as much in projects ceaselessly revised and then abandoned as in his finished works. From 1829 to 1841 he contemplated a work entitled *Almèh* (Bonnefoy suggests that Vigny preceded, and may have advised Hugo). Only the four chapters of the work, published in the *Revue des Deux-Mondes* in April and May of 1831, have survived. The work introduces a Hindu figure, along with a variety of notions and ritual implements and gestures that reveal at least some concern for documentation of Brahmanism. In Vigny's work, as in that of others, Buddhism did not take shape until after the contributions of Hodgson and Burnouf.

Amid a good many ideas for works, which frequently revolved around the history of religions, Vigny's unpublished journal summarized a plan for a poem that would depict the successive crumbling of temples in all climes, particularly India.[1] In 1832 the outline recurred in explicit form in *Stello:* in chapter 36, for no other reason than to humble the West in the face of the Orient, three pages accorded to Brahmanism, with reference to the Veda and Brahmanic practices, complemented the scene from *Almèh*. In 1838, under the shock of Strauss's *Life of Jesus*, which probably struck him through Quinet's article in the *Revue des Deux-Mondes* for December, Vigny undertook a major project that was closely linked with Quinet's work: the *Daphné* that Vigny would work on intermittently for years but never complete, perhaps because, valuing it so highly, he wished it to contain everything, the history of both human restlessness and his own. *Daphné* is conspicuously an idea inspired by the Oriental Renaissance. This is the case not only because in 1859 in one of the later versions the hero, Julian the Apostate, must learn, all over again, about the transmigration of souls and the anguish of the wheel of existence from a Brahman, and then learn about deliverance through Nirvana from Shakyamuni himself, but especially because of the very design of the work, its axis and scope. Fernand Gregh, who wrote the preface to this work when it appeared posthumously, rightly indicated that it is "in a sense a cyclic work, a grand overview of the history of humanity," which was to have been represented in the second consultation with Doctor Noir. The first had dealt, through three tragic, but random, anecdotes, only with the misfortune of poetry; the second was to confront all the inadequate solutions that religion had proposed to the riddle of the world.

Coming after Quinet's *Ahasvérus*, at the same time as *La chute d'un Ange*, and before Hugo's *Dieu*, *Daphné* was a novelistic transposition of the philosophy of religion. Why novelistic and not poetic? Because Vigny, as he stated in defense of *Cinq Mars*, had misgivings about the epic possibilities of modern poetry. *Ahasvérus, Chute d'un Ange, Daphné, Dieu, The Temptation of Saint Anthony*—these are the titles of works produced by the Pleiades of the Oriental Renaissance. That there was less success and less continuity in many of them than in the works of Ronsard and his heirs perhaps, as must be reiterated, stemmed from the fact that the second Renaissance posed differently vast, internal, and difficult questions to its adepts. The extent to which such questions created fraternal activities among these adepts can be seen in a few shared obsessions with problems: there is, for example, the problem of evil, personified by Lamartine's fallen archangel, by Quinet and Flaubert's devil, and by Vigny and Hugo's Satan (and Lilith). During the period from 1831 to 1837, when the Orient seemed absent from his published works, Vigny was nonetheless continuing to prepare for his encounters there by overstressing questions of destiny and of the eternal nature of sorrow, questions that always obsessed him. Swept along by the first of these problems, he more than once investigated Islam, attracted no doubt by the picturesqueness that prevailed regarding Islam during the period, but even more by a fascination with fatalism. By 1819, the year of his encounter with Bruguière, one finds excerpts from the Koran in his papers. Between 1841 and 1847, possibly because of Desgranges, Vigny again turned toward India. "When," according to Flottes in his *La pensée politique et sociale d'Alfred de Vigny*, "after 1848, Vigny finally reentered 'the fortress of his conscience,' the Buddhist Orient appeared to him, as the Muslim Orient had twenty years earlier, but with a deeper consolation." He only drew from it notes for his journal, and yet he had never been "more likely to develop, at least from time to time, a Buddhist soul."

In 1859, at the same time as the India of *Daphné*, there appeared in Vigny's journal a plan for a poem to be entitled *Le Char de Brahma* ("Brahma's Chariot,") in which Vigny expressed a longing, which could only have been transitory, for the blind faith of the zealot. In the same year Vigny discovered Burnouf's *Bhagavata Purana* and proclaimed it "an admirable source of poetry and feeling." He was particularly moved by chapter 31 of book 4, which dealt with "the progress of the individual soul." He noted the passage in his journal and referred to it when writing to Dr. Brierre de Boismont.

Here new encounters with people and new readings began to have a permanent effect. The years from 1843 to Vigny's death in 1863 were twenty years of close, nearly familial intimacy with the philosopher and orientalist Adolphe Franck, one of those who publicly endorsed the Oriental Renaissance. Vigny's association with Franck began at the time Franck was translating and annotating the cabala. Here, after Bruguière de Sorsum and Pauthier, was a new advisor in oriental studies. But, following a rule that no longer surprises us, it was Barthélemy Saint-Hilaire who especially gave Vigny access to the India that suited him best, the Buddhist India newly opened by scholarly research—particularly the works of Burnouf and Foucaux, including *Introduction au Buddhisme indien* (1840), the *Bhagavata Purana* (first volume 1844) and the *Lalita Vistara* (1847–48, after the Tibetan version; a translation based on the Sanskrit text did not appear until 1884). Vigny does not seem to have noticed or studied these essential texts until he was guided to them by Saint-Hilaire's study, *Le Bouddha*, which did not appear until 1858; from that time on he engaged in his journal in a long, solitary dialogue with the timid and suspect interpreter. (However, we should remember that as early as March of 1855 Vigny wrote in his journal, "J'ai l'esprit occupé de Bouddha," "My mind is filled with Buddha").[2]

Before then it had been his deadlock with Brahmanism which had aroused uneasiness: he wrote in his journal on April 17, 1842, "Do not fear Indic absorption; your perfected soul cannot perish." Immediately, then, India was encountered in the field of paramount interest: with Lamartine and Hugo the question of India indisputably touched on their attitudes toward the soul (Lamartine's were, perhaps, more spiritual and Hugo's more intellectual); but this was, one might say, of secondary importance—the primary consideration was one of poetic principles: their India was primarily its poetry. Vigny was the poet among them for whom a life in poetry was most conspicuously a philosophical problem. I do not mean to say that he was a better philosopher: the best poet is infallibly the best philosopher, but for Vigny's philosophy, poetry was not enough. Poetic satisfaction could never, in itself, become an explanation of the world, and although for Vigny poetry could come from philosophy, philosophy could never come from poetry. Thus to Vigny India posed the doctrinal problem with the most vital sense of urgency. And, consequently, Vigny gave it less translation into poetry. Hence in Vigny's work, the second Renaissance appears as a completely interior event, not one given formal expression.

Seven months after the first Hindu notation in the journal, November 8, 1842, there is an early draft of "La maison du berger" which contains a verse later eliminated. That the plan should surpass the finished work now seems natural, since Vigny was describing particularly interior events:

> Si ce soir tu gémis rêvant à la mort, viens,
> Roulons notre maison dans l'Orient splendide.
> L'Orient, ce berceau des hommes et des Dieux,
> L'Orient a nourri les sombres jalousies,
> Qui dévoraient des cœurs grands et silencieux.

> If tonight you wail, dreaming of death, come,
> Let us move our house to the resplendent Orient.
> The Orient, cradle of men and gods,
> The Orient has nourished the dark jealousies
> Which devoured great and silent hearts.

Similarly, twenty years later, at the end of his path from Brahma to Buddha, there was on the one hand the final quatrain of silence publicly added to *The Mount of Olives* and, on the other hand, this note in Vigny's journal that complemented it: "The silence of God. Be like Buddha: keep silent about Him who never speaks."[3]

Vigny pursued his dual disputation with Buddha and Saint-Hilaire in his journal, where on March 5, 1858 he had set these two terms in opposition: "A single hope, annihilation in Pantheism. The Nirvana of Buddha, without divinity." The entries for 1859 are strewn with questions and vacillations: Buddhism, which did not promise "heavenly rewards," was "a religion too pure for the human race and too ideal for the common coarseness of the Celtic races." It lacked "the egoism" of Christianity—a direct response to Saint-Hilaire, who only brandished India to cast it down at the feet of Christianity. On August 29 Vigny returned to this subject a third time: "The perfection of the Buddha is more beautiful than that of Christianity, because it is more disinterested." But a set of scales does not produce faith anywhere; by weighing and reweighing the pros and cons of each system, Vigny returned to point zero. Citing Saint-Hilaire, Vigny still did not, as a thinker, espouse his complaint against "a soulless spiritualism," but he did balk at "a religion of despair" lacking Christian rapture and "the idea of God, which the entire Buddhist system *does not mention a single time*."

Vigny had further changes of mind and hesitations on this topic: in September, referring to the *Bhagavata Purana*, he noted, "The love of abstract contemplation has never been extended further than in this book." Two or three fundamental questions kept revolving in his mind, and the question of reward and punishment always returned to the fore. On February 20, 1861 Vigny reversed the position I have just quoted: in a note intended for his folder on *Daphné*, Vigny reproached Brahmanism for its renunciation of action and its denial of works, the reasons Julian ultimately moved back toward Christ.

But the end of these debates was approaching, dictated by a terrible master. In 1862 Vigny was confined to his room, tortured by the long beginning of his death. It is then that he came to his despairing conclusion about divine silence; it was then that his doubt, always suspended behind his quest, and his endeavor was professed. The argument that rekindled his doubt was the absence of rewards. February 1, 1862: *"Religions.* All religions, without exception, have committed the same error, that of drawing from the *same* source, by which I mean the puerile notion of *punishments and rewards*, worthy, at best, of a school where competition is stimulated by canes and candy." And further on: "Budhha alone did not speak at all about heavenly rewards. *Charity* is the soul of his religion, the most profound self-abnegation, and he does not even utter the uncertain name of God. He consoles the Orient by disposing of Brahmanism's idea of an eternal metempsychosis and successive incarnations and he says, 'Be charitable, give everything, and you will finally have rest in nirvana.'[4] Does this mean union with God or with nothingness? That is the question."

It is not surprising that Vigny concluded with a question mark. India had been a testing ground for Vigny, a cruel mirror of his own estate. Here is the final note, written March 9, 1863, six months before his death and eight days after signing his poetic testament with "L'esprit pur": "After having demonstrated that *Doubt*, man's true destiny, is not the same thing as *skepticism*, it is necessary to define it clearly and to show that it is *Universal Doubt* alone that complies with the Creator's designs, since He has remained silent to our cries and has willed that man derive no *unquestionable idea* from Him." A craving for the absolute, a feeling of human honor which rebelled at a theology of sanctions and, enduring above all, a congenital doubt that came to seem a law of the world—these varied and simultaneous aspects of Vigny's peculiar religious thought never changed except in appearance. The dogma of a doubt that is not skepticism is particularly characteristic of his religious thinking, submission through doubt to the will of a Creator who is doubtful himself. This position, in which the response of a human challenge to the divine challenge would no longer be to rebel but, on the contrary, to obey—simply dignified obedience—was original to the point of being disconcerting.

It was a conclusion, but also a closure of a humanism regenerated but self-enclosed. Vigny is a symbolic character who was not to shrink from the new Renaissance: his various companions found in it a ground for reviving mankind's religious hopes, and for them cyclic images could lead to expansive ones. What Vigny found in the second Renaissance was the ruin of his final hope; for him the circle was that of a prison courtyard.

Amiel

The stumbling block for Vigny was a point in Hindu spirituality that the West denounced as stubbornly as India upheld it: what the one charged was a law of passivity the other remonstrated was a principle of the highest form of action. The Western way of life was one that in his turn the Buddhist condemned as a deceptive semblance of action, whereas his own way seemed to him the only true and valid activity, a perpetual striving toward a higher state of existence.

Toward the middle of the nineteenth century, European scholarship considered quietism an indisputable fact of oriental and especially Buddhist thought. Vigny himself, who was better qualified, it seems, to see such a view as an episode in the endless dispute between the active and contemplative dispositions, took a stance in 1861 against this supposed doctrine of inertia. On March 18, 1869 Amiel showed himself sensitive to the first contacts with this distant religion. He wrote in his *Journal intime*, "From reget, from disillusionment, I have drifted up to Buddhism, up to universal lassitude." Doesn't this amount to confusing the label with the contents? Wasn't it a failure to recognize the unrestrained revolt against the painful illusion of the world that such a religion implies, the work it demands in composing one's being and approaching one's essence? Amiel's interior colloquy between Buddhism and Christianity may appear rather similar to Vigny's, but there is a fundamental difference: to the same extent that the balance wheel returned to equipoise with Vigny, the pendulum continually demanded further oscillation with Amiel, who was the kind of man who is always ready to disengage himself from any commitment—a consciousness trained only to break down responded fully to a temperament equipped only to waver.

The possible nature of faith was another question that involved them all. Ultimately, Vigny showed no trace of an appeal to the childlike state that the Gospels require before everything else. For Amiel, on the contrary, as he wrote in his journal on April 24, 1869, "One thing alone is necessary: surrender to God." It is true that he repeated this to himself a great deal, more, perhaps, than he would have if he did not doubt it, but the very repetition amounted to an effort to make it so. It is as difficult to determine to what extent this tormented Protestant went beyond a superficial concept of India as it is to determine to what extent the imperturbable Catholic Saint-Hilaire did. Despite the stigma of India's supposed lethargy, Amiel suspected a great richness of spiritual unity there; he reconsidered Buddhism through the circuitous expedient of calling on Schopenhauer: "I am impressed, and almost frightened, by the depiction of Schopenhauer's idea of man. What I continue to appreciate in this misanthrope from Frankfurt is his antipathy toward everyday prejudices, toward European clichés, toward the hypocrisies of Westerners, and toward superficial success. Schopenhauer is a great disillusioned thinker who professes Buddhism right in the middle of Germany, absolutely detached in the midst of the nineteenth-century orgy" (August 16, 1869). Here was a different aspect of revenge for the Persian Wars. Morally and intellectually estranged, those who remained undefiled in the midst of the orgy were hoping that an oriental bath would wash the Europe of the Second Empire clean.

Four months later, on December 8, Amiel again approvingly united the philosophies of Germany and India in his thought, this time à propos Eduard von Hartmann, whose confirmation of Buddhism in his *Philosophie des Unbewussten (Philosophy of the Unconscious)*, published in Berlin in 1870, brought him to the desolate thesis: "Creation is a mistake; existence, such as it is, is not worth nothingness." Amiel, like Vigny, and they were not the only ones, adopted the Indic solution through its denying aspect, for the pivotal metaphysical role ascribed to the problem of evil and the "suffering of the world." "Egypt and Judea had noted that fact, but Buddha alone provided the key to understanding it: individual life is a nothingness unaware of itself," etc. (June 9, 1870).

These would remain the two poles of his exploration: on the one hand, the pseudo-ataraxia of Buddhism; on the other, the deliverance from evils that was, for Amiel, the positive prerogative of Hindu wisdom: "My Occidental conscience, imbued with Christian moralism, has always persecuted my Oriental quietism and my Buddhist inclination" (October 14, 1872). And finally as his own death on January 5, 1881 drew near, Amiel, like Vigny, experienced an uplifting in which Hindu thought returned in a language that resembled stoicism and evangelism at once: "Let us slough off our own skins; we will not be denuded. He who has given his life can look death in the face: what more can death take from him? The abolition of desire and the practice of charity is the whole method of Buddha, it is the entire art of deliverance." The whole method? Perhaps. But is the whole content of the doctrine to be equated with its least utilitarian aspect, its transcendent value? Thus as always an individual case again reveals to us another nuance in the totality of incompatibilities and approximations that make up the history of the relations between India and the West: "Christian moralism"—"Buddhist inclination."

CHAPTER SIXTEEN

Michelet Answered by India

The Threefold Revolution in Historial Studies

NO one paid more attention to the widening of horizons that integral humanism afforded for meditation than Michelet. When he arrived on the scene, historical study was expanding in three dimensions simultaneously. First, its range was expanding through the *spatial* multiplications of pasts that resulted from the opening of the oriental regions. Second, it was expanding in *depth* through the extension of chronology that resulted from the discovery of remote epochs. Finally, history was expanding in *density*, if I may state it this way, as a result of the adoption of material references culled from the most varied sources—excavations, missions, museums—that were used to verify written documents, which ceased to reign solely and absolutely.

The advent of archaeological methodology powerfully enhanced the authority and efficacy of history. If the quarrel between the ancients and the moderns dissolved into thin air in the nineteenth century, it was because life was everywhere being sought in its successive guises: suddenly the ancients were ourselves. The museum was no longer so much the repository of models as the warehouse of information; the masterpiece, which had but lately been only the source of pleasure and the arbiter of taste, now had to share its place with the domestic relic and was placed side by side with the commercial object on the exhibit table; it broke free from a cast of aeroliths and was assigned a serial number. Thus the masterpiece descended from its absolute position in the relativity of periods and conditions. This was a great innovation and coincided with the reign of this new tenet: the immemorial and social variants of humanity were identical and interdependent. To pass beyond written accounts was no less revolutionary; what contemporaries stated about an event or what its inhabitants stated about a city was checked against the still tangible remains of things they had touched. The object was matched against the text, the inscription against the narrative, and the writ of the king against the king's legend.

This revolution, which moved quickly, was linked to the evolution of oriental studies: on November 18, 1837, when Michelet was a candidate to the Collège de France, the question arose whether the chair of archaeology should be eliminated or retained. Salvandy, the Minister of Public Instruction, wrote to Sacy, the administrator of the Collège, that they could not, for the following reason, "abandon" archaeology: "It has taken on too much importance through the development of criticism over the last fifty years, through the works of oriental scholars, through the conquests of Champollion, and, thanks to our armies in Egypt, Greece, and Asia, through the discovery of so many monuments." Thus archaeology was not thought of so much as medieval or classical as oriental. Of course, when one is the top official one gives any imaginable reason to justify an administrative decision except the real one. Hence it is all the more instructive to see that the successes of archaeology in the Orient were given as incontrovertible proof. We have already seen, in the prospectus aimed at launching the *Revue Archéologique*, the place they held in the preoccupations of the times.

Through archaeology, posterity came to be in a better position to judge the meaning of a given period than the period itself would have been, to consider the turns of historical fate, and to compensate for the abiding injustice which is its law. The *ethics of compensation* was the personal meaning, vital to Michelet, which he introduced into the philosophy of history. Of all the historians, Michelet was the one for whom history was the great remunerator. This motivating idea, which crystalized his program of historical restoration, occurred to him as the result of the excitement of an archeologist; he frequently declared that he had sensed his vocation in the presence of the monuments collected by Alexandre Lenoir, which were to him more alive than written records. Through his extended contacts with the simulacra of ancient lives, Michelet's awareness of accounts to settle on behalf of those who had lived before him deepened.

In addition to the effects produced by the development of history in density are those of its development in amplitude and depth. Comparison now stretched beyond the surface of chronological cross-sections; the effect of each civilization upon its neighbors throughout an endless sweep became the general rule of comparison. In defiance of time, a single chorus of all sages, saints, heroes, and gods assembled. And in the feverish midst of growth, the other sciences as well spoke only of unity, and in turn the events demanded of the historain that his account be their legal

brief. This is the source of Michelet's new sense of the historian's responsibility.

From it the wonderful vision *in perpetuum ver* burst forth: "The historian
. . . often sees in his dreams a throng of people weeping and lamenting,
a throng composed of those who have not lived enough, who would like
to live again. . . . It is not merely a burial urn and tears that these dead
ask of you; it is not enough to recompense their sighing. It is not a *Nenia*
or a weeper they require, it is a diviner, a *vates*. Until they have him, they
will wander around their poorly sealed graves and have no rest."[1]

A vitality that burst forth everywhere coincided with the fortunate results of research projects, methodological maturity, and the accumulation
of materials. In the very beginning of the century an unrestrained urge to
know, to explain, which bordered on a rage for enjoyment, replaced the
rage for destruction. There was, under the Directoire and the Consulat, a
gluttonous urge to feed the mind, which had gone hungry for years.
Michelet, very attentive to alimentary reports, thoroughly convinces us that
France had stomach cramps in those days—but she also had intellectual
cramps and even cramps of the soul. During these periods it was *time* that
was being attacked; one fired pointblank at the notion of time, one thought
of what had been and was no more. Time was the aspect of the human
condition that one fought. And from all sides treasures that time had ignored were resurfacing and tumbling out. How could great thought *not*
have been directed toward historical studies, the fascinating discipline that
rescued time and, for better or worse, contradicted its finiteness.

"An exceedingly beautiful movement of serious studies succeeded the
revolutionary effervescence almost without pause," Augustin Thierry
claimed, alluding to his first decade as a historian, from 1817 to 1827.[2] First
there had been, from Marengo to Austerlitz, what Michelet termed "the
triumph of ennui." But directly after the Reign of Terror, even before Bonaparte patronized antiquity and the sciences, there had been an astounding ferment: "There was an appeal from the provinces to Paris, a
universal appeal to everyone, by the poor, for advanced studies. It was
an admirable ascent of living forces. . . . Most of the poor people who
arrived were madmen, crazed with work, men like Bichat and Biot, like
Cuvier and soon Dupuytren. . . . It is like the first days of the world,"
Michelet writes, "it is a *Genesis* we are reading, the week of Creation . . .
twelve chairs at the Ecole normale and twelve more at the Museum of
Natural History were established. On December 4, the three medical
schools. And finally the central schools (or lycées) on February 25, 1795."

There was the same animation in the arts: "The young people arrived
in a flutter from the provinces, ready to absorb the immeasurable creations housed in the museums and libraries." The Louvre was opened in

1793, the Museum of French Monuments in 1795. "The figures of Gothic art, of the Renaissance, were at home there, thrived and became established there. . . . I can see it all again. For those of us who were children of Paris, these museums and gardens were our education. When, leaving the dark neighborhoods and black streets behind us, we went there on Sundays to dream in front of so many beautiful enigmas, how many things we felt instinctively, through our hearts! Did we understand? Not everything. But in the chiaroscuro of these things made out only imperfectly, we gained all the more a strong, penetrating consciousness of life. I returned from them brimming over with dreams." It was there "and nowhere else," Michelet later stated, "I first received the living impression of history." In this way Michelet came from sculpted monuments to the written document. "I was seeking, what? I do not know—probably the life of those days and the genius of those times. I was not totally convinced that all the marble sleepers stretched out on their tombs lived no more." Hence archaeology became the inevitable path to resurrection, reverie on the tangible forms of the past created an ever-present life out of elapsed times. At the very moment past civilizations were multiplying, the dead of history were coming to life, and the classical presentiment of human identity would assume its full meaning.

Chateaubriand's cry "Pharamond! Pharamond!" filled the heads of the young. Like Guizot, Thierry discovered *Les Martyrs* and said of *Génie du Christianisme,* according to Jullian, "few books are less characterized by the spirit of exactitide and analysis that is the condition of history, yet few books have had greater influence on the fortunes of history." "In 1814 a generation of great historians" came of age—Guizot, born 1787; Thierry, born 1795; and Michelet, born 1798. 1814 was also the year of the first Sanskrit and Chinese university chairs. There was, then, around the cradle of oriental studies, the blessing of knowing and dreaming, a pullulation of creations and initiatives.

When writing of his education, Michelet always associated the Museum of Natural History and the Lenoir Museum as his two poles.[3] Following the readjustment of the time scale that these museums required, the Botonical Gardens required a reorientation of horizons, the images of islands and tropics following the evocation of the dead. And also the new presences of Lamarck and Lavoisier required new spaces in the biological arena. With Michelet the need for universal explanation encountered the lessons of the natural sciences in a fundamental way. Reflecting in old age, Michelet framed his life's work within the adventure of a single question: "Everyone, friend and enemy alike, said 'It was alive.' But what are the real, indisputable signs of life?" He was proud of having posed the historical question squarely "as a resurrection of integral life, not its outer aspects but its deep, inner organisms." Thierry, Michelet's precursor, had undoubtedly, as Renan notes, provided "a sense of the immediacy of past life," but without Michelet's passion for hypothesis and synthesis that is characteristic of scientific genius and that startled even Michelet himself.

An Autobiographical India

Michelet seized any opportunity to introduce India into the corners of pages where his allegiance was perhaps most convincing. Just as he depicted Virgil as "Indic in his love of nature, Christian in his love of humanity," Heine defined Michelet himself as "a kind of Indian, immersed in universal life."[4] In his quasi-testamentary *History of the Nineteenth Century,* Michelet made a point of proclaiming his debt and rendering homage to Sir William Jones: "His *Institutes of Hindu Law* was once one of my favorite books." Indeed, it was though the laws of Manu that Michelet approached India. In September 1828, at Quinet's repeated invitation, he went to Heidelberg, where he was in daily contact with Creuzer and saw Tieck and Görres, who was at that time working on the myths of Asia. He missed Schlosser and did not manage to meet Jakob Grimm, whose anthologies were then the mainstay of his reading. At Bonn, Wilhelm Schlegel's standoffishness furnished little hospitality, but Lassen, Schlegel's young assistant, made the reception easier to bear. On his return to Paris a fascinated Michelet immersed himself once more in Görres and Grimm in preparation for his study of Luther. Quinet sent him Grimm's *Deutsche Rechtsalterthümer,* published in 1829, and Michelet wrote Grimm an enthusiastic letter. Michelet's *Origines du Droit français (Origins of French Law),* published in 1837, resulted directly from his reading of Grimm's book. Grimm frequently gave Michelet guidance while he was writing the work, and Grimm and Burnouf edited the proofs. It was in Grimm that Michelet discovered Jones, later citing Jones's *Institutes of Hindu Laws.* He later stated, in his preface to *Nos Fils,* that Luther and Grimm had made him a new man and confirmed his religion of liberty in the one and his theme of constant survival in the other.

Michelet was preoccupied from the outset with linguistic questions. In this too he was a child of his century. In 1819, at the age of twenty-one, he conceived "A History of Customs and Peoples as Found in Their Vocabularies" and contemplated a polyglot dictionary to aid in this inquiry. Another one! One part of the work outlined an idea that remained central for Michelet, "A History of the Species Considered as an Individual"—a title true to the spirit of Cuvier. He returned to this theme in 1824 for the lecture delivered at Sainte-Barbe, developing Pascal's thought on "the entire sequence of mankind." In passages pointing out the strong link between the historical and exact sciences, Michelet stressed the importance of subjects pertaining to languages.

In 1829 Michelet's chair of "histoire-philosophie" at the Ecole normale was divided; philosophy was taken away from him, and thus his remarks on this lost half were delayed. At the same time, he took a keen interest in the work of Rémusat, Klaproth, and Champollion, and his admiring friendship with Burnouf, his colleague at the Ecole, was developing. During the year he was so greatly influenced by Grimm, he also continuously praised Creuzer, "patriarch of scholarship and philosophy," Görres, "the greatest genius in Germany," and Herder, who "had caught sight of Asia" and "inspired the appreciation for the philosophy of history." He read Hugo's *Orientales*, whose preface proclaimed the new Renaissance, and *Cromwell*, whose preface reflected Herderian ideas. In 1831 Eckstein frequently came to see him and praised his *Introduction to Universal History*, which in part developed ideas Michelet had presented in his lecture at Sainte-Barbe, in his *L'Avenir*. Eichoff, another Indic scholar, showed an equally favorable opinion. Michelet was named to the Collège de France in 1831, and when Burnouf arrived there in 1832 their conversations became a daily occurrence. More and more, a collector's India was being transformed into an India of great thoughts. Through Quinet everything widened and grew feverish; he and Michelet shared a passion for Asia and "the Church of the Future." Cloistered in his work during the following decade, seeing almost no one except Burnouf, Ballanche, Dargaud, Ravaisson, Eckstein, and Montalembert (significant names), Michelet experienced, according to Monod, his "crisis of the soul." In 1839 he lost his first wife, and in 1842 he saw Madame Dumesnil die after a prolonged period of suffering; he had broken with Catholicism and did not know what to rebuild his strengh around. At that time Quinet, who had returned from Lyon and was still filled with enthusiasm from his *Génie des religions*, was close to him. Soon after that it was Mickiewicz and Polish messianism. During that period Michelet feverishly read and reread works ranging from Vico to the Saint-Simonians. Then he turned to "metaphysical mysticism" and sought new faith in a philosophy of history in which a transposed metempsychosis survived.

The recourse to musing on the Orient was tied to his inner necessities: *the Orient became autobiographical for him.* He set down in his journal the following thought that would reappear in 1864 in his *Bible de l'Humanité,* inverted but essentially the same: "The tiny ruins of the Mediterranean world no longer fill the need for ruins that my ravaged heart feels. I need the desolations, the cataclysms, of the Orient, the vast destruction of races, the deserts. . . . The hall of the Nibelungen is not enough for me. I need the great plain of the Indic world where the Gourous and Panons fall by the hundreds of thousands—or else the absolute desert, the last man of Grainville."[5] Desolations or consolations—sometimes it would be the one, sometimes the other, but from that time forward what Michelet, like Lamartine, was to derive from India was the discovery of *his own mental dimensions*. Even if the great breathing images that came from the plain of the world and its poetic infinity spoke of catastrophe, they were curative nevertheless.

Origines du Droit français, the title of Michelet's 1837 book, (unfortunately substituted, at the publisher's request, for the title *Origines poétiques des civilisations*, which was magnificent) revealed, if anything, that it was not a true indication of the contents of the work. The book is altogether a work of the Oriental Renaissance. In it Michelet illuminates with short strokes (as he later would with armfuls) the traditions and relics of societies, each reflecting the other. The dogma of historical unity, here taken up for the third time in thirteen years, was becoming ever more explicit. Michelet's preparatory notes for his public course in 1849 are unimpeachable sources of information on the role India played in the development of his thought. At the height of his emotional and spiritual crisis Michelet called on Hindu poetry and doctrine for help; India was no longer to touch only his intellect but his soul. In 1846 in *Le peuple*, his most autobiographical work, Michelet bridged the two halves of his life: again, as in the notes for the 1849 course and his 1846 *Bible*, Michelet hailed the *Ramayana* and the *Mahabharata* as "gigantic pyramids before which our small Western works should remain humble and respectful."

India, an elevating sort of abyss, served to help Michelet forget his own inner chasm. India became the mother who delivered and diverted us from "this contentious Occident." Although he still knew few of the texts, the historian recognized a land without antinomies. India was part of his substitute food, a necessary part of his emotional life. Thirty-five years elapsed between Michelet's first contact with Jones and Manu and the publication of *La Bible de l'Humanité* in 1864; India received attestations and tendernesses meanwhile in his *Sorcière*, *La femme*, and *Histoire du XIXe siècle*. India was linked with his love for Athénaïs Mialaret, whose father he venerated as a "brahman," and with his growing concern for animals. But it was in *Bible de l'Humanité* that a long-standing belief, enriched by a thousand encounters, experiences, and compensations, burst forth.

In *Jules Michelet* Daniel Halévy has underscored, in an unprecedented way, the circumstantial nature of this book: the stir caused in August 1863 by Renan's *Life of Jesus* and the primacy it accorded to Semitic origins provoked in Michelet a "response that would not be a critique of Renan but rather one book set in opposition to another." Once again the Vedas and the *Avesta* were contrasted with the Bible: it was in honor of them that Renan's adversary rose to his feet. Yet it cannot be said that these "Aryan antiquities" would "remain the domain of scholars," nor that Michelet's masterpiece passed without comment. The proof that these kinds of questions touched a sensitive spot in the opinion of the times is provided, at the least, by Charles de Mazade's notable article defending the positions of the *Revue des Deux-Mondes* (February 1, 1865) against "The Biblical Musings of Michelet," exactly as Lèbre had defended them against *Génie des Religions* twenty-four years earlier.

Michelet's unpublished correspondence shows that Fauche sent him a kind of public regret that Renan's book "had not been undertaken" by Michelet. "Well, sir! The life of Jesus remains to be done." As a matter of fact, these same documents contain earlier notes, taken from Indic readings. But refreshing his memory before setting down to work, Michelet drew his strength from "the book in which there is assuredly the world's greatest goodness, the divine *Ramayana*." (He was referring here to Fauche's translation, of which he later called for, and brought to a successful conclusion, a standard edition). Michelet immersed himself in this work at the end of August 1863, when Renan's book had just appeared; in October, 1864, he published his *Bible*. The unpaginated manuscript was not free from confusion; the documentation gathered together ardent, lively, and spasmodic notes.[6] Above all, this historical poem was "dictated by the heart," which accounts for its extraordinary tone.

Michelet arrived at the hope that history would be the locus not only of all fields of learning but also of all imaginations. He arrived at this hope through a mental duality, one side archivist, the other poet. Catalog-history and poetry-history—it was the dual activity of the century itself. Nothing adumbrates Taine's methodology better than Michelet's *Origins of French Law*. "Minor occurrences" are calmly aligned and, with a wave of the wand, the deep tendency, the progress of which these instances are the overlay, springs into relief. A row of documentary shop windows would always provide the solid ground floor for the aerial architectures of Michelet's work; the former squared with the realism of an archaeological era, the latter with the new disproportionateness of the past. The transmutation from the factual to the lyrical was most discernible in the cases of Persia and India; there history broadened into the magisterial art of reliving all differences possessed of incantatory characteristics. Then this faculty, which Sainte-Beuve, referring to Michelet's *History of France*, called "the ardor of a witches' dance," was exercised on the millennia. Michelet responded admirably: "This kind of ardor does an injustice to human works. And yet I do not know whether there should be any work without it. Life itself seems a kind of ardor which, by the grace of heaven, we get over sooner or later."[7] It was from Chateaubriand that Michelet, like Hugo, learned the secret of the rhythm that swept the great historical prose of Romanticism along, the attack of lyrical commentary on strings of names and events. This is the great approbation of *a lyrical truth* as dependent on a kind of warmth as on a sense of accuracy, the degree of accent having the value of proof. History springs into existence only through a rhythm. The historian penetrates series of events in order to extract a cadence from them. What good is a registrar at imbuing actual experiences with life? That requires a musician.

Thus the philosophy of history, after a period of savagery among barbarians who were proud to be so, returned to the position from which Bossuet and Voltaire had read the world their lesson. Their successors, however, returned there via the epic; consequently the enumerations in which the dossiers of mankind became repositories of vocables multiplied and were simplified to compose an immense portable ideography. Their successors had rediscovered, after the manner of Monsieur Jourdain, that all learning is eloquence. No period, I believe, other than that of integral humanism with its vast landscapes of the past was able to demonstrate to historians the enormous distance that exists between a conformity to the letter of the subject and a fidelity to its spirit.

From Biology to Social Mystique

In his 1824 discourse, Michelet stated, "Science is one: languages, literature, and history; physics, mathematics, and philosophy, the branches of knowledge that are furthest apart in appearance are, in reality, related, or rather they form one system." Even in childhood he had associated his appreciation of the Bible with his propensity toward the exact and natural sciences. In his twentieth year he was attracted by medicine; in 1868 conversations with his physician Edwards prompted him to note in his journal the links between embryogeny and the history of languages. Later he recalled that Edwards' "truly encyclopedic mind" was "greatly admired by Burnouf, who had also begun with the physical sciences before becoming the world's first linguist." He could judiciously point to his "powerful attraction" for Geoffroy Saint-Hilaire, to whom he turned in the darkest hours of his crisis. This crisis "brewed for a long time" in him, he said, until he perceived the confluence between the sciences of nature and the sciences of mankind. Thus "the veil of Isis" covering "the mystery of our origins" lifted from his eyes. From 1855 to 1865 he pursued his own studies in the two spheres in tandem. Recalling his youthful excitement,

Michelet wrote retrospectively in his *History of the Nineteenth Century*, "How interdependent this world is! Science combines with action, with great social movement! . . . Chemistry is not merely a science but a language that is spoken by the man on the street. Its concepts have infiltrated everywhere. One senses its influence even in political language." A lucid observation, hardly touched on by others, which must have been a striking one in the days of the linguists. All such series of associations led intellectual reflection into its temptation—politics.

To characterize the historian recomposing "a period, an individuality" on the basis of a collection of slight indications, Michelet's widow would later compare him, inevitably, to Cuvier. Like Balzac and Hugo, Michelet overlapped Cuvier, but with Hugo's political bias rather than Balzac's. Thus Michelet reveals to us the culmination of the linguistics-biology parallelism in action. An enthusiastic supporter of transformism, Michelet was in the camp that rejected both theology and dictatorship. "Around 1800," Michelet wrote, "a young man, Cuvier, found his way into the Museum of Natural History and, little by little, made himself its master." Cuvier seconded Bonaparte's despotism by attacking Lamarck through Laplace: "This ingenious Cuvier, as skillful a draftsman as he is an elegant writer, forbids by his example any speculation concerning the *transformation* of species, the spontaneous movement of life, and so reduces natural history to a study of the *correlation of forms* which can account for functions, and even habits, in extinct animals." Michelet compared Cuvier's system to the dictatorial constitution of the year VIII.

The chain of hypotheses by which the thought of the period postulated a general theory of life passed from fossils and cuneiforms to the Lenoir Museum and the Museum of Natural History, and did not stop there. Michelet underscored the link between the mystique of science and the social mystique: "Saint-Simon's weak spot was to believe not only in science but in scientists personally. He was their courtier and particularly enthusiastic about the mathematics of his time; he greatly admired Lagrange, the young Laplace, and before long even Poisson." Saint-Simon even went to see Lavoisier with the intention of working out agrarian reform on a mathematical basis. "In 1803," when Bonaparte was reopening the Catholic Church, Saint-Simon wanted "to found the universal church of the planet upon the tomb of Newton." In an ecstatic delirium in his prison at Luxembourg, he received from God the mission to accept as priests only the learned. Newton would govern the planets, represented on earth by an elect council consisting of twenty artists and scholars. One senses here the roots of the hierarchies of his student Comte.

Thierry, who referred to Saint-Simon as his adopted father, was the first to proclaim that history had not yet truly been written, since the history of the masses had never been told. It was while meditating on William Jones that Michelet, according to Monod, confirmed "one of his favorite ideas: the identity of the human race." When he prayed in his journal for the coming of human unity while preparing his courses of 1842, 1848, and 1849, Michelet set the term India opposite the term Christendom, comprehending from an overall viewpoint the great alternative that India brought to Western consciousness. In the winter of 1842 Michelet reexamined Vico and Herder, conversed with the Saint-Simonians, and sought his own personal formula of "inner chemistry" between the systematic thought of a thinker like Herder and the fluctuating thought of one like Quinet. For the first time he wrote of "Asia as a medicine for the soul. Impression from the end of the *Mahabharata*," adding, "which leads the course forward." He was referring to the public course, the outline of which carried the following explicit reference: "Identity always pursued. The soul's perpetuity. End of the *Mahabharata*."[8] One cannot overstress the intimate nature of oriental ideas in Michelet's work. His hopes to reconcile all religions in a strange way rose simultaneously with his amorous ecstasy; he no longer distinguished between religions and Athénaïs Mialaret. On January 2, 1849 he wrote, "O my fiancée, I am making a marvelous bouquet of flowers for you. . . . Tomorrow I will break open the gates that separate *religions*." This letter remained clipped to the manuscript of the lecture that outlined exactly how this would be done; the lecture of the following day affirmed a quest for unity in which one cannot determine the point at which sex and history separated.

During all these years, Michelet kept a close watch on the metempsychosis adapted by Jean Reynaud. Twenty years later, he had not forgotten it, referring to Reynaud and to Dumesnil's *Foi nouvelle* as "a ray of light" in "the dark night." This reference occurred in *La sorcière*, whose epilogue, in an adjuring tone characteristic of the author, recapitulated, outside any demarcated doctrine, a favorite theme of the previous half century, no different from religious hope: "Gods pass away, but not God. On the contrary, the more they pass away, the more He becomes evident." Lamennais's *Essai sur l'indifférence* had not at all contradicted this. It could have been Hugo writing in *Dieu* or *Religions et religion*. And the following is almost the preamble to *Ahasvérus:* "He is like an occulting light that each time returns more luminous. . . . This religious dawn is so near that I continually thought I saw it appearing over the desert in which I completed this book." He heralded the approaching sun: "Let us hopefully await the recollection." In 1862 such a profession of faith carried the conviction of twenty years during which Michelet was fusing Vico's eternal return, Pascal's humanity-as-individual, Polish messianism, and the concept of great men as a "successive Messiah," "a successive incarnation of eternal truth."[9] These visions advanced from a tenet of universal identity to one of perpetual Revolution. He had inferred from the events of 1830 a concept of history as an "eternal July," that is to say, a history avenging all the obscure deaths that had occurred during great historical days, history written by a nation of anonymous writers. The intuition of several English poets, of whom Blake was most prominent, had been close to this, transposing the events of 1789 into a spiritual eternity. This symbolism was also to be found in Ballanche: one of the books of his "Mystical City" was to have been entitled "The French Revolution Seen as a Cosmogonic Phase."

This myth would blossom above all in *La Fin de Satan* in the character of the Angel of Liberty. It is significant that Michelet insisted that only the century of ideas liberated since 1789 could have been the proper time to proclaim universal identity. A final indication is that India was enlisted for this construct, which was at once historical, poetic, political, and religious. It is Hugo who offers us final proof through his agreement with Michelet: in the exchange of letters following *Bible de l'Humanité*, he defined this work as "clearing a swath between Brahma and Robespierre," along which he declared he could walk with his friend. In times when, under the pressure of the philosophy of history, "peoples" tended to be identified with "the people," one is tempted to say that "peoples" is to "people" as "India" is to "Revolution."

The Collective Men

By 1808 Friedrich Schlegel had detected in Indic systems "the apotheosis of extraordinary men." The theme of "representative men" came into widespread use throughout European and American Romanticism. Sometimes exalted, sometimes lowered again in his mind, this theme was consistently central for Michelet: it seemed to him that a spiritual mission, over the sweep of the ages, was relayed from one genius to another—and it was from this idea of the human that he viewed reincarnation. A collection of privileged heads symbolizing human destinies extended from Chateaubriand's Equals and Hugo's Magi to Baudelaire's Phares or beacons—and this vision had already allowed the German metaphysicians to secularize the biblical prophets. It haunted historical summae such as *Génie des religions*. The poets combined the entire adventures of peoples *en bloc* beneath banners bearing a string of proper names that had become collective nouns. The moralists drew from this practice an alternative to lost religions: Emerson and Carlyle demonstrated which new sect, what earthly mystique, dedicated to Buddha, Zoroaster, Confucius, or Muhammad, cleared the way for the arrival of the Magi kings.

These allegories were not entirely gratuitous: sages were summoned together to be transformed into diviners, diviners became legislators, and through that juncture the mythic was brigaded into the revolutionary. The mechanism is clear: in a period when one was suddenly confronted with the infinity of language, each Romantic writer with a parcel of genius became aware of his subversive power and assumed that speech was what altered reality. Every society is at the mercy of the inventors of forms, and no society more so than the one into which they are born—from which issues an idolatry of all those exceptional men who have broken and remade the rules. This would ultimately lead to the conception of a Superman in whom all the powers of rupture would be united and who would be, in his entirety, nothing but rupture. In the ordinary course of things, the names of heroes are the instruments of poetry; after Romanticism they were much more—the symbol of revolts and reforms on the one hand and the intermittent localization of the divine on the other. These two values, the one political, the other spiritual, produced a compound messianism; indeed, it amounted to coining the Messiah.

Michelet found his justification in lending his life's blood to all societies that had ever existed. Would he merely glorify the blazing names of a few leaders, or would it not be essential to redeem the vast body of the unnamed? He seemed to incline toward one or the other alternately. In his *Histoire romaine* he had already outlined a reconciliation which, here again, Ballanche had envisaged: genius was valued for the voice it gave to the speechless masses. This resembled, if not the Germanic teachings, at least Vico's idea concerning the Homeric question: highlighted by figureheads, who were the mouthpieces, history as well as poetry contained an impersonal sublime. Yet Michelet did not resign himself to forgetting the personality within the collectivity, reproaching Leroux for consenting to do so, and refused to allow himself to be lulled back to sleep by a new religion of social classes according to which "the individual is powerless." On May 17, 1842 he noted, "The soul, far from losing itself in a vague generality, must (from what we can see of the ascendant ladder of beings) take on increasingly individualized characteristics." Here was a feverishly sought position very similar to Hugo's, drawn simultaneously from a vestige of metempsychosis and an awareness of the quality of genius. Here the exceptional being was no longer interpreted as a representative of unexpressed humanity but rather as a representative of the collective soul exerting itself to become, through successive incarnations, the animating principle of an increasingly perfect individual. For a century the West wrongheadedly strained its ingenuity over *samsara*. Friedrich Schlegel himself applied a remembrance of euhemerism and the "symbolism" of the times to what he gleaned of the doctrine. Quinet, whose *Genius of Religions* Michelet was rereading at this time, wrote in it, "At the origin of human revolutions, India made, earlier than anyone, what could be termed *the declaration of the rights of the Being*." He underscored these words in which the unbroken thread attaching the Revolution to pantheism is visible. "This divine self, this society of the infinite and the self combined, here indeed is the foundation, the root of all life, all history, all religions, and every individual society." This may appear obscure, but nothing can better demonstrate how a sort of oriental free-thinking seemed to justify to the men of 1840 the strange but sincere mysticism that they were diverting from religion to politics.

Later it became one of the prime movers of an entire period. Long before the appearance of Hugo's *William Shakespeare,* Michelet's journal (June 1842) was agreeing with its principal points: "Yes, a man's destiny, when one probes it, is more than the life of a nation.[10] Nations are universals, a sort of middle ground between the true life of the individual and the true life of the human race." Both the poet and the historian were aware of the exceptional powers through which the prophetic man clarified the otherwise obscure meaning of beings and things. Hugo attached paramount importance to "named geniuses," having his own reasons for believing in beings who, since they could not be "erased," could not have a mortal soul; Michelet believed that all signed manifestations were more vast and significant, for he was certain he was the one who would transfigure the past of peoples—and consequently their future—into something they would never have been without him. In the end they were very close to each other. Hugo would conceive his successive epics on three principles: faith in a perpetual human identity (from which *La légende des siècles* grew), belief in an ascending progression of religions toward an ineffable God (out of which the poem *Dieu* sprang), and the quest for a solution to the problem of evil through a revolutionary metaphysics of Liberty *(Fin de Satan)*.

Emerson and the Representatives of Humanity

Michelet "insists that life comes from the people, until the great man, until the great individual or collective force that carries out divine thought."[11] Thus he was opposed to messianism, Mickiewicz's or Blanc Saint-Bonnet's as much as Emerson's. Nonetheless, there are some striking similarities between Michelet and Emerson. Emerson wrote in his es-

say "History," "The primeval world,—the Fore-World as the Germans say—
I can dive to it in myself as well as grope for it with searching fingers in
catacombs, libraries, and the broken reliefs and torsos of ruined villas."
Michelet asked himself in his journals, "What is history made up of if not
myself?" We have seen how deeply the American thinker was marked by
his remembrance of India, where, he felt, he could perhaps discover the
secret of the world, if only he sought it there. This question is raised in
the Upanishads, and Emerson knowingly ascribed the understanding of
Identity to the orientals.

Michelet and Quinet took an interest in those ideas of Emerson's that
bordered their own. Quinet's notes from his reading of Emerson include
Emerson's statements, "Of the universal mind each individual man is one
more incarnation" and "How easily these old worships of Moses, of Zoroaster, of Menu, of Socrates, domesticate themselves in the mind. I cannot find any antiquity in them. They are mine as much as theirs."

In May 1848, three years after Michelet had mentioned him in his journals, Emerson, passing through Paris en route to visit Carlyle, attended
one of Michelet's lectures. As it happened, the topic was India. Emerson
left the lecture disappointed. Had he not understood the French in which
it was delivered, or was it Michelet that he did not understand? It seemed
to Emerson that the Orient had been treated with the sort of levity which,
outside France, is taken to be typically French. "I went to hear Michelet
lecture on philosophy, but the sublime creed of the Indian Buddhists was
not meant for a Frenchman to analyze and crack his joke and make his
grimace upon." Perhaps Michelet had two approaches to India, one that
he used when writing and one that he used when lecturing. Apparently
the American was accusing the Frenchman of using the very religiosity,
which Emerson refused to accord the worship of great men, to demean
the spirituality that, for his own part, Emerson drew from Buddhism.

In 1845 Emerson delivered the lectures that he would collect in *Representative Men*. Applying himself to a close examination of the theory of
human identity, Emerson showed great men to be successive incarnations
of the same phase of the human soul. Religion embodied the spirit of the
universe, and history was the memorial of this universal agent. What then
is the difference between Emerson and Michelet? What Emerson retained
of his lost church and what had caused him to lose it mixed into his oriental nostrums an ingredient that was from the outset connected with the
cause of Indianism: the faith in inner revelation. Such subjectivism, after
proclaiming the individual the arbiter of his faith, yet makes the historian
the great judge of things past; Michelet himself had sought the lesson in
Luther and associated it with his memory of Grimm. Emerson, for his part,
rejoined the Germany of Carlyle. In 1837 Carlyle had extolled the theory

set forth in Fichte's work, according to which, since a "Divine Idea" permeated the visible universe, "the Man of Letters is sent hither specially
that he may discern for himself, and make manifest to us, this same Divine Idea. . . . Men of Letters are a perpetual Priesthood, from age to
age, teaching all men that a God is still present in their life."

The philosophies of Herder, Schelling, and especially Schleiermacher,
had prepared Carlyle for *On Heroes and Hero Worship*. He had delivered
these lectures in 1840, five years before those of Emerson. In transforming
the poet into the *vates*, Carlyle made use of Fichte's *Uber des Wesen des
Gelehrten*, and in 1827 he had declared "as I take it, Universal History . . .
is at bottom the History of the Great Men." This great question of the age
regarding those connections which, having been those between the human and the ultra-human, were becoming those between the human and
the superhuman, was bursting out on every side. Emerson stated it more
clearly than anyone when he gave these two propositions in his essay
"History." On the one hand, "there is properly no history, only biography," a logical corollary of the identity principle. On the other hand, "All
inquiry into antiquity, all curiosity respecting the Pyramids, the excavated
cities, Stonehenge, the Ohio Circles, Mexico, Memphis,—is the desire to
do away with this wild, savage and preposterous There and Then, and
introduce in its place the Here and the Now." Who would better infer the
ultimate meaning of the Oriental Renaissance, the absolute equality of all
races and ages? Hence "elsewhere" and "formerly" needed to become
"ours" and "presently."

CHAPTER SEVENTEEN
From Historical Poetry
to Poetical History

An Antiquity of Redemption: The Doctrine of Leconte de Lisle

THE dream of a global history, by which Hugo regarded himself filled, Leconte de Lisle detailed in multiple soliloquies—what had been elements of an interior vocabulary became detached episodes. Quite naturally, for Hugo such a pullulation of the millenarian, a limitless mythology, although often reduced to the magic of the name, produced countless direct correspondences with his visions. Leconte de Lisle made a point of stating that thereafter there would be no poetry except humanistic poetry. A cold consciousness replaced "spirited" naïveté; history was no longer the faith of poets but the refuge of skeptics who were resolutely artists of knowledge rather than artists of nature. "Archaeologist" was a title whose iciness did not displease them, its merit outweighing whatever bitter or withered quality it implied.

In response to Hugo's preface to *Orientales*, Leconte de Lisle's preface to *Poèmes antiques* in 1852 referred modern poetry to a knowledge of remote eras: "Science and art have now turned toward their common origins. This movement will soon be unanimous." "The genius and tasks of this century," said Hugo in almost the same words Anquetil had used when he reclaimed the archives of the human race, "is to rediscover and reunite the family titles of human intelligence." Leconte de Lisle wrote, "Art has lost this intuitive spontaneity, or rather exhausted it; it is scholarship that must remind art of the meaning of its forgotten traditions." Yet the perspicacity of learning could not supply the lost intuition by which a young poet "offered no resistance" to "the poetry that came." Now the newcomer was raking through tombs, grasping bits of treasure. By introducing the *Bhagavad Gita*, a Hindu poem, alongside the resurrected Greco-Latin ones, by knowledgeably grouping all this intercontinental past under the title *Poèmes antiques*, Leconte de Lisle sanctioned the extension of the term "antiquity." Here there were multiple antiquities. He saw clearly that this would open "a new path."

In 1855 the preface to *Poèmes et poésies* recommended a poetry of generalized erudition in the hope that in the long run it would set pure science apart from industrial science. Regardless of how the poet "turned his eye on the past," he could still see it only "through the smoke of burning coal, billowing into the sky in clouds." His rationality demanded that a chance remain open for those who would sing of "historical origins," of times "when mankind and the earth were young." At the time Leconte de Lisle himself projected a large-scale poem retracing, "in a series of actions and heroic recitals, the history of the sacerdotal and heroic era of one of the mysterious races that came from the ancient Orient to people the deserts of Europe."

This attitude, which would later characterize the Parnassians, post-dated, by about a generation, the enthusiasms for India of the great Romantics, whether Lamartine in France, Rückert in Germany, the Lake Poets, or in America Emerson (I am thinking of the initial period of each of these). Partly it was because of the prestige of the French school of poetry that this attitude remained, if not the only one, the most widely known. Perhaps it was because it preferred surface interests that the attitude had interested the largest surface-area of humanity. And also because it was in league with the adventure of the moderns. After Romanticism, a writer accepted, or hoped, that the fictions of his pen would be for him a life of compensations; after the Parnassians, the lode of archaism almost automatically provided something to compensate for a world whose prosaic-ness was directly proportional to its scientific progress. The tip given us by Leconte de Lisle was that *a redeemed world* could be attained through the most extensive displacement into the past. This was something that he had in common with Flaubert and that would be passed on to the Symbolists. Entire generations were born who believed that they could remain shielded from and uncontaminated by their age by living in it as little as possible. And the elsewhere, the "anywhere out of the world," would always be a past. From that time on there was *a cult of former times*, by no means dilettantism but rather *an approximation of lost religion:* this characteristic of the sacred is highly visible in the doctrines central to Leconte de Lisle and Flaubert. Such a distorted form of the philosophy of history and religions should have interested sociologists. An entire literature of disengagement, alienated from the present, accusatory toward its time, following the paradox of progress from its past to its culmination, is necessary to explain the clamorous revenge of today's engaged literature, which murders ascetics and is well versed in accounting.

A good many moderns became convinced that Truth was one, and thus more accessible to the youth of humanity. Diderot and Rousseau with their savage and Herder with his exotic conjured up primitive homelands. Goethe demanded of Saadi that he isolate him from his own age. The Pre-Raphaelites demanded blinkers from their Quattrocento Celtism. One could lengthen the list by enumerating each fetish. What was altogether novel was that *the discovery of the Different introduced a therapy of the Different*. This would have been inconceivable to a classical mind: one proceeded infallibly, euphorically, from the same to the same. Throughout the entire Greco-Latin Renaissance, *the antique was something identical*, something permanent. Can one imagine Fénelon seeking escape in Calypso? At that time the rotation of the Past within a confined Mediterranean orbit made it appear to be a stay-at-home. And there, since nothing uproots us, it was less the object of positive science than the subject of personal meditation; it was less an existence in itself than an enrichment of the general notion of an existence in which Romans and Hebrews wore the dress of Louis XIV. In short, until the Romantics the past was less an experiential representation than a moral reflection.

This prejudice was abruptly turned around, so much so that one can speak of *a Renaissance of the archaic*. In the middle of the nineteenth-century a poet for whom the only learning was that which derived from the tombs and oblivions of Qain and Bhagavat arranged Asiatic, Celtic, and Scandinavian specimens into a self-evident equality. It was an attempt to found another classicism, one in which the principle of the perfect and the unchangeable would be replaced by the prestige of the abrupt and the unpredictable. Until then the sons had been challenged to equal the fathers; now the elders were humiliated in the eyes of the children. One agitates for the nascent, the intact, the ground-zero of civilizations. One no longer looked back to the security of time-honored filters and of successive alembics, but rather toward guaranteed bedrocks and matrices. "Among peoples who cultivate the arts," Voltaire said in *Siècle de Louis XIV*, "many years are required to refine the language and sense of taste"—a trite application of Boileau's rule that before the reign of reason "all men obeyed their grosser natures." Hereafter they would be glorified; one would seek in them a model. The beautiful was no longer at the point of arrival but at the point of departure. A period of green fruit was beginning.

Baudelaire: The Principle of Wonder

Since we are changing Renaissances, the problem, in effect, is to determine in what fundamental way the second Renaissance differed from the first.

In all compartments of history an interbreeding had taken place among all the fluctuations of taste. At first it was undoubtedly the vogue for the Middle Ages, along with the prestige of the Gothic, that had accredited what had long been excluded for the crime of barbarism. It was the basis by which the predilection for the anticlassical encroached upon the Greek museum itself, the basis by which the notion of the "hyper-antique," recently abhorred by Fauvel, displaced the Elgin marbles with those of Aegina, which were installed (retouched, it is true, by Thorwaldsen) in 1831 in the museum of sculpture at Munich. Returning from viewing them, and recounting that access to them led through halls in which a "Brahma" and a Buddha were displayed, Fortoul declared in the *Revue des Deux-Mondes*, September 15, 1839, that it was necessary "to renovate the entire theory of Greek art."

On November 26, 1863, *Figaro* began Baudelaire's magisterial series of articles, collected in *Art romantique*, entitled "The Painter of Modern Life." In these articles the life of a thousand years ago became present-day life. His "modernism," which like that of the most ancient of the classics is a modernism of the eternal, refers to the "Ninevite" monuments that had so impressed his friend Delacroix when they were installed in the Louvre. By an impact analogous to that of the Hindu epics, which were again teaching the poets the grand scale, Babylonian architectures taught hierarchy to the artists. Just as a taste for Valmiki developed among poets, one for the images of Sardanapalus developed among artists. The impact produced upon literature by Sanskrit was produced upon art by Khorsabad (not, I repeat, by Luxor). Among the existing accounts of this impact, Delacroix's is one of the clearest and most memorable: for him Nineveh became the natural standard for comparison. With Baudelaire nothing is so simple. He repudiated and even reversed the judgments of scale. Archaism reached him through another seduction: he is the first who, through his aptitude for transforming a normal disposition into affectation and provocation, drew from an already banal deference toward the primitive a fresh veneration of the childish.

What he was seeking from archaeological excavations was an explanation of genius by means of childhood—"a childhood retrieved at will." Appraising all art in terms of its premeditation, and even its artifice, he turned the weapons of history against the intention of those who had founded its philosophy: the savage was, in his eyes, exactly the opposite of what he himself loathed and termed, underscoring his horror, *simple nature*. A precursor, Baudelaire pointed out those arbitrary and conventional elements that the future would, to a steadily increasing extent, trace to the supposed naturalness of the past: "Through their innocent yearning for the sparkling, for variegated feathers and shimmering materials, for the superlative majesty of artificial forms, the savage and the baby display their disgust for the real; thus they unwittingly prove the immateriality of their souls." An admirable lucidity pierces this polemical mischief. Baudelaire was taking the opposite view from the Herderian theorists who postulated spontaneous creation of the works of remote antiquity. He presented a sounder hypothesis, one that a century would consider true. He brought the variety of the Sioux to the primitives who were the coddled compensation of the Parnassian school. Doesn't this anticipate the conclusion of Indic scholars that the Vedic hymns, which they had but lately viewed as the standard model of natural improvisation, revealed all the marks of sacerdotal formalism and scholarly artifice?

What the individual qualified by Baudelaire as Romantic sought everywhere was a recourse against the tendency of the outer world toward monotony, repetition, and saturation—and he sought it in the interior world's faculty of playfulness and passion. The daily problem was to flee the enemy—spleen. Living was an incessant craving for wonder, "the faculty of wonder which is one of the great delights created by art and literature." Here was the principle laid down by the innovators, the "moderns." In the face of the formulated art of the classics, accidental art was exalted. "I will go still further. . . . The beautiful is always bizarre." Hence childhood was considered the great judge of art, since it tended to see "everything in a new light," to be "always intoxicated," a state "in which no aspect of life is *dulled*." Next came a reference to supreme art, which was that art which the success of oriental excavations had made known to people in the 1850s; there each detail had been seen in all its salience. Arising from this confusion of detail is a superior grace, guaranteeing through its angles and crudities that the memory of personal emotions would dominate the power of the real (there, in essence, was the magic: the being or object became possession or prize): "I want to speak about an inevitable barbarism, synthetic and childlike, which often remains perceptible in a perfect art (Mexican, Egyptian, Ninevite) and which arises from the need to see things on a grand scale, to consider them, above all, in their total effect."

For the first time the modern sense of the word "primitive," no longer that of Herder or Quinet, appears. It was, but in a different way, a question of the pre-Adamic. Revolutions in art are always questions of paradises lost. While Delacroix denounced "the abuse and excess of learning" as pernicious to creativity, for Baudelaire the youth of the earliest historical periods scoured the world clean of time-worn anthologies. With an obstinate coherence Baudelaire carried out maneuvers on behalf of a certain kind of poetry, a certain kind of music, a certain kind of painting: the notion of the authoritative was replaced by one of the original, perfection was replaced by character, and sentiment was replaced by will, above all, as in the world of the child, by the will to surprise and be surprised. Thus the primitive and the modern could, through their crudities, be made equivalent. Originality was no longer a miracle but archetypal trickery; the barbaric was the production of a sort of sacred comedian. All this was, with good reason, called Romanticism, the romantic result of a disproportionate history.

Nearly retrospective as it was, Baudelaire's work was a syllabus for *an era of the Archaic*. Today "archaism" is no longer a pejorative term except, at the most, among grammarians. This has not long been the case, but who can remember when it was not so? Throughout the final period of classicism the epithets "archaic," "Gothic," "oriental," and "barbarian" carried a synonymous pejorative sense of the indecent or the outrageous. Then here they were, completely accepted as a letter of recommendation. Until about the year 1800 one's position depended on being born after somebody or other; suddenly one's merits came from being born before someone or something. Until Romanticism origins remained an interdiction or a mockery: one whitewashed what we would scrape away, one buried what we would excavate. The gnarled was proscribed by the unctuous; one enjoyed the habitual, while we have come to applaud only the dis-ordered.

One would only archaize while winking at the onlookers, or while smiling at the old-fashioned. Thereafter it would be necessary to go from the archaic to the even more archaic. One paltry strike of the pickax carried us to layers of buried cities ever closer to the original darkness. Bad historical periods are like children whose mothers complain that although they do nothing they consume more than the other children. Decadent periods have a need for the ultra-ancient endlessly intensified by the consumption of the formerly new; only the ends of things are truly interested in the beginnings of things.

Outside of time, a realm of the archaic was established where through their ageless characteristics the Khmer is brother to the Byzantine, the Sumerian to the Roman, the icon to the fetish. The "primitive" acquired a spatial aspect as well: it was no longer a period but a type. A complete displacement of enthusiasm coincided with the raising of the blockade of Mediterranean culture: there was amazement, as we have seen, in response to the Aeginetan monuments just as there had been in response to the Hindu. A great many unknown dead, a great many cursed beauties, including the Parthenon, had to be rehabilitated before it could admitted that there were tribes on earth to be rediscovered, and uncatalogued riches.

Greco-Roman antiquity itself had waited underground for ten centuries. This bath of youth enabled it to return to dazzle four of our centuries through the prerogative accorded "grand centuries," although there were, in historical fact, only three of them. In actual fact this antiquity usurped its title: it was a "middle ground," a middle age par excellence. Furthermore, it had implanted a complacency for the well-rounded. In 1827, the year Langlois published his *Monuments littéraires de l'Inde*, Stendhal burst out laughing at Michelangelo. Moderns and ancients alike continued to assess the beautiful according to its conformity with Rome-Versailles standards. We know perfectly well that there are people who will never be *l'archaïque de personne*, aware of the archaic as it actually was. But before restoring its transcience to the first known antiquity, it was necessary, in order to perceive that the gulf of the past was as broad as that of the future, to measure the full disproportion.

CHAPTER EIGHTEEN

An External Orient: Exoticism

Local Color and the Orient of the Painters

BETWEEN 1824 and 1827, when Hugo was composing *Orientales*, the entire left-wing element of his audience was composed not of poets but of painters, young people expecting Hugo to deliver them from Greco-Latin formalism. And this was the service rendered by the second book of poems by an adolescent whom all considered a master. To listen to his verses, Hugo took his audience behind the gates of Montparnasse, a landscape upon which he superimposed his Orient. Thus it would, in large part, be an Orient done by painters in the suburbs to whom he gave subjects and settings. Probably there was interchange between his divination, which lost no opportunity, and the pressure of a clientèle waiting for a cause to devote themselves to.

It is a curious fact that the travels undertaken by painters turned out well only when they were brief. Distant explorations only gave them imagery; being chamber naturalists, painters did not export themselves. In 1832 Delacroix landed in Morocco with the Comte Mornay; like Delacroix, his colleagues Marilhat, Decamps, Fromentin, Chassériau, and Dehodencq limited their excursions, albeit with cries of admiration, to the Levant or North Africa. These were very short-range outings, except for Flandin's to explore Persepolis in 1840–41. Orientalism reprovisioned by coastal trading. Was there ever such a thing as an orientalist painter—wasn't it necessary to be either one or the other?

Blaze, not without reason, denied that the Orient of the *Orientales* had any reality, saying in so many words that it was the Orient of Decamps (or even that of Delacroix). There was an Orient common to the plastic arts and literature that was Mediterranean and almost lake-dwelling rather than maritime. The traditional voyage to the Orient followed the itinerary of Lamartine, Chateaubriand, Gautier, Nerval, Flaubert, and Renan, vacillating between the Holy Sepulcher and the pyramids. It would, until

Barrès, be a nostalgia for the Crusades, unless it resulted from an Egyptian or Algerian expedition like that undertaken by the old chevalier Jaubert, which in 1840 excited Maxime de Camp, who said: "to make up the *Orientales* without knowing the Orient is like making rabbit stew without the rabbit."

Since this meager, picturesque Orient was, unfortunately, more than adequate for an entire period of literary history, it should be at least mentioned. For some artists formal creation is so vital that it monopolizes all their activity. For them no doctrine is worthwhile that is not contained in their own art or inferred from it. As soon as someone asks what part the Orient played in nineteenth-century French literature, everyone names Gautier, Leconte de Lisle, and Flaubert—but that is a misunderstanding. The more superficial used the Orient primarily for costumes, the more profound as fancy dress for the soul. It is true that this was dazzling publicity. It is, by universal consent, in them that the Orient was embodied; they furnished a pocket-size edition, homeopathic doses, of the cumbersome and disquieting scholarship. But some confusion undoubtedly remains concerning what their genius gained from the Orient and what gain it created for the Orient.

Pagodas and Fakirs: Théophile Gautier and Gérard de Nerval

Art for art's sake again demanded an Orient appreciated less for itself than as a diversion. In his tales and novels, particularly *Avatar*, Théophile Gautier seems to have taken the oriental revelation to heart. His sorcerer declared, "I departed for India, hoping to find the answer to the riddle in this country of ancient wisdom. I learned Sanskrit and Pacrit [*sic*], the learned and vernacular idioms; I was able to converse with the pandits and brahmans." But we have already encountered this tone of voice in the antiquarian in *La peau de chagrin* who mistook Arabic for Sanskrit. Here the essential concerns come under two headings: local color and the German taste for the fantastic.

There had been only a smattering of a vague India in *Fortunio* in 1837. That novel ended with a letter written upon the protagonist's return to India, a letter that could have been a sequel to *Les lettres persanes*. On January 10, 1840, while working on the short story to be entitled "The Pavilion on the Water," Gautier wrote to the director of the *Musée des Familles*, "I have to read a few books to smear myself with some local color, and I need to poke my nose into a good many pots from Japan and elsewhere."

Gautier was doubtless accumulating information. For his article on Gérard's *Chariot* he seems to have read Wilson's volumes on Indic theater thoroughly. His tales made use of the notes that Chézy appended to his translation of *Shakuntala*. Gautier's integrity is not at question, any more than the pleasure one can receive from both his prose and poetry; what is at question are the images of the Orient that he formulates. The physician Cherbonneau, the magus in *Avatar*, is presented like "a character out of E. T. A. Hoffmann," for which he advances as his authorities Armin, Brentano, and Chamisso, whom he confuses with La Motte-Fouque. (It was likewise more than a slip in vocabulary in *The Mummy's Foot* to call the Egyptians "the hieroglyphic race.") In three or four pages on India there is, along with all the author's good faith in the magical elements of the Orient, a strikingly apparent gift for painting generalized pictures. The theme of the orientals' superiority in contemplation can be found there, along with his views on the initiatory tradition. But the author's failure in regard to the major question—that of the Different—is just as apparent. The inclination toward contemplation is again connected with world-weariness and called "a chronic impossibility to live." There is no more distinction made between Mount Meru and the Brocken than between yoga and spleen; over and over "sorcery" is attributed to encounters with brahmans and pandits.

In *La partie carrée* (1848), a sort of detective novel in which an escape by Napoleon and an anticipation of the submarine are outlined, Gautier's acceptance of an India of secret societies proved useful: it is the India of the Thugs, deliberately distorted here as "Sainte-Vehme." Nevertheless Gautier's opportune placement of remembered legends, writings, and rituals suggests an author with a rather broad range of knowledge at his disposal; he does not seem to have wasted his time in this area on items that did any more than enrich his poetic vocabulary with names evocative of gods and plants, or replenish it with singular scenery or episodes, such as the temple of Shiva or the rite of conjuration. It seems probable that Gautier, Méry, and Nerval carried on some sort of intermittent dialogue on an India that, although rather imaginary, was documented nonetheless. But aside from Wilson, *Shakuntala*, and the *Laws of Manu*, did the documenting look much further than fellow travelers and other novelists?

As a poet (and his poetic works are, in my opinion, his best), Gautier contributed greatly to the diffusion of the oriental *presence*, surrounding other poets with familiar images: he had a talent for returning to the world the joy in images he had such an outstanding talent for receiving. Even his composites or incongruous images, his Indian, his Persian, and especially his Chinese, entered into the composition of a philtre that would rise to the unconscious of the century, in the works of Mallarmé and his successors, and the works of Hugo himself. Gautier's daughter Judith in her turn would again convey this characteristic touch, whether in the

"Poèmes de la Libellule" in *Livre de jade*, translated with a Chinese house-boy, in *Iskender*, modeled on Firdausi, or in all that part of her work which would render the Orient of the novelists more veracious. A piece like "La Marguerite," which appeared in *Poésies diverses* in 1865, is entirely anec-dotal and limited to coloration, yet what a power of poetic transmission in its simple perfection!

> Les poètes chinois, épris des anciens rites,
> Ainsi que Li-Tai-Pé, quand il faisait des vers,
> Mettent sur leur pupitre un pot de marguerites
> Dans leurs disques montrant l'or de leurs cœurs ouverts . . .

> The Chinese poets, infatuated with ancient rites,
> Like Li Po when he wrote his verses,
> Placed on their desks a vase of daisies
> Whose centers showed the gold of their open hearts.

Elaborated and selected in this way, the China of the scholars, like that of Hervey Saint-Denys, was one in which such chimerical vegetation would proliferate.

> Imiter le Chinois au cœur limpide et fin
> De qui l'extase pure est de peindre la fin
> Sur ses tasses de neige à la lune ravie
> D'une bizarre fleur qui parfume sa vie . . .

> Imitate the Chinese with his heart limpid and fine
> Whose pure ecstasy is to paint on its sea of snow,
> By the light of the entranced moon, the end
> Of a strange flower that perfumes his life.

When one encounters a "Ghazel" in *Poésies nouvelles*, one is reminded of Nicolas Martin dedicating his 1860 study of Platen "to Théophile Gautier. When writing this, my dear poet, I remembered that you had once asked me to translate more of Platen." Thus, entering the competition, Gautier kept himself up to date on the adaptations of oriental poetry being made in Germany. Undoubtedly, ghazals and pantuns would, in the meticu-lousness of their formal requirements, be only too dear to the Parnas-sians; undoubtedly such preciosities, like the parodic lyricism of "Nostal-gies d'obélisques" (*Emaux et Camées*), are only too much the oriental curio and bagatelle; and yet didn't that in itself leave active deposits in the memories of creators, among whom we shall see Laforgue and Verlaine numbered?

This blend of oriental curiosities and German reminiscences was also an important component of Nerval's work. In his *Histoire du Romantisme*, Gautier wrote of Nerval, "The legends of the Orient could not have failed to exert a major influence upon his easily aroused imagination, one that the Sanskrit scholarship of the Schlegels, the *Divan* of Goethe, the ghazals of Rückert and Platen had, moreover, long since prepared for such poetic wizardries." This faithful abridgment of a bibliography may have been supplied by Nerval himself; in any event it confirms the contacts supposed above. Even more certain here is the contamination of occultism. As Balzac's mother had done for him, an uncle introduced Gérard, as a child, to a collection of esoteric books designed to set young minds spinning. Nerval said he never forgot them, and his reading in this domain is well documented. Afterwards he met, in the course of several trips, the poets, artists, and philosophers of Germany. He is credited with having astounded his contemporaries by citing Bhavabuti familiarly, along with Maimonides, and with having revealed the Hindu theater—which he had discovered, like so many others, through Wilson—to throngs of Parisians in 1850 with his *Chariot d'enfant*.

In 1841, in an autobiographical letter to Cavé that Richter cites,[1] Nerval availed himself of fifteen years of oriental studies, extracting from them some strange hypotheses on the history of races, in which one can recognize the deformation of linguistic theories originating in Germany. According to Gautier's review, *La Bohême galante* showed Nerval a young pupil of Friedrich Schlegel on the subject of popular poetry. Nerval's memoir goes back to the years when this subject was the life of Hugo's conversations with Eckstein. The original and the intuitive, after the manner of the times, coalesed in his mind: "religious inspiration" and "new poetry." And the fascination with the Orient was mingled with it, magnified by the new learning and renewed musings that had been in the air at the time. *La Bohême galante* was interlarded, following Herder's recipe, with medieval and Illyrian songs. *Les Illuminés* considered Indic and Celtic gods to be identical. Because he saw Prince Pückler-Muskau pass by in a coach in Vienna with an Abyssinian woman seated alongside the coachman, he "hit upon the idea of traveling through Africa and Asia," as he states in the dedication of *Souvenirs d'Allemagne*. Accompanied to the Orient by the Egyptologist Théodore de Fonfrède, he learned a great deal from the physician Perron, whom we have glimpsed in the Egyptian escapade of the Saint-Simonians. It was from Perron that Nerval adapted his theories, theories in which he perceived "the Indians, the Persians, and the Trojans" in the Merovingians. Nerval had studied and used d'Herbelot, Langlès, Garcin de Tassy, Quatremère, Regnaud and, for the Druses, Sacy. However, India, of which his friends considered him such a persuasive connoisseur, appeared only furtively in his works. The Orient that fertilized his imagination was, as for so many others, the Islamic one.

One also recognizes Friedrich Schlegel's teachings, along with those of Fabre d'Olivet, in "Isis" in *Les Filles du Feu:* "Orpheus and Moses, both initiated into the mysteries of Isis, preached sublime truths simply to diverse races—truths gradually altered later by differences of custom and language and the passage of time, and then entirely transformed. Today it seems that Catholicism itself has had, depending on the country, a response analogous to that which took place during the last years of polytheism." But after Hamann such discoveries were being hauled in from everywhere, wherever the German influence reached. They had been revived by the Görres-Creuzer circle, and even cropped up on Lamennais's very doorstep. To the extent that Nerval was an original dreamer, his learning retained something of the twice-told, the borrowed: "I shall certainly take precautions not to draw the same conclusions from these rapprochements that Volney and Dupuis did. On the contrary, in the eyes of a philosopher, if not a theologian, might it not seem that there has been within all intelligent creeds a certain share of the divine revelation? . . . A new evolution of dogmas might enable the religious accounts of diverse times to reach an accord on certain points." That is truly what it meant to discover Asia in those days! But he found an admirable formula to sum up, in symbolic language, the spirit of the beginning of the century in which he blossomed: "Material man yearned to receive from the hands of the beautiful Isis the bouquet of roses that was to regenerate him."

Flaubert

For Flaubert, as can be seen early on in the letters he wrote as a young man to Louise Colet, the Orient was a story one told oneself—but there are some stories that one lives. On March 18, 1839, at the age of eighteen, he wrote to Ernest Chevalier that *The Temptation of Saint Anthony* was already a "long-abandoned project," sketching a Satan carrying the hero "on winged horses to the banks of the Ganges." Could he have possibly been unaware of Quinet's *Ahasvérus,* published six years earlier, in which a similar image had appeared? When actually written, the scene was only vaguely localized: this vagueness of a decorative India would become, in the definitive work, only an indeterminate landscape of the spirit. Flaubert's vision especially needed settings of barbarians and distant antiquities to compensate, as in Baudelaire's work, for the *dullness* of everyday thought, and as in the work of Leconte de Lisle, to give a purified universal value to the modern world. Flaubert's barbarian was a compensation for a suffocating interior cage, the consequence of an inability to go outside himself. The need to link the barbarian with the oriental so that both words might benefit from the same prestige is significant. Historical and geographical localization was one of those concrete particulars he was eager for, since for him there was no escape until he first knew, unless he could name, see, and touch beforehand, the place he would land. Documentation was the footbridge over which he could escape.

In his first writings, such as "Novembre," the Orient was a child's rendezvous with itself: "I was, in the diversity of my being, like an immense Indian forest where life throbs in every atom . . . the mysterious and unformed gods were hidden in the hollows of caves amid huge piles of gold." "There are, then, no more of these divine youths of old upon the earth! Neither a Bacchus nor an Apollo!" "To take my departure, to leave, to leave so as never to return, to go anywhere so long as I quit my country!" "Oh, India, India above all! The blue mountains filled with pagodas and idols." In *Mémoires d'un fou* he writes, "I sought beauty in the infinite, but I find only doubt there." This statement seems an epitome, anticipating *The Temptation*. This notion of India is tantamount to Baudelaire's "leaving for the sake of leaving" and his "Anywhere out of the world."

With Quinet the autobiographical and symbolic Wandering Jew incarnated world-weariness. Flaubert picked up the dual significance, but almost completely the wrong way round; in using it he destroyed it. For Quinet the stations of faith remained the objective of peregrination; for Flaubert it was the advance of nihilism. The jostling of aborted beliefs seems to parody the historic philosophy of religions—a negative reversal, the final, completely exhausted appearance of the philosophy of history, which several generations had applied to religions and which all but served them as spirituality itself. Not even Renan would appear, like Flaubert, to have returned from all the soul's voyages beforehand; the horde of texts with which he gorged himself, even his own, were an opiate. Sainte-Beuve did him an injustice by supposing his reconstructions contained an element of jest, but they did contain an element of betting, a wager backing human forces against man: since the ironic shadows of Bouvard and Pecuchet lengthen behind Anthony, we have a hint, as much of unintentional farce as of truncated drama, beneath the festoons of *The Temptation*.

The design of such a book implies yielding all hope to a supreme idolatry—art. Not only is the survey of all beliefs sterilized by a preliminary despair, but a religion of beauty is made out in advance to be one of lifeless beauties. In the end art alone would be the object of conviction. To the full extent that the supremacy of genius crushes Quinet beneath comparison with it, Flaubert's own prodigious talent achieved the immobility of the evocation. The long period between 1839 and 1874, over which the successive drafts of *The Temptation* were spread, was the same period that had as its landmarks *Génie des religions* and *Bible de l'Humanité*, works whose material Flaubert adopted and whose tone he contradicted. The whirlwind of exhumed civilizations that had stirred up unprecedented ardor in Romantic youth resolves into a spiraling vertigo in the case of Anthony. The disenchantment of those who had turned from Christianity was projected onto the pagan past: this is what Vigny projected onto neighboring times in *Daphné* by taking Julian the Apostate as his hero. It is the piercing element in Flaubert's response to Sainte-Beuve concerning *Salammbô*, in which Flaubert exonerated Schahabarim by attacking "the good old boys of Port-Royal." This sort of general twilight of the gods seems to have been conceived, prior to Quinet and Flaubert, by Heine in *The North Sea* in 1825–26. The piece entitled "The Gods of Greece" is like a parody of the symbolism in vogue in Germany at the time, and which Heine knew well. I believe I can recognize in it not only the central theme of Banville's *Exilés*, but the Greco-Roman cloak-room of *The Temptation*.

However much Flaubert's scrupulous preparations may attest to his unlimited honesty, he inhabited all these countries and dogmas only evasively. Burnouf's masterpieces, Franck's *Etudes orientales*, Foucaux's *Lalita Vistara*, the works of Reinaud, Maury, and the older Görres were among his research materials, but his Gymnosophist, like "the Absolute of the Brahmans," remains a projected shadow, his Buddha a parade god. The richest element in this Orient was his melancholy.

The need for concrete images, for a visual quality, caused the Africa of his travels to hold sway in his work, the image of Africa that would be the backdrop for *Salammbô*. It was, again, the Levantine Orient of the painters. Here Flaubert's personal myth of the "barbarian" (which was not too far removed from that of the "boy") blossomed. The novel did a great deal to create, in bookstores, journalism, and conversation, a taste for a more or less agreed-on, or at least commonplace, Orient. Flaubert's prose introduced the same innovation as Leconte de Lisle's poetry: archaeological modernity. The archaeological novel is inconceivable before the period of rediscovered writings; neither the travesties of *Télémaque* nor the pedagogics of *Anacharsis* had succeeded in linking the visionary with the documentary, nor in disengaging fiction from moral compromises.

The Parnassians and the Symbolists

Leconte de Lisle's elephants and marbles sprang from Burnouf, Wilson, Langlois, and Fauche (as well as Lamairesse and Marlès) in the same way. Is it from these that his thoughts about gazelles and stucco sometimes come?

How pink and gray this India of bronze and basalt is! "It is the prome-
nade of a dilettante rather than the progress of an initiate. . . . For him
the idea bends under the weight of the image." He shows little more than
"the negative and most trite aspects of doctrine; he intoxicates himself
primarily with its forms and colors, and the nature that at times sends
him into an ecstatic trance is a collection of semblances, not the spiritual
power of the Brahman." When all is said and done, "faced with the treasures revealed by the new humanism, Leconte de Lisle did not experience
the thrill that, on reading the masterpieces of Greece and Rome, had
gripped his predecessors, the poets of the Renaissance. He made only a
rather circumspect use of these literary, and particularly philosophical,
riches."[2]

The most trenchant remark was made, as might be expected, by another poet: Jules Laforgue saw Leconte de Lisle flattened "beneath his over-
stuffed, glaring poems." It is no more a question of doubting an artist's
sincerity than it was of doubting Flaubert's verbal genius. We should remember that de Lisle did not study the India of the metaphysicians, and
that Western readers received from him a different India, one of art for
art's sake. The poet drew the ancient wisdom into his personal code of
aesthetic impassiveness. His Vedic fabric was a large one, a new beauty
in French, but both Leconte de Lisle and his drapery remain outside the
very subject that moved them. Leconte de Lisle the nihilist did not share
the same interests as Indian thinkers any more than Flaubert the nihilist
did. The attitude was adopted by all poets, provided they were French,
nineteenth-century, and Parnassian.

The striking thing about this poetry was that it knew it could not rediscover nature except through learning. Born in Réunion, Leconte de Lisle
took pleasure in saying, when he succeeded Hugo, that he had found the
Orient in *Les Orientales* that his native landscape had never taught him
about. From this a poetry of bookishness, of human old age, and of the
century of history overtly showed itself. Answering its call and following
its example, generations to come would find their surest sources in this
quarter. The Parnassian school made the philosophy of history tractable,
and Symbolism made it legal tender. Not only elements of faded orientalism but also elements of generalized philology could be found there.
Through writers like Heredia and Samain the results of resurrecting Iran,
India, Assyria, Scandinavia, and the Americas, which had created around
modern life a multifarious retinue of parallel lives, became ostentatious.

Leconte de Lisle always thought in terms of grandeur, and he sometimes attained it. Thus he was able to put vast images of the Hindu pantheon, on the whole acceptable, into our mental habits. He did not, in the
final analysis, distort them any more than most of the poets in other

countries who believed themselves capable of capitalizing on their course of Indic instruction. His influence was visible in the poems of a novice: in 1867 Verlaine's first work, *Poèmes saturniens*, opened with a Prologue which, after the manner of the master, used legendary India to provide a professional symbol of the French poets: "Along the Ganges," we see bowing down

> Les guerriers saints devant les Poètes sacrés

> The holy warriors before the sacred poets.

Bound together are

> Le Kchatrya serein au Chanteur calme,
> Valmiki l'excellent à l'excellent Rama

> The serene Kshatriya and the calm Singer,
> Valmiki the excellent to the excellent Rama.

These figures illustrate a lesson taken from another precursor, only recently dead, the Vigny of

> Un monde où l'action n'est pas la soeur du rêve.
> Aujourd'hui, l'Action et le Rêve ont brisé
> Le pacte primitif par les siècles usé

> A world where action is not sister to dream.
> Today action and dream have broken
> The primitive pact by reason worn away by the centuries.

Further on, the poem "Savitri" introduced a brief moral taken from the poet of *Montreurs:*

> Ainsi que Çavitrî faisons-nous impassibles

> Like Savitri, let us make ourselves impassive.

The commentators remind us that, according to Lepelletier, who was close to him, Verlaine reportedly spent his secondary school vacations "plunging into Hindu mythology," thus easing the hatred he had in those days for the Church and the Bible. It is unfortunate that an error in the epigraph of the poem was consistently reprinted (with variations); it seems to be a slack student who would write "Maharhabatta." After Leconte de Lisle and Vigny, Verlaine's pastiches made use of Baudelaire and Banville: from the one he took the "saturnien" of his title; from the other, the author of "Exilés," he borrowed the theme of his poem "Dieux":

> Du Coran, des Védas et du Deutéronome,
> De tous les dogmes, pleins de rage, tous les dieux
> Sont sortis en campagne: Alerte! et veillons mieux.

> From the Koran, the Vedas, Deuteronomy,
> From all the dogmas, all the gods, filled with rage,
> Have taken the field: To arms! let us keep a better watch.

Neither in the poetry of Mallarmé nor that of Rimbaud did the oriental allusions deviate from Parnassian practice: more contorted in the work of the former, more abrupt in the work of the latter, the distant backdrop was there, like a propitiation offered to the Chimera.

Mallarmé educated himself on India, well enough, at least, to adapt material from George W. Cox's *Myth of the Aryan Nations* and from the prefaces to several other of Cox's popularizations, which Mallarmé published as his own *Dieux antiques* (1880); he also extracted "Contes indiens" from an anthology by Mary Summer (wife of the Indic scholar Foucaux). To begin with, Jean Lahor (Dr. Cazalis), one of the westerners who had tried to live in India, had been his close friend from 1862 to 1896. Mallarmé wrote to him on June 18, 1888, after receiving his *Histoire de la littérature hindoue*, "I took your book with me to the country. . . . It is a textbook, and it is poetry at the same time; I understood it all the better for living in a different palace, or summer house, from you. What is wonderful to me is that your Orient arises completely from your soul, because that is your nature, and you have simply juxtaposed an exotic malady against your own thought, as a proof or illustration; but even your voice, and a certain rich monotony that veils your lyricism, elucidates this remoteness in ourselves—entrancing, sad, broad—that loses itself in the sacred river of annihilation. You appear to me there in each age with that. The intimate *thou* brings back many of the hours that we shared."

This passage seems essential to me because it provides the key to a complete poetic use of the Orient rather than because it gives an inkling of previous conversations in which Indian images were perhaps mentioned; here is the secret that impelled Gautier to seek *le mal du siècle* in yoga, as so many others had satisfied themselves with "an exotic malady," the secret by which the greatest, Lamartine and Michelet, took upon themselves, as a personal event, an India that arose entirely from the soul. "This remoteness in ourselves—entrancing, sad, broad—that loses itself in the sacred river of annihilation" is a beautiful phrase, one that conveys, with the occult crudity of music, the cynical usage that the thought of the pure poets reserved for the thought of an entire world. Another perfect condensation appeared in the 1876 preface to *Vathek:* I believe that no one managed better than Mallarmé, by light touches and immersions, to get at the literary metamorphosis created by the Oriental Renaissance: "A veil placed over political or moral abstractions, to make them more visible, like the muslin fabrics from India in the eighteenth century, when the *conte oriental* was prevalent. And now, according to scholarship, such a genre is raising up peopled cities from the authentic ashes of history, immortalized by the *Roman de la Momie* and *Salammbô.* Except in *The Temptation of Saint Anthony,* an ideal that mingles epochs and races in a lavish feast, like the final flash of the Orient, seek! In no-longer-fashionable books, from pages where nothing of whole synthesis remains but obliteration and anachronism, there brews a storm of fragrances that has not yet thundered."

In Rimbaud's work the difficulty is that mystery is very nearly casual. Gengoux, one of his biographers, believed that his occult science came exclusively from Eliphas Lévi. According to Rolland de Renéville, the keenest critics of "Lettre du voyant" call particular attention to a similarity of experience, the oblique transmission of a message at most, in Rimbaud's allusions to the oriental tradition. However, it seems to me farfetched to seek an echo of the *Bhagavad Gita* in his statement "Je est un autre." Rimbaud's "several other lives seem due to me" appears to have a much greater resemblance to Hugo's "He senses that he is reliving other lives."

Nothing better shows the artful nonchalance that treasured the useful vagueness of a particular mental landscape than a verse such as this: "Dans une magnifique demeure cernée par *l'Orient entier,* j'ai accompli mon immense oeuvre et passé mon illustre retraite" (In a magnificent dwelling encircled by *the entire Orient,* I completed my immense work and passed my illustrious retreat). I italicize *the entire Orient.* This time the echo is of Racine and his "Orient désert"—a sublime discovery and a pompous parody. With the ultra-selfconsciousness of the fire-stealer, Rimbaud, having written, "I returned to the Orient and to the first and eternal wisdom," took exception with himself: "It seems a dream of vulgar idleness." Ah, yes, again the Orient of Mallarmé's Romantic Chinese "Weary of the bitter repose that is the offense of my idleness." A magic region, and even more a magic word, the Orient was the unfailing "Open, Sesame" to the cavern of images: "O the vast avenues of that holy land, the terraces of the temple! Where the Brahman to explicate the Book of Proverbs for me? . . . I recall hours of silver and of sunlight near the rivers, the hand of my companion on my shoulder and, standing on the spice-scented plain, our caresses." Isn't the echo here of Thomas de Quincey's Malay-Hindu which the traveler Rimbaud brought back from London? It has always been demanded that exoticism serve as the mechanism of dreams. "Exiled here, I have had a stage on which to perform the dramatic masterworks of all literatures."

It is by no means insignificant that the violins of the masters sounded the tune of an Orient as "primitive homeland." The Renaissance produced one final fruit that the misconceptions of genius were to ripen: something that neither a Rückert nor an Emerson, studying India with other scruples, could derive would be provided by the falsifications of a Rimbaud (following on those of Gautier and Flaubert), which established a new creative atmosphere in the West, subsumed under the term "Orient" but, above all, poetry.

The final product of this acclimatization, or this diversion, was the Buddhism of Jules Laforgue. Francis de Miomandre has recalled that "the entire first part of [Laforgue's] lyric output" was "inspired by Buddhism," having been conceived under the influence of *Oiseaux s'envolent*, Elémir Bourges' most Buddhistic work. Indeed, his *Complaintes* was dedicated, as was Lahor's *Littérature hindoue*, to Paul Bourget, the other leader of the same group. At first the impression is that the taste for parody that we detected in Verlaine's poetry, if not in Rimbaud's, is becoming more marked. The poet declares himself "a good Buddhist in his shrine," cries out "O Robe of Maya, O Skirt of Mama," and speaks of "Holy Buddhist nannies" and "the good Buddha of exiles." But this cryptographic irony needs to be deciphered. We are guided, by the "thoughts and paradoxes" revealed in Laforgue's *Mélanges posthumes*, to an understanding that restores the clarity of the author's intentions which their fulfillment concealed. Here was a vital seriousness, completely akin to the pursuits of Rimbaud: "I have spent my night meditating in the air of Sinai." The book to write, said Laforgue, is the very one that neither Leconte de Lisle, who was too "bourgeois," nor Lahor, "too much of a dilettante," nor Madame Ackermann, who was "not artistic enough," wrote. These three names were not cited at random. Pantheists and pessimists haunted by India, these three poets stood surety for the theme of universal illusion that was to inspire *Le sanglot de la terre*. To remove our last doubts we have "The Sage of the New Humanity: A Pessimistic Catechism"—almost a title by Lahor; "Breviary of a Pessimist"; and "Two Proposed Solutions: Buddha and Venerable India—Schopenhauer and Hartmann." Shortly afterward one sees the pitch of seriousness to which melancholy was carried in pages where, following his invocations of—significantly—Michelet and Carlyle, the poet promises himself that, in order to interpret deceptive "universal reality," he will revive in his turn global history, so that he may "see all the pain of the planet" and "bleed for all mankind." The dilemma he faces is clear to him: "Nirvana or love."

Thus the Oriental Renaissance ended. Thus we can see the dream, even if it was at first to all appearances gratuitous, the poetry, even if it had come close to art for art's sake, being led, even though it was along the pathways of the picturesque, toward an impenetrable element dominated by India. After the detour of the Parnassians and the Symbolists, the Renaissance returned to the mystical "primitive" of the Romantics. The Orient of Rimbaud or Laforgue, a remedy for the dullness of daily life, an escape hatch, furnished a cure that was not much different from the one that Coleridge, De Quincey, and Wordsworth had imagined. At the same time, only Elémir Bourges drew this romantic escapism back to the solidity of metaphysical doctrine in the Buddhistic hymn that concludes *Oiseaux*. There, in 1893, and later in *La Nef* (1904–22), it was no longer a question of an arbitrary, oriental gateway of dreams; rather it was one of the many solutions and techniques that India proposed for the Pain of the World.

Part Six

DETOURS AND CONTINUATIONS

CHAPTER NINETEEN
The India of Schopenhauer

ON being introduced to the *Oupnek'hat* by Maier at the age of twenty-five, Schopenhauer immediately announced that no philosophy would be acceptable unless it was in agreement with Vedantic doctrine; throughout his life he celebrated the blessings that he ceaselessly derived from it. Two points are worth stressing: first, his faithfulness extended to the point of beginning to draft an Indic bibliography, although he accused Indic studies of concealing Asia beneath European dress; and second, in 1844 he supplemented his 1818 *World as Will and Idea* with a second volume that bristled with polemics. India became the bludgeon with which to slay all monsters, all traitors to philosophy, such as Hegel and above all an even worse enemy, if that were possible—the Semitic tradition.

The first period: it was to the Vedanta that Schopenhauer traced the origin of his own system, uniting "empirical realism" with "transcendental idealism." Central themes, such as the declaration of the will to live, a therapeutic measure against the Pain of the World, and the illusion of existence and personality, could have come from no other climate; for India individuation was no more than a specimen to which nature, interested only in the species, was indifferent. This notion is connected with Michelet's sense of history: "In all innocence, it declares the great truth to us in this way: ideas alone, not individuals, have a proper reality, for they alone are a genuine objective realization of the will."

The second phase: Schopenhauer's encounter with Buddhist doctrine would confirm and harden these principles. "You will arrive at Nirvana, where you will no longer find these four things: birth, old age, sickness, and death." Conclusion: "Never has myth come closer to the truth, nor will it." The propaganda of "the English clergy or the lies of the Moravian Brethern" on this point aroused Schopenhauer's indignation, and he was jubilant at the failure of their missions: "Our religions are not taking nor will they take root in India; the primitive wisdom of the human race will not allow itself to be diverted from its course by some escapade that occurred in Galilee."

In this way anti-occidentalism and anti-biblicalism grew stronger. Each time a Western thought excited him, this philosopher would undertake to demonstrate that it could have originated only in the land of "primitive wisdom" where his compatriots had already placed the original purity of those languages and races of which they had appointed themselves the universal heirs. No sooner were the "prodigious writings" of Meister Eckhart edited in 1857 than they were compared, along with those of Angelus Silesius, to the lessons of the Vedanta. The same was true for Giordano Bruno and Spinoza: "The true homeland of such geniuses is the sacred banks of the Ganges." And Raymond Lull was placed side by side with a Hindu doctor.

By the end of the forty-year period separating the two parts of *The World as Will and Idea*, Buddhism had been elucidated, and during the 1850s reverberated throughout Europe in revelations from Hodgson and Prinsep and in the works of Burnouf and Spence Hardy. It passed to the forefront of Schopenhauer's arguments, and it is largely due to his influence that these years were decisive in the spread of Buddhism. His strategy, distinguished from similar ones only by its forcefulness, aimed at dissociating the two testaments of the Bible in order to redeem Aryan purity, recognizable in the Christian tradition, from a Jewish monopoly. If the New Testament, but not the Old, acknowledged immortality, it was because New Testament Christianity "is Indian in spirit, and therefore more than probably also of Indian origin, although only indirectly, through Egypt. But to the Jewish stems upon which that Indian wisdom had to be grafted in the Holy Land, such a doctrine is as little suited as the freedom of the will to its determinism."[1] In his chapter "On the Doctrine of the Denial of the Will to Live," a sort of world society of mystics reunited Boehme and the Sufis, Plotinus, Eckhart, and Madame Guyon; the deep meaning of the Gospels was a lesson originating in India and excluding the Old Testament. It was the mistaken Clement of Alexandria who had misled us by preferring "Christian Judaism" to "Indian asceticism." In reality, "Judaism . . . is not related to Christianity as regards its spirit and ethical tendency, but Brahmanism and Buddhism are."[2]

To establish these theses, Schopenhauer proceeds to analyze Christian and Indo-Iranian origins: "Although Christianity, in essential respects, taught only what all Asia knew long before, and even better, yet for Europe it was a new and great revelation, in consequence of which the spiritual tendency of the European nations was therefore entirely transformed. For it disclosed to them the metaphysical significance of existence, and therefore taught them to look away from the narrow, paltry, ephemeral life of earth, and to regard it no longer as an end in itself, but as a condition of suffering, guilt, trial, conflict, and purification, out of which, by means of moral achievements, difficult renunciation, and denial of oneself, one may rise to a better existence, which is inconceivable by us."[3]

The dialogue "On Religion" in the 1851 *Parerga and Paralipomena,* which provoked a number of reactions, extended the attack on the Bible; after reading the Septuagint, Schopenhauer regretted that Nebuchadnezzar had been so gentle with the Jews. Of all their crimes, it is monotheism he indicts: "I must add, . . . to render homage to the truth, that the fanatic atrocities perpetrated in the name of religion are in reality attributable only to the adherents of monotheistic religions, that is to say, to Judaism and its two branches, Christianity and Islam. There is no question of anything resembling it among the Hindus and the Buddhists." Exonerating India's polytheism was no longer necessary. Voltaire had been a forerunner in this inverted trial: but what a sonority the denunciation acquired beneath the lofty vaults of the philosophy of religions buttressed by Indology! Thereafter the paradox became commonplace: now and then we will again hear of those unsociable people who shut themselves up in ghettos and those provocateurs who call themselves martyrs. For example, if "the Jews alone have been the object of religious persecutions, it is because they alone were monotheists." And "their intransigent monotheism" had begun "through preventing them from tolerating cults addressed to gods other than their own." The Bible is hardly in agreement with Schopenhauer concerning their intransigence; otherwise Moses would have seen Canaan. According to Pirenne, "The persecutions that were undertaken against the Christians during the first three centuries of our era were the expression of the same tragic conflict between the monotheists—necessarily intransigent in their faith—and the pantheists, who by the very fact of such intransigence regarded them only as enemies of the gods and of humanity."[4]

Other innovations from Schopenhauer's short religious tracts were included in *Parerga.* Indian civilization was reproached for giving an impression of being an amnesiac who has forgotten his own history. Schopenhauer, on the contrary, made an observation whose consequences would be worth exploring: "Christianity has the particular disadvantage of not being, like other religions, a pure *doctrine;* its essential characteristic is that it is a story . . . and it is this story which comprises the dogma one must believe in to be saved." Again one can readily sense the argument drawn from this against the happenstances of exportation, an argument that could have come only from a mind that had taken a stance against the Western soul and its needs, which were fulfilled by personal and historical divinity. Likewise charity toward animals and metempsychosis were preferable to the human limitations of Christian salvation, which was considered an aberration that perpetuated "the scene of installation into the garden of paradise."

These efforts intended to disrupt the unity of Western religion were presented under the title "The Old and New Testament." Judaism had absorbed the pessimistic Ahriman of the *Avesta* but had subordinated him to an Ormuzd transformed into an optimistic and realistic Jehovah, whereas Brahmanism and Buddhism were idealistic and pessimistic. "The New Testament, on the contrary, must have some sort of Hindu origin; its ethics, which translate morals into asceticism, its pessimism, and its *avatar* all attest to such an origin. All of which places it in decided opposition to the Old Testmment, so that the story of the fall of man is the only possible point of connection between the two." What with some sort of Hindu origin, a Christian avatar, and all the rest, why wait any longer to state that "Christian doctrine, born of Hindu wisdom, has completely covered the old trunk of a grosser Judaism completely uncongenial to it." Do we insist on proof? The demonstrator has a dauntless hypothesis: "The wheel of birth" is in the Epistle of James (3:6); Jesus, reared during the flight to Egypt by disciples from India, received his moral science from them and then adapted the concept of the avatar to Jewish theophanies. Critics who were also Indic scholars were invited to draw inspiration from such comparisons in order to finish demonstrating the Christian-Hindu "relationship."

The history of mankind is a complex and implacable meteorology. The concept of Indic primacy that seemed a godsend for Germany returned triumphant through the instrument of metaphysics, always very powerful in Germany, and, at that moment, throughout Europe. Schopenhauer's voice, which had fallen on deaf ears for forty years, suddenly aroused the world at a time when, furthermore, Germany's martial materialism coincided with Gobineau's encouraging fabrications.

In *Revue des Deux-Mondes*, July–August 1856, during the Congress of Paris, Saint-René Taillandier, a disciple of Quinet, presented a picture of political Germany as well as the first outline in French of Schopenhauer's system. In the eyes of this singular onlooker the most salient feature of Europe in the decade before Sadova was the eclipse of Prussian prestige. It was a bad mistake to banish Prussia, the victim of cruel distrust, from the concert of powers; but in Prussia the confusion between a lost, lamented mysticism and a debilitating materialism was growing stronger. The name of Schopenhauer made, tardily, a flashing mark in this interregnum of the spirit. Germany's new master thinker—and he was not alone—brought her some long-awaited recompense: the confiscation of the Orient and the fulfillment of her pantheistic destiny, while by other means her cravings for empire and drama were channeled into a tough military realism. Taillendier himself cited "this incomparable title" of the work of a certain J. Kruger: "The Primitive History of the Indo-Germanic Race: The Conquest of High Asia, Egypt, and Greece by the Indo-Germans." After which he waxed fatuous over the blessing it would be for the world when Germany was cured "forever of the enervating folly of mysticism" by a rediscovered taste for "the active life." Without lingering over Germany's favorite forms of "the active life," let us marvel over the number of chance occurrences that contrived to bring the dream of the Orient, cherished since Herder, to maturity.

If Young in 1813 had not crystallized the linguistic affinities envisaged as early as 1785 by Jones into the term "Indo-European," if in 1816 Bopp had not scientifically confirmed them, if in 1823 Klaproth had not confiscated the idea by substituting the label "Indo-Germanic," if a dogma of Aryan supremacy had not blossomed all the way down to Pictet, neither would Schopenhauer have demanded, on behalf of the pure ancestors, the place usurped by the Semite and the Christian, nor would the Oriental Renaissance have been able to end by installing the concept that most negated its own humanism—the inequality of races. Schopenhauer's impact is parallel to Gobineau's, whose celebrated essay *On the Inequality of Human Races* (1853–55) he considered a work of major importance, quoting passages from it, unaware he had long lived in the same city as the author.

The Inequality of Races

Born in 1816, Gobineau was educated in Switzerland, where he acquired a taste for oriental languages he subsequently continued to study thoroughly with his father. In 1844 he organized a group of young people as "The Cousins of Isis," a name reminiscent of Novalis and Nerval. The leading theme of his *Les religions et les philosophies dans l'Asie centrale* (1865) was the axiom that all European thought originated in Asia. This was an exact correspondence as well as a further systematic enlargement of what Schopenhauer was affirming in the ontological and theological realms. It was a grave turn for the new Renaissance.

Proceeding via Germany and Bismarck, Gobineau traveled to Persia in 1855 to verify the foundations of his doctrine. In 1854, in the dedication to the king of Hanover in his first edition (Gobineau was chargé d'affaires in Hanover in 1851 and in Frankfurt in 1854), he introduced the instruments of oriental studies into the arsenal of ethnic propaganda, openly paving the way for partisan exploitation of historical philosophy. For an entire page, among others, he musters both Assyria and "the Iran of Zoroaster" (on the authority of Burnouf), as well as Vedic India in a mobilization of trenchant conjectures and imperturbable horoscopes on the destinies and duties of Europe and civilization. The tendency becomes more marked as the book proceeds. And one has the impression that it does so through the perspective of a great historian, added to the pains of a great craftsman. Devoting three long and remarkable chapters, the first three of book 2, to Brahmanic and Buddhist India, Gobineau does not fail to expose the error of the alleged Indo-Germanic: "The languages of the white race are no more Hindu than Celtic, and I consider them much less Germanic than Greek. The sooner we forget such geographical appellations the better." And here he specifies that "long before they arrived in India, the Aryans ceased to have anything in common with the nations that were to become European," a fact that had eluded "scholars of the first rank." But the same postulate he rejects when it comes to languages, he turns into a dogma in the domain of races, an even more romantic one whose hypothesis had gained credence only because of the fabrications of linguists. He clung unswervingly to the term "Aryans." For him it meant the nobility of mankind, and he saw a cognate in the German word *Ehre*. It was, of course, a question of tall blonds. In the final book of *On the Inequality of Human Races*, entitled "The Capacity of the Native German Races," the Germanic Aryan is sacred, the race of the lords of the earth. And in the general conclusion Gobineau states, "The Germanic race has been furnished with all the energy of the Aryan variety. . . . After it the white species had nothing powerful and active to offer." It was the Germanic race that completed the discovery of the globe, "no nook" eluding them; it was the Germanic race that poured "the last drops of Aryan essence into the womb of diverse populations." Subsequently pure Aryans were no longer to be seen: the world had no further need of them! Hence everything that would be observed about contemporary nations would be rubbish, and doubtless incapable of demonstrating the gratuity of the hypothesis.

The position is strengthened by Gobineau's *Treatise on Cuneiform Writings* (1864), less known but perhaps more important than *On the Inequality of Human Races*. His *Philosophies and Religions* had already denounced the partition of the diverse forms of human dialectic created by the absolute reign of Greek logic. According to Paul Masson-Oursel, it was in opposition to this basis of consciousness that a deep European unconscious had given rise to Romanticism. "Whereas we pursue the ideal of clear ideas . . . the Orientals have never included in a priori essences standard models of correct thought. This was Gobineau's thought when, without expressing it so explicitly, he denounced the Asiatic mentality for 'the immoderate use of the inductive method.' . . . The opposition between under-standing and imagination does not exist, any more than the opposition between feeling and intellect. The fact is that thought always operates au-tonomously and creatively, except that it uncovers guidelines in the can-ons of action which we westerners pride ourselves on reaching in the per-fection of ideas. What Gobineau failed to grasp here was that the philosophies of the Orient spring from ritual practices, not from arbitrary myths, and not from an entirely dialectical agility."

This serious lacuna is also evident in Schopenhauer, where it allowed a good many affirmations of primacy as well as of origins to be advanced. At the extremity of the Gobineau line of ideas would be the reaction of a Vacher de Lapouge in 1898: "The role of Western nations must be re-garded as ended." We will hear the same thing, in one form or another, until Toynbee. It is not without significance that we can see the broad outline appearing of Gobineau's contacts with the three German innova-tors: Schopenhauer, Wagner, and Nietzsche.

The inequality of races! In this way, for the first time, one had suc-ceeded in splicing together the disparate threads of human knowledge, in reconstituting "the archives of the human race," only to deduce from them an antagonism alongside which the Persian Wars were merely pacifistic games. But such was the tragic denouement that German Romanticism could not do without. The inequality of races was a providential medica-tion to at last extract the bone stuck sideways in the German throat: the prestige restored to the France of kings by her revolution. The too-ob-vious shock that France created in the world destroyed the claim that Eu-rope had not received and could not receive any watchword, any su-preme principle, any organizing power, that did not originate with the Germanic invaders. Now, against the Declaration of Equality of the rights of all people, which had stirred nations everywhere and battered Prussia on all sides, they could oppose, and soon substitute, something that had philosophy and science on its side, something that had always tempted the heart of mankind in a much more natural way: the Declaration of In-equality. A declaration of the rights of those who proposed it. It was enough to make the Oriental Renaissance stand for the opposite of its content and its justification.

A curious apotheosis. By rewriting the history of the world for the ben-efit of the superior races, Germany mobilized the Orient and the Roman-tic movement against the fundamentals of revolutionary France, just as it had done against classical and absolutist France—and at the same time the great French thinkers for their part were enlisting the Orient and the Romantic movement in the cause of eternal revolution. Again it strikes us that two camps had begun to divide the world into something beyond mere nations; even in ethnology, even in oriental studies, in Romanticism, it would always be, no matter what happened, a dispute between the right and the left. Renaissances marched off to religious wars. Various countries sought alliances with defunct Asian empires in order to give success to their national specialities: in France it was the cause of the Revolution, with Michelet marking 1789 as the starting point of the reign of individual intuition, allowing history to become the conscience of humanity; with Quinet ascribing to India "a Declaration of the Rights of Being," confusing metaphysical liberty with political liberty; and with Hugo transfiguring the Revolution into an angel. In Germany, according to Bréhier, the cause of Germanic primacy, "the German people considered as an eternal essence," held the same position that the Revolution, considered an "eternal July," did in France. From then on the oriental was appreciated in relation to the German as the universal was in relation to the oriental.

Obstinate in exalting the race, ever avenging the ancestral humiliation it had suffered, Aryanism resembled a local deformation of "histoire-poésie": the collective life was summoned from the dream to govern there. This accounts for the somnambulistic aspects of the racist world: orders dictated in a trance, and which established the trance; victims waiting to see if they will wake from the nightmare; haggard leaders, doped or dumbfounded, who take furtive, flashing, nocturnal, mechanical steps; the very idea of the State as a machinelike something abounding in gears bound by new gears, its servants more and more like the Sorcerer's Apprentice. Here, in Hugo's phrase, was the encounter of consciousness-of-self and unconsciousness, "where India ultimately became Germany." Today no one needs to be reminded of the backlash of that idea, of the antimonies that were suddenly revived between the two states of mind of the Greek agora and the Mongol tent.

CHAPTER TWENTY
The Iran of Nietzsche

APART from the Spenglers and the Shuberts, art in Germany offered two other apotheoses of the German Oriental Renaissance—Wagnerism and Nietzscheanism, both of which bore, to a greater or lesser extent, the dual mark of Schopenhauer and Gobineau.

Because what they contained was more fluid than fixed, such novelties were bound to affect the most turbulent personalities. To oppose a Dionysian Asia to an Apollonian Hellenism amounted to backing certain ethnic priorities in a new manner. Attention was turned back to the Presocratics, because one now had presentiments of the Asia behind them. Brandishing a certain Orient against Judeo-Christianity amounted to indicting the latter for having stopped or diverted historical and spiritual currents; such a move would probably not have occurred if the old supremacies of Greek reason and the Mesopotamian Bible had not already been undermined.

What is there in *Thus Spake Zarathustra* that is Iranian? It is a debated question. Bianquis, speaking for one camp, says that the name, personality, and clime were adopted only on fortuitous evidence and superficial preferences, and that neither the historical figure of the prophet nor the true meaning of his teaching are involved. Others point out occurrences of authentic Mazdean themes. Even if Zoroaster had started as only an alias for Nietzsche the poet, Nietzsche the scholar may have been advising him in matters oriental. When a great creator is at the same time a sound philologist, perhaps less of the documented personage escapes his understanding than he might think; his pen allows more precision than his conscious mind presents to his will. Nietzsche hesitated for some time over the character and native land of the spokesman he would choose. Then he went back to the classical Iranian sources already brought together by Barnabé Brissot and Thomas Hyde, did some specialized reading in the library at Basel between 1875 and 1878, and familiarized himself with recent translations of the *Avesta*. Duchesne-Guillemin, who has gone back over this question, detects the flavor of *gathas* in Nietzsche's work.

The lesson of Nietzsche's book runs counter to Zoroastrian teaching by setting man against the world, by replacing the dogma of the final reconciliation of light and darkness, good and evil, with a dogma of a sovereign revolt, to begin in this world, against the ethics of compensation. Speaking more broadly, the principle of Nietzsche's new teaching, through derision of all kingdoms not of this earth, would annihilate all eschatology by sanctioning "the death of God." Wasn't this the sudden windfall for which the Germany of dreamers was waiting to enable it to join forces with the Germany of materialists? Brilliantly rejuvenated, the genre of the aphorism would thus be borrowed from Zoroaster only in order to underscore a liberation from his essential message: the promise of reward. The future victory of a luminous divinity was a lure to be replaced with the announcement of a dawn that was close at hand and completely human. Instead of being subdued by his desire for salvation from the order of the world, man was set against any previous or transcendent order. Furthermore, wasn't the Iranian locale chosen to indicate disapproval of the old counsel of humility that the captive Hebrews addressed to the Persian kings? For the first time, morals and sympathies for these two camps changed sides: the longing for Marathon, another fruit of oriental studies, was transferred to Mesopotamia. Set in opposition against an Israel that offered eternal life to the man who would make himself small in this life was the invention of an age in which man would be more than man, and of a here that no longer had a hereafter. Logically, the inventor had to conclude that the Judeo-Christians had led their heirs astray, not by betraying a Hindu origin but by rejecting a separate Aryan tradition encountered in the Persia of the Babylonian Captivity. (And the school of Gobineau accused the Jews of having strangled or perverted that tradition.) Above all it was the very root of this unquestioned dualism, whose most conspicuous image had been the Ormuzd-Ahriman dichotomy, that Nietzsche attacked. We are reminded by Leibrich that before his insanity in, Nietzsche had at times signed himself "Dionysos" and at others "Der Gekreuzigte" ("The Crucified One"), likewise extending these two aliases beyond good and evil. By turns he ceaselessly flattened the God of the sickly, the poor, and the failures beneath the serene strength of the Presocratics or expressed an "almost unreserved sympathy" for "the very person of Christ," a recluse announcing "a new way of life." He let no messianic figure slip past without appropriating it, and his Zarathustra was perhaps a means of not completely, nor suddenly, pronouncing the real name of Him whom he would presently believe himself to be.

Quinot, a specialist in Nietzsche studies, points out in *Pages mystiques de Nietzsche* the Iranian connections and fidelities in the detail of his images, such as the worship of fire and the highest light, such as symbolic animals and the battle of the celestial Eagle against the Ahrimanian reptile. "Furthermore, Nietzsche implicitly acknowledged a relationship in his works, especially those of the Zarathustrian cycle, which unites them with that Muslim literature permeated by Sufism, whose representative best known to him seems to have been Hafiz." The result is "a semi-pantheistic inclination to be lost in the sacred immanence of things" or a tendency "to be God or at least the Fool of God."

Indic thought entered these slippery confines: "On more than one occasion, Zarathustra, the poetry, and the posthumous fragments call to mind the religious lyric poetry of India. Dionysos recollects having been the Indian Bacchus. What his initiate says of him the devotees of Shiva have frequently said of their God: is he not the emerald God, the God who from one cosmic day to another becomes, dies, and is reborn, the God of the orgiastic, the Creator, the Guide, and the Destroyer, the God who dances and makes the worlds dance ceaselessly from their morning to their evening?" One of the "last scholarly works Nietzsche seriously studied" was the *System of Vedanta* by his friend Paul Deussen. "It is impossible not to be aware of its influence in Nietzsche's work after 1883, particularly as regards the deification of the creative philosopher and his identification with the supreme principle of universal life."[1] Nietzsche's friendship with Deussen both preceded and passed beyond the book, and revealed the Vedanta to him. Nietzsche's informant, one of the modern masters of German Indic studies, had Schopenhauer's weakness for points of similarity between Hindu metaphysics and certain European systems; perhaps this was the reason his correspondent drew away. In the exchange of letters between 1875 and 1888, Nietzsche seems to have wavered between contempt and sympathy for India, the latter marked during the composition of *Zarathustra*. Ultimately, however, it is a rather conventional and "median" image of Asia that seems to prevail. It is for us that the dance of Zarathustra recalls Shiva's dance.[2]

CHAPTER TWENTY-ONE

The Buddhism of Wagner

HAVING escaped Wagnerian idolatry, Nietzsche also tore himself away from the influence of Gobineau; he violently repudiated the racism of his brother-in-law Forster, and even dealt a hard blow to Wagner's antisemitism by claiming that the real manuscript of Wagner's autobiography, *My Life,* began with the confession "I am the son of Louis Geyer," later sacrificed to his wife's revisions. But it was Wagner himself who, at the end of his life, rushed more and more into Gobineau's arms: he had found there his least soothing idol, the aspect of joy-in-destruction of the Oriental Renaissance. It was Wagner who insisted on being the first Gobineau fanatic in Germany: he met the count as early as 1876, although the movement did not take hold in Germany until 1883. In 1881, one year before the death of the historian and the premiere of *Parsifal,* Wagner published his "Introduction" to the works of Gobineau. Fate had led him there along two paths: the execration of Meyerbeer and the revelation of Schopenhauer, the latter ushering in another, more significant exploration of Buddhist thought.

In India, as in the Germanic epic, Wagner sought the substance of his inspiration: here was a diet that nourished his personality and gave recourse against his dissatisfaction with contemporary art and the agitation caused by his presentiments of other forms. But for Wagner too, and especially for him, it was above all a choice against the Latin tradition. Wagner's point of departure by 1850 was to destroy routine Italian-French opera. Later, when he was on the point of creating, in all its fullness, the art of the future, and by then aware that this could be done only by linking it with Germanic epic, Wagner suspended all other work in order to unburden himself, in *Opera and Drama,* of his need for systematization.

This central passage from Wagner's writings is in the pure Schlegel tradition: Wagner deplored the fact that the language of opera was still based "according to the conventions, at once religious, historical, and political," established by French logic "at the order of the Académie and under the tyranny of the conventions embodied by Louis XIV." Against this he set the national arguments of *Naturpoesie* and the laws, which were scarcely less national, of inner meaning. Moreover, it had previously been demonstrated that European theater had, as a whole, until then, been misled by "Roman Catholicism." Since Shakespeare himself produced only "hybrids," the conditions for true liberation could be found only in a return to the unalterable source of purity—Germanic paganism. Thus "the national *Saga* of modern European peoples, especially the *Germans,*" would better revive the competition against "Christian myth" than warmed-over Greek mythology had done. This program calls to mind a good many known elements: once again   their finest hour—the Nibelungen were to defend from the usurpers the legitimacy of a true Europe, which was Germanic, which is to say the flower of ancient Asia, who had transmitted supreme art, inaccessible to the Latins, and virile faith, forbidden to the Christians. Hence Wagner the poet and musician was the fulfillment, at last complete, the most lasting result of German Romanticism. He was so through his choice of subjects and atmosphere, through his basic objective, and most of all through a pantheist mysticism, even before he implemented his methods in his work. It was predestination that would finally be confirmed by his formal, enthusiastic adherence to the Orient of the new Renaissance.

The chronology of Wagner's intellectual adventures demonstrates the importance of his encounter with India. After 1844 he had studied the myth of Siegfried like a madman. In 1848 he wrote *Siegfried's Death*, together with a narrative in prose entitled *The Myth of the Nibelungens, or Project for a Drama*, in which he condensed the whole cycle of legends. He drew *The Young Siegfried* from the prose outline in 1851, the year following *Opera and Drama*, and drew *The Valkyrie* and *Rhinegold* from it in 1852. Around Christmas, 1852, he read the completed *Ring of the Nibelungens* to his friends: fifty copies of the text were printed in 1853 but were not circulated until 1863, and it would be still longer before he composed the score for it. As Wagner recounts in *My Life*,[1] it was while working on the orchestration of *Die Walküre* in 1855 that the event occurred which could not fail to fulfill his destiny: "Burnouf's Introduction to the *History of Indian Buddhism* interested me most among my books, and I found material in it for a dramatic poem, which has stayed in my mind ever since, though only vaguely sketched. I may still perhaps work it out. I gave it the title *Die Sieger (The Victor)*." (The rough draft was included in Wagner's collected works.) Wagner outlined its subject hurriedly and added, "For to the mind of Buddha the past life (in a former incarnation) of every being who appears before him stands revealed as plainly as the present."

There are abundant indications of the extent to which this new world was linked with Wagner's life and thought, notably—a significant placement—in his letters to Mathilde Wesendonk, the grand passion who would nourish the metaphysics of love in *Tristan* and *Parsifal* and who was correspondingly exalted by the major themes of these works. This entire progression was likewise synchronized with Wagner's readings and meditations in which Buddhism, a discovery for which he chose Mathilde as his confidante, was singularly important.

His October 1, 1858 entry in his diary which he kept for Mathilde during his stay in Venice includes thoughts on the sufferings of animals, "with death alone for liberation; a liberation which goes to prove that it would have been better had they never arrived at existence at all. Wherefore if there be any purpose at all in this suffering, it can only be the awakening of pity in Man; who thereby takes the animal's failed existence up into himself, and becomes redeemer of the world inasmuch as he recognizes the error of existence in general." It was an entry filled with Buddhist charity for animals, for which Wagner himself indicated the next outlet: "The meaning will become clear to thee some day from the third act of Parzival, Good Friday morning." In this way the pantheistic underpinnings of his ideas on redemption are revealed. The same week, on October 5, Buddhist thought filled six pages of the diary he was keeping for Mathilde. Wagner had just received a small Chinese Buddha whose image he found as inadequate as the one in Köppen's *History of the Buddhist Religion*, a work he had read with considerably less enthusiasm than Taine would. The point is that he was defending his pure, profound concept of Shakyamuni against the commentators. At the end of another two or three years he revised *The Victor* extensively: "The most difficult thing," he later stated, "was to lend a dramatic, indeed even musical form to that human being delivered from all his desires, the Buddha himself."

Yet this figure of nonbeing corresponded with a fundamental part of Wagner's nature. Buddha, Mathilde, and the Grail gave him, slightly intermingled with negation of his impurity, release from his acridity, from all the inner gnawings that he was always turning against the exterior world—a charity toward sheep balancing a carnivorous destiny. Since this atonement was unable to spring to life under the names Buddha, Ananda, or Savitri, with which the entry was strewn, Wagner cursed art and his genius: "Were this strange gift not within me, this strong predominance of plastic phantasy, clear insight might make me obey my heart's dictate, and—turn into a saint; and as saint I durst bid thee, Come, quit all that holds thee, burst the bonds of nature: at that price do I point out to thee the open road to healing." To be sure, he could not hope that the two of them would become Ananda and Savitri. Yet India, to the extent it could enter the life of a great artist of himself, had penetrated his innermost fiber. In the end, *Tristan and Isolde*, followed by *Parsifal*, would be charged with being what neither *The Victor* nor Richard and Mathilde could be. The part of the man that needed purgation, non-turmoil, antivulcanism was eased there—in *Tristan* and in *Parsifal*, as in a two-act play, the drama of the will-not-to-live was performed. This Buddhism of withdrawal from the world wavered in the back of his consciousness. "Everything is strange to me, and I often cast a nostalgic glance toward the country of Nirvana. *But for me Nirvana again becomes, very quickly, Tristan."* The confession deserves to be italicized as the consciousness of one condemned to create. It was also the consciousness of a living being. Concerning a major decision in his career, Wagner unaffectedly wrote (May 2, 1860), "Well, my mind has grown clear as to the choice which now faces me, but not yet as to how I ought to choose—nor will that choice, apparently depend at all on me; but *It* will choose, *the Brahm,* the neuter." A pleasantry? Men who live to communicate are not masters of those pleasantries in which one discerns an alien notion naturalized in their code of expression.

From 1852 to 1858 Wagner's amorous liaison followed an ascending curve to a brutal separation: around 1854 Schopenhauer, whom the poet Herwegh revealed to Wagner, became his great comfort at a time he was wearying of any friendship, the one who transformed suffering into understanding, who revealed him to himself, and who unveiled the world to him. Shortly thereafter India was introduced to Wagner and came to alternate with the cult of Schopenhauer. The composer would ask each source how to resolve the problems of unhappy or impossible love, and then he would inscribe in his work the alternations, acquired as much from life as from books, of his experience. It is not a question of reducing Wagner to a dialogue between India and Schopenhauer; but one of the major keys to Wagner's work is to know that it voiced the answers and conclusions of that dialogue, and that the questions came to a significant extent from a shattered love affair. Day after day *Parsifal* made a breach between *The Victor* and *Tristan:* Parsifal first appeared in 1854 as a possible figure in the Tristan opera, but was removed from it in 1857. The poem *Parsifal* was completed in 1877, orchestrated in 1880, and given its first performance in 1882, at Bayreuth. Hence its growth took place in the period when Wagner's correspondence with Mathilde was at its most Buddhistic, and it accompanied his full maturity. Let us come to the precise point where Hinduism impregnated this indissoluble mass of works, thoughts, and life.

The entry of October 1858 had not lied: in it Mathilde had been implored to await the Good Friday scene in order to understand it better. But—a typical, unimpeachable piece of evidence—has it ever been observed that the episode in the drama that marks Parsifal's first appearance draws on two Hindu sources simultaneously—one pertaining to the life of the author, the other to the *Ramayana?* The hero, guileless and pure, is preceded, when he first appears to the Knights of the Grail, who are appalled by his cruel deed, by the fall of the swan that he has shot with his arrow: by killing the sacred bird he has transgressed the rule protecting animals, and this is why, tarnished by this profanation, the fool later fails at first to cure the king Amfortas of the evil spell that holds him. This evokes a magical principle that goes back to the beginning of time (compare the legend of Orpheus, the marriage of pure love with resurrection and pantheism), a principle frequently employed in oriental literature (see Hugo's "Sultan Murad"), consonant, above all, with a thousand Buddhist fables, but already, and nothing less than, the very principle of Brahmanic *samsara*. Why did Wagner declare that Parsifal would make his Indianesque religion concerning animals understandable? The answer is given clearly at the beginning of the entry—and this is the *personal source* of the episode presented in the theater:

The other day, in the street, my eye chanced to light on a poulterer's stall; unconsciously I was looking at the heaped-up wares, all neatly and appetisingly dressed, when, as a man at one side was busy plucking a fowl, another thrust his hand into a cage, dragged out a live hen, and tore off its head. The bird's horrible shriek, its pitiful clucking while being overcome, sent a shudder through my soul.— Often as I had experienced the impression before, I haven't got rid of it since.—It is ghastly, the bottomless abyss of inhumanest misery on which our existence, for the most part bent on pleasure, is really poised!

When one notes in the next portion of the entry the full and serious reflections that this incident produced, when one perceives the rigid obsession that brought back to Wagner all his past associations with Buddhism, one can appreciate the value of the impression he hadn't "got rid of since." The chance incident in the street was the small decisive shock, immediately after which Parsifal was consigned the task of rendering butchery detestable.

Here the *exterior source* came into play: Wagner found in the *Ramayana* the symbolic episode that the hero Parsifal would be made to reenact: Wagner's drama would begin with an imitation of the famous scene to which India assigns the invention of epic verse. In the second song of the first book of the *Ramayana* two curlews, "a pair delightful to the eye," come and go under the gaze of Valmiki himself, the author of the poem. An unseen hunter, as Parsifal would be to Wagner's audience, shoots the male of the pair with his arrow; a curse against the hunter, set to the rhythm of the female's wailing, rises spontaneously to the Brahman's lips. Astounded by the sound of the distich that has occurred to him, he makes a note of its movement and declares it a "shloka" (a play on the word "shoka," which means grief), which will, thereafter, be the noble verse of great poetry.

Wagner substitutes Gurnemanz for Valmiki as the murderer's accuser; he takes into account the pain of the female swan toward which, he indicates, the slain male was flying. These are traces of direct borrowing. Also common to the two texts is the idea of an inexpiable sin: all the symbolism of blood, of which the whole first act of Wagner's drama is entirely composed, issues from Parsifal's criminal deed. Because he has spread the offending crimson over the white plumage, the young hero fails, at his first attempt, to stem the flow of blood which, as it begins to seep again from the royal wound, enshadows the theater in a final crimson. A symbolism symmetrical with that of gold in Wagner's work, and one with a similar universal value, is concerned with animal sacrifice and the chase, which render all men's violations of the law of love tangible: the hero will be cleansed of his sin, and be made fit to staunch the flow of royal blood that issues from the pain of the world, only when he becomes initiated into the mystery of cosmic charity on Good Friday. What could be truer to the Indic lesson? How can Wagner's underlying intention be understood unless one is familiar with its Indic origin? It is the third panel of a triptych: the other two are the law of renunciation of materialism or gold, shown in the *Ring* cycle, and the transgression of individual love by death in the carnal world, shown in *Tristan*.

The mystery of Good Friday, and the dialogue between Parsifal and Kundry, turns on this essential choice, either the adoption of a single being or species, and consequently the negation of the others, or a knowledge of the world obtained through participation in all the pain, all the legitimacy, of created beings. The young man has difficulty in finding the way of universal love; so long as he remains blinded by carnal, individual love, he lays himself open to the sorceries of Klingsor. The conflict is not resolved until, by a dramatic turn of events, having seized the lance the magician hurled at him, Parsifal traces with it the sign of the redeeming cross. Could one show more clearly the necessity to rise, by means of the soul's force, from profane to mystical love? Replacing the symbol of the wheel with that of the cross seems, in comformity with the Germanic taste that Schopenhauer had recently best sated, to voice once more the original link between them. The Good Friday scene may have been an attempt to extend the evengelical good news even unto animals and plants. The peripeteia of the Hindu poem is here translated into Christian terms: in the former Brahma himself descended to Valmiki to ratify the purification his invention of the shloka achieved for the murder of the curlew. In *Parsifal* the link between the events is underscored by Gurnemanz, representing the unconscious, which will be the healing agent: "Do you see who it is? It is he who killed the swan." Redeemed by the grace of the Cross, the perpetrator of the Offense becomes the one predestined to save the sick man; the ransom for the blood spilled on the swan is the blood stopped in the wound.

This apotheosis of the genius of the Oriental Renaissance through the genius of Wagner was no accident. All of Germany's turmoil drove the temptation of a salutary Orient inevitably into his hands. In his youth Wagner had already thought of escaping from Bordeaux to Asia in order to end his affair with Jessie Laussot, which preceded that with Mathilde Wesendonk. The first time Judith Gautier—the sister of *Avatar* and *Fortunio*—went to see her idol at Tribschen in 1869 she heard Cosima reading him the story of Nala and Damayanti, translating it into German (probably, that is to say, from Bopp's then-famous *Nalus*). Around the same time, Gautier says elsewhere, Wagner was linked with Munich through Count Friedrich von Schack, a rich collector and polyglot who had learned Arabic, Persian, and Sanskrit, and who had translated Firdausi. Wagner was planning to extract a drama from the *Shah Namah,* as well as from *Stimmen von Ganges (Voices of the Ganges),* one of Schack's anthologies. In 1876 Judith Gautier sent Wagner copies of the *Bhagavad Gita,* the *Bhagavata Purana,* and the *Mahabharata* (he must already have been familiar with the *Ramayana*); but when she later visited him and asked him how far he had progressed with *The Victor,* he replied that he had settled instead on *Parsifal.* Thus it could not have been long since he had made up his mind, and the prevailing atmosphere within which he reached his decision is quite clear.

Had he, for that matter, ever abandoned his Hindu reveries? A strange piece by Judith Gautier implies that even in the name given to his chosen home he was admitting a revealing symbolism. Describing *Wahnfried,* she explained this mysterious word, based on the probable confidences of its proprietor, as translating "illusion of peace," a recollection of *maya.*

The legends of the North, the fog-bound mythologies, were moving and grandiose; yet that was not all, for the Orient still remained to be won over: Persia, India, the splendors of the *Ramayana,* the gentle words of the meditative Buddha. But how would such luminous creations be understood through the veil of mist that the gloomy Norns had woven over our cold lands? One would have to see the sun, the true sun, which scatters heat and light lavishly, which gives birth to splendid blossomings and great forests. Well? India is not so far away after all!

Wahnfried! this word, which at first seemed to me to contain a sense of sorrow, perhaps on the contrary embodies a sense of hope.[2]

Germany's "New Adventure"

"What aspect of Indianism was accessible to the great Germans from Goethe to Nietzsche?" Masson-Oursel wonders in *Recherches philosophiques*, having inferred from an affinity between the languages "a fundamental relationship between the metaphysical attitudes of India and those of Romantic Germany." It is a question of two "independent traditions," both of which "were, among all mankind, perhaps where metaphysics has grown its broadest foliage." It was certainly on Bopp's linguistic foundation that the ediface of a Romantic Germano-Asianism was confidently erected. How much stability did it have? Goethe frolicked on the poetic surface of oriental thought; Schopenhauer failed to recognize the true esotericism of the Upanishads; Nietzsche's only contact with them was through Deussen, someone else who did not perceive their profound originality, improperly reconciling India with Plato. Not even Hermann Oldenberg could undeceive Nietzsche, who ultimately rejected Asia as the homeland of his own bugaboos: pessimism, asceticism, sterile negation. Wagner made Buddhism an appendage to a mystery cycle of the Christian Middle Ages.

Friedrich Schlegel voiced a broadly German truth when he wrote to Goethe that he was turning toward Asia in search of "a new adventure." The Lutheran Reformation was comparable to Hindu schisms insofar as it thrust religious activities in the direction of philosophical activities and did not cut off the individual quest for salvation from orthodoxy. This spiritual reformation sought its roots in metaphysics and its outlet in action: there was no more difference in this West between "to believe" and "to know" than there was in the Orient—where neither "have any reward except by doing." This is the way in which the notion of becoming was postulated. The difference between the continents is that Goethe's said "Become what you are" and Nachiketas' said "Be what you become."

Masson-Oursel, a lucid historian, shows that the supposed staticism of Asia is in fact an endless movement in which the individual dissolves: the beat of events is transmuted into the rhythm of a collective spirit and thus tends toward symbol. History has its reality less in dated and localized facts than in legendary emanations and strives for a magical efficacy. Moreover, knowledge, the estate of human masses spread over the illusory course of time sanctions a perpetual scholasticism. All these factors worked to eliminate any sense of cultural displacement from Germanic Romanticism. The two interlocutors even came to an agreement on the paradox of "representative men," who in the Occident contradicted the basis of the Homeric hero and who in the Orient contradicted the denunciation of all egotism. Sylvain Lévi has stressed the importance of "great men in the history of India," and Masson-Oursel has reminded us that they were restored to her through "a sustained labor" on the part of scholarly Europe. Reconciling the worship of saints or heroes with the affirmation that "thou" is merely a mask of the "self" may pose a problem for Greek logic without posing one for oriental dialectics.

The paradox is resolved by the fundamental unity that the principle of action provides: ascetic heroism frees the individual from his personal limitations and at the same time liberates him from inherent evil. Might not one thereafter see in the homage rendered to a succession of perfected individuals the consecration of states or stages acquired for the benefit of humanity-as-individuals, or even nature-as-entity? It is true that European Romanticism was inclined, like Michelet, to make this acquisition the lot of an abstraction, Social Progress, or, like Nietzsche, the privilege of a future zoological phylum, the Superman. It was another matter to make it, as India did, the attribute of a Being with neither qualities nor resolve. But it presented Masson-Oursel with an opportunity to say that "The most Romantic *Weltanschauung* was not that of German Romanticism but that of the followers of Mahavira or Buddha," for the latter condemns reason itself along with the natural universe. Similarly, both curse intellectualism: Germany replaces it with intuition and inspiration; India uses it only as a tool "to dissociate the web of existence," after which the work of truth begins. Two currents merged during the reaction to the Aufklärung: the first, running "through Leibniz and Eckhart, comes from pseudo-Dionysius and the Alexandrians"; the second, "attached to an ascetic tradition reflecting a tendency that might have been Neoplatonic, likewise postulates illumination; both draw heavily from the solar religions of Iran." Thus the acclamations of the generations revived by Boehme when they arrived in the presence of their relatives rediscovered by Jones and Colebrooke were rendered intelligible.

The agitation, striking in Latin eyes, of this *furor teutonicus* that burst forth in the works of Fichte, Schopenhauer, and Feuerbach, in Wagner and Nietzsche, was merely the reverse of the intellectual principle of action, a new manifestation of a kind of alchemical vocation that needs, at all times, to be changing the world: the yogi transforms it through inner action, while the Superman carries internal action to its extreme external limit. Even in the mission that the Germans willingly assigned themselves, that of disruptive thought and action, the essential principle remained clear: Being has no point of rest. Yet there remained a rather broad difference between Asia, the supposed original, and Germany, its supposed descendant: the space reclaimed by glorifying the barbarians (in the historical sense of the term). That unforgotten transition comes to mind when we apply Masson-Oursel's operative formula "The static is merely an abstraction of the dynamic." (We know what a fertile play on words on Aristotle and his "virtual" Masson-Oursel exploited in his notion of dynamism.) In ancient India as well, no knowledge had any value except insofar as it reinvented the world:

What rapture Hebbel, Hölderlin, and Novalis would have experienced if they had known the creative frenzy of the Yogacaras who discovered supraintelligible worlds, or simply the Vaishnava lyric poetry of Bengal, which resolved all enigmas, which fulfilled any duty with sighs of love! And Nietzsche, who ventured this profession of faith: "I would only believe in a God who knew how to dance," why was he not present at the dance of Shiva! [Would it not be more appropriate to ask: why did he not want to be present?]

The subordination of being to action was the basis of the two "mentalities." . . . In nostalgia or hope, Germany aspired; in joy or despair, India worked on. The obsession with "going beyond," regressive on this side, progressive on the other, demonstrated that no state, no existence could satisfy them. Rebelling against the finite, repulsed by the infinite they considered closed, both consecrated themselves to the indefinite.

These are strong and revealing views. Yet has reality always placed in ideas that which philosophy considers to lie beneath words? One can easily understand how the transient nature of appearances, proclaimed by the final chorus of *Faust*, could be invoked or implied even in Germany's political theories. But didn't this deep Romanticism remain theoretical and contradictory there? It is a bizarre achievement if, having produced in India the passivity of the yogi and universal love, it then sanctioned in Germany the will to power and ethnic hatred and caused Hartmann's collective suicide to coincide with Feuerbach's aggressive materialism. The principle of acting upon the world might be common to these two climates, India and Germany, but the tools and objectives are glaringly different. And among the metaphysicians themselves, wasn't Schopenhauer's polemical use of Buddhism a betrayal of that spiritual homeland where all beliefs and differences merged?

Concerning this principle, Masson-Oursel, who confines himself to principle, removes an uncertainty: an entire German school, instead of denouncing the West's old contract with Greek wisdom, undertook to renovate it by wrapping the defined in the limitless. Here Nietzsche's legerdemain becomes clear: he forced the Presocratic to become the Dionysian. But this provocation (or trompe-l'oeil) had no result, since the true path for true Germanism was "to surpass logic to the same extent that it denied chaos."

For its part Indic thought, whose viewpoint is, so we are told, the only one in all human thought analogous to that of the German school, does not lead to definition but rather to efficacy, not to textbooks but to rituals.

It does not enjoin classroom lessons but rather an *interminable* activity. It does not calculate measurable quantities, it does not pursue a geometry of the spirit, but merely uses all categories as footbridges and stepping stones which it destroys behind itself. It still remains to ask ourselves whether, by use of the term "activities," we are actually speaking of the same results that the power of the spirit attains. In India the result is the transmutation of temporal values into a world beyond; here it is a simple, all too human aggrandizement of the human empire.

"The magic of Novalis," according to Masson-Oursel,

is evidence of designs more analogous to those of the Brahmans and to Tantra than to any Western theory or technique; between the third and the seventh centuries, the powerful Buddhist idealism of Maitreya, Asanga, and Dijnaga accomplished in advance the imposing tasks assigned by Fichte and Schelling and undertaken by those titans Wagner and Nietzsche. . . . It was enough to have life at their command, but having laid this foundation, they sought to build a spiritual life upon it. Perhaps they conceived this ambition precisely because they did not consider themselves, as the ancients and the moderns did in accordance with classicism or Christianity, endowed by nature with an immaterial soul. When one believes oneself to possess that transcendent value, one is less inclined to promote it than if one only dreams of acquiring it. Development can be cultivated; being cannot. Wherever it has been rife, spiritualistic ontology has sterilized religion and philosophy. But the quest for the Holy Grail and the attainment of Nirvana have demanded an immense effort to realize the spirit.

We have had occasion to remark that in the European history of Becoming, the absence of preoccupation with the immaterial at the point of departure does not necessarily guarantee its presence at the point of arrival. A certain Titanism ended in a single grandiosity, that of assassination. There remain, in the realm of transcendence, a good many encounters. The Hegel who began his own work amid the intoxications of the Orient during the last years of the eighteenth century, as his colleagues Schelling, Fichte, and Schlegel also did, ended in 1830 by allotting the lion's share to the historical Orient. But didn't he, on the other hand, put forward the Western intellectual system closest to Vedanta, one most parallel to it in denying the principle of contradiction?

CHAPTER TWENTY-TWO
Russian Orientalism and Nonviolence

Tolstoy was the only force in the world powerful enough to overcome
the influence of Greece.

—T. E. Lawrence
(Letter to his mother)

WHETHER owing to location or blood, to historical or structural traits, proximity to the Asiatic temperament was more evident in the Slavic than in the Germanic nature; it was not nourished by the same exchanges, did not vibrate at the same depth, and by no means culminated in comparable practices—its yield of moral applications contained something both more natural and more accurate. A peculiar affinity between the Russian soul and the Hindu has frequently been underscored. M. I. Markovitch pointed this out, supporting his own findings with a few memorable authorities: Burnouf translating "Nirvana" as "Nihilism," Vogüé and Gorky rediscovering passivity and contempt for logic in each climate, Berdyaev making an inclination for the universal a characteristic of his nation. These marks, especially a preference for the spiritual rather than the active world and a penchant for humility balanced by "the legitimate pride of a soul in dialogue with its Creator," also fit the figure of Tolstoy at his most photogenic.

We have glimpsed the precocity, or predestination, with which Russia prepared for linguistics at the end of the eighteenth century. Looking naturally to Asian languages, she was at first particularly interested in those that served commercial or political interests. The fire of curiosity that the Calcutta Society sparked touched her at an early date: in 1810 and 1818 we see Uvarov, rector of the University of Saint Petersburg and later a government minister, planning an Asiatic Academy and inaugurating the instruction of oriental languages, with preferential attention to Sanskrit. It was the decade in which the first chair of Sanskrit was created for Chézy in Paris and in which Joseph de Maistre, ambassador to Russia from the king of Sardinia, pampered by Alexander I, pondered his *Soirées de Saint-Pétersbourg* and discovered the *Asiatic Researches* and Jones's Manu.

Russia began by adopting the foreign specialists who were breaking new paths, most of whom came from Germany, like Pallas, Catherine the Great's collaborator. One of the first was Friedrich Adelung, nephew and successor to the author of *Mithridates;* a councilor of state, he directed the oriental institute of the Ministry of Foreign Relations beginning in 1823. Turning his attention to lexicography, he produced the first *Bibliotheca Sanscrita* (1830–37) while confessing that he hardly knew the language; yet his initiative would prove fruitful. Böhtlingk and Roth, the authors of the great Sanskrit Lexicon (1852–75), were German by nationality. Otto Böhtlingk was born in Saint Petersburg in 1815 of a Dutch family that lived in Lübeck; he spent many years in the German universities, reconciling the positions of the Indic scholars of Bonn and Berlin. Rudolf von Roth was born in Stuttgart in 1821 and died a professor at Tübingen in 1895; he was a student of Burnouf and Wilson. I. J. Schmidt (1779–1847) traveled among the Kalmyks in 1804 and became a member of the Russian Academy in 1825; an explorer of the Mongol and Tibetan worlds, he published translations in German at Saint Petersburg as well as the first Mongolian grammar (1831). Although its scientific value was not of the first rank, it was widely quoted in the rest of Europe, notably by Schopenhauer. Like the merchant Afanasii Nikitin, who visited India in the fifteenth century and seems to have spoken at least Hindustani, the musician Gerasim Lebedev happened to be drawn outside Europe by a Russian embassy and passed twelve years, from 1785 to 1797, in India; arriving at the time the Calcutta Society was opening new perspectives, he studied both Sanskrit and modern vernaculars. I have already mentioned the grammar he published on his return to England in 1801. He also set up a Sanskrit printing house in the Russian capital at the request of the tsar and in 1805 printed *La contemplation impassible des systèmes des Brahmanes de l'Inde orientale.*

In its first stages Russian scholarship and research naturally concentrated on Mongolia, Siberia, and Turkestan; and, as in other Christian countries, university doors were opened to the languages of the Bible and Islam before those of the Far East. Under the rectorship of Musin-Pushkin (1826–45), the University of Kazan crystallized its teaching of oriental languages, among which, after 1841, a chair of Sanskrit, occupied by Petrov, figures prominently. Among other long-planned institutions, only a college of oriental languages founded in Saint Petersburg in 1854 managed to materialize. In 1852 Petrov transferred his courses to Moscow, where he continued until 1875.[1] Now at Kazan, during the 1840s, when the interest in remote languages must have been quickening, we find a young student, still practically a child, attracted to these new interests: at the age of fifteen or sixteen Tolstoy enrolled in the course in oriental languages. In 1847, at the age of nineteen, he had a second providential encounter, one that he recorded in his private journal: he had to be hospitalized, and in the bed next to him was a Buddhist lama whose conversations he found edifying. Around 1870, between *War and Peace* and *Anna Karenina*, he became interested in Indian and Arabian tales. Six years later, at the time of his moral crisis, having fruitlessly sought the meaning of the universe in Western thought, he plunged headlong into an examination of Christian and oriental religions. In his *Confessions* he compared his own anxious quest for a code of living to that of the tormented prince who would become the Buddha. "There is not a one of Tolstoy's works written after this period," Markovitch concludes, "which is not inspired, in part, by Hindu thought. Although he turned toward the Gospels in the end, his was a Christianity underpinned by the great Hindu doctrines, confirmed by the Buddha, from which he drew."

Here was someone who, like Rammohun Roy, wished to corroborate the words of Jesus in the Upanishads and rediscover the same lessons by a reading of Vivekananda's *Yoga*. Like Wagner, Tolstoy introduced himself to oriental thought through Burnouf and Schopenhauer; he contemplated the *Bhagavad Gita*, as all the Romantics had done, and accumulated the oriental texts that were being emphasized. He would proclaim repeatedly his profound debt to the Indian sages, whose thought he adapted to the modern world. He borrowed from them extensively for his own books of doctrine, but did so not according to literary principles but according to moral and religious necessity. At the end of his life a delegation from the Arya Samaj visited him. By means of an indirect influence, it seems likely that Tolstoy was, in his turn, Romain Rolland's initial reason for seeking India, which would find in Rolland its best agent for "the order of Ramakrishna."

Tolstoy doubtless remains the most striking example, among a great many, of those who sought a cure for the Western spirit in India—one of the most contagious, in the end for India as well. The Vedanta of Shankara enabled him knowingly to deny all the alleged European scholarship; a composite reflection extending from the Upanishads to Ramakrishna guided him in his revision of spiritual values. It was Buddhism in particular that set him on the path of his moral principle of nonviolence; probably nothing else was better equipped to resolve his personal and national problems in the direction they were waiting to be resolved. It was the Slavic shaping of "ahimsa" that would afterward impress the custodians of the faith: in return, Gandhi sought his own personal inspiration in Tolstoy and through him rediscovered his path toward the law of love and passivity. Writing Tolstoy from London in 1909, Gandhi signed himself "Your humble disciple," and received back the advice to read *Letter to a Hindu*, where the connection was more explicit and whose decisive effect on his thought Gandhi later acknowledged.

CHAPTER TWENTY-THREE

The Dialogue Between Creeds on the Question of the Soul

TO write history is to retrace changes in habit. The first idea the Occident had while gathering information on India was to bring those who did not think in Christian terms to their senses; the condition of the pagans seemed more anomalous than contagious. Voltaire himself made light of all that "something else" and had not the least fear of being converted. Feelings, first of superiority, then of tranquillity, were supported by the prolonging of ignorance or ambiguity. Soon, step by step, one word and then another became acclimated, and behind those words ideas were at work. Around the end of the eighteenth century, while the knowledge of languages was progressing, oriental doctrines came into favor because of their apparent likeness to the philosophies being extolled at the time in the West—one more reason to shunt aside the distinctions that the similarities masked. In the course of the nineteenth and twentieth centuries three divergent trends developed: strict schools of technicians, philologists and philosophers alike, pursuing rigorous studies, alienating hasty adepts; circles of ideologists or initiates grafting foreign products onto local experience; and the old missionary spirit reappearing among the theologians, raising scruples about both science and conscience. This three-fold interest explains why, as never before, such a numerous clientele passed from one civilization to another.

No consequence of the oriental revelations stirred things up quite so much as religious comparativism; no chapter counted for so much in the history of the spirit as this new confrontation between two spiritual techniques, a history insufficiently known because official history represses, as a specialty, that which touches only the soul. The history of religions, born late, imparted a change of direction to the history of religion. All the beliefs that suddenly appeared from other times and places created a pressure on the inquisitive to ask what lay behind belief. One now knew all that had been believed, for it lived on in those who still believed. The Credo had some scores to settle with credos which had been ignorant of it, and which it could no longer ignore. If there is but one Truth, is it because the others are insignificant? Or is it because they are suddenly no different from it? Faith had never before experienced such a need for a reference point. Furthermore, it was not merely a matter of a faith's content. The novelty of competition between different aptitudes for the inner life had to be considered. In his *Fragments de l'Almeh* in 1831 Vigny wrote (and this is but one example among many): "In spite of their fanatical love of a false faith, the orientals have a natural need—I would almost venture to say instinct—for religion that would put Christians to shame." He was referring to Muslims in particular, but this attitude would increasingly prevail, and to a much greater extent, regarding the Hindus.

It was the Hindus who posed the fundamental questions to Europe. Of course Zoroastrianism had been the first to come forward, thanks to Anquetil, after whom it would no longer be possible to study dualistic or salvationist religions wihout allotting this one the full attention that its closeness to Hebrew religion demanded. But the past history of this Exile remained among the dead pasts, since the Parsi relic lacked any power of expansion. With India, on the contrary, Christianity encountered a heterodoxy millennia old yet still very much alive, and for the first time Christendom ceased automatically to consider gentiles idolators. Instead of opposing a unique form of certitude against the certitude of universal error, one began to seek an original principle of commonality within foreign beliefs. This was, at the beginning of the nineteenth-century, the business of symbolism (symbolism and syncretism date from the Romantic period): Friedrich Schlegel and Eckstein were pursuing in India the most intact trace of a universal revelation. A hesitancy to curse all paganisms was a major event.

Faith and Comparativism

Thus spirituality, the inmost circumference of a certain world, was reached by the encyclopedic spirit and critical activity, the general hallmarks of modern times. Thenceforward the spirituality thus created would not advance without taking its precursors and competitors into account; there was risk involved here, but the possibility of a new maturity as well.

Never before, it seems, had debates over religious confessions been less exempt from external considerations, not even in the Rome of Plotinus, which comes most readily to mind. The analogies between his time and ours today are explicit: the second century witnessed an extraordinary

vogue for oriental philosophies, especially those from India, whose brahmans obsessed metaphysicians and even Church Fathers. Intellectual activity in the West focused on compilation, an admission of impotence, and
on hopes steeped in misgivings, a revelation of vacuity. The truism current during the Empire that all philosophy was born in the Orient came
from Germanism. The tendency to associate the brahmans with the druids
came from Romanticism. Furthermore, one steadfastly assumed "the
priority of the barbarians." As for occultisms, "the classical lands of occultism are credited with legendary knowledge: Egypt, with subterranean
temples propitious for sorceries; Chaldea, land of star-gazers; Persia, home
of Magian magicians; and, finally, India, paradise of fakirs."[1] Here are Fabre
d'Olivet and Balzac.

This is not to maintain, of course, that today each believer is holding a
dialogue, based on either parish practice or his own conviction, with Buddha, or that he even always suspects his existence. Rather it is to say that
Christianity, precisely to the extent that it is the voice of the West, is led
by this *other* spirituality to new self-assertions, which are comparative. Series of studies with titles such as "What Are We to Make of Quetzal-
coatl?" or "Why We Are Dervishes" are more and more abundant. Just
as the genius of literature, the plastic arts, and music has fragmented into
fifty entities, so all the fragments of religion are forming a vestibule to
religion for those who do not yet have a religion or no longer have one
entirely. This current has propelled those who have no doubts about their
religion to create a movement out of their certitude.

Nothing is more instructive than to examine *L'étude comparée des religions* by Father Pinard de la Boullaye, a work written from a dogmatic point
of view, side by side with one written from a sociological point of view,
Chantepie de la Saussaye's *Lehrbuch der Religionsgeschichte*. It is in the former that one finds the most detailed account of the new field. Pinard de
la Boullaye postulates it began as early as the works of de Brosses and
Gébelin. "A new series of discoveries . . . marks the beginning" of the
period that was dawning. "We are obtaining the sacred books of ancient
religions; we are exhuming their monuments, covered with inscriptions;
we are deciphering their respective languages; their relationships to each
other are being established, based on reliable standards." The first efforts
were tentative. At the time of Hyde orientalism was groping in the dark.
Then came Anquetil, whose book spread into German territory through
the translation by Kleuker. Finally Jones's contribution revived biblical
questions and established the hypothesis of multiple bibles.

Straightway there would be an effort to expropriate the theological element for the benefit of idealism, certain aspects of which cause one to think
of a return to rationalism; such was Hegel's enterprise: Pinard de la Boul-

laye outlines Hegel's idea thus: "The human mind which discerns the universal is itself universal reason; we are in the midst of pantheism. If the mind is the sole reality, then all that is rational is real, and all that is real is rational; otherwise it would not exist. The most strict determinism presides over the development of history." Pinard has good grounds for stressing Hegel, who needed the contributions of oriental studies not only for his pro-Germanic organization of history but to construct his ontology; it was a vision of a universal and perpetual totality that allowed for a doctrine that applied evolution "even to God: God is a constant becoming." This represents an ultralogical outcome of the religious hopes of German Romanticism. "The category of the totality, the universal and determinant predominance of the whole over the parts," would also constitute, according to Georg Lukács, "the very essence of the method Marx took over from Hegel and transformed in such a way as to make it the original foundation of an entirely new science." In passing we can only indicate what had been waiting through all human history to become unified, and who was dependent on it: "It is the point of view of totality," Lukács specified, and not "the prevalence of economic motifs in the interpretation of history, which most clearly distinguishes Marxism from bourgeois science." The German genius for the systematic and the measurable devoted itself to these historical quanta with relish. For Hegel, Pinard states, "each religion marks a moment, a moment that is necessary in the evolution of the Idea, a transitory form in which the Idea is conceived. . . . Hegel classifies them according to their ascending perfection, from magic, the most unrefined, to Christianity." In the second division—religions of nature—he places "Religions of consciousness divided from itself, or material religions," China, Brahmanism, Buddhism. In the other two sections he places the religion of the Parsis, Syria and, Egypt; and Judea, Greece, and Rome, respectively.

Chantepie reproduces other classifications after that of Hegel. In his chapter "The Division of Religions," Chantepie outlines Von Hartmann's classification of types of religions. Under the second major heading, "supernaturalism," is "Abstract Monism, or the idealistic religion of salvation" with its two subdivisions: "a) Akosmism (Brahmans) and b) Absolute Illusionism (Buddhists)." Such ingenious classifications have continued to multiply. In his excellent introduction to his French translation of Chantepie, Hubert refrains from attempting a historical evaluation of the work, which would require, he says, "a thick book." But among the origins of questions subordinate to the history of religions he lists "the invention of comparative grammar, the study of the Vedas and Sanskrit literature, the restoration of Germanic folklore and mythology, the excavation of Mesopotamian texts, and the establishment of scientific ethnography." These were the very elements of the Oriental Renaissance. Chantepie traced the new discipline back to Hegel's lectures of 1821–31, although the notion had been around since Vico, the true founder of "folk psychology," wrote his *Scienza Nuova* in 1725, followed by Voltaire's *Essai sur les moeurs* (1756), Lessing's *Erziehung des Menschengeschlects* (1784) and Herder's *Ideen zur Geschichte der Menschheit* (1784)—all creators of the philosophy of history. "But these frameworks had to be filled." That is what the decipherers of writings subsequently made possible, orientalism clearing the way for linguistics, which opened up ethnography; ultimately great religious criticism, formed by Sanskrit under the hand of Burnouf, blossomed in Max Müller.

Pinard depicts this climactic age of the soul: "We have reached the middle of the nineteenth century. The reader can readily appreciate the importance of the work accomplished and the progress achieved in the course of the past fifty-odd years." An ambiguous progress. Faith had lost its solitude. "Like a reading room whose anxiously awaited opening is continuously postponed, the Orient is finally 'Open to the Public.' Persia, India, and Egypt are already represented by extensive sections," which would be extended as far as the eye could see. When all was said and done, the revolt of the eighteenth century against rationalism would end by producing two extreme tendencies, both of them heterodox: the deification of tradition against reason (or authority), as with Lamennais, and the deification of interior feeling, as with German Romanticism. The Catholics were working to uphold the dogmas of the Church; the Protestants were caught up in subjectivism and relativism. All the same, the former could not ignore what the latter advanced. But, as Pinard pointed out, "the more one reconciles religious meaning with asthetic or moral meaning, the more obvious it becomes that identical, or at least very similar, opinions can be found in the heart of all *religions*. From there it but remains to consider them as equally legitimate forms of *Religion*, to affirm there is but one religion despite the diversity of its historical manifestations. There is only one threshold, and all of them have crossed it." Here was an important confirmation, penned by a Catholic, of the important innovations brought about by the convergence of orientalized humanism and Romantic religiosity.

"Christianity," Pinard continues, "far from being set against 'natural religion,' was regarded as its most perfect expression. However, if we take history into account, we must admit that comparativism transformed the entire religious vocabulary. The supernatural, revelation, miracle, prophecy, all these words took on a new meaning. Christian dogmas received an altogether new interpretation, which the symbolists termed focus and the conservatives termed a profound deformation." Here in its veritable fullness, and without exaggeration, was the whole occurrence whereby orientalism divided the Christian era. Pinard left it to a Protestant author, Edmond Schérer, to denounce the notion that the God to which the astonishing reformation aspired could be nothing but "the conscience and reason of humanity personified." After that, "would not religion, under the pretext of becoming more religious, cease to exist"? This was precisely the objection that Lanjuinais had immediately made to Eckstein. In his eyes the attempts at Indo-Christian unity could yield nothing more than "a Christianity entirely human."

The Universalism of Lamennais

On November 5, 1823, Lamennais asked Eckstein for oriental documents "on man's original degradation and his expectation of a redeemer." Two months later he asked for documents concerning "the anticipation of a liberator before Jesus Christ" and "the original fall of mankind."[2] For more than fifteen years he had been taking notes on the doctrines of Iran and India, meditating on how to reconcile all the churches. In 1817, along with the first volume of his *Essai sur l'indifférence* had appeared his plan to establish the truth of a single religion, incontestable in its universality (he had been born two years before the Calcutta Society). Eckstein's public response in *Le Catholique* revealed that he had found Hindu doctrines concerning original sin—at this point in time that was how the faithful argued amid the confusions brought about by the anti-Christianity of Voltaire, who had drawn his arguments from Holwell and Dow. Such oriental mainstays were essential to the framework of a construct for which Lamennais would brave censure and would, for the time being, be abandoned by Eckstein himself. Lamennais embodied a rebellion born of the Oriental Renaissance, symmetrical to the Reformation, which had once been associated with the Hellenic Renaissance. Lacordaire later discerned in it "a Protestantism more vast and profound than the old one."[3]

According to Burtin, "The last three books of the *Essai sur l'indifférence,* particularly the chapter 'Unity as a Characteristic of Christianity,' represent, with a few slight differences of meaning, not only the thought of Eckstein but his method and parade of learning as well." A typical quotation from Lamennais: "Christians believe in everything the human race has believed, and the human race has believed in everything Christians believe." This rush to extract a universal church from a provisional science fired some believers and alarmed others, Lacordaire above all. He poked fun at it in a letter to his friend Foisset on September 24, 1827: "Jesus Christ truly did a poor job of presenting his ideas; he should have hidden his Gospel in the hut of some Brahman who would not have been able to read it, and who would have burned half of it and left the other half to the Calcutta Society." Here the cause of much excess is clearly shown. Lacordaire adopted a definite position against Lamennais in his famous *Considérations sur le système philosophique de M. de La Mennais* (1834), which opened several perspectives on the oriental foundations of the debate.

The discovery that had precipitated the extraordinary success of the first volume of the *Essai sur l'indifférence* (in 1817, still the Chézy period) was, for Lacordaire, something his former friend had lost: proof of religion through philosophy that rooted both in the Cartesian principle of evidence. From then on *"universality* and *perpetuity"*—that is, still, the criterion of totality—embodied "the distinctive characteristic of the truth. Now, where is universality if not in the belief of all peoples? Where is perpetuity if not in beliefs of all the centuries?" (One can understand the affinities between a writer like Lamennais and the future author of *Legénde des siècles*—an astonishing consistency of periods!) "The human race is thus the repository of the truth, its unerring oracle. . . . Whoever prefers his own thought to that of all peoples and all times is a madman who denies his own reason by denying that of humanity; he leaves the church of understanding." This was the church of the historians, almost that of the linguists. The watermark of the Oriental Renaissance is apparent behind all the patents that the mind claimed throughout this period. Lacordaire made no secret of having reflected for ten years on the reinterpretations that the new doctrines demanded. Ultimately the inadmissible offense would be to replace the authority of the Church with another. "Lamennais's great mistake, whatever else his philosophy may have been, was to try to establish a philosophical school and to hope that this school would be the link between minds, the basis of religions, and the salvation of society." One discerns in the second volume of Lamennais's *Essai* an intention to superimpose a massive foreign authority onto the unique interior authority; thus two factors seemed called on to consolidate faith: idolatry itself and the human quantum. Isn't Lamennais too resorting to the equation peoples = People?

"Where is the human race?" asked Lacordaire. "Who has heard it? What is its voice?" There can be only a Catholic response to such questions: "Set in the world's most famous place, it is the Father of the Christians, the Vicar of Jesus Christ, who raises the voice that the savage in his forest, the Chinaman at the ends of the earth, the Indian on the banks of his rivers, hears." Lacordaire seems to have detected how Lamennais connived with the many daydreams of the period. Lacordaire's analysis underscores—in keeping with the concept of humanity inherited from the

eighteenth century and with the new humanism inaugurated by the nineteenth—the need for belief. Nor did he deny the documentary value of
the case his adversary argued; the texts that Lamennais cited seemed to
him "clear, in general, like the medallions of a primitive revelation." What
he disputed was the adherence of the very people who might possess the
revelation. There may have been among the infidels a partial faith in fundamental dogmas that confirmed the positive beliefs of the faithful, but
for the latter, the profession of faith and reference to the Church remained the only solid ground (hence there was no question at all of an
"Aryan Bible"). Lacordaire most condemned the concept that "Christianity floats in the midst of the human race, which surpasses it in grandeur,
just as sixty centuries are greater than eighteen, just as the sweep of the
Old and New World surpasses that of the Church." This quarrel over extension was basic: it had been inconceivable so long as world history remained within the framework established by Bousset. And suddenly, like
a detective on the trail of the collusions of the times, Lacordaire points the
finger of scorn at the typical heresy—Saint-Simonianism. More than anyone it was the Saint-Simonians who had utter faith in "humanity, which
they proclaimed infallible, in mankind's past, and in the present hope of
the human race." It was they who made no secret of awaiting a "fourth
revelation." It was they who announced the absolute unity of "good and
evil, mind and matter, of God, man and woman, rich and poor, king and
subject, all and everything, everyone and everyone." This stirs together a
good many amalgams. Was it pure coincidence that Lacordaire's *Considérations* was published in 1834, following the Colebrooke-Pauthier outburst still echoing through the Collège de Juilly?

Rapprochements: Brahman Rammohun Roy and
Pastor Bochinger

"A traveling Brahman who comes to England to publish works he has
written with a view toward combating Indian polytheism—this is a sin-
gularity that understandably provokes surprise in people who, recognizing how difficult it is to bring Hindus to renounce their ancient beliefs in
order to adopt those of Europe, become accustomed to regarding such a
change as forever impossible." So wrote Burnouf in the *Journal Asiatique*
at about the same time Roy was in England. We have already seen that
for him the danger of comparativism was the great hope: through it each
faith could recover an awareness of a common aspiration and find its way
again, for the way is one. On this point we must return to the distinction
that Burnouf supplied, for none has been clearer: "In the mind of an In-

dian, the universal soul is almost the sum total of the individual souls which are its detached parts, parts that subsist individually only for the duration of the mortal body that confines and limits them. The destiny of the soul is to cross those barriers, even during life, and to be reunited through thought with the soul of the world, for the individual soul is no different than the universal soul. The soul of the individual is God himself, an assertion that leads directly to the most exaggerated mysticism, and that is an assertion a Christian would reject as blasphemy."

Roy's position vis-à-vis his coreligionists is comprable to Lamennais's vis-à-vis Christianity: they opposed him by defending the worship of divinity in all its attributes, the primordial value of their observances and of a ritual of purification. Roy proclaimed a knowledge of God independent of practices, denouncing adoration of his attributes as idolatry and establishing the truth of his religion not by its distinctions but by what it held in common with others. Occidentalism came to the fore in the very methods of the reformer's work. "The European aspects of his line of argument stand out in the most unequivocal way by their contrast with the Indic methods that his adversaries follow," Burnouf noted. Indeed, their comparisons, their images, their "words and expressions scarcely conceal their lack of rigor in ideas and substance; a fine-spun false dialectic, but bold and fascinating," the habits still those of the Upanishads. "There are a good many centuries between this form and that of Aristotelian argument." Centuries or temperaments? we may ask.

Burnouf took up the question again in his preface to the *Bhagavata Purana*:

Philosophical fragments . . . should not be confused with dogmatic passages, and one should not seek in them what we in the West understand, strictly speaking, as philosophy. . . . I do not know if I am deluding myself, but this mixture of poetry and metaphysics has something striking about it that is as least as interesting as it is surprising. . . . It is not yet a question of knowing what the knowledge of this country will supply us that might be applicable to our intellectual condition, of use for the future progress of our ideas. . . . Is it not a fact deserving the full attention of philosophy that there once existed and there still exists, before our very eyes, a society for which poems such as the *Bhagavata* serve, if I may express myself in this way, as intellectual food? Is it not surprising to our so practical and so matter-of-fact common sense that a great nation, rich in all the gifts of the spirit, blessed with sagacity and a marvelous penetration, would seem to devote all its powers to the examination of forever insoluble questions in which a sense of strength is aroused only when the object that excites it is among those that cannot be attained?

Admirable lucidity; an equally luminous gift for exposition. This great difference in the magnetization of thoughts, and this discovery of another mental hemisphere, were, upon the discovery of India, precisely what would give Europe, whether in the form of amazement or uneasiness, a sudden start. Here the meaning of the formula that had already inspired the poet Vigny was made explicit by the scholar: an exotic aptitude for a contemplation that was at once religion, philosophy, and poetry. The time was ripe for Burnouf to speak of it with the respect thinkers held for these three hierarchies; a few years later they were speaking of "the primitive mentality."

The third of Roy's published defenses of his system bore the strange title *An Apology for the Pursuit of Final Beatitude, independently of Brahmunical Observances.* For him that said everything; more than one Europe understood it. We have seen, fifteen years earlier, Lebedev's title *La contemplation impassible des systèmes des Brahmanes.* Eleven years later (1831), we will see Pastor Bochinger publish *La vie contemplative, ascetique et monastique chez les Indous et chez les peuples bouddhistes.* Above I mentioned attitudes declared to be Protestant regarding other religious confessions; Bochinger's was one that acknowledged being so (one could rethink this position today by reading Albert Schweitzer).

Engaging, noble characteristics foreshadowed by a premature death mark Jean-Jacques Bochinger, born in 1802 in Strasbourg where, as Quinet's and Bergmann's histories show, a taste for things oriental flowed in from Germany. Bochinger himself had gone, during the same years as Quinet, to hear the masters of theology and oriental studies at Heidelberg and Göttingen; Bochinger completed his studies of these two fields in Paris.

He pursued them concurrently for the rest of his brief career. He completed his initial course in theology and then went on to obtain his bachelor's degree with a thesis on Origen (1829–30). He first published, in German, at Tübingen, an *Introduction to the Reading of the Holy Scriptures,* which was translated into French by Laure at Nîmes in 1840. After 1830 he served as pastor of the Church of Saint Nicholas at Strasbourg. "Always with a pen in hand," according to the *Dictionary of Famous Men of Alsace,* "he had, on June 23, 1831, just completed the additions to his latest work, 'On the Connections between the Contemplative Life among the Indic and Buddhist Peoples and the similar Phenomena in the History of Islam and Christianity' (59 quarto pages), when death struck him down on August 12, 1831." In 1826 he had founded a Sociète Théologique and a Société Philosophique in Strasbourg with his friend Edouard Reuss, two years his junior, a student of Sacy who would leave behind the best accounts of him.

Bochinger's documentation elaborated with a great deal of discernment on what was available at the time. After mentioning the first authorities on Indic studies, he immediately qualified Friedrich Schlegel, Polier, Dow, and Ward as secondary authorities in the field of beliefs and practices; in his opinion Colebrooke, Othmar Frank, Ellis and, particularly Rammohun Roy were more important—and Jones and the *Asiatic Researches* were the starting point. Although lacking the necessary tools, Bochinger also studied Sanskrit; regarding Buddhism he turned to Hodgson's first Nepalese studies and provided praiseworthy Jain bibliographies. With a clarity not commonplace at the time he distinguished between primitive Vedism and the literature of commentary, between popular Brahmanism "and the religion of the sages, between practical religion and mystical religion." On the one side were polytheism and ritualism, on the other pantheism and contemplation. The pioneering English scholars had begun to employ these classifications, and they gained ground wherever *Asiatic Researches* penetrated. Colebrooke, following Wilkins, had clarified the field, but it was Bochinger who, after the confused encyclopedism of Friedrich Schlegel, revived the traditions of Anquetil by sanctioning the idea of equality between the two spiritual worlds.

Bochinger preferred to trace the initiative for this idea to the German schools whence he had come, marking the separation between the periods clearly in his preface to *La vie contemplative:* "A theologian formerly did not dare to speak of non-Christian religious systems except with disdain tinged with horror." But here was an idea that rejoined Lamennais's "Protestantism," all the more readily since the "theology" here is German: "In agreement with the philosophers, the theologians have been obliged to acknowledge that the human race, from its very origin, forms in all its developments but one immense moral and intellectual organism, all parts of which deserve to be examined." His own study of Indian contemplation was rooted in a consideration of the importance of its mysticism, and monasticism in general, *for the Christian.* For although Protestantism had no experience "of the monastic life, mysticism in its diverse forms concerns it powerfully. A bold philosophy based on pantheism, and a spirit reacting against the incredulity of later generations, support religious ideas that, if rigorously applied, would necessarily lead to the ascetic and contemplative life." One could not record and serve with more seriousness the linkage of interests that extended from the Boehme revived by Jacobi and Schelling to the India to be revived; nor could one frame in a more logical form the lesson that more than one spiritual European had gone to seek in India. Once more intuition came forward to lead scholarship; since the initial linguistic period had passed, it was thanks to its religion and philosophy that India occupied, "today, more than ever, the attention of scholars" who set out to determine whether an Asiatic mysticism distributed from the Buddhists through the Muslims to the Christians had originated in India, or whether several independent undertakings had culminated in converging results (which remains a great question).

Again Bochinger echoed Anquetil's attitudes, and almost his expressions, when he implored his readers to go beyond appearances; it was essential "to differentiate carefully the periods, the schools of philosophy, and the religious sects. It is because this has not been done that, in the process of constructing systems based on the religions of India, one has sometimes set about it like a pandit who, ignorant of the languages and history of European peoples, might assemble as a body of doctrine anything that happenstance might have taught him about any of their systems and beliefs," from the Greeks to the moderns, "and who would then present this strange combination to his compatriots as the religious system of the people of the Occident."

In Bochinger's examination of "The Source from Which We Can Draw an Understanding of the Brahmanic System" (as he entitled his fourth chapter, speaking of the records available at that time on Indian sects, to which he devoted the second part of his book), the criticism of the materials was as well balanced, as consistently impartial if not even sympathetic, as the precise inventory of Indian thought he pursued. For all that, Bochinger did not allow himself to be drawn into a universal philosophy of history or religions, calling instead for serious consideration of the connections glimpsed from India to Egypt and between the Sufis, the Gnostics, and the Greek philosophers. Yet he suspected that the ramifications of Indian mysticism, "which at times seem borrowed word for word from Indian authors," extended into China, Japan, Tibet, Persia, and central Asia, echoing through the Manicheans and coming to affect Pythagoras, Plato, and subsequently Neoplatonism, reappearing in Philo. Even the very principle of asceticism might have come from the Asian subcontinent to the anchorites and cenobites of the first Christian centuries.

Bunsen

Another thirty years elasped. The age of grand historical syntheses was coming to a close, and one of the many consequences it left behind, one of the most conspicuous, became the culmination of the trend: a student of Sacy, a German, the universal Baron Christian Karl Bunsen (1791–1860) had been, since his twenty-fifth year, meditating a plan for the history of spirituality that had haunted so many contemporary minds. Before his death he published *Christianity and Mankind* (1854; *Gott in der Geschichte*, 1857–58), a reference to Rowland Williams' *Christianity and Hinduism*, which had preceded it. Bunsen had wanted to go to India to study its religious forms on the spot but broke off his journey in Rome, where he succeeded Nie-buhr as Prussian ambassador. There he met Champollion, who left his imprint on him. Subsequently, his *Aegyptens Stelle in der Weltgeschichte (Egypt's Place in World History)* (1845), as Henri Martin remarked in his preface to the French translation, ascribed to Egypt the primacy that Eck-stein ascribed to India. Nevertheless, the entire third book is reserved for "The Aryans of the Indus and the Ganges," a study of Vedism, Brahman-ism, and Buddhism backed by copious and diligent research. Bunsen had been linked with Schleiermacher and would be even closer to Schelling. The metaphysical aspirations of Romantic Germany, in which the mem-ory of Herder persisted, seem to have in part determined Bunsen's work; his conclusions, arrived at during the same years, tallied with those of Schopenhauer. As Martin points out, "For Bunsen the essential element of history was the dual development of Semitic and Aryan religions, ul-timately united in Christ, the center of history. He thought that although the Bible was the work of the Semites, the Aryan spirit alone had discov-ered the Bible's universal and historical meaning."

Written along lines with which we are familiar, his venture joined, by a different path, the aims of Lamennais: each historical home, each stage of human consciousness, revealed an identity of needs and manifesta-tions, upon which one could build a sort of pan-theology. For his part Bunsen worked to materialize the religious fact. Hence the reproach for denying reality that he addressed particularly against Brahmanism, which he accused, in the habitual way, of producing "inert despair" and "glacial indifference." Buddhism offered his inquiring hope a better reward. He took great pains as a westerner to defend both religions against the sus-picion of atheism. He extended this zeal truly far on behalf of Buddhism: once again one wonders whether an inadequate analysis of the vocabu-lary isn't simply an excuse for an exchange of courtesies motivated by the desire for concord.

A continuation, a descendant, appeared on Bunsen's very heels in the work of Jacques Milsand, one of those inventive thinkers whom fame has unfairly undervalued. His collection *Littérature anglaise et philosophie*, which was published only posthumously in 1893, includes an article first pub-lished in 1859 in the *Revue des Deux-Mondes* entitled "Modern Protestant-ism in the Philosophy of History." In it Milsand compared two works, Bunsen's *Christianity and Mankind*, which had captured the attention of heedful thinkers, and *Histoire des trois premiers siècles de l'Eglise chrétienne* by Edmond de Pressensé, one of the leaders of liberal Protestantism. Mil-sand credits Bunsen with having written a veritable "general treatise of comparative philology," for "it is from the complete range of Asian and European idioms that he wishes to cull the intellectual origins of our race," a reference to the reconciliation, strongly emphasized in Bunsen's work, of Aryan and Semitic thought. Milsand found the same consideration of the history of languages a means of elucidating the history of people and beliefs in Pressensé; India in particular held a privileged place in the collections and arguments. Using these materials, Milsand quickly retraced the diverse theories that general interpretations of religious need, sentiment, or fact inferred from linguistic advances. Thus he surveyed the half century that moved forward from Schleiermacher to Schelling, from Herder to Creuzer, touching on Dupuis, Benjamin Constant, and Lamennais in passing.

Pressensé's education was partly Germanic, which gave Milsand the opportunity to trace the evolution of German Protestantism: his account again brings a good many features into relief, notably the coincidence between the advent of personal intuition in the Romantic West and the accession, thanks to the new philology, of an oriental form of thought previously undreamt of. He only touches on this, lacking any real grounds for dwelling on it, but his entire intensely interesting study reveals that the decipherments had repercussions no smaller in reform circles than among Catholics.

A "Second Legitimacy" in the Orient?

A few words will suffice to indicate the kinds of consequences that the notion of an open world was to have in the spiritual realm. We know that many of the minds in the West who ventured to connect themselves with the Hindu tradition interpreted it in a Unitarian sense. Without judging the principles of the Unitarian movement, one must remember its extent, first exemplified by Romain Rolland and more recently by Rene Guénon, Ananda Coomaraswamy, and Jean Herbert, among others. On the side of orthodoxy, although inclinations and conclusions varied, there are abundant signs of a deep interest. Just as in the past one read this sort of thing in Vigny, today one reads it in *Apologétique: Nos raisons de croire, réponses aux objections,* a handbook of apologetics by Brillant and Nédoncelle: "The Indians clearly seem to be the most naturally religious of all peoples, and apply themselves to eternal realities more than anyone else." A great number of careful and very thorough studies have been produced by admirable specialists such as Lacombe, Monchanin, Father Johanns, Father Dandoy, and Father Taymans d'Eypernon. In a work that received widespread attention through its publication in *Le Catholicisme,* Father de Lubac, assuming for the Church "responsibility for the entire human race," recalled Saint Augustine's beautiful expression "Duo justi, alter sit in Oriente, alter in Occidente, secum sunt, quia in Deo sunt" (Two just men—even if one is in the East, the other in the West—are together because both are in God"). He could have linked it with the remark from the Vulgate, "Dico autem vobis, quod multi ab Oriente et Occidente venient, et recumbent cum Abraham, et Isaac, et Jacob in regno coelorum" ("But I say unto you, many will come from the East and the West, and will recline with Abraham, with Isaac and Jacob in the Kingdom of heaven"). Studies were taken from one hemisphere to the other; it goes without saying that since it was the points of juncture that were sought out, the borders of essential dogma were not being effaced.

Among the philosophers, Bergson gave one chapter of his book *Deux sources* the title "Oriental Mysticism," only to acknowledge ultimately "complete mysticism" only in "the great Christian mystics." The objections Bergson raised against India are typical: the mystical there had been constantly mixed with the dialectical, and both had "reciprocally" prevented each other "from seeing it through." Buddhism treats "men and gods as beings of the same species, subject to the same fate and having the same need for deliverance." Since use of *soma* or the practice of yoga did not allow one to go beyond "the more popular form of mystical contemplation," such contemplation did not, as in Greek philosophy, result in "the infinitely extensible knowledge that Hellenic science already had." This was because, for the Greeks, "knowledge was always . . . a means rather than an end." For the Hindu it was a question of "escaping from life." The analysis of both Brahmanism and Buddhism concluded in their radical inferiority: a charity endowed with "warmth," "the total and mysterious gift of oneself," was missing.

In their turn the spokesmen for Buddhism denounced the West's inability to get rid of its prejudice. According to *The Listener* (November 20, 1947), Dr. B. Rajan, speaking on the BBC, added to earlier examples of incomprehension (which included Blake), T. S. Eliot, Yeats, and Aldous Huxley (whose perennial philosophy established a sort of syncretism among all the mysticisms while cutting them off from any dogmatism). In 1935 Entai Tomomatsu, a Japanese Buddhist, published a statement of his beliefs for the French public. After raising the question of racial prejudice, he then moved closer to the heart of the matter by pointing out that the accusations against Buddhism of quietism frequently emanated from studies that were too brief to interpret correctly "the negation of the present life." When he subsequently ventures to say that since "the horrors of the Great War" (by which he means that of 1914–18), Buddhism "was to become one of the spiritual nourishments of Europe," one thinks that the lion does not paint the man any better than the man paints the lion. Of course, as he recognized, illogical intuition may be genuinely attractive as a retaliation against Greek logic, as may a religion lacking belief in the immortality of the soul, for certain souls; but is it not, for occidentals, most often a matter of provisionally dismissing problems they are weary of but will not dispense with for long? The author defines both Western faith, as it seems to him, and his own faith, as the West fails to explain it. Nothing that he adduces seems gratuitous, yet the whole article and his conclusions call to mind the peculiar opportunities for dialogue that differences of vocabulary provide among foreigners.

The most obvious attraction of oriental doctrines, from the historical viewpoint, seems apparent: in the battle between faith and reason, the rickety position of deism seemed, at the close of the eighteenth century, to be favored. Suddenly Brahmanism and Buddhism supplied an undreamt of solution—something, so it seemed, like a religion of salvation that would rule out hope. The immortal soul and God-the-Creator would be avoided; the arguments of philosophical idealism could be recognized without losing the air of spirituality. A fresh advantage was the elimination of the problem of evil and the problem of matter; one was assured and engulfed. The great All towards which pre-Romanticism, seeking one original cause for the universe, was groping, appeared here in a form that seemed antipathetic to the Occident but proved exceedingly misleading: that of dissolution. For a writer like Vigny, it was a bitter satisfaction to have done with the calculus of retribution. It was as if there were a kind of unknown guarantee in a divinity so completely purged of anthropomorphism, a faith so abstract, a morality so free from recompense. A religion whose divine genealogies could be forgotten, so that one could make nothing but metaphysics out of it; a religion that retained all the attraction of the indeterminate—it was this that the West had hardly experienced before.

The Jansenist Pascal had said, "The real conversion consists in knowing there is an invincible opposition between God and us." This amounted to stating in European terms, that is to say through antimony, the problem which, in Asiatic terms, was stated in a unitary form; but the Self there is not the same as Him here. One admired the natural talent, nowhere else so widespread, for the unity of life, through which the least daily act was integrated into the faith. There was no longer any profane territory, any meaningless gesture. The breath of each moment was linked to consequences in the world beyond—and it was so much a question of a world beyond that it ceased to be a question of a different world. On the other hand, in that universe where nothing begins nor finishes, in that proliferation of paraphrases and those winding interpolations which are the office of each individual, fidelity appears the essential characteristic which, in its tangle of limbs and its deification of the multiple, startles and disconcerts the Western mind, which made Hugo recoil in apprehension from the abyss where the Hellenic tradition of selection and the Asian tradition of multiplication again found themselves most irreducibly at odds. Two contrary rules, two opposed necessities, the one born of small numbers and the final appeal to reason, the other born of large numbers and the final appeal to imagination. For one of our contemporaries, Lanza del Vasto, the attitude of the Hindu soul is "something like a separate sex." For another, René Grousset, "the revelation of Indian and Chinese thought is tantamount for us to the discovery of different humanities, inhabiting different planets."

Conclusion

WHAT REMAINS

CHAPTER TWENTY-FOUR

An Age of Relativism

SURELY no one will any longer assume that the Oriental Renaissance was a gratuitous dream or a passing fancy. But still it will be asked, what lasting result did it have? In what way are its results comparable to those of the other Renaissance? The obvious fact is this: an immense mental displacement has occurred. The air of the times contained the necessity; chance created its reality. Will it still be possible to speak of Romanticism, of the nineteenth-century, of the modern soul, without recording the consequences of the Oriental Renaissance in all provinces of the mind?

From that time forward complete panoramas of ideological geography expanded with each glance and contracted with each question. In the process of considering humanity, the whole expanse of time had to be traversed, all inhabited space had to be covered, the whole world of speech sounded. Ideas on poetry, revealed religion, and architecture wavered, for neither Homer nor the Bible nor the basilicas were, now, historically unique. The new Renaissance Man was one who no longer approached solutions to eternal problems without adding up the global balance sheet. The Romantic intelligence was no longer satisfied with anything less than totality, and this was, in large part, due to the Oriental past. The ultimate value of the classics was not their totality but rather their traditionality, that is to say their time-honored selectivity. Subsequent to the Oriental Renaissance the study of the masses would prevail: the mind applied its attention to migrations rather than to states. Initially it was origins, which were viewed as widely divergent, that were most exciting; then even origins lost their fixity and one would have eyes only for evolution.

The modern era has a triple rhythm in which two centuries in a fixed universe are followed by a century of expansion (the thirteenth, sixteenth, and nineteenth), as if two centuries of classifiers are needed in order to deal with each century of innovators. The expansive power of the nineteenth century seems unprecedented and was linked to the newest of inventions—the decipherment of writing. This time there had been no school proclaiming, I am the Renaissance. The movement rose like the tide. The new humanism had many fathers other than the Orient, just as its predecessor, which was, in any case, destined to cause the notion of experience and the principle of criticism to triumph, had had many other fathers besides the Byzantine scholiasts. Upon its arrival the second Renaissance too found several nearly full-grown innovations and transformed them in an unprecedented way, thereby furthering its own development. But these parallels should not extend the symmetry too far: the second Renaissance was less flattering to the European mentality and perhaps obsessed it more, in exact ratio to the extent that it disordered it. A major distinction is that the second Renaissance was almost entirely verbal rather than plastic. Asian thought endeavored to mingle with the vital current of the occidental mind, where Greco-Latin thought had hitherto flowed virtually alone. This Renaissance was the introduction, in a massive dosage, of a foreign body into the organism. The way for Hellenism had been prepared—as that for Indianism was not—by time-honored precedent, an entire past of natural affinities and well-preserved relics; thus the luxuries in the realms of the spirit, the arts, and even literature, were little disturbed by Indianism. The necessities of the soul, on the other hand, were attacked at their very root. India arrived with the power of lost tribes whose essential traits could be rediscovered, and the bite of the unexpected favored an event that could not have occurred twice in human history—the encounter with an entire tradition that provided solutions to the same problems that were simultaneously different and related. India offered a different course toward the same goal toward which Judea had aspired, and a different use of the same rationality that Greece had employed.

Thus by both its nature and its date, Greco-Latin culture was not merely something worn out by immemorial abrasions; it was, in reality, the prerogative of restricted groups, the property of an elite, a feature of class luxury that would be removed only with extreme difficulty. For inverse reasons Indian culture, worn out and yet new to Europe, immediately became, symbolically, food for all hungers. Not since an Aristotelianism revived by Avicenna had provisioned a scholasticism destined for an entire society had anything questioned what the soul considered most urgent so much as Hindu thought did. Doubtless access to it was not immediately available either in the same degree or to the man in the street, but when a thing concerns the destiny of everyone, even if through the work of a few, everyone inevitably knows about it in the end. It is a little like what is happening only today in matters Hindu in the form of a new Hinduism wherein the West is seeking its own well-being. For 150 years now, matters Mediterranean, known by almost everyone and vital to a certain number, have been confronted by a universal concern known to a few but perceptible by all.

Montaigne's village knew nothing of Seneca, and yet Seneca is a hundred times closer to its mental rhythm than Vivekananda adopted by Romain Rolland could be; but Vivekananda stood for a reconsideration, in question form, of the problems of life that were no longer known except in the form of solutions. The entire Greco-Latin canon was one of common sense, of good sense—that was no longer debated; but here was en entire culture that had dispensed with it, suddenly arriving from afar to contest the mind's old audacities that had become its habits. Possibly, however, it fell on a ground better prepared than was apparent: Christianity had adapted Hellenic thought to Semitic religious sentiment, and its disciples would be interested by a world where, as if by a gift of Nature, the metaphysical was inseparable from the religious, the dialectical from the mystical, and the logical from the irrational. In the end, how many in our streets ever wonder whether their code of conduct is preferable to those they have seen attributed to the sages and fools, the saints and revolutionaries, of Asia? Asia has entered European thought like an invisible interlocutor.

The first Renaissance thrust us back onto the known so that we could know it better; it gave us counterparts which became reassuring; it immortalized the dispute between the ancients and the moderns, an examination for which different centuries had proposed different candidates rather than different criteria—an examination, in short, that had always taken place within the same school. The second Renaissance challenged us, as if it were juxtaposing us with another us, forcing us to revise the known. An unknown seized us which, since it would perhaps always have to remain unknown, became mysterious—mysterious within every mind. Yes, here our horizons were opened—and our wounds as well. At Pompeii one saw only the place of former lives; one touched worn objects. Paganism was the same museum. But Brahma or Buddha, those of the old days, are not the Jupiters of a bygone time. At the moment the West was so belatedly recording their first steps on the Earth, steps that were themselves without dates, Brahma and Buddha continued to mark the same rhythm, to strike the same resonances; they were not dead gods toward whom the living glanced back over their shoulders, even if it was with veneration. Rather, here was the divinity of the living, which had come to speak, face to face, with our divinity and our lives. As in oriental tales where the king's sons, grown old, meet again at the crossroads to compare their adventures, the sons of Adam asked each other what they had made from their treasure of hopes and heritage of anxieties. Amid the diversity of responses, the analogy in their routes, rather than their resting places, became dazzlingly clear. It was not only in the titles of poems that nineteenth-century religion wondered about its plurality.

The term "Renaissance" means the marriage of rediscovered knowledges and unprecedented creations; never before had it been so clearly *a multiplication of points of comparison*. The old religious hope of a global community was revived under the name of comparativism. The billboards in the interior of the mind were changed; intellectual habits altered along with verbal repertoires. The terminological invention Eurasia seemed to pedantize the syntheses Romanticism contemplated endlessly. Without devising "an assimilation of doctrines," each retaining "certain elements of a radical originality intransmissible to the other," one could, according to Emile Bréhier, in *La philosophie comparée*, "grasp the common circumstances of Eurasian thought." But India presented itself as if it sought "efficacy" rather than formal knowledge, as if it engaged "the whole individual in philosophical research." From then on would it not be the rational West that would be invited to justify itself? To Masson-Oursel, a few key texts reveal identical methods of spiritual teaching in India and Greece. It is no longer the Orient but the Occident that becomes difficult to localize, to identify. In *Civilization on Trial* Toynbee not only maintains that "the whole habitable world has now been unified into a single great society," but that among nineteen civilizations that have appeared in six thousand years, and of which only five remain, those of Asia had "better lives . . . than our own Western Christendom." For "the present Western ascendency in the world is certain not to last. . . . The western component will gradually be relegated to the modest place which is all that it can expect to retain in virtue of its intrinsic worth by comparison with those other cultures—surviving and extinct—which the Western society, through its modern expansion, has brought into association with itself and with one another." I confess my own distrust of statistical prophecies. This inquiry into "intrinsic worth," this attempt to bring into contact so many differences among those societies and with one's own—was it not the lowly culture of the "western component" that alone was able, or rather had the need, to do so? Which was not the effect but the cause of its "expansion." Would it not be a kind of superiority that, under the immodest name of genius, would secure for itself a shameless destiny which, nonetheless, no other was able or wished to claim? In short, such seductive estimates are possible if and only if one sums up the mass with the lever. In that vast autobiography that the nineteenth-century West had begun to entitle "Civilization," would there really remain nothing more of itself than a brief chapter called "Local History"? Prejudices are never so enticing as when they are reversed.

During the 1940s, René Guénon called on the "modern world" to seek the only way out of its mortal "crisis" by a return to oriental sources of contemplation. The agnostic Koestler, finding only the type of the yogi to oppose against the type of Commisar of the People, boldly wrote, "Contemplation survives only in the East and to learn it we have to turn to the East."[1] A "Sur-romantic" had already thought along these lines; in *Une Saison en enfer*, Rimbaud stated, "I will return to the Orient and to the first and eternal wisdom." One can see at the least that the expansion of the principle of comparativism had, in all domains, disconcerted Western absolutes and given rise to a crisis of absolutes in the diverse regions of the mind.

The initial phenomenon, at the turn of the eighteenth-century, had been the discovery of passages for the linguistic circumnavigation of the globe: the first voyage round the spoken world became possible at the very moment everyone was seeking to explain mind, society, and almost faith (as in Bonald) by means of language. One soon despaired of landing on any linguistic virgin shore; in linguistics, as in other fields, one never reached an irreducible primitive but rather only sediments more or less eroded. There, one suspected, the absolute was only a little-known relative; one gave up hope of rediscovering the cosmic egg. The unique work of science is to analyze processes; getting at substances is the concern of belief. History, that insatiable invader, stopped short of crossing the boundary of faith: this symbolic act discretely marked the foundation of comparative grammar, an act repeated by the division of grammatical studies into those concerned with languages and those concerned with language. The historical terrain that had been so magnified and adored was *deconsecrated*. The event was significant: the linguists believed they had found the answer to Babel, the poets expected the return of Eden; a passion for origins rose up in the hearts of men with each new archaeological excavation, a little as if, with each new formula produced by a chemist came the illusion that he had created new life: the postulate of a mother tongue produced linguistics by parthenogenesis. But the notion of the primitive could be confirmed only by distorting it; it could no longer be regarded as the starting point of history, but only as an increasingly lower point on its scale. It was movable and it therefore brought into play notions about change; history no longer provided a bulwark for all time, and certainly it could not provide a foundation. At the same time, both aesthetic canons and scientific theories renounced their claims to permanence; each worker in what had been the ancient verities felt that he had been betrayed if he pursued or acquired anything durable. The Romantic aesthetic movement, the biological dogma of evolution, the imperialism of language in the intellectual empires, these were now the new and important things that one could agree upon. In our day, the heirs of the poets of instability, the metaphysicians of the unconscious, and the doctors of myth, the most revolutionary manipulators of language and literature, speak of "free words" as of a "spiritual experience"—they are confirming without knowing it Burnouf's formula *Nomina numina*.

CHAPTER TWENTY-FIVE

Aesthetic Incompatibilities

IT was in the realm of the plastic arts, which mark the end of both the rationed and the rational, that oriental studies were, as I suggested, assimilated with the most difficulty. Is Hindu art widely appreciated even today? The Guimet Museum was not founded at Lyon until 1879 (it was moved to Paris in 1885). In *Apollo* in 1904 Salomon Reinach excluded India and China from "a general history of the plastic arts" on the pretext of chronology; yet this posed no barrier to the Assyrian monuments. It is true that Mahabalipuram and, for a long time, even Angkor could not be transported as Khorsabad was. But, most imporant, Nineveh was less troubling, insofar as it was territory known from the biblical prophets— and it was truly past. One could engage its works in dialogue but not its artists; it is India's misfortune that there are no more Assyrians, and, further, that the living ritual, the unalterable tradition of cultures, is concentrated in ornamental codes. Faced with the Indian monuments, the old student of the Greeks was frightened by something inextricable where possibilities live on harmoniously. There, in essence, a seminal mystery replaced the practice of expurgation. It was there that the conflict arose, between agglutinative fecundity and reductive discipline.

Schelling had already enlisted Hindu art in support of his mistaken theory of an art based on imitation of the vegetable kingdom. In 1823 Sacy proposed to the Société Asiatique the creation of a special museum. In 1947 an exhibition of Indian art opened in London, and K. de B. Codrington, a member of its organizing committee, recalled: "Unfortunately, when the Honourable [East India] Company was abolished after the Mutiny, the Government of India was not willing to maintain the India Museum in London, and the objects were eventually divided between the Bristol Museum and the South Kensington." Codrington also states, "One of the most interesting things in the Exhibition is a volume of paintings from Archbishop Laud's library, which he must have acquired before 1630," around the time of Henry Lord. "Both Rembrandt and our own Sir Joshua Reynolds, the first president of the Academy, had seen Indian paintings. . . . The need for an India Museum in London has often been voiced by the Royal India Society, and the Royal Asiatic Society, but in point of fact, nothing could be done. . . . Ruskin damned Indian art as being artificial and without significance; all he had seen was the bric-a-brac retired Indian officials brought back from India. Indian sculpture and painting only became known slowly to Western artists, first to Rodin in Paris, later to Will Rothenstein, Walter Crane, Augustus John and Epstein, all of whom spoke and wrote enthusiastically of it."[1] Furthermore, only the German sensibility, always closer to the philological documentation, had early on acknowledged the position of Hindu art in the great world tradition.

All the same, it was Goethe who gave strongest expression to the West's terror in the face of the multiform gods with diverse gestures that seemed a striking proclamation of contraries. It was because of them that Western custom avoided, as long as possible, what threatened to enter both its homes and minds and to attack its comfortable repertoire of images. Because of its power of perpetual metamorphosis and its erudite iconography of attributes and symbols, that teeming population of divinities long remained unfathomable. It was difficult to discover what secret order, so different from our own, here, through so many multiples, gave expression to the One. There is no scandal so violent as that which touches a man's eyes. Until that time Western man had been able to take his own body with its limbs balanced in sets of two, with its whole symmetrical skeleton already matched to a council of dichotomic wisdom, as the perfect model. How could he respond to gods to whom one could always add another appendage intended to divert it into various adjacent, but contradictory, actions? Not only was his whole rhetoric at issue, but his whole organic foundation was in peril. Moreover, the Asian, with a natural agility further sharpened by centuries of devoted exercise, read his plastic arts as if from an open book and was at ease in the tangled fretwork to which he was the son and witness. Christianity had, since the end of the Middle Ages, lost the faculty of reading bibles of stone, those signs having been supplanted by the monopoly of the book. If India abounded in people unable to read the written word, the West had a prodigious number who were illiterate when it came to images, incapable of spontaneously deciphering architecture and drawing edification from it. Such examples fully illustrate the major conflict between the two civilizations, the two modes of reason, the two souls. One of the very rare instances in which a European painter submitted himself to authentic Asiatic influence is Gauguin. But to what extent do experts acknowledge this?

Only to the extent that Gauguin abandoned the two axioms of Western painting—perspective and distribution of light and shade. In other words, perception is redressed by logic, and sense experience is shielded by convention.

CHAPTER TWENTY-SIX

The Orient, the Supreme Romanticism

Tout ce qui est incompréhensible ne laisse pas d'être.
　　　　　　　　　　　　　　　　　　　　　—Pascal

SUDDENLY energing in the nineteenth century as a sign of separation, was Romanticism itself anything other than an oriental irruption of the intellect? Its adventure is not restricted to any particular seg-
ment of time, but rather is one of the manifestations of a perpetual question.
The relation between the Orient and Romanticism is less a local and temporal one than an essential one.

A Europe where a good many intellectual and spiritual veins were pe-
tering out and which had had enough of the rationalizations of reason
was looking for anything, provided it was something different. Even before knowing what that something different would be, it called out, from
the depths of its confused memory, to Asia, which it had so often cursed
and which it had always, though with difficulty, forgotten. And Asia came.
An entire Asia, of all times, which Europe almost began to consider an
Asia of all places. The departures of Anquetil and Jones were not much
of an accident. What followed was nearly inevitable. What followed was
governed by two converging laws, one fate, a physical law of accident,
the other necessity, the result of the human will. The one dictates that in
any realm of sufficient size a given event will encounter its moment: we
can call this *the odds of the ages*. This is represented by, for example, factors
of births, accumulations of matching events. The other law, after placing
something within a few minds, proceeds, step by step, to introduce it into
a body of thought, thus causing a shared feeling of a period in which to
act on coincidences: we can call this *the mission of the generations*.

Germany required an enormous alternative with which to checkmate
Cartesian absolutism. The last excesses of academicism and the recent
bloodshed of civil war had left a deadly vacuum in France. Almost alone

amid the natural and physical sciences, and before the literary awakening, oriental studies made gigantic strides. A new age would be promoted both by an extension of the encyclopedic curiosity characteristic of periods deprived of creativity and by a plenitude of happy discoveries characteristic of times in which scholarship and invention were in equilibrium. Yet, at bottom, something had been irremediably transformed: through the vacuum, a whole chain of systems, an entire intellectual tendency and habit, was toppled by its opposite. The other chain, which would become Romanticism, owed a great deal to the *activity* through which Germany became the privileged destroyer of ancient values. This can be seen quite clearly, since Germany's new values were also taken from French innovators—but it was Germany that armed them with their philosophical detonator. The French are well suited for social and artistic revolutions, the Germans for theological ones; with the former there is an early need to let the wheel rest, and with the latter an aptitude for putting their shoulder to it. Migrants and bearers of a nomadic spirit, great handlers of the wheel, the "barbarians" who were one day to raise its standard knew how to make "a tragic phenomenon" out of spiritual joy. It was through them that Asia first became, as Elie Faure called it, "our interior life." India appeared to the West as an entirely different means of thought: a place where prescription scorned experience, where a higher sense of order dominated life and where dogmatics were preexistent to judgment. In the holy work of reuniting the world, all of mankind's proud use of intellect was—for India—merely a subordinate means and an inconclusive approximation.

For the West the term "to think" presupposes the faculty to create a reality, and thus speech stands for a sort of unfettered magic. In India the magic is closely bound. Certainly no less active, the word is thus bound by the terms of an opposite action and opposite proprieties—by returning the unreality of the thinker to a central reality, unique and diffuse, over which he has power by a title older and other than "thinker," a reality that is, at the same time, complete negation. All Hellenic reflection had been a march toward thought-as-absolute; in the Vedas, far from being autonomous, thought was merely the reference point of Being-in-itself. Greece had worked to separate the rational from the mythical as best it could; India had worked to reunite the human with a divine that is the Universe and the negation of the universe. In that elevated theocracy where to shift a syllable, an intonation, is to upset a particle of the infinite Event, doctrine remained a fluctuating mass whose elasticities and incompatibilities everyone appraised, but for which no one could translate a list of articles into an invariable catechism. The life of the poet or the theologian—and every believer is, without breaking the caste rules, his own theologian and hence his own poet—is bound by an incomparable inter-weaving of commandments, received wisdoms, and practices; but he is allowed, even invited, to insert into each text a thousand interpolations that are like a spiritual autobiography and that are absorbed directly into the floating orthodoxy. In the dense fabric of rituals and the overgrowth of glosses, the disparity of his own unprecedented meditation constitutes his true faith. Thus he moves in an extraordinarily abundant emptiness—an unreality that opens from all sides into a reality beyond. Many Euro-peans were to come to a recognition of themselves within this system that was also irrational, inside this destiny of burgeoning aggregation, this very scholasticism at once imperious, taking complete charge of one, and shift-ing, that is to say volatizing the old trap of believing only in what one can touch. Profound, very profound—and more profound than it seemed, so long as one had not explored its depth. It was in this Orient, so Friedrich Schlegel's saying went, that we must seek the highest Romanticism. His compatriots were at last exploring the promised counterwisdom. There the Unconscious of the individual, which had become the Inner Conscious-ness of the world, awaited them, a disincarnate Unconscious, at once col-lective and scattered, indivisible and dissolved, the only certitude and all ideality.

Within the enchanted mirror of the unconscious the Hindu Orient ap-peared as the unfathomable, the nocturnal figure of the mind, the pres-ence of the chaos that the West had warded off. A new army of the mind entered the battlefield where everyone seemed to have fallen asleep. Yes, there were many-headed Indian gods, but there were Assyrian cherubim and Chinese dragons as well. The elemental called the organic to account, just as the tumultuous had the Olympian; a Titan about whom Greece had maintained a remarkable silence rose up from beneath Mount Ida. One can discern among the great inhabitants of Romanticism, Goethe, Hugo, Michelet, a concealed drama, an attraction to and withdrawal from the breath of the abyss, a fear of forbidden influences, an obsession with making a sense of calm prevail over a sense of panic. Which of them thrived on it and which of them was completely undone? The question almost boils down to this: did the events take place anywhere but in the mind? At the beginning of the nineteenth century, in the eternal left hand of the mind, the conspicuous episode of orientalism coincided with the interior event of Romanticism. From the primitive homeland where heresy cease-lessly became orthodoxy, a strong incentive to make use of their here-siarchs reached Western reason and arts.

Calling for a whole world, Romanticism could not be one of the three ages of humanity so famous in the German school. It no longer said no to certain things; instead it said yes, it is possible, to all things, aligning itself with an Orient where one did not have to choose between yes and no. Either/or was the paramount question for the Greeks: sophistry was the perfect exploitation of the principle of contradiction. If you say white, you cannot say black (although the genius of Socrates did its utmost to place the semblance of an interlocutor before that wall). Indian casuistry, no less indefatigable, had as a law and satisfaction venturing through walls: if you do not say black and white together, I and Thou, then you say nothing. In the Mediterranean tradition the individual or the idea is challenged at all crossroads over the description inscribed in its passport; one settles down into a world of appurtenances. From the Indian perspective, whether one be man or god, the highest sort of identity is the power of transmutation or indefinition; the statue can always grow another limb, the limb another attribute, the monument another decoration, the idea another circuitry, the poem another bundle of verses. The soul's desire is not to make sure that it will always be the same, but rather, amid an infinite series of moltings, to set its sights on just that one that will change it enough to give it, finally and forever, sufficient capacity for all the changes. There is nothing, not even a literary genre, that is anything other than a fragment, neutral in itself, of a multivalent whole. Discrimination intervenes, without doubt and without end, only to destroy all permanences one after another.

When the doctrines had moved beyond a merely ornamental profusion, they struck Europe with a flood of compounds and pedagogical dilutions. "The practices more or less suited to produce union with God," observes D'Souza, today's "leader of Catholics from India," allow one to consider that "the dogmatic contents of religion are of secondary importance." This nearly verbatim repetition of Schleiermacher and his friends sheds light on the union of oriental studies and Romanticism. In the West the ultimate aim of mentation had been a position; in India it had been an attitude. This difference seems to have been the border of their common ground, for could it not be said that *Romanticism was a sanctification of attitudes that was substituted for the sanctification of positions?*

It was a marvel that the cipher disc that cryptographers of genius suddenly set into place over an immemorial coded message should have so vitalized the issue of human limitations. The arrival of India brought about something like an unexpected peopling of the three domains of science, art, and faith. What oppressive or exalting thing did that arrival bring for Man—in the sense that the West had so patiently forged for that word? All the experiences that he had long since dismissed from his councils now battered against the island of the rational, which from then on found itself isolated in the ocean of time. Must the duel between cosmos and chaos be played out again? All he had rejected protested, as if life itself had been refused the prize that he bestowed on his creations. No longer is the unconscious alone a candidate for the title of the natural; the monstrous is a candidate as well. This is the fault not of oriental studies but of a vast meshing that we may term the cosmology of history. The chapter in which civilizations were the work of small countries is closed; David and Solomon are no longer the sole arbiters. Closed too is the chapter in which learned society, itself insular in the tide of illiterates, demanded a small-town literature and the arts of the regime. A centuries-long calm, with the poverties and richnesses of calm periods, is also at an end. Goethe perceived a systolic pulsation of several centuries, followed by a diastolic century. Now I feel I understand the images, so dear to Romanticism, of thoracic expansion under orientalized heavens. This is how what we call open civilizations should be described, with the stress that can be placed on them only by those to whom they are closed again.

$\mathcal{N}$otes

DEFINITIONS

1. In this translation "Orient" and "the East" have been used interchangably as synonyms for all of Asia, and where possible the terms Orient, oriental, orientalism and the like have been left intact, since they are important to Schwab's arguments.

2. Max Müller, *Lectures on the Science of Language*, 1:91. Originally delivered at the Royal Institution of Great Britain in April, May, and June 1861. Schwab takes most of the material in this paragraph from Müller's third lecture.

3. Sylvain Lévi, "Abel Bergaigne et l'indianisme," in *Mémorial Sylvain Lévi*, p. 10.

4. André Festugière, *La révélation d'Hermès Trismégiste*, and Jean Filliozat, "La doctrine du brahmisme d'apres S. Hippolyte." These points will be dealt with more thoroughly later when we encounter "the question of the soul." [Schwab]

5. Paul Jean Oltramare, *L'histoire des idées théosophiques dans l'Inde* 2:iii. Oltramare shows that modern theosophy did not actually originate in India but "in the ancient tradition of Judaism and the Renaissance." [Schwab]

1. THERE IS AN ORIENTAL RENAISSANCE

1. There are two epigraphs from Eckstein, appearing at the head of chapter 46, "Les caprices du sort font naître, des causes les moins aperçues, d'important circonstances, ou dérangent le cours des choses" ("The whims of fate engender, from the least perceptible causes, significant events, and sometimes alter the course of things"), and at the head of chapter 50, "Il n'y a d'aveugle que la puissance du mal, qui ignore le but, quoiqu'elle sache parfaitement raisonner ses intentions et combiner ses moyens" (The only blindness is the power of evil, which knows nothing of its purpose, although it is very adept at arguing its intentions and marshaling its forces).

2. For further discussion on this point see Henri Baudet, *Paradise on Earth*.

2. ESTABLISHING THE TEXTS

1. Maxime du Camp, *Souvenirs littéraires*, 2:108.

2. The correct view is that of Vasillii Vladimirovitch Bartold in *La découverte de*

l'Asie (tr. Nikitine), p. 41: "The nineteenth century's infatuation with Egypt *replaced* its infatuation with India." [Schwab]

3. The English founded an East India Company in 1599, the Dutch in 1602. The French company was reorganized by Colbert in 1664. Before Nobili, there were reports that in Goa in 1597 an English Jesuit, Thomas Stevens, spoke a local dialect in which he may have written a biblical history for neophytes, and he may have known Sanskrit. [Schwab]

4. Pierre Villey-Desmesrets, *Les sources des idées*.

5. "Sir William Jones had proposed to government the compilation of an extensive code, of both Mohammedan and Hindu law, arranged after the method of Justinian's Pandects, with extracts from the native authorities. Sir William died before he could do much more than plan the work, and it was carried on by a pandit, Jagannatha. The important task of translating this great work was undertaken by Colebrooke." Sir Leslie Stephen and Sir Sidney Lee, eds., *Dictionary of National Biography* (Oxford: Oxford University Press, 1973), 4:739.

6. Louis Mathieu Langlès, *Recherches asiatiques*, preface.

7. See *Sir William Jones. Bicentenary of his birth*, and *Proceedings of the Sir William Jones Bicentenary Conference*.

8. See Sir T. E. Colebrooke, *The Life of H. T. Colebrooke, by his son* (London: Trubner, 1873).

9. Abel Rémusat, "Discours sur la littérature orientale," in *Mélanges posthumes*, p. 255.

10. H. H. Wilson's *History of British India from 1805 to 1835* was written as a continuation of James Mill's *The History of British India*.

11. Gustave Dugat, *Histoire des orientalistes*, 1:159.

12. Silvestre de Sacy, *Mélanges*, p. 67.

13. James Darmesteter, *Essais orientaux*, pp. 1–4 passim.

14. Sylvain Lévi, "Les origines d'une chair: l'entrée du sanskrit au Collège du France," in *Mémorial*, p. 150.

15. Salomon Reinach, *Manuel philologie classique*, 1:19.

3. EUROPE LEARNS SANSKRIT

1. Joseph Guigniaut, *Religions de l'antiquité*, 1:606.

2. It is no surprise when a note in Volney's *Ruins* (1791) extols the Indianists of Calcutta. [Schwab]

3. Francois Joseph Picavet, *Les Idéologues*, p. 98.

4. Comtesse de Pange, *Auguste-Guillaume Schlegel et Madame de Staël*, p. 126.

5. Goethe wrote Schiller on February 19, 1802: "I have now read 'Gita Govinda' in English and I am sorry to say I must accuse our good Dahlberg of inept trash. Jones says in his introduction that he first of all made a literal translation of this poem and then omitted what seemed to him too lascivious and too bold for his nation. And now the German translator not only again omits what seems to him suspect along these lines, he also fails to understand very fine, innocent passages and translates them wrongly. Perhaps I shall make a translation of the end, which

chiefly has been withered by this German blight, so that the old poet can at least appear before you in whatever beauty the English Translator could leave to him." M. von Herzfeld and C. Melvil Sym, trs., *Letters from Goethe* (Edinburgh: Edinburgh University Press, 1957), p. 316.

6. It was through Kosegarten that Goethe became personally acquainted with Sacy, for whom Goethe added a dedicatory poem to the *Divan*. [Schwab]

7. Alphonse de Lamartine, *Cours familier de littérature*, 3:338.

8. Published by Langlès in 1807 in the *Magazin Encyclopédique*. After his return to England, Hamilton published *The Hitopadesa in the Sanscrita Language* (London: Library, East India House, 1810), *Terms of Sanscrit Grammar* (London: Cox and Baylis, 1814), and *A Key to the Chronology of the Hindus* (2 vols., Cambridge: Rivington, 1820). [Schwab]

In her *Alexander Hamilton (1762–1824): A Chapter in the Early History of Sanskrit Philology*, Rosane Rocher convincingly sets forth reasons why this last-named work, originally published only with the initials A. H. and ascribed to Hamilton by a cataloger in the British Museum, should be considered "an apocrypha."

9. August Wilhelm Schlegel, *Réflexions sur l'étude des langages asiatiques*, p. 97.

10. Quoted in Albert Garreau, *Clément Brentano*, p. 71.

11. Benjamin Constant, *Journal intime*, p. 78.

12. Before he was known as an orientalist in Germany, Mackintosh had gained recognition in France for his refutation of Burke; in 1792 the Assemblée Législative bestowed on him the title of "Citizen." [Schwab]

13. At the College de France, auditorium 4, called "des langues," is where Sacy, Champollion, Burnouf, and Renan taught. [Schwab]

14. Besides that of Angelo de Gubernatis at Florence, Italy also established in the course of the nineteenth-century chairs of Sanskrit (or comparative linguistics) at Milan, Naples, and Pisa. [Schwab]

4. THE ERA OF DECIPHERINGS AND THE EXPANSION OF THE KNOWN WORLD

1. This journal followed *Asiatic Researches* and these were both followed in 1839 by the *Journal of the Asiatic Society of Bengal*; in 1841 by the *Journal of the Bombay Branch*; in 1844 by the *Calcutta Review*; and in 1847 by the *Zeitschrift der Deutschen Morgenländischen Gesellschaft* [Schwab].

2. In his "Discours introductif" to the *Encyclopédie*, in 1751, d'Alembert proclaimed that the time had come to replace Latin with French as the language of learning, it "having spread over all of Europe." Moreover, under Frederick the Great the Academy of Sciences of Berlin, which had been presided over by the French down to 1786, employed French as its first language, ahead of Latin. It was Louis XIV, the bogeyman of young Germany, who had arbitrarily replaced Latin with French each chance he could. [Schwab]

3. Elme Marie Caro, *Mélanges et Portraits*, 1:90.

4. In 1840, at Burnouf's request, Guizot allotted funds to reproduce a new Vedic collection, under Prinsep's supervision (Filloźat, *Catalogue fonds Sanskrit*, Biblio-

thèque Nationale). See also Loiseleur-Deslongchamps, *Lois de Manou*, p. 380, n. 2. [Schwab]

5. A part of Pauthier's translation of Colebrooke (concerning the Vedas) was reproduced by Loiseleur-Deslongchamps at the end of his *Lois de Manou*, which has been continuously reprinted in the series Classiques Garnier. [Schwab]

6. Mlle M.-L. Dufrénoy has established (*Journal de la Société de Statistique de Paris*, November–December 1945) the most autocatalytic curves (with abscissas and asymptotes) of the oriental publications (eighteenth-century fiction). [Schwab]

7. For Germany see Benfey's 356 double-column page article "India" in Johann Ersch and J. G. Gruber's *Allegemeine Encyklopadie die Wissenschaften und Kunste* (Leipzig: F. A. Brockhaus, 1850–51). [Schwab]

8. Paul Hazard, *La pensée européenne au XVIIIᵉ siècle*, 3:143.

5. THE PROGRESS OF ORIENTAL STUDIES

1. For details see Alfred Foucher, *La vie du Bouddha*, pp. 14–15.

2. Joseph Guigniaut, *Religions de l'antiquité*, 1:576 ff.

3. I admit I cannot read Saint-Hilaire's name any more calmly—but for different reasons—than Hugo could. To my way of thinking this devotee of Victor Cousin must lay to his conscience a great many fripperies, such as the following: "The Buddha was one of those naïve and blind thinkers who, leaving being to attain nothingness, never felt the overwhelming weight of this untenable contradiction, who lose themselves in their own thought for lack of a sufficient examination of its principles" (*Le Bouddha et sa religion*, p. 23). Losing himself in his own thought was a peril which posed little threat to Saint-Hilaire. Even the essay on Sankhya bestowed on the doctrine discussed the honor of this concluding dictum: "We condemn it unreservedly." [Schwab]

4. Burnouf's manuscript is preserved among his papers in the Bibliothèque Nationale. [Schwab]

5. Ernest Renan, *Nouvelles lettres intimes*, p. 168.

6. H. G. Rawlinson, "India in European Literature and Thought," pp. 35–36.

6. THE DOCTRINAL STAGES

1. New verification, concerning Buddhism this time, may be found in Alfred Foucher's *Vie du Bouddha*, p. 21. [Schwab]

2. Friedrich Christoph Schlosser, *Universalhistorische ubersicht der Geschichte der alten Welt und ihrer Cultur*; the French translation by de Golbéry to which Schwab refers is *Histoire universelle de l'antiquité*.

3. Also published under the title *Essai sur les Dogmes de la Métempsychose et du Purgatoire enseignés par les Bramins de l'Indostan*, Berne, 1771. There were four editions and a German translation. [Schwab]

4. Joseph Guigniaut, *Religions de l'antiquité*, 1:140.

5. *Ibid.*, 1:654.
6. *Ibid.*, 1:569.

7. THE BIRTH OF LINGUISTICS

1. Yvon Belaval, "Leibniz et la langue allemande," pp. 121–32.

2. There were enormous surveys: Hervas' *Catalogo delle lingue conoscuite (Catalog of Known Languages)*, published in 1784, which also appeared in a 6-volume Spanish edition between 1800 and 1805; Adelung's *Mithradates*, in four volumes, 1806–17; and the *Glossarium comparativum totius orbis* of Pallas and Catherine the Great, which appeared from 1787 to 1817. [Schwab]

3. *Catalogo*, 1784 (Italian); subsequent edition, in Spanish, 6 volumes, 1800–5. See also the importance of the question for Ballanche, in Barchou's "Essai d'une formule générale." [Schwab]

4. Ernest Renan, *De l'origine du langage*, esp. 2:76, 156.

5. Joseph Vendryes, *Le langage*, p. 6.

6. He became professor of foreign literature at once, and later dean. Just as there was already a school of Indic studies at Nancy, there would continue to exist at Strasbourg an active, excellent center of Semitic studies in a Protestant milieu, during periods when these studies were not represented elsewhere in France. Reuss later excelled there, at the time of Bergmann, and in the 1830s the young pastor Bochinger, showed great promise in the study of Hindu religions, a promise he died too young to fulfill. [Schwab]

7. Klaproth had been the first to remark that the birch is the only tree whose name is found in both Sanskrit and in the Slavic languages. Pictet made a great deal of this remark (which had first appeared in the *Journal Asiatique* in 1830), which he considered of great importance. [Schwab]

8. Jean Edouard Spenlé's *La pensée allemand de Luther à Nietzsche* contains these edifying quotations: from Schiller, "Each people has its day in history. The day for the Germans will be the harvest of all the past centuries." From Fichte: "We alone are the living People. We are the original People, das Urvolk, the true People of God." By contrast and inference, the others, notably the French, are the "non-people," "not because of language nor of history, nor of race, but by virtue of a metaphysical necessity." [Schwab]

8. REPERCUSSIONS IN LITERATURE

1. For the original English versions see Thomas Roe, *The journal of Sir Thomas Roe*, and John Ovington, *A voyage in Suratt in the year 1689*.

2. H. G. Rawlinson, "India in European Literature and Thought," pp. 27–28.

3. I leave aside the question of industrial and artistic activities in India which had led Michelet to remark, "The English make no fuss about saying that they are the ones who have killed India" *(Bible de l'Humanité)*. This has been a matter for much discussion, and for harsh words. [Schwab]

4. Quoted by G. T. Garratt, "Indo-British Civilization," p. 400.

5. Quoted in *ibid.*, pp. 401–2.

6. *Ibid.*, pp. 411–12.

7. Charles Edwyn Vaughan, *The Romantic Revolt.*

8. Curtis Hidden Page, *The Chief American Poets*, p. 88n.

9. Edward Carpenter, *Days with Walt Whitman.* Carpenter's own interest in India is evidenced in *From Adam's Peak to Elephanta: Sketches in Ceylon and India* (London: S. Sonnenschein, 1892; New York: Macmillan, 1892) and his edition of Ponnambalam Arunachalan, *Light from the East: Being letters on Gnanam, the divine knowledge* (London: Allen and Unwin, 1927).

10. Here I am following Maryla Falk's *I "Misteri" di Novalis*, in which the subject was revived. [Schwab]

11. Baron Henri Blaze, who provided a great many valuable particulars in *Ecrivains et poètes le l'Allemagne*, still felt obliged to excuse philology for this poetry, which was produced through the necessity of making a living. [Schwab]

12. Max Rouché in *Johann Gottfried Herder: Une autre philosophie de l'histoire* (tr., with notes and introduction, Paris: Aubier, Editions Montaigne, 1943).

13. For further details see René Guignard, "Le groupe romantique de Heidelberg," *Revue des cours et conférences*, 1936–37. [Schwab]

14. For Friedrich Schlegel, Christianity was "an event that had scarcely begun." According to Viatte, Joseph de Maistre accepted the idea of "a third revelation," and the Saint-Simonians would later speak of a fourth. On the other hand, one must trace back to Lessing the idea that all religions are each but a moment in the history of the same religious sentiment. Finally, what Heidelberg and Görres did for the German Catholic revival is well known. [Schwab]

15. Karl Hillebrand, "De la philologie en Allemagne dans la première moitié du siècle."

16. Leo Jourbert, *Essais de critique et d'histoire.*

17. Emile Bréhier, *Schelling.*

18. Elme Marie Caro, *Du mysticisme au XVIIIe siècle.*

19. Henri Lichtenberger, trs., Johann Wolfgang von Goethe, *Divan occidental-oriental [West-Ostlicher Divan].*

20. Alfred Schlagdenhauffen, *Frédéric Schlegel et son groupe.*

21. Once again, an idea shared by the group: "Schelling . . . a poet and philosopher, teaches that philosophy, born of poetry in the early days of the human race, must, after reaching full maturity, immerse itself once more, via the intermediary of the new mythology, in the ocean of poetry, and that Christianity, in its most recent inspiration, is a product of the oriental spirit that brought forth the religion of India and in this way penetrated the entire Orient. Hence for the *choryphées* of Romanticism the Orient is gradually becoming . . . the homeland of that magical idealism that they dreamed of establishing. It was there that they hoped to find the fullness of life, primitive mankind, the original religion that they are making every effort to trace. Frederick Schlegel in particular works tirelessly in this direction." (H. Lichtenberger) [Schwab]

22. The skeptic Jacquemont had made the same comparison in an insolent dic-

tum: "Don't the absurd of Benares and the absurd of Germany bear a striking family resemblance?" [Schwab]

23. Antoine Frédéric Ozanam, *Lettres*, 1:7, 16n1.

9. WELL-PREPARED GROUND

1. Charles Nodier, *Mademoiselle de Marsan*, and Pauline de Pange, *Madame de Staël et la découverte de l'Allemagne*.

2. Jules Barbey d'Aurevilly, *Dix-neuvieme siècle*, 2d series. The first series (1860) ran to 26 volumes.

3. ". . . This marvelous Germany, the ultimate homeland of the West's poetic traditions and beliefs" (*Le Peintre de Salsbourg*, preface, 1840). Cf. publisher's note for *Jean Sbogar*: for German literature Mme de Staël "awakens curiosity, Nodier excited passions." See also, in Nodier, *Mademoiselle de Marsan*, the ideas of Dr. Fabricius, "an exalted spiritualism, a speculative theory uniting principles of Swedenborg, Saint-Martin, and perhaps Weishaupt." [Schwab]

4. Ozanam, *Lettres*, 1:5.

5. Albert Beguin, "Poésie et occultisme."

6. Charles Baudelaire, *Les fleurs du Mal*, ed. by Jacques Crepet (Paris: L. Conard, 1922), p. 457.

7. Jean Blum, *Johann August Starck*, p. 73.

8. *Ibid.*, p. 27.

9. Quoted in Sébastien Charléty, *Histoire du Saint-Simonisme*.

10. Adrienne Moore, *Rammohun Roy and America*, p. 7.

11. Compare Taine with André Festugière, *La révélation d'Hermès Trismégiste*. See esp. *L'astrologie et les sciences occultes*, 1:477 ff.

12. Egger, who, as we have seen, influenced both Eckstein and Burnouf, analyzed Fauriel's course in the *Journal de l'Instruction Publique* in twelve articles that diffused these ideas within learned circles. Ozanam makes errors in detail in his discussion of the students influenced by Hamilton. [Schwab]

10. THE MOVING SPIRITS

1. I am indebted for the principal traits in this portrait and, save for indications to the contrary, for my citations, to Père Nicholas Burtin, *Un semeur d'idées au temps de la restauration*. [Schwab]

2. Philarète Chasles, *Memoirs*, 1:270.

3. Burtin, *Un semeur d'idées*, p. 320.

4. *Ibid.*, p. 354.

5. Emile Egger, *Mémoires de littérature ancienne*, p. 510.

6. Alfred Marquiset, *Ballanche et Madame d'Hautefeuille*, p. 11.

7. Ottmar de Mohl, ed., *Correspondance de Fauriel et Mary Clarke*, p. 393.

8. For Michelet's deference to Eckstein see the unpublished letters in the Bibliothèque Historique, Paris. [Schwab]

9. Maurice Souriau's introduction to Hugo's *Le préface de Cromwell*, pp. xvi and 23.

10. Hugo later changed his opinion, although probably somewhat belatedly. The cruel—and accurate—note to *Choses vues* published in the *Figaro Littéraire* (December 31, 1849) is unfortunately not dated. In it Eckstein is compared to the moon "never visible except from the briefly lighted side"; "his ideas are a teeming army, but one that straggles along and always seems to have just been routed. His brain is encumbered with notes, erasures, cross-references, and brackets. He will never manage to edit his mind." There is no appeal to the charge; but it does not mean that the young Hugo did not benefit from those notes and references. Cf. Lamennais's phrase stating that Eckstein "had all the keys, but he opened nothing." [Schwab]

11. Burtin, *Un semeur d'idées*, p. 103.

12. Ernest Renan, *Etudes d'histoire religieuse*, pp. 75 and 175.

13. Burtin, *Un semeur d'idées*, p. 65.

14. *Ibid.*, p. 125.

15. Jozef Maria Hoene-Wroński, *Messianisme*, pp. 45n, 125, 128, 254. Compare Auguste Viatte, *Les sources occultes du Romanticisme*, 2:258, and Alexandre Erdan, *La France mystique*, 2:389–478.

16. Hermoine Quinet, *Edgar Quinet avant l'exile*, p. 173. Unless otherwise indicated, the quotations in this section are from this book or its companion volume, *Cinquante ans d'amitié*. It should be remembered, however, that these accounts by Quinet, and especially those by his second wife, are frequently debatable. [Schwab]

17. Jean Boudout, "Faust et Ahasvérus."

18. Henry Michel, et al., *Edgar Quinet*, p. 27.

19. Sylvain Lévi, "Les parts respectives des nations occidentales dans les progrès de l'indianisme," in *Mémorial*, p. 116. (Reprinted from *Scientia* [January 1924], pp. 21–34.)

20. Hermoine Quinet, *Edgar Quinet*, pp. 307 ff.

21. Edgar Quinet, *Le génie des religions*, pp. 77–78.

22. Joseph Buche, *L'école mystique de Lyon*.

11. FOUNDERS AND INTERMEDIARIES

1. There were three philologists with the name Burnouf: Jean-Louis (1775–1844) the Latinist and translator of Tacitus and Pliny the Younger and a student of Sanskrit under Chézy before his son Eugene. His nephew Emile-Louis, born in 1821, was also a serious Indic scholar and a Hellenist by profession; Emile founded the Ecole Indianiste at Nancy and was later director of the Ecole d'Athènes. One is surprised to find René Guénon, in *Introduction générale a l'étude des doctrines hindoues*, confusing Eugene with Emile Burnouf when he attacks *La science des religions*, which was the work of the latter. Jean-Louis, born in 1775 near Valognes (the son of a weaver), was a professor of Latin oratory at the Collège de France in 1817, a friend of Bopp and Chézy, and a character in the tradition of Postel. [Schwab]

2. Michelet notes: "Many Englishmen were in contact with him, not only for his scholarship, but for the trust his character inspired." Jules Michelet, *Histoire*

du XIXe siècle (3 vols.; Paris: C. Marpon and E. Flammarion, 1880), 3:306. [Schwab]

3. Quoted in Ernest Windisch, *Geschichte der Sanskritphilologie und indischen Altertumskunde.*

4. Prosper Mérimée, *Correspondance générale.*

5. Ernest Renan, *Oeuvres complètes,* 1:121–26.

6. Joseph Guigniaut, *Religions de l'antiquité,* 1:607, and Léon Feer, *Papiers d'Eugène Burnouf.*

7. Same observation as for the Burnoufs: even in the bibliographies, Silvestre de Sacy (Antoine-Isaac) the orientalist was frequently confused with his son, Samuel-Uztazade. [Schwab]

8. Abel Bergaigne and Paul Lehugeur, *Sacountala.*

9. Louis Madelin, *La nation sous l'Empereur.*

10. Burtin, *Un semeur d'idées,* p. 230.

11. Pierre Moreau, *Le romantisme,* p. 440.

12. Anatole Cerfbeer and Jules Christophe, *Répertoire de la Comédie humaine de Honoré de Balzac,* pp. 292–93.

13. The "famous debate" [provoked by Laurencet's and Meyranx's essay] between Cuvier and Geoffroy Saint-Hilaire at the Académie des sciences in 1830, the "successive stages of which were recorded by the political press, and which intrigued Goethe" (Caullery), had to do with the quasi-cosmogonic postulate of the unit of structure *(l'unité d'organisation).* Consequently, the polemics of exegetes was revived among biologists, and one could, by contrasting Geoffroy to the finalist Cuvier, again characterize the former as a pantheist and point to his proximity to German *Naturphilosophie.* [Schwab]

14. In his translation, Herbert J. Hunt footnotes this passage thus: "The supposed text of the original, given above, is in Arabic translated for Balzac by the orientalist Baron von Hammer-Purgstall" (New York: Penguin Books, 1977), 51*n.*

15. Marie Jeanne Durry, *La vieillesse de Chateaubriand,* 1:480, 2:360.

16. See Terrick Hamilton, *Antar, a Bedoueen romance: Translated from the Arabic* (London: J. Murray, 1819) and Etienne-Jean Delécluze, *Antar, roman bédouin d'Abou Sa'ìd Abd al-Malik ibn Zoraib al-Asma'ì, traduit de l'arabe par Terric-Hamilton* (3 vols.; Paris: A. Bertrand, 1819).

17. Georges Goyau, *Ozanam.*

18. Christian Maréchal, *La jeunesse de La Mennais.*

19. Cited in Pierre Harispe, *Lamennais et Gerbet.* See also Harispe, *Lamennais.*

20. The same year he was exasperated by V. Parisot's *Ramayana,* Barbey d'Aurevilly lashed out against Pauthier, whom he styled a pedant in a white frock coat, in a letter to his friend and publisher, Trébutien, himself an orientalist (November 21–22, 1857). [Schwab]

21. Théodore Pavie translated, from the *Mahabharata,* Savitri in 1831, and the abduction of Draupadi in 1833. *Fragments du Mahâ Bhârata* appeared in the *Journal Asiatique* in 1839–41, and in the bookstores in 1844; *Krishna et sa doctrine* was published in 1852. It was Pavie who, after the death of Burnouf, ensured the publication of *Lotus de la bonne loi.* [Schwab]

22. René Bazin, *Paysages et pays d'Anjou.*

23. Henri Alexandre Wallon, *Eloges académiques,* 1:61.

12. CHRONICLERS AND NOVELISTS

1. One of his publications is entitled *Bramanical Fraud detected* (1812). [Schwab]

2. My list is by no means exhaustive: Anquetil, and then Schlosser, also cited, among others, Malcolm, J. Mill, Hermann, Dalrymple, Guyon, and La Croze as historians of India. B. Saint-Hilaire, in Franck's *Dictionnaire des sciences philosophique*, is lenient with Ward. [Schwab]

3. Chateaubriand's grand embroideries of India are attributed to his readings, the most important (but including Raynal) being Sonnerat, d'Anville, Tavernier, and the Abbé Dubois, who, "having lived thirty years in India was from 1823 to 1848 director of the Séminaire des Missions Etrangères, Rue du Bac." (*Mémoires d'Outre-Tombe*, n 2 of 1.3, chap. 11). To these influences should be added the impact of his exile in England. [Schwab]

4. In the *Asiatic Researches* of 1822 (vol. 14) Duvaucel is cosignatory of a communiqué concerning a still unclassified animal species. [Schwab]

5. Louis Jacolliot wrote a series of such works: *Voyage au pays des Brahmes* (Paris: E. Dentu, 1878), *Voyage aux ruines de Golconde et à la cité des morts* (Paris: E. Dentu, 1879), *Voyage aux pays des fakirs charmeurs* (Paris: E. Dentu, 1881), and *Voyage au pays des jungles: Les femmes de l'Inde* (Paris: E. Dentu, 1889). Pierre Eugène Lamairesse wrote two such works: *L'Inde avant le Bouddha* (Paris: G. Carre, 1891) and *L'Inde après le Bouddha* (Paris: G. Carre, 1892). In addition to his *L'Inde des Rajahs: Voyage dans l'Inde centrale et dans les présidences de Bombay et du Bengale, 1864–68* (Paris: Hachette, 1875), Louis Rousselet also wrote *Chants populaires du sud de l'Inde* (Paris: Librairie internationale, 1868).

6. This subject had interested Montaigne, who cited Propertius on suttee, as well as Quintus Curtius on the gymnosophists, in his essay "Of Virtue." [Schwab]

7. Abel François Villemain, "Du génie anglais dans l'Inde."

13. INDIA AND THE BLOSSOMING OF LAMARTINE

1. Maurice Levaillant, ed. *Lamartine: Oeuvres choisies*.

2. "A subtle critic, Jules Lemaître, has shown *La chute d'un Ange* to have many analogies to Brahmanical thought"; Camille Latreille, *Les dernières années de Lamartine*, p. 148. [Schwab]

3. Louis Renou has pointed out to me that another episode had an analogous meaning: that of Yajnadatta from the *Ramayana*. It was an episode known early on in Romantic Europe, particularly in France; Chézy had translated it in 1814 and republished it in 1826 in the notes to his *Shakuntala*. [Schwab]

14. HUGO TROUBLED BY INDIA

1. Louis Guimbaud, *Les "Orientales" de Victor Hugo*.

2. A book that was of paramount importance to Hugo: he told Stapfer that, in the book, one sentence "contains the explanation of the universe" (P. Stapfer, *Victor*

Hugo à Guernesey, p. 140). He was referring to the migration of souls and "what the occult science of the Persians had sought, in the name of magic." It was the period when Hugo was moving from deism to a quasi-pantheism; at first glance, it would seem that he must have been attracted to oriental doctrines. [Schwab]

3. By Jean-Marie Carré, *Michelet et son temps*, pp. 40–70. "There are not," the author so rightly observes, "in nineteenth-century French literature, two imaginations more comparable, two sensibilities more fraternal." Not long ago, I might add in confirmation, Georges Victor-Hugo showed me two sentences Michelet had written, heart to heart, and Hugo always kept before him on his worktable. [Schwab]

15. VIGNY TEMPTED BY INDIA

1. Vera A. Summers, *L'orientalisme d'Alfred de Vigny*, p. 134.

2. There had previously appeared, in the *Revue des Deux-Mondes* of June 15, 1837, an article by Ampère entitled *L'Histoire du bouddhisme*; in the July 15, 1854 edition there was an article by Pavie on the *Rig Veda* and *Les livres sacrés des Hindous*. [Schwab]

3. Quoted in Marc Citoleux, *Alfred de Vigny*, p. 321.

4. In *La pensée religieuse et morale d'Alfred de Vigny* (p. 317), Bonnefoy states, regarding Vigny's reading of the *Gita*, that "in fact, thenceforth he would buttress his critique of Christianity with arguments drawn from the Hindu poems. Christianity, conceived as a religion of hope and desire, was impurity itself; a poetry of corporeal desire unable to resign itself to death, it ignored renunciation, the sole virtue. . . . Purity of duty and purity of thought—these were the tendencies that were confirmed here." [Schwab]

16. MICHELET ANSWERED BY INDIA

1. Dated January 30, 1842. Cited in Gabriel Monod, *La vie et la pensée de Jules Michelet*, 2:73.

2. Augustin Thierry, "Considérations sur l'histoire de France."

3. His is not an isolated instance; in 1802 Fauriel frequented the Museum, perhap because he met his beloved Madame Condorcet there. [Schwab]

4. Quoted in Pierre Moreau, *Le romantisme*, p. 351.

5. *Sic*; Monod, *Vie de Michelet*, 2:224. The terms should, of course, read Kurus and Pandus; nowadays, Indic scholars prefer to write them as *Kauravas* and *Pandavas*, the names of the two factions brought together in the *Mahabharata*. [Schwab]

6. For the Vedas, Michelet used the translations of Wilson, Rosen, Langlois, Emile Burnouf, and Max Müller; for the epics, Fauche and Gorresio; for the *Laws of Manu*, he now had at his disposal the Loiseleur-Deslongchamps translation. The phrase that Michelet used to describe his work when he sent it to Hugo, that it was "a miserable, an execrable thing," was not empty of sincerity. The work was not all that he would have hoped for, all that he would have liked to say about Asia. [Schwab]

7. Quoted in Marie Jeanne Durry, *La vieillesse de Chateaubriand*, 2:328.

8. Quoted in Monod, *Vie de Michelet*, 2:780.

9. *Ibid.*, 2:95.

10. Hugo remarked, "The self of an individual is vaster and more profound than the self of a people." [Schwab]

11. Monod, *Vie de Michelet*, 2:95.

18. AN EXTERNAL ORIENT: EXOTICISM

1. Jean Richter, *Gérard de Nerval et les doctrines ésotériques*.

2. E. Carcassonne, "Leconte de Lisle et la philosophie indienne."

19. THE INDIA OF SCHOPENHAUER

1. Schopenhauer, *The World as Will and Idea*, from the 1883 Haldane-Kemp translation, 3:281.

2. *Ibid.*, 3:445.

3. *Ibid.*, 3:451.

4. Pirenne, *Les grands courants*, preface to vol. 3.

20. THE IRAN OF NIETZSCHE

1. Lou Andreas-Salomé, *Frédéric Nietzsche*.

2. It is more difficult to believe that the notion of Eternal Return evoked no recollection in Nietzsche's mind, however indirect, of yugas and samsara. [Schwab]

21. THE BUDDHISM OF WAGNER

1. Richard Wagner, *My Life* (2 vols.; New York: Dodd, Mead, 1911), 2:638.

2. Judith Gautier, *Auprès de Richard Wagner*, p. 229.

22. RUSSIAN ORIENTALISM AND NONVIOLENCE

1. In his supplementary bibliography to his translation of Vassili Barthold's *La découverte de l'Asie* (Paris: Payot, 1947), Basile Nikitine cited Karl Marx's "Lettres sur l'Inde," preface by D. Riasanov, *Annales du Marxisme*, vol. 3 (Leningrad, 1927).

23. THE DIALOGUE BETWEEN CREEDS ON THE QUESTION OF THE SOUL

1. André Festugière, *La révélation d'Hermès Trismégiste*, p. 37.

2. Père Nicholas Burtin, *Un semeur d'idées*, p. 81.

3. Jean Baptiste Henri Dominique Lacordaire, *Considérations sur le système philosophique de M. de La Mennais*, p. 175.

24. AN AGE OF RELATIVISM

1. Arthur Koestler, *The Yogi and the Commissar and Other Essays* (New York: Macmillan, 1945), p. 246. Koestler's sentence continues, "but we need qualified interpreters and above all a re-interpretation in the terms and symbols of Western thought."

25. AESTHETIC INCOMPATIBILITIES

1. Eric Newton, art critic of the *Manchester Guardian* and himself a painter.

Bibliography

This bibliography is not intended to encompass all titles to which Schwab makes reference in his text, but rather confines itself to those works Schwab indicated to be of importance to his own research. Entries published after 1950, the date of the original publication of *La Renaissance orientale*, have been added by the translators. Readers interested in French translations of English titles used by Schwab are referred to his bibliography in the original French edition.

Aarsleff, Hans. *The Study of Language in England, 1780–1860.* Princeton: Princeton University Press, 1967.

Adelung, Friedrich von. *An Historical Sketch of Sanskrit Literature.* Oxford, 1832.

—— *Versuch einer Literatur der Sanskrit-Sprache.* Saint Petersburg, 1830.

Adelung, Johann Christoph. *Mithridates, oder Allegemeine sprachenkunde.* 4 vols. Berlin: Vosische buchhandlung, 1806–17. Johann Adelung died in 1806 and this work was seen through the press by Friedrich von Adelung.

Allemand, Maurice. *Sainte-Beuve et "Volupté."* Paris: Société française d'éditions littéraires et techniques, Edgar Malfère, 1935.

Ampère, André-Marie and Jean-Jacques. *Correspondance et souvenirs (de 1805 à 1864). Recueillis par Madame H. C.* 2d ed. 2 vols. Paris: J. Hetzel, 1875. See also *Correspondance et souvenirs (de 1793 à 1805),* Paris: J. Hetzel, 1873.

Ampère, Jean-Jacques. "Des bardes chez Gaulois et chez les autres nations celtiques." *Revue des Deux-Mondes* (July 1, 1836), 7:419–46.

—— "Histoire du Bouddhisme. Relations des Royaumes bouddhiques. Traduite du chinois et accompagnée d'un Commentaire, par Abel Rémusat." *Revue des Deux-Mondes* (June 15, 1837), 9:731–51.

—— "Histoire littéraire de la France avant le XIIᵉ siècle." *Revue des Deux-Mondes* (January 1, 1836), 5:24–38.

—— "Littérature orientale: Antiquités de la Perse—Travaux de M. E. Burnouf." *Revue des Deux-Mondes* (October 1, 1836), 8:575–94.

Ancelot, Marguerite. *Les salons de Paris*. Paris: J. Tardieu, 1858.

Andler, Charles. *Nietzsche, sa vie et sa pensée*. 6 vols. Paris: Editions Bossard, 1920–31.

Andreas-Salomé, Louis. *Frédéric Nietzsche, traduit de l'allemand et précédé d'une introduction par Jacques Benoist-Méchin*. Paris: B. Grasset, 1932.

Anquetil-Duperron, Abraham Hyacinthe. *Législation orientale, ouvrage dans lequel, en montrant quels sont en Turquie, en Perse et dans l'Indoustan, les principes fondamentaux du gouvernement*. Amsterdam: M. M. Rey, 1778.

——, tr. *Oupenek'hat (id est, Secretum tegendum)*. Strasbourg, 1801.

—— *Recherches historique et géographiques sur l'Inde*. 2 vols. Berlin: P. Bourdeaux, 1786–87.

——, tr. *Zend-Avesta, ouvrage de Zoroastre*. Paris, 1771.

Anstett, Jean Jacques. *La pensée religieuse de Frédéric Schlegel*. Paris: Société d'édition Les Belles Lettres, 1941.

Les Appels de l'Orient. Special edition of *Cahiers du mois*. Paris: Emile-Paul Frères, 1925.

Approches de l'Inde. Special edition of *Cahiers du Sud*, 1949, edited by Jacques Masui.

Arberry, Arthur John. *Asiatic Jones: The Life and Influence of Sir William Jones (1746–1794), Pioneer of Indian Studies*. London and New York: Longmans, Green, 1946.

—— *British Contributions to Persian Studies*. London: Longmans, Green, 1942.

—— *British Orientalists*. London: W. Collins, 1943.

—— "The Founder: William Jones." In *Oriental Essays: Portraits of Seven Scholars*, pp. 46–86. London: George Allen and Unwin, 1960.

Audiat, Pierre. *Ainsi vécut Victor Hugo*. Paris: Hachette, 1947.

Babbitt, Irving. "Romanticism and the Orient." In *On Being Creative and Other Essays*. Boston: Houghton Mifflin, 1932. Reprinted from *The Bookman* (December 1931), 74(4):349–57.

Bailly, Auguste. *La Fontaine*. Paris: A. Fayard, 1937.

Bailly, Jean Sylvain. *Lettres sur l'origine des sciences et sur celle des peuples de l'Asie, adressées à M. Voltaire*. Paris, 1777.

Baldensperger, Fernand. *L'appel de la fiction orientale chez Honoré de Balzac*. Oxford: Clarendon Press, 1927.

—— *Orientations étrangères chez Honoré de Balzac*. Paris: H. Champion, 1927.

—— "Un informateur de Balzac: Barchou de Penhoën." *Mercure de France* (July 1, 1949), no. 1031, pp. 431–42.

Bamboat, Zenobia. *Voyageurs français dans l'Inde aux XVIIe et XVIIIe siècles*. Introduction by A. Martineau. Paris: Société de l'histoire des colonies françaises, 1933.

Barbey d'Aurevilly, Jules. *Dix-neuvieme siècle. Les Oeuvres et les Hommes*. 2d series, Littérature etrangère. Paris: A. Lemerre, 1890.

Barchou de Penhoën, Baron Auguste. "Essai d'une formule générale de l'histoire de l'humanité, d'après les idées de M. Ballanche." *Revue des Deux-Mondes* (1831), 526–60.

Barth, Auguste. *Quarante ans d'indianisme: Oeuvres, recueillés à l'occasion son quatre-vingtième anniversaire.* 5 vols. Paris: E. Leroux, 1914–27.

—— *Les religions de l'Inde.* Paris: G. Fischbacher, 1879. Reprinted from *Encyclopédie des sciences religieuses.*

Barthold, Vasilli Vladimirovitch. *La découverte de l'Asie: Histoire de l'orientalisme en Europe et en Russe.* French translation by Basile Nikitine. Paris: Payot, 1947.

Baruzi, Joseph. *Le rêve d'un siècle.* Paris: Calmann-Lévy, 1904.

Baschet, Robert. *Etienne Jean Delécluze, témoin de son temps, 1781–1863.* Paris: Bovin, 1942.

Baudet, Henri. *Paradise on Earth: Some Thoughts on European Images of Non-European Man.* English translation by Elizabeth Wentholt. New Haven and London: Yale University Press, 1965.

Bazin, René. *Paysages et pays d'Anjou.* Paris: Calmann-Levy, 1930.

de Beaumont, Adalbert. "Les arts décoratifs en Orient et en France: Une visite à l'Orient à l'exposition universelle." *Revue des Deux-Mondes* (November 1, 1867), 72:138–60.

Bédier, Joseph and Paul Hazard, eds. *Histoire de la littérature française.* Paris: Larousse, 1923–24.

Béguin, Albert. "Poésie et occultisme: Les sources initiatiques de Nerval et de Rimbaud." *Critique* (December 1947), 3 (19):483–93.

Belaval, Yvon. "Leibniz et la langue allemande." *Etudes germaniques* (January–March 1947), 2:121–32.

Benfey, Theodor. *Geschichte der Sprachwissenschaft un orientalischen Philogie in Deutschland seit dem Anfange des 19 Jahrhunderts mit einem Rückblick auf die früheren Zeiten.* Munich, 1869. Rpt., New York: Johnson Reprint, 1965.

Bergaigne, Abel. *Les dieux souverains de la religion védique.* Paris: F. Viewig, 1877. Rev. ed. published under the title *Les dieux antiques,* 1925.

Bergaigne, Abel and Paul Lehuguer, trs. *Sacountala: Drame en sept actes mêlé de prose et de vers.* Paris: Librairie des bibliophiles, 1884.

Bernoulli, Jean. *Description historique et géographique de l'Inde.* 3 vols. Berlin, 1786–89.

Berret, Paul. *Le moyen âge européen dans La légende des siècles et les sources de Victor Hugo.* Paris: H. Paulin, 1911.

—— *La philosophie de Victor Hugo (1854–1859), et deux mythes de La légende des siècles: La satyre—Pleine mer—plein ciel.* Paris: H. Paulin, 1910.

Bianquis, Geneviève. *Nietzsche en France: l'Influence de Nietzsche sur la pensée française.* Paris: F. Alcan, 1929.

Biot, Jean Baptiste. *Etudes sur l'astronomie indienne et sur l'astronomie chinoise* (1862). Rpt., Paris: A. Blanchard, 1969.

Biriukov, Pavel Ivanovich. *Tolstoi und der Orient.* Zurich and Leipzig: Rotapfel-Verlag, 1925.

Blaze de Bury, Henri. *Ecrivains et poètes de l'Allemagne.* Paris: Michel Levy frères, 1851.

Blum, Jean. *Johann August von Starck et la querelle du crypto-catholicisme en Allemagne, 1785–1789.* Paris: F. Alcan, 1912.

—— *La vie et l'oeuvre de Johann Georg Hamann, le "mage du Nord," 1730–1788.* Paris: F. Alcan, 1912.

Bochinger, Johann Jacob. *La vie contemplative, ascétique et monastique chez les Indous et chez les peuples bouddhistes.* Strasbourg: F. G. Levrault, 1831.

Bonnefoy, Georges. *La pensée religieuse et morale d'Alfred de Vigny.* Paris: Hachette, 1944.

Bonnet, Charles. *La palingénésie philosophique: ou, Idées sur l'état passé et sur l'état futur des êtres vivants.* Amsterdam: M. M. Rey, 1769.

Bopp, Franz. *Die Sündflut nebst drei anderen der wichtigsten Episoden des Maha-Bharata. Ans der Ursprache übersetzt.* Berlin, 1829.

—— *Uber das Conjugationssystem der Sanskritsprache in Vergleichung mit jenem der griechischen, perischen und germanischen Sprache.* Frankfurt, 1816.

—— *Vergleichende Grammatik des Sanskrit, Zend, Griechischen, Lateinischen, Litthausischen, Gothischen und Deutschen.* Berlin: F. Dummler, 1833. See also *A Comparative Grammar of the Sanskrit, Zend, Greek, Latin, Lithuanian, Gothic, German and Slavonic Languages. Translated from the German principally by Lieutenant Eastwick. Conducted through the press by H. H. Wilson.* 3 vols. London: Madden and Malcolm, 1845–53. And *Grammaire comparée des langues indo-européennes.* Introduction by Michel Bréal. 5 vols. Paris: Imprimerie impériale, 1866–74.

Boudout, Jean. "Faust et Ahasvérus." *Revue de littérature comparée* (October–December 1936), 16:691–709.

Brandt, Gustav. *Herder und Görres, 1797–1807.* Berlin: Friedrich-Wilhelms Universität, 1939.

Bréal, Michel. "Volney orientaliste et historien." *Journal des Savants* (February 1899), 98–107 and (May 1899) 261–71.

Brehier, Emile. *Histoire de la philosophie allemande.* Paris: Payot, 1921.

—— *Schelling.* Paris: F. Alcan, 1912.

Brillant, Maurice and Abbé Nédoncelle, eds. *Apologétique: Nos raisons de croire, réponses aux objections.* Paris: Bloud et Gay, 1937.

Bruguière, Antoine Andre, Baron de Sorsum. "Lettres inédites." *Revue de littérature comparée* (1927), 7:146–64.

Brun, André. "Le Baron d'Eckstein: Policier et journaliste marseillais." *Revue de littérature comparée* (1947), 21:481–96.

Brunetière, Ferdinand. "L'Orient dans la littérature française." In *Etudes critiques sur l'histoire de la littérature française*, 8:183–212. 8 vols. Paris: Hachette, 1896–1910.

Brunschwig, Henri. *La crise de l'Etat prussien à la fin du XVIIIe siècle et la genèse de la mentalité romantique*. Paris: Presses universitaires de France, 1947. Reprinted as *Enlightenment and Romanticism in Eighteenth Century Prussia*. Translated by Frank Jellinek. Chicago: University of Chicago Press, 1974.

Buche, Joseph. *L'Ecole mystique de Lyon, 1776–1847: Le grand Ampère, Ballanche, Cl.-Julien Bredin, Victor de Laprade, Blanc Saint-Bonnet, Paul Chenavard*. Paris: F. Alcan, 1935.

Burnouf, Eugène. *Choix de lettres d'Eugène Burnouf, 1825–1852, suivi d'une bibliographie*. Edited by Laure Burnouf Delisle. Paris: H. Champion, 1891.

——, tr. *Le lotus de la bonne loi*. Edited by Théodore Pavie. Paris, 1852.

Burtin, Père Nicholas. *Un semeur d'idées au temps de la restauration: Le baron d'Eckstein*. Paris: Editions de Boccard, 1931.

Cameron, Kenneth Walker. *Emerson's "Indian Superstition," with Studies in his Poetry, Bibliography and Early Orientalism*. Hartford: Transcendental Books, 1977.

du Camp, Maxime. *Les Beaux-Arts à l'Exposition universelle de 1855*. Paris: Librairie nouvelle, 1855.

—— *Orient et Italie, souvenirs de voyage et de lectures*. Paris: Didier, 1868.

—— *Souvenirs littéraires*. 2 vols. Paris: Hachette, 1882–83.

Cannon, Garland. "The Literary Place of Sir William Jones (1746–1794)." *Journal of the Asiatic Society of Bengal* (1960), 2(1):47–61.

—— *Oriental Jones: A Biography of Sir William Jones (1746–1794)*. New York: Asia Publishing House, 1964.

—— *Sir William Jones, Orientalist: An Annotated Bibliography of his Works*. Honolulu: University of Hawaii Press, 1952.

Cannon, Garland and Siddheshwar Pandey. "Sir William Jones Revisited: On his Translation of the *Sakuntala*." *Journal of the American Oriental Society* (1976), 96:528–35.

Carcassone, Emile. "Leconte de Lisle et la philosophie indienne." *Revue de littérature comparée* (1931), 11:618–46.

Caro, Elme Marie. *Du mysticisme au XVIIIe siècle. Essai sur la vie et la doctrine de Saint-Martin, le philosophe inconnu*. Paris: Hachette, 1852.

—— *Mélanges et portraits*. 2 vols. Paris: Hachette, 1888.

Carpenter, Edward. *Days with Walt Whitman, with some notes on his life and work*. London: G. Allen, 1906.

Carpenter, Frederick Ives. *Emerson and Asia*. Cambridge: Harvard University Press, 1930.

Carré, Jean Marie. *Les écrivains français et le mirage allemand, 1800–1940*. Paris: Boivin, 1947.

—— "L'Egypte antique dans l'oeuvre de Théophile Gautier." *Revue de littérature comparée* (1932), 12:765–800.

—— *Michelet et son temps, avec de nombreux documents inédits*. Paris: Perrin, 1926. Rpt., Ann Arbor: University Microfilms, 1976.

—— *Voyageurs et écrivains francais en Egypte*. 2 vols. Cairo: Imprimerie de l'Institut français d'archéologie orientale, 1932.

Caullery, Maurice. *Historie des sciences biologiques*. Paris: Plon-Nourrit, 1924.

Cerfbeer, Anatole and Jules Christophe. *Repértoire de la Comédie humaine de Honoré de Balzac*. Paris: C. Levy, 1888.

Chamberlain, Houston Stewart. *Richard Wagner*. Translated from the German by G. Ainslie Hight and revised by the author. Philadelphia: J. B. Lippincott, 1897.

Chambers, William. "Some Account of the Sculptures and Ruins at Mavalipuram, a Place a few Miles north of Sadras, and known to seamen by the name of the Seven Pagodas." Reprinted from *Asiatic Researches* (1784), vol. 1, in *Descriptive and Historical Papers Relating to the Seven Pagodas on the Coromandel Coast*, pp. 1–29. Edited by Mark William Carr. Madras, 1869.

Champollion, Jean François. *Précis du système hiéroglyphique des anciens Egyptiens: ou, Recherches sur les éléments premiers de cette écriture sacrée*. Paris: Truettel et Wurtz, 1924.

Chantepie de la Saussaye, Pierre Daniel. *Lehrbuch der Religionsgeschichte*. 2 vols. Freiburg: Mohr, 1887–89. See also *Manual of the Science of Religion*. Translated by Beatrice Colyer-Fergusson. London and New York: Longmans, Green, 1891. And *Manuel d'histoire des religions*. Translated from the 2d German edition under the direction of Henri Hubert and Isidore Lévy. Paris: A. Colin, 1904.

Chardin, Sir John. *Journal du voiage du Chevalier Chardin en Perse et aux Indies Orientales*. Amsterdam: J. Wolters and Y. Haring, 1686. See also *Sir John Chardin's Travels in Persia. Never before translated into English*. London, 1720.

Chari, V. K. *Whitman in the Light of Vedantic Mysticism*. Lincoln: University of Nebraska Press, 1964.

Charléty, Sébastien. *Histoire du Saint-Simonisme (1825–1864)*. 1896. Rpt., Paris: P. Hartmann, 1931.

Chasles, Philarète. *Mémoirs*. 2 vols. Paris: G. Charpentier, 1876.

Chassay, Frédéric Edouard, Abbé. *Conclusion des dèmonstrations évangéliques*. Edited by Jacques Paul. 20 vols. Paris, 1843–62.

Chateaubriand, René de. *Le génie du Christianisme, ou beautés de la religion chrétienne*. Brussels: Demat, 1835. See also *The Genius of Christianity: or, The Spirit and Beauty of the Christian Religion*. Translated, with biography and notes, by Charles I. White. Baltimore: J. Murphy, 1856.

—— *Mémoires d'outre-tombe* (1849). Edited by Maurice Levaillant and Georges Moulinier. Paris: Gallimand, 1946.

Chatterjee, Sir Atul Chandra and Sir Richard Burn. *British Contributions to Indian Studies*. London and New York: Longmans, Green, 1943.

Chauvin, Victor. *Bibliographie des ouvrages arabes ou relatifs aux Arabes publiés dans l'Europe chrétienne de 1810 à 1885*. Liege, 1892–1932.

Chazin, Maurice. "Extracts from Emerson by Edgar Quinet (1844–1845)." *Revue de littérature comparée* (1935), 15:136–39.

Chesne, Chesnier du. "La candidature de Lamartine a l'Académie en 1824." *Mercure du France* (1934), 250:287–304.

—— "Lamartine académicien: Documents inédits." *Mercure de France* (1931), 232:86–100.

Chinard, Gilbert. *L'exotisme américain dans l'oeuvre de Chateaubriand*. Paris: Hachette, 1918.

Christy, Arthur. *The Orient in American Transcendentalism*. 1932. Rpt., New York: Octagon Books, 1969.

Citoleux, Marc. *Alfred de Vigny, persistances classiques et affinités étrangères*. Paris: Champion, 1924.

—— *La poésie philosophique au XIXe siècle: Lamartine*. Paris: Plon-Nourrit, 1906.

des Cognets, Jean. *La vie intérieur de Lamartine, d'après les souvenirs inédits de son plus intime ami, J. M. Dargaud, et les travaux les plus récents*. Paris: E. Arrault, 1913.

Colebrooke, Henry Thomas. *Essays on the Religion and Philosophy of the Hindus*. 2 vols. London: W. H. Allen, 1837.

Colebrooke, Thomas Edward, ed. *Miscellaneous Essays by Henry Thomas Colebrooke, with a life of the author*. London: Trübner, 1873.

Constant de Rebecque, Henri Benjamin. *Journal intime et lettres à sa famille et à ses amis*. Paris: Ollendorff, 1895.

Cook, Stanley A. "The Rediscovery of the Ancient Orient." In *Actes 20e Congrès orientale*. Paris, 1940.

Coomaraswamy, Ananda K. *Hinduism and Buddhism*. New York: Philosophical Library, 1943.

Cordier, Henri. "Un orientaliste allemand: Jules Klaproth." In *Mélanges d'historie et de géographie orientales*. 4 vols. Paris: J. Maisonneuve et fils, 1914–23.

Cournot, Antoine Augustin. *Traité de l'enchaînement des idées fondamentales dans les sciences et dans l'histoire*. Paris: Hachette, 1861.

Courtillier, Gaston. *Les anciennes civilizations de l'Inde*. Paris: A. Colin, 1930.

Cousin, Victor. *Premiers essais de philosophie.* Paris: Librairie nouvelle, 1855.

Creuzer, Friedrich. *Symbolik und Mythologie der alten Volker, besonders der Griechen.* 4 vols. Leipzig and Darmstadt, 1810–12.

Cuénot, Gaston. "L'origine des 'Contes Indiens' de Mallarmé." *Mercure de France* (November 15, 1939), 970:117–26.

Das Gupta, R. K. "Schopenhauer and Indian Thought." *East and West* (March 1962), n.s. 13 (1):32–40.

Darmesteter, James. *Essais orientaux.* Paris: A. Levy, 1883. See especially "De la parté de la France dans les grandes decouvertes de l'orientalisme moderne."

Dauer, Dorothea W. "Early Romanticism and India as Seen by Herder and Novalis." *Kentucky Foreign Language Quarterly* (1965), 12:218–24.

David, Henri. "L'exotisme hindou chez Théophile Gautier." *Revue de littérature comparée* (1929), 9:515–64.

Debidour, Antonin. "L'Indianisme de Voltaire." *Revue de littérature comparée* (1924), 4:26–40.

Deherain, Henri. *Silvestre de Sacy et ses correspondants.* Paris: Hachette, 1919.

—— *Silvestre de Sacy, ses contemporains et ses disciples.* Paris: P. Geuthner, 1938.

Delécluze, Etienne-Jean. *Antar, roman bédouin d'Abou Sa'ìd Abd al-Malik ibn Zoraib al-Asma'ì, traduit de l'arabe par Terric-Hamilton . . . imité de l'anglais.* 3 vols. Paris: A. Bertrand, 1819. See also Terrick Hamilton, *Antar, a Bedoueen romance. Translated from the Arabic.* London: J. Murray, 1819.

—— *Dante Alighieri: ou, La poésie amoureuse.* Paris: Amyot, 1848.

—— *Souvenirs de soixante années.* Paris: Michel Lévy frères, 1862.

Dermenghem, Emile. *Joseph de Maistre, mystique: Ses rapports avec le martinisme, l'illuminisme, et la franc-maconnerie, l'influence des doctrines mystiques et occultes sur sa pensée religieuse.* 1928. Rpt., Paris: La Columbe, 1946.

Dillon, Peter. *Narrative and successful result of a voyage in the South Seas, performed by order of the government of British India, to ascertain the actual fate of La Perouse's expedition.* London: Hurst, Chance, 1829. Translated as *Voyage aux îles de la mer du Sud.* 2 vols. Paris: Pillet aîné, 1830.

Dubois, Jean Antoine, Abbé. *A Description of the Character, Manners and Customs of the People of India.* London, 1816.

Dubois, Paul François. *Fragments littéraires . . . Articles extraits du Globe.* 2 vols. Paris: E. Thorin, 1879.

Duchesne-Guillemin, Jacques. *Zoroastre: Etude critique, avec une traduction commentée des Gâthâ.* Paris: G. P. Maisonneuve, 1948.

Dugat, Gustave. *Histoire des orientalistes de l'Europe du XIIᵉ au XIXᵉ siècle précédée d'une esquisse historique des études orientales.* 2 vols. Paris: Maisonneuve, 1868–70.

Duka, Theodore. *Life and Works of Alexander Csoma de Koros.* London: Trübner, 1885.

Durry, Marie Jeanne. *La vieillesse de Chateaubriand, 1830–1848.* 2 vols. Paris: Le Divan, 1933.

Dussand, René. *La nouvelle Académie des Inscriptions et Belles-Lettres, 1795–1914.* 2 vols. Paris: P. Geuthner, 1946–47.

Dussieux, Louis-Etienne. *Essai sur l'histoire de l'érudition orientale.* Paris: de Bourgogne et Martinet, 1842.

Eckstein, Ferdinand. *Des études sanscrites.* Paris: Imprimerie de S. Racon, n.d.

Egger, Emile. *Mémoires de littérature ancienne.* Paris: A. Durrand, 1862.

—— *Notions élémentaires de grammaire comparée.* Paris: A. Durrand, 1852.

Emery, Léon. *Vision et pensée chez Victor Hugo.* Lyon: Imprimerie Audin, 1939.

Erdan, Alexandre [pseud. Alexandre-Andre Jacob]. *La France mystique, tableau des excentricités religieuses de ce temps.* 2 vols. Paris: Coulon-Pineau, 1855.

Ersch, Johann Samuel and J. G. Gruber. *Allgemeine Encyklopädie der Wissenschaften und Künste.* Leipzig: F. A. Brockhaus, 1850–51.

L'Ezour Vedam ou Ancient Commentaire de Vedam, contenant l'exposition des opinions religieuses et philsophiques des Indiens. Traduit de Samscretan par un Brame. Yverdon, 1778. See also *Ezour-Vedam, oder die Geschichte, Religion und Philsophie der Indier.* Translated by J. Ith. Leipzig, 1779.

Falk, Maryla. *I "Misteri" di Novalis.* Naples: Casa editrice Rondinello Alfredo, 1938.

Falshaw, Gladys. *Leconte de Lisle et l'Inde.* Paris: H. d'Arthez, 1923.

Faral, Edmond. *La Chanson de Roland, étude et analyse.* Paris: Mellottee, 1934.

Fauche, Hippolyte. *Le Maha-bharata, poème épique de Krishna-Dwaipayana plus communément appelé Veda-vyasa, c'est-à-dire le compilateur et l'ordonnateur des Védas: Traduit complètement pour la première fois du Sanscrit en français.* 10 vols. Paris: A. Durrand et B. Duprat, 1863–70.

Faure, Elie. "Orient et Occident." *Mercure de France* (July 15, 1931), 794:257–77.

Feer, Léon. *Papiers d'Eugène Burnouf conservés à la Bibliothèque nationale; catalogue dressé par M. Léon Feer, bibliothécaire au Département des manuscrits.* Paris: H. Champion, 1899.

Festugière, André. *La révélation d'Hermès Trimégiste, avec un appendic sur l'hermétisme arabe par Louis Massignon.* 4 vols. Paris: Lecoffre, J. Gabalda, 1949–54.

Fichte, Johann Gottlieb. *Die Anweisung zu einem seligen Leben, oder auch die Religionslehre.* Berlin, 1806.

—— *Discours à la nation allemands. Traduits pour la première fois en français par Léon Philippe.* Paris: Librairie C. Delagrave, 1895. [Translation of *Reden an die deutsche nation.*]

Filliozat, Jean. "Débuts de l'Indianisme." *Journal Asiatique*, April–June 1937.

—— "La doctrine du brahmisme d'après S. Hippolyte." *Revue d'histoire des religions* (1947).

—— "Les échanges de l'Inde et l'empire romaine." *Revue histoirique* (1949) 201:1–29.

—— "La France et l'Inde dans la création de l'Indianisme." *France-Orient,* January 1947.

Flottes, Pierre. *La pensée politique et sociale d'Alfred de Vigny.* Paris: Société d'édition, 1927.

Foucaux, Philippe Edouard. *Doctrine des bouddhistes sur le nirvana.* Paris: Benjamin Duprat, 1864.

—— *Le Mahabharata: Onze episodes tirés de ce poème épique, traduits pour la premiere fois du sanscrit en francais.* Paris: B. Duprat, 1862.

—— *La reconnaissance de Sakountala, drame en sept actes de Kalidasa, traduit du sanscrit.* Paris: E. Picard, 1867.

Foucher, Alfred. *L'art gréco-bouddhique du Gandhara: Etude sur les origines de l'influence classique dans l'art bouddhique de l'Inde et de l'Extrême-Orient.* 2 vols. Paris: E. Leroux, 1905–22.

—— *La vie du Bouddha, d'après les textes et les monuments de l'Inde.* Paris: Payot, 1949.

Fourquet, J. "Vers un renouvellement de l'étude du germanique." *Etudes germaniques* (January–March 1947), 2:1–21.

Fourtol, Henri. "De l'art grec: Les marbres d'Egine." *Revue des Deux-Mondes* (September 15, 1839), 806–48.

Frilly, G. *L'Inde, la littérature sanscrite, avec un essai sur l'Inde et l'Occident par Charles Simond.* Paris: L. Michaud, 1909.

Galley, Jean Baptiste. *Claude Fauriel, membre de l'Institut, 1772–1843.* Saint-Etienne: Imprimerie de la "Loire républicaine," 1909.

Gandhi, Mohandas K. *An Autobiography: or, The Story of My Experiments with Truth.* Ahmedabad: Navajivan Publishing House, 1940.

Garratt, G. T. "Indo-British Civilization." In *The Legacy of India.* Edited by G. T. Garratt. Oxford: Clarendon Press, 1937.

Garreau, Albert. *Clément Brentano.* Paris: Desclée de Brouwer, 1921.

Gaulmier, Jean. *L'idéologue Volney, 1757–1820: Contribution à l'histoire de l'orientalisme en France.* Beyrouth, 1951.

Gautier, Judith. *Auprès de Richard Wagner, souvenirs (1861–1882).* Paris: Mercure de France, 1943.

Gengoux, Jacques. *La symbolique de Rimbaud: Le système, ses sources.* Paris: La Colombe, 1947.

Gérard, René. *L'Orient et la pensée romantique allemand.* Paris: Didier, 1963.

Gildemeister, Johann. *Bibliothecae Sanskritae sive recensvs librorvm sanskritorvm hvevsqv typis vel lapide exscriptorvm critici specimen.* Bonn: H. B. Koenig, 1847.

Girard, William. *Du Transcendentalisme considéré essentiellement dans sa définition et ses origines françaises.* Berkeley: University of California Press, 1916.

—— *Du Transcendantalisme considéré sous son aspect social.* Berkeley: University of California Press, 1918.

Glasenapp, Helmuth von. *Das Indienbild deutscher Denker.* Stuttgart: Koehler, 1960.

—— *Die Literaturen Indiens von ihren anfangen bis zur gegenwart.* Wildpark-Potsdam: Akademisch Verlagsgesellschaft Athenaion, 1929.

—— *Die Philosophie der Inder, eine Einfuhrung in ihre Geschichte und ihre Lehren.* Stuttgart: A. Kröner, 1949.

Goethe, Johann Wolfgang von. *West-Ostlicher Divan.* Stuttgart: Inder Cottaischen Buchhandlung, 1819. Translated, with introduction and notes, by John Weiss as *Goethe's West-Easterly Divan.* Boston: Roberts Brothers, 1877. Translated, with preface and annotations, by Henri Lichtenberger as *Divan occidental-orientale.* Paris: Aubier, 1940.

Görres, Joseph. *Mythengeschichte der asiatischen Welt.* 2 vols. Heidelberg, 1810.

Goyau, Georges. *Ozanam.* Paris: E. Flammarion, 1931.

Gregh, Fernand. *L'Oeuvre de Victor Hugo.* Paris: E. Flammarion, 1933.

Grousset, René. *Bilan de l'histoire.* Paris: Plon, 1946.

—— *Les civilizations de l'Orient.* Paris: Les editions G. Cres, 1929. See also *The Civilizations of the East.* Translated by Catherine Alison Phillips. 4 vols. New York: Alfred A. Knopf, 1931.

—— *Histoire de la philosophie orientale: Inde, Chine, Japon.* Paris: Nouvelle librairie nationale, 1923.

—— *L'Inde.* Paris: Plon, 1949.

Gubernatis, Angelo. *Cenni sopra alcuni Indianisti viventi.* Florence, 1872.

—— *Dante e l'India.* Rome, 1889.

—— *Méteriaux pour servir à l'histoire des études orientales en Italie.* Paris: E. Leroux, 1876.

—— *Le type indien du Lucifer chez le Dante.* Leiden, 1895.

Guenon, René. *La crise du monde moderne.* Paris: Gallimand, 1946.

—— *Introduction générale à l'étude des doctrines hindoues.* Paris: M. Rivière, 1921.

de Guignes, Joseph. *Recherches historiques sur la religion indienne,* 1776.

Guigniaut, Joseph Daniel, tr. *Religions de l'antiquité, considérées principale-*

ment dans leurs formes symboliques et mythologiques. 4 vols. Paris: Treuttel et Würtz, 1825–51. [Translation of Creuzer's *Symbolik.*]

Guillemin, Henri. *Le Jocelyn de Lamartine: Etude historique et critique, avec des documents inédits.* Paris: Boivin, 1936.

Guimbaud, Louis. *Les "Orientales" de Victor Hugo.* Amiens: Editions Edgar Malfère, 1928.

Halévy, Daniel. *Jules Michelet.* Paris: Hachette, 1928.

Halhed, Nathaniel Brassey. *A Code of Gentoo Laws: or, Ordinations of the Pundits, from a Persian translation, made from the original, written in the Shanscrit language.* London, 1776. See also *Code des loix des Gentoux.* Paris: Imprimerie de Stoupe, 1778.

Hardy, R. Spence. *A Manual of Buddhism, in its modern development: Translated from Singhalese manuscripts.* London: Partridge and Oakley, 1853.

—— *The Legends and Theories of the Buddhists Compared with History and Science.* London: Williams and Norgate, 1866.

Harispe, Pierre. *Lamennais: Drame de sa vie sacerdotale.* Paris: Editions de l'Abeille d'or, 1924.

—— *Lamennais et Gerbet: Edition ornée de 15 portraits et manuscrits hors texte et contenant des lettres inédites de Lamennais et Lacordaire.* Paris: Société d'Edition Française et Etrangère, 1909.

Haym, Rudolf. *Die romantische Schule.* Berlin: R. Gaertner, 1870.

Hazard, Paul. "Les influences étrangères chez Lamartine." *Revue des cours et conférences,* 1922–24.

—— *La pensée européene au XVIIIe siècle, de Montesquieu à Lessing.* 3 vols. Paris: Boivin, 1946.

Hecker, Max. *Schopenhauer und die indische Philosophie.* Cologne: Hübscher und Teufel, 1897.

Herbert, Jean. *Spiritualité hindoue.* Paris: A. Michel, 1947.

Herold, J. Christopher. *Bonaparte in Egypt.* New York: Harper and Row, 1962.

Hervás y Panduro, Lorenzo. *Catálogo de las lenguas de las naciones conocidas, y numeración, división, y clases de éstas según la diversidad de sus idiomas y dialectos.* 6 vols. Madrid: Ranz, 1800–5.

—— *Catalogo delle lingue conosciute e notizia della loro affinità, e diversità.* Cesena: G. Biasini, 1784.

Hillebrand, Karl. "De la philologie en Allemagne dans la première moitié du siècle. L'école historique." *Revue moderne* (1865), 33:239–68.

Hodgson, Brian Houghton. *Essays on the Languages, Literature, and Religion of Nepal and Tibet.* London: Trübner, 1874.

Hoene-Wronski, Jozef. *Messianisme, union finale de la philosophie et de la religion, constituant la philosophie absolue.* Paris: Bureau de l'Union antinomienne, 1831.

Huch, Ricarda. *Blutezeit der Romantik.* 1899. See also *Les Romantiques allemands,* translated by André Babelon. Paris: B. Grasset, 1933.

—— *Die Romantik.* 2 vols. Leipzig: H. Haessel, 1902–5.

Hugo, Victor. *Les contemplations. Nouvelle édition publiée d'après les manuscrits et les éditions originales avec des variantes.* Edited by Joseph Vianey. Paris: Hachette, 1922.

—— *La légende des siècles.* Edited by Paul Berret. New variorum edition. Paris: Hachette, 1920.

—— *Les Orientales.* Paris: Hetzel. 1820.

—— *Han d'Islande.* Paris: Chez Persan, 1823.

Hunter, Sir William Wilson. *Life of Brian Houghton Hodgson.* London: John Murray, 1896.

Iversen, Erik. *The Myth of Egypt and Its Hieroglyphs in European Tradition.* Copenhagen: Gec Gad Publishers, 1961.

Jacquemont, Victor. *Correspondance de Victor Jacquemont avec sa famille et plusieurs de ses amis, pendant son voyage dans l'Inde (1828–1832).* Paris: H. Fournier, 1833. Translated as *Letters from India: Describing a Journey in the British Dominions of India, Tibet, Lahore and Cashmere.* London: E. Churton, 1834.

Jankelvitch, Vladimir. *L'odyssée de la conscience dans la dernière philosophie de Schelling.* Paris: Alcan, 1933.

Jasinski, René. *Les années romantiques de Théophile Gautier.* Paris: Vuibert, 1929.

—— *Histoire de la littérature française.* Paris: Boivin, 1947.

Jeanroy, Alfred. *Voyage au purgatoire de St. Patrice. Visions de Tindal et de St. Paul. Textes languedociens du quinzième siècle.* Toulouse: E. Privat, 1903.

Jones, Sir William. *The Letters of Sir William Jones.* Edited by Garland Cannon. 2 vols. Oxford: Clarendon Press, 1970.

—— *The Works of Sir William Jones, with the life of the author by Lord Teignmouth.* 13 vols. London: John Stockdale and John Walker, 1807.

Sir William Jones: Bicentenary of his birth. Commemorative volume, 1746–1946. Calcutta: Royal Asiatic Society of Bengal, 1948.

Joubert, Leo. *Essais de critique et d'histoire.* Paris: Firmin-Didot, 1863.

Jourda, Pierre. *L'exotisme dans la littérature français depuis Chateaubriand.* 2 vols. Paris: Boivin, 1938–56.

Jullian, Camille. *Questions historiques. De l'influence de l'Egypte sur le monde antique.* Paris: Imprimerie de E. Capiomont, n.d.

Körner, Josef. *Die Botschaft der deutschen Romantik an Europa.* Augsburg: B. Filser, 1929.

La Brière, Léon de. *Champollion inconnu: Lettres inédites.* Paris: Plon, 1897.

Lach, Donald. "Leibniz and China." *Journal of the History of Ideas* (1945), 6:436–55.

—— *The Preface to Leibniz' Novissima Sinica: Commentary, Translation, Text.* Honolulu: University of Hawaii Press, 1957.

Lacordaire, Jean Baptiste. *Considérations sur le système philosophique de M. de La Mennais.* Louvain: C. J. Fonteyn, 1847.

Lacôte, Felix. "L'Indianisme." In *Société asiatique: Livre du centenaire,* pp. 219–49. Paris: La Société asiatique, 1922.

Laffitte, Pierre. *Les grands types de l'humanité: Appréciation systématique des principaux agents de l'évolution humaine.* 2 vols. Paris: E. Leroux, 1875–76.

Lamartine, Alphonse. *Cours familier de littérature.* Paris: privately printed, 1856.

—— *Oeuvres choisies.* Edited by Maurice Levaillant. Paris: Librairie A. Hatier, 1925.

Lammenais, Félicité Robert de. *Essai d'un systeme de philosophie catholique.* Edited by Christian Maréchal. Paris: Bloud, 1906.

—— *Essai sur l'indifférence en matière de religion.* 4 vols. Paris, 1817–23.

Langlès, Louis Mathieu. *Recherches asiatiques: ou, Mémoires de la Société.* Paris: Imprimerie imperiale, 1805.

Langlois, Alexandre. *Monuments littéraires de l'Inde: ou, Mélanges de littérature sanscrite.* Paris: Lefevre, 1827.

Lanjuinais, Jean-Denis. *Oeuvres.* 4 vols. Paris: Dondey-Dupré, 1832.

—— *La religion des Indoux selon les Védah: ou, Analyse de l'Oupnek'hat, publié par M. Anquetil Du Perron en 1802.* Paris: Dondey-Dupré, 1823.

Lanson, Gustave. "Deux voyages en angleterre: Voltaire et César de Saussure." *Revue d'historie littéraire de la France* (1906), 13:693–97.

—— Review of *L'Orient dans la littérature française au XVIIe et au XVIIIe siècle,* by Pierre Martino, in *Revue d'historie littéraire de la France* (1906) 13:545–47.

de Launay, Louis. *Le grand Ampère, d'après des documents inédits.* Paris: Perrin, 1925.

—— *Un amoureux de Madame Récamier: Le journal de Jean-Jacques Ampère.* Paris: H. Champion, 1927.

Latreille, Camille. *Les dernières années de Lamartine, 1852–1869, d'après les documents inédits.* Paris: Perrin, 1925.

La Vallée-Poussin, Louis de. *Indo-Européens et Indo-Iraniens: L'Inde jusque vers 300 ans avant Jésus-Christ.* As part of *Histoire du monde.* Edited by M. E. Cavaignac. 3 vols. Paris: E. de Boccard, 1924.

Lebedev, Gerasim. *La contemplation impassible des sytèmes des Brahmanes de l'Inde orientale.* Saint Petersburg, 1805.

Lebre, Andre. "Du *Génie des Religions* par M. E. Quinet." *Revue des Deux-Mondes* (April 15, 1842), 15:201–28.

Lee, Sarah. *Mémoires de baron Georges Cuvier, publiés en anglais par Mistress Lee, et en français par Théodore Lacordaire.* London: Longman, Rees, Orme, Brown, Green, and Longman, 1833; and Paris: H. Fournier, 1833.

Lefranc, Abel. *Ernest Renan en Italie: Sa mission scientifique et littéraire (juillet 1849–juillet 1850), d'après sa correspondance, et vingt lettres inédites.* Paris, 1938.

Lefranc, Abel and Pierre Langevin, eds. *Le Collège de France (1530–1930): Livre jubilaire composé à l'occasion de son quatrième centenaire.* Paris: Presses Universitaires de France, 1932.

Leibrich, Louis. "Présentation de Karl Jaspers: Nietzsche und das Christentum." *Etudes germaniques* (January–March, 1947), 2:95–98.

Lemierre, Antoine. *La veuve du Malabar: ou, L'empire des coutumes.* Paris, 1780. See also Mariana Starke, *The Widow of Malabar. A tragedy. As it is performed at the Theatre-Royal, Covent Garden.* Philadelphia: E. Story, 1791.

Lenormant, Charles. *Beaux-arts et voyages.* 2 vols. Paris: Michel Lévy frères, 1861.

Leroux, Pierre. "De l'influence philosophique des études orientales." *Revue Encyclopédique* (April 1832).

Lettres édifiantes et curieuses écrits des missions étrangères. 8 vols. Paris, 1703–8.

Lévi, Sylvain. *L'Inde et le monde.* Paris: H. Champion, 1928.

—— *L'Indianisme.* Paris: Larousse, 1915.

—— *Mémorial Sylvain Lévi.* Paris: P. Hartmann, 1937.

Loiseleur-Deslongchamps, Auguste. *Lois de Manou, comprenant les institutions religieuses, morales et civiles des Indiens.* Paris: Imprimerie de Crapelet, 1833.

de Lubac, Henri. *La rencontre du bouddhisme et de l'occident.* Paris: Aubier, 1952.

McCrindle, John Watson. *Ancient India as Described in Classical Literature.* Westminster: A. Constable, 1901.

Maes, Pierre. *Un ami de Stendhal, Victor Jacquemont.* Paris: Desclée de Brouwer, 1934.

Madelin, Louis. *La nation sous l'Empereur.* Paris: Hachette, 1948.

Magnin, Charles. "*Ahasvérus, Mystère;* et de la nature du génie poétique." *Revue des Deux-Mondes* (December 1, 1833), 533–76.

Maier, Friedrich. *Allgemeines mythologisches Lexicon aus original-quellen bearbeitet.* 2 vols. Weimar, 1803–4.

Maréchal, Christian. *La jeunesse de La Mennais.* Paris: Perrin, 1933.

Marie, Aristide. *Bibliographie des oeuvres de Gérard de Nerval.* Paris: H. Champion, 1925.

—— *Gérard de Nerval, le poète, l'homme, d'après des manuscrits et documents inédits.* Paris: Hachette, 1914.

Markovitch, Milan. *Tolstoi et Gandhi*. Paris: H. Champion, 1928.

Marquiset, Alfred. *Ballanche et Madame d'Hautefeuille. Lettres inédits de Ballanche, Chateaubriand, Sainte-Beuve, Madame Récamier, Madame Swetchine, etc.* Paris: H. Champion, 1912.

Martin, Nicolas. *Poètes contemporains en Allemagne*. Paris: Poulet-Malassis et De Broise, 1860.

Martineau, René. "Ernest Fouinet et 'Les Orientales.' " *Mercure de France* (June 16, 1916), 432:648–59.

Martino, Pierre. "Le carnet du *Voyage en Orient* de Gérard de Nerval." *Revue de littérature comparée* (1933), 13:140–73.

—— *L'Orient dans la littérature française aux XVIIᵉ au XVIIIᵉ siècle.* Paris: Hachette, 1906.

Massé, Henri. *Essai sur le poète Saadi*. Paris: P. Geuthner, 1919.

—— *Firdousi et l'épopée nationale*. Paris: Perrin, 1935.

Masson, Charles. *Narrative of a journey to Kalat, including an account of the insurrection at that place in 1840 and a memoir on Eastern Balochistan.* London: R. Bentley, 1843.

—— *Narrative of various journeys in Balochistan, Afghanistan and the Punjab, including a residence in those countries from 1826 to 1838.* 3 vols. London: R. Bentley, 1842.

Masson-Oursel, Paul. "Bibliographie sommaire de l'indianisme." *Isis* (1920), 3:171–218.

—— *Esquisse d'une histoire de la philosophie indienne*. Paris: P. Geuthner, 1923.

—— *La philosophie comparée*. Paris: F. Alcan, 1923. Translated as *Comparative Philosophy*. New York: Harcourt, Brace, 1926.

—— *La philosophie en Orient*. Paris: F. Alcan, 1938.

Masson-Oursel, Paul, Helena Willman-Grabowska, and Philippe Stern. *L'Inde antique et la civilisation indienne*. Paris: La Renaissance du Livre, 1933.

Master, Alfred. "The influence of Sir William Jones upon Sanskrit studies." *Bulletin of the School of Oriental and African Studies* (1946), 9:798–806.

Maury, Alfred. *Les académies d'autrefois: l'Ancienne Académie des Inscriptions et Belles-Lettres*. Paris: Didier, 1864.

Maury, Fernand. *Etude sur la vie et les oeuvres de Bernardin de St. Pierre*. Paris: Hachette, 1892.

Maynial, Edouard. "Flaubert orientaliste et le *Livre posthume* de Maxime du Camp." *Revue de littérature comparée* (1923), 3:78–108.

de Meester, Marie E. *Oriental Influences in the English Literature of the Nineteenth Century*. Heidelberg: C. Winter, 1915.

Meillet, Antoine. "Ce que la linguistique doit aux savants allemands." *Scientia* (1923), 33:263–70.

—— *Introduction à l'étude comparative des langues indo-européennes.* 1903. 8th ed., Paris: Hachette, 1937.

Mérimée, Prosper. *Correspondance générale.* Edited by Maurice Parturier, Pierre Josserand, and Jean Mallion. 17 vols. Paris: Le Divan, 1941–64.

Mesnard, P. "Dialogue avec Schleiermacher." *Vie intellectuelle,* May 1947.

Michaud, Joseph François. *Biographie universelle, ancienne et moderne.* Paris: Madame C. Desplaces, 1854–65.

Michaud, Regis. *Autobiographie d'Emerson, d'après son "Journal intime."* 2 vols. Paris: Colin, 1914–18.

—— *Panorama de la littérature américaine contemporaine.* Paris: Kra, 1928.

Michel, Henry, Daniel Halévy, and Gabriel Trarieux. *Edgar Quinet.* Paris: Cahiers de la quinzaine, 1903.

Mohl, Julius. *Vingt-sept ans d'histoire des études orientales: Rapports faits à la Société Asiatique de Paris de 1840 à 1867.* 2 vols. Paris: Reinwald, 1879–80.

Mohl, Ottmar, ed. *Correspondance de Fauriel et Mary Clarke.* Paris: Plon-Nourrit, 1911.

Mommsen, Katharina. *Goethe und der Islam.* Stuttgart: Goethe Gesellschaft, 1964

Mommsen, Momme. *Studien zum West-Ostlichen Divan.* Berlin: Akademie Verlag, 1962.

Mondor, Henri. *Vie de Mallarmé.* 2 vols. Paris: Gallimand, 1941–42.

Monod, Gabriel. *La vie et la pensée de Jules Michelet, 1798–1852.* Paris: E. Champion, 1923.

Moor, Edward. *Hindoo Pantheon.* London, 1810.

Moore, Adrienne. *Rammohun Roy and America.* Calcutta: Satis Chandra Chakravarti, 1942.

Moreau, Louis. *Le philosophe inconnu. Réflexions sur les idées de Louis-Claude de Saint-Martin le théosophe.* Paris: J. Lecoffre, 1850.

Moreau, Pierre. *Le romantisme.* Paris: J. de Gigord, 1932.

Mueller, Roger C. "Transcendental periodicals and the Orient." *Emerson Society Quarterly* (1969), 57:52–57.

Mukherjee, Soumyendra Nath. *Sir William Jones: A Study in Eighteenth-Century British Attitudes to India.* London: Cambridge University Press, 1968.

Müller, Friedrich Max. *Lectures on the Science of Language.* 2 vols. London: Longman, Green, Longman and Roberts, 1861–64.

Müller, Niklas. *Glauben, Wissen und Kunst der alten Hindus und im Gewande der Symbolik.* Mainz, 1822.

Mungello, David E. *Leibniz and Confucianism: The Search for Accord.* Honolulu: University Press of Hawaii, 1977.

Naudet, Joseph. "Notice historique sur MM. Burnouf, père et fils." *Mé-*

moires du Académie des inscriptions et belles-lettres (1861), 20:285–337.

Nerval, Gérard de. [Gérarad Labrunie.] *Voyage en Orient.* Edited by Henri Clouard. 3 vols. Paris: Le Divan, 1927.

Nodier, Charles. *Mademoiselle de Marsan.* Paris: E. Renduel 1832.

Oltramare, Paul Jean. *L'histoire des idées théosophiques dans l'Inde.* 2 vols. Paris: E. Leroux, 1906–23.

O'Meara, Kathleen. *Madame Mohl, her salon and her friends: A study of social life in Paris.* London: R. Bentley and Son, 1885.

Oppenberg, Ursula. *Quellenstudien zu Friedrich Schlegels Übersetzungen aus dem Sanskrit.* Marburg: Elwert, 1965.

Ovington, John. *A voyage to Suratt in the year 1689. Giving a large account of that city, and its inhabitants, and of the English factory there.* London: J. Tonson, 1696. An edition prepared by H. G. Rawlinson was published by Oxford University Press, 1929.

Ozanam, Antoine Frédéric. *Lettres de Frédéric Ozanam, 1831–1853.* 2 vols. Paris: Librairie Victor Lecoffre, 1891.

—— *Mélanges.* 2 vols. Paris, 1855.

Page, Curtis Hidden. *The Chief American Poets.* Boston: Houghton Mifflin, 1905.

de Pange, Comtesse Pauline de Broglie. *Auguste-Guillaume Schlegel et Madame de Staël, d'après des documents inédits.* Paris: Editions Albert, 1938.

—— "Les voyages de Herder en France." *Etudes germaniques* (January–March 1947), 2:42–58.

—— *Madame de Staël et la découverte de l'Allemagne.* Paris: E. Malfere, 1929.

Parrot, André. *Archéologie mésopotamienne.* Paris: A. Michel, 1946.

Pavie, André. *Médaillons romantiques: Lettres inédites de Sainte-Beuve, David d'Angers, Madame Victor Hugo, Madame Ménessier-Nodier, Paul Foucher, Victor Pavie, etc.* Paris: Emile-Paul, 1909.

Pavie, Théodore. *Fragments du Mahabharata traduits en français sur le texte sanscrit de Calcutta.* Paris: B. Duprat, 1844.

—— "Littérature Indienne: Le Rig-Véda et les livres sacrés des Hindous." *Revue des Deux-Mondes* (July 15, 1854), 252–82.

—— *Victor Pavie, sa jeunesse, ses relations littéraires.* Angers: Lachèse et Dolbeau, 1887.

Pavie, Victor. *Oeuvres choisies, précédées d'une notice biographique par René Bazin.* 2 vols. Paris: Perrin, 1887.

Pedersen, Holger. *The Discovery of Language: Linguistic Science in the 19th Century.* 1931. Rpt., Bloomington & London: Indiana University Press, 1962. (Translation by John Webster Spargo of *Sprogvidenskaben i det Nittende Aarhundrede: Metoder og Resultater.* Copenhagen: Gyldendalske Boghandel, 1924.)

Petit, Léon. "Madame de la Sablière et François Bernier." *Mercure de France* (April 1, 1950), 1040:670–83.

Picavet, François Joseph. *Les idéologues: essai sur l'histoire des idées et des théories scientifiques, philosophiques, religieuses, etc, en France depuis 1789.* Paris: F. Alcan, 1891.

Pichois, Claude. "Sainte-Beuve et Philarète Chasles, d'après des documents inédits." *Mercure de France* (March 1, 1950), 1039:471–83.

Pilon, Edmond. "Le salon de Cuvier au jardin des plantes." *Revue des Deux-Mondes* (July 15, 1932), 382–94.

Pinard de La Boullaye, Henri. *L'étude comparée des religions, essai critique.* 2 vols. Paris: G. Beauchesne, 1922–25.

Pirenne, Jacques. *Les grands courants de l'histoire universelle.* 7 vols. Neuchâtel: Editions de la Baconnière, 1944–56.

Pottier, Edmond. *Les antiquités assyriennes.* Paris: Gaston Braun, 1917.

Prinsep, James. *Essay on Indian Antiquities, historic, numismatic, and palaeographic of the late James Prinsep.* London: J. Murray, 1858.

Proceedings of the Sir William Jones Bicentenary Conference held at University College, Oxford, September 2–6, 1946. London: Royal India Society, 1946.

Quinet, Edgar. *Le génie des religions: De l'origine des dieux.* Paris: Pagnerre, 1857.

—— *Histoire de mes idées, autobiographie.* Paris: Germer-Baillière, 1878.

—— *Oeuvres complètes.* 11 vols. Paris: Pagnerre, 1857–70. A later edition, in 26 volumes, was published in Paris by Germer-Baillière, 1878–80.

Quinet, Hermione. *Cinquante ans d'amitié: Michelet-Quinet (1827–1875).* Paris: A. Colin, 1899.

—— *Edgar Quinet avant l'exile.* Paris: C. Lévy, 1887.

Quinot, A. *Pages mystiques de Nietzsche; extraits traduits et accompagnés d'éclaircissements.* 5th ed. Paris: R. Laffont, 1945.

Rajan, B. "India and the English mystics." *The Listener* (November 20, 1947), 38:901–2.

Rawlinson, H. G. "India in European Literature and Thought." In *The Legacy of India,* edited by G. T. Garratt. Oxford: Clarendon Press, 1937. Pp. 1–37.

Reinach, Salomon. *Manuel philologie classique d'après le Triennium philologicum de W. Freund et les derniers travaux de l'érudition.* 2 vols. Paris: Hachette, 1880–84.

Rémusat, Abel. *Mélanges asiatiques: ou, Choix de morceaux critiques et de mémoires relatifs aux religions, aux sciences, aux coutumes, à l'histoire et à la géographie des nations orientales.* Paris: Dondey-Dupré, 1825–26.

—— *Mélanges posthumes d'histoire et de littérature orientales.* Paris: Imprimerie royale, 1843.

—— *Nouveaux mélanges asiatiques: ou, Recueil de morceaux de critiques et mémoires*. 2 vols. Paris: Schubart et Heideloff, 1829.

Remy, Arthur F. J. "The Influence of India and Persia on the Poetry of Germany." Dissertation, Columbia University, 1901.

Renan, Ernest. *L'avenir de la science, pensées de 1848*. Paris: Calmann-Lévy, 1890.

—— *Correspondance, 1847–1892*. Paris: Calmann-Lévy, 1898.

—— *Etudes d'histoire religieuse*. Paris: Michel Lévy, 1857.

—— *Lettres intimes, 1842–45*. Edited by Henriette Renan. Paris: Calmann-Lévy, 1896.

—— *Mélanges religieux et historiques*. Paris: Calmann-Lévy, 1904.

—— *Nouvelles lettres intimes, 1846–1850*. Edited by Henriette Renan. Paris: Calmann-Lévy, 1923.

—— *Oeuvres complètes. Edition définitive établie par Henriette Psichari*. 7 vols. Paris: Calmann-Lévy, 1947.

—— *De l'origine du langage*. Paris: Au bureau de la Revue . . . et chez Toubert, 1848. 2d ed., Paris: Michel Lévy frères, 1858.

—— *Questions contemporaines*. Paris: Michel Lévy frères, 1868.

Renan, Ernest and Henriette Renan. *Brother and sister: A memoir and the letters of Ernest and Henriette Renan*. Translated by Lady Mary Loyd. London: W. Heinemann, 1896.

Rennell, James. *A treatise on the comparative geography of western Asia, accompanied with an atlas of maps*. London: C. J. G. & F. Rivington, 1831.

Renou, Louis. *Anthologie sanskrite: Textes de l'Inde ancienne*. Paris: Payot, 1947.

—— *Littérature sanskrite, avec en appendice une table de concordance du Rigveda*. Paris: Maisonneuve, 1946.

—— *Les maîtres de la philologie védique*. Paris: P. Geuthner, 1928.

—— *La poésie religieuse de l'Inde antique*. Paris: Presses universitaires de France, 1942.

—— "Raymond Schwab et les études orientales." *Mercure de France* (December 1956), 1120:657–62.

—— *Sanskrite et culture, l'apport de l'Inde à la civilisation humaine*. Paris: Payot, 1950.

Renou, Louis, et al. *L'Inde classique, manuel des études indiennes*. Paris: Payot, 1949.

Restoux, Daniel. *Notes sur Guillaume Postel*. Paris: Mortain, 1930.

Reynaud, Jean. *Philosophie religieuse: Terre et ciel*. 2d ed. Paris: Furne, 1854.

Reynaud, Louis. *L'influence allemande en France au XVIIIe et au XIXe siècle*. Paris: Hachette, 1922.

—— *Le romantisme: Ses origines anglo-germaniques; influences étrangères et traditions nationales; le réveil du génie français*. Paris: A. Colin, 1926.

Richardson, Joanna. *Théophile Gautier: His life and times.* London: Max Reinhardt, 1958.

Richer, Jean. *Gérard de Nerval et les doctrines ésotériques. Avec des textes et des documents inédits.* Paris: Editions du Griffon d'or, 1947.

Riepe, Dale. *The Philosophy of India and its Impact on American Thought.* Springfield, Il: Charles C. Thomas, 1970.

Robertson, William. *An historical disquisition concerning the knowledge which the Ancients had of India.* London, 1791.

Roche, Louis. *La vie de Jean de La Fontaine.* 3d ed. Paris: Plon, 1913.

Roche, Maurice. *Alfred de Vigny et l'ésotérisme.* Blois: Editions du Jardin de la France, 1948.

Rocher, Rosane. *Alexander Hamilton (1762–1824): A Chapter in the Early History of Sanskrit Philology.* New Haven: American Oriental Society, 1968.

Rod, Edouard. *Les unis.* Paris: E. Fasquelle, 1909. Originally published in *Revue des Deux Mondes*, February–March, 1909.

Roe, Sir Thomas. *The journal of Sir Thomas Roe, ambassador from His Majesty King James the First of England, to Ichan Guire, the mighty Emperor of India, commonly called the Great Mogul.* In *Pilgrimes*, edited by Samuel Purchas. London, 1625.

Rolland, Romain. *Essai sur la mystique et l'action de l'Inde vivante.* 3 vols. Paris: Stock, Delamain and Boutelleau, 1929–30.

—— *Mahatma Gandhi. Edition nouvelle augmentée d'une postface.* Paris: Delamain, Boutelleau, 1924.

Rouché, Max, tr. *Une autre philosophie de l'histoire, pour contribuer à l'éducation de l'humanité.* Paris: Aubier, 1943. Translation, with notes and introduction, of Johann Gottfried von Herder's *Auch eine Philosophie der Geschichte.*

Rouge, Julien. *Les écrivains allemands de la première génération romantique et l'histoire générale de la littérature.* Paris: H. Champion, 1930.

—— *Frédéric Schlegel et la genèse du romantisme allemand (1791–1797).* Paris: A. Fontemoing, 1904.

Rousseaux, André. "Raymond Schwab et l'humanisme integral." *Mercure de France* (December 1956), 1120:663–71.

Rückert, Friedrich. *Brahmanische Erzählungen.* Leipzig: Weidmann, 1839.

—— *Die Weisheit des Brahmanen, ein Lehrgedicht in Bruchstücken.* 2 vols. Leipzig: Weidmann, 1838–40.

Sacy, Silvestre de. *Mélanges de littérature orientale.* Paris: E. Docrocq, 1861.

Said, Edward W. *Orientalism.* New York: Pantheon, 1978.

—— "Renan's Philological Laboratory." In *Art, Politics, and Will: Essays in Honor of Lionel Trilling,* pp. 59–98. Edited by Quentin Anderson, et al. New York: Basic Books, 1977.

Sainte-Beuve, Charles Augustin. *Correspondance générale.* Edited by Jean Bonnerot. Paris: Stock, 1935.

—— *Portraits contemporains.* 3 vols. Paris: Didier, 1846.

—— *Premiers Lundis.* 3 vols. Paris: Michel Lévy frères, 1874–75.

Samsami, Nayereh. *L'Iran dans la littérature française.* Paris: Presses universitaires de France, 1936.

Sarrazin, Gabriel. *La renaissance de la poésie anglaise, 1798–1889.* Paris: Perrin, 1889.

Saurat, Denis. *La religion de Victor Hugo.* Paris: Hachette, 1929.

Schack, Adolf Friedrich. *Stimmen von Ganges. Eine sammlung indischer sagen.* Berlin: W. Hertz (Sesser), 1857.

Schelling, Friedrich Wilhelm. *Einleitung in der Philosophie der Mythologie.* Stuttgart: J. G. Cotta, 1856–57.

—— *Philosophie der Mythologie* (1842). Munich: C. H. Beck, 1943.

—— *Philosophie und Religion.* Tübingen: Cotta, 1804.

—— *System des transscendentalen idealismus.* Tübingen: Cotta, 1800. See also *Système de l'idéalisme transcendental.* Translated by Paul Grimblot. Paris, 1842.

Scherer, James. "Notes sur les 'Contes Indiens' de Mallarmé." *Mercure de France* (January 1, 1938), 955:102–16.

Schlagdenhauffen, Alfred. *Frédéric Schlegel et son groupe: La doctrine de l'Athenaeum (1798–1800).* Paris: Les Belles-lettres, 1934.

Schlegel, August Wilhelm. *Indische bibliothek: eine Zeitschrift.* Bonn: E. Weber, 1820–30.

—— *Refléxions sur l'étude des langues asiatiques, adressées à Sir James Mackintosh, suivies d'une lettre à M. Horace Hayman Wilson.* Bonn: E. Weber, 1832.

Schlegel, Friedrich. *Cours d'histoire universelle (1805–1806).* Edited by Jean-Jacques Anstett. Trévoux: Imprimerie G. Patissier, 1939. First printing of Schlegel's manuscript.

—— *Friedrich Schlegels Briefe an seinen Bruder August Wilhelm.* Edited by Oskar F. Walzel. Berlin: Speyer und Peters, 1890.

—— *Uber die Sprache und Weisheit der Indier.* Heidelberg, 1808. See also "On the Language and Wisdom of the Indians," translated by E. J. Millington. In *The Aesthetic and Miscellaneous Works of Friedrich von Schlegel.* London, 1849.

Schleiermacher, Friedrich. *Uber die Religion. Reden an die Gebildeten unter ihren Verächtern.* Berlin, 1799.

Schlosser, Friedrich Christoph. *Universalhistorische übersicht der Geschichte der alten Welt und ihrer Cultur.* 9 vols. Frankfurt: Bey F. Varrentrapp, 1826–34. For de Golbéry's translation see *Histoire universelle de l'antiquité.* 3 vols. Paris: F. G. Levrault, 1828.

Schopenhauer, Arthur. *Parerga und Paralipomena: Kleine philosophische Schriften.* 2 vols. Stuttgart: Cotta, 1850. Translated by J-A Contacuzène as *Parerga et Paralipomena: Aphorismes sur la sagesse dans la vie.* 9th ed. Paris: F. Alcan, 1901.

—— *Die Welt als Wille und Vorstellung.* Leipzig: F. A. Brockhaus, 1819. Translated by R. B. Haldane and J. Kemp as *The World as Will and Idea.* 3 vols. London: Trübner, 1883–86.

Schwab, Raymond. *L'auteur des Mille et une Nuits: Vie d'Antoine Galland.* Paris: Mercure de France, 1964.

—— "Hugo troublé par l'Inde." *Revue de littérature comparée* (1947), 21:497–511.

—— *Vie d'Anquetil-Duperron, suivie des Usages civils et religieux des Parses par Anquetil-Duperron.* With a preface by Sylvain Lévi and two essays by Sir Jivanji Jamshedji Modi. Paris: E. Leroux, 1934.

Schwartz, W. L. *The Imaginative Interpretation of the Far East in Modern French Literature, 1800–1925.* Paris, 1927.

Schweitzer, Albert. *Die Weltanschauung der Indischen Denker.* Munich: C. H. Beck, 1935. Translated by Mrs. Charles E. B. Russell as *Indian Thought and Its Development.* London: Hodder and Stoughton, 1936.

Sebeok, Thomas A. *Portraits of Linguists: A Biographical Sourcebook for the History of Western Linguistics, 1746–1963.* Volume 1, *From Sir William Jones to Karl Brugmann.* Bloomington and London: Indiana University Press, 1966.

Séché, Léon. *Educateurs et moralistes.* Paris, 1893.

Seillière, Ernest. *Barbey d'Aurévilly, ses idées et son oeuvre.* Paris: Bloud, 1910.

—— *Le comte Gobineau et l'aryanisme historique.* Paris: Plon-Nourrit, 1903.

—— "La philosophie religieuse de Gobineau." *Nouvelle Revue Française* (1934), 42:223–28.

Sencourt, Robert. *India in English Literature.* London: Simpkin, Marshall, Hamilton, Kent, 1925.

Sepp, Johann Nepamuk. *Görres.* Berlin: E. Hofmann, 1896.

Silvestre de Sacy, Antoine Isaac. "Balzac, G. Saint-Hilaire et l'unité de composition." *Mercure de France* (June–July 1948).

—— *Mélanges de littérature orientale.* Paris: E. Docrocq, 1861.

—— *Mémoires d'histoire et de littérature orientale.* Paris: Academie des Inscriptions et Belles-Lettres, 1823–32.

Simpson, Mary. *Letters and recollections of Julius and Mary Mohl.* London: K. Paul, Trench, 1887.

Singh, Iqbal. *Rammohun Roy: A Biographical Inquiry into the Making of Modern India.* London: Asia Publishing House, 1958.

Smith, Byron P. *Islam in English Literature.* Beirut: American Press, 1939.

Smith, Marion Elmina. *Une anglaise intellectuelle en France sous la Restauration*. Paris: H. Champion, 1927.

Société Asiatique. *Le livre du centenaire (1822–1922): Cent ans d'orientalisme en France*. Paris: Geuthner, 1922.

Sola Pinto, Victor de. "Sir William Jones and English Literature." *Bulletin of the School of Oriental and African Studies* (University of London) (1946), 14:686–94.

Sonnerat, Pierre. *Voyage aux Indes Orientales*. 2 vols. Paris, 1782.

Souriau, Maurice. *Le préface de Cromwell (Introduction, texte et notes)*. Paris: Société française d'imprimerie et de librairie, 1897.

Spenlé, Jean Edouard. *Novalis, essai sur l'idéalisme romantique en Allemagne*. Paris: Hachette, 1903.

—— *La pensée allemande de Luther à Nietzsche*. 1924. 4th ed., rev., Paris: A. Colin, 1949.

Stapfer, Paul. *Victor Hugo à Guernesey: Souvenirs personnels*. Paris: Société française d'imprimerie et de librairie, 1905.

Stein, William B. "A Bibliography of Hindu and Buddhist Literature Available to Thoreau through 1854." *Emerson Society Quarterly* (1967), 47:52–56.

Sucher, Paul. *Aus dem Leben eines Taugenichts*. 1826. Rpt., Berlin: Simion, 1842. Translated by Joseph Eichendorff as *Vie d'un propre à rien*. Paris: Editions Montaigne, 1941. See also *Memoirs of a Good-for-Nothing*. Translated by Charles Godfrey Leland. New York: Leypoldt and Holt, 1866.

Summers, Vera A. *L'orientalisme d'Alfred de Vigny*. Paris: H. Champion, 1930.

Susini, Eugène. *Franz von Baader et le romantisme mystique*. Paris: J. Vrin, 1942.

Téchoueyres, Emile. *A la recherche de l'unité: Essais de philosophie scientifique et medicale*. Paris: Librairie J. B. Baillière et fils, 1937.

Thevenot, Jean. *Relation d'un voyage fait au Levant*. Paris: L. Bilaine, 1664.

—— *Voyages de M. de Thevenot contenant la relation de l'Indostan, des nouveaux Mogols et des autres peuples et pays des Indies*. Paris: V. Biestkins, 1684.

Thierry, Augustin. "Considérations sur l'histoire de France." His preface to *Récits des temps merovingiens* in Volume 4 of his *Oeuvres*. 5 vols. Paris: Jouvet, 1866–82.

van Tieghem, Paul. *Le mouvement romantique (Angleterre—Allemagne—Italie—France)*. 2d ed. Paris: Hachette, 1923.

—— *Le préromantisme, études d'histoire littéraire européenne*. 3 vols. Paris: F. Rieder, 1924–47. Volume 1: *La notion de vraie poésie. La mythologie et la poésie scandinaves*. Volume 2: *La poésie de la nuit et des tombeaux. Les idylles de Gessner et le rêve pastoral.* Volume 3: *La découverte de Shakespeare sur le continent.*

—— *Le romantisme dans la littérature européenne.* Paris: A. Michel, 1948.

Tomomatsu, Entai. *Le Bouddhisme.* Translated by Kuni Matsuo. Paris: F. Alcan, 1935. See also *The Buddha's Words.* Translated by Kaneko and L. Bush. Tokyo: International Buddhist Society, 1939.

Tonnelat, Ernest. "Paradoxe sur Herder." *Etudes germaniques* (January–March 1946), 1:26–70.

Toynbee, Arnold. *Civilization on Trial.* New York: Oxford University Press, 1948.

Tronchon, Henri. *Allemagne—France—Angleterre: Le jeune Edgar Quinet, ou l'aventure d'un enthousiaste.* Paris: Les belles lettres, 1937.

—— *La fortune intellectuelle de Herder en France, bibliographie critique.* Paris: F. Rieder, 1920.

—— "Historiens allemands et français: Trois lettres inédites." *Revue de litterature comparée* (1932), 12:401–8. (Letters of Creuzer and Schlosser to Quinet.)

—— *Romantisme et préromantisme.* Paris: Les Belles-lettres, 1930.

Valle, Pietro della. *Viaggi cioè la Turchia, la Persia, e l'Inde.* Rome, 1650.

Vassilief, Vasilii Pavlovich. *Le bouddisme, son histoire et sa litérature.* Translated by G. A. La Comme. Paris: A. Durand, 1865.

Vaughan, Charles Edwyn. *The Romantic Revolt.* Edinburgh: W. Blackwood & Sons, 1907.

Vendryes, Joseph. *Le langage: Introduction linguistique à l'histoire.* Paris: Renaissance du livre, 1921.

Vianey, Joseph. *Les sources de Leconte de Lisle.* Montpellier: Coulet et fils, 1907.

Viatte, Auguste. *Le catholicisme chez les romantiques.* Paris: E. de Boccard, 1922.

—— *L'Extrême-Orient et nous.* Montréal: Editions de l'Arbre, 1942.

—— *Victor Hugo et les Illuminés de son temps.* Montréal: Editions de l'Abre, 1942.

—— "Notes sur les sources de Victor Hugo." *Revue d'histoire littéraire de la France* (1932), 434–43.

—— *Les sources occultes du romantisme: Illuminisme—théosophie, 1770–1820.* 2 vols. Paris: H. Champion, 1928. Volume 1: *Le préromantisme.* Volume 2: *La génération de l'Empire.*

Vigny, Alfred. *Correspondance.* Edited by Fernand Baldensperger. Paris: L. Conrad, 1933.

Villemain, Abel François. "Du génie anglais dans l'Inde: Sir William Jones, Grand-juge dans l'Inde—Le très révérend Réginald Heber, Lord Evêque de Calcutta." *Revue des Deux-Mondes* (December 15, 1857), 810–25.

Villey-Desmeserets, Pierre. *Les sources des idées, textes choisis et commentés.* Paris: Plon-Nourrit, 1912.

Vitet, L. "Un mot sur l'archéologie orientale." *Revue des Deux-Mondes* (June 1, 1868), 746–55.

Wallon, Henri Alexandre. *Eloges académiques.* 2 vols. Paris: Hachette, 1882.

Ward, William. *A view of the history, literature and religion of the Hindoos, including a minute description of their manners and customs, and translations from their principal works.* 2 vols. London: Black, Parbury, and Allen, Booksellers to the Hon. East India Co., 1817.

Weber, Albrecht. *Akademische Vorlesungen über indische Literaturgeschichte.* Berlin: F. Dummler, 1852.

—— *Indische Studien: Beiträge für die Kunde des indischen Alterthums.* 18 vols. Berlin: F. Dümmler, 1850–63; Leipzig: F. A. Brockhaus, 1865–98.

Weidle, Vladimir. "La philosophie de l'histoire d'Arnold Toynebee." *Critique* (1949), 5:721–37.

Welbon, Guy Richard. *The Buddhist Nirvana and Its Western Interpreters.* Chicago: University of Chicago Press, 1967.

von Wesendonk, O. G. "Nietzsche und seine iran Quellen." *Preussiche Jahrbuch* (July 1933), 233:56–62.

Wilford, Francis. *Essai sur l'origine et la décadence de la religion chrétienne dans l'Inde.* Translation by J. Daniélo of "The origin and decline of the Christian religion in India." from *Asiatic Researches.* Paris: B. Duprat, 1847.

Willson, A. Leslie. "Herder and India: The Genesis of a Mythical Image." *PMLA* (1955), 70:1049–58.

—— *A Mythical Image: The Ideal of India in German Romanticism.* Durham: Duke University Press, 1964.

Wilson, Horace Hayman. *The History of British India from 1805 to 1835.* 2 vols. London: J. Madden and Co, 1845–46. Written as a continuation of James Mills' *The History of British India.* 3 vols. London: Baldwin, Cradock and Joy, 1817.

Wincklemann, Johann Joachim. *Geschichte der Kunst des Alterhums.* Dresden: Walther, 1764.

Windisch, Ernst. *Geschichte der Sanskrit-philologie und indischen Altertumskunde.* 2 vols. Strasbourg: K. J. Trubner, 1917–20.

Windischmann, Karl Joseph. *Die Philosophie im Fortgang der Weltgeschichte.* 2 vols. Bonn: A. Marcus, 1827–29.

Winternitz, Moriz. *Geschichte der indischen Literatur.* 3 vols. Leipzig: C. F. Amelang, 1908–22.

Zenker, Julius Theodor. *Bibliotheca orientalis: Manuel de bibliographie orientale.* 2 vols. Leipzig: G. Engelmann, 1846–61.

Index